Realizing the Purpose and Benefits of Juvenile Transfer to Criminal Court

Joseph B. Sanborn, Jr.
University of Central Florida (Retired), USA

A volume in the Advances in Criminology, Criminal Justice, and Penology (ACCJP) Book Series

IGI Global
PUBLISHER of TIMELY KNOWLEDGE

Published in the United States of America by
IGI Global
Information Science Reference (an imprint of IGI Global)
701 E. Chocolate Avenue
Hershey PA, USA 17033
Tel: 717-533-8845
Fax: 717-533-8661
E-mail: cust@igi-global.com
Web site: http://www.igi-global.com

Library of Congress Cataloging-in-Publication Data

Names: Sanborn, Joseph B., Jr., author.
Title: Realizing the purpose and benefits of juvenile transfer to criminal court / by Joseph B. Sanborn.
Description: Hershey, PA : Information Science Reference, (an imprint of IGI Global), 2023. | Includes bibliographical references and index. | Summary: "This book provides an in-depth examination of the most important decision made in juvenile court: transfer of a juvenile's case to criminal court"-- Provided by publisher.
Identifiers: LCCN 2022024515 (print) | LCCN 2022024516 (ebook) | ISBN 9781799879237 (hardcover) | ISBN 9781799879244 (paperback) | ISBN 9781799879251 (ebook)
Subjects: LCSH: Juvenile delinquents--United States. | Prosecution--United States. | Criminal courts--United States.
Classification: LCC KF9812 .S26 2023 (print) | LCC KF9812 (ebook) | DDC 345.73/08--dc23/eng/20220801
LC record available at https://lccn.loc.gov/2022024515
LC ebook record available at https://lccn.loc.gov/2022024516

This book is published in the IGI Global book series Advances in Criminology, Criminal Justice, and Penology (ACCJP) (ISSN: pending; eISSN: pending)

British Cataloguing in Publication Data
A Cataloguing in Publication record for this book is available from the British Library.

Advances in Criminology, Criminal Justice, and Penology (ACCJP) Book Series

Liam J. Leonard
Winchester University, UK

ISSN:pending
EISSN:pending

Mission

Criminology has never been more relevant. Violence, serial murder, crime and victimization continue to remain an unfortunate staple of society. Crime is a key issue globally, nationally, and regionally. Law enforcement personnel within the criminal justice system must keep pace with ever changing modes of crime. As officials work to predict and prevent crimes, as well as apprehend offenders, they will need to devise new tools and strategies to preserve the safety of society and ensure proper justice is served.

The **Advances in Criminology, Criminal Justice, and Penology (ACCJP)** Book Series explores emerging research behind crime control strategies, crime motivation, new methods and the utilization of technology for committing illegal acts, criminal justice and reform strategies, and the effects of crime on society and its victims. The publications contained within this series are valuable resources for government officials, law enforcement officers, corrections officers, prison management, criminologists, sociologists, psychologists, forensic scientists, security specialists, academicians, researchers, and students seeking current research on international crime.

Coverage

- Drug Trafficking
- Gaming
- Social Media and Crime
- Prisons
- Criminal Rehabilitation
- Gang Violence
- Hate Crimes
- Criminology
- Law
- Hacking

IGI Global is currently accepting manuscripts for publication within this series. To submit a proposal for a volume in this series, please contact our Acquisition Editors at acquisitions@igi-global.com or visit: https://www.igi-global.com/publish/.

The Advances in Criminology, Criminal Justice, and Penology (ACCJP) Book Series (ISSN pending) is published by IGI Global, 701 E. Chocolate Avenue, Hershey, PA 17033-1240, USA, www.igi-global.com. This series is composed of titles available for purchase individually; each title is edited to be contextually exclusive from any other title within the series. For pricing and ordering information please visit https://www.igi-global.com/book-series/advances-criminology-criminal-justice-penology/212650. Postmaster: Send all address changes to above address.

Titles in this Series

For a list of additional titles in this series, please visit:
www.igi-global.com/book-series/advances-criminology-criminal-justice-penology/212650

Cases on Crimes, Investigations, and Media Coverage
Liam James Leonard (University of Winchster, UK)
Information Science Reference • ©2023 • 254pp • H/C (ISBN: 9781799896685) • US $215.00

Paths to the Prevention and Detection of Human Trafficking
Sharon K. Andrews (University of Houston-Clear Lake, USA) and Caroline M. Crawford (University of Houston-Clear ake, USA)
Information Science Reference • ©2022 • 422pp • H/C (ISBN: 9781668439265) • US $215.00

Comparative Criminology Across Western and African Perspectives
Simeon P. Sungi (United States International University-Africa, Kenya) and Nabil Ouassini (Prairie View A&M University, USA)
Information Science Reference • ©2022 • 322pp • H/C (ISBN: 9781799828563) • US $250.00

Handbook of Research on Present and Future Paradigms in Human Trafficking
Essien D. Essien (University of Uyo, Nigeria)
Information Science Reference • ©2022 • 488pp • H/C (ISBN: 9781799892823) • US $295.00

Global Perspectives on Reforming the Criminal Justice System
Michael Pittaro (American Military University, USA)
Information Science Reference • ©2021 • 380pp • H/C (ISBN: 9781799868842) • US $215.00

Interventions, Training, and Technologies for Improved Police Well-Being and Performance
Eamonn Patrick Arble (Department of Psychology, Eastern Michigan University, USA) and Bengt B. Arnetz (College of Human Medicine, Michigan State University, USA)
Information Science Reference • ©2021 • 278pp • H/C (ISBN: 9781799868200) • US $215.00

Invisible Victims and the Pursuit of Justice Analyzing Frequently Victimized Yet Rarely Discussed Populations
Raleigh Blasdell (North Central College, USA) Laura Krieger-Sample (Southeast Missouri State University, USA) and Michelle Kilburn (Southeast Missouri State University, USA)
Information Science Reference • ©2021 • 474pp • H/C (ISBN: 9781799873488) • US $215.00

IGI Global
PUBLISHER of TIMELY KNOWLEDGE

701 East Chocolate Avenue, Hershey, PA 17033, USA
Tel: 717-533-8845 x100 • Fax: 717-533-8661
E-Mail: cust@igi-global.com • www.igi-global.com

Table of Contents

RESPONDING TO THE VIOLENT OFFENSES OF YOUTHS WHO
HAVE NO FEAR
IS DAUNTING.

RESPONDING TO THE VIOLENT OFFENSES OF YOUTHS WITH
NOTHING TO FEAR
IS TERRIFYING.

Preface: Putting the Book in Context

When thinking of whose (and what) crimes we want juvenile court to address, there is an analogy to the family, appropriately enough.

When offenses are neither particularly serious/violent nor chronic we don't feel nervous about letting the family take care of the problem. In this context, juvenile court is properly seen as a court of last resort.

But at some point, the seriousness/violence or repetitiveness of a juvenile's criminality suggests the family should relinquish control, and that society will not/should not entrust the problem to the attention and limited resources of the family. In this context, responsibility for addressing and controlling/correcting the problem youth belongs to a "higher" power, namely, the juvenile court.

The same can be said of juvenile court and the limits society wants to bestow upon that institution. Juvenile court may be a court of last resort, but it surely is not a court of our only resort.

At some point, (due to its nature/limited resources) juvenile court should relinquish control and follow the lead of the family when particularly serious/violent, chronic offending is involved. In this context, responsibility for controlling/punishing that behavior belongs to a yet "higher" power, namely, the criminal court.

This book was written with that focus in mind. Society needs to rely upon criminal court to prosecute some chronic and violent juvenile offenders. There are, indeed, myriad benefits stemming from -- and purposes served by -- the prosecution of these youths' occurring in criminal court. These benefits/purposes are not voiced elsewhere. They need to be disclosed to inform the debate/consideration surrounding this vital topic. It is hoped that this work will indeed provide that critic information.

SECTION 1: PUTTING JUVENILE COURT (JC) AND TRANSFER TO CRIMINAL COURT (CC) INTO CONTEXT

Section 1 launches the discussion of transfer to *criminal court* (hereinafter, CC) by disclosing the lack of theory construction in the area. After Chapter 1 documents that dearth of theory, Chapter 2 assists the discussion of transfer to CC and the development of the book by suggesting numerous theories surrounded the introduction of both the *juvenile court* (hereinafter, JC) the original theory of transfer to CC. Chapter 3 completes Section 1 with a most important explanation of exactly what transfer to criminal court does and does not involve.

Chapter 1 has four objectives. The first objective is to set a foundation for what is at stake in transferring juvenile offenders to CC. The second is to address an *Anti-Transfer Crowd* (ATC)[1] criticism that transfer to CC exists in a theoretical vacuum, explained by something other than reason and logic. This chapter begins to provide a theoretical explanation for and defense of transfer to CC, revealing its logic and reason. This is the major focus of the work. The third objective is to explain that, although a good deal of the purpose of and benefits derived from transfer cannot be "proved" by social science research, that does not mean the purpose and benefits lack tangible and discernable outcomes that help maintain JC's existence. The fourth and final objective of this chapter is to lay out the organization and overall mission of the book.

Chapter 2 addresses the (Anti-Transfer Crowd's) ATC's claim that JCs were founded primarily to be diversion outlets for CCs. Although the current purpose of JCs might legitimately be identified in that manner, diversion from CC was not the exclusive, or even primary, motivation of the JC founders in promoting the JC's introduction in 1899 or in later explaining its critical role in resolving social problems in the first half of the Twentieth Century. Instead, as disclosed in this chapter, there were at least 20 other purposes that were as important, if not more important, than simply diverting juvenile offenders from CC. Understanding these 20 typically ignored "other" purposes helps the reader to put the original JCs and their operation into context. It also helps explain why transfer to CC would have been mostly irrelevant to the original JCs, which would remain the case for decades.

Chapter 3 accomplishes a critical exercise for this book and the field of transfer to CC. That exercise entails specifying what transfer *is and what it is not*, as well as *how it works and how it doesn't work*. Although this should be a relative no-brainer, this task has been complicated by misleading statutory wording, and by misrepresentations of the phenomenon in the literature. Before attacking *or* defending transfer to CC, it is essential that everyone be on the same page. It is (or should be) impossible to research and analyze transfer when there is serious variation in how it is defined. This chapter carefully details the *two* (and not three or more) *types of transfer* that exist, and the difference between transfer (or discretionary exclusion) from mandatory exclusion. The latter is often misunderstood and falsely portrayed as an example of transfer. It isn't, as this chapter explains.

SECTION 2: THE DISINFORMATION CAMPAIGN: FALSE ALLEGATIONS CONCERNING TRANSFER TO CC

The campaign to largely limit, if not completely eliminate, transfer has been extensive and all-inclusive. Virtually every aspect of transfer has been attacked, ranging from misreporting its (and JC's) history to misrepresenting nearly every aspect of its identity, elements, and operation. This Section is divided into three major parts. The first part, covered in Chapters 4 and 5 detail the very beginnings of JC operation and how its offender population changed dramatically by the 1960s; both chapters rely upon data from Philadelphia's JC. Chapters 6 and 7 explain the varied and numerous ways in which the transfer subject has been misunderstood and misreported; both the relevant terminology of transfer and its operation are considered here.

Finally, Section 2 details the (Anti-Transfer Camp's) ATC's initiative to reduce, if not eliminate, transfer to CC. While Chapters 8 and 9 address the ATC's movement to insist why juvenile offenders *should not be transferred to CC* (Chapter 8) or *cannot be prosecuted in CC* (Chapter 9), the last two chapters disclose how the ATC seeks to limit transfer (should its elimination prove impossible) by either minimizing those offenders eligible for transfer (Chapter 10) and/or permitting only judges to make the critical transfer decision (Chapter 11).

Specifically, the next eight chapters in Section II will address and debunk:

- the purported original design and purposes of JC (Chapter 4);
- how JC became a clone of criminal court, but long before the spike in violent juvenile crime in the mid-1990s (Chapter 5);
- the various incorrect ways in which terminology is utilized regarding transfer (Chapter 6);
- how transfer works, and, more important, perhaps, how it does not work (Chapter 7); and,
- at whom transfer should be directed and in which way transfer should be practiced (Chapters 8-11).

Unless and until these criticisms and complaints about transfer to CC are resolved, legislatures and appellate courts will remain misinformed and subject to the manipulation of the ATC.

Chapter 4 details the nature of the original JC via data from Philadelphia. Although all the data are from Philadelphia, the elements corroborate the declarations from national JC proponents, covered in Chapter 2. In other words, Philadelphia's JC likely operated very similarly to urban JCs across the country. The JC from the first few decades of the Twentieth Century bears little, if any, comparison to the JC of today. The chapter reveals a very young offender population committing obnoxious "offenses" rather than serious crimes. The original JC was committed to a morality crusade to maintain the chastity of girls, treating similarly behaving boys differently, and to informally resolving as many disputes as possible in the community, without direct JC involvement. JC was portrayed as the ultimate parent, denying defendants rights, while committing very few "offenders" and only to benign facilities/clinics. JCs were engaged in cleaning up families and communities.

Chapter 5 utilizes data from Philadelphia's JC to detail the ways in which JC evolved from a would-be clinic (with a family/community focus) to a criminal court (with younger defendants committing real crimes) from the 1940s to later in the century. Perhaps the most critical development was adding 16- and 17- year-olds to the jurisdiction, which became a common trait among JCs during the first few decades after JC was founded. The older youths brought more numerous and serious crimes with them to JC. This time period also experienced a decline in the use of benign facilities, and a corresponding use of delinquent institutions to house juveniles. Meanwhile, JC became more official, dependent upon trials, and rights-oriented. The JC became criminalized or much more like its CC counterpart during this time as Chapter 5 discloses. These changes in JC's nature resulted in making transfer to CC more relevant and necessary.

Chapter 6 begins to undo the damage done by the numerous ways in which transfer has been misidentified and mishandled; offense exclusion (OE) is the type of transfer that is most often and extensively mischaracterized. The literature guilty of spreading this disinformation is massive, which the tables included in this chapter reveal. The most prevalent misidentification is probably the most understandable, namely, that transfer means juveniles are being tried *as adults*. The first mission of the Chapter is to lay this notion to rest. Juveniles are not chronically transformed due to being transferred to criminal court (CC). There are actual transformations that do occur and they are explained fully. The second and more sustained objective is to remedy the many misidentifications of OE; there are at least nine of these. This chapter also details the two types of mandatory exclusion (ME) and distinguishes them from transfer, which often doesn't happen in both research and literature.

Chapter 7 continues unraveling the confusion in the transfer literature. This ATC misinformation deals with misrepresenting the effect of transfer, exaggerating its reach, and distorting its operation. Chapter

7 shows prosecutors' transfer powers are never unreviewable beyond the charging itself; excessiveness on the prosecutor's part is subject to nullification by a judge and/or jury at trial. The chapter explains how, contrary to ATC assertions, transfer is not sentencing; it is charging. Similarly, granting prosecutors transfer authority is not a violation of the separation of powers; actually, granting judges this authority arguably is. Although prosecutorial transfer (PT) certainly means the offenders' best interests are not paramount, that does not mean they are irrelevant. Even still, PT is not a rejection of JC, nor does it contribute to the criminalization of JC. Finally, Chapter 7 explains why transfer is neither inextricably tied to a crime rate nor acts primarily like a safety valve.

Chapter 8 addresses a popular ATC tactic in arguing for the elimination of transfer. The ATC has employed a couple of maneuvers, here. The first move is contending that a singular case that suggests or shows the possible inappropriateness of transfer is sufficient to claim that all transfers are wrong. Specifically, the ATC says that since juveniles are generally (more) amenable to treatment, and are less mature (i.e., culpable) and less deterrable than adults, they ***should not*** see CC. This chapter exposes the corrupt use of converting the singular and relative cases to establish a false categorical. The ATC also moves in the opposite direction in claiming that a categorical (e.g., OE) establishes the wrongfulness of transfer applied to a particular juvenile. Since violent behavior is supposedly normal juvenile behavior, this normal juvenile behavior should not qualify for transfer. This chapter debunks both false conversions.

Chapter 9 deals with the part of the ATC campaign that argues juvenile offenders ***cannot go to*** CC for two reasons. The first is the ATC claim that the best interests (BI) of juvenile offenders must always prevail, which, impliedly, means transfer can never occur. This chapter reveals how both segments of the sentence are incorrect. Nowhere in JC history has any reasonable authority asserted that the juveniles BI were sacrosanct and that *all* offenders must be prosecuted in JC. Also ironic is that there are occasions in which the juveniles' BI would be served by transfer. The second alleged obstacle is that juveniles, *en masse*, are incompetent to stand trial (IST) due to the same characteristics we saw in Chapter 8 that were engineered to establish their lesser culpability. Chapter 9 debunks this contention, including a thorough critique of the concepts and research relied upon by the ATC to make their claim.

Chapter 10 deals with the ATC tactic of limiting the reach of transfer to CC, assuming its elimination proves unattainable. The ATC mission, here, is to limit the target of transfer, especially in terms of age, offense, and disposition. A common claim is that only older (typically 16 and 17) delinquents should be transfer eligible. Inasmuch as the vast majority of transfers involves youths of this age the claim is mostly moot. Another argument is that only violent and person-related crimes should be transferred. This chapter emphasizes that the chronic offender, the most prevalent subject of transfer, would very likely be beyond transfer's reach under this formula, which was probably the ATC's goal. Finally, the ATC demands that transfer be limited to youths who "require" a sentence longer than that available to JC. Although this is a critical reason for transfer, it is far from the only/primary reason to transfer.

Chapter 11's focus is also on the ATC's transfer-limitation-mission, this time addressing the claim that Judicial Transfer (JT) is only the permissible method. To establish this position, the ATC falsely floats the idea that JT is a constitutional requirement. Chapter 11 establishes that since there is no constitutional right to prosecution in JC, there is no constitutional right to JT prior to prosecution in CC. Some ATC members strongly object to the amenability-to-treatment considerations inherent in JT, however, due to the nebulous and ambiguous criteria employed and the potential discriminatory outcomes invited. Although all ATC folks prefer JT to PT, then, only some are willing to embrace traditional JT. Stripping amenability from JT, nevertheless, leaves judges with the solitary chore of gauging offenses, which prosecutors can do well and better. The bottom line is that the ATC demands JT because they know certainly that judges are less inclined than prosecutors to transfer.

SECTION 3: ANALYSIS

Chapter 12 addresses the research that has purportedly examined transfer to CC. Just about all research has been limited to gauging deterrence. The research results have been mixed; some studies have found greater deterrence served by transfer, others have found less. Other studies have found sentences in CC that were longer than what JC could have imposed, others have found sentence shorter than the maximum JC disposition. The ATC uses the latter situation to "prove" that transfer is unnecessary. This chapter discloses the shortsightedness of the research, plus the serious methodological problems that compromise the findings, especially in matched-pair studies. Also identified are the very relevant factors that are typically ignored in the research. The chapter explains the promise of better constructed propensity-score research, which controls more factors and has found greater deterrence through transfer. The chapter finishes on a cautionary note to pro-transfer types not to expect stellar results from transfer.

SECTION 4: BENEFACTORS OF TRANSFER TO CRIMINAL COURT (CC): THE CASE FOR TRANSFER

This Section identifies the benefits attending transfer for JCs (Chapter 13), defendants (Chapter 14), and society (Chapter 15). In addition, the situations in which transfer to CC is not only appropriate but also necessary are identified. Jurisprudential rationales and principled legal answers in support of transfer and stating which youths should be prosecuted "as adults" are provided as well.

Chapter 13 details how transfer to CC benefits JCs. The first benefit deals with JCs' maintaining a positive public image (and acceptance). Simply put, transfer allows JC to avoid claims of being a never-ending-revolving-door for juvenile offenders or a place where juveniles get away with murder. Unlike CCs, JCs need that positive image because they are not indispensable. As important, transfer helps JCs' operation by preventing them from becoming even more punitive (and criminalized), which would likely require an increase in the rights afforded to defendants. Transfer also helps the image of rehabilitation, critical to the preservation of JCs; it allows rehabilitation (a reward of sorts) to be denied to rapists and murderers (among others). Rehabilitation's operation is also benefitted by not losing resources that would be spent for increased rights in JC, and by not having violent and chronic offenders clogging up facilities and compromising the treatment of salvageable youths.

Chapter 14 demonstrates the myriad ways in which transfer benefits juvenile offenders, especially, but not only, those retained in JC. The ATC *completely ignores* the fate of these juveniles; the ATC's focus, instead, is towards transfers exclusively. The JJ system remains more able to be committed to offering rehabilitative services because the worst of the worst, in terms of violent and chronic offending, are denied those services. Retained youths benefit from this. Jurisdictions' practicing OE offer retained offenders the potential benefit of facing a reduced charge that was arranged to keep the case in JC. Contrary to ATC assertions, some offenders will benefit from transfer, especially because of the increase in due process protections they should experience in CC; some youths might transfer themselves. Some adult defendants can also benefit by not looking as chronic and/or violent in their offending, and could experience greater opportunities for leniency as a result.

Chapter 15 itemizes the benefits transfer offers society. Like the benefits associated with JC and defendants, the benefits society realizes are mostly, if not completely immeasurable and, not surprisingly, have not been researched. One critical benefit is that transfer allows for a balance of society's and the juvenile's best interests (BI). If the no-transfer policy prevails and JC becomes all and only about juvenile offenders, there is little likelihood that the juveniles' BI will be operationalized in JC. Transfer allows a realistic prospect that JCs' and retained juveniles' BI can co-exist, which, in turn, serves society's BI. Transfer also promotes community protection, with the ability for CC to impose lengthy sentences for the severely violent and seriously chronic juvenile offender. Transfer and prosecution in CC also serves numerous important concepts and pursuits, such as justice, moral condemnation, proportionality, incapacitation, deterrence and retribution. The chapter concludes by explaining how prosecutors benefit by transfer.

SECTION 5: POLICY DEVELOPMENT

A popular R&B song from the early 1970s, written by Philly's Gamble and Huff, "Now That We Found Love What Are We Gonna Do With It?" was recorded by Philly-based The O'Jays on their Ship Ahoy album (reprised by both Third World and Heavy D & the Boyz). So, with the viability and the desirability of CC transfer established, what are we gonna do with it?

Chapter 16 begins by very briefly revisiting the misinformation that dominates the transfer literature (see Chapters 6-11), and by briefly reaffirming the dimensions of transfer identified in Chapter 3. The chapter then explains the three tasks associated with developing transfer policy: 1) choosing an option, such as no transfer, no transfer, but serious modifications to JC, selective transfer, or total transfer (abolition of JC); 2) selecting a transfer method, such as PT and/or JT (assuming transfer is the option chosen); and, 3) discussing implications associated with the available policies. The chapter concludes by attempting to accomplish reconciliations in three contexts: whether there is a lack of fit between transfer and CC/CJ System outcomes; whether transfer should be backwards-looking (based on current offense and/or delinquent/treatment record) or forward-looking (based on future behavior forecasts, such as future dangerousness or desistance from crime); and, whether reverse transfer from CC should be available.

Joseph B. Sanborn, Jr.
University of Central Florida (Retired), USA

Acknowledgment

To the Thousands of Juvenile Court Workers from Philadelphia, Delaware, and Chester Counties (PA) (from 1974-1994):

from whom I learned a great deal,

with whom I witnessed so much, and,

to whom I dedicate this book,

Thank you for making this "outsider" always feel welcome during twenty years of work and research in your courts, and,

Thank you for your service!!

To the three professors who were most responsible for my selecting a major, a graduate program, a dissertation topic, a career, and a focus on juvenile justice. First, Dr. James McKenna of Villanova University, who recommended my pursuing a Ph.D. at Albany State. After I told him I did not want to relocate to Georgia, he corrected me and directed me instead to the New York version (SUNYA). Dr. Donald J Newman and Professor Fred Cohen from SUNY Albany (U. Albany, today) steered me towards studying and eventually researching juvenile court. The former had conducted the first comprehensive study of plea bargaining in criminal court, while the latter had specialized in juvenile justice matters. Together, they prompted me to conduct the first (and only) comprehensive study of plea bargaining in juvenile court. My gratitude to these three true academics cannot be overstated. Thank you, professors, and may all three of you rest in peace. You did good, guys!

A special thank you to Lisa Harvey. Lisa was the former juvenile unit chief in Philadelphia's Juvenile Court. Currently, she is the Juvenile Court Administrator. Lisa filled me in on the current practices in the transfer process in the juvenile court, confirming that the criminal court charging unit acts as a centralizing force in determining whether an excluded offense will be charged as such (sending the case directly to criminal court) or reduced in severity to retain the case in juvenile court.

I would also like to thank the reviewer who offered cogent recommendations in how to improve the book.

Finally, a special thanks to Michael Brehm at IGI Global for his guiding the publication of this book through its final stages. His help was critical, and sometimes life-saving.

Introduction

TWO INTRODUCTORY CAVEATS

As pointed out, deservedly and well by the reviewer, two important items need to be addressed prior to launching into the substance of this book.

The first concerns the focus of the text. It is primarily academic, especially with respect to disclosing the state of the *transfer to criminal court literature* and the misinformation contained therein. Nevertheless, the hope is that the practical arena, particularly those making the transfer decision as well as those contesting this decision, can and will benefit from a more comprehensive awareness of what is at stake in this critical issue. If nothing else, this book reveals a very comprehensive consideration of the pros and cons of transferring juvenile offenders to criminal court to stand trial. Those occupying the practical world need exposure to these pros and cons, as do those in the academic world. Thus far, that exposure has not materialized in either world, which inspired the development of this book. Also revealed in this book is that the decision to grant or deny transfer has serious practical consequences that require those making the decision to give it equally serious deliberation. Thus far, those in the practical world have been instructed by those in the academic world to consider only the potential negatives surrounding *transferring any juvenile offenders* to criminal court. This book concedes the presence of those negatives, but, unlike previous works, it also identifies the very practical negatives resulting from *not transferring some juvenile offenders* to criminal court.

The second item involves the potential impact of the principle of equity on transfer to criminal court. Equity is a huge concern today. Equity and its elements go far beyond the parameters of the transfer phenomenon. Whereas transfer and the desire for equal protection insist upon the "equal" handling of two "equal" juvenile offenders (by virtue of offense and record, at least), equity dives deeply into social and economic considerations on a societal, if not global, level. The latter considerations defy identification, as they could and should vary from one jurisdiction to the next (and from one judge/prosecutor to the next). Although valid and important/influential, these considerations can be neither predicted nor precisely gauged by any one observer. Consequently, this book will not attempt to account for national, let alone local, variations in the evaluation and exercise of the equity principle and its connection to the transfer decision.

Suffice it to say that this book was conceived and written from "neutral" offender behavioral and juvenile/criminal justice system principles. Equity concerns could certainly influence legislatures in drafting transfer policies and judges/prosecutors in operationalizing those principles. Both sources could decide that equity concerns trump one of more of the benefits associated with the transfer practice as identified in this book. While it is believed that the equity principle should not alter the dimensions of the benefits of transferring some juvenile offenders to criminal court, its precise impact on the future of transfer remains to be determined and disclosed in another book that remains to be written.

Section 1
Putting Juvenile Court (JC) and Transfer to Criminal Court (CC) Into Context

Section 1 launches the discussion of transfer to criminal court (hereinafter, CC) by disclosing the lack of theory construction in the area. After Chapter 1 documents that dearth of theory, Chapter 2 assists the discussion of transfer to CC and the development of the book by suggesting numerous theories surrounded the introduction of both the juvenile court (hereinafter, JC) and the original theory of transfer to CC. Chapter 3 completes Section 1 with a most important explanation of exactly what transfer to criminal court does and does not involve.

Chapter 1
Initiating the Transfer to CC Discussion

ABSTRACT

Chapter 1 has four objectives. The first objective is to set a foundation for what is at stake in transferring juvenile offenders to criminal court (CC). The second is to address an anti-transfer crowd (ATC)1 criticism that transfer to CC exists in a theoretical vacuum, explained by something other than reason and logic. This chapter begins to provide a theoretical explanation for and defense of transfer to CC, revealing its logic and reason. This is the major focus of the work. The third objective is to explain that, although a good deal of the purpose of and benefits derived from transfer cannot be "proved" by social science research, it does not mean the purpose and benefits lack tangible and discernable outcomes that help maintain juvenile court's (JC's) existence. The fourth and final objective of this chapter is to lay out the organization and overall mission of the book.

PART 1: THE DEARTH OF THEORY BEHIND THE TRANSFER DEBATE

Excluding defendants who are chronological juveniles from prosecution in the JCs that were founded to address their misbehaviors is a critical decision.[2] Elsewhere, exclusion has been called "the most intriguing and contentious topic pertaining to the juvenile justice system.... (and) an emotionally charged issue.... (Sanborn, 2003, p.198)." Prosecution in JC has serious advantages, such as relatively brief, rehabilitation-oriented sanctions, most likely situated in the community or, at worse, at an institution that could be nicer than the youth's home/community, and will most often operate more like a school than as a prison (Sanborn & Salerno, 2005).

Those excluded youths will most likely face trial instead in CC. The potential outcome awaiting a CC conviction is significant, although it can no longer result in a death sentence. The death penalty for juvenile murderers was abolished by the U.S. Supreme Court in 2005 (*Roper v. Simmons*). Nevertheless, most other CC sentencing options are still available equally to both adults and chronological juveniles convicted there. Assuming conviction, the youth will likely experience a punitive and lengthy sanction. If prison is involved, the youth will likely be incarcerated with adult, hard-core criminals (Sanborn & Salerno, 2005).

DOI: 10.4018/978-1-7998-7923-7.ch001

Whereas a juvenile court adjudication does not entail civil disabilities and can expire or be sealed when the youths reach adulthood (assuming no more arrests/convictions), a CC conviction is likely to be long lasting, if not permanent, and to be replete with civil disabilities, such as voting and licensing disqualifications (Sanborn & Salerno, 2005).

The high stakes involved in the decision to prosecute juvenile offenders in CC help explain the contention and emotion attending the issue, and account for the immense amount of disinformation and misrepresentation found in the literature on exclusion. Virtually every aspect of the phenomenon has been falsely portrayed, ranging from its history (as well as the history of JC's — see Chapters 4 and 5) to transfer's nature and effect, among other elements.

Transfer to CC (also called waiver and certification), a major way in which exclusion occurs (see chapter 3),[3] has received nearly all the attention of critics/researchers. It has been particularly vilified and misrepresented; this topic is the primary focus of the book. The literature attacking transfer by the ATC has been so voluminous and misinformative that any explanation of the benefits derived from and purposes served by it cannot occur until there is a lengthy and complete examination of the anti-transfer accounts (see chapters 6-11).

Defenses of transfer or minimal pro-transfer comments are rare, if not non-existent, at least among juvenile/criminal justice professionals and academics. The fact that all 51 jurisdictions in the United States (50 states and Washington, D.C.) provide for transfer partly explains this absence of support; no applause by pro-transfer practitioners seems needed when it is permitted in every state. Another explanation is that any academics who comment on the wisdom or necessity of transfer (unless this support occurs in the most limited capacity) are disinclined to do so because: they have a biased view of the phenomenon (transfer does not fit their ideology); they have consulted only a one-sided narrative of transfer in the literature (i.e., there are not aware of any positive features); or they believe (correctly) that defending transfer puts them at risk of being equated with those who support child abuse (literally) or domestic violence. Transfer advocates have cited only a limited number of reasons some juvenile offenders warrant prosecution in CC. This book intends to fill that substantive void.

Many critics of transfer have gone as far as to allege that transfer lacks validity and rationality. They often accuse transfer supporters of having nefarious motives. Beyond asserting that transfer is immoral and never permissible under any circumstances, the ATC's fallback strategy centers mostly around granting transfer the narrowest legitimacy and then arranging the research, complete with appropriately selected findings, that conclusively proves transfer fails to accomplish any positive objective (see Chapter 12); this default strategy is brilliant, if not disingenuous. The anti-transfer wagons have been strategically positioned and defy breaching.

Franklin Zimring and Jeffrey Fagan, two prominent representatives from the ATC, fault both sides of the controversy and claim the topic lacks "principled and sustained analysis." Even worse, "there has been almost no thoughtful analysis of the transfer problems…" (2000, p. 408). They reveal their bias as they criticize the shortcomings of their ATC compatriots' approach:

Those who strongly support juvenile courts have approached the waiver (i.e., transfer) issue by believing that youth welfare is always better served in juvenile courts than in criminal courts, so that the task of drafting standards or laws is to hold the practice to an absolute minimal level. Under such circumstances, it might not have been considered a profit-able enterprise to inquire about the appropriate principles to decide when transfer to criminal court should be chosen because many youth advocates believed there were no such appropriate cases… (Id.).

Implicit in this criticism is the suggestion that only ATC members strongly support JCs; in other words, to support transfer is oppose JCs. It is ironic that the exact opposite can be the case (see chapter 13).[4] Zimring and Fagan are searching for principles, just not neutral ones.

Zimring and Fagan continued their "analysis" of the transfer debate by alleging that pro-transfer people also have not contributed to the transfer debate:

For the last twenty years, there has been strong interest group support for substantial increases in the number of juveniles sent to criminal court. Has the arrival of protransfer interest groups led to principled dialogue on what sort of cases justify criminal court treatment? No, it has not; and one reason for the lack of principled analysis in recent years is that the protransfer groups are just as result oriented as their opponents (Zimring & Fagan, 2000, p. 409).

Although it is unclear as to exactly whom Zimring and Fagan were referring, it is highly unlikely that the remarkable expansion of transfer eligibility that took place in the latter half of the 1990s (which bothers them most) occurred without those seeking that expansion explaining to legislatures the need for (if not the theory of) facilitating the transfer of older, chronic, and violent juvenile offenders to CC (see Sanborn, 1996b). Nevertheless, it is almost certain there were no detailed etiologies or theories offered by the pro-transfer individuals as to why expansion was necessary. Again, this book intends to fill that void by providing numerous justifications, and theories, as to why maintaining transfer to CC is vital, especially for JC.

Zimring and Fagan concluded their account of the transfer debate by claiming both the ATC and the pro-transfer folks are guilty of having engaged in merely and "only an exchange of preferred outcomes... (2000, p. 409)." Critical of both camps, Zimring and Fagan contended:

The difference of opinion is really just about the desirability of serious punishment for adolescent offenders, not about the reasons for such outcomes. So the different preferences do not produce different principles for decision; instead, these two camps assume the correctness of their contrasting assumptions toward getting tough on juveniles and make any debate on waiver or legislative transfer into nothing more than a referendum on toughness. The prospects that such a shouting match will provide jurisprudential insights are pretty slight. There has been little or no reasoned elaboration about transfer policy in the legislative process (Id.).

While supposedly criticizing both camps in a fair and balanced way, Zimring and Fagan have ingeniously narrowed the debate to simply and only a matter of "serious punishment." This book will demonstrate that *serious punishment* is merely the tip of the transfer iceberg.

Theory-absent transfer practices have continued, as Zimring complained a decade later:

(W)hat justifies separate treatment for adolescent offenders should be an important and jurisprudentially thick discourse, but it is not.

*****

Transfer...is a jurisprudential wasteland. The gap between theory and practice in decision-making is huge....

*****

For the entire existence of the juvenile court, the waiver of some serious cases into a criminal court has been a practice in search of a theory... (Zimring, 2010, pp. 1-2).

Zimring and Fagan have not been alone in decrying the state of the art in the dialogue surrounding transfer to CC. Decades ago, ATC members Krisberg and Austin observed:

(T)he juvenile justice system lacks a coherent and consistent perspective on how to define those children who should be handled in special juvenile courts and those who require adult court referrals... (Krisberg & Austin, 1993, p. 6).[5]

This book provides a coherent and consistent perspective regarding the critical decision to transfer chronic and violent juvenile offenders to CC, historically absent in the transfer debate.

PART 2: THE REALITIES/LIMITS OF TRANSFER RESEARCH AND POLICY

Complicating matters even further (beyond the supposed lack of a supporting theory) is the ability to conduct research and to develop policy in the transfer arena. In the contemporary world of juvenile justice (JJ) and criminal justice (CJ) for any policy to pass muster it must produce a significant, tangible payback, which can be documented via research. The research, in turn, can yield *Best Practices,* telling us what is right about and what is wrong with the policy. Policies (and theories) that do not produce tangible and measurable utilitarian outcomes are considered suspect and vulnerable (see Howell, Lipsey, & Wilson, 2014; Lipsey, Howell, Kelly, Chapman, & Carver, 2010; Myers, 2013, 2016).

The literature/studies surrounding transfer policy follow this pattern. The ATC folks have dominated the transfer arena; pro-transfer types have been mostly silent. Not surprising, then, the policy linked with transfer has been extremely limited to give transfer as little applicability and relevance as possible. Thus, the literature and research in the area have tended to identify and examine only one possible, tangible payback obtained by the criminal prosecution of juvenile offenders. That is the potential for reducing recidivism via the longer sentences that can be imposed on those convicted in CC compared to dispositions and outcomes possible in JC. In turn, this focus has led to a policy argument that the only youths who should be transferred are those who require longer periods of incarceration than are permissible in the JJ system.[6] Although this perspective/approach is not incorrect, it is excessively narrow and shortchanges the benefits derived from transfer. It has also contributed to the dearth of transfer theory development.

As we will see (see chapters 13-15), there is an abundance of reasons/benefits to support the transfer of chronic and violent juvenile offenders to CC. However, some reasons are mostly, or completely, immeasurable, making research of the reasons often implausible, if not impossible: transfer's assisting/

improving the image of JC and its mission of rehabilitation are prime examples. This means that a good deal of the reasons favoring transfer require logic and a well-rounded perspective, if not a modicum of faith. This also violates the psyche of social scientists who demand the *sound theory to sound research to sound policy* trilogy.

In the previous section, we addressed the absence of theory in the transfer to CC field. While policy requires research that requires theory, theory, in turn, requires sound definitions and understandings of the phenomena. Transfer to CC has existed since the beginning of JC. Virtually every element currently associated with the prosecution of juvenile offenders in CC has existed for more than a century. Despite this, there is still confusion and distortion surrounding the identification and research of what is an easily understood phenomenon (see Section II).

****

THE OVERALL ORGANIZATION AND MISSION OF THE BOOK

The first objective of the book is to provide a clear theoretical understanding of the early years of the JCs and their original purposes. This understanding is critical to putting the history of transfer in context. The second mission is to detail specifically what transfer to CC is, and more important, what is it not (chapter 3). The third objective of the book is to correct the countless myths and misrepresentations concerning the original JC and its evolution (Chapters 4-5), and how/why transfer to CC did not factor into the original JC. The next mission is correcting the mischaracterizations and misrepresentations surrounding the transfer of juvenile offenders to CC, some of which will disclose what transfer is not (Chapters 6-7).

The next four chapters address the ATC campaign to eliminate, or at least to minimize the scope of transfer. Elimination is demanded because juvenile offenders either *should not go* to CC (Chapter 8) or *cannot go* to CC (Chapter 9) for a variety of reasons. Minimization is desired by either reducing the number of juvenile offenders who are eligible for transfer (Chapter 10) or by eliminating the two variations of prosecutorial and permitting only judicial transfer (Chapter 11).

Following an analysis of the research that has been conducted to date in the area (chapter 12), an exhaustive examination of the myriad reasons behind and purposes served by transfer to CC will be discussed (chapters 13-15). Finally, Chapter 16 develops a coherent and consistent policy of transfer and integrates how JCs and CCs respond to offenders overlapping the systems.

Importantly, this book expands the considerations in addressing transfer. The one-sided nature of the issue found in the literature does a serious disservice to a vast majority of juveniles and to all JCs. The big picture represented in transfer needs to be understood and reconciled. These considerations are critical for legislatures and courts to review in making decisions concerning the future viability of transfer.[7]

As two authorities noted years ago:

The ongoing debate about juvenile and criminal court line drawing must be informed by an appreciation of what is at stake for the system... (Bishop & Frazier, 2000, p. 228).

REFERENCES

Bishop, D. M., & Frazier, C. E. (2000). Consequences of transfer. In J. Fagan & F. E. Zimring (Eds.), *The changing borders of juvenile justice: Transfer of adolescents to criminal court* (pp. 227–276). University of Chicago Press.

Howell, J. C., Lipsey, M. W., & Wilson, J. J. (2014). *A handbook for evidence-based juvenile justice systems*. Lexington Books.

Krisberg, B., & Austin, J. (1993). *Reinventing juvenile justice*. Sage Publications. doi:10.4135/9781483326450

Lipsey, M. W., Howell, J. C., Kelly, M., Chapman, G., & Carver, D. (2010). *Improving the effectiveness of juvenile justice programs: A new perspective on evidence-based practice*. Center for Juvenile Justice Reform.

Myers, D. L. (2013). Accountability and evidence-based approaches: Theory and research for juvenile justice. *Criminal Justice Studies*, *26*(2), 197–212. doi:10.1080/1478601X.2012.709853

Myers, D. L. (2016). Juvenile transfer to adult court: Ongoing search for scientific support. *Criminology & Public Policy*, *15*(3), 927–938. doi:10.1111/1745-9133.12232

Roper v. Simmons. (2005). 543 U.S. 551.

Sanborn, J. B. Jr. (1996b). Policies regarding the prosecution of juvenile murderers: Which system and who should decide? *Law & Policy*, *18*(1-2), 151–178. doi:10.1111/j.1467-9930.1996.tb00168.x

Sanborn, J. B. Jr. (2003). Hard choices or obvious ones: Developing policy for excluding youth from juvenile court. *Youth Violence and Juvenile Justice*, *1*(2), 198–214. doi:10.1177/1541204002250879

Sanborn, J. B. Jr, & Salerno, A. W. (2005). *The juvenile justice system: Law and process*. Roxbury Publishing Company. Oxford University Publishing.

Zane, S. N., Welsh, B. C., & Mears, D. P. (2016). Juvenile transfer and the specific deterrence hypothesis: Systematic review and meta-analysis. *Criminology & Public Policy*, *15*(3), 901–925. doi:10.1111/1745-9133.12222

Zimring, F. E. (2010). The power politics of juvenile court transfer: A mildly revisionist history of the 1990s. *Louisiana Law Review*, *71*, 1–15.

Zimring, F. E., & Fagan, J. (2000). Transfer policy and law reform. In J. Fagan & F. E. Zimring (Eds.), *The changing borders of juvenile justice: Transfer of adolescents to the criminal court* (pp. 407–424). University of Chicago Press.

ENDNOTES

1 The ATC includes anyone who either completely rejects the validity or necessity of transfer to CC or accepts it in only very narrow circumstances, much narrower than is currently permitted and practiced.

2 A *juvenile* in this book is anyone younger than eighteen years of age.

3 Besides waiver and certification, transfer is also known as fitness, bindover, referral, decline, relinquishment, removed or designated (see Sanborn & Salerno, 2005, Chapter 12).

4 Zimring and Fagan granted their ATC compatriots a free pass: it is understandable ATC folks did not develop principles because the cause was hopeless since pro-transfer types have held all the power. ATC members *can be faulted* with having an overly narrow perspective in considering what is at stake in transfer (ignoring any impact upon JC and retained offenders). In Chapter 14, we will also see that the proposition that "youth welfare is always better served in JCs than in CCs" is both inaccurate and very dependent upon which youths are being considered.

5 Zane, Welsh, & Mears, 2016, also contended that we lack a coherent and rational transfer policy.

6 Not finding longer sentences in CC and/or a lack of reduction in recidivism rates among transfers are declared examples of the failure in transfer policy. Narrowing the policy discussion aids the claim that transfer to CC can be eliminated without negative repercussions.

7 Myers noted: "There may come a time … when the Supreme Court chooses to reexamine the constitutionality of juvenile transfer to criminal court (2016, p. 932)."

Chapter 2
Developing JC and Transfer to CC Theories/Propositions (T/Ps):
Original JCs

ABSTRACT

Chapter two addresses the anti-transfer crowd's (ATC's) claim that juvenile court (JCs) were founded primarily to be diversion outlets for criminal courts (CCs). Although the current purpose of JCs might legitimately be identified in that manner, diversion from CC was not the exclusive, or even primary, motivation of the JC founders in promoting the JC's introduction in 1899, or in later explaining its critical role in resolving social problems in the first half of the twentieth century. Instead, as disclosed in this chapter, there were at least 20 other purposes that were as important, if not more important, than simply diverting juvenile offenders from CC. Understanding these 20 typically ignored "other" purposes helps the reader to put the original JCs and their operation into context. It also helps explain why transfer to CC would have been mostly irrelevant to the original JCs, which would remain the case for decades.

INTRODUCTION: THEORIES/PROPOSITIONS (T/Ps): ORIGINAL JCs

One criticism of transfer concerns "the paucity of careful attention to matters of theory when discussing transfer policy…" (Fagan & Zimring, 2000, p. 3).[1] The overarching *Theory/Proposition* (hereinafter T/P) is:

Transfer to criminal court is designed to remove young offenders, who, due to their problems or behavior, are considered by a judge or a prosecutor to be too chronic, too old and/or too violent to be rehabilitated or punished within the sanctions/treatment programs available to the system (Sanborn, 1994a. p. 267).[2]

DOI: 10.4018/978-1-7998-7923-7.ch002

These juvenile offenders do not deserve immunity from criminal prosecution; they deserve to be transferred to CC. Not all juvenile offenders deserve relatively benevolent JC treatment.

The Original Purposes of JC And Transfer To CC

Proponents claimed that JCs were developed to address and remedy "the inadequacy and barbarity of our methods of dealing with the helpless and erring little ones," "to stop the spiritual slaughter of the innocents," (Schoff, 1904, p. 133). Society needed a JC that "protects and fosters helpless, unprotected childhood" who were

victims of environment, neglect, or bad homes.... Society ignores them. The churches giving millions to missions, yet blind, unconscious of the need at their very doors. No mother thought for those little ones; only the cold legal procedure of the criminal court (Id., p. 135).[3]

The ATC contends that JC was created to remove juvenile offenders from the harsh outcomes of prosecution in CC. JC's prime directive, then, was to serve as diversion of from CC.

Where once the juvenile court was to be a diversion from the punitive and rigid institutions of criminal justice, we have now been at work to divert youths from this first great diversion... (Zimring 1998a, p. 193).

*****

[T]he juvenile justice system provided alternatives to the harsher penalties meted out by criminal courts... (Sabo, 1996, p. 2431).

*****

[T]he juvenile court was founded not mainly as a means of facilitating intervention in the lives of young offenders but rather as a means of diverting juveniles under arrest from the harms inflicted by jails and criminal courts.... (Zimring, 2019, p. 31; see, also, Zimring, 2002; Fagan, Kupchik, & Liberman, 2007).[4]

Transfer to CC is portrayed, then, as a betrayal or refutation of what JCs were created to do. If accurate, this diversion purpose would seem to challenge the validity of transfer to CC.

There had been child-centered reform experiments preceding JCs, aimed at sparing a handful of juvenile offenders from the rigors of CC. Some CC judges imposed diversion-like measures on some juvenile offenders before JCs were created. To promote physical separation between juvenile and adult criminals, separate trial dockets were adopted within the CC. These initiatives were insufficient, however. To bring about meaningful child-saving an entire, self-contained system needed to be created. This new JC was child-focused: *comprehensive* in addressing *all* problems affecting youths, and *completely ameliorative* in solving those problems. The JC plan of wide-spread care and improvement of child, family, and neighborhood was essential in giving youths a chance to succeed in life as well as in erasing the causes of juvenile delinquency. None of this critical reform was plausible or permitted within the halls of CCs.

Thus, JCs were created not to impose *less punishment* than would be imposed by CCs, but rather to impose *no punishment*. JCs were created to allow some offenders to avoid the harsh conditions and soul-crushing experiences witnessed in jails and prisons. But the primary focus of JCs was to provide mostly non-offenders proper home-like experiences and parental rearing they were currently denied. JCs were created as youth/family/community rehabilitation agencies.

Punishment does not accomplish (developing the child). Education, help, love, and patient stimulation of the better instincts can alone develop that germ (of good). We do not consider the crime, we consider the child, and we have saved those whom even the reform schools feared to take, considering them prodigies of crime...(Schoff, 1904, p. 142).

Another JC attribute that speaks against its having a primary-diversion mission is that JCs were built in full preparation of having to accommodate single-offense youths on a sustained basis, and even more relevant, countless repeat customers. JCs were not "one and done" experiences the way typical diversion programs operate. Although JC founders were optimistic in believing they had the remedy to juvenile misbehavior, they were aware that some youths would require more than one or two or even three JC treatment attempts. Soon JCs experienced multiple recidivists within a single year (see Chapter 4). JCs remained faithful to permitting "obviously incorrigible" juveniles to witness mostly mild JC sanctions. Even if diversion from CC would have been thought appropriate in a particular case, it would never have granted repetitive applications of diverting a case. Only a separate court system, offering levels of increasing supervision and constituting something *categorically different and unique*, would be capable of such continual displays of mercy and leniency. JCs were created to fit the bill.[5]

While a diversionary purpose was not irrelevant to JC founders, it mostly was. If that was the primary objective of the progressive movement, that could have been accomplished from within CCs. There were 20 other *original* purposes (T/Ps, below) that were *more* essential to original JC operations. They explain that JCs were created as a Progressive effort at human and social engineering. The Progressives saw social problems as societal in scope, beyond that of an individual miscreant. The solution was viewed as requiring a societal-wide, deeply grass-rooted intervention designed to produce a massive renovation of individuals, homes, and communities. These 20 purposes, combined with the structure of the original JCs, made both *transfer to CC* and *diversion from CC* practically unnecessary and essentially irrelevant to the original JC.

There were two missions in the Progressives' ideology that JCs were to operationalize. The first was the ways in which JCs were to advance the cause of "crime" fighting. Nearly all JCs' attention was directed at pre-/non-criminal situations and activities that, if unaddressed, might eventually evolve into crimes. The statuses/behaviors were not criminal and did not constitute grounds for state regulation/intervention; CCs could not have addressed or sanctioned them. The second was the ways in which JCs were to engage in human and social engineering. Advances in the social engineering category would eventually reduce, if not eliminate, the individual, familial, and social problems associated with the former.

PART 1: JC'S "CRIME" FIGHTING PURPOSE

T/P #1: JC's *Control "Offenders" Typically Ignored by CC* Purpose

Creating JC was necessary due to society's neglecting juveniles charged with crime.

[T]heir menace to the order of society which disregarded them could not permanently be ignored.... (Lathrop, 1925, p. 290).

****

[O]ften they were let off because often justices could neither tolerate sending children to the bridewell nor bear to be themselves guilty of the harsh folly of compelling poverty-stricken parents to pay fines. No exchange of court records existed and the same children could be in and out of various police stations an indefinite number of times, more hardened and more skillful with each experience (Id., p. 291).

JCs enabled the founders to address and correct youth who had committed acts that CCs ***could not*** (younger than criminal liability; non-criminal conditions and misbehaviors); or, ***would not*** (very young offenders; very minimal offenses) ***address and correct.***

JC mostly addressed behavior that was being ignored by CC by necessity, if not by choice. JC enabled workers to apply some discipline in cases that would have been ignored and uncorrected. Most "offenders" would not have been brought to CC, let alone experience CC conviction or harsh consequences. They were not transfer-to-CC material, let alone subjects to be diverted from CC. For example, the original JC Act identified delinquency to include any child who

is incorrigible or knowingly associates with thieves, vicious or immoral persons; ... or is growing up in idleness or crime; or knowingly frequents any policy shop or place where any gaming device is operated; or frequents any saloon or draw shop where any intoxicating liquors are sold or patronizes or visits any public pool room or bucket shop; or wanders about the streets in the night time without being on any lawful business or lawful occupation; ... or uses vile, obscene, vulgar, profane or indecent language in any public place or about any schoolhouse; or is guilty of indecent or lascivious conduct (Illinois Juvenile Court Act, 1899, p.131; see, also, Tuthill, 1904, p. 2).

This statute was copied by all other states adopting JCs. Virtually every possible street-related behavior or entry into an unsavory location/business became fodder for JC legislation in every state (see Appendix, 1904). JCs created new "crimes" for which youths could not be forced to face prosecution in CCs.

The most intriguing juvenile "offense" did not require any behavior: idleness.

The boy who does nothing is a loafer and is cheating all his brothers and sisters in the world of the food he eats... (Murphy, 1904, p. 13).

JCs were designed to *clean up the urban streets*. To achieve this, the jurisdiction of JC ranged from attitude problems (such as incorrigibility) to obnoxious misbehaviors (such as drinking, gambling and playing ball in the street) to outright traditional criminal behavior (such as burglary, robbery, rape, and homicide). All of these situations called for the court's intervention and discipline. JC Acts suggested the intent was to apply to every child ever born.[6]

The corrective mission was furthered by JCs' addressing status situations, well beyond the purview of CCs. These youths were categorized as dependent or neglected; they presented a lack of proper parenting, coupled with the absence of adequate correction of misbehavior. Poor parenting would lead not only to improperly socialized/prepared adults but also to future criminals due to a lack of proper parental discipline. Both current delinquents and delinquents-in-the-making needed to be within the jurisdiction of JC. JCs represented "an attempt to restore their birthright to the children of misfortune," (Lathrop, 1925, p. 296).

JCs were to have the best of both worlds: superpowers to deal in myriad ways with all sorts of troubled youths with the caveat that truly criminal youths could be shipped off to CC.

Yet we realize that there are exceptional cases of depravity and viciousness among the young, and the State retains the right, by one section of the juvenile law, to consider any one of these (16 years or under) ***a proper subject for the criminal courts****, and may elect, in accordance with the procedure prescribed,* ***to prosecute such case in the criminal court****, subject to* ***all the rules and penalties of the criminal law*** *(Lindsey, 1904, p. 63, emphases added).*[7]

T/P #2: JC's *Prevention and Development* Purpose

Perhaps more than any other purpose *prevention* was the keystone of the JC movement.

The fundamental duty of society is to prevent the child from going wrong... (Mack, 1925, p. 318).

JCs determined whether the juvenile becomes "a good citizen or a criminal," (Schoff, 1904: 136).

The only effective way to check crime is at its source, and that is at the very first downward step in childhood. Wise treatment at this time will save the child, but unwise treatment or neglect will develop all the bad qualities, and the result will be a criminal against whom society must protect itself and for whose support it will be largely taxed (Id.).

Prevention was more important than punishment, which was not a successful reaction to crime since crime was on the increase, especially among the young. It was known "that the seeds of criminality in the great majority of cases are planted in youth," (Lindsey, 1904, p. 28); most in prison "are there largely because of uncorrected delinquency in childhood," (Id., p. 53). JC's

purpose is of course to prevent crime ***before crime is actually committed****; to correct, to aid, and assist those who might be criminals, or who might do a criminal act, to avoid falling into either misfortune. It deals only with children and those responsible for the fault of children. It realizes we can not have good men and women unless we start with good children... (Id., pp. 30-31, emphasis added).*

****

[T]he inception of crime is in the waywardness of misdirected children. It would take care of these children in adolescence, when character is plastic and can be molded as clay in the potter's hands. It would help to form character and not postpone the evil day in a bungling attempt to reform it. It is being done in some cities. It is a strenuous life... (Id., p. 31).

****

(JC) has every advantage while character is plastic, in the golden period of adolescence, to redeem ***a possible offender of the future*** *to good citizenship* ***before he has really become an offender at all...*** *(Id., pp. 51-52, emphases added).*[8]

JCs were geared to prevent the development of criminal behavior, or, failing that, the continuation or worsening of a criminal career. The goal was not to shield offenders from harsh CC punishment. It was to ensure that CCs remained irrelevant to juvenile offenders.[9]

JCs were charged with properly socializing youths whose parents were failing at that critical job. JCs developed youths into becoming model citizens, benefitting the parents who

soon come to understand they are to be more benefitted than anyone else by having their disobedient and bad boy transform into a good man, honest and industrious, the pride and support of their old age (Tuthill, 1904, p. 3).[10]

Criminal parents and mischievous children/merchants needed to be controlled. Inaction would exacerbate the ills of the urban area (e.g., "cheap dives and saloons of the lowest order") and its children (who scored weapons and alcohol, etc.). Nonintervention meant "anarchy."[11]

T/P #3: JC's *Repudiation of Criminal Law and CCs* Purpose

JCs operated very differently. CCs focused on the behavior that triggered their authority over the offender and in punishing that conduct. JCs focused on the conditions surrounding the youth that required more intensive and longer interventions. CCs were mostly backward-looking with a nod to future sanctions, JCs were mostly forward-looking with a nod to past misbehavior.

The PA JC Act emphasized the distinction.

(I)t is important that the powers of the (juvenile) courts in respect to the care, treatment, and control over dependent, neglected, delinquent, and incorrigible children should be clearly distinguished from the powers exercised in the administration of the criminal law (Appendix, 1904, p. 182).

JCs represented a parting of the ways with and repudiation of CCs.

The traditional administration of criminal justice is characterized by the theories of retribution, of determent, and of law as an inflexible body of rules. This attitude of hostility toward the lawbreaker and this supposedly impartial and impersonal character of justice... provide no principles for the eradication of crime, (or) for returning the delinquent to normal social relations... They are the causes of many absurdities and distortions in the criminal law. They accomplish neither legal justice nor social good.

This is why the traditional administration of criminal justice...spectacularly fails in the repression and suppression of crime (Lou, 1927, p. 1).[12]

JCs were willing to err on the side of intervening into juveniles' lives when *unnecessary*.

The court experience and realization of the restraining hand of the law,the lesson learned as to where fun ends and the law begins, is entirely sufficient; and while probably most of such city boys would become good men if simply left to home training, ***even without this court experience****, yet it is certain a large per cent would not. No one knows what boys will make up this per cent; consequently all must be amenable to the law.* ***We should make no distinctions.*** *It is indeed the satisfaction ofnatural desires unlawfully among children that is the very inception of criminality, and if permitted to continue unchecked is sure to produce evil results... (Lindsey, 1904, p. 95, emphases added).*[13]

This over-reach would not have been plausible in CC. A child is not protected "by discharging him because *there is no legal evidence to convict, as would be done in a criminal case* when we know he has committed the offense..." (Lindsey, 1904, p. 107, emphasis added). [14]

CCs were cumbersome/inefficient (rights), wrongheaded (punishment only), reactive only (no prevention measures), corruption breeders with misplaced priorities (focused on older criminal offenders only). CCs waited too late to apply ineffective punitive responses to confirmed criminals who had been ignored until after a criminal personality/lifestyle had been adopted. Society was falling apart; a *completely innovative* response to social ills was needed.

We must proceed on the theory that we can not overcome the waywardness of children by punishment and force. We must overcome falsehood with truth, dishonor with honor, impurity with purity, unrighteousness with righteousness, evil with good. This is and must continue to be the doctrine of the juvenile court. There must be love at the foundation of it all, and with this there must be justice... (T)here is no justice without love. ***The State in the past has not done this...*** *(Lindsey, 1904, p. 120, emphasis added).*[15]

The essence of JC marked a severe demarcation from CC.; Judge Lindsey (1904) explained:

The old process is changed. Instead of coming to destroy we come to rescue. Instead of coming to punish we come to uplift. Instead of coming to hate we come to love (p. 49).

****

(JC) has required more firmness and less brutality, more discipline and less retribution, more earnest interest and less indifference, more strength and less ignorant authority than ever before (Id.).

JCs sought to distance themselves from any connection to both criminal law and CCs.

The juvenile court is conspicuously a response to the ***modern spirit of social justice****. It is perhaps the first legal tribunal where law and science, especially the science of medicine and those sciences which deal with human behavior, such as biology, sociology, and psychology, work side by side. It recognizes the fact that the law unaided is incompetent to decide what is adequate treatment of delinquency and* *crime. It under-takes to* ***define and readjust social situations*** *without the sentiment of prejudice. Its approach to the problem which the child presents is scientific, objective, and dispassionate. The methods it uses are those of social case work, in which every child is studied and treated as an individual (Lou, 1927, p. 2, emphases added).*[16]

JCs were the epicenter of child saving and social reform, which required a separate court with plenary powers absent in CCs.[17] Prevention called for disregarding CCs (and their criminal law) because they required waiting for a crime to be committed. The CCs opened the door for guilty offenders to escape the system and to not receive the treatment they sorely need, until it was too late, assuming the treatment ever happened.[18]

T/P #4: JC's *Critical No-Rights Policy/Practice* Purpose

It was no mistake that JCs were granted plenary, if not shocking, powers.[19] Relocating juveniles into a completely different forum enabled JCs to operate without any legal constraints. The first JC Acts provided for jury trial and defense counsel, probably due to a fear that a total no-rights-approach could not pass constitutional scrutiny. Nevertheless, the expectation was that these rights would never be requested (Lindsey, 1904, p. 64). Any speculation about the ability of juvenile offenders to claim rights in their new forum was quickly and universally put to rest.

The Pennsylvania Supreme Court declared the *parens patriae* doctrine enabled the JCs to operate without providing constitutional rights. In *Commonwealth v. Fisher* (1905), Pennsylvania's highest court held that youths could be brought to JCs "without any process at all." Although *parens patriae* was completely inapplicable to what JCs were doing (see Sanborn, 2017), *Fisher* was thereafter cited as precedent by all state appellate courts in upholding a no-rights policy in JC. A decision without a legitimate foundation served as the foundation for all appellate courts' endorsing the no-rights formula.

Founders feared rights would interfere with JCs' objectives. An absence of rights might have been the *top priority* since, arguably, many of the founders' objectives could have been achieved within CC, *but for* the existence of rights. JC-sanctioned facilities could have been constructed to receive young offenders prosecuted and convicted in CC. Relying upon CCs, however, undermined the correction mission since many *could not or would not* have been convicted there. Moreover, a no-rights JC could correct youth crimes over which CCs had jurisdiction, but were actions CCs

most likely would not have been able *(having to prove guilt via trial) to* ***address or correct.*** [20]

Judge Lindsey (1904) proclaimed that JCs "never appoint attorneys to defend children. The court is their defender and protector as well as corrector," (p. 64). [21] The no-rights formula extended beyond the demands of trial procedure. The more prominent CC complaint was its tendency to either ignore juvenile misbehavior completely or to react to with only "a reprimand (that was) too lenient to command respect for the law… (Murphy, 1904, p. 11). The lenient outcomes far exceeded the harsh ones in the number of incidents, and this bothered the founders. Consequently, also pivotal to the child-saving cause were the potential length and malleability of JC dispositions that were not as likely, if even possible, in CC. An important aspect of the JCs' corrective agenda was the indeterminate sentence, which granted JCs much longer control over its offenders than would have been likely or possible in CC. With a maximum original jurisdictional age of 15 and a typical retention age of 21, virtually all youths were eligible for five years or more of control by the system. Non-offenses and simple violations could result in years of incarceration that would be unheard of, or illegal in, CC; even five or six (or more) years of potential incarceration for crimes, such as burglary, would have been unlikely in CC.[22] Rather than sparing offenders from harsh CC punishment, JC allowed for dispositions that could be much longer, if not "harsher," than CC sentences. Also, adjusting the disposition was invaluable and necessary for rehabilitation to succeed.[23] There were

no rules *for the period of probation. It depends on each individual case, on the home, the neighborhood, the environment, as well as the particular type of boy. A great many things must enter into the case, and it would be absurd, in our opinion, to attempt to enforce* ***definite rules…*** *(Lindsey, 1904, p. 92, emphases added).*[24]

T/P #5: JC's *Vital Operation in Secrecy* Purpose

JCs were to operate outside the scrutiny of the public and media, denying a right to public trial. Publicity was the enemy of rehabilitation; JC privacy ran until transfer to CC or adulthood.

To save children from lifelong consequences of childish errors, to check their feet at the entrance of the downward road and to set them upon the gently graded pathway leading to usefulness and happiness, to let them expiate a fault at their own homes under the surveillance of kindly probation officers, and to accomplish these ends without the publicity that tends to blast later attempts at well-doing, as well as to save young souls from the taint of contact with matured criminals, these were the purposes sought to be accomplished in the establishment of the juvenile court of Buffalo (Murphy, 1904, p. 10).

Guaranteeing the anonymity of juvenile offenders went well beyond any diversion from CC purposes.

T/P #6: JC's *What Happens in JC, Stays in JC* Purpose

Records of delinquency would be expunged following the youths' final contact with JC. youths who continued their criminality as adults would do so on a clean slate in CC. JC records were not directly factored into CC sentences. It is unlikely that a JC record achieved as a diversion from CC (let alone a JC record of many such "diversions") would have been similarly disregarded.

T/P #7: JC's *Recasting the State as Friend and not as Adversary* Purpose

The founders recast the state *as the friend of* the juvenile. The founders saw themselves as the ultimate parent to all wayward children, but they also viewed the JC as more than just a foster parent. The JC, as the State's representative, was the embodiment of love and affection for children.

[T]he care, custody, and discipline of the child shall approximate as nearly as may be that which should be given by his parents, and that, as far practicable, any delinquent child shall be treated not as a criminal, but as misdirected and misguided and needing aid, encouragement, and assistance (Lindsey, 1904, pp. 66-67).

JC judges were benevolently motivated due to experiencing a "moral awakening" that

caused a revulsion against the carelessness and indifference which formerly characterized the State in its dealing with children offenders... [The awakening] compelled us to realize that the attitude of the State in the care and correction of the child should be as nearly parental as possible.... It has awakened the State to see with clearer vision that the child is not to be reformed, but to be formed.... This should be accomplished as a wise and loving parent would accomplish it, not with leniency on the one hand or brutality on the other, but with charity, patience, interest, and what is most important of all, a firmness that commands respect, love, and obedience, and does not produce hate or ill-will... (Lindsey, 1904, pp. 51-52).[25]

T/P #8: JC's *Diversion from Rather Than Diversion To* Purpose

Allowing that JCs were created, in part, to serve as diversion from CCs, the question that is begged is: diversion to what? Diversion to a court system with a jurisdiction, procedure, sentencing ideology, and institutional network separate from and alien to CC? Diversion typically involves a satellite program providing services associated with and answerable to the relevant court, whether JC or CC. Diversion has not traditionally involved a referral to an independent and self-sustained court system, which, in turn, has its own array of programs to utilize as a post-conviction remedy, and employing its *own comprehensive diversionary system* as well. JCs certainly received some juvenile offenders who otherwise would have been bound for CC prosecution (and could be seen as having been diverted from CC). But not only were the majority of JCs' clientele ineligible for CCs, but also the CC "eligible" minority were intended to be *diverted from* JC itself. The latter case, according to the JC-as-diversion argument, would seem to constitute a *double diversion* in a single case. JCs were designed more to be the distributor of diversion than to be the recipient of such from CCs.

JCs were established as courts of last resort. Only when the home and school had failed would the JC intervene. "It should never be resorted to until necessary," (Lindsey, 1904, p. 54).[26]

Whenever the home is not criminal the child is returned home under the care of the probation officer. That is always the first choice. If the home is absolutely unsuitable, the second choice is to provide the child a home in a family rather than in an institution. The reform school and the institution are the last resort, only to be used when other methods have proved unavailing (Schoff, 1904, p. 141).[27]

T/P #9: JC's *Embrace of Probation and Enshrinement of the Probation Officer (PO)* Purpose

JC's diversionary mission was made possible by the unique role of the PO. POs were the essential feature of all JCs (Barrows, 1904, p. xii); they were surrogate parents. They achieved in the home/community what judges could not personally. Some of the first POs were "volunteers"

who can afford to give a little time to the boy or girl who may be placed in their charge. They are clergymen, doctors, lawyers, and business men, and broad-minded, charitable women (Stubbs, 1904, p. 150).[28]

The probation period sufficed in a "large majority of cases," making a return visit to JC unnecessary (Mack, 1911: 5).[29] The key to success was a positive "personal touch" by the judge and/or the PO (Lindsey, 1904: 151). The priority was to avoid institutionalization, as Judge Lindsey explained:

The principal purpose of the probation system is to keep the child in the home and keep it out of institutions. No institution is better than a home. It is better than thousands of miserable places of habitation for children, mistakenly called homes. The best institutions are those nearest like the ideal home (Lindsey, 1904, p. 123; see, also Mack, 1911, p. 5).[30]

T/P #10: JC's *Efficient and Effective Administration of Justice* Purpose

JCs had a positive, financial aspect. POs resolved cases without hearings. That was "convincing evidence of the wisdom, efficiency, and economy of such a course of treatment."

The fact that in a large majority of cases this treatment by probation officers, wisely and faithfully persisted in, has so resulted that it has been found unnecessary to have the child brought into court again is convincing evidence of the wisdom, efficiency, and economy of such a course of treatment... (Tuthill, 1904, p. 4; see, also, Mack, 1925, p. 317).[31]

T/P #11: JC's *Separation From all Adults* Purpose

The JC founders borrowed Nineteenth Century House of Refuge ideology (see Sanborn & Salerno, 2005) that held it was critical for juveniles to be separated from adults. JC founders expanded that separation in two ways: JCs would help *all* youths with problems (and not just mis- or undirected poor kids); and JCs built a court system (and not simply substitute housing facilities) that guaranteed a firmer foundation and an all-inclusive net from which no juvenile needing help would escape. JCs avoided "the contaminating influence of the jails *and the criminal courts,"* (Lindsey, 1904, p. 29, emphasis added).

Separation from adults within CCs still allowed for proximity to adults, and there were myriad other problems associated with separate trial dockets (see Murphy, 1904, p. 11), ranging from CC procedure to inappropriate sanctions. An entire court system dedicated to juvenile "offenders" exclusively was required to advance the cause of child saving.

The only way for JCs to operate effectively as substitute parents was to separate youths from their parents/families. JC tasks, including diagnosis and treatment, were accomplished without interference or contamination of parents/adults (see Lathrop, 1925; Skinner, 1904).

T/P #12: JC's *Only the Young Will Attend* Purpose

JCs kept older juveniles, more likely to be both chronic and violent offenders, apart from younger youths. The latter were less likely to be committed to a life of crime and were more susceptible to prevention efforts. Since the greatest mischievous age was perceived as between 12 and 14 (see Lindsey, 1904, p. 127), JCs were tailor-made to the audience most deserving of the JC's preventive measures; they were equally likely to be ignored by CCs. Moreover, a major part of the JC jurisdiction involved offenses due to one's age, such as truancy and running away that were irrelevant to older juveniles. The primary focus of JC did not apply to older youths.

It is very telling, then, that the states containing the three most populated centers in the country during the early years, New York, Chicago, and Philadelphia, created their JCs with a maximum age of fifteen.[32] The three states involved (NY, IL, PA) were among the first to embrace JC. It strains credulity to suggest that JCs were designed to spare "juveniles" from harsh CC treatment when *all sixteen- and seventeen-year-olds*, the ones most likely to be transferred to CC originally were eliminated from JC jurisdiction and purposely forced to continue facing CC prosecution and punishment, *regardless of crime and record*. These older serious offenders are the very ones that criminal courts were *least likely to ignore and were most likely to be subjected to harsh punishment*. JCs obviously were not created to spare them of harsh CC outcomes.[33]

T/P #13: JC's *Informal Community Conflict Resolution Center* Purpose

JCs helped establish informal resolution centers to settle disputes/conflicts in the family, the school, and the neighborhood. Informal complaints (ICs) involving minor neighborhood problems, such as broken windows, were prevalent. ICs were submitted to POs who typically reached a result that satisfied all parties. JC's attention was averted, unless an agreement was not reached or was violated. Formal hearings would occur in failed negotiations. Parents, relatives, neighbors, and schools, were frequent users of this more informal method of solving problems at home/school.[34]

This JC feature promoted efficiency/economy. POs settled complaints informally so that

the complaining victims of such lawlessness are spared the mortification of a more formal proceeding, and saved the expense of filing court cases and the trial thereof (Lindsey, 1904, p. 113).

PART 2: JC's 'HUMAN/SOCIAL ENGINEERING AND HEALTH MANDATE' PURPOSE

JCs were created to make humans better and to make better humans. "(T)he juvenile court rightly understood is something of an effort at man-building — character building," (Lindsey, 1904. p. 47). JCs tried to "improve and strengthen character," (Id., p. 54), and to promote "child betterment," while

the home, the school, and religious influences, supplemented by all the great social agencies that build up a community, is caring for and protecting the child life of this nation better than it ever has before. It is producing the noblest citizenship the world has ever known. These great movements for the betterment of our children are simply typical of the noblest spirit of this age, the Christ spirit of unselfish love, of hope and joy... (Id., p. 49).[35]

JCs were the critical lynchpin in coordinating a societal response to improvement in the conditions of children and the community as well as the critical inspiration for the expansion and development of social agencies that were geared to accomplish the same important mission.

T/P #14: JC's *Ultimate/Substitute Parent* Purpose

Parents frequently were identified by the founders as the cause of the juvenile problem due to a lack of "proper parental care or guardianship." JC judges cast the State as the supreme parent.[36]

[S]ince the State is placed above the parent and made the judge, as it often is, as to the proper discharge of the parental function, if it may assume it, as it often must, where the parent fails, then at least as great responsibility devolves upon the State as upon the parent to properly discharge every function, act, or duty toward the child, and as wisely and well (Lindsey, 1904, pp. 48-49).[37]

JC judges used parental power as they were "standing in *loco parentis* to the child."

I have always felt and endeavored to act in each case I would were it my own son that was before me in the library at home charged with misconduct... (Tuthill, 1904, p. 3; see also Hurley, 1904).

****

The facts are considered merely as evidence tending to show whether the boy is in a condition of delinquency, so that the State, standing in loco parentis to the child, ought to enter upon the exercise of its parental care over him (Tuthill, 1904, p.3).

Judge Cabot (1925) noted his "powers of the super-parent"[38] and that "the fathers and mothers have failed, or the child has no business there," (pp. 248-249). Under this guide/obligation, JCs adopted thousands of kids.

The founders believed youths had to be taught "to respect authority, to respect the rights of others, for their own good as well as that of others (Lindsey, 1904, p. 29)."

If the home in which this duty rests can not do it, the state must; and in performing this function, a purely parental one, it must frequently, deal with the home, the parent, and the child. The state must handle the problem as a wise parent should. It never has and never can do this through jails, prisons, and criminal courts. These things may be all right for adults. They are monstrous for children," (Id.). [39]

JCs served as a constant notice and threat that parental rights were not absolute. Parents realized "that if they do not take care of their children there are others who will," (Murphy, 1904, p. 15).

T/P #15: JC's *Operationalizing Contemporary Criminology Theory* Purpose

Part of JC's focus and purpose was:

- to operationalize positivism, which perceived offenders more as victims than perpetrators and society as a contributor to crime; poor parenting, delinquent associates, truancy, idleness and not working, various societal temptations (gambling, drinking, sexual promiscuity) were sources of or gateways to crime;

- to counteract what some (perhaps most) founders viewed as the societal threats posed by increased urbanization, societal modernization, poverty, immigration;
- to compensate for, if not eliminate, unfortunate hereditary characteristics of a changing and threatening poor urban/immigrant population;
- to avoid the labeling/stigmatization of offenders represented in derogatory titles, such as arrest, conviction, criminal and sentence, etc.; and,
- to attack and resolve all social problems through the wisdom and humanity gleaned through modern scientific tools, such as psychology and sociology.

JCs would "minister to the needs of those who suffer as the victims of heredity, environ-mental or broadly stated, social conditions," (Hoffman, 1925, p. 258), to effect a "correction of children without stigmatizing them with crime upon the threshold of life," (Lindsey, 1904, p. 120).

Poor parenting (or "wretched parents" as per Eliot, 1904, p. 164) caused problems.

It is really astonishing how little care and attention is given by many parents to their children. It is troublesome and tiresome very often for them to do their duty. The law awakens them to a realizing sense of their responsibility to the child and if not done voluntarily that it can be enforced by statute in a most salutary manner. If you read the section defining delinquency you will observe that there is hardly any kind of offense that a child can commit that the parent or others cannot be held responsible for (Lindsey, 1904, p. 68).

The community was also condemned.[40] Life was deleterious in cities: "thousands" of kids "go down to destruction every year in the cities of this nation," (Lindsey, 1904, p.71). Delinquents were considered blameless and not part of a "criminal class." "A child's environment, lack of home care, and neglect may lead him into crime…" (Schoff, 1904, p. 142).[41] Offenders were raised "in poverty, yielding to the glare and the life and joy of the roadhouses…" (Mack, 1925, p. 316).

[T]he fundamental duty of society is to recognize the causes that lead to the wrongdoing. The fundamental duty of society is to see what the economic basis is that brings the children into court and correct the economic wrong. Tear down your hovels and your slums… (Id., p. 318).[42]

Societal ills also explained the failures of the JJ system, such as unsuccessful probation.

Of course many are returned (to JC), but when one considers the squalor of the homes to which the children must return from the court, the vice, drunkenness, and criminality with which they are brought in constant contact, the evil surroundings and the natural weakness of youth, one can not wonder that many more don't slip and fall (Tuthill, 1904, p. 4-5).

JC proponents embraced other positivist criminology perspectives regarding crime:

[T]he child who has done something against the laws of the state is no longer treated as a criminal. The state no longer stigmatizes the child first and then attempts to save it, but takes it in hand as a wise parent deals with his child. Such a parent does not stigmatize his child by marking it with the brand of

criminality that will remain throughout life; he attempts to shield it, not without correction, not without care, but with correcting care (Mack, 1911, p. 678; see, also, Skinner, 1904).

Fortunately, modern times also produced the solution to social problems: social science.

Law is a living social institution, and there is no reason why it should not keep pace with the progress of the modern social sciences and incorporate and utilize the ideas, the methods, and the morals developed therein. It would seem strange if our criminal law, our law courts, and court procedures were still clinging to the medieval sentiments of vengeance despite the tremendous advances that have been made in these sciences. With the advent of the sociological school of jurisprudence of the present century, which advocates the unification of all social sciences, of which law is just one, law is no longer regarded as a self-centered, self-sufficing science, isolated from the other social sciences. We are realizing more and more that law should be conceived as a means toward social ends. This new conception of law compels us to take account of social causes and social effects in relation to social conditions and social progress. This is sometimes called social justice (Lou, 1927, p. 1).[43]

T/P #16: JC's *Multiple Targets* Purpose

JCs targeted more than just the juvenile. Essential JC features were exacting penalties against parents as well as against third parties, such as bar owners, etc. for the role they played in contaminating juveniles and society (Hurley, 1904, p. 9). JC had a societal reach, particularly in renovating the community (and the family). JCs placed "responsibility for the delinquency upon the parent and the home," (Lindsey, 1904, p. 48). Judge Lindsey noted that "parents and other citizens responsible are often fined and sent to jail for the faults of children," (Id.). He claimed within the first four years several hundred parents and others have been either fined or sent to jail (Id., p. 62). This accountability was "just" and reached the "root of the problem," (Id., p, 68).[44]

Parents and civilians sent boys to "saloons, gambling houses, and other evil resorts (Lindsey, 1904, p. 70)." At these places, youths would see men "engaged in immorality," (Id., p. 71).

In these cases, little can be done without a change of environment. But the conception of parental and social responsibility has led to the passing of a law in Colorado holding parents and others responsible for the moral delinquency of children. This law not only covers cases of parents criminally neglecting their children, or saloon keepers selling liquors to minors, but other forms of theft and depredation... (Barrows, 1904, p. xvi).[45]

The JC mission was aimed at benefitting the community while teaching youths the

rights of others and the respect they owe to the law intended for theprotection of all and their duty as little citizens to keep their neighborhood clean and its reputation above reproach, to banish lawlessness from their midst... (Lindsey, 1904, p. 95).[46]

T/P #17: JC's *Multiple Party Team Participation* Purpose

JCs required a team effort. The founders recognized their limitations. JC simply *cannot do the work of the home nor of the school; it cannot counteract the effect, even by heavy penalties, of parental neglect, of intemperance, overcrowding in the slums, the lack of playgrounds, amusements, and industrial training for children. Every investigator into the causes of juvenile delinquency has felt that in the work of child saving preventive work must be enlarged and strengthened... (Barrows, 1904, p. xvii).*

****

[JC] needs and demands the help, assistance and cooperation of the parent and the school, and with their aid, brings to bear such additional power as it may wield in the life of a child, to correct its evil tendencies... (Lindsey, 1904, p. 54).

Many juveniles referred themselves to the court; after a visit to JC, some youths returned to school and brought more offending youths into JCs (Lindsey, 1904, p. 114).[47] More than 150 boys over a two-year span confessed to Judge Lyndsey, without having been arrested, and turned in many other accomplices and troublemakers (see Barrows, 1904, p. xv).

JC work truly required the contribution of all.[48] JCs could not succeed

unless intelligent women give to the subject the same thought and care that wise, loving mothers give to the rearing of their children. Unfortunately childhood must suffer unless women recognize that a larger motherhood is required of them to care only for their own children. Until they give to every subject affecting childhood the mother thought and care, we shall see the same old system which has marred thousands of lives and made criminals of children who might just as easily have been made into good citizens (Schoff, 1904, p. 136).[49]

T/P #18: JC's *Clinic* Purpose

JCs diagnosed the medical, physical, and mental health conditions of youths.[50] JCs addressed the youths' physical nourishment and helped buy clothes and food (Lindsey, 1904). The clinic aspect of JC was a priority. JC Judges ensured that there had been a broad inquiry.

(There was) a proper examination made of the boy, physically, mentally, morally, as a whole personality, we want him to build up that personality, we want him to get into proper mental control, we want a whole personality...(Cabot, 1925, p. 250; see, also, Schoff, 1904, p. 142).

The founders saw a connection between physical condition and delinquent behavior.

By this system physical defects are often found to be the cause of moral delinquency, and so we have a physical department in connection with the juvenile court. Johnny has been a stupid, dull boy, and brought poor reports. We find that his eyes are poor, his vision defective. They said he was "poor" or "bad" because no one was interested enough to find out; no one cared... (Lindsey, 1904, pp. 87-88).[51]

The founders were concerned with juveniles' physical welfare as well.

The lack of physical nourishment, proper food, cleanliness, wholesome sanitary conditions, and sufficient clothing is hot only responsible for a great deal of unhappiness and suffering among children, but directly contributes to their delinquency... (Id., pp. 117-118).

Serious health and physical problems often resulted in hospital commitments.

JCs' incredibly broad jurisdiction and powers helped its workers reach a population of children unreachable and unassisted by CCs.

T/P #19: JC's *Educative/Rehabilitative* Purpose

JCs reinforced compulsory education laws by imposing sanctions for truancy. Youths on probation would report periodically, presenting a report from the teacher each time; JCs were partners of school (Lindsey, 1904, p. 32-33). JC law "furnished a connecting link between school and court whereby the school helped the court and the court helped the school," (Lindsey, 1925, p. 276). Lindsey (1904) proclaimed that the JC "should be regarded rather in light of a school than a court," (p. 119). JCs were a backup because "(i)t will not do merely to enact compulsory-education laws, to send the children to school, and to endeavor to make them learn," (Mack, 1911, p. 680).

There is no more important adjunct to the juvenile court in Denver than the compulsory school law and the aid rendered by the school officials.... The law, as is at present stands, is the joint result of the teachers' association and the juvenile court of Denver (Lindsey, 1904, p. 72).

JCs promoted job training and ensured that boys had manual work to complement and supplement school.[52] JC also imposed therapeutic-oriented interventions that sought to "cure" youth suffering from various afflictions and behavior issues. They improved the youths' lives and assisted in their becoming productive adults. The emergence of psychology bolstered the workers' confidence in their mission to cure juveniles (see Sanborn, 2003; Sanborn and Salerno, 2005; Sanborn, 2009a). Often, JCs issued warnings without other restrictions, keeping the youth in the community. Some were placed in foster homes, hospitals, child-serving/delinquent institutions.

The mission was to improve the living conditions of the offender, which often did occur. Education, rehabilitation, and non-punitive measures were not then available in the CJ system. Even industrial schools for juveniles, the juvenile prisons of the era, were dubbed "educational institutions maintained by the State and declared by law to be educational and not penal..." (Lindsey, 1904, p. 66).

T/P #20: JC's *Religious Crusade/Morality Enforcement, War Against Girls* Purpose

The founders' desire to enforce morality required JCs. The PA JC Act explained that

the ordinary process of the criminal law does not provide such treatment and care and moral encouragement as are essential to all children in the formative period of life, but endangers the whole future of the child... (Appendix, 1904, p. 182).

JCs were "one great moral improvement association," (Lindsey, 1904, p. 119), as well as "an aid to the home and the school in the moral training of the child," (Id., p. 54); JCs promoted

the moral welfare of its children. The value of the future citizen to the State depends upon a great deal more upon how well and how carefully his morals are guarded than how wisely his money is spent (Id., p. 63).

Accordingly, JCs were designed to ensure that the delinquent

is impressed with the idea that he must overcome evil with good and make up for his delinquency by being as decent and good as he can in the home, the neighborhood, and the school. (Id., p. 79).[53]

JCs were also representatives in a religious crusade.

The personal work is the main thing. It is said that St. Paul in arming the Christian soldier placed sincerity and enthusiasm above all things. Thus armed should be the juvenile-court worker. He or she should have the magnetism of Moses, the patience of Job, the firmness and love of our Lord and Master (Id, p. 48).

****

These great movements for the betterment of our children are simply typical of the noblest spirit of this age, the Christ spirit of unselfish love, of hope and joy... (Id., p. 49).[54]

JCs reined in young girls whose nearly every "misbehavior" was seen as immorality. While boys were treated as delinquent due to exuberance, girls were handled as immoral due to incorrigibility. Behavior was not required of girls; a status/condition would suffice. JCs spent a disproportionate amount of time labelling female delinquency as girls' acting immorally or in danger of becoming such. Similar behavior by boys was neither labelled as nor responded to that way.[55]

THE OVERALL ORIGINAL PURPOSE OF JCs

JCs were created to do work CCs *could not* do, *would not* do, or *would fail* in doing. That is why JCs needed to be created as brand-new forums separate and distinct from CCs. Contrary to the assertions of some, JCs were not all-inclusive, come-one-come-all forums, even for juveniles. Instead, JCs were selective in the offenders to whom they would offer their treatment efforts. JCs formally eschewed punishment and offered rehabilitation/salvation for "offenders." That 16- and 17-years-old criminals were omitted from that offer is neither puzzling nor cruel.

Finally, although it was not among the original purposes of JC, another aspect of the JC's original design also speaks against the argument that the primary, if not exclusive, purpose was diversion to spare young criminals from facing harsh CC punishment. Transfer to CC was available to JC from the very beginning (see Bonnie, 1989; Feld, 1987; Flicker, 1981, 1983; Fox, 1970; Hamparian, 1981; Kurlychek, 2016; Loughran, Mulvey, Schubert, Chassin, Steinberg, Piquero, Cota-Robles, Cauffman, & Losoya, 2010; Snyder & Sickmund, 1995; Stamm, 1973; Tannenhaus, 2000, 2004; Whitebread & Batey, 1981; Wizner, 1984; Zane et al., 2016).

Despite the incredible optimism with which JCs were founded (see Lindsey, 1904; Mack, 1909; Lou,1927), the most serious and the most chronic offenders were subject to being transferred to CCs from the very first days, thus removing from JCs the responsibility of addressing their crimes; the older ones did not even belong to the club.[56]

The 20 original purposes of JC identified here speak dramatically against the argument that JC was exclusively, or even primarily, created to serve as a diversionary outlet for CC. Contrary to Zimring's and others' assertions, then, the evidence is abundantly clear that the juvenile court *was* indeed founded "mainly as a means of facilitating intervention in the lives of young offenders" and certainly not mostly "as a means of diverting juveniles under arrest from the harms inflicted by jails and criminal courts," (Zimring, 2019, p. 31). Only a revisionist spin on history could support the diversionary primacy supposition.

REFERENCES

Appendix. (1904). In Barrows, S. J. (Ed.), *Children's courts in the United States: Their origins, development, and results* (pp. 165–198). U.S. Government Printing Office.

Barrows, S. J. (1904). Introduction. In S. J. Barrows (Ed.), *Children's courts in the United States: Their origins, development, and results* (pp. ix–xvii). U.S. Government Printing Office.

Bonnie, R. J. (1989). Juvenile homicide: A study in legal ambivalence. In E. P. Benedek & D. G. Cornell (Eds.), *Juvenile homicide* (pp. 185–217). American Psychiatric Press.

Bowen, M. J. T. (1925). The early days of the juvenile court. In Addams, J. (Ed.), The child, the clinic, and the court: A group of papers (pp. 298-309). The New Republic Inc.

Cabot, F. P. (1925). The Detention of children as a part of treatment. In J. Addams (Ed.), *The child, the clinic, and the court: A group of papers* (pp. 246–254). The New Republic Inc.

Commonwealth v. Fisher. (1905). 62 A 198. Pennsylvania Supreme Court.

Eliot, C. C. (1904). The change wrought by the juvenile probation system in St. Louis. In S. J. Barrows (Ed.), *Children's courts in the United States: Their origins, development, and results* (pp. 162–164). U.S. Government Printing Office.

Fagan, J., Kupchik, A., & Liberman, A. (2007). Be careful what you wish for: Legal sanctions and public safety among adolescent offenders in juvenile and criminal court. *Columbia Law School, Public Law Research Paper* 03-61.

Fagan, J., & Zimring, F. E. (2000). Editors' Introduction. In Fagan, J., & Zimring, F.E. (Eds.), The changing borders of juvenile justice: Transfer of adolescents to the criminal court (pp. 1-10). University of Chicago Press.

Feld, B. C. (1987). The juvenile court meets the principle of the offense: Legislative changes in juvenile waiver statutes. *The Journal of Criminal Law & Criminology*, *78*(3), 471–533. doi:10.2307/1143567

Flicker, B. (1981). Prosecuting juveniles as adults: A symptom of a crisis in the juvenile courts. In J. C. Hall, D. M. Hamparian, J. M. Pettibone, & J. L. White (Eds.), *Major issues in juvenile justice information and training: Readings in public policy* (pp. 351–377). Academy for Contemporary Problems.

Flicker, B. (1983). *Transferring juveniles to adult court for trial.* Institute of Judicial Administration.

Fox, S. J. (1970). Juvenile justice reform: A historical perspective. *Stanford Law Review, 22*(6), 1187–1239. doi:10.2307/1227960

Hamparian, D. M. (1981). Introduction. In J. C. Hall, D. M. Hamparian, J. M. Pettibone, & J. L. White (Eds.), *Major issues in juvenile justice information and training: Readings in public policy* (pp. 169–177). Academy for Contemporary Problems.

Hoffman, C. W. (1925). Organization of family courts, with special reference to the juvenile court. In J. Adams (Ed.), *The child, the clinic, and the court: A group of papers* (pp. 255–266). The New Republic Inc.

Hunter, J. D. (1925). The history and development of institutes for the study of children. In J. Addams (Ed.), *The child, the clinic, and the court: A group of papers* (pp. 204–214). The New Republic Inc.

Hurley, T. D. (1904). Development of the juvenile-court idea. In S. J. Barrows (Ed.), *Children's courts in the United States: Their origins, development, and results* (pp. 7–9). U.S. Government Printing Office.

Hurley, T. D. (1925). Origin of the Illinois juvenile court law. In J. Addams (Ed.), *The child, the clinic, and the court: A group of papers* (pp. 320–330). The New Republic Inc.

Illinois Juvenile Court Act. (1899). An act to regulate the treatment and control of dependent, neglected and delinquent children. *Illinois Laws*, 133-137.

In re Gault. (1967). 387 U.S. 1.

Kurlychek, M. C. (2016). Effectiveness of juvenile transfer to adult court: Implications from current research and directions for future study. *Criminology & Public Policy, 15*(3), 897–900. doi:10.1111/1745-9133.12240

Lathrop, J. C. (1925). The background of the juvenile court in Illinois. In J. Addams (Ed.), *The child, the clinic, and the court: A group of papers* (pp. 290–297). The New Republic Inc.

Lindsey, B. B. (1904). The juvenile court of Denver. In S. J. Barrows (Ed.), *Children's courts in the United States: Their origins, development, and results* (pp. 28–132). U.S. Government Printing Office.

Lou, H. (1927). *Juvenile courts in the United States.* University of North Carolina Press.

Loughran, T. A., Mulvey, E. P., Schubert, C. A., Chassin, L. A., Steinberg, L., Piquero, A. R., Cota-Robles, S., & Cauffman, E. (2010). Differential effects of adult court transfer on juvenile offender recidivism. *Law and Human Behavior, 24*(6), 476–488. doi:10.100710979-009-9210-z PMID:20195895

Mack, J. W. (1909). The juvenile court. *Harvard Law Review, 23*(2), 104–122. doi:10.2307/1325042

Mack, J. W. (1911). The state and the child. *Proceedings of the Academy of Political Science in the City of New York, 1*(4), 676–681. doi:10.2307/1172077

Mack, J. W. (1925). The chancery procedure in juvenile court. In J. Addams (Ed.), *The child, the clinic, and the court: A group of papers* (pp. 310–319). The New Republic Inc.

Mayer, J. M. (1904). The child of the large city. In S. J. Barrows (Ed.), *Children's courts in the United States: Their origins, development, and results* (pp. 16–24). U.S. Government Printing Office.

Murphy, T. (1904). History of the Juvenile Court in Buffalo. In S. J. Barrows (Ed.), *Children's courts in the United States: Their origins, development, and results* (pp. 10–16). U.S. Government Printing Office.

Pennsylvania Juvenile Court Act. (1903). No. 205, April 23, 1903, P.L. 274.

Pound, R. (1937). *Pauline V. Young, Social treatment in probation and delinquency (Forward).* McGraw-Hill.

Rogers, H. W. (1904). The Probation System of the Juvenile Court of Indianapolis. In S. J. Barrows (Ed.), *Children's courts of the United States: Their origins, development, and results* (pp. 153–161). U.S. Government Printing Office.

Sabo, S. (1996). Rights of passage: An analysis of waiver of juvenile court jurisdiction. *Fordham Law Review, 64*, 2425–2454.

Sanborn, J. B. Jr. (1994a). Certification to criminal court: The important policy questions of how, when, and why. *Crime and Delinquency, 40*(2), 262–281. doi:10.1177/0011128794040002007

Sanborn, J. B. Jr. (2003). Hard choices or obvious ones: Developing policy for excluding youth from juvenile court. *Youth Violence and Juvenile Justice, 1*(2), 198–214. doi:10.1177/1541204002250879

Sanborn, J. B. Jr, & Salerno, A. W. (2005). *The juvenile justice system: Law and process.* Roxbury Publishing Company. Oxford University Publishing.

Schoff, H. K. (1904). A campaign for childhood. In S. J. Barrows (Ed.), *Children's courts in the United States: Their origins, development, and results* (pp. 133–143). U.S. Government Printing Office.

Skinner, A. F. (1904). History of the Children's Court in Newark. In S. J. Barrows (Ed.), *Children's courts in the United States: Their origins, development, and results* (pp. 147–148). U.S. Government Printing Office.

Snyder, H. N., & Sickmund, M. (1995). *Juvenile offenders and victims: A national report.* U.S. Department of Justice, Office of Justice Programs, Office of Juvenile Justice and Delinquency Prevention.

Stamm, M. J. (1973). Transfer of jurisdiction in juvenile court: An A\analysis of the proceeding, its role in the administration of justice, and A proposal for the reform of Kentucky law. *Kentucky Law Journal (Lexington, Ky.), 62*, 122–199.

Stubbs, G. W. (1904). The mission of the juvenile court of Indianapolis. In S. J. Barrows (Ed.), *Children's Courts in the United States: Their Origins, Development, and Results* (pp. 149–153). U.S. Government Printing Office.

Tanenhaus, D. S. (2000). The evolution of transfer out of the juvenile court. In J. Fagan & F. E. Zimring (Eds.), *The changing borders of juvenile justice: Transfer of adolescents to the criminal court* (pp. 13–43). University of Chicago Press.

Tanenhaus, D. S. (2004). *Juvenile justice in the making*. Oxford University Press.

Tuthill, R. S. (1904). History of the children's court in Chicago. In S. J. Barrows (Ed.), *Children's courts in the United States: Their origins, development, and results* (pp. 1–6). U.S. Government Printing Office.

Whitebread, C. H., & Batey, R. (1981). The role of waiver in the juvenile court: Questions of philosophy and function. In J. C. Hall, D. M. Hamparian, J. M. Pettibone, & J. L. White (Eds.), *Major Issues in Juvenile Justice Information and Training: Readings in Public Policy* (pp. 207–226). Academy for Contemporary Problems.

Wilkin, R. J. (1904). History of the children's court, social division, borough of Brooklyn, city of New York. In S. J. Barrows (Ed.), *Children's courts in the United States: Their origins, development, and results* (pp. 25–27). U.S. Government Printing Office.

Wizner, S. (1984). Discretionary waiver of juvenile court jurisdiction: An invitation to procedural arbitrariness. *Criminal Justice Ethics*, *3*(2), 41–50. doi:10.1080/0731129X.1984.9991757

Zane, S. N., Welsh, B. C., & Mears, D. P. (2016). Juvenile transfer and the specific deterrence hypothesis: Systematic review and meta-analysis. *Criminology & Public Policy*, *15*(3), 901–925. doi:10.1111/1745-9133.12222

Zimring, F. E. (1998a). *American youth violence*. Oxford University Press.

Zimring, F. E. (2002). The common thread: Diversion in the jurisprudence of juvenile courts. In Tanenhaus, D. S., Rosenheim, M. K., Zimring, F. E., Tanenhaus, D.S., & Dohrn, B. (Eds.), A century of juvenile justice (pp. 142-157). University of Chicago Press.

Zimring, F. E. (2010). The power politics of juvenile court transfer: A mildly revisionist history of the 1990s. *Louisiana Law Review*, *71*, 1–15.

Zimring, F. E. (2019). *American Juvenile Justice* (2nd ed.). Oxford University Press.

ENDNOTES

1 Similarly, Zimring (2010) later argued: *The gap between theory and practice in transfer decision-making is huge at every branch of state government, and the poverty of judicial performance in waiver decisions and appeals is a particular disappointment.... For the entire existence of the juvenile court, the waiver of some serious cases into a criminal court has been a practice in search of a theory...* (pp. 1-2).

2 Transfer currently operates this way; it is more necessary because JCs prosecute older juveniles who commit more serious/violent crimes than in the JC's first years. Transfer imposes criminal liability on juveniles who do not deserve immunity from criminal prosecution.

3 Similarly, Denver's first JC Judge Lindsey (1904), explained: *That the State is simply devising a method of dealing with its wards, not as criminals, but as misguided and misdirected; as those who might be criminals some day, but in childhood not yet responsible, still in the formative period, and as needing the care, help, and assistance of the State rather than its punishment...* (pp. 62-63). The Preamble of the Pennsylvania JC Act (1903) shows the founders, believing youths lacked "proper

parental care or guardianship," wanted them to have no "contact with crime and criminals," and to provide juveniles "treatment and care and moral encouragement" so that, "their evil tendencies may be checked and their better instincts may be strengthened…." (No. 205, April 23, 1903, P.L. 274, in JCAR, 1917, pp. 197-98).

4 The debate over whether JC was originally interventionist or diversionary is mostly irrelevant today. It is unwise to ignore history, but it is unwise to revise it, too. It is also unwise to be restricted to it. Contemporary policies need to be connected to contemporary realities rather than to be anchored in romantic and nostalgic (not to mention, inaccurate) accounts of the past.

5 JCs were to stand specifically in opposition to the *punishment and repression* of CC: *It must not be supposed that the juvenile court is only a smaller court for smaller offenders or simply a court holding separate sessions for such offenders; it represents an altogether different principle. The juvenile court is a life-saving institute in society…* (Barrows, 1904, p. ix).

* * * * * * * * * *

What has been most significant in developing children's courts in this country is the moral awakening of the community to a new consciousness of its duty to the child… (Id., p. xi).

6 In Manhattan/Bronx, mischievous youths were those who were: *arraigned because they engage in playing shinny (a form of street hockey), football, baseball, and other innocent games on public thoroughfares or build bonfires on the asphalt or other pavements. These acts are, of course, innocent in themselves, but are prohibited in the interest of the safety of life, limb, or property in our crowded streets…* (Mayer, 1904, p. 16). In Brooklyn, the "troublesome child" was one who: *teases and annoys the smaller children of the neighborhood…destroys the daily newspaper…uses the bean shooter...doing petty, annoying acts which make them a nuisance in the community* (Wilkin, 1904, pp. 25-26).

7 Moreover, JCs in many states, did not need to prosecute murder or even indictable offenses; CC prosecutors were given "first crack" at juvenile offenders (see, e.g., Skinner, 1904; Appendix, 1904). A maximum JC age of 15 also helped keep these numbers to a minimum.

8 Similarly, Judge Julian Mack (1911), an original Cook County JC Judge, observed: *One hopeful method of preventing men from becoming criminals is the method of the juvenile court. We are trying to save the child, so as to prevent the growth of adult crime* (p. 676; see, also, Hurley, 1904, pp. 325-326; Mack 1925, p. 314).

9 The Pennsylvania Supreme Court also noted this objective (and others) in *Commonwealth v. Fisher* (1905), the first state appellate court to uphold JC operations: *To save a child from becoming a criminal, or from continuing a career in crime, to end in mature years in public punishment and disgrace, the Legislature surely may provide for the salvation of such a child, if its parents or guardians be unable or unwilling to do so by bringing it into one of the courts of the state without any process at all, for the purpose of subjecting it to the state's guardianship and protection…. When the child gets there, and the court, with the power to save it, determines on its salvation, and not its punishment, it is immaterial how it got there. The act simply provides how children who ought to be saved may reach the court to be saved* (p. 200).

JC "stands for prevention" in order "that children by the cold processes of science can be saved from pauperism and crime and the fate of a wretched existence…" (Hoffman, 1925, p. 260).

10 JCs were invented to "protect the rights of others," and "to overcome lawlessness, secure obedience from the child, and respect for the law," (Lindsey, 1904, p. 54).

11 JC Judge Lindsey (1904) explained: *In this way incipient anarchy is checked. Until one has studied this question and observed the alarming numbers of such cases in the cities there can not begin to be any just appreciation of the tremendous importance of this one detail of the child problem* (p. 98).

* * * * * * * * * *

This source of degradation and pollution to childhood is almost impossible to eradicate, but of course it is generally confined to that portion of the city where the population is congested and opportunities for association and observation of crooks and criminals is constantly present. The only hope generally is to lift the child out of it... (Id., p. 99).

Growing up in the city meant juveniles' "little souls are absolutely stunted, deformed," (Id.).

12 Herbert Lou (1927) continued: *These principles upon which the juvenile court acts are radically different from those of the criminal courts. In place of judicial tribunals, restrained by antiquated procedure, saturated in an atmosphere of hostility, trying cases for determining guilt and inflicting punishment according to inflexible rules of law, we have now juvenile courts, in which the relations of the child to his parents or other adults and to the state or society are defined and are adjusted summarily according to the scientific findings about the child and his environments.... (W)e have now probation officers, physicians, psychologists, and psychiatrists, who search for the social, physiological, psychological, and mental backgrounds of the child in order to arrive at reasonable and just solutions of individual cases... (W)e tear down primitive prejudice, hatred, and hostility toward the lawbreaker in that most hide-bound of all human institutions, the court of law, and we attempt, as far as possible, to administer justice in the name of truth, love, and understanding* (p. 2).

13 Judge Lindsey (1904) further explained: *It will be observed that we pay very little attention to the rules of evidence. The whole proceeding is in the interest of the child and not to degrade him or even to punish him. We do not protect the child by discharging him because* **there is no legal evidence to convict, as would be done in a criminal case** *when we know he has committed the offense. This is to do him a great injury, for he is simply encouraged in a prevalent opinion among city children, and adults also, for that matter, that it is all right to lie all they can, to cheat all they can, to steal all they can, so long as they "do not get caught," or that you have "no proof" ....(W)e pay absolutely no attention to the rules of evidence. We get the truth and we are always sure we get the truth and nothing but the truth* (pp. 106-107, emphasis added). The focus in JC was to discover "every condition surrounding the life of the child," (Rogers, 1904, pp. 154-155). Misbehavior was "a mere symptom that a pathological condition exists..." (Id.).

14 Police wanted to remove the child from the community and not the causes of delinquency (Rogers, 1904).

15 Judge Lindsey (1904) criticized the "abuses, mistakes, and failures" of criminal law (p. 54). JCs relieved "some of the distressing conditions imposed by the criminal law," (Id., p. 31). *Because of infancy both the constitution and laws of the State and public sentiment will justify methods of dealing with children which would not be tolerated in dealing with adults...* (Lindsey, 1904, p. 31). Similarly, Cincinnati Domestic Relations Judge Hoffman (1925) proclaimed: (T)*he juvenile court was the first attempt in the history of jurisprudence to eliminate from the law the element of hostility toward the law-breaker and to substitute therefore a social objective* (p. 263). Chicago JC Judge Hurley (1925) also expressed disdain for CCs: *In the preparation of the (JC) bill, great care was taken to eliminate in every way the idea of a criminal procedure. The law was*

expressly framed to avoid treating a child as a criminal. To this end the proceedings were divested of all features which attach to a criminal proceeding (p. 327).

16 JCs marked a severe departure from CCs: *The true function of the court is educational. It educates the child, but it is also educating the community. Heretofore the child at a tender age has been amenable to the State; hereafter the State is to be in an important sense amenable to the child. In this great judicial, social, and educational work represented by the juvenile court, marking a distinctive departure in criminal procedure, the truth of the prophecy has been fulfilled: "A little child shall lead them" (Barrows, 1904, p. xvii).*

17 As JC Judge Hurley (1904) explained: *The principal feature of the juvenile-court law… is to transfer the care and custody of the person of the child to* **a court of original and unlimited jurisdiction,** *so that the court shall have* **sufficient powers** *to deal with the difficulties that surround the particular child, not only at the time it is brought into court and becomes a ward of the court, but at any time when it may be brought into court in the future to have its growing wants supplied by the court standing* in loco parentis (pp. 8-9, emphases added).

18 Often, complainants were unwilling to proceed, preventing CC prosecution. Police would simply release a youth. JCs were not hampered by these or other handicaps. The JC law in St. Louis required police report arrests to a PO. The mandatory reporting ended premature, dangerous releases of delinquents, and complainants were contacted at home by a PO. As a result, "(c)hildren who are thus drifting into evil ways are checked and restrained…" (Eliot, 1904, p. 164).

19 The Star Chamber's powers were inferior to the powers of JCs (Pound, 1937, p. xxvii).

20 Potential offenses were all-inclusive. Crimes and some juvenile offenses (truancy) were specific. Other misbehaviors, such as incorrigibility or "nuisance," lacked specificity and allowed JC workers to interpret any behavior as misbehavior. JC founders wanted no substantive (any behavior qualifies) or procedural (no rights/trial) obstacles to extending treatment.

21 JCs protected juveniles; they did not need protection from that protection. Rights were costly, taking resources away from rehabilitation; they allowed youths to escape treatment; and they are linked with crime not with delinquencies (Sanborn & Salerno, 2005, pp. 24-25).

22 *In re Gault* (1967) is an example. Fifteen-year-old Gault, adjudicated of making an obscene phone call, was institutionalized for up to five years in a juvenile facility for an offense that could not have exceeded two months in jail in CC. CCs either ignored delinquents or engaged in "cruel barbarism" by confining them with adults, disregarding their exposure to corrupt adult offenders. JCs prevented both extremes: delinquents would be neither ignored nor corrupted.

23 As Judge Mack (1911) explained: *The state intervenes for the good of the state and for the good of the child. The child is taken in hand by the state for an indeterminate period. This may in some cases extend until it reaches the age of majority. It may be for a very much shorter period. No attempt is made at the time the child comes before the court to determine how long the supervision shall last, because it is humanly impossible to know at that time how long that child is going to need the care of the state* (p. 677).

24 "A boy from half a home or no home, bad environment, constantly beset by temptations, and surrounded by evil influences," (Lindsey, 1904, p. 92) might not be "excused" from probation, even if all reports have been positive. A sentence could be ended early, assuming rehabilitation occurred. Early release enabled work with youths back in the community. These youths could be sent to foster homes or assisted in finding/learning to work (see Stubbs, 1904).

25 Judge Lindsey (1904) emphasized youths were expected to cooperate or face the consequences. JCs aimed to contain the spread of a juvenile misbehavior disease. *If the child can not be corrected at home, for its own good and for the good of society at large it is simply sent to a State public school, where discipline is superior to that of the home and where it is intended to correct its waywardness, and also, in so far as it may, serve as an example to prevent the waywardness in others. The purpose is in delinquent cases, to inspire and receive obedience, to improve and strengthen character.... We never release a boy upon probation until he is impressed with the idea that he must obey. It is explained what the consequences will be if he does not obey and keep his word. It is kindly but firmly impressed why all this is so, and why after all he is the one we are most interested in, and that it is for him we are working and not against him. We want him to work with us and not against us. He must, to do this, obey in the house, in the school, and of course he must obey the laws of the land and respect the rights of others...* (pp. 54-55). JC Judge Tuthill expressed similar thoughts and concerns (see Tuthill, 1904, p. 3).

26 In New York, JCs sent youths and parents home after they were properly instructed (Mayer, 1904, p. 17). "Monition and admonition are given to the child and to the parents as well..." (Tuthill, 1904, p. 4). Unlike CCs, multiple diversions/probations were possible in JCs.

27 JC founders disdained both adult and juvenile correctional facilities. Even the latter ended in youths "handicapped in life by the stigma of reform school odor," (Lindsey, 1904, p. 55).

28 Cook County JC Judge Tuthill (1904) revealed the vital role POs served in the JC: *The probation officer visits the home at frequent periods or requires the child to report from time to time at a designated place. This probation officer acts as a parent, and does in each case what seems wisest and best for him to do...* (p. 4) JC Judge Lindsey (1904) echoed this sentiment (p. 30; see, also, Rogers, 1904, p. 155).

29 Judge Lindsey (1904) claimed a 95% success rate in the first four years of Denver's JC operation (Id., pp. 50-55). JC Judge Stubbs, from Indianapolis, cited a greater than 90% probation success rate (see Stubbs, 1904, p. 151); a greater than 92% rate was cited in St. Louis (see Eliot, 1904, p. 164). Each PO had three youths to supervise at home/community (Rogers, 1904, pp. 156-157).

30 *Juveniles left to their own had little or no chance in life, but when assigned to a PO, a kindly hearted, broad-minded man of affairs, a man of character and standing, and a new world is opened to him. He has never known that there was anything better in life for him than the treatment he is so painfully familiar with....* (I)*f the kindly, thoughtful supervision is only kept up that boy can be saved and developed into a good citizen in nine cases out of ten...* (Stubbs, 1904, p. 150; see, also, Mack, 1925, p. 316; Rogers, 1904, p. 160; Schoff, 1904, p.141).

31 Philadelphia JC Judge Harry Davis relied on JCs' prevention mission to save funds. *The prevention of crime is more economical than either its suppression or punishment. The association of children with crime in the dock, in the van, or in cells can not fail to develop a class of men and women detrimental to citizenship and an expense to the treasury of the county* (Appendix, 1904, pp. 193-194). "The economic gain has been great" in Denver, according to Barrows (1904): *Judge Lindsey... found (savings) in one case to be $839, and in another case to be $1,036.76. An expenditure of $11.99 has been sufficient to take boys of the same class and by a change of environment under the probation system to make good citizens of them. The cost of sending boys through probation is small compared with sending them to institutions. The saving of expense in Denver in proportion to the number of trials and commitments made has exceeded $100,000* (p. xvi, citing Lindsey, 1904, pp. 33, 55).

32 By 1910, eight of the 14 largest cities (New York, Chicago, Philadelphia, Baltimore, Pittsburgh, Buffalo, San Francisco, and Newark) and 12 states had a maximum JC age of 15 for boys. The other six largest cities (Detroit, Cincinnati, Cleveland, St. Louis, Boston, and, Milwaukee) had an upper age limit of 16 for boys; 16 states and D.C. observed this age limit. Only Louisiana, Nebraska, and Oregon had a maximum age of 17 (Tanenhaus, 2000, pp. 20-21, fn. 20, pg. 41).

33 Founders thought their principles would fail with adults. JC was about *true children. The hope of the future is in the children. If we will concentrate in trying to save them, we can afford, for the time being, to neglect some of the problems applicable to the adult* (Mack, 1925, p. 318).

34 Those living in urban areas could not easily approach neighbors and seek a friendly resolution of problems caused by the neighbors' kids. JC provided an amicable resolution. Poor urban parents, suffering from "industrial conditions," needed the help of JC ambassadors to work with their children. Poor urban youths needed an understanding corrector of delinquent behavior (Lindsey, 1904, pp. 93-94). Most of the obnoxious non-criminal misbehavior arose due to the complexities of urban living; playing ball in the street was an example of mischievous behavior that presented danger to both the ball player and pedestrians (and eventually motorists).

35 Similarly, Schoff (1904) observed: *Love for the child, patience, insight, and comprehension of child nature and its needs applied to the life of each child will revolutionize the world* (p. 142). Judge Martin, Philadelphia's first JC Judge, expressed similar thoughts: *My experience in administering the law in the juvenile court leads me to the firm conviction that the establishment of the tribunal is of inestimable value as a civilizing factor in the community* (Appendix, 1904, p. 194). JC was part of "the movement of human betterment," (Lindsey, 1925, p. 274). While on probation, "the child appears before the probation officer weekly with his hands and face washed, his hair brushed, and oh, marvel of improvement! — even his shoes shined…" (Murphy, 1904, p. 14).

36 This perspective, stemming from the *parens patriae* doctrine, was introduced by the Pennsylvania Supreme Court in 1839 (*Ex parte Crouse*). The doctrine was manipulated (see Sanborn, 2017) to let the state assume responsibility as the ultimate parent, substituting its version of parenting for natural parents alleged to be failing. The substitution was not always forced. As in *Crouse,* parents often referred children to JC, dumping their children on the system.

37 Similarly, Philadelphia JC Judge Beitler commented: *The juvenile court supplies the rational method of dealing with juvenile delinquencies — the method adopted in the family — correction and oversight. It is the ounce of prevention. It gives the boy another, a new, and a better chance. It gives him, often, the first chance he has ever had to get into the straight path. It supplements the parents' efforts, often doing what the parent would like to do, but through ignorance fails to do…* (Appendix, 1904, pp. 194-195).

38 JC Judge Cabot (1925) also noted: *The court is empowered and has the duty to act as a parent should for the welfare of the child, and the court must exercise these powers through intimate talks with the child…* (p. 246).

* * * * * * * * * *

The true function of the court is to act really as a parent from the moment you first have the child, to inspire confidence and trust, not sentimental confidences, but faith that they are going to get through and get through whole… (Id., p. 252).

* * * * * * * * * *

(I)*f it is to proceed as a wise, understanding parent, if it is to have an understanding of the child in various relationships: in relationship to himself — that is to his physical, mental and moral make-up — his characteristics, his history and development. It should have an understanding of the child in relationship to his family, guardian and others; an understanding of mutual duties, services, privileges; an understanding of the child in relation to his former education, to school, to his work; an understanding of the child in relationship to the use of his leisure time, to his reading, his play, his companionship, his friends, his clothes; an understanding of him in relationship to his aims and his ideals, his spiritual aspirations...* (Id., p. 247).

Judge Mack (1911) from Cook County JC uttered similar thoughts (p. 676; see, also, Mack, 1925, p. 312).

39 Parents could not solve the problems of their children due to homelessness/poverty or due to being "intemperate, shiftless, or dishonest … thieves, beggars, or vagrants," (Mayer, 1904, p. 20).

40 As JC Judge Hurley (1904) proclaimed: *Reformers throughout the United States realized that the worm in the bed, the poison that was destroying the life of good citizenship, the moth that was gnawing at the fabric of human society until it was becoming tattered and disreputable was the fact that the rising generation was growing up surrounded by seasoned vice and hardened criminality. They realized, too, that if the crime disease should ever be destroyed the work of fumigation must begin in the homes and with the children, and they must be cured by being educated and loved out of their ignorance and desolation* (p. 7)

Other observers echoed these thoughts: *Another result of juvenile courts has been to reveal the sources of contamination of child life as they were never revealed before. It has been found that the children returned to court and committed are delinquents owing largely to evil surroundings and the vice and drunkenness with which they are brought into contact...* (Barrows, 1904, p. xvi).

* * * * * * * * * *

A boy who has lived in an environment of vice and degradation, who has been repeatedly sent to the nearest saloon after a bucket of beer which is consumed in his presence by the family, who listens to quarrels and often witnesses a fight between his father and mother, who is kicked and cuffed out of the house and often ordered to steal coal for the kitchen stove, which sometimes affords the only heat in the house, such a boy has but a poor chance in life without some outside assistance... (Stubbs, 1904, p. 150).

* * * * * * * * * *

(T)*he violation of social law... is produced mainly through association with lawlessness and vice, so regeneration can be wrought only through close and persistent contact with integrity and purity...* (Rogers, 1904, p. 156).

41 Urban life was threatened. JCs were "intended primarily for the large cities where the problem of the children is very different from that of the smaller towns," (Lindsey, 1904, p. 62).

42 The pursuit of equity was a duty of society that could and would be furthered by JCs. *The aim, object and purpose of the State is, primarily, to adjust the differences existing between its citizens, and to provide for the wants and necessities of its dependents...* (Hurley, 1925, p. 320).

43 Herbert Lou (1927) continued: *The juvenile court is conspicuously a response to the modern spirit of social justice. It is perhaps the first legal tribunal where law and science, especially the science of medicine and those sciences which deal with human behavior, such as biology, sociology, and psychology, work side by side. It recognizes the fact that the law unaided is incompetent to decide what is adequate treatment of delinquency and crime. It undertakes to define and readjust social situations without the sentiment of prejudice. Its approach to the problem which*

the child presents is scientific, objective, and dispassionate. The methods it uses are those of social case work, in which every child is studied and treated as an individual (p. 2).
"Scientific" advances led to optimism that social problems were solvable. Probation was designed to determine not only the facts but also the causes of delinquency. It was believed,
to be the humanitarian and ethical method as well, because it seeks to remove those causes through the uplifting power of healthy, human influence. We believe that a juvenile court without a thorough probation system is both unscientific and unhumanitarian… The probation system was one of the first steps for the scientific treatment of criminality…(Rogers, 1904, pp. 160-161).
Idleness and truancy were viewed as precursors to committing crime.
Truancy leads to a dangerous form of idleness, deception, and disobedience in child life, and is, therefore, one of the chief causes of crime… (Lindsey, 1904, p. 74).
Juveniles' engaging in "useful trade or valuable work with the hands (will) do more to prevent delinquency than any other one thing…" (Id., p. 77). Lindsey (1904) noted he saw grounds,
for alarm at the failure of boys, in particular between 14 and 16 years of age, to do any kind of useful work… One of the greatest difficulties…is idleness. If not employed at some useful thing they are generally on the streets or in the alleys, the downtown public pool rooms and bowling alleys, engaged not always in wholesome play, but too often in the most demoralizing character of dawdling, idling, cigarette smoking, or dirty story-telling with absolutely no thought of work or the serious side of life. They are too constantly occupied with thoughts of "having a good time" and some rather perverted notions of what a good time is. Too many of our boys thus reach the age of moral and legal responsibility without the slightest conception of work…(p. 77).

44 Judge Lindsey (1904) explained: *To correct the child we must often begin by correcting the parent, improving the environment in which the child lives, and adding, as far as possible, good opportunities to its life. If the parent is careless and negligent, punishment is rather for the parent than the child. If the parent is helpless, or if the environment is such as to seriously hamper the honest effort of the parent, as is often the case; … then the State simply comes to the aid of the parent and the child* (p. 52; see, also, id., pp. 63-64). JCs also provided "help and instruction for ignorant, careless parents," (Schoff, 1904, p. 142). JCs, *made a continuous effort to educate parents to raise the standards of the home, and to keep children from committing the various crimes and misdemeanors which take them to police stations*(Bowen, 1925, p. 299). Dilapidated urban areas were the cause of delinquency and the targets for improvement: (I)*f we expect the child to reform it is only just and fair to improve such conditions as far as we can. I have visited the tenements and homes of the children of the poor in our largest cities…. The dirt upon the floors was actually deep enough to plant seeds in; the bed-clothing was grimy and filthy, and vermin more plentiful in the children's heads than anywhere else, while the atmosphere was fairly reeking…. The father deserted and gone, no one knows where; the mother soured, cynical, and melancholy, slaving all day as a scrub woman, and living, practically, in a hell on earth. Is it strange that these boys do not stay at home nights and are attracted by the bright lights and music of the cheap theaters and dance halls? Is it strange that they will steal money to enter such places, which are to them heaven on earth?…* (Lindsey, 1904, p. 118).

45 Barrows (1904) went on to explain: *The act as first drawn only permitted the punishment of* **parents,** *by fine or imprisonment, while they were responsible for the habitual truancy of their children. The present act makes not only parents but all other persons responsible either for the truancy or delinquency of the child. It provides that all parents, guardians, or other persons by*

any act or in any manner causing, encouraging, or contributing to the delinquency of any child... shall be guilty of a misdemeanor, and punished by a fine not to exceed $1,000 or imprisonment not to exceed a year, or both... (p. xvi, quoting Lindsey, 1904, p. 32; emphasis in original). Of the more than 100 parents that had been brought to JC over their children's truancy charges, fewer than five failed to become "regular school attendees" (Id). JCs "were holding parents to a rigid accountability for the faults of their children," (Lindsey, 1904, p. 32). A youth sent to a bar to purchase beer could result in legal trouble for the youth, the parent, and the saloon keeper.

46 The community was the target of but also the benefactor of JC intervention; urban areas were to become cleaner, more orderly, and safer. JCs would affect all these changes.

47 During a two-year period in Denver, 150 boys voluntarily came to JC and turned in many accomplices and other juveniles (Lindsey, 1904, p. 34). Lindsey reported 200 boys freely came to his JC; some were brought by other delinquents (Id., p. 127). Two boys brought in 16 others, who, in turn, brought in many more parents and offending civilians (e.g., bar owners). Another four boys "rounded up 44 others" and another 6 or 7 boys "rounded up 52 others," (Id., p. 114). Many JC clients served as neighborhood ambassadors, helping police find delinquents (Id., p. 106). Of the 1,000 girls in JC, more than 700 had submitted to the court's attention and help (Lindsey, 1925, p. 285). Lindsey was hailed as a "moral dynamo" (Barrows, 1904, p. xii).

48 Judge Mack (1925) saw it as,
the duty of the juvenile court judge to go out into his community, if not into the larger community of the country at large, and stimulate and arouse the people to a sense of their obligation to the wards who come into his immediate care.... If he or others would but go out and awaken the fine men and women to a sense of obligation to take unto themselves the care and protection of but one child and to give that child the kind of thought that a parent ought to give his own child, we would solve the problem (p. 316).

49 This viewpoint could be the origins of "it takes a village" and neighborhood watch.

50 An early major work about JC was titled: *The Child, the Clinic, and the Court.* The superior placement of clinic vis-à-vis court was not a misstep. The publication included papers presented by prominent individuals from JC and related professions who were jointly celebrating the 25th anniversary of the first JC as well as the 15th anniversary of the first Psychopathic Institute. Psychopathic Institutes had direct or indirect connections to JCs (see Hunter, 1925).

51 Judge Mack (1911) explained: *It may sound sensational to say that adenoids lead to the penitentiary, but they do. Take a youngster from a neglected home, or from an uninformed home, and suffering from adenoid growths. The schoolroom of course is over-crowded. ... (T)he teacher has more than she can attend to, and cannot give individual care to the child. The boy, nervous because of his defective breathing power, cannot do the ordinary tasks that are set for the children; naturally he gets out of harmony with his surroundings and begins to " bum " from school. There is not much fun in bumming alone, so he draws two or three others away with him. Mere bumming is not sufficient; it is more fun to break open a sealed car and to take things than to pick up things on the track, which might naturally be considered derelict property. The boy comes into contact with the police, and if, as has been possible only during the last ten or twelve years, he gets into the juvenile court, there is a chance that his physical defect may be observed and corrected. But if there be no juvenile court, and the boy gets into the police court, is found guilty of larceny and sentenced to a short term in jail, during which he mingles with adult criminals, the state is starting him on a path that too often leads to the commission of more desperate acts and ultimately lands him in the penitentiary,*

-and all through a failure to demand a correction of physical ailments in his youth (pp. 680-681). Judge Mack (1925) claimed juveniles needed a thorough examination: heredity, environment, physical, mental, and psychical make-up, before seeing a judge, who "must reach into the soul-life of the child…" (p. 315). Judge Tuthill (1904) saw juveniles suffering from contagious diseases, and other problems; he backed the JC's commitment to remedy these ailments (p. 5).

52 As Judge Lindsey (1904) explained: *We need ungraded rooms in a number of schools, and, in my judgment, more manual and industrial work. I know that this will largely reduce delinquency and truancy in certain neighborhoods…* (p. 122).

53 Numerous JC judges believed in the morality crusade.

The boy is sick — not physically, but morally…. We have before us an individual as the chrysalis, being formed. We want to assist in the formation…. His morals, his soul, his future as a citizen, and possibly a parent, are a great deal more important (than physical ailments) …. (A)nd so a morally sick child is of infinitely more importance, demands infinitely more attention, care, solicitude, patience, kindness, and firmness than a physically sick child…. (M)oral ailments have not only been neglected, but brutally treated (Lindsey, 1904, p. 87; see, also, Schoff, 1904, p. 141).

****

Should not the State safeguard the interests of its helpless citizens and provide adequately and wisely for their development physically, morally, and intellectually?... (Schoff, 1904, p. 135).

54 Judge Lindsey was not alone in perceiving a religious purpose in JCs.

(A)*ll men are brothers and all boys and girls (are the State's) children…. They deserve to be treated accordingly. It is only in this way that we shall come nearer to the teachings of our Lord and Master…* (Schoff, 1904, p. 120).

****

It is God's own work to uplift the weak and the fallen, and in this pro-bation care the more nearly it resembles His love and His patience for His children the more nearly will it approach the standard it should attain… (Id., p. 142).

****

(E)*ach one a child of the God who said, "It is not the will of your father in heaven that one of these little ones should perish…." The treatment given at this time will decide the future of their immortal soul….* (Id., p. 135).

****

It is well known that there is the taint of savagery in most of us, and though it is smothered and kept down by civilization, education, and the influence of our blessed Christian religion, yet let these be deadened and how easily we drift into vice and crime… (Stubbs, 1904, p. 153).

Most original juvenile justice (JJ) facilities had a religious foundation and operation (see Chapter 4).

55 The disorderly/incorrigible categories were interpreted uniquely for girls. Girls were only rarely actual criminals (see Chapters 4 and 5), but were "morally led astray," and were brought to JC by parents because "(s)uch a child must be saved against herself…" (Mayer, 1904, p. 22). And, although their "offenses" were trivial or nonexistent, girls were often committed to a delinquent facility or child-caring institution: *(F)reedom and the opportunity to be abroad either when going to or coming from work or school present ordinarily too many dangers upon which to experiment with the parole system…* (Id., pp. 22-23; see also, Wilken, 1904).

[56] In the 1920s-30s, progressive child advocates sought to eliminate transfer, which failed. As compromise, states agreed to raise their JC maximum age limit to 17. Legislatures also began to exclude serious offenses, such as murder and crimes punishable by death/life sentences (see Tanenhaus, 2000, p. 25); many other states had already excluded these offenses. It was understood and accepted early in the day that JCs were not expected to adjudicate all juveniles.

Chapter 3
Current Dimensions of the Criminal Prosecution of Juvenile Offenders

ABSTRACT

Chapter 3 accomplishes a critical exercise for this book and the field of transfer to criminal court (CC). That exercise entails specifying what transfer is and what it is not, as well as how it works and how it doesn't work. Although this should be a relative no-brainer, this task has been complicated by misleading statutory wording, and by misrepresentations of the phenomenon in the literature. Before attacking or defending transfer to CC, it is essential that everyone be on the same page. It is (or should be) impossible to research and analyze transfer when there is serious variation in how it is defined. This chapter carefully details the two (and not three or more) types of transfer that exist, and the difference between transfer (or discretionary exclusion) from mandatory exclusion. The latter is often misunderstood and falsely portrayed as an example of transfer. It isn't, as this chapter explains.

INTRODUCTION

The criminal prosecution of juvenile offenders (defined here as anyone under the age of eighteen) requires their *exclusion from juvenile court (JC)*. Youths can end up in CC only if they have been removed from the forum created to address their misbehavior, the JC. Due to the variety of the ways in which it can occur (i.e., the topic is broader than transfer), it is best to call the removal of youths from JC (or denial of entrance to JC) as *exclusion* from that forum.[1] Although this topic is straightforward and not complex, the exclusion of youths from JC has been misrepresented in the literature. The resulting confusion and misidentification of the material is so extensive that it is essential to first explain *what exclusion and transfer are and what they are not.*

DOI: 10.4018/978-1-7998-7923-7.ch003

MANDATORY EXCLUSION (ME)

Simply put, not all exclusion is created equal. There are two vastly different versions of it, each having its own rationale/justification, and each having unique implications for juvenile offenders. The first type is *mandatory exclusion* (hereinafter ME) where the choice of selecting a court in which to prosecute the juvenile was made *before* the youth committed the offense at issue. There is *no choice* in selecting the court, which is why this exclusion must be considered *mandatory* in nature. What has happened in this situation is that the "juvenile" has been redefined to be on a level legally equal to that of an adult (at least with respect to being prosecuted for crimes), and this transpired *prior to* the current criminal incident. When these juveniles left their homes the day of the current crime, they had already been converted to an adult-like status. Thus, there is only one forum in which these "juveniles" can be prosecuted, namely CC. Since mandatory exclusion does not involve any relocation of a case from one forum to another (the trial has only one place in which it can occur), it is not a matter of, and should never be referred to as, transfer.

There are two major ways in which mandatory exclusion can occur. The first is practiced in three states that have adopted a maximum JC age of sixteen instead of the more customary maximum age of seventeen. The thinking in these few states appears to be that seventeen-year-old offenders across the board deserve to be prosecuted for all offenses in CC; they apparently deserve to be denied any advantages potentially stemming from a JC prosecution.

The plain and simple truth is that it is the prerogative of a state's legislature to decide the proper parameters of or boundaries between JCs and CCs, and even whether to maintain a JC in the first place. Whether the boundary decision of an age younger than seventeen is wise or appropriate is a matter of personal/political judgment. Unlike transfer, this method of exclusion has been ignored in the way of research or discussion/debate.

Historically, this method of exclusion accounted for the vast majority of defendants younger than eighteen who were subjected to criminal prosecution. This is easy to understand since this type of exclusion means *every criminal offense* committed by individuals of these ages must be resolved in CC.[2] This exclusion is mandatory and is not an example of transfer. Rather, the charges have *only one path* that can be taken. Nevertheless, this brand of mandatory exclusion has been incorrectly labelled transfer (see Chapter 6 and Table 38 I). Most important, resolving any problems related to transfer (including its elimination) will have no effect whatsoever on this example of mandatory exclusion.[3]

The second brand of mandatory exclusion has been adopted by most jurisdictions. It involves considering all juveniles who previously have been transferred to and convicted in CC as having been permanently removed from JC jurisdiction for any crimes committed by them from that point forward.[4] This approach represents a "you can't go home again" attitude towards offenders upon whom JC has given up on trying to help.[5] By 2020, at least 34 states and Washington, D.C. had adopted it (Szymanski, 1996; OJJDP, 2020).

These youths are in the same legal context as those "juveniles" whose age is higher than the JC's maximum age. By virtue of their previous record, they are permanently regarded as criminals once they have achieved that CC conviction. Trial for these offenders' future criminal actions *must* occur in CC. Their cases have not been transferred to CC; JC never had jurisdiction over these current charges. These cases have been incorrectly referred to as transfer (see Chapter 6 and Table 38 J).

In this version of mandatory exclusion, some very young juveniles can end up being CC candidates for life. How young the minimum age is can be dependent on how young a jurisdiction allows transfer and how soon the youth can be convicted in CC (after transfer) and then commit a subsequent crime. This category has implications for the validity of research (see Chapter 12).

DISCRETIONARY EXCLUSION (OR TRANSFER)

The second type of exclusion is *discretionary*, which means the exclusion *does not have to happen* and is going to require *someone's choice* to transfer the case. That someone is a judge or a prosecutor. *Discretionary exclusion* is a synonym for *transfer.* The criminal case that could have gone to JC was sent or moved instead to CC. There has been a redirection or relocation (or transfer) of the case. These are juveniles; they left their homes the day of the crime legally defined as juveniles in every sense of the term, but, following the commission of the current crime, a judge or a prosecutor has selected CC as the proper location for trial.

Any case in this context *would have gone* (*would have to have gone*) to JC for trial, *but for* the decision made by the court official to transfer it to CC. Here, only JC had jurisdiction over the case due to the juvenile status of the defendants; CC lacked original jurisdiction over the case, meaning the case could not go directly there (as with mandatory exclusion cases). Rather, someone (i.e., a judge or a prosecutor) had to channel (redirect, relocate, or transfer) it there.

Although words such as *automatic* and *mandatory* have been associated with this version of exclusion (see Chapter 6 and Table 38 D), this is wrong since neither judges nor prosecutors can be forced to transfer any youth; legislatures cannot mandate such. Legislatures can mandate that the presence of certain conditions when *found or charged* by a judge or prosecutor (such as a specified age, offense, or record) can require a case be transferred to CC (making it appear as though the transfer is mandatory). For example, a legislature may mandate that JC *has no jurisdiction* over *first-degree felonies committed by anyone sixteen years of age or older* and that these crimes *must be prosecuted*, if at all, in CC. CC would have original jurisdiction over this type of case. That sure sounds mandatory.

Important, however, that mandate identifies a crime situation that must be *interpreted*. A first-degree felony does not exist until the prosecutor charges it as such. A particularly brutal rape may have all the markings of a first-degree felony. That does not guarantee that a first-degree classification will emanate from this brutal offense. If the prosecutor charges a second-degree felony, the mandate has been negated. Trial for that lesser charge would occur in JC. The same would apply if all murders were mandatorily excluded from JC jurisdiction such that murder could be prosecuted only in CC. That seems to be mandatory. But it takes more than a dead body and an intent to kill for that offense to end up in CC. A prosecutor must charge murder rather than a lesser included offense, such as manslaughter. Charging the latter offense would mean the case remains in JC.

In the two contexts, above, the legislature has necessarily left the transfer decision to the discretion/judgment of the prosecutor. In other situations, the legislature has left the discretion in the hands of the judge. Legislatures cannot transfer anyone by themselves even though they may employ language that makes it sound as though they are transferring certain juvenile offenders.[6] Instead, to move a juvenile's case to CC, legislatures must empower someone to personally or individually decide the transfer issue; the case/offender must be ushered to CC, which means judges or prosecutors must serve as the escorts.

PRIMARY TRANSFER TARGETS

Transfer, historically, has been aimed primarily at two groups of juvenile offenders. The first category can be called the *beyond-treatment* group. In other words, these youths are regarded as having issues or treatment needs that exceed what JC has to offer; the issue could relate to a matter of time and/or the availability of treatment regimens in the JJ system. A JC judge is typically the person who decides whether the youth is beyond treatment. This type of transfer has existed from the first days of JC and traditionally has been the dominant method of transfer; that dominant situation would change in the 1990s.

The juveniles included here *either* have been chronic in their offending (e.g., a fifteenth burglary or nineth auto theft) *and/or* have not benefitted from previous JC treatment efforts (e.g., exhausting *every* treatment program JC has to offer), *or* committed one or more serious offenses leading to the belief that JC is not equipped to deal with it/them (e.g., a murder or brutal rape), *or* the juveniles are old (i.e., close to the maximum retention age of JC), meaning there is only a limited amount of time that the JC has to rehabilitate the offenders (see Bishop & Frazier, 2000; Furdella & Puzzanchera, 2015, p. 3; Hockenberry, 2018, p. 3, 2019a, p. 3, 2019b, p. 3; Hyland, 2018, p. 3; Tanenhaus, 2000, p. 29). Very chronic or older juvenile offenders could present a situation in which the severity of the current offense is largely irrelevant. The Anti-Transfer Crowd (ATC) has mostly ignored or misrepresented the *beyond treatment* reason to transfer (see Chapter 12); these youths are rarely identified by the ATC as a proper candidate for transfer.

The second category of targeted transfers is the *greater-punishment* group. These offenders are regarded as having committed one or more crimes that call(s) for punishment that exceeds the JC's dispositional authority (see Zimring, 2000a, 2000b). Incapacitating the offender for a longer period could also be the objective. A prosecutor is often the person who decides whether the youth merits greater CC punishment (see *prosecutorial transfer--hereinafter PT*, below), but judges can be called upon to make the choice, here, if prosecutors lack the power to do so.

The juveniles typically included here either have been charged with committing a serious/violent offense over which only CC has jurisdiction, meaning charging that offense guarantees transfer (as in the examples above), or the prosecutor simply has been granted the discretion to decide whether to pursue a prosecution of the case in *either* juvenile *or* CC.

Although the chronic serious offender could boast of membership in both groups, it is important to understand that these two populations do not necessarily overlap. For example, the first-time violent offender who could qualify for CC greater punishment is not automatically beyond the treatment capacity of JC, while the perpetual thief who has not been rehabilitated despite several efforts is neither targeted for nor guaranteed greater punishment if transferred.

TWO TYPES OF TRANSFER

Judicial Transfer (JT)

There are two types of transfer; each is named after the court official who has been authorized to make the transfer decision. The first type is *judicial transfer (hereinafter JT)*, which usually involves a judge's determination that the youth is beyond the rehabilitative measures of the juvenile justice (JJ) system. Most often this transfer will not occur unless the youths have experienced previous treatment failures.

These chronic offenders may not have committed a particularly serious offense. Instead, it could be the judge's motivation to transfer is solely not to waste valuable JJ treatment resources rather than to pursue longer sentences of incarceration via a CC conviction. Moreover, the judge could fear that placing a chronic offender in a facility will compromise the treatment offered to other, more salvageable youths. It is also possible that the severity or violent nature of the current (even first) offense is so serious that the judge will conclude the youth is beyond the help of the system and requires a sentence of considerable duration, which requires a CC conviction.

This type of transfer has existed from the first days of JC. Until the 1990s it was the dominant method of transfer to CC; it remains the only way transfer will occur in some states.

Not surprising, JT requires a hearing in JC. It is possible that the legislature has mandated a transfer hearing, given the presence of certain crimes and conditions (e.g., age or record). As with the previous seemingly mandatory situations, this sounds as though the transfer has been made mandatory and has been misunderstood and misidentified as such (see Chapter 6).[7]

The transfer hearing is usually divided into two stages. In the first stage, the prosecutor presents evidence that establishes probable cause to believe the juvenile committed the required offense. This is likely to be called the *probable cause* stage, which is a preliminary hearing. The second stage is likely to be called the *amenability* stage,[8] where the judge determines the youth's amenability to JC treatment; is the youth able to be rehabilitated by available JJ programs?[9]

There are two versions of JT. The first can be considered *traditional*, or perhaps *regular*, wherein the amenability burden is on the state (i.e., a probation officer or prosecutor).[10] That is, the party pursuing transfer must prove to the judge that JC cannot help the accused. Prosecutors will seek this transfer due to lacking the authority to directly transfer the case. In this situation, prosecutors must rely upon *both* a "favorable" report from the PO, indicating that transfer is recommended for whatever reason(s), *and* the ultimate decision by the judge that agrees with the report. It would not be unusual for POs themselves to initiate the transfer request. A preponderance of evidence should suffice to satisfy this burden of proof.

The second version of JT is called *presumptive*. This transfer places the amenability burden on the defendant.[11] It typically is limited to older/more chronic defendants or to serious offenses, and where prosecutorial transfer is unavailable. Defendants must prove that they can be rehabilitated in the JJ system. A preponderance of evidence should suffice to satisfy this burden of proof.

Prosecutorial Transfer (PT)

The second version of discretionary exclusion is prosecutorial transfer, which always involves this official's decision to charge the youth as a criminal and not as a delinquent. Charging is necessarily a discretionary decision. Usually there are limits to the prosecutor's charging power such that a minimum age and level of offense, and possibly a prior delinquent record, could be required before the prosecutor can personally transfer the case to CC (see Sanborn & Salerno, 2005).

Offense Exclusion (OE)

There are two types of PT. The first form of PT is *offense-oriented* and is best referred to as *offense exclusion*. Here, the offense has been excluded from JC jurisdiction.[12] This version typically requires very violent or serious offenses for the prosecutor to be able to determine where the trial will take place. The two scenarios mentioned at the beginning of this Chapter are examples of offense exclusion. So, mandating that murder charges go to CC for prosecution is offense exclusion. Although discretionary, OE very frequently has been misrepresented as automatic, mandatory, and non-discretionary (see Chapter 6 and Table 38 D). This is wrong, nevertheless.

For example, if murder (or any other Class A or 1st degree felony) is the only offense that is excluded from JC jurisdiction, then a charge of manslaughter (or any other Class B or 2nd degree felony) would be subject to prosecution in JC. Charging crimes is necessarily a discretionary act, and prosecutors can choose to keep any case in JC by selecting a non-excluded offense for prosecution. No one can force a prosecutor to charge an excluded offense.

Legislatures have contributed to the confusion surrounding OE by identifying the concept in at least 11 different sets of wording in statutes (see Sanborn & Salerno, 2005, p. 279):

- Jurisdiction, child, delinquency ≠ excluded offense;
- Excluded offense = adult;
- Juvenile court does not have jurisdiction;
- Juvenile court has jurisdiction unless/except;
- Offenses are excluded from juvenile court jurisdiction;
- Juvenile court jurisdiction is excluded/divested;
- Criminal court has original jurisdiction;
- Juvenile must be charged or prosecuted as adult;
- Prosecutor shall direct file;
- Mandatory direct file;
- Juvenile court shall transfer or waive.

It is little wonder that so much confusion has resulted in interpreting this uncomplicated term (see Chapter 6). The last provision, the JC shall transfer has been misinterpreted as a form of JT, namely, "mandatory JT" (see Chapter 6).[13] Actually, it is PT since the prosecutor's showing probable cause for the excluded crime mandates transfer to CC. It is the mirror image of the "CC has original jurisdiction." The solitary difference between the two is that, with the former the preliminary hearing occurs in JC, while, in the latter, the preliminary hearing occurs in CC. In addition, the two *direct file* references are especially confusing since direct file is ordinarily completely discretionary in selecting charges *and* the proper forum. The transfer in these two scenarios is also discretionary, nevertheless. The prosecutor merely must charge a lesser-included offense to remove it from the "mandatory/shall" commands, if selecting the JC forum is desired. Choosing an offense within the statutory criteria does compel the prosecutor to pursue criminal prosecution (just as in "regular" OE). In other words, "mandatory direct file" is offense exclusion, with different wording. All of these statutory terms exclude the catalogued offenses from JC jurisdiction and share one critical component: the presence of probable cause for an offense identified within the parameters of these 11 sets of terms empowers the prosecutor to initiate the criminal prosecution of the juvenile offender, assuming any age and/or record requirements have been met.

Direct File (DF)/Concurrent Jurisdiction

The second form of PT is *forum-oriented* and is known as *direct file* (hereinafter DF) or *concurrent jurisdiction*. Concurrent jurisdiction involves exactly what it suggests. *Both* JC *and* CC share (or have concurrent) jurisdiction over the crimes committed by certain juveniles (depending upon age, offense, and record); prosecutors have the authority to direct file the case in CC (or in JC, if they so decide). This version might involve serious offenses, but unlike the typical OE provision, DF might focus more on older juveniles committing virtually any felony offense (see Sanborn & Salerno, 2005: chapter 12). Although DF is probably the term most frequently used to identify this type of PT, it might be safer to refer to it as concurrent jurisdiction. The problem with DF is that that term has also been wrongly used to refer to OE since in OE prosecutors are authorized to "directly file" charges against youths in CC (see PA Judges, 2018, p. 110; Chapter 6)

Appellate courts have upheld the validity of both forms of PT (see Feld, 2000, p. 144). Although not as prevalent as today, both forms have existed since the first days of JC (see Tanenhaus, 2000: 21-23). Altogether, more than 40 jurisdictions currently provide for PT; some employ both forms of it (see Sanborn & Salerno, 2005, Chapter 12).

The two types of PT differ enough that many experts see categorical differences between the two; they are very mistaken. Offense exclusion has been described as "a less obvious grant of power to prosecutors" (Zimring, 2010, p. 9). But the only element that is "less obvious" is critics' understanding it and its relationship to DF. While DF is almost always acknowledged as discretionary, OE usually is not and tends to be referred to as automatic, mandatory, and non-discretionary (see Chapter 6). OE is even likely to be mislabeled as *legislative* transfer (see Chapter 6) apparently because it is the legislature that has specifically excluded certain identified offenses from JC jurisdiction. It appears it is the legislature itself that is transferring the offense/case to CC, but it is not and cannot transfer a case.

OE is no more or less legislative than are DF and both types of JT. Transfer to CC is no more or less legislative than ME. OE is also every bit as discretionary and every bit as much an example of transfer as is DF. In both OE and DF, the prosecutor is determining whether the juvenile/case belongs in CC or should remain in JC; does the case call for transfer to CC or not?

Having said that, there is one crucial difference between the two types of PT. In OE, the prosecutor *cannot* charge the excluded offense *and* retain the case in JC. Prosecutors have a sensitive charging choice to make since selecting an excluded offense *simultaneously selects* the forum for the prosecution. OE can be regarded as necessitating an *interdependent* or a *two-in-one decision* because *choosing a crime* to be charged *also chooses a court*; the first decision *determines* the second decision. With concurrent jurisdiction, however, charging a particular crime is not as sensitive a decision since both courts are authorized to hear the case. The prosecutor's choice here can be regarded as *independent* or *sequential*. First, the prosecutor commits to what exactly should be the charge. Second, the prosecutor then determines whether JC or CC should be the location of the trial; the charging decision *does not determine* the forum decision. Despite this crucial difference, both OE and DF are examples of PT and are discretionary decisions; neither is automatic, mandatory, or non-discretionary (or legislative).

Although the prosecutor's motivation to transfer often is seeking a longer sentence in CC, there could be many other considerations that have been taken into account (see Section IV). Contrary to some accounts (see Bishop & Frazier, 1991), the prosecutor's decision could be based on a belief that the offender just cannot be helped by JC (see Sanborn, 1994a). This conclusion could be due to the offense, the repetition of crimes or the offender's attitude, maturity, or age. The prosecutor could be aware of a lengthy delinquent history of the juvenile, coupled with previous failures at various JJ treatment programs, and determine that yet another placement at a juvenile facility would be a waste of resources, or worse. The prosecutor could also believe that rehabilitation is simply an inappropriate response to the youth/offense; perhaps justice is thought to demand a different response. In these situations, a longer sentence in CC could be irrelevant to or at least not the driving force behind the prosecutor's decision.

The legislature is the source of all exclusion and transfer power. In adopting transfer, they have decided that the commission of certain offenses by certain youths and being charged as such by prosecutors and/or the lack of amenability to JC treatment and being found as such by a JC judge qualifies for transfer to CC.[14] The power to transfer a case to CC has been granted to a judge and/or a prosecutor in every jurisdiction in this country; indeed, the vast majority of states and the District of Columbia practice both (one or both versions of each) JT and PT. Where the two types of transfer coexist, the tendency is to give judges transfer power over younger youths who could still be perceived as being beyond rehabilitation due to chronic or violent behavior, while prosecutors typically are permitted to determine the fate of more violent/serious offenders and those juveniles of advanced age (see Sanborn & Salerno, 2005, Chapter 12).

Previous research has disclosed that JC workers overwhelmingly endorse the need for transfer of at least some chronic and violent juvenile offenders to CC; only defense attorneys tended to object to its existence. The explanation provided by defense attorneys was that they usually were willing to trade the better justice of CC for the more lenient dispositions/sentences (and court record) of JC (see Sanborn, 1994a, p. 270).

In the end, it is important to realize that there is never anything automatic or mandatory about transfer. Rather, transfer, by definition, is necessarily discretionary because it is a judgment call completely within the decision-making power of an official. Simply put, if juveniles leave their homes to commit a crime and are legally defined as juveniles prior to that commission of an offense, the only way in which they can end up facing trial in CC for that offense is to be *redefined* as criminal defendants. That cannot happen automatically; that redefinition requires the input of a decision-maker. That someone (and that can be only a judge or a prosecutor) must take responsibility for creating the redefinition.

Another lesson to remember here is that while all transfer is a matter of exclusion, not all exclusion is discretionary or transfer-oriented. Most of the literature has not observed these parameters and has unnecessarily confused and distorted the topic (see Chapter 6).

The intent of this book is to address the purposes and benefits attending the transfer of violent and chronic juvenile offenders to CC. The relative merits of JT and PT are not part of the focus, although some purposes/benefits might be better served by one type of transfer versus the other. Suffice it to say that this book assumes and defends the existence of both types of transfer. Also important to note is that none of the purposes and benefits identified in this work has any necessary connection to either version of mandatory exclusion. Whether there are benefits and purposes realized in this brand of exclusion awaits the efforts of another book.

This book will also not address the pros and cons of the use of blended sentences to bridge the sentencing gap between juvenile and criminal courts. There are benefits to be derived from and problems attending this brand of sentencing, but they will not be explored in this book.

REFERENCES

Bishop, D. M., & Frazier, C. E. (1991). Transfer of juveniles to criminal court: A case study and analysis of prosecutorial waiver. *Notre Dame Journal of Law, Ethics & Public Policy*, *5*, 281–302.

Bishop, D. M., & Frazier, C. E. (2000). Consequences of transfer. In J. Fagan & F. E. Zimring (Eds.), *The changing borders of juvenile justice: Transfer of adolescents to criminal court* (pp. 227–276). University of Chicago Press.

Feld, B. C. (2000). Legislative exclusion of offenses from juvenile court jurisdiction: A history and critique. In J. Fagan & F. E. Zimring (Eds.), *The changing borders of juvenile justice: Transfer of adolescents to the criminal court* (pp. 83–144). University of Chicago Press.

Furdella, J., & Puzzanchera, C. (2015). *Delinquency cases in juvenile court, 2013*. Office of Juvenile Justice and Delinquency Prevention.

Griffin, P., Torbet, P., & Syzmanski, L. (1998). *Trying juveniles in adult court: An analysis of state transfer provisions*. Office of Juvenile Justice and Delinquency Prevention, Office of Justice Programs, U.S. Department of Justice.

Hockenberry, S. (2018). *Delinquency cases in juvenile court, 2015*. Office of Juvenile Justice and Delinquency Prevention.

Hockenberry, S. (2019a). *Delinquency cases in juvenile court, 2016*. Office of Juvenile Justice and Delinquency Prevention.

Hockenberry, S. (2019b). *Delinquency cases in juvenile court, 2017*. Office of Juvenile Justice and Delinquency Prevention.

Hyland, N. (2018). *Delinquency cases in juvenile court, 2014*. Office of Juvenile Justice and Delinquency Prevention.

In re Gault. (1967). 387 U.S. 1.

OJJDP. (2020). *Statistical briefing book. Provisions for imposing adult sanctions on juvenile offenders, 2018*. Office of Juvenile Justice and Delinquency Prevention. https:/www.ojjdp.gov/ojstagg/structure-process/qa04113.asp?qadate=2018

PA Judges. (2018). *PA judges benchbook*. Pennsylvania Juvenile Court Judges' Commission.

Sanborn, J. B. Jr. (1994a). Certification to criminal court: The important policy questions of how, when, and why. *Crime and Delinquency*, *40*(2), 262–281. doi:10.1177/0011128794040002007

Sanborn, J. B. Jr, & Salerno, A. W. (2005). *The juvenile justice system: Law and process*. Roxbury Publishing Company. Oxford University Publishing.

Szymanski, L. A. (1996). *Specialized waiver provisions: Reverse waiver and once an adult/always an adult. NCJJ Snapshot, 1(3)*. National Center for Juvenile Justice.

Szymanski, L. A. (2007). *"Once an adult/always an adult" (2007 update). NCJJ Snapshot 12(4)*. National Center for Juvenile Justice.

Szymanski, L. A. (2008). *Once an adult/always an adult (2008 update). NCJJ Snapshot 13(4)*. National Center for Juvenile Justice.

Szymanski, L. A. (2009). *Once an adult/always an adult (2009 update). NCJJ Snapshot 14(5)*. National Center for Juvenile Justice.

Szymanski, L. A. (2010a). *Can juveniles transferred for criminal prosecution be held for pre-trial detention in adult jails? NCJJ Snapshot 15(8)*. National Center for Juvenile Justice.

Tanenhaus, D. S. (2000). The evolution of transfer out of the juvenile court. In J. Fagan & F. E. Zimring (Eds.), *The changing borders of juvenile justice: Transfer of adolescents to the criminal court* (pp. 13–43). University of Chicago Press.

Zimring, F. E. (2000a). Penal proportionality for the young offender: Notes on immaturity, capacity, and diminished responsibility. In T. Grisso & R. G. Schwartz (Eds.), *Youth on Trial: A Developmental Perspective on Juvenile Justice* (pp. 271–289). University of Chicago Press.

Zimring, F. E. (2000b). The punitive necessity of waiver. In J. Fagan & F. E. Zimring (Eds.), *The Changing Borders of Juvenile Justice: Transfer of adolescents to the criminal court* (pp. 207–224). University of Chicago Press.

Zimring, F. E. (2010). The power politics of juvenile court transfer: A mildly revisionist history of the 1990s. *Louisiana Law Review*, *71*, 1–15.

ENDNOTES

1 Some states allow juvenile defendants to transfer themselves to CC.

2 Not long ago, 13 states had a maximum JC age of fifteen/sixteen years of age. The number of "juveniles" mandatorily subjected to criminal prosecution was enormous (see Sanborn & Salerno, 2005). As of 2022, only Georgia, Texas, and Wisconsin have a maximum JC below 17.

3 Most states and Washington, D.C. have chosen 18 as the initiation of *guaranteed* criminal liability.

4 For a detailed account of these ME conditions, see Sanborn & Salerno (2005).

5 In the literature/research, these youths are called: *"Once an Adult, Always an Adult."* These transfers/convicts are not converted or equal to adults in any legal sense other than criminal liability. They are not legally permitted to vote, smoke, consume alcohol or enter into contracts, etc. There is a change in legal status, however. Instead of enjoying delinquent status, they are criminal defendants/convicts and are permanently considered as such henceforth. So, the proper and more accurate title for them is: *"Once a Criminal, Always a Criminal."*

6 Legislators do not intervene into local jurisdictions to transfer any juvenile or to charge any criminal. Legislatures authorize local prosecutors and judges to make the decision.

7 Three realities refute this transfer's being considered mandatory. The *only* mandatory aspect is holding the hearing. The prosecutor's discretionary charging powers (the need to interpret the case and charge specified crimes) mean there is nothing mandatory about this. Judges cannot be forced to transfer unless certain findings are made, requiring interpretation.

8 See Sanborn & Salerno (2005) for a detailed account of the transfer hearing.

9 A recent innovation, adopted in Massachusetts and New Mexico, provides a CC-like trial when the prosecutor petitions for transfer. If there is a conviction, the judge decides whether it will be juvenile or criminal at sentencing. This procedure has been described as an example of PT (Griffin, Torbet, & Szymanski, 1998). It is actually a *delayed JT*. Instead of the judge's making the transfer decision prior to trial, it has been delayed until after conviction (see Sanborn & Salerno, 2005). The prosecutor, meanwhile, has no direct control over the designation.

10 Before *In Re Gault* (1967), POs asked judges to transfer. *Gault* made defense attorneys and prosecutors relevant to JC. Prosecutors have likely assumed this responsibility since the *Gault* decision.

11 Presumptive JT has also been identified as: *nonculpability burden on the defendant*; *crime or factor weighs in favor of transfer*; and *no amenability burden* at all (see Sanborn & Salerno, 2005, Table 12.1). Traditional transfer has also added more crimes/factors that *broaden* the transfer targets. These changes have not made transfer presumptive/more expected per se. Unless the burden is eliminated or switched to the defendant, the JT is not actually presumptive.

12 Under OE, prosecutors must prove PC for the excluded offense to a JC judge, which would then guarantee that transfer to CC (where JC has original jurisdiction), or to prove the same to a CC judge to keep the transferred case in CC (where CC has original jurisdiction).

13 Another confusing aspect of transfer statutes involves presumptive JT. Three ways it is represented are clear: amenability burden is placed on the defendant; a nonculpability burden is placed on the defendant; and, a certain charge or factor weighs in favor of transfer. Much less clear is when there is "no amenability burden." That could mean this is another statutory version of OE and to effect a transfer the prosecutor simply needs to prove PC for the offense. However, it is unclear whether the defense can still fight to retain the case in JC, even when the prosecutor holds no amenability burden. Should that be the case, then the transfer decision would truly be judicial, albeit presumptive, in nature (see Sanborn & Salerno, 2005, p. 279).

14 Legislatures are the ultimate arbiter whether JCs exist and under which conditions: *It is well-established law that a juvenile has neither a constitutional right nor a common law right nor a fundamental right to adjudication in juvenile court. Treatment as a juvenile is not an inherent right but one granted by the state legislature and, therefore, the legislature may restrict or qualify that right as it sees fit, as long as no arbitrary or discriminatory classification is involved* (Szymanski, 2007, p. 1; see also Szymanski, 2008, p.1; 2009, p. 1; 2010a, p. 1).

Section 2

The Disinformation Campaign: False Allegations Concerning Transfer to CC

The campaign to limit, if not eliminate, transfer has been extensive and all-inclusive. Virtually every aspect of transfer has been attacked, ranging from misreporting its (and JC's) history to misrepresenting nearly every aspect of its identity, elements, and operation. This Section is divided into three major parts. The first part (misreporting history), covered in Chapters 4 and 5, details the very beginnings of JC operation and how its offender population changed dramatically by the 1960s; both Chapters rely upon data from Philadelphia's JC. The second part (misidentifications and mischaracterizations) is Chapters 6 and 7, which explain the varied and numerous ways in which the transfer subject has been misunderstood and misreported; both the relevant terminology of transfer and its operation are considered here. Finally, the third part (misrepresentations of proper transfer targets) details the anti-transfer camp's (ATC's) initiative to reduce, if not eliminate, transfer to CC. While chapters 8 and 9 address the ATC's campaign to prove juvenile offenders should not be transferred to criminal court (CC) (Chapter 8) or cannot be prosecuted in CC (Chapter 9), the last two Chapters disclose how the ATC seeks to limit transfer (should its elimination prove impossible) by either minimizing those offenders eligible for transfer (Chapter 10) and/or permitting only judges to make the critical transfer decision (Chapter 11).

Specifically, the next eight chapters in Section 2 address and debunk:

- the purported original design and purposes of JC (Chapter 4);
- how JC became a clone of criminal court, but long before the spike in violent juvenile crime in the mid-1990s (Chapter 5);
- the various incorrect ways in which terminology is utilized regarding transfer (Chapter 6);
- how transfer works, and, more important, perhaps, how it does not work (Chapter 7); and,
- at whom transfer should be directed and in which way transfer should be practiced (Chapters 8-11).

Unless and until these criticisms and complaints about transfer to CC are resolved, legislatures and appellate courts will remain misinformed and subject to the ATC's manipulation.

Chapter 4
The Juvenile Court (JC):
The Original Design – The Philadelphia Version

ABSTRACT

Chapter 4 details the nature of the original juvenile court (JC) via data from Philadelphia. Although all the data are from Philadelphia, the elements corroborate the declarations from national JC proponents, covered in Chapter 2. In other words, Philadelphia's JC likely operated very similarly to urban JCs across the country. The JC from the first few decades of the twentieth century bears little, if any, comparison to the JC of today. The chapter reveals a very young offender population committing obnoxious "offenses" rather than serious crimes. The original JC was committed to a morality crusade to maintain the chastity of girls, treating similarly behaving boys differently, and to informally resolving as many disputes as possible in the community, without direct JC involvement. JC was portrayed as the ultimate parent, denying defendants rights, while committing very few "offenders," and only to benign facilities/clinics. JCs were engaged in cleaning up families and communities.

INTRODUCTION

The ATC has relied substantially on an assertion that JC was founded to remove juvenile offenders from exposure to the harsh results of CC prosecution (see Sabo, 1995, p. 2431; Zimring, 1998a, p. 193; Zimring, 2019, p. 31); that original design, in turn, supposedly repudiates transfer. If the JC was founded to accomplish this task, returning juvenile offenders to CC is not only wrong, but also illogical, counterintuitive, disloyal, and unfaithful.

Assuming JC was meant to remove juvenile offenders from CC, why is that position so sacred and unadjustable? Numerous aspects of the original JC have been found to be problematic or simply inadvisable and are no longer part of its operation. The now discarded, fundamental original aspects include:

- "criminalizing" behaviors that were not crimes or even illegal actions;
- "criminalizing" behaviors that were mere ordinance violations;

DOI: 10.4018/978-1-7998-7923-7.ch004

- "criminalizing" conditions/status that did not require behavior;
- exercising jurisdiction/control over incredibly young "offenders;"
- divesting JCs of the responsibility to deal with older teenagers;
- detaining thousands of young people without accusation of crime;
- imposing judgmental labels of immorality against girls;
- fostering a religious crusade as part of JC's reason for intervention;
- investing probation officers (POs) and judges with unlimited powers;
- operationalizing complete informality and flexibility;
- forgoing trials in "proving" misbehavior, denying basically all rights;
- adopting a clinic-like approach to all juvenile misbehavior;
- preventing a record of juvenile misbehavior from trailing youths into CC;
- directing JC's reform/rehabilitative efforts at society at large;
- engaging in gender discrimination (probable class/religious/ethnic, too);
- removing from home and institutionalizing thousands of poor kids; and,
- incarcerating for long periods kids who committed no/minor crimes.[1]

JC has evolved to be virtually a clone of CC, unrecognizable in early 20th Century JC terms, but it certainly did not start out that way.

First, it helps to consider the major aspects of Philadelphia's version of the original JC.[2]

MAJOR JC FEATURES DURING ITS ORIGINAL, FORMATIVE YEARS[3]

Back in the day, JC bore little resemblance to CC; ATC acknowledgment of this is rare:

At a broad level, extreme delinquents do not fit neatly within traditional juvenile justice processes originally designed to handle relatively nonserious delinquents and status offenders (Trulson, Caudell, Belshaw, & DeLisi, 2011, p. 264).

It is possible that the ATC sees a benefit in pretending that the original and contemporary JCs are essentially the same. Comparability might assist the anti-transfer argument: since JCs today are designed to be similar to the original version (which is inaccurate), the fact that the original JC survived without transfer to CC means the current JC can persist without having transfer (which is also inaccurate). Illinois, the birthplace of JC implemented judicial transfer in 1907, before JC was a decade old. Even prior to that date, prosecutors exercised transfer power over serious offenders (see Bonnie, 1989, p. 187; Geraghty, 1997, p. 215; Tanenhaus, 2000). The ATC's reasoning shows that a specious premise leads to a specious conclusion.

A. Very Young "Offenders" Separated from Adults and Even Older Juveniles

To be convicted of a crime, two elements are required: *mens rea* (i.e., intent) and *actus reus* (i.e., an act). These two elements are necessary to be *responsible* for one's behavior, which is required before one can be *punished* for committing a crime. Under common law, offenders younger than the age of seven *could not be prosecuted* for criminal behavior. The so-called *infancy defense* prevented these prosecutions because before this age no one could form the necessary *mens rea*. For those between the ages of seven and fourteen there was a presumption of *mens rea* incapacity, but a prosecutor could overcome that. For defendants in this age group, prosecutors had an additional burden: to prove *both* that the youth had committed the offense *and* that the youth was sufficiently precocious to have been able to form intent. Youths over the age of fourteen were grouped with adults and were presumed to be able to form *mens rea*.

We have seen that JCs were created to prevent children from developing into criminals. They wanted to address and assist youths before their misbehavior became criminal in nature. JC was designed to halt criminal careers *before* youths wanted to become career criminals. This required JC to address the behavior of potential offenders at a very young age. It was believed that JC intervention could not begin too soon on a path of misbehavior or at too young an age. This required the abolition of the infancy defense in JC. Following the start of JC, the infancy defense was available only to those younger than 14 who were prosecuted in CC.

Justification for abolishing the infancy defense was straight forward. The vast majority of misbehavior within JC jurisdiction involved behaviors that were *not crimes*. Second, when actual crime was at issue, it was categorized as *delinquency*. Third, punishment was not imposed in JC. Benevolent rehabilitation was offered to delinquent youths when "crimes" were involved. Fourth, the absence of punishment made the concept of responsibility (and *mens rea*) irrelevant. Juvenile offenders were regarded as irresponsible, which is what necessitated JC intervention.

Through the first half of the Twentieth Century, JC practice included remarkably young participants. Table 1 discloses the ages of JC "delinquency" defendants' cases in Philadelphia for the 18 years between 1920 and 1939 (no ages were reported in 1922).[4] In the six years between 1918 and 1924 (again, no 1922 report), there were three three-years-old, five four-years-old, 18 five-years-old, and 80 six-years-old brought into JC. 1921 had the most shocking figures: one one-year-old girl; four two-years-old girls; one three-years-old girl; two boy and eight girl four-years-old; eight boy and three girl five-years-old; and 11 boy and 13 girl six-years-old. All of these cases were introduced to JC as *informal complaints* (hereinafter ICs) and were identified as such separately in these years' *JC annual report* (hereinafter JCAR). It is unknown just how many other years involved "defendants" this young.[5]

The annual reports explained that very young boys and girls were brought to JC due to being witnesses to (likely victims of) rape or other sexual-oriented offenses, assumedly in the home (JCAR, 1924, Table 6, p. 55, fn. 3). Just how much of a witness they could be at some of these ages is questionable, and perhaps most confusing is that these children were brought to the delinquency rather than the dependent or neglected side of the jurisdiction. Nearly all of the very young had their cases adjusted, without securing a delinquent record. Not all experienced this outcome, however, especially if they *appeared* to be delinquent; perhaps they enjoyed or even initiated the sexual contact. Moreover, even those initially released without a delinquent record still earned a JC record (they were "known to the court"), meaning the initial contact could affect subsequent court findings of misbehavior.

The 1919 JCAR provides an extremely rare insight into the crimes committed by specific ages. The five five-years-old boys were linked with two larcenies, one vagrancy, one running away from home, and one fornication/bastardy (presumably as a product thereof); there were no recidivists in this group. The nine six-years-old boys were charged with: larceny (2); burglary (2); incorrigibility (1); running from an institution (1); and malicious mischief (3); the lone recidivist was the runner. The youngest girl (seven) was charged with running away from home. The 41 seven-years-old boys charged mostly involved larceny (11) or burglary (7), but eight were recidivists. Not surprising, as the ages of the boys increased so did the number of recidivists.[6]

Between 1919 and 1938 boy defendants younger than 14 comprised the majority (ranging 52.0%-58.3%), except for 1934 (49.2%) and 1936 (48.6%). They were also a majority in 1939 (54.4%), if the 443 newly admitted 16/17-year-olds are disregarded. So, for most of the early years of JC, the boy defendant population was mostly under the age of 14. The overall percentage of younger than 14-year-olds during this era was 55.2%. The original JC was truly meant for young defendants.

Not only was JC created to keep juveniles away from adults (originally defined as 16- and 17-year-olds and older), but also to keep detained younger juveniles away from older juveniles.

To secure freedom from moral contamination, proper classification is made so that the older and more experienced children do not have an opportunity to associate with the younger and more impressionable ones, and constant supervision of all groups is maintained (JCAR, 1919, p. 227).

B. A Majority of Very Innocuous "Offenses" Prosecuted in the Original JC

If the term, *delinquency*, was meant to connote mostly non-criminal behavior committed by irresponsible young children who lacked proper parental guidance, JCs were adequately created and designed, while employing appropriate terminology. The original JC was truly a court of delinquency where most youths were damaging themselves, if anyone, and certainly more so than inflicting damage on others or their property in the community. That original JC bears little, if any, resemblance to today's JC.

It is possible to calculate the number of children prosecuted in JC who *could not have been prosecuted* in CC (i.e., under the age of seven and those committing noncriminal acts). Determining the number of youths who *likely would have been ignored* by CC due to a young age and/or insignificant crime would require speculation. Similarly, it is impossible to discern how many youths were placed under the JC's supervision, with or without an adjudication, that *would not have been convicted* in CCs, especially if any constitutional rights had been provided.

Ironically, one very notable example of a "delinquent" who would not have been convicted in criminal court is the youth from *Commonwealth v. Fisher* (1905). He had been adjudicated delinquent of a larceny in JC and was committed to a delinquent facility for the act. A critic of the constitutional irregularities in JC operation commented in 1930:

After Fisher had been committed to the house of refuge his case came up in the court of quarter sessions. The judge, taking the position that conviction was not essential to the interests of the state, ordered a verdict of acquittal. Thus Fisher was acquitted in the criminal court, but his "sentence," if it may be called such, to the house of refuge was unaffected (Shenton, 1930, p. 52, fn. 14).

There is no way in which to pinpoint how many other juveniles were "included" within the jurisdiction of JC despite what could/would have been or was an acquittal in CC. The design of JC would allow no obstacles to assuming jurisdiction over a youth that was perceived to need the court's care.

The commitment to addressing only non-serious offenses was represented in the first Pennsylvania JC Act (1903) that explained indictable offenses could be processed in JC only when the judge certified the transfer and the prosecutor signed off on it. Not only were older juveniles excluded from JC, so were many, if not most, serious offenses committed by those 15 years-of-age and younger.

Table 2 provides examples of the minor crimes and non-offenses that dominated processing for the first several decades of JC. Many, if not most, involved behaviors that virtually every urban juvenile has experienced, such as playing ball in the streets, trespassing, and larceny. Some misbehaviors were never defined and potentially were all-encompassing, including whatever mom or dad or any other interested party alleged they meant (such as incorrigible). Thousands of juveniles were brought to JC for loafing or vagrancy; begging also constituted an offense. Minor questionable misbehaviors were the norm in the original JC.

For some of the 1930s, the JCAR offered a rare offense profile, by age. Table 3 catalogues the number of youths younger than 10 years of age who were charged with auto theft; as the depression was ramping up, 1930 became a prolific crime year for all age groups. In that decade, the JCAR also reported dispositions by age for non-dismissed cases (see Table 4).

There were major differences between the way in which JC regarded boys versus girls. The best way to phrase the primary difference is that boys disturbed the community; girls were disturbed in the community. For boys, the concern was the condition in which they left the neighborhood; for girls it was the condition in which they were found in the home/community.

Most of the offenses committed by boys during the beginning decades were either not offenses or were very minor in nature;[7] for girls more than 80% of their conduct were purported examples of immorality (see Section C, below) and/or were not crimes. Reports offered accounts of the difference between boys and girls and their offenses. Boys outnumbered girls, but

(t)his larger proportion of boys' cases is due in part to the fact that the offenses committed by boys are often of a less serious character than are those committed by girls, and it is often felt that bringing a boy into court will do him no harm but may give him a good scare (JCAR, 1922, p. 70).

* * * * * * * * *

The greater number of boys' cases is due in part to differences in the character of the offenses, as boys are often brought to court for childish pranks, or gang depredations, while girls are usually brought in for serious immorality, which necessitates immediate and vigorous action… (JCAR, 1924, p. 17).

Back in the day, boys' offenses were not only overwhelmingly minor but also grossly outnumbered "Big-10" crimes (i.e., burglary, robbery, indecent assault, rape, assault and battery, homicide, carrying weapons, drug offenses, auto theft, and arson). Table 5 provides a profile of boys between 1917 and 1923, showing minor crimes were much more prevalent than Big-10 crimes.[8] Although there were juveniles who committed actual, serious crimes, the vast majority of supposed delinquents during the beginning decades were hurting themselves, and not others.

C. The Morality Crusade (MC) Launched Against Young Girls in the Original JC (The Original and Very Real Moral Panic)

Not only were girls seriously underrepresented in committing crimes, virtually all of their behavior involved perceived immoral or immorality-threatening conduct. There were four "offenses" that were viewed as examples of girls' immoral tendencies or indicators of their being in danger of becoming immoral. These four were: running away from home, incorrigibility, sex offenses, and their being so-called witnesses (primarily) to rape (or other sexual misconduct).[9]

The four girl "offenses" that represented this affront to morality were first combined in 1922. That year runaway and incorrigibility were added to sex immorality (i.e., "sex offenses and witness to rape cases;" JCAR, 1922, p. 52) because they were believed to be linked to situations "which often indicate suspected sex immorality or the danger of its development," (JCAR, 1922, p. 24, footnote omitted). What made JC intervention necessary is that, according to JC workers,

(t)here is also a greater unwillingness on the part of parents and others to bring a girl into court and thereby acknowledge or expose her waywardness. When a girl is brought in it is usually because the situation demands immediate action (JCAR, 1922, p. 71).

Beginning in 1923 (and continuing every year until 1951), the court explained (using the same wording every year, with only the number of relevant offenses and page numbers changing):

Pronounced differences exist in the nature of the offenses charged against boys and girls. The most common offense among boys was stealing — 33.1 per cent of all boys being charged with this offense, while among the girls, only 9.9 percent were brought in on this charge. Over one-half (53.2 per cent) of the girls were charged with offenses indicating either suspected sex immorality or the danger of its development, such as running away from home (27.6 per cent), incorrigibility (12.2 per cent), sex offenses (7.6 per cent), and witnesses in rape cases (5.8 per cent) … (JCAR, 1923, p. 14-15).

The situation never seemed to improve as one year later the alarm was sounded that "girls are usually brought in for serious immorality, which necessitates immediate and vigorous action…" (JCAR, 1924, p. 17). Table 6 indicates the number of girls captured in this JC-initiated morality crusade (MC) between 1920 and 1939, as well as the percentage of morality crusade cases within the total of overall girls' cases.

Combined, these "misbehaviors" of girls ignited a full-blown crusade by JC. The sex offenses were very innocuous. In none of them was there a victim other than the girl in court (see Table 7).[10] Even the sex "offenses" typically involved living conditions and fornication; prostitution, itself, was rarely charged, but all girls were younger than 16. Just living in a house of prostitution (or a so-called bawdy house) could result in a finding of delinquency and a probation or commitment disposition.

The witness category was focused overwhelmingly on girls.[11] These cases supposedly involved situations in which girls were literally witnesses to rape or other serious sexual assaults. Although that was the definition supplied in the annual reports, it was never completely clear whether the girls were considered truly as witnesses or victims; alternatively, they could have been seen as co-defendants (perhaps willing participants?) or future offenders.[12]

Most often, witness cases were adjusted and dismissed, with warnings to all parties. Some girls were found delinquent, however, and, as seen in Table 8, were placed on probation or experienced a delinquent commitment; this finding seems to have been limited to those girls who "looked to be delinquent." Table 8 shows the greater tendency for girls' morality crusade cases and truancy to result in probation/commitment compared to boys' cases. In other morality crusade and truancy cases, placement in child-placing agencies, child-care institutions or other "safer-than-home" living arrangements followed a finding of delinquency for these girls (who required the court's protection).

There is no doubt as to how seriously JC responded to girls' alleged actual or potential immorality, as the JCAR (1917) reported:

[S]ome girls are under the closest kind of supervision from day to day for several years, every detail of their lives, health, work, play, dress and company being planned so that they may have the best possible chance of a wholesome and happy future, in spite of the overwhelming obstacles of heredity and early environment that they have encountered (p. 115).

Table 9 indicates how disproportionately probation and commitment resources were dedicated to the morality crusade (together with running from an institution and truancy).[13]

D. The Original JC's Different Responses to Boys versus Girls

There was a serious difference in the way boys and girls were handled by JC. Overall, JC was more willing to impose no change in the status of a boy. JC was more willing to dismiss boys' cases without detaining them or continuing probation; just scaring boys was the norm. Girls were far more likely to be placed on probation or to be removed from home and committed.

Table 10 demonstrates that the no-status-change result was much more common for boys (66.4%) compared to girls (43.4%). Probation was much more likely the outcome for girls (32%) than it was for boys (19%). Commitments had similar discrepancies for girls (24.1%) versus boys (12.8%). Girls were more likely to be newly placed under the JC's supervision (56.1%) than boys (31.8%). It was not severity of "crime" that steered those differences.

Differences were most marked in the perceived morality-related situations. JC seemed concerned for the chastity of boys: fornication and obscenity were disapproved, while sodomy appears to have thrown JC workers into turmoil. But there was not an equivalency in perceived threats when it came to boys' running away and incorrigibility (see Table 10).[14]

E. Dearth of Serious Crimes Prosecuted by the Original JC

Serious crimes did not characterize the original JC's operation. The first JCAR (1917) revealed boys committed less than 9% of Big-10 offenses (i.e., burglary, robbery, indecent assault, rape, assault and battery, homicide, carrying weapons, drug offenses, auto theft, and arson) processed in JC. When JC emerged in Philadelphia in 1903, the amount of these offenses was very probably incredibly low. Table 11 discloses that, although the extent of these most serious crimes increased pretty steadily every year after 1917, as late as 1939, Big-10 crimes were less than one-fourth of the JC's caseload. Between 1917 and 1939, Big-10 crimes accounted for an average of 17.2% of JC's caseload.[15]

Girls committed even fewer Big-10 crimes. Between 1923-1945, girls were involved in 13,941 cases (17,463 when witness cases are included). As to Big-10 crimes, girls were charged with 27 auto thefts (.2% of cases); 124 burglaries (.9%); 99 robberies (.7%); and, 367 assault and batteries (including homicides, 2.6%). The girls' total Big-10 crimes numbered 617 for a total of 3.5% of all girls' cases. In addition, there were 1,270 stealing charges (=1,887 charges or 10.8%), and 1,162 "careless" charges (such as disorderly conduct and mischief) (=3,049 charges or 17.5%). Otherwise, JC was focused on the morality crusade for girls; obviously, the vast majority of JC's attention to girls was dedicated to the morality crusade!

Even sex crimes were mostly innocuous or merely offensive. Although juveniles committed sex crimes, such as rape/indecent assault, most sex "crimes" were harmless.[16]

Also interesting, it was not until 1924 that an appreciable percentage of Big-10 crimes went to trial, as opposed to being adjusted by the PO. That informal case resolution method lends further support that JC was not regarding even Big-10 crimes as ultra-serious juvenile offenses in the beginning years; roughly two-thirds of these cases were adjusted until 1924 (see Table 12).[17]

The outcomes for boys' Big-10 crimes through the 1920s were relatively benign as well. Table 13 shows the relatively few correctional commitments that were dedicated to boys' major crimes. In 1920, only 26 of 80 commits involved Big-10 offenses; in 1921, only 23 of 68 commits involved Big-10 crimes. That demonstrates delinquent facilities were dominated by non-serious offenders. During the 1930s, there were 3,026 commitments. Of these, 902 (or 29.8%) were *R*unning away from home, *I*ncorrigibility, *T*ruancy (hereinafter, *RIT*) offenses, 810 (or 27.7%) were larcenies, and 181 (or 6%) were careless offenses; these 3 areas of delinquency accounted for 1,893 correctional commitments (or 62.6%) during this decade. Delinquent facilities had a different population during the original JC years compared to today.

F. Informal Complaints (ICs) Serve as the Original JC's Neighborhood Resolution Center

The original JC relied heavily upon an informal method in resolving cases. The "official" court typically was reserved for cases appearing to require an intervention more serious than probation. The PO could impose community-oriented outcomes. In the beginning years, as much as two-thirds of the petitioned cases ended up being adjusted, sometimes even involving serious charges. Adjustments most often resulted in neither an adjudication of delinquency nor a formal disposition, per se; reprimands and threats of worse outcomes for recidivating usually sufficed. Youths (and parents) who refused to accept the PO's findings and offer of an adjustment could demand a judicial hearing. Otherwise, POs were authorized to enter a finding of delinquency. Judges' signatures were required for these findings and for outcomes involving probation, but the process in obtaining the signature was pro forma. Potential commitment cases required a hearing presided by a judge; the judge, alone, was authorized to remove the youth from the home.

Philadelphia's JC took the IC system one step further. Instead of filing a petition with the court, those with a grievance against a juvenile could submit an IC to the probation department. This opportunity began in 1919. The process served as a sifting device: for issues over which the court did not have jurisdiction (complainant was referred to the proper outside agency); and, for matters belonging in the court (the hope was that the issue could be resolved informally without requiring a hearing and draining the court's resources). This process was seen as an effective forum for resolving neighborhood disputes/squabbles; JC was a neighborhood resolution or mediation center. ICs also enabled citizens to report kids and families that had raised concerns among neighbors. Table 14 indicates how much parents/relatives and neighbors relied upon ICs.

This method of investigation and adjustment of informal complaints frequently relieves difficult situations by bringing a better understanding between complainants, parents, and children. Many trivial cases and neighborhood quarrels are disposed of and the expense and inconvenience of court appearances are avoided. Some complaints merely require advice or reference to some social agency which is equipped to handle such problems. Others bring to the attention of the court children who are seriously in need of help. Frequently probation officers are able to do preventive work by handling situations in their incipient stages instead of letting them develop into conditions which might require official court action (JCAR, 1941, p. 6).[18]

The high number of ICs suggests that the community was aware of the court's serving in this dispute resolution capacity. Besides parents, relatives and neighbors, the police and prosecutors were frequent sources of the ICs, especially in witness cases. The likelihood, here, is that criminal cases involving an adult offender and a juvenile victim/witness/co-defendant led to police and prosecutors' referring the juvenile part of the offense to JC via an IC. Table 15 discloses there was a sizable caseload that involved ICs between 1921 and 1939.

G. Majority of Cases Adjusted, Avoiding Use of Formal Procedures in the Original JC

After JC had been operating a decade or so, hearings before a judge were averted constantly. Not only most ICs, but also most misbehaviors and full-fledged crimes introduced to JC via an arrest were adjusted, especially for boys. The dominance of moral concerns in girls' misconduct brought about an elevated concern for their welfare, which likely explains the fewer adjustments for girls. Most of the witness to rape cases were brought to court via ICs. Assuming there was not an underlying delinquent tendency found in the girl (calling for some type of placement outside of the home), these cases were regularly adjusted by POs.

As explained in the JCAR (1919):

The general trivial nature of the offenses committed by boys is shown by the fact that 80.9 per cent of the 3,731 boys' cases brought in and adjusted were discharged as to the offense charged. Of those 3,020 cases discharged as to the offense charged, 2,313 cases were discharged outright, 440 were discharged but owing to the fact that they were on probation, were continued on probation... (pp. 36-37).

* * * * * * *

Most boys are handled "out of court," that is, given lectures or reprimands by the interviewers at the House of Detention, without trial, than are handled through the process of court hearing. This is done partly to avoid the stigma of a trial and court record, and partly to reduce the volume of business before the Judge.... (The high number of adjusted cases) makes manifest the large proportion of children who have been spared a court record, and is suggestive of the amount of time and attention which the Judge is able to devote to the more serious cases, as well as the immense savings in dollars and cents to the taxpayers for court hearings and other expenses attached to trials. The savings to the families and children concerned can only be appreciated; it cannot be measured in terms of money (p. 241).[19]

Table 16 shows how popular adjustment of cases was in the original JC. Its popularity, nevertheless, would decline severely in later decades (see Chapter 5).

H. The Substitute/Ultimate Parental Role of the Original JC: Improving Living Conditions

JC was founded, in part, to compensate for the failures of parenting in the community, as expressed in the original Pennsylvania JC Act (as well as JC's education/treatment/prevention missions):

Experience has shown that children, lacking proper parental care or guardianship, are led into courses of life which may render them liable to the pains and penalties of the criminal law of the State, although in fact the real interests of such child or children require that they be not incarcerated in penitentiaries and jails, as members of the criminal class, but be subjected to a wise care, treatment and control, that their evil tendencies may be checked and their better instincts may be strengthened... (PA Juvenile Court Act of April 23, 1903, P.L. 274, Preamble).

Regardless of the disposition, the JC's objective was to improve the youth's situation.[20] There were basically no limits to the children who would benefit from the JC's intervention. Accompanying the broad spectrum of "misbehaviors" that were included within JC's delinquency jurisdiction were four categories of youths: dependent, neglected, mental defects, and custody matters. Table 17 catalogues the large number of children in these categories brought into JC between 1914 and 1939. Most interesting, perhaps, is that the JC's involvement in the lives of these children began shortly after the child's birth as detailed in Table 18. Much as with delinquency matters, the availability of ICs for these youths gradually declined through the 1930s and 1940s.

I. The Benign Facilities Utilized by the Original JC

Due, in no small part, to the prevalence of non-serious misconduct, dispositions in the original JC were mostly benign and were designed to improve the youth's lot in life. There was an abundance of child-placing opportunities, mainly via the Department of Public Welfare (DPW), together with child caring/dependent institutions. Table 19 illustrates the number of facilities utilized by the original JC, which were able to remove many youths from bad homes to child-caring locations. These facilities were renamed dependent in 1925; commitments to these facilities were impossible via CC. Otherwise, delinquents were sent to institutions for mental defectives (especially boys) and hospitals (especially girls).

Table 20 discloses how many delinquents were committed to the non-delinquent institutions. The number of delinquents sent to actual delinquent facilities by the original JC was relatively small. By the mid-1920s, however, commitments to delinquent facilities became the norm; these facilities had doubled in number by 1931.

There was considerable overlap between delinquent and dependent/neglected kids in both delinquent and dependent facilities. The latter were able to house "delinquent" kids that would not have fared well in delinquent facilities and would not have been incarcerated in adult institutions. These commitments decreased significantly during the 1930s. Over-active dependent youths were housed in delinquent facilities; none could have placed in CJ institutions.

J. Thousands of Very Young "Offenders" Detained by the Original JC

Complementing the thousands of minor "offenders" that were put on probation and institutionalized (see Tables 8, 9, and 16), the original JC detained thousands more "offenders." Table 21 discloses the thousands of juveniles who were detained, at least overnight, by the original JC between 1925 and 1951. Most critical, the numbers reported in that Table do not include any years prior to 1924, as well as in 1929 and 1943! Almost all of the nearly two thousand boys and girls younger than 10 who were detained between 1925 and 1951 likely would not have been held in the criminal justice (CJ) system; the same can be said for the thousands of other youths younger than 15.

Detention served three JC purposes. First, these youths could be analyzed for medical, mental, and physical issues, and could be provided for immediately:

One of the most valuable features of the detention of delinquent children is the opportunity which is thus afforded to make careful and detailed physical and mental examinations.Shortly after the arrival of a child at the House of Detention, he is given a thorough physical examination, and if he is found to have any defects which should be remedied, the parents' consent is requested. If such consent is obtained, the child is taken to the proper hospital. In venereal cases examinations and hospital treatment are given when necessary and are closely followed up by probation officers after discharge from the hospital (JCAR, 1919, p. 226).

* * * * * * * * * *

Regular school work, together with supervised play and recreation, keep the children's minds and hands so occupied that only a minimum amount of discipline is necessary. Their physical welfare is provided for by supervised play and games in the fresh air, daily setting-up exercises and calisthenics, clean and well-aired dormitories, and ample bathing facilities. The children's clothes are fumigated and suitable clean house clothing is provided during their stay in detention (Id., p. 227).

Second, detention provided JC a chance to operationalize their substitute parental role:

The food served is simple, but well prepared, and is chosen with due regard to preserving a proper balance of foodstuffs and providing the necessary variety. Traveling branches of the public library, lectures illustrated with the stereopticon, and the phonograph are used for the entertainment of the children. In fact every endeavor is made to put the child in the proper frame of mind toward himself and those who placed him in detention and at the same to guard against the possibility of alienating him from his own home (JCAR, 1919, p. 227).

Third, detention could provide a "taste" of JC "punishment" that would hopefully deter offenders from recidivating. Detention could accommodate many more youths than long-term facilities because the time was shorter, and the services (and their costs) were markedly curtailed. The temporary deprivation of liberty was designed to convince youths to not return to the juvenile justice (JJ) system.

K. The Original JC's Immigrant/Religious Focus

JCs also disproportionately addressed the situations of poor immigrants. The juveniles

most affected by juvenile court intervention are poor and ignorant kids being put upon by the dominant social class who can't fight the system (Lindsey, E., 1914, p. 140; see, also, Shenton, 1930, p.52)

JCs intervened mostly into the lives of Italian Catholics (followed by Irish and Polish youths):

The nativity of children, however, is not so significant an indication of their social background as the nativity of their parents. The children of foreign or mixed parentage contributed more than their share of delinquency, dependency and neglect cases. Sixty-three in every 100 delinquent white children, 63 in every 100 dependent white children, and 57 in every 100 neglected white children were of foreign or mixed parentage, while among the white child population 7 to 15 years of age in Philadelphia, 55.2 per cent were of foreign or mixed parentage. Among the delinquent white boys, 64.7 per cent were of foreign or mixed parentage as compared with 53.9 per cent of the white girls (JCAR, 1923, pp. 26-27).

Table 22 details the percentage of white Protestant versus white Catholic boys and girls. Philadelphia JC was concerned with the ethnic ghettoes and kids gathering in groups there.

L. The Original JC's Family/Clinic Focus

The original JC was more of a clinic than a court. That statement no longer applies and has not for decades. But the entire original JC experience was geared to adopt a comprehensive, family-oriented, health-first approach to juveniles' problems. Even POs were under this obligation in the community:

The aim of the department is not only to see that at least a minimum standard of care is given the child place on probation, but to do constructive work for the entire family. Emphasis is placed on intensive educational work. The health is supervised, advice is given regarding bathing, fresh air, sleeping arrangements. Institutional care is urged for feeble-minded, insane, active tubercular and syphilitic cases. Suggestions are made to the mother regarding the care of the home, especially as to the proper buying and preparation of food... (JCAR, 1917, p.94).

From the beginning, the purpose of the JC was to conduct a thorough and incredibly comprehensive living condition/social examination of all children believed to have a problem.

The fundamental purpose of Juvenile Court procedure in delinquency cases is to discover whether he is a subject for special protectiocare, and guardianship by the community in the same degree as the child which is neglected or homeless.

* * * * * * * * * *

Since the juvenile offender is not considered a criminal, but a child in need of protection, it is essential that legal evidence be accompanied by social evidence. The Probation Department, therefore, makes a thorough and impartial investigation of the child's family history and circumstances, parental history and characteristics, and the Medical Department makes an examination of his physical and mental condition. The results of these investigations and examinations are recorded, filed, and summarized, so that they may be utilized by the Judge in determining the proper procedure for the children concerned (JCAR, 1919, pp. 212, 213).[21]

The clinic-like responsibilities of JC were widespread and intensive:

About 3 in every 5 (58.5 per cent) children brought in on new charges were examined physically — 68.3 per cent of the delinquent children, 51.3 per cent of the dependent children, and 47.0 per cent of the neglected children.

Of the 2,112 children examined, 1,432 or 67.8 per cent, were found to be defective. About one-half (51.3 per cent) of the delinquent children examined were found to be physically defective as compared with 91.4 per cent of the dependent children, and 86.8 per cent of the neglected children.

Defective teeth was the most common defect noted in the physical examinations; 312 had defective teeth, 156 had defective eyes, 107 had phimosis. Other common defects and the number of children found to be defective, were: Bronchitis, 77; defective hearing, 56; malnutrition, 44; pediculosis, 42; gonorrhea, 41; diseased tonsils, 40.

Nearly one-half (48.1 per cent) of the children brought in on new charges and disposed of were examined mentally — 57.2 per cent of the delinquent children, 42.5 per cent of the dependent children, and 35.9 per cent of the neglected children. Over one-half (56 per cent) of the delinquent children examined were found to be mentally defective—52.4 per cent of the boys and 68.1 per cent of the girls (JCAR, 1923, pp. 27, 28).[22]

M. The Original JC's Denial of Rights Approach

The original JC relied heavily on an informal setting and informal procedures. Constitutional rights afforded the accused would sabotage the entire inquiry into the juveniles' situations and interfere with potentially necessary outcomes. Additionally, rights would restrict the powers of JC workers (especially judges and POs), and perhaps prevent them from doing the right thing. The absence of rights also allowed the expediting of the court process to reach children quickly and cheaply. Resources could be both preserved and dedicated to treatment.

Informality and adjustments ruled the early JC. Trials and substantive rights were denied.

Whenever it seems unnecessary or inadvisable to bring the child personally into court, a summary of the findings is presented to the Judge, who if he approve the recommendation, signs the transcript to this effect, by which the recommendation becomes a legal disposition... (JCAR, 1917, p. 99).

Although critical to the mission, the early annual reports from Philadelphia's JC did not emphasize the lack of rights in JC. There would have been countless adjudications and dispositions lost or later voided by the allowance of rights; JC would have been severely compromised. One of the few acknowledgements of this reality was noted in the 1941 JCAR.

Privacy in the hearing of juvenile cases is essential to create an atmosphere of understanding between the judges on the bench and the child. The child must not feel that he stands before the bar of a court as an indicted criminal; instead he should be and is made to feel that the judge is a friendly person who seeks to protect the child as well as the community... (p. 9).

In a nutshell, rights were denied to juvenile defendants for myriad reasons. The explanations and defense of this no-rights policy/practice were comprehensive:

Unnecessary: youths did not need protection against the JC's protective efforts; JC was rehabilitating, not punishing youthful offenders;
Inappropriate: JC was examining the youth's condition (clinic), not conduct;
Undeserved: juveniles were entitled to protective custody, not liberty;
Harmful: rights would be costly and deprive the court of valuable resources; rights could lead to the wrongful acquittal of a needy offender; rights would suggest that JC was hurting and not helping youths; right to a public/jury trial would stigmatize the youth; and, rights would interfere with both inquiring into and developing the solution to the youth's problems;
Inapplicable: JCs used a different terminology and perspective. Juvenile offenders were not arrested, convicted or punished. Instead, they were taken into custody, adjudicated, and rehabilitated. The titles and classification would both stigmatize less and expand the powers of juvenile court workers (no crime/punishment=no rights) (see Sanborn and Salerno, 2005, pp. 24-25).

The overall benevolent mission of JC regarding delinquents, bolstered by its jurisdictional inclusion of dependent and neglected juveniles, likely contributed to the no-rights formula being seen as reasonable and even legitimate. That perception lasted for six plus decades, until the U.S. Supreme Court intervened into JC operation in the *In re Gault* decision (1967).

N. The JC's Original Design Worked Against the Relevance and Necessity of Transfer

In the end, the original JC was truly a court of *delinquency* where the vast majority of juvenile "offenses" were not even offenses, let alone crimes, and where the vast majority of "offenders" were mostly damaging themselves and not others. Perhaps it is no surprise, then, that

(o)riginally, juvenile courts characterized young people as vulnerable and morally incapable of committing a crime... (Feld, 1999, p. 242).[19]

The original JC was not created primarily to spare juvenile criminals the harsh outcomes of CC. Most, if not all, of the Theories/Propositions (T/Ps) suggested in Chapter 2 have been confirmed by the experiences of Philadelphia's JC in its early and formative years.

Philadelphia's JC would change dramatically and permanently after 16- and 17-year-olds were added to its jurisdiction. The original JC would not survive the 1950s, as we will see in Chapter 5.

REFERENCES

Bonnie, R. J. (1989). Juvenile homicide: A study in legal ambivalence. In E. P. Benedek & D. G. Cornell (Eds.), *Juvenile homicide* (pp. 185–217). American Psychiatric Press.

Claghorn, K. H. (1931). *Statistical department of the municipal court of Philadelphia*. Thomas Skelton Harrison Foundation.

Commonwealth v. Fisher. (1905). 62 A. 198. Pennsylvania Supreme Court.

Feld, B. C. (1999). *Bad kids: Race and the transformation of the juvenile court*. Oxford University Press.

Geraghty, T. F. (1997). Justice for children: How do we get there? *The Journal of Criminal Law & Criminology*, *88*(1), 190–241. doi:10.2307/1144077

In re Gault. (1967). 387 U.S. 1.

JCAR. (1917-1978). *Juvenile court annual report*. Municipal Court of Philadelphia (1917-1959); County Court of Philadelphia (1960-1967); Court of Common Pleas, Juvenile Division (1968-1978).

Jeter, H. R. (1922). *Bureau Publication no. 104*. The Chicago juvenile court, U.S. Children's Bureau.

Lindsey, E. (1914, March). The juvenile court movement from a lawyer's standpoint. *The Annals of the American Academy of Political and Social Science*, *LII*(1), 140–148. doi:10.1177/000271621405200117

Mansfield's Case. (1903). 22 Pa Super. 224. Pennsylvania Superior Court.

Packel, L. (1975). A Guide to Pennsylvania Delinquency Law. *Villanova Law Review*, *21*, 1–71.

Pennsylvania Juvenile Court Act. (1903). No. 205, April 23, 1903, P.L. 274.

Sanborn, J. B. Jr, & Salerno, A. W. (2005). *The juvenile justice system: Law and process*. Roxbury Publishing Company. Oxford University Publishing.

Shenton, C. G. (1930). *History and function of the Municipal Court of Philadelphia*. Thomas Skelton Harrison Foundation.

Tanenhaus, D. S. (2000). The evolution of transfer out of the juvenile court. In J. Fagan & F. E. Zimring (Eds.), *The changing borders of juvenile justice: Transfer of adolescents to the criminal court* (pp. 13–43). University of Chicago Press.

Trulson, C. R., Caudill, J. W., Belshaw, S. H., & DeLisi, M. (2011). A problem of fit: Extreme delinquents, blended sentencing, and the determinants of continued adult sanctions. *Criminal Justice Policy Review*, *23*(3), 263–284. doi:10.1177/0887403410370618

Zimring, F. E. (1998a). *American youth violence*. Oxford University Press.

Zimring, F. E. (2019). *American Juvenile Justice* (2nd ed.). Oxford University Press.

ENDNOTES

1 The original Pennsylvania Juvenile Court Act (1901) was declared unconstitutional by the state's intermediate appellate court (*Mansfield's Case*, 1903) because the Act authorized incarceration until the age of 21 for mere violations (a fine was the most serious penalty for violations in CC), and defendants in JCs were denied a right to jury trial The legislature responded within three months and passed a second JC act in 1903 where "only those children deemed appropriate for such disposition were to be referred to the juvenile court… (Packel, 1975, p. 5)." That act was upheld by the state's Supreme Court in 1905 (*Commonwealth v. Fisher*). In 1923, JCs were finally given exclusive jurisdiction over juvenile crimes (Packel, 1975, p. 7).

2 The contention is the dynamics of the JC's operation in Philadelphia would be found as well in other urban areas (see, e.g., Chapter 1, fn. 7) during the first years of JCs; these major urban areas accounted for most youths processed by JCs during that era. Those dynamics include: the maximum age limit; the breadth of JC jurisdiction; the young age of "offenders;" the non-criminal behavior dominance of the docket; the absence of constitutional rights; the campaign against the alleged immorality of girls; and, the virtually unlimited powers of POs and judges.

3 The annual reports from Philadelphia's JC began in 1917. Between 1917 and 1923, some indictable offenses committed by those younger than sixteen went directly to CC, which could then send the case to JC, except murder charges that had to remain in CC (Shenton, 1930, pp. 48-49). During this time, Philadelphia's JC enjoyed much less autonomy over its jurisdiction. There is a strong likelihood that the characteristics of the original, non-reported JC (1903-1916) in Philadelphia were even more distinguishable from the CC than are revealed in this chapter.

4 Table 1 underreports the actual numbers of cases for the age groups subjected to JC intervention in these two decades. Besides the absence of 1922 data, only one-half of 1924's numbers were reported, some years reported the number of defendants and not cases, some years reported no informal complaints (ICs) (see subsection on ICs), and some years reported no ages related to cases in which girls were witnesses to sex crimes (see subsection on girls' immorality).

5 These numbers were reported in Table 45, p. 138 of the 1921 JCAR. There were not age breakdowns in the IC category in other early years of the annual report. ICs involved most of the very young JC "defendants" during the court's earliest years. These cases allowed parents, relatives, neighbors, and others to submit sensitive and minor issues to the court typically without triggering a formal process or the court's official attention (see subsection C, *infra.*).

6 The numbers for recidivists in the other (age) groups were: 21 of 93 (eight); 57 of 176 (nine); 79 of 292 (ten); 146 of 406 (eleven); 209 of 561 (twelve); 273 of 663 (thirteen); 321 of 816 (fourteen); The proportion of recidivists per age group also ascended with age, except for those 10 and 14 years-old and, 372 of 855 (fifteen). Similar age breakdowns with respect to numbers of offenses committed, and recidivists were reported in the 1921, 1923, 1924, and, 1925 annual reports. Later reports failed to cover this material by specific ages.

7 Boys' offenses were typically very minor and were regarded and treated that way: *One of the interesting features for 1918 was the work done by the referees on trolley cases. Whenever a boy was arrested for stealing a ride on trolley cars, he was given a severe reprimand and allowed to go home until a further date, when he was again summoned to appear, together with other like offenders. On this second hearing the referees would explain at length to parents and children the danger of the practice of stealing rides on the cars and the object of the arrests — that is, preserving of*

the children's lives and limbs, so that Philadelphia may have in the future, strong, healthy, sound citizens. These talks of the referees would be further supplemented by a talk from the "Safety First Lady" employed by the Philadelphia Rapid Transit Company. During the year 1918, there were 193 cases of this type and only two children repeated the offense during the year (JCAR, 1918, p. 139).

8 JCs was getting tired of boys' trivial acts; the titles of these acts evolved with a change in tone:
• Disturbing the peace (1919);
• Offenses due to carelessness or spirit of play (1920);
• Offenses due to carelessness or spirit of play or mischief (1923);
• Acts of carelessness or mischief (1925); and, years later,
• Malicious mischief (1964)

9 Boys who ran away or who were incorrigible were not seen as immoral creatures.

10 Between 1922 and 1929, there were two indecent assault and one indecent exposure girl cases. During the 1930s the annual reports did not itemize sex offenses for boys or girls.

11 One or two boys sometimes were mentioned in this category; most years had none.

12 A complaint was lodged against including *witness cases* among *delinquencies*: "If a witness has not committed an offense, he is not an offender; if he or she has committed an offense — for example, if a girl held as a witness in a sex offense is also considered enough of an offender to be placed on probation — he or she should be classified under some offense and not as a witness (Claghorn, 1931, p. 21, footnote omitted)." The footnote explained: "The statistical clerks now examine the records of cases of witnesses and decide from the recorded data whether the child is simply a witness, a protection case, in danger of becoming immoral, or an offender (Id.)." Starting with the 1926 Annual Report, witness cases were recorded separately from delinquent cases.

13 This segment of the morality crusade ended by 1956. From the late 1960s on the minimum age of female sex offenders was very rarely below 11 years of age. The morality crusade had run out of steam.

14 JC authorities reacted to an increase in delinquency rates in 1918. Besides WW1, the fact that mothers were tempted away from their homes into employment where they sought to take advantage of the high wages due to industrial activities. These were the chief factors decreasing home and parental control, and made for increasing delinquency and dependency... (JCAR, 1918, p. 92).

15 There was a yearly average: 3.2 homicides (range: 0 (4 times) to 9 (once)); and 13 carrying weapons (range: 2-27) between 1917 and 1939, while there were 5.1 indecent assaults (range: 0-22); and, 11.5 rapes (range: 2-21) between 1917 and 1929.

16 Examples of innocuous sex crimes included:
• Disorderly child (staying out overnight, disregarding parental commands): nearly all girls (20/year during the 1920s);
• Associating with dissolute/vicious persons: almost all girls; (36 cases in 1923, and joined with disorderly child in 1924);
• Bastardy: both genders (four boy and 49 girl cases between 1917 and 1924);
• Fornication: both genders (124 boy and 166 girl cases between 1923 and 1929);
• Incest: (one boy and three girl cases between 1923 and 1929);
• Sodomy: nearly all boys (124 boy and four girl cases between 1917 and 1929);
• Obscene pictures; all boys (10 cases between 1917 and 1929);
• Immorality (13 boy cases in 1918);

- Inmate of bawdy/disorderly house: (19 boy and 68 girl cases during the 1920s);
- Danger of becoming immoral: (eight boy and 45 girl cases between 1923 and 1929);
- Insulting persons of the other sex: (4 four boy cases in 1929);
- Witness of rape/other sex crime: almost all girls (see Table 6); and,
- Indecent exposure: (54 boy and two girl cases during the 1920s).

17 High numbers of adjustments/discharges in serious cases suggests several possible causes: (1) high tolerance of misbehavior; 2) tangential connection to the crime; 3) JC as a last resort; 4) informal handling effective; 5) POs' over-charging; 6) reduce AH caseload; or, 7) desire to avoid stigma.

18 The 1964 report repeated this statement and then added: *Not every child about whom a complaint has been made needs to appear before the juvenile court judge. Also, from a practical standpoint, the number of cases of alleged delinquency is so large that some method of sifting out cases before they come to the judge is necessary* (JCAR, 1964, p. 34).

19 The JCAR (1922) cited a Chicago report favoring avoidance of formal court action: *Court action should be avoided for a number of reasons. First and foremost is the wish to spare the child a court record, for the trial of dependent and delinquent cases in the same court has resulted in attaching a stigma even to dependency proceedings. In the second place, the moral effect of a voluntary arrangement is thought to be happier than that produced by the order of the judge, and even if that order is with the consent of the parents, the flexibility of an informal disposition is often to be preferred to the rigidity of a court order. In the third place, it is imperative that the overburdened judge shall not waste his time and energy on unnecessary cases. A fourth consideration is the saving of taxpayers' money; every case heard in court involves a certain expense...* (JCAR, 1922, p. 18, citing Jeter, 1922, pp. 42-43).

Similarly, the JCAR (1941) explained:

On the day following the arrest, the child appears for a preliminary, informal interview, the main purpose of which is to adjust cases too trivial and inconsequential to warrant court action; cases, for example, involving playing ball in the streets, stealing rides, "malicious" mischief, and other minor offenses which occur daily in a large industrial city like Philadelphia, having a population of about 270,000 children of juvenile-court age (p. 7).

* * * * * * * * *

If the facts brought out at this conference show that it is for the best interests and welfare of the child to settle that case then and there, this is done and the child is discharged from custody. If the interviewers believe that the child will not further offend and may profit by a short period of supervision by a probation officer, probation is recommended. All decisions as to adjustment or probation must be confirmed by the judge (Id.).

20 As explained in the JCAR (1941): *"Probation" in juvenile work connotes more than is ordinarily understood by the term. The court worker's friendly supervision of the child on probation consists in frequent home and school visits and interviews with the child, his parents, the teacher, the principal, or the school counselor. The probation officer, having once established personal contact with the child and parents, endeavors to discover the cause or causes of the child's difficulties. He tries to ascertain his needs and desires. He endeavors to re-establish the child's self-confidence which might have been shaken by his failure in school or lack of understanding and appreciation at home. The worker helps the child to join a recreation center, playground*

association or boys' club.... The institutions, both public and private, to which juveniles are committed, are founded on the idea that their training and education should enable the child to find a place in the community.

** * * * * * * * * **

The promotion of the best interests and welfare of the child is paramount concern of the court. Whenever possible, this aim is achieved through the co-operation of the parents. If, however, the parents are unwilling or unable to co-operate, the judge can use the authority of his position and of the law (sometimes against the will of the parents) in order to safe-guard the permanent welfare of the child. The State has not only the right but the duty to override the formal rights of the parents if the welfare of the child demands it (pp. 10, 12).

21 This concern and dedication on JC's part continued for decades: *The complete case record is before the judge at the hearing of the case, giving a detailed picture of the family relationships; the home and neighborhood; the economic status of the parents; the personal history of the child, including other conduct difficulties, control, and supervision; school report; religious training; impressions of personality; interests; recreation; and associates. It is an established rule of the court that every child under 16 whose case is to be heard by the court must have a thorough physical and mental examination, including an intelligence test. These examinations are conducted by the medical department of the court, under the supervision of a competent staff of physicians, psychologists, psychiatrists, and nurses* (JCAR, 1941, pp. 8-9).

22 The 1920 results of physical exams of boys: 1,588 defects: Teeth: 808 or 50.9%; Circumcision: 276 or 17.4%; Throat: 161 or 10.1%; Eyes: 134 or 8.4%; Physical Upbringing: 67 or 4.2%; Skin: 36 or 2.3%; Nose: 30 or 1.9%; Ears: 18 or 1.1%; Speech: 18 or 1.1%; Hernia: 17 or 1.1%; Heart: 11 or .7%; Lungs: 8 or .5%; Varicocele: 2 or .1%; Hydrocele: 1 or .1%. and, Urethritis: 1 or .1% (JCAR, 1920, p. 49). There were also administered: 363 B and 150 G for syphilis; 1888 for gonorrhea and 150 G examined for rape. The last report on venereal disease and IQ appeared in 1954. For mental exams in 1920 there were 970 boys/ 743 girls tested with the following results: Normal 595/243; Normal Dull 219/471; Border Line 15/4; Moron 6/4; Imbecile 1/1; Doubtful Cases 134/19; Border line or below 51/8; Normal/Normal Dull 83/11 (JCAR, 1920, p. 50). *[O]f the 612 children distributed between the first grade and high school only 66 were in grades normal for their respective ages. Two children were above normal in their scholastic standing and 540 were retarded. In other words, 98 per cent of the children who came before the Juvenile Court are retarded by comparison with approximately 250,000 public school children in the City at large. Doubtless those who charge all delinquency to mental defects will find proof for their theory in these figures. It remains, however, for the Court to make more thorough and more systematic neuropsychiatric tests of the children who came in contact with the probation department* (JCAR, 1918, pp. 96-97).

CHAPTER 4 TABLES

*Table 1. Cases of juveniles, by age, processed in Philadelphia's juvenile court, 1920-1939**

Age	#Boys/Girls Cases	Average # Boys/Girls Cases	% Boys/Girls Cases
< 7	468/369	26.0/20.5	.5/2.7
7-9	7,206/919	400.3/51.1	8.2/6.7
<10	7,674/1,288	383.7/64.4	8.7/9.4
10-11	14,968/1,284	831.6/71.3	17.1/9.4
<12	22,642/2,572	1,132.1/128.6	25.8/18.9
12	11,534/1,116	640.8/62.0	13.1/8.2
13	14,286/1,909	793.7/106.1	16.3/14.0
<14	48,462/5,597	2,423.1/279.85	55.2/41.0
14	18,613/3,303	1034.1/183.5	21.2/24.2
15	20,648/4,736	1,147.1/263.1	23.5/34.7
Total	87,723/13,636	4,873.5/757.6	99.9/99.9

Note: This Table reports cases involving new charges only; it omits relatively few 16- and 17-years-old defendants that had been adjudicated delinquent while fifteen years of age or younger and had to appear before juvenile court due usually to a Violation of Probation or review of the disposition/commitment.

* The data presented in Tables 1-37 are derived from JCAR (1917-1939). *Juvenile court annual report.* Municipal Court of Philadelphia (1917-1959); County Court of Philadelphia (1960-1967); Court of Common Pleas, Juvenile Division (1968-1978).

Table 2. Examples/Numbers of < 16 Boys' Minor Crimes/Acts of Carelessness/Status Offenses, 1917-1939

Offense Type	Years Reported	Number Reported	Average	Range
Larceny/theft[i]	1917-1939	23,502	1,021.8	561-1427
Malicious Mischief[ii]	1917-1939	23,057	1,002.5	324-1720
Trespassing	1917-1939	7,860	341.7	81-795
Disorderly Conduct[iii]	1917-1939	6,025	262.0	6-703
City Ordinance	1917-1929	498	38.3	5-73
Running-Institution	1917-1939	1,789	77.8	4-245
Delinquency[iv]	1919-1925	473	67.6	11-213
Auto Violations[v]	1923-1939	631	37.1	6-94
Non-violent Sex Crimes[vi]	1917-1929	447	34.4	4-90
Food/Coal Stealing[vii]	1923-1939	743	43.7	3-181
Home Stealing[viii]	1921-1939	245	12.9	3-45
Gambling	1917-1939	1,127	49.0	10-148
Play Ball in Street	1921-1939	260	13.7	2-34
Fighting	1925-1939	200	13.3	1-36
Stealing Rides	1917-1939	1,706	74.2	14-266
Throw Stones	1917-1939	599	2.6	3-89
Swim Nude	1923-1939	68	4.0	0-15
Begging	1921-1939	115	6.1	2-21
Loafing/Vagrancy	1917-1939	2,575	112.0	33-60
Drunkenness/ Intoxication	1917-1939	137	6.0	1-16
Child Labor	1921-1939	111	6.5	1-13
Truancy	1917-1939	7,259	315.6	130-677
Runaway Home	1917-1939	13,273	577.0	411-728
Incorrigible	1917-1939	6,898	300.0	134-541
TOTAL	1917-1939	99,695	4,334.6	81.4%

[i] The thefts include all larceny, shoplifting, receiving stolen property, fraud, and embezzlement charges.

[ii] Destroying property first appeared in 1925. Between 1925 and 1933 malicious mischief and destroying property were reported separately; they were joined as one in 1934. The two offenses are joined as one from 1925-1939 in this table.

[iii] Disorderly conduct was identified from 1917 until 1923. From 1924 until 1932, disorderly conduct was replaced by disturbing the peace, which, in turn was replaced by creating a disturbance in 1933. All three offenses are reported under disorderly conduct in this table.

[iv] A generic "delinquency" charge was available for a brief time. It served as a trashcan for offenses that did not seem to fit anywhere else. Perhaps the only amazing thing about this is that it lasted only a brief time.

[v] Auto violations include stealing automobile accessories and motor vehicle violations.

[vi] Non-violent sex-related offenses include sodomy, fornication, indecent exposure, bastardy, living in a bawdy house, in danger of becoming immoral, incest, and obscenity.

[vii] This form of theft was described in the reports as stealing food or coal for the residents of the home.

[viii] This form of theft was described as stealing from another member of the home.

Table 3. Number of Delinquent Charges against Boys/Girls (B/G), Ages: <10; 10/11; 12/13; 14/15; 1930; 1932-1936; 1939

Year	Burglary	Robbery	Other Stealing	Assault & Battery	Acts of Carelessness	Auto Theft	Incorrigibility	Truancy	Runaway	Sex Offenses	Other/ Misc.	Total Number
B/G < 10 Offenses												
1930	74/0	13/0	128/10	11/0	316/23	6/0	44/3	4/0	54/3	14/4	5/1	669/44
1932	43/1	1/0	54/4	6/0	236/44	5/0	28/10	8/0	64/5	13/3	4/1	462/67
1933	44/0	0/0	58/1	10/0	273/24	5/0	45/4	10/2	56/3	16/4	4/1	521/39
1934	51/0	1/0	41/0	7/1	151/18	2/0	24/4	11/4	52/5	3/7	2/0	345/39
1935	22/0	1/0	44/1	8/1	179/12	3/0	29/2	7/0	56/2	8/5	0/0	357/23
1936	30/2	0/0	25/0	7/1	116/11	1/0	25/2	6/1	29/2	10/3	2/0	251/22
1939	18/0	1/0	41/0	29/4	159/6	0/0	18/6	8/0	46/7	9/3	1/0	330/26
B/G 10 & 11 Offenses												
1930	131/2	24/0	229/9	17/0	470/20	13/0	52/14	18/0	132/11	8/5	8/3	1102/64
1932	89/1	1/0	176/4	14/2	478/21	10/0	32/13	13/0	83/19	13/2	9/0	918/62
1933	117/0	2/0	146/9	14/2	506/14	16/0	49/11	12/2	79/9	14/5	4/0	959/52
1934	123/1	20/	149/14	6/2	378/20	12/0	54/14	28/0	111/9	6/4	3/1	881/65
1935	73/0	2/0	123/6	20/0	415/10	10/0	31/10	13/1	152/18	8/2	1/1	848/48
1936	72/2	5/0	109/7	17/4	285/7	6/0	37/12	14/1	102/4	10/7	5/0	662/44
1939	83/0	2/0	119/8	46/9	306/8	11/1	25/6	11/0	105/13	15/3	5/0	728/48
B/G 12 & 13 Offenses												
1930	186/0	46/0	419/23	42/2	784/53	44/1	84/47	28/6	192/74	21/18	44/4	1890/228
1932	173/0	7/0	322/39	20/4	846/39	26/0	64/34	41/2	114/39	17/11	43/1	1673/154
1933	192/2	10/0	311/17	26/6	759/32	26/0	57/53	39/4	97/30	15/10	30/1	1562/155
1934	242/0	9/0	307/23	41/1	667/23	28/0	57/45	32/8	170/39	11/15	13/0	1577/154
1935	172/1	11/0	303/17	27/5	615/27	19/0	51/40	43/4	172/35	16/14	7/1	1436/144
1936	143/1	7/1	224/17	31/4	423/17	10/0	62/36	32/3	132/32	16/14	13/2	1093/127
1939	152/4	12/0	258/18	43/11	483/11	31/0	58/30	37/4	160/35	17/9	13/0	1264/122
B/G 14 & 15 Offenses												
1930	247/2	47/1	514/40	85/4	1018/45	159/1	134/163	116/19	172/207	39/51	222/8	2753/541
1932	198/5	8/1	469/40	45/10	1134/48	106/0	95/171	116/32	132/147	32/47	161/12	2496/513
1933	293/0	23/0	476/34	70/6	1310/57	105/0	101/144	125/47	111/82	38/30	121/13	2773/413
1934	370/2	12/0	473/34	55/1	1237/40	97/0	100/128	142/45	296/110	31/43	83/4	2896/407
1935	273/0	29/0	457/30	28/14	954/55	70/1	97/117	148/30	265/98	28/45	59/7	2436/397
1936	234/1	23/0	347/18	54/5	765/21	60/0	96/104	129/37	254/118	54/28	91/5	2122/337
1939	262/0	17/0	343/24	61/14	660/20	99/0	98/103	120/32	220/93	29/32	35/1	1944/319

Table 4. Dispositions for Non-Dismissed Delinquent Cases for Boys/Girls (B/G), Ages: <10, 10/11, 12/13, 14/15; 1930-1936 B/G <10

Year	Probation	Commit Agency/ Individual	Correctional Commit	Dependent Institution	Hospital/ Feeble	Runaway Returned	Restitution
1930	53/2	23/2	16/0	8/0	4/0	30/1	36/0
1931	30/4	6/3	7/0	4/1	0/0	30/3	12/0
1932[1]	50/2	6/2	22/1	-------	--------	?	10/1
1933	47/7	16/0	10/0	14/0	2/0	38/1	7/0
1934	23/4	11/10	8/1	7/1	1/0	?	9/0
1935	22/3	11/2	10/0	2/0	2/1	50/2	3/0
1936	40/2	10/3	9/0	0/3	2/0	24/1	6/0
B/G 10/11							
1930	140/7	35/3	47/3	4/3	8/0	80/5	45/0
1931	122/17	24/2	38/1	7/1	3/1	74/6	25/0
1932	92/4	16/5	44/4	--------	-------	?	23/0
1933	102/9	20/1	27/2	2/0	7/0	59/8	24/0
1934	101/12	38/6	41/4	8/0	1/0	?	17/3
1935	101/6	20/7	39/4	2/3	6/0	122/9	12/0
1936	129/9	23/7	55/3	7/1	4/0	74/2	2/0
B/G 12/13							
1930	220/58	19/11	124/19	4/3	12/5	117/34	84/0
1931	187/25	25/15	106/5	1/ 2	7/4	100/18	41/2
1932	205/26	27/9	112/15	--------	--------	?	39/3
1933	201/30	45/12	66/9	3/0	12/3	66/14	46/0
1934	207/40	37/13	88/9	1/ 4	2/1	?	50/1
1935	216/39	34/6	136/17	4/1	11/4	134/19	15/1
1936	237/45	26/8	102/7	5/2	7/4	98/17	11/0
B/G 14/15							
1930	321/120	22/46	169/40	2/12	7/10	111/80	63/0
1931	276/125	23/22	162/48	2/4	11/15	113/85	60/1
1932	258/162	63/41	174/55	--------	--------	?	55/4
1933	269/94	107/43	124/30	1/1	21/5	73/38	68/1
1934	294/107	94/38	184/41	0/0	21/18	?	53/1
1935	411/111	54/43	231/39	4/3	21/15	221/36	23/0
1936	450/95	33/29	214/43	2/0	33/15	217/51	10/1

Table 5. Early Juvenile Court Profile of < 16 Boys' Delinquent Charges, 1917-1923

1917: 3.75x as many Larceny charges (1,920) as *all* Big 10 charges (506) (see Table 4-SSS); 2.1x as many Runaway-Home (H) *and* Incorrigible charges (1,078) as *all* Big 10 (506); 2.4x as many Runaway-H, Incorrigible and Truancy (RIT) charges (1,208) as *all* Big 10 (506); More Vagrancy/Gambling/Stealing Rides (181) than Robbery *and* Assault & Battery (A&B) (173); More Disorderly Conduct (DC) and Trespass (TR) charges (294) than Robbery *and* A&B (173); More Vagrancy/Gambling/Stealing Rides/City Ordinance (CO) (247) than Big 10 w/o Burglary (202); More Vagrancy (V) and Gambling (G) (127) than Robbery (83), Rape (11), Indecent Assault (4), Carrying Concealed Weapon (Carry) (12), *and* Homicide (2) (combined 112 total); As many Lost (L) (2) and Reckless Auto (RA) (2) charges as Homicide charges (2); More Malicious Mischief (MM) charges (324) than Burglary charges (304); More Fire Alarms charges (FA) (12) than Rape charges (11); and, All non-Big 10 thefts+RIT+Run-Institution (RI)+TR+DC+V+G+CO+FA+RA+Stealing Rides (SR)+ Throwing Stones (TS)+Nuisance (N) = 3,844 = 81.4% of new charges. (With MM=4,168=88.2%).
1918: More Gambling charges (111) than A&B charges (110); Almost 3x as many Larceny charges (1,838) as *all* Big 10 charges (622) (see Table 4-SSS); More Malicious Mischief charges (458) than Burglary charges (402); More of each V (47), CO (46), SR (35) and TS (33) charges than Carry (22) *and* Rape (9) charges; 1.7x as many RIT charges (1,054) as *all* Big 10 charges (622); and, All non-Big 10 thefts+RIT+R-I+TR+DC+V+G+SR+CO+FA+ST+N+TS+RA = 3,653 = 76.5% of new charges. (With MM = 4,111 = 86.1%).
1919: More Adjudicatory Hearings (AHs) for Runaway (H and I) (232) than *all* Big 10 AH (209); 2.1x as many Larceny charges (1,193) than *all* Big 10 charges (562) (see Table 4-SSS); 1.4x as many RIT charges (812) as *all* Big 10 charges (562); More Vagrancy charges (79) than Robbery charges (71); 1.8x as many RIT AHs (369) as *all* Big 10 AHs (209); More AHs for Runaway-home (164) and Truancy (165) than #1 AHs in Big 10: Burglary (139); and, All non-Big 10 thefts+RIT+Run-I+DC+G+V+TR+TS+CO+SR+Delinquency (D) = 3,210 = 72.3% of new charges. (With MM = 3,848 = 86.7%).
1920: 1.53x as many AHs for Larceny charges (356) as for *all* Big 10 charges (233); More AH for Incorrigibility (59) than for Robbery (23), A&B (18), Rape (4), *and* Carry (4); As many AHs for Vagrancy as for Robbery (23); More AHs for Runaway-H (139) *and* Truancy (138) (277) than for *all* Big 10 AHs (233); More Correctional Commits (CCs) for Larceny (29) than for *all* Big 10 CCs (26); As many/more CCs for Runaway-H (5), Incorrigibility (3), and Truancy (4) as/than for Rape (2), A&B (3) and Robbery (3); and, All non-Big 10 thefts+RIT+Run-I+DC+D+G+V+CO+SR+TR+FA+TS = 3,407 = 73.3% of new charges. (With MM = 3,869 = 83.3%).
1921: 1.5x as many Larceny charges (1,095) as *all* Big 10 charges (713) (see Table 4-SSS). 1.7x as many RIT charges (1,183) as *all* Big 10 charges (713) (1.8x as many when R-I added). More AHs for Truancy (259) than for *all* of the Big 10 AHs (216); More AHs for Larceny (190) than for Burglary AHs (150); More AHs for Incorrigibility (66) than for all Big 10, except Burglary (all others = 63); Almost as many AHs for Vagrancy and Disorderly Conduct (DC) (15 each) as for Robbery (19) and A&B (16) and more than Rape (10), and almost 2x as many as Auto Theft (8) and Carry (8); More CCs for Larceny (14) *and* Runaway-H (12) than for *all* Big 10 CCs (22); 13x as many CCs for Larceny and Runaway-H (26) as for Robbery (2); and, All non-Big 10 thefts+RIT+Run-I+DC+V+TR+CO+D+TS+SR+Begging (B)+Play Ball (PB)+Child Labor (CL)+Drunkenness (DR) = 3,378 = 68.9% of new charges. (With MM=3,977=81.2%).

continued on following page

Table 5. Continued

1922: More Larceny charges (824) than *all* Big 10 charges (795) (see Table 4-SSS); 1.6x as many RIT charges (1,258) as *all* Big 10 charges (795) (1.9x as many when R-I added); More AHs for both Larceny (239) and Truancy (336) than for *all* Big 10 AHs (213); More AHs for Runaway-H (149) than for Burglary (147); More AHs for both Incorrigibility (103) and Run-I (92) than for all Big 10 AH w/o Burglary (66); More AHs for both MM (36) and DC (28) than for Robbery (23) and A&B (25); CCs for Truancy (33), Run-H (20), Run-I (18), and Incorrigibility (17) = 43.1% of all CCs; and, All non-Big 10 thefts+RIT+Run-I+ST+TR+SR+PB+DC+V+DR+G+D+CO+CL+B= 3,231 = 67.8% of new charges. (With MM = 3,769 = 79.0%).
1923: 1.2x as many all non-Big 10 thefts (1,197) as *all* Big 10 charges (976) (see Table 4-SSS); 1.9x as many RIT charges (1,837) as *all* Big 10 charges (976) (2.1x as many when R-I added); More AHs for Truancy (392) than all Big 10 (324); More AHs for Larceny (244) and Incorrigibility (105) (total 349) than *all* Big 10 (324); 1.5x as many AHs for Larceny (244) as for Burglary (168); More AHs for Incorrigibility (244) and Runaway-H (192) than each Big 10 (Burglary highest at 168); More AHs for Run-I (102) than for Robbery (31) *and* Auto Theft (67); More AHs for Vagrancy (10) than Rape (8), Homicide (7), Indecent Assault (4), Arson (2), Carry (0); As many AHs for Drunkenness/Begging/Child Labor/Receiving Stolen Goods/Stealing Rides as Arson (2); More AHs for Home Stealing (18) than Rape *and* Homicide *and* Arson (17); and, All non-Big 10 thefts+RIT+Run-I+V+G+DC+DR+SR+TR+B+CL+PB+CO+FA+TS+ Motor Vehicle+Swim Nude = 4,238 = 67.8% of new charges. (With MM = 5,032 = 80.5%).
For 60 months (1919-23), Juvenile Court Judges presided at AHs over the following charges: 15 Homicides, 35 Rapes, 4 Indecent Assaults, and 20 Carrying Concealed Weapons charges. *Versus* 81 Vagrancy, 8 Begging; 21 City Ordinance, 807 Runaways-H, 1,290 Truants, 346 Run-I, 10 Gambling, 373 Incorrigibility, 1,376 Larceny/theft, 33 Home Stealing, 29 Trespassing, and 24 Shoplifting charges. (Home Stealing, Begging, and Shoplifting were first reported in 1921)

Table 6. Number & Percentage of Girls' Cases involved in the Morality Crusade (MC),[i] 1920-1939

Year	Total Cases	Run Away[ii]	Incorrigibility	Sex Offenses	Witness Cases[iii]	Total MC#	Total MC (%)
1920	835	235	166	16	72	489	58.6
1921	913	198	166	32	167	563	61.7
1922	928	174	185	64	139	562	60.5
1923	1033	215	178	72	158	623	60.3
1924	914	191	174	51	177	593	64.9
1925	880	161	186	52	152	551	62.6
1926	980	144	207	150[iv]	150	651	66.4
1927	955	205	202	49	199	655	68.6
1928	947	249	230	31	158	668	70.5
1929	1038	306	247	39	172	764	73.6
1930	1100	287	228	78	212	805	73.2
1931	1024	242	235	65	158	700	68.4
1932	992	211	228	64	179	682	68.8
1933	840	127	212	50	172	561	66.8
1934	829	166	193	69	153	581	70.1
1935	779	147	169	67	162	545	70.0
1936	697	150	154	52	166	522	74.9
1937	801	199	171	77	159	606	75.7
1938	769	168	166	39	183	556	72.3
1939	718	148	147	47	200	542	75.5
Total	17,856	3,923	3,844	1,164	3,288	12,219	68.4

[i] The morality-based cases were not the only examples of girls' innocuous behavior during this time. Between 1920 and 1939, 350 cases (or an average of 17.5/year) of*running away from an institution or* agency (which, in some years, was counted as another example of purported immorality) and 923 cases (or an average of 46.2/year) of *truancy* joined the victimless morality-related offenses to provide a profile of girl-offenses that criminal court would have had to ignore. Adding these offenses to the morality-oriented ones yields 13,376 cases or 74.9% of the girls' caseload for those years. Adding these two offenses to the girls' caseload raises the percentage of cases dedicated to non-offenses to a range between a low of 62.4 (in 1920) to a high of 83.9 (1938). Between 1936 and 1939, the percentages of girls' cases involving these six offenses were the highest in the 1920-1939 period: 81.8, 83.9, 80.1, and, 81.5. respectively. In 1940, the percentage rose to 82.6, but there was a slight decline in the percentages of the five following years: 73.4; 67.7; 72.6; 79.5; and, 78.2, respectively. Perhaps the most intriguing aspect involving girls' running away from an institution or agency is that while there were 29 charges in 1929, the numbers decreased in the 10 years between 1930 and 1939 to: 15, 9, 9, 4, 2, 7, 6, 9, 12, and 7, respectively. The depression seems to have had a significant impact on girls' willingness to abandon their current living conditions. World War 2 did not seem to have a similar impact, however. For the next 6 years (1940-1945), the numbers rose to: 25, 48, 26, 22, 23, and, 38, respectively.

[ii] The runaway cases, here, are only those from home/foster home, and not those who ran from an institution/agency. Some annual reports included the latter among the youths who triggered morality concerns; not all did include them, however, and they were not counted in this group

[iii] In 1926, witness offenses were officially removed from the new charges of delinquency category; they were given a separate recording location in the annual reports. That move was intended to reflect that these girls were usually not considered to be actual delinquents. Important, that was not always the case, however. The Total Cases reported in column 1 include both the new delinquency charges and the witness cases for all years.

[iv] The spike in sex offenses in 1926 included 110 charges of fornication. Previous and subsequent years had relatively few fornication charges levelled against girls: 1919: 7; 1921: 2; 1922: 11; 1923: 3; 1924: 3; 1925: 16; 1927: 31; 1928: 3; and, 1929: 0. Seemingly, either girls were especially horny or there was something in Philadelphia's water that year (some of which had started the year before and some of which was left over for the next year).

Table 7. Girls' Sex Offenses, 1922-1929

Year	Disorderly Child[i]	Bastardy	Fornication	Associate[ii]	Danger[iii]	Sodomy/ Indecent Assault	Incest/ Indecent Exposure	Inmate[iv]	Other
1922	7	14	11						
1923		15	3	36	16		1 (I)	1 (B)	
1924	21	15	3		6	1 (IA)		5 (B)	
1925	20		16		6	3 (S); 1 (IA)		4 (B)	2
1926	10		110		8	1 (S)	1 (IE)	20 (P)	
1927	6		31					7(P)	5
1928	24		3					2 (P)	2
1929	19				8			12 (B)	

[i] Although the statute declared that offenders in this category were those not under the age of 16, this category was routinely applied to girl juvenile offenders. It was meant to include all children, "deserting their homes without good and sufficient cause, or keeping company with dissolute or vicious persons, against the lawful commands of their fathers, mothers, or guardians, or other persons standing in the place of parent… (JCAR, 1929, p. 13, Table 4, fn. 5)."

[ii] The illegal association here was with dissolute or vicious persons (which is also the definition of a disorderly child).

[iii] The danger involved becoming an immoral person.

[iv] The illegal residences (as an inmate) were called either a Bawdy house or house of prostitution.

Table 8. Percentage of Boys'/Girls' Cases Resulting in Probation or Commitment, 1924-1939

Year	Runaway	Incorrigibility	Sex Offenses	Truancy	Witness Cases[i]
1924	65.3/70.7	75.4/71.3	64.5/70.6	81.3/70.9	38.4
1925	78.2/67.1	65.8/62.9	74.3/69.2	80.2/68.4	31.6
1926	69.5/60.4	83.2/44.4	67.1/75.3[ii]	89.6/78.3	15.3
1927	65.9/62.0	42.3/36.1	52.6/69.4	77.2/54.3	24.1
1928	70.6/71.2	48.2/46.1	48.3/71.0	62.6/64.9	24.7
1929	50.7/66.4	46.2/49.4	42.9/59.0	58.3/63.0	27.9
1930	30.1/51.7[iii]	33.6/39.9	16.5/52.6	52.1/44.0	15.6
1931	24.5/41.0[iii]	18.2/37.9	30.5/49.2	43.2/24.4	20.9
1932	25.0/64.7	33.0/43.0	19.7/46.9	68.5/61.8	20.1
1933	21.5/55.0	33.1/40.6	12.9/46.0	72.7/61.8	15.7
1934	17.3/68.4	25.8/46.6	21.6/56.5	71.0/64.4	17.0
1935	21.7/65.5	44.5/53.8	20.0/71.6	71.4/61.8	31.8
1936	27.2/66.1	45.9/50.6	44.0/84.6	68.5/71.4	31.3
1937	23.3/60.4	41.8/48.0	45.5/48.1	70.9/71.9	28.9
1938	27.1/50.7	42.5/41.6	35.2/79.5	65.7/68.8	27.5
1939[iv]	24.7/49.6	43.0/54.9	34.8/58.9	66.3/61.1	27.5

[i] There were so few boys' witness cases that only the girls' dispositions are reported here.

[ii] The spike in the percentage of sex offenses resulting in probation/commitment is attributable to 84 of the 110 fornication cases being given these dispositions.

[iii] For 1930-1931, only, runaways included those from institutions/agencies. That inclusion would result in a slight decrease in the percentages of probation and commitments since most of these youths were simply returned to their institution/agency.

[iv] For this year only, all probation and commitment percentages include sixteen- and seventeen-years-old youths.

Table 9. Number/Percentage of Dispositions Dedicated to 6 Girls' Offenses: RISW,[i] Runaway Institution/Agency, Truancy,1925-1939

Year	Probation	Delinquent Commitment	Other Institution/Agency Commitment	Total[ii]
1925				384/487 (78.9%)
1926				375/451 (83.1%)
1927				285/348 (81.9%)
1928				354/436 (81.2%)
1929				404/496 (81.5%)
1930	181/212 (85.4%)	58/64 (90.6%)	93/101 (92.1%)	332/377 (88.1%)
1931	131/155 (84.5%)	46/58 (79.3%)	91/97 (93.8%)	268/310 (86.5%)
1932	184/221 (83.3%)	55/58 (94.8%)	76/85 (89.4%)	315/364 (86.5%)
1933	130/160 (81.3%)	36/43 (83.7%)	67/72 (93.1%)	233/275 (84.7%)
1934	135/178 (75.8%)	53/59 (89.8%)	101/124 (81.5%)	289/361 (80.1%)
1935	150/187 (80.2%)	52/62 (83.9%)	83/95 (87.4%)	285/344 (82.8%)
1936	151/185 (81.6%)	54/57 (94.7%)	83/87 (95.4%)	288/329 (87.5%)
1937	177/205 (86.3%)	41/42 (97.6%)	85/92 (92.4%)	303/339 (89.4%)
1938	123/170 (72.4%)	34/41 (82.9%)	86/102 (84.3%)	243/313 (72.6%)
1939	148/189 (78.3%)	51/60 (85.0%)	72/85 (84.7%)	271/334 (81.1%)

[i] *RISW* means *R*unaway from home, *I*ncorrigibility, *S*ex offenses, and, *W*itness cases, the four morality-based offenses.

[ii] For the first five years in this Table, only a combined probation/commitment disposition was reported. There was no differentiation among the three dispositions so only the cumulative number/percentage is reported.

Table 10. Number & Percentage of Boys'/Girls' (Total) Cases' Resulting in Referrals to Other Courts, Dismissals, Probation & Commitment, 1923-1945[i]

Outcome	Boys	Girls
Referral to Other Court	134	18
Dismiss	71,974	5,851
Dismiss (continue probation)	2,829	204
Total # and % Dismiss, etc.	74,803 (66.4%)	6,055 (43.5%)
# and % of Probation Cases	21,468 (19%)	4,457 (32%)
Commitments: Delinquent	7,997	1,395
Commitments: Other Institutions	1,834	584
Commitments: Agency/Individual	4,564	1,369
# and % of Commitments	14,395 (12.8%)	3,348 (24.1%)
Total # and % of Supervision Cases	35,863 (31.8%)	7,805 (56.1%)
Total Cases	112,740	13,910

[i] Local boys who ran away were 1 ½ times more likely than girls to have their cases dismissed, incorrigible boys two times more likely than girls to experience dismissals, and boy sex offenders were two to three times more likely to have cases dismissed. Compared to boys, girls were two to four times more likely to get probation in runaway cases; probation was one and ½ to two times more likely for girls in both sex and incorrigible cases. Similarly, compared to boys, girls were one and ½ to two times more likely to be committed in runaway cases; commitment was one and ½ times more likely for girls in sex cases and one and ½ times more likely in incorrigible cases.

Table 11. Number & Percent of <16 Boys' Big 10 Serious Offense Cases, & Number of Transfers, 1917-1939

Year	Burglary	Robbery[i]	Indecent Assault/ & Rape	A&B/ Homicide	Carrying Weapon	Drug Offenses	Auto Theft	Arson	Transfers	Total Number & Percent[iii]
1917	304	83	4/11	90/2	12	----	----	----		506/8.9
1918	402	74	0/9	115/0	22	----	----	-----		622/11.0
1919	377	71	0/11	84/0	19	----	----	----		562/10.6
1920	392	48	0/8	109/3	22	----	----	5	3	587/12.6
1921	441	76	7/19	111/3	25	----	30	2	6	714/14.6
1922	462	121	4/19	130/4	14	----	41	----	1	795/16.7
1923	556	73	8/21	176/7	14	----	114	7	3	976/15.6
1924	491	90	20/17	139/4	2	----	61	----	6	824/14.0
1925	412	138	22/12	160/9	17	----	61	----	2	831/15.9
1926	536	191	21/14	126/4	27	----	228	----	6	1,147/21.7
1927	478	103	0/5	95/0	15	----	215	1	1	912/16.9
1928	495	132	0/2	103/2	16	----	242	2	0	994/18.4
1929	512	233	0/2	115/1	11	----	257	6	3	1,13718.7
1930	649	167	85[ii]	157/1	12	0	203	----	4	1,274/19.2
1931	669	42	59	137/5	6	0	170	----	2	1,088/16.7
1932	507	56	76	85/0	5	0	119	----	0	848/14.4
1933	648	81	85	117/4	7	1	134	----	0	1,077/17.6
1934	791	85	51	118/5	6	0	127	----	1	1,183/20.4
1935	545	131	60	109/3	10	0	100	----	1	958/18.7
1936	483	89	91	125/1	10	0	74	----	1	873/21.0
1937	625	86	110	156/7	4	0	138	----	2	1,126/24.0
1938	518	103	71	124/7	9	0	116	----	3	948/24.2
1939	580	123	80	207/2	14	2	145	----	2	1,153/24.4
Total	11,873	2,396	1,004	2,888/74	299	3	2,575	23		21,135/17.2

[i] Robbery and pick pocketing were originally reported separately but were joined in the 1940s. For consistency, both offenses were joined under robbery in this Table. Eventually, purse snatching was identified separately and then later joined with these two offenses.

[ii] During the 1930s, sex offenses were not itemized. This number and the remaining ones in this column include all rapes, indecent assaults, and other sex-related offenses. Thus, these numbers exaggerate, at times considerably, the actual cases of rape/indecent assault. The percentages of boys' cases resulting in probation or commitment dispositions during the 1930s (see Table 8) (and the numbers from previous years) suggest the number of rape and indecent assault charges against boys during this decade is seriously exaggerated among the 1930s' sex offenses. The same applies to total number and percentage of 1930s' Big 10 crimes. The number of arsons was not specified in the 1930s as well; thus, Big 10 crimes in this category were also underreported during this time, but likely not by as much as the rape/indecent assaults were overreported.

[iii] Comparing Table 2 to this Table reveals some interesting results: compared to the Big-10 crimes (21,135) committed between 1917 and 1939, there were 1.1 times as many Larceny/Theft charges (23,502), and Malicious Mischief (MM) charges (23, 057); 1.3 times as many Runaway, Incorrigibility, Truancy (RIT) charges (27,430); and, more Trespass, Disorderly Conduct, Gambling, Stealing Rides, Loafing/Vagrancy, and Begging charges (21,197).

Table 12. Percentage of < 16 Boys' Big 10 Cases Resolved by Trial (AH) & Adjustment (Adj). Percentage of Adjudicatory Hearings & Adjustments Containing Boy's Big 10 Offenses, 1919-1939

Year	% of Big 10 Cases Resolved by AH	% of Big 10 Cases Resolved by Adj	% of AH with Big 10 Offenses	% of Adj with Big 10 Offenses
1919	37.2	62.8	9.4	11.4
1920	39.8	60.2	18.7	10.4
1921	30.3	68.4	18.5	13.3
1922	26.8	73.2	15.8	17.0
1923	33.2	66.8	20.3	14.0
1924	73.8	26.2	17.6	8.9
1925	72.3	27.7	19.7	11.5
1926	81.3	18.7	29.9	9.9
1927	76.3	23.7	24.8	10.3
1928	81.9	18.1	28.6	7.0
1929	82.8	17.2	31.8	6.3
1930	68.8	31.2	38.3	9.2
1931	48.3	51.7	35.6	11.1
1932	49.3	50.7	33.0	9.3
1933	50.9	49.1	38.0	11.3
1934	50.4	49.6	43.9	13.3
1935	60.5	39.5	41.9	10.1
1936	69.6	30.4	45.2	9.4
1937	71.0	29.0	46.5	11.0
1938	75.5	24.5	47.1	9.7
1939	68.2	31.8	43.6	12.6

Table 13. Number of Correctional Commitments, by Offense, <16 Boys, 1920, 1921, 1929-1931, 1933-1939

Offense	1920	1921	1929[i]	1930	1931	1933	1934	1935	1936	1937	1938	1939
Larceny	31	15	244[ii]	205	75[iii]	38	77	125	73	89	54	74
Burglary	17	18	-----	----	73	56	99	106	124	106	73	114
Robbery	3	2	-----	----	4	9	11	16	19	7	9	9
Auto Theft	0	0	-----	-----	15	10	8	11	9	14	16	23
A&B	3	0	2	6	4	7	9	8	19	11	8	19
Rape	2	0	----	----	----	----	----	----	----	----	----	----
Run-Home	5	12	49[iv]	46	47	19	18	31	20	27	14	28
Run-Institution	1	4	-----	----	-----	5	7	6	4	2	1	0
Incorrigible	3	5	35	26	26	24	18	19	24	24	19	18
Truancy	4	3	22	44	54	38	52	52	50	63	57	44
Careless[v]	5	4	37	18	13	18	20	35	30	19	8	20
Sex	----	----	6	5	5	1	0	4	6	9	4	9
Other	6	5	8	8	0	4	3	5	5	2	2	4
Total	80	68	403	358	316	229	322	418	383	373	265	362

[i] Between 1922 and 1928, probation and commitment dispositions were grouped so that there is no way to determine which offenses ended in a commitment disposition.

[ii] The 1929 and 1930 JCARs did not itemize the types of stealing so all larcenies, auto thefts, burglaries and robberies are included within the larceny category in this Table entry. In 1929 and throughout the 1930s sex offenses were not itemized.

[iii] From 1931 on, all non-burglary/robbery/auto theft thefts were grouped as all other stealing and are identified in this table as larceny.

[iv] Between 1929 and 1931, runaways were not divided into the two possible categories.

[v] The careless offense category includes malicious mischief, carrying a concealed weapon, and delinquency.

Table 14. Number of <16 Boys'/Girls' Adjusted Informal Complaints (ICs) on New Charges Brought by Parents/Relatives & Neighbors, 1921-1922, 1926-1939

Year	Parents/Relatives[i]	Neighbors
1920	-------	-------
1921	(246/116)	(24/19)
1922	(396)	(33)
1923	-------	-------
1924	-------	-------
1925	-------	-------
1926	94/91	281/98
1927	103/99	282/88
1928	81/76	253/65
1929	91/75	280/80
1930	101/89	313/91
1931	98/87	212/76
1932	80/68	243/102
1933	76/71	168/67
1934	85/68	191/50
1935	68/57	180/47
1936	-------	-------
1937	92/78	136/29
1938	59/62	141/61
1939	97/69	181/30

[i] The sources of the Informal Complaints (ICs) were not recorded in 1920, 1923-1925, and 1936. In 1921 and 1922, only the whole numbers of Parents/Relatives and Neighbors as sources were reported; the numbers in parentheses do not reflect how many cases in each category were adjusted, per se.

Table 15. Number of Boys'/Girls' New Delinquent Charges as Informal Complaints (ICs), 1921-1939

Year	Theft	Careless[i]	Runaway[ii]	Incorrigible	Truancy	A&B	Other Big 10	Non-Violent Sex Offenses[iii]	Witness to Rape	Other	Total
1921	37/7	159/64	27/27	165/99	29/14	28/11	16/0	3/8	0/145	13/7	477/382
1922	37/5	134/40	47/34	204/122	29/16	53/23	0/0	2/37	0/137	25/31	531/445
1923	33/8	173/46	31/26	150/98	19/5	60/21	2/1	3/20	0/118	1/4	472/347
1924	14/2	66/13	18/16	59/33	13/4	39/14	1/1	5/8	0/98	14/10	229/199
1925	28/5	189/53	11/12	101/45	9/7	27/4	4/1	1/7	1/92	13/5	384/231
1926	15/5	312/101	11/17	98/96	9/6	37/11	5/0	6/9	0/124[iv]	29/17	522/386
1927	26/4	283/77	12/17	96/96	8/4	4/1	1/0	9/3	0/129	1/0	440/331
1928	9/6	236/52	1/8	96/89	3/2	0/2	0/1	8/0	1/94	1/0	355/254
1929	16/3	245/54	6/10	107/99	7/0	16/0	0/0	0/0	0/100	0/0	397/266
1930	27/3	282/82	2/8	100/92	5/2	0/0	0/0	19/4	2/148	0/0	437/339
1931	8/0	234/71	2/4	96/94	6/5	1/0	4/0	3/0	6/101	0/0	360/275
1932	6/0	231/92	3/0	86/77	15/3	0/0	0/0	11/2	1/115	0/0	353/289
1933	3/3	181/57	2/2	73/75	5/3	0/0	0/0	21/3	3/126	0/0	288/274
1934	15/3	177/42	4/0	82/69	1/1	3/1	3/0	5/6	1/115	0/0	291/237
1935	12/3	163/37	2/2	59/61	1/2	15/1	1/0	8/5	7/110	0/0	268/221
1936	15/1	133/31	2/3	71/62	4/0	13/4	1/0	6/1	2/97	0/0	247/199
1937	10/2	125/24	0/2	85/75	6/3	5/2	5/0	21/9	1/104	1/1	258/118
1938	11/1	128/52	0/4	57/72	4/0	10/7	0/1	6/0	0/115	0/0	216/252
1939[v]	15/4	105/13	5/1	92/63	3/2	66/17	7/1	13/3	0/120	0/0	306/224

[i] Careless charges include: disorderly conduct, malicious mischief, throwing stones, gambling, trespassing, etc.

[ii] Runaways are both from home and institutions.

[iii] Non-violent sex offenses include bastardy, disorderly child, obscenity, sodomy, fornication, incest, associating with dissolute persons, in danger of becoming immoral, and, indecent exposure.

[iv] Starting in 1926, witness cases were not counted among the official girls' (or boys') offenses. They are added to the official total of ICs in all the years in this table

[v] In 1939, there were 3 ICs (2 boys and 1 girl) involving 16- and 17-year-olds, but the charges were not indicated; those 3 are included in this table.

Table 16.[i] *Number of (<16) Boys'/Girls' Disposed New Charges: Adjusted Informal Complaints, Adjusted Arrests, & Court Hearings, 1917-1939. Probation & Commitment Dispositions, 1920-1939.*

Year	Adjusted Informal Complaints	Adjusted Arrest Cases	Total Adjusted Cases Without Court Hearing	Court Hearings	Probation & Commitment Dispositions
1917	------	2,615[ii]	2,615	3,127/587	--------
1918	------	3,087[ii]	3,087	2,588/626	--------
1919	------	3,102[ii]	3,102	2,219/693	--------
1920	893[iii]	3,400/328	4,621	1,245/188	2,228/340
1921	669[iii]	3,731/247	4,647	1,170/273	2,363/332
1922	366/306	3,419/246	3,785/552	1,349/349	2,372/380
1923	472/347	4,187/324	4,659/671	1,593/362	2,104/364
1924	229/199	2,211/110	2,440/309	3,452/605	3,397/453
1925	384/231	1,691/71	2,075/302	3,145/578	2,817/406
1926[iv]	522/262 (124)	1,651/67 (1)	2,173/329 (125)	3,122/501 (25)	2,419/428
1927	440/202 (129)	2,148/114	2,588/316 (129)	2,808/440 (70)	2,102/324
1928	354/160 (94)	2,214/101	2,568/261 (94)	2,843/528 (64)	2,162/397
1929	397/166 (100)	2,734/110 (2)	3,131/276 (102)	2,958/590 (70)	2,075/448
1930	435/191 (148)	3,904/180 (2)	4,339/371 (150)	2,290/543 (62)	1,410/357
1931	354/174 (101)	4,692/253	5,046/427 (101)	1,478/439 (57)	1,127/314
1932	352/174 (115)	4,280/247	4,632/421 (115)	1,266/392 (64)	1,081/329
1933	285/148 (126)	4,390/226	4,675/374 (126)	1,444/294 (46)	1,102/248
1934	290/122 (115)	4,137/219	4,427/341 (115)	1,358/335 (38)	1,173/316
1935	261/111 (110)	3,473/196	3,734/307 (110)	1,384/310 (52)	1,341/309
1936	245/102 (97)	2,567/164	2,812/266 (97)	1,345/265 (69)	1,349/266
1937	258/118 (104)	2,715/223 (1)	2,973/341 (105)	1,720/298 (54)	1,511/282
1938	216/137 (115)	2,185/178 (2)	2,401/315 (117)	1,520/271 (66)	1,371/262
1939	304/103 (120)	2,607/157 (2)	2,911/260 (122)	1,375/258 (78)	1,384/237
Total[v]	12,577	74,911	87,488	46,799/9,725 (815)	36,888/6,792

[i] JCAR, 1939 p. 62, Table 5, explains that the numbers for 1924 and 1925 Adjusted Arrest Cases and Court Hearings "are not comparable to other years because of changes in juvenile court procedure in effect during the greater part of 1924 and 1925 (1939, p. 62)." The numbers in the 1939 report often differ slightly from the ones in this Table, which are the numbers reported in each year's annual report. The 1939 report adjusted numbers (e.g., removed witness cases).

[ii] JCAR, 1919. p. 267, Table 2, indicates that none of the girls' delinquent cases were adjusted between 1917 and 1919. Instead, all girls' cases were disposed of by the judge. Whether all of these cases resulted in a hearing as opposed to an adjustment by a PO that was merely later signed off by a judge is unclear. 1919 was the first year in which adjusted cases were identified. The early reports were more oriented to disclosing characteristics of offenders and their families than in disclosing the methods of case resolution.

[iii] The 1920 and 1921 JCARs do not give a gender breakdown for adjusted informal complaints for those years.

[iv] From 1926 on, witness to rape cases (all girls, here) were reported separately in all annual reports. In this Table, the numbers associated with these cases are indicated in the parentheses of each relevant column.

[v] Due to inconsistencies in the reporting of gender association with case resolution, the numbers in the first three columns of the Total are cumulative, without gender differentiations. The number of court hearings in the fourth column is divided by gender, with the number of court hearings in witness cases reported in parenthesis.

Table 17. Dependency, Neglect, Mental, & Custody Cases Disposed, 1914-1939[i]

Court Dispositions							
Year	**Dependent**	**Neglected**	**Mental**	**Custody**	**Total**	**Informal Complaints**	**Cases Placed under Supervision or Committed**
1914	----	----	----	----	2,729	----	----
1915	----	----	----	----	3,188	----	----
1916	----	----	----	----	2,149	----	----
1917	----	----	----	----	1,810	----	----
1918	----	----	----	----	1,964	----	----
1919	----	----	----	----	1,980	726	----
1920	----	----	----	----	1,486	1,768	1,150
1921	1,406	409	64	41	1,920	1,231	1,647
1922	910	960	82	29	2,056	1,694	1,802
1923	1,050	841	61	37	2,122	1,901	1,790
1924	1,654	756	103	42	3,080	1,086	2,407
1925	1,364	999	103	35	2,508	1,488	2,254
1926	1,431	1,078	113	37	2,659	1,419	2,534
1927	1,444	838	151	37	2,470	1,441	2,052
1928	1,157	1,101	152	30	2,440	1,533	2,092
1929	1,351	1,303	166	35	2,855	1,042	2,580
1930	1,548	953	154	40	2,695	1,585	2,485
1931	1,712	956	145	15	2,828	1,157	2,516
1932	1,226	589	149	12	1,976	1,251	1,730
1933	766	491	113	16	1,386	1,187	1,244
1934	1,006	556	104	13	1,679	1,010	1,531
1935	828	679	80	22	1,609	768	1,460
1936	880	808	104	17	1,809	872	1,575
1937	885	936	94	23	1,938	677	1,823
1938	781	772	85	41	1,679	598	1,569
1939	864	757	103	21	1,745	481	1,609
					81,675	24,915	37,850

[i] This Table was derived, in part, from JCAR, 1939, p. 86, Table 27, and JCAR, 1949, p. 104, Table 26.

Table 18. Number of Boys & Girls Dependent/Neglected/Mental Defect (MD)/Custody/Physical Defect Children/Cases[i] by Age, 1918-1921-1923-1939[ii]

Year	Age in Years										
	<1	1	2	3	4	5	6	7	8	9	10
1918	66	125	241	222	260	231	267	260	290	268	254
1919	59	129	182	185	194	248	240	225	247	212	193
1920[iii]	44	88	86	128	120	134	136	122	114	109	93
1921	119	104	132	125	147	160	167	180	144	126	136
1923	130	121	157	171	142	139	174	179	160	141	122
1924	147	184	211	201	190	212	196	209	217	182	162
1925	188	236	253	285	300	257	250	257	272	243	239
1926	176	241	313	280	269	324	282	247	232	278	263
1927	196	234	273	283	266	280	270	320	256	228	233
1928	183	251	273	300	267	293	283	341	280	244	197
1929	100	128	139	138	131	138	148	154	136	131	101
1930	258	298	287	288	313	303	345	298	327	293	261
1931	260	284	282	254	275	271	273	290	293	285	273
1932	172	201	234	216	202	273	234	246	237	212	192
1933	152	166	161	170	161	187	186	214	180	179	151
1934	180	168	153	149	167	160	177	206	198	203	193
1935	169	131	122	131	158	135	158	186	184	156	167
1936	164	153	157	157	176	192	201	189	181	205	172
1937	196	148	155	180	151	159	173	191	199	178	194
1938	165	141	143	132	135	152	125	176	178	130	150
1939	198	142	127	138	131	152	127	144	164	157	150
Total	3,322	3,673	4,081	4,133	4,155	4,400	4,412	4,604	4,489	4,160	3,896
MD Cases[iv]	11	39	75	107	117	119	158	183	211	178	174
1940[v]	179	137	126	126	124	127	119	137	113	139	110
1941	216	150	155	144	145	159	138	130	122	119	111
1942	207	132	148	144	124	158	136	128	108	109	119
1943	269	189	206	165	177	169	171	157	147	134	134
1944	261	216	369		308		322		296		
1945	261	217	404		365		332		331		
1946	330	249	218	221	227	189	229	173	163	170	135
1947	350	213	201	215	248	190	200	194	168	160	157
1948	315	204	198	212	170	209	190	168	148	160	124
1949	316	207	220	191	185	168	191	158	164	146	141

[i] The annual reports varied in reporting children or cases in the dependency/neglect area. This Table reflects the numbers that were contained in the Tables in the annual reports.

[ii] The 1922 JCAR contained no age information. In 1918 and 1919, only dependency was reported. In 1921, neglect was added. In 1926, mental and physical defects were added; physical defects were no longer identified after 1930. In 1931, custody was added.

[iii]The 1920 numbers are seriously underreported because no ages were identified for all the Informal Complaints.

[iv]The numbers in this row represent the total number of mental defect cases (by age) reported between 1926 (when mental defect cases were first reported) and 1939.

[v]The years from 1940 on are reported here to show how juvenile court responded to the dependency/neglect area post-depression and then post-World War 2. A new energy was dedicated to this area after both world-wide challenges were finished. In 1944 and 1945, 2 and 3, 4 and 5, 6 and 7, 8 and 9, and 10 and 11 ages were combined; the last duo (10/11) was not reported in this Table.

Table 19. Number of Commitment Facilities Available for Delinquents < 16 Boys & Girls, 1917-1939

Year	Child-Placing-out	Child-Caring/ Dependent	Correctional	Mental Defective	Physical Defective	Hospital
1917	12	20	6	3	4	1
1918	8	33	9	2	2	2
1919	6 (6)[1]	34 (17)	9	2	2	2
1920	8 (5)	41 (10)	9	4 (2)	4 (1)	2 (2)
1921	10 (6)	44 (11)	8	5 (1)	5 (1)	4 (4)
1922	9 (6)	37 (30)	8	6 (4)	4 (0)	3 (3)
1923	9 (9)	41 (12)	7	6 (3)	2 (0)	2 (2)
1924	9 (9)	45 (21)	9	5 (2)	5 (2)	3 (3)
1925	9(9)	37 (16)	9	5 (4)	2 (1)	5 (5)
1926	11 (9)	40 (11)	9	5 (4)	5 (1)	5 (5)
1927	11 (10)	35 (10)	10	5 (3)	3 (0)	5 (5)
1928	13 (11)	34 (9)	10	5 (3)	4 (1)	7 (5)
1929	11 (8)	32 (8)	10	5 (5)	4 (1)	5 (5)
1930	10 (8)	29 (10)	11	7 (5)	3 (1)	4 (4)
1931	12 (7)	35 (12)	12	7 (4)	4 (0)	4 (4)
1932	10 (8)	29 (9)	11	4 (3)	4 (0)	4 (4)
1933	10 (8)	30 (7)	10	5 (4)	3 (0)	4 (3)
1934	10 (9)	26 (10)	12	5 (4)	6 (1)	5 (5)
1935	12 (8)	28 (13)	12	5 (5)	3 (0)	4 (4)
1936	11 (10)	25 (6)	12	7 (4)	2 (0)	4 (4)
1937	12 (7)	35 (12)	12	7 (4)	4 (0)	4 (4)
1938	11 (11)	29 (8)	13	8 (6)	2 (0)	5 (3)
1939	11 (9)	27 (8)	14	9 (8)	2 (0)	6 (3)

Note: The numbers in parentheses are the number of agencies/facilities that accepted boy and/or girl delinquent referrals in the categories and years indicated.

Table 20. Number & Percentage of <16 Boys'/Girls' Delinquent Commitments Cases, 1919-1939

Year	Private & Public Placing Agency[i]	Child Caring Inst.[ii]	Delinquent Facility[iii]	Mental Defective[iv]	Physical Defective[v]	Hospital	Percent Delinquent Facility
1919	53/21	238/18	104/51	1/0	0/0	2/7	26.1/52.6
1920	67/25	174/17	66/34	2/1	1/1	3/9	21.1/39.1
1921	40/24	180/7	47/41	4/0	1/0	0/26	17.3/28.1
1922	67/49	144/25	209/54	6/3	----	10/15	47.9/40.0
1923	83/63	156/9	243/67	8/1	----	16/13	48.0/43.8
1924	129/65	160/29	493/134	9/10	0/2	12/16	61.4/52.3
1925	120/90	62/11	470/97	8/3	1/0	14/20	69.6/43.9
1926	170/92	52/8	578/86	14/8	0/1	7/26	70.4/38.9
1927	161/81	38/13	418/65	8/3	----	14/21	65.4/35.5
1928	129/72	42/2	501/95	8/5	0/1	14/16	72.2/49.7
1929	141/87	35/15	510/87	10/8	1/0	2/24	76.8/39.4
1930	128/64	31/20	484/85	26/8	3/0	15/23	70.5/42.5
1931	97/52	29/11	383/79	18/11	----	13/25	70.9/44.6
1932	61/41	20/7	290/62	30/9	----	16/13	69.5/43.7
1933	56/24	29/3	307/57	41/9	----	11/11	61.5/54.8
1934	92/53	23/11	390/73	32/13	1/0	5/16	71.8/44.0
1935	63/57	15/14	503/81	48/15	----	6/16	79.2/44.3
1936	83/59	15/6	504/96	50/19	----	10/18	76.1/48.5
1937	107/62	18/5	460/73	49/25	----	8/8	71.7/42.2
1938	109/69	10/6	370/81	77/31	----	3/6	65.0/42.0
1939	94/45	12/7	432/93	78/27	----	0/16	70.1/49.5

[i] Placing out agencies were not divided into private versus public: Department of Public Welfare and Department of Public Health until 1925.

[ii] Child Caring Institutions became known as Institutions for Dependent Children beginning in 1925.

[iii] Institutions for Delinquent Children were first called Reform Institutions and Agencies until 1919 and then Correctional Institutions until 1925.

[iv] Institutions for Mental Defectives became known as Institutions for Feeble-Minded or Epileptic Children in 1925.

[v] Institutions for Physical Defectives became known as Institutions for Physically Handicapped Children in 1925.

Table 21. Numbers & Yearly Averages of < 16 Boys/Girls Detained by Juvenile Court, 1925-1951[i]

Age	1925-1928	1930-1942	1944-1951	1925-1951 (25 years)
<10	378/25 94.5/6.3	757/67 58.2/5.2	602/71 75.5/8.9	1,737/163 69.5/6.5
10/11	869/69 217.3/17.3	1,970/218 151.5/16.8	1,310/143 163.8/17.9	4,149/430 166/17.2
12/13	1,483/219 370.8/54.8	3,584/858 275.7/66	2,466/749 308.3/93.6	7,533/1,826 301.3/73,.0
14/15	2,100/607 525/151.8	6,375/2,516 490.4/193.5	4,414/1,391 551.8/173.9	12,889/4,514 515.6/180.6
<12	1,247/94 311.8/23.5	2,727/285 209.8/21.9	1,912/214 239/26.8	5,886/593 235.4/23.7
<14	2,730/313 682.5/78.3	6,311/1,143 485.5/87.9	4,378/963 547.3/120.4	13,419/2,419 536.8/96.8
<16	4,830/920 1207.5/230	12,686/3,659 975.8/281.5	8,792/2,354 1,099/294.3	26,308/6,933 1,052.3/277.3

[i] The first annual report to disclose age-related detention figures was 1924. That report did not mention defendants younger than 10 years old and was not included in this Table. The numbers from that 1924 report are: <12: 203/19; 12/13: 256/42; and 14/15: 273/112. There are no age-related detention figures mentioned in the 1929 and 1943 JCARs.

Table 22. Percentage (& Difference) of White Protestant vs. White Catholic Boys' & Girls' Delinquency & Dependency Charges, 1931-1949

Year	Boys' Delinquency	Girls' Delinquency	Boys'+Girls' Dependency
1931	17.4 vs 69.5 (52.1)	23.2 vs 69.3 (51.3)	25,7 vs 64.5 (38.8)
1932	16.9 vs 68.2 (51.3)	20.0 vs 68.2 (51.0)	27.9 vs 61.3 (33.4)
1933	17.0 vs 68.6 (51.6)	23.8 vs 68.5 (50.9)	24.1 vs 63.8 (39.7)
1934	19.0 vs 72.4 (53.4)	23.6 vs 71.8 (52.4)	26.7 vs 62.0 (35.3)
1935	21.3 vs 70.7 (49.4)	27.3 vs 70.3 (48.5)	29.2 vs 60.6 (31.4)
1936	21.3 vs 70.4 (49.1)	19.6 vs 70.6 (49.4)	26.2 vs 64.6 (38.4)
1937	24.1 vs 69.6 (45.5)	33.0 vs 68.7 43.7)	28.3 vs 62.6 (34.3)
1938	23.7 vs 69.6 (45.9)	29.5 vs 68.9 (44.5)	28.1 vs 62.9 (37.8)
1939	27.3 vs 66.2 (38.9)	29.0 vs 66.1 (38.7)	25.3 vs 67.4 (42.1)
1940	25.9 vs 68.5 (42.6)	26.1 vs 68.2 (42.3)	32.3 vs 56.7 (24.4)
1941	24.8 vs 69.2 (44.4)	29.1 vs 68.5 (43.0)	30.5 vs 57.0 (26.5)
1942	26.5 vs 68.0 (41.5)	37.8 vs 65.9 (37.6)	31.4 vs 59.2 (27.8)
1943	28.5 vs 66.7 (38.2)	36.5 vs 65.6 (36.0)	32.5 vs 60.5 (28.0)
1944	28.8 vs 66.3 (37.5)	35.1 vs 65.5 (35.8)	33.5 vs 57.5 (24.0)
1945	28.2 vs 66.1 (37.7)	38.6 vs 65.0 (35.4)	34.4 vs 58.0 (23.6)
1946	29.9 vs 65.8 (35.9)	38.5 vs 64.7 (33.7)	30.7 vs 61.9 (31.2)
1947	33.0 vs 62.9 (29.9)	42.2 vs 60.5 (26.1)	34.8 vs 59.4 (24.6)
1948	30.8 vs 64.9 (34.1)	37.0 vs 64.0 (32.4)	30.9 vs 64.6 (33.7)
1949	29.7 vs 65.3 (35.6)	36.3 64.7 (26.0)	28.6 vs 65.9 (37.3)
Average Differences for White Boys (B) & Girls (G) Protestant vs Catholic Delinquent & Dependency Charges, 1931-1949 Delinquent Delinquent Dependent			
1931-36	51.2% more Catholic B	45.0% more Catholic G	36.2% more Catholic B & G
1937-42	43.1% more Catholic B	31.3% more Catholic G	32.1% more Catholic B & G
1943-49	35.6% more Catholic B	19.5% more Catholic G	28.9% more Catholic B & G
Average Differences for White Boys & Girls Protestant vs Catholic Delinquent Charges, 1931-1949			
1931-36	50.6% more Catholic Boys *and* Girls		
1937-42	35.7% more Catholic Boys *and* girls		
1943-49	31.6% more Catholic Boys *and* Girls		

Note: The Catholic group is being offered as a proxy for ethnicity (i.e., Italian, Irish, and Polish). Blacks were omitted from this Table to highlight the ethnic (apart from any racial) focus of the JC. Also omitted were Jewish and Greek Catholic kids.

Chapter 5
How Juvenile Court Became a Criminal Court With Younger Defendants:
The Philadelphia Version

ABSTRACT

Chapter 5 utilizes data from Philadelphia's juvenile court (JC) to detail the ways in which JC evolved from a would-be clinic (with a family/community focus) to a criminal court (with younger defendants committing real crimes) from the 1940s to later in the century. Perhaps the most critical development was adding 16- and 17- year-olds to the jurisdiction, which became a common trait among JCs during the first few decades after JC was founded. The older youths brought more numerous and serious crimes with them to JC. This time period also experienced a decline in the use of benign facilities, and a corresponding use of delinquent institutions to house juveniles. Meanwhile, JC became more official, dependent upon trials, and rights-oriented. The JC became criminalized, or much more like its criminal court (CC) counterpart during this time as Chapter 5 discloses. These changes in JC's nature resulted in making transfer to CC more relevant and necessary.

INTRODUCTION

Chapter 5 utilizes data from Philadelphia's JC to detail the ways in which JC evolved from a would-be clinic (with a family/community focus) to a criminal court (with younger defendants committing real crimes) from the 1940s to later in the century. Perhaps the most critical development was adding 16- and 17- year-olds to the jurisdiction, which became a common trait among JCs during the first few decades after JC was founded. The older youths brought more numerous and serious crimes with them to JC. This time period also experienced a decline in the use of benign facilities, and a corresponding use of delinquent institutions to house juveniles. Meanwhile, JC became more official, dependent upon trials, and rights-oriented. The JC became criminalized or much more like its CC counterpart during this time

DOI: 10.4018/978-1-7998-7923-7.ch005

as Chapter 5 discloses. These changes in JC's nature resulted in making transfer to CC more relevant and necessary.

JCs relied heavily upon the judge and probation officer (PO) to serve as family to troubled youths. There were constant proclamations among the early JC advocates that judges and POs were to act as though their own children were before the court (see Barrows, 1904; Lindsey, 1904; Tuthill, 1904). Perhaps the handwriting was on the wall when Barrows noted the "personality of the judge, as well as that of the probation officer, is an element of vast importance in the success of any juvenile court (Barrows, 1904, p. xiii). One had to wonder how long this could last.

THE EVOLVED/CURRENT PURPOSE OF JC TRANSFER TO CC

The ***evolved*** purpose of JC is not the same as its several original ones. History has disclosed that most of the original theories/purposes (T/Ps in Chapter 2) have been adjusted to various degrees (#1, #3-6, #8-9, and, #14-17), if not abandoned (#7, #12-13, #18 and #20); only #2, #10-11 and #19 currently seem to be receiving emphasis similar to the beginning days. JC's character, mission, and operation have evolved dramatically from the early decades of the 20th Century.

Warnings of the potential demise of the original JC soon surfaced. A JC advocate lamented that the local Chicago detention home had changed from a family dwelling to one that

has every appearance of being a jail, with its barred windows and lockedbdoors. Its attendants do not understand the psychology of childhood; theynknow very little about dependents and delinquents; their idea seems to benthat every child in the institution is there for punishment and that they are all potential criminals... (Bowen, 1925, p. 309).

While the ATC acknowledges the evolutionary changes in JC, they attribute the metamorphosis mostly to the U. S. Supreme Court's intervention into the system via the granting constitutional rights to defendants facing trial in JC (*In re Gault*, 1967; *In re Winship*, 1970). While the legalization of the adjudicatory hearing (AH) contributed to the *criminalization of JC* (see Feld, 1984a, 1990, 1991), other more critical factors explain how JC became a CC with just younger offenders.[1] These factors contributed to the need for the Supreme Court's intervention.

Several Theories/Propositions (T/Ps) account for the changes that transpired in JC. They complement the 20 original T/Ps and add to the debate regarding the theory surrounding the transfer controversy.

T/P #21: JC Evolved into A CC Via Numerous Modifications

The evolution of JC was marked by several developments during the mid-20th Century decades and later that transformed its essence to increasingly mirror its CC counterpart:

- increase in the minimum age required for prosecution in JC;
- increase in the average age of juvenile defendants;
- increase in the maximum age of JC jurisdiction;
- increase in the volume and severity of crimes committed by juveniles;
- decreased reliance upon POs to informally resolve cases;

- increased use of adjudicatory hearings (AHs) to determine offenders' outcomes;
- increase in the use of delinquent facilities to rehabilitate juvenile criminals;
- increase in the number of recidivists coming to JC;
- abandonment of clinic-like concerns and methods;
- extension of constitutional rights to defendants in JC;
- revisions of JC purpose clauses; and,
- removal of non-criminal behavior from JC's jurisdiction.

JC had changed dramatically and was becoming a CC clone, especially in terms of crimes committed by its population, independent of any decision by the Supreme Court to renovate JC's operation. These developments have combined to make the transfer to CC even more relevant.[2] Despite these developments, JCs are still dedicated primarily (but no longer, if ever, exclusively) to pursue the rehabilitation of those offenders processed there (Sanborn and Salerno, 2005).

It is certainly defensible to maintain that the *current primary* purpose of JC is to serve *largely*, but *still not exclusively*, as a diversionary outlet for CC. That purpose would appear to be in sync with sparing most juvenile offenders from harsh CC punishment. Nevertheless, the ATC has adopted a position that transfer to CC is inconsistent with JC's current purpose as *either* a diversion outlet *or* a shield against harsh CC punishment. The only way in which this contention could have merit is if JC 's current purpose is to address *all the offenses* committed by *all chronological juveniles*. That simply is not the current purpose, nor has it ever been such.

While under such legislation the child is not deemed a criminal, nevertheless the law recognizes the fact that some children under seventeen or eighteen are criminals in whatever sense you may define the word criminal; and the power is therefore given to the judge of the juvenile court to determine, as to any child, whether or not it shall be dealt with in the juvenile court or turned over to the criminal court. It sometimes but very rarely happens that a child at sixteen has become a habitual criminal, and it must be dealt with as such (Mack, 1911, p. 678).

T/P #22: JC Changes Made Transfer to CC More Necessary

Accepting JC's current purpose does not lead to regarding transfer to CC as contradictory or unnecessary. Prosecution in the contemporary JC is legitimately perceived as *immunity from criminal prosecution*. Actually, JC prosecution has *always* amounted to immunity for offenders, at least for those juveniles older than seven who have committed crimes. In 1935, this aspect was recognized by the Illinois Supreme Court while deliberating the appeal of a 15-year-old murderer:

It was not intended by the Legislature that the juvenile court should be made a haven of refuge where a delinquent child of the age recognized by law as capable of committing a crime should be immune from punishment for the violation of the criminal laws of the state (People v. Lattimore, 1935).

In the same year, a New Jersey appellate court noted similarly that "it is inconceivable that the Legislature intended to make the juvenile court a sanctuary for juvenile felons (here, murderers) (*Ex parte Daniecki*, 1935, p. 92, cited in Tanenhaus, 2000, p. 28).[3]

Thus, transfer to CC is legitimately perceived as denying immunity to juvenile offenders sent there due to chronic or violent offenses, which have become much more numerous in today's JC compared to the beginning years of operation.[4]

T/P #23: JC Changes Made Transfer to CC More Appropriate

The current JC is not populated only (or even largely) by young, irresponsible youths committing mostly mere obnoxious acts. The entire tenor of the JC has evolved such that the youths' being committed to its care and correction have dramatically altered their behavior. Gone from the delinquent court's purview are truancy and running away from home, playing ball in the street or stealing rides on conveyances. In their place are many acts of violence and serious crime. The youths are no longer predominantly younger than 14 years old. Instead, the majority of juvenile "delinquents" are 16- and 17-years-old (the primary target of transfer). To look at the current JC from a lens manufactured in the early 20th Century is a distortion of current reality.

Had the current profile of juvenile offending existed in 1899, the JC founders would most likely have had an impossible task in convincing the Cook County legislature to pass the original JC act. It is also highly unlikely that the JC movement would have experienced such a rapid spread across the country. Alternatively, a maximum JC age of twelve or thirteen likely would have been permanently adopted. It is nearly impossible to believe that the cause of diverting or sparring older and chronic/violent offenders from the harsh consequences of CC would have gained much traction or that creating JC would be regarded as either necessary or an improvement.[5]

THE CURRENT PURPOSE OF (AND THE RESULTS OF RESEARCHING) TRANSFER TO CC

The ATC contends that research has demonstrated that transfer is a failure as a crime control policy. Their argument is twofold: first, transfer to CC does not guarantee longer sentences for transfers in CC than could/would have been secured in JC (the ATC's supposed top, and maybe only, target for transfer, assuming transfer is permitted/possible at all); second, transfer does not decrease recidivism among transfers compared to allegedly comparable youths retained in JC (the supposed only true utilitarian benefit the ATC recognizes for transfer), meaning that transfer to CC does not deter crimes among transfers. There are numerous rebuttals to the ATC's determination of transfer problems detailed in Sections III-IV.

T/P#24: The Goal of Transfer to CC Is Not Limited to Pursuing Longer Sentences

The pursuit of longer CC sentences that exceed possible JC dispositions is a valuable aim of transfer. It is simply *not the only* valuable aim, never has been the only aim, and would be irrelevant in many, if not most, transfer situations. This T/P will be fully explicated in Chapters 13-15.

T/P #25: Deterrence Is Not Transfer to CC's Only Utilitarian Benefit

Much like the pursuit of longer sentences, deterring crime is also a valuable aim of transfer; it is simply *not the only* valuable aim, and, concededly, will not occur in some situations. The same complaint about the lack of deterrence via prosecution in CC can be made against JC, itself. It is possible that almost *nothing* will deter crime among some young offenders. Moreover, the complicity of CC has been ignored (such as continued leniency in CC). This T/P is explicated in Chapter 16.

T/P #26: Researching Transfer to CC Has Been Woefully Deficient

Most of the research, to date, has been deficient as to the factors taken into consideration and controlled, and has suffered from other methodological problems, when examining the outcome of transfer to CC. This T/P will be more fully explicated in Chapter 12.

T/P #27: Researching Transfer to CC Has Not Yielded Consistent Results

Although some studies have found a lack of deterrence, other studies have found greater deterrence via transfer to CC. This T/P will be more fully explicated in Chapter 12.

Finally, the main pitch put forth by the ATC is that transfer to CC does a disservice to everything and everybody, especially to juvenile offenders who are supposed transfer "victims." Not only is this contention wrong about some transferred youths, but the true disservice is also that put upon both JC and the offenders prosecuted there when transfer to CC is unavailable (see Chapter14).

T/P #28: Transfer to CC Serves The Best Interests (BI) Of Numerous Parties

Chapters 13-15 will fully disclose how the transfer of chronic and violent juvenile offenders to CC serves the *best interests* (BI) of the JC, society, and the vast majority of juvenile offenders, perhaps most obviously those retained in JC, but also for some of the transferred offenders; even adult defendants can benefit from the practice (see Chapter 14).

It would be interesting to go back to the late 1800s/early 1900s and ask the founders two questions. First, would they proceed with their reform movement if that were to mean all juvenile offenders (those younger than eighteen) had to be processed by and dealt with within the parameters of JC and juvenile justice (JJ), regardless of the severity of and/or the violence in the current offense and regardless of prior record as well? Of course, these elements would need to be measured in contemporary terms and not by what was typical juvenile misconduct in their time. An interesting follow up question would be whether they would launch their reform movement within the current: adjustments to their jurisdictional reach; changes in procedural requirements; revamped nature of rehabilitative interventions; shortage of institutional options; inability of service providers to stem the tide of juvenile offending; changes in the natures of juveniles/families/neighborhoods/communities; and, limits on both the team participants behind and multiple targets of JC intervention (compare Chapter 2).

THE CONTEMPORARY JC: HOW WE GOT HERE: THE PHILADELPHIA JC STORY

On the same day that the Nazis invaded Poland, September 1, 1939, Pennsylvania began adding 16- and 17-years-old offenders to the jurisdiction of their JCs. The initial reaction to this inclusion was very telling, nearly as dramatic as the world's response to Nazi Germany.

THE INITIAL REACTION TO ADDING OLDER DELINQUENTS TO THE JC JURISDICTION

The initial reaction was cold, if not harsh. Whereas boys 16/17 were treated more severely than boys younger than 16, the situation for girls was mixed, as revealed in Table 23. Table 24 provides a rare glimpse of the remarkable discrepancies between the percentage of cases adjusted for the two age groups between 1940 and 1946, ranging from the most serious charges (such as indecent assault) to the least serious ones (such as playing ball in the street). Hardly any charges were adjusted for the older boys.

Resolutions of crimes were not the only distinguishing feature of JC's reactions to the addition of 16 and 17 years old. The older age group was detained and institutionalized separately; the intake stage and trials or adjudicatory hearings (AHs) were conducted separately as well (see 1941 JCAR references below).

From 1940 to 1954, hundreds of youths younger than 16 went to the Youth Studies Center (hereinafter YSC) for detention; a handful of juveniles between 14 and 16 headed to county prison, instead, due to being unmanageable.[6] Hundreds of the older youths went to county prison for detention, while only about 40 went to the YSC. The crossover provided JC the same flexibility it had had with the dependent/delinquent dichotomy. "Bad" younger youths could be detained in the county prison, while "vulnerable" older youths could be detained in the YSC.

Within two years of the introduction of the older youths to JC, the state opened Camp Hill/White Hill to house older delinquents; some young adults were also committed to this facility by CC. Again, separation of the two age groups was the theme. Table 25 shows the marked separation between the two groups in relevant commitment facilities. Crossover was possible with those younger than 16 being sent to "older" youths' placements when a very serious charge/record was at hand, or a previous disposition had not worked out and the case had to be reopened. Some vulnerable or less serious/chronic older offenders were able to be placed in the institutions geared for younger juveniles. The "older" youth facilities gave JC an opportunity to avoid transfer to CC for younger offenders, while mixed-population institutions (older juveniles and younger adults), such as Camp Hill/White Hill gave JC an opportunity to avoid transfer to CC for older delinquents.[7]

Complete separation from youth younger than 16 from the original young adult offenders (16/17-year-olds) existed from the very start of the jurisdictional joinder. For example, two years after the merger, the 1941 Annual Report explained:

Owing to the limited facilities of the House of Detention for children, as well as the inadvisability of housing more serious and older offenders with younger children, boys 16 and 17 years of age are received at the Municipal Court's branch of the County Sheriff's office...and are interviewed by the probation officer of the boys' misdemeanants' division....

* * * * * * * *

Arrest cases of children under 16 may be disposed of informally at interviews held at the House of Detention; informal complaints in all cases may be adjusted by field workers subject to the approval of the probation officer in charge. But arrest cases of children under 16 and complaint cases which require extensive investigation and judicial disposal and ***all arrest cases of children between 16 and 18 years of age*** *are referred to juvenile court for formal hearing before the judge.*[1] *The method to be followed in cases of children under 16 years depends upon the interviews at the House of Detention, the investigations made by the probation officers, and the attitude of the complainants (JCAR, 1941, pp. 4, 5-6, emphasis added).*

[1]Regular sessions of the juvenile court are held on Wednesdays for the hearing of cases of dependency and neglect; on Fridays for the hearing of cases of delinquent children under 16 years of age; on Tuesdays for the hearing of cases of delinquent boys 16 and 17 years of age; and on Thursdays for the hearing of cases of delinquent girls 16 and 17 years of age (Id., p. 5).

* * * * * * * * * *

As soon as a formal hearing is decided upon the case goes to the probation department for investigation. In any case, whether begun by an informal complaint, or an arrest, if the complainant insists upon filing a petition at once, the case is listed for court hearing far enough ahead to permit the probation department to make a preliminary investigation.[1]

[1]In order to avoid increasing the already heavy pressure on the juvenile division, it was deemed advisable to place the investigation and supervision of cases of boys 16 and 17 years of age under the boys' misdemeanants' division and of girls 16 and 17 years of age under the women's misdemeanants' division. These two divisions have had previous experience with these older children and this arrangement also has the advantage of making possible ***a differentiation in treatment of the older from the younger offender,*** *although the procedure is definitely patterned after the procedure in the juvenile division (Id., p. 8, emphasis added).*

THE TRANSFORMATION OF THE ORIGINAL JC

It took years and significant changes in the nature and operation of JC for its original brand to have been largely discarded. Nevertheless, JC gradually became truly criminalized via internal revisions to its procedures and the evolution of the nature of their juvenile clientele.

A. The Increase in the Average Age of Juvenile Offenders

Even after the 16/17-year-olds were added full-time in 1940, the 7-13- and 14/15-year-old groups *each* accounted for low to mid-30% of the caseload each year until 1957. Table 26 shows that, together, these two age groups constituted two-thirds of the defendants processed by JC (range 63.7% to 69.8%, mean = 67.1%) during that time. Until 1964, the percentage of the younger-than-16-group ranged from 59.1 to 64.8%. From 1965 through 1973 this group experienced a constant decline, such that finally, in 1974, the 16/17-year-olds were most of the defendants processed by JC; they have not been a minority since then. The number of 16- and 17-years old youths climbed from 1,685 in 1940 to 7,937 in 1974, an increase of 471%.

Thus, most defendants headed to the delinquent jurisdiction of JC from the mid-1970s until today are the very ones originally left remaining in CC. While the total number of boys processed by JC mostly declined throughout the remainder of the 20th century (to 6,206 in 1999), the number of boys younger than 14 decreased as well. The one-time bread and butter of JC, these younger offenders that dominated the JC population during the 1920s and 1930s consistently was reduced from the 1940s through the rest of the century; by 1981, the younger-than-14 age-group constituted a mere 12.1% of the JC delinquent population.

The delinquent ratio per 1,000 juveniles for both boys and girls rose in each age group. Not surprising, there was also an increase in the percentage of the population that was delinquent. Table 27 discloses the gradual increases in these ratios. The ratios for the 16/17 age group were most pronounced, increasing from 25/1,000 in 1940 to 83/1,000 in 1974.

B. The Increase in Volume and Severity of Boys' Offenses; The Decrease in/Removal of Non-Crimes

Accompanying the increase in the ages of juvenile defendants was a marked rise in Big-10 offenses (i.e., burglary, robbery, indecent assault, rape, assault and battery, homicide, carrying weapons, drug offenses, auto theft, and arson) committed by boys. What began as only 506 Big-10 crimes in 1917 (or 8.9% of the caseload; see Table 11 in Chapter 4) swelled to more than ten thousand in 1971 and to 74.1% of the caseload in both 1981 and 1985. The 1971 number (10, 254) of boys' Big-10 crimes was 11 times the average annual number of Big-10 offenses (918.9) committed between 1917 and 1939. Table 28 catalogues the rise in boys' Big-10 crimes committed between 1940 and 1985. Special mention deserves to be made of boys' drug offenses that experienced incredible increases, starting in 1966. Table 27 also shows the steep increase in the number of boys' transfers to CC. While there were a mere 3 transfers in 1941, there were a whopping 234 in 1981.

The average annual number of burglary charges against boys between 1917 and 1939 (516.2) increased five times that amount in 1971, 1974, 1978, and 1981. Similarly, the average annual number of robbery charges (104.2) between 1917 and 1939 increased more than 20 times that amount in 1981. Table 29 discloses the increases in the annual number of eight of the boys' Big-10 crimes, comparing the 1917-1939 versus 1940-1985 periods. There were more homicide charges against boys in 1969 (134), 1970 (136), 1971 (126),1972 (122), and 1973 (77) than all homicide charges between 1917 and 1939 (74). Homicides doubled or more in number from one year to the next several times: 10-22 (1941-1942); 11-28 (1944-1945); 19-39 (1959-1960); 21-44 (1961-1962); 67-134 (1968-1969); between 1955 and 1956 the increase was four times greater. In 1970, homicide charges were 42 times the annual average between 1917 and 1939 (3.2).

There were more rape charges against boys in 1971 (174), and 1972 (175) than 1917-1929 combined (150); similarly, there were more rape charges in 1973 (253) and 1974 (286) than the 1917-29 (150) *and* 1943-1949 (87) periods' cumulative numbers. There were more than two times as many indecent assault charges against boys in 1954 (146) than all of 1917-1929 (66). This crime was 22 times more prevalent in 1954 than the annual average between 1917 and 1929 (6.6).

Arson charges against boys increased from zero (1940-1949) to 186 (1973); similarly, drug offenses against boys increased from no charges (1940, 1945-1947) to 1,040 (1974). There were more carrying concealed weapons charges against boys each year 1955-56, 1960-1974 (see Table 26) than all such charges cumulatively between 1917-1939 (299). In 1971, the carrying weapons charges against boys (805) were 61 times the average for that offense between 1917 and 1939 (13). The male juvenile offender population became well armed, especially after 1945.[8]

Not only was the assault and battery charge against boys (2,180) 17 times more prevalent in 1971 than the annual average between 1917 and 1939 (125.6), but also assault and battery on a police officer, as well as aggravated assault and battery on a police officer became sufficiently numerous by 1961 and 1968, respectively, to earn separate calculation in the JCAR.[9]

There were 99,990 Big-10 charges against boys between 1960 and 1974 (annual average 6,666 charges). There were more than three times Big-10 cases on *average each year* between 1960 and 1974 than the *total number of all Big-10 charges* against boys between 1917-1939.

Not only was there a serious increase in serious offenses, the number of boys sent to JC also consistently rose from 5,269 in 1940 to 15,387 in 1974 (high of 16,832 in 1972),

At the other end of the offense spectrum, JC gradually shred its jurisdiction of the true delinquencies that were the hallmark of its original operation. The witness to rape, etc. category faded from existence by the mid-1950s. By 1964, acts of carelessness were more serious and were renamed *malicious mischief*, which was limited to acts such as vandalism, arson, and resisting an officer. Fornication and bastardy were relocated from to Misdemeanants' Court in the early 1970s. Truancy was "de-criminalized" and incorrigibility was restricted to runaways and promiscuous girls in 1972 (Packel, 1975). Shortly after that, the (runaway, incorrigible, truancy *(RIT)* category was abandoned.

After reaching a high of 74.1% in 1985, there was a decrease in both the absolute numbers of Big 10 offenses as well as their percentage in the overall crime profile. Each of the major offenses experienced a decline. This decline in the Big 10 offenses lasted until the mid-90s explosion in violence. Some of the decline after the mid-90s is most likely explained by prosecutors' being given direct transfer power at that time over most of the Big-10 offenses.

From the end of the 1970s, just about the entire boys' caseload was occupied by *true crimes,* serious or otherwise, due to the removal of the *RIT* category, among other "offenses," from JC jurisprudence. The only "fluff" charge remaining from previous eras was running away from an institution, which numbered between 150-300 charges per year. JC had become a CC clone in terms of the illegal behaviors processed there.

C. The Increase in the Percentage of Boy/Girl Recidivists

Age and the severity of crimes were not the only areas affected by the modernization of JC. Percentage increases were also witnessed in the number of boy and girl recidivists. The rise was true for both overall cases petitioned in JC and cases resulting in an AH. Table 30 shows the percentage increases in both categories. Table 31 demonstrates the lower percentages for boys and girls in both categories between 1920 and 1939. Male juvenile offenders were not only older and more serious, but they were also more chronic in their offending from the 1940s on. The percentages of recidivist boys and girls appearing at AHs in 1971 (86% and 77%, respectively) and 1972 (86% and 83%, respectively) were staggering. It is entirely likely that these high numbers convinced the compilers of the JCAR to stop reporting this category after 1972.

For several years, the JCAR documented the first or multiple arrests experienced by boys and girls during a single year. Table 32 details just how often rearrests and reappearances occurred for boys and girls at intake or adjudicatory hearings. Boys were especially prolific in this category during these years.

D. The Decrease in/Elimination of Informal Complaints (ICs) and Adjusted Cases

ICs virtually disappeared by 1960. Boys particularly had been the focus of ICs. In the 17 years between 1923 and 1939 a total of 5,793 cases involving boys younger than 16-years-of- age (an average of 340.8 cases a year) were ICs (see Tables 14 and 15 in Chapter 4). The decline in boys' ICs was steady from 265 in 1940 to 171 in 1945. By 1960, that number for boys dropped to 12; for girls (disregarding the witness cases) the number dropped from 262 ICs in 1926 to 37 in 1951. Not surprising, then, 1960 marked the last year data for ICs were reported.

Accompanying the disappearance of ICs was the reduction in the number of adjusted cases; this method of case resolution was a mainstay in the original JC (see Table 16 in Chapter 4). Table 33 reports the gradual decline in the use of adjustments, as well as the gradual rise in the use of court hearings in JC. The decrease in adjustments for boys was marked.[10]

Between the decreases in ICs and adjusted cases, JC was becoming increasingly formal in the way cases were resolved. Due in no small part to the increase in the severity of crimes, the number of AHs for boys increased significantly, especially for the most serious crimes. Table 34 documents the percentage of boys' Big-10 offenses that were resolved by trial (versus adjustments) and the percentage of boys' AHs (and adjustments) that involved Big-10 crimes. This Table shows that the boys' Big-10 crimes dominated AHs between 1960 and 1974; of the 99,900 Big-10 charges, 80,070 went to trial or to a transfer hearing. [11]

E. The Increase in the Use of Delinquent Facilities in Delinquent Commitments

The number of delinquent institutions increased from the eight to 10 available in the 1920s (11 to 14 during the 1930s) to 17 to 23 from the 1960s on. Table 35 captures this evolution of the delinquent facility commitments for boys. This increase was likely necessary due to the significant increase in the number of serious/chronic delinquents (especially boys) that needed to be placed in a delinquent facility. The character/nature of the juvenile offender population in these delinquent facilities changed dramatically as well. Largely or soon to be mostly gone from these institutions were the larceny, runaway, incorrigible and truancy offenders to be replaced by a majority of burglars, robbers, auto thieves and rapists (drug offenders became prevalent commitments later in the 1970s).[12]

While older juvenile offenders were mostly separated from younger offenders until the mid-1970s, they were typically comingled following that time. The nature and character of committed juvenile offenders changed even more after that.

The range of the percentage of commitments to delinquent facilities for boys rose constantly from less than 80% (until 1945) to 80-90% from 1946-1957 to a pretty consistent 90% (plus) from 1959 to 1974, as revealed in Table 36.

F. The Disappearance of "Benign" Facilities

With the increase in boys' serious and violent crimes and the increase in the percentage of commitments to delinquent institutions, it should come as no surprise, perhaps, that eventually there was a sharp decline in both private placing-out agencies from nine or 10 throughout the 1920s and the 1930s to between four and six by the latter half of the 1960s. Additionally, child-caring institutions/dependent facilities shrank from a range of 20-45 throughout the 1920s and 1930s (see Table 19 in Chapter 4) to between four to six by the latter half of the 1960s. Meanwhile, correctional facilities increased from 13 in 1943 to 23 in the 1960s. Table 37 details the rise and fall in the numbers of the facilities to which juvenile offenders were committed between 1943 and 1970.

G. How the Transformation of the JC Has Impacted Transfer to CC

It is accurate to hold that the JC that has existed since the 1960s/1970s bears little, if any, resemblance to the original JC. One could confidently assert that it is not your (let alone your grandfather's) JC any longer. Increasingly, through the 1960s and thereafter JC judges were encountering older, more chronic, and more serious/violent offenders at the AH and throughout the juvenile justice (JJ) system. Contrary to the assertions of the ATC, transfer to CC was not mostly a response to the significant spike in juvenile violence in the late 1980s and early 1990s. Due to the nature of the JC's clientele prior to this period, as demonstrated in this Chapter, an abundance of juvenile offenders amply qualified for transfer to CC long before the final decade of the Twentieth Century. What did occur during that decade was a serious increase in transfers due to the serious increase in the number of those serious juvenile offenders. While transfer to CC had long been relevant and necessary, it simply became much more so in both contexts at that time. That significant increase in the availability and imposition of transfer, in turn, elicited a tremendous rise in the number of criticisms and attacks on transfer by the ATC.[13]

JC eventually evolved into a true of clone of CC where only true crimes were prosecuted against a population only slightly younger than those who automatically and necessarily qualify for CC by virtue of age, alone. In fact, most of today's juvenile offenders were purposely excluded from the original JC. It is very unlikely, virtually impossible, that the decision to include these older juvenile, quasi-adult offenders within JC's jurisdiction would be made again today, if transfer to CC were no longer an option.

JC began as a clinic where struggling families were rescued from urban blight, boys from downward paths and girls from moral degradation. It evolved into a forum considered to constitute immunity from criminal prosecution, or, in other words, as a diversion from CC.

Having said that, there is still much to distinguish JC from CC, especially in terms of sincere rehabilitation efforts and the best interests (BI) of defendants, as well as a commitment to not ruin the life chances of those defendants. The evolution of the JC into a veritable clone of CC does not mean we should either return to JC's original operation or abandon its current one. Maintaining transfer to CC will allow JC to retain what remains of its commitment to rehabilitation and the BI of the vast majority of juvenile offenders. The reasons why transfer should be retained will be explored at greater length in Chapters 13-15. Before that, the mighty disinformation crusade that has been vigorously mounted by the ATC has to be met and derailed (see Chapters 6-11).

REFERENCES

Barrows, S. J. (1904). Introduction. In S. J. Barrows (Ed.), *Children's courts in the United States: Their origins, development, and results* (pp. ix–xvii). U.S. Government Printing Office.

Bowen, M. J. T. (1925). The early days of the juvenile court. In J. Addams, (Ed.), The child, the clinic, and the court: A group of papers (pp. 298-309). The New Republic Inc.

Ex parte Daniecki. (1935). 117 N.J. Eq. 527, 177 Atl. 91. N. J. Court of Errors and Appeals.

Feld, B. C. (1984a). Criminalizing juvenile justice: Rules of procedure for the juvenile court. *Minnesota Law Review*, *69*, 141–276.

Feld, B. C. (1990). The punitive juvenile court and the quality of procedural justice: Disjunctions between rhetoric and reality. *Crime and Delinquency*, *36*(4), 443–466. doi:10.1177/0011128790036004002

Feld, B. C. (1991). The transformation of the juvenile court. *Minnesota Law Review*, *75*, 691–725.

In re Gault. (1967). 387 U.S. 1.

In re Winship. (1970). 397 U.S. 358.

JCAR. (1917-1978). *Juvenile court annual report*. Municipal Court of Philadelphia (1917-1959); County Court of Philadelphia (1960-1967); Court of Common Pleas, Juvenile Division (1968-1978).

Lindsey, B. B. (1904). The juvenile court of Denver. In S. J. Barrows (Ed.), *Children's courts in the United States: Their origins, development, and results* (pp. 28–132). U.S. Government Printing Office.

Mack, J. W. (1911). The state and the child. *Proceedings of the Academy of Political Science in the City of New York*, *1*(4), 676–681. doi:10.2307/1172077

Packel, L. (1975). A Guide to Pennsylvania Delinquency Law. *Villanova Law Review*, *21*, 1–71.

People v. Lattimore. (1935). 362 Ill. 206, 199 N.E. 275. Illinois Supreme Court.

Sanborn, J. B. Jr. (1994d). The juvenile, the court, or the community: Whose best interests are currently being promoted in juvenile court? *Justice System Journal*, *17*(2), 249–266. doi:10.1080/23277556.1994.10871207

Sanborn, J. B. Jr, & Salerno, A. W. (2005). *The juvenile justice system: Law and process*. Roxbury Publishing Company. Oxford University Publishing.

Tanenhaus, D. S. (2000). The evolution of transfer out of the juvenile court. In J. Fagan & F. E. Zimring (Eds.), *The changing borders of juvenile justice: Transfer of adolescents to the criminal court* (pp. 13–43). University of Chicago Press.

Tuthill, R. S. (1904). History of the children's court in Chicago. In S. J. Barrows (Ed.), *Children's courts in the United States: Their origins, development, and results* (pp. 1–6). U.S. Government Printing Office.

Wigmore, J. H. (1926). Juvenile court vs. criminal court. *Illinois Law Review*, *21*, 375.

ENDNOTES

1 The criminalization effect involves critical changes to the JC character/operation that occurred before the spike in violent juvenile crime in the mid-1990s. A premise of this book is that JC had already undergone a significant metamorphosis prior to that spike in violence; it had already become a CC with younger defendants. The ATC credits the mid-1990s juvenile crime numbers as essentially destroying the traditional JC; previous spikes in juvenile crime during the 1970s were important but did not result in large renovations in JJ. The claim of destruction is largely connected to the significant increase in the numbers of juveniles who became potential targets of transfer (especially by prosecutors). Since then, the extent of juvenile violent crime has decreased somewhat, with periodic increases. The ATC contention is: since transfer was expanded in response to the spike in violent crime (which also supposedly expanded criminalization) now that the violent crime has decreased so should the availability of transfer (see Chapter 7). Although not part of the court's operation, the JC's purpose clauses experienced revisions following the changes noted in this Chapter. Before these changes (i.e., pre-1980s and pre-*Gault* and *Winship*) the purpose clauses identified the juvenile's and the family's BI as the JC's focus. Following alterations in the JC crime profile and the expansion of constitutional rights, the purpose clauses were much more CC-like: punishment to fit the crime/record; vindicating the victim; protecting society; holding youths accountable, etc. (see Sanborn, 1994d). Following that mid-1990s outbreak there was yet another wave of reforms that increased the criminalization effect: granting prosecutors increased control over charging decisions, including diversion; increasing the situations in which juveniles can experience pre-trial detention; opening AHs to the public; adopting harsher disposition/sentencing options; and, making it more difficult to expunge JC records (see Sanborn & Salerno, 2005, Sections III-V).

2 The JCARs (1917-1978) show changes in JC's character that explain how it became a mini-CC long before the mid-1990s spike in juvenile violence (i.e., T/Ps #21-28 in this Chapter).

3 Some authorities decried that fact that many serious offenders were retained in JC contrary to both the BI and protection of society (see Wigmore, 1926).

4 The *rate* of offending does not drive the need for transfer (see Chapter 7).

5 Even after 16- and 17-year-olds were first added to JC jurisdiction, the primary objective was not to shield them from harsh CC punishment. JC workers likely thought that JCs could rehabilitate these older offenders much as they had done, to some extent, with younger offenders. It took time before the offenses of the older youths became very serious, chronic and violent (see *infra.*).

6 By 1954, no youth younger than 16 could be sent to jail. All juveniles were detained in the YSC unless they were unmanageable, or the YSC was overcrowded.

7 By the 1960s the two age groups were mostly joined at detention and commitment.

8 Weapons charges increased dramatically during this period:

- Never <100 charges after 1945 (except 74 in 1948);
- Never <200 charges after 1952;
- Never < 300 charges after 1955 (except 298 in 1957, and 296 in 1959);
- Never < 500 charges after 1968; and,
- Never < 600 after 1969.

And boys' choice of weapons increased in severity, too:

- 1961: 119 pistols or handguns/27 rifles or shotguns;

- 1962: 195/32;
- 1963: 138/27;
- 1964: 222/24;
- 1965: 157/28;
- 1966: 146/22;
- 1967: 133/30;
- 1968: 258/27;
- 1969: 237/69; and,
- 1970: 252/75.

9 Both genders were accused of this offense. The assault & battery (hereinafter A&B) charges on police officer breakdown for boys/girls between 1961 and 1973 is:

- 1961: 55/15;
- 1962: 72/17;
- 1963: 95/23;
- 1964: 128/15;
- 1965: 107/24;
- 1966: 124/35;
- 1967: 196/31;
- 1968: 231/38;
- 1969: 282/39;
- 1970: 277/60;
- 1971: 233/23;
- 1972: 247/50;
- 1973: 153/31.

The aggravated A&B on police officer breakdown for boys/girls between 1968 and 1973 is:

- 1968: 25/4;
- 1969: 42/16;
- 1970: 55/9;
- 1971: 31/2;
- 1972: 9/5;

10 The number of Informal Complaints (ICs) rapidly declined during these years.

- 1972:< 6,000;
- 1976: <5,000;
- 1977: <3,000;
- 1978: <2,000;
- 1985: <700;
- 1987: <600; and,
- 1990: <200.

11 The numbers for the Big-10 offenses breaks down as follows for Adjudicatory Hearings (AH) and Transfer Hearings (TH):

- 987 homicide charges (65.8 per year), 985 (99.8%) went to AH/TH;
- 1,958 rape charges (130.5 per year), 1,909 (97.5%) went to AH/TH;
- 16,254 auto theft charges (1,083.6 per year), 14,851 (91.4%) went to AH/TH;
- 14,743 robbery charges (982.9 per year), 12,402 (84.1%) went to AH/TH;

- 1,354 indecent assault charges (90.3 per year), 1,089 (80.4%) went to AH/TH;
- 1,307 arson charges (87.1 per year), 1,041 (79.6%) went to AH/TH;
- 28,974 burglary charges (1,931.6 per year), 22,891 (79.0%) went to AH/TH;
- 7,884 carry weapon charges (525.6 per year), 5,957 (75.6%) went to AH/TH;
- 22,327 A&B charges (1,531.6 per year), 16,588 (74.3%) went to AH/TH;
- 4,202 drug charges (280.1 per year), 2,357 (56.1%) went to AH/TH.

12 The percentage of delinquent commitments that were dedicated to boy's Big-10 offenses rose steadily from the 1960s on.

- In 1961, 1,019 of 1,589 = 64.1%
- In 1962, 1,272 of 1,827 = 69.6%
- In 1963, 1,143 of 1,634 = 70.0%
- In 1964, 1,458 of 1,958 = 74.5%
- In 1965, 1,327 of 1,882 = 70.5%
- In 1966, 1,046 of 1,565 = 66.8%
- In 1967, 719 of 1,023 = 70.3%
- In 1968, 697 of 909 = 76.7%
- In 1969, 893 of 1,198 = 74.5%
- In 1971, 775 of 955 = 81.2%
- In 1972, 601 of 751 = 80.0%
- In 1973, 599 of 735 =81.5%

13 There was also a serious increase in the ATC's misinterpretations of these varied transfer measures as well as the adoption/launching of a campaign to misrepresent the impact of transfer outcomes (see Chapters 6 and 7).

CHAPTER 5 TABLES

Table 23. Percentage of Resolutions in Boys' & Girls' Cases, <16 versus 16/17-Year-Olds 1940-1949

	Resolutions										
Gender & Number Of Cases	Dismiss	Dismiss, continue Probation	Medical Probation	Feeble-Minded Commit	Hospital Commit	Probation	Delinquent Commit	Agency/ Individual Commit	Restitution	Adjudicated Delinquent	Transferred (# of Cases)
Boys Percentage of Resolved Cases											
<16 42,203	66.5	3.2	.2	.8	.1	17.2	9.1	2.5	.5	29.4	.04 (18)
16/17 20,879	53.0	2.4	.4	.5	.9	23.4	17.1	.4	.9	42.9	1.0 (216)
Girls											
<16 7,217	46.1	2.5	1.2	1.8	1.6	27.7	10.1	8.8	.2	46.8	0
16/17 3,606	38.5	1.1	2.6	5.9	12.9	22.1	13.0	3.1	.4	39.0	.44 (16)

Table 24. Number & Percentage of Adjusted Cases for <16 vs. 16/17-Year-Olds, 1940-1946

Offense	<16 # Adjustments/Charges; %	16/17 #Adjustments/Charges; %
Auto Theft	230/1,110; 20.7%	3/1,716; .2%
Burglary	1,342/4,563; 29.4%	14/1,276; 1.1%
Robbery	251/721; 34.8%	1/454; .2%
Vagrancy	463/509; 91%	6/1,008; .6%
Fireworks	6/8; 75%	0/17; 0%
Ball in Street	25/25; 100%	2/18; 11.1%
Smoking	17/17; 100%	0/67; 0%
Assault & Battery	426/895; 47.6%	37/1,110; 3.3%
Rape	8/16; 50%	0/25; 0%
Indecent Assault	45/98; 45.9%	0/84; 0%
Sodomy	98/153; 64.1%	2/47; 4.3%
Shoplifting	151/321; 47%	1/59; 1.7%
Create Disturbance	2,759/2,997; 92.1%	33/2,628; 1.3%
Malicious Mischief	2,698/3,243; 83.2%	51/620; 8.2%
Trespassing	2,500/2,674; 93.5%	15/468; 3.2%
Incorrigibility	990/1,704; 58.1%	119/497; 23.9%
Carrying Weapon	106/216; 49.1%	0/295; 0%
Fighting	139/142; 97.9%	8/63; 12.7%
Gambling	186/192; 96.9%	2/485; 4.1%
Steal Rides	277/288; 96.2%	2/56; 3.6%
Drunkenness	39/47; 88.6%	1/298; .3%
Acts of Carelessness	9,519/10,749; 88.6%	126/5,404; 2.3%
Throwing Stones	285/304; 93.8%	3/31; 9.7%
Fire Alarm	75/83; 90.4%	0/5; 0%
Total	22,635/31,075; 72.8%	426/16,731; 2.5%

Table 25. Number of Boys' <16 & 16/17 Commitments by Facility, 1940-1951, 1954

Year	House of Correction/ County Prison	Pennypack House	Pomeroy Farm	Huntington Industrial Reformatory	Glen Mills	La Salle School	Philadelphia Protectory Phoenixville	Elliott House	Shallcross	Camp Hill/ White Hill Industrial School[i]
1940	3/153	10/28	----	48/159	92/5	43/1	76/3	32/0	21/0	0/0
1941	3/117	15/50	----	45/114[ii]	105/3	66/1	47/1	19/0	23/0	11/33
1942	1/114	6/44	----	26/4	83/4	77/2	45/4	25/0	23/	29/55
1943	0/114	14/81	54/0	36/85	93/2	121/2	46/6	29/5	31/1	25/44
1944	0/9	18/200	36/0	27/63	136/1	127/0	53/2	34/0	46/0	42/79
1945	0/4	30/258	25/0	17/37	169/2	130/1	77/5	26/0	73/0	58/159
1946	0/2	16/161	20/0	52/36	131/0	128/0	70/7	0/0	38/1	42/127
1947	0/4	31/244	18/1	25/46	182/3	95/1	83/4	0/0	27/0	45/165
1948	0/1	52/247	33/0	27/32	171/4	122/1	75/2	0/0	45/0	39/102
1949	0/1	43/254	39/0	17/35	141/4	67/1	79/5	0/0	29/0	48/97
1950	0/0	35/242	29/0	27/27	139/4	81/0	79/6	0/0	26/0	47/119
1951	1/2	19/178	32/1	11/13	139/8	61/0	78/6	0/0	18/0	23/88
1954[iii]	0/1	38/359	9/1	14/34	201/5	38/0	116/9	0/0	22/0	52/159

[i]Camp Hill was opened on May 1, 1941, shortly after the September 1, 1939 introduction of 16- and 17-year-olds to juvenile court jurisdiction. Camp Hill, also known as White Hill, served as the primary destination for older/chronic/serious juvenile delinquents until its closing in 1975. It housed both juvenile delinquents adjudicated in juvenile court and young adults convicted in criminal court. Between 1940 and 1942, it was identified in the annual reports as Camp Hill; White Hill replaced Camp Hill as the title between 1943 and 1960 (no institutions were identified between 1961 and 1963). Camp Hill reemerged as the title of the facility in the annual reports in 1964 and remained that way until 1975. At that time of its closing a Philadelphia Juvenile Court Judge observed that she would be much more likely to transfer older, more serious offenders to criminal court now that this multi-age facility, where extended sentences were possible, was no longer available for her dispositions.

[ii]Huntington received both normal and defective delinquents until May 1, 1941. From that date on only defective delinquents and borderline cases were committed there. The changed target of the facility likely explains why there was no longer a serious disparity in the ages of the delinquents committed there.

[iii]By 1957, annual reports no longer detailed the ages of delinquents committed to the various facilities. The 1952, 1953, 1955, and 1956 JCARs were unavailable to the author.

Table 26.Number & Percentage of Boys' Delinquent Cases per Age Group, 1940-1957,[i] 1959-1974

	Boys' Ages					
Year	**<7**	**<13**	**14/15**	**<16**	**16/17**	**Total # Cases**
1940	8	1845 (35%)	1739 (33%)	3584 (68%)	1685 (32%)	5,269
1941	8	1993 (36.7%)	1780 (32.8%)	3773 (69.8%)	1636 (30.2%)	5,409
1942	7	1892 (32.9%)	2064 (35.6%)	3956 (69.1%)	1772 (30.9%)	5,728
1943	9	2490 (33%)	2333 (31%)	4823 (64.1%)	2697 (35.9%)	7,520
1944	13	2438 (31.9%)	2405 (31.5%)	4843 (63.6%)	2776 (36.4%)	7,619
1945	10	2512 (31.6%)	2562 (32.2%)	5074 (63.7%)	2886 (36.3%)	7,960
1946	10	2245 (33.6%)	2275 (34%)	4520 (67.6%)	2166 (32.4%)	6,686
1947	13	1911 (34.2%)	1843 (33%)	3754 (67.2%)	1831 (32.8%)	5,585
1948	12	2016 (34.7%)	1913 (32.9%)	3929 (67.5%)	1889 (32.5%)	5,818
1949	8	2077 (36.9%)	1824 (32.4%)	3901 (69.3%)	1730 (30.7%)	5,631
1950	8	1907 (36.6%)	1612 (30.9%)	3519 (67.5%)	1694 (32.5%)	5,213
1951	3	1837 (34.8%)	1665 (31.5%)	3502 (66.3%)	1777 (33.7%)	5,279
1952	---	-----	-----	4001 (69.8%)	1730 (30.2%)	5,731
1953	---	-----	-----	4773 (67.4%)	2290 (32.6%)	7,033
1954	2	2700 (33.8%)	2703 (33.8%)	5403 (67.6%)	2593 (32.4%)	7,996
1955	---	-----	-----	5783 (68.1%)	2705 (31.9%)	8,488
1956	---	-----	-----	6291 (65.1%)	3379 (34.9%)	9,670
1957	2	2740 (31.3%)	3025 (34.5%)	5765 (65.8%)	3003 (34.2%)	8,768
1959	0	2186 (28.6%)	2493 (31.9%)	4625 (60.5%)	3025 (39.5%)	7,650
1960	3	2419 (30.1%)	2567 (31.9%)	4986 (62%)	3061 (38%)	8,047
1961	2	2458 (29.2%)	2932 (34.9%)	5390 (64.1%)	3015 (35.9%)	8,405
1962	1	2758 (27.4%)	3764 (37.4%)	6522 (64.8%)	3538 (35.2%)	10,060
1963	3	2235 (24.6%)	3141 (34.5%)	5376 (59.1%)	3725 (40.9%)	9,101
1964	3	3092 (26.3%)	3976 (33.8%)	7068 (60%)	4692 (40%)	11,760
1965	1	2237 (24%)	3172 (34%)	5409 (58%)	3927 (42.1%)	9,336
1966	3	2616 (25.7%)	3383 (33.2%)	5999 (58.9%)	4188 (41.1%)	10,187
1967	0	2663 (26%)	3364 (33%)	6027 (59%)	4198 (42%)	10,225
1968	0	2879 (23%)	4340 (35%)	7219 (58%)	5219 (41.5%)	12,438
1969	0	3280 (23%)	5059 (35.5%)	8339 (58.5%)	5907 (41.5%)	14,246
1970	0	3111 (20.8%)	5237 (35%)	8348 (55.8%)	6625 (44.2%)	14,973
1971	0	3255 (19.3%)	5731 (34%)	8986 (53.4%)	7846 (46.6%)	16,832
1972	0	2606 (19.2%)	4553 (33.6%)	7159 (52.8%)	6405 (47.2%)	13,564
1973	0	2861 (19.1%)	4786 (31.9%)	7647 (50.9%)	7368 (49.1%)	15,015
1974	0	2544 (16.5%)	4906 (31.9%)	7450 (48.4%)	7937 (51.6%)	15,387

[i]There was no annual report produced in 1958, nor were the numbers from 1958 printed in later years. The 1952, 1953, 1955, and 1956 JCARs were unavailable to the author; only the numbers for the <16 and the 16/17 age groups could be discerned from reports from later years.

Table 27. Ratio of Boy/Girl Delinquents per 1,000 Juveniles, by Age Group; & Percentage of Boy/Girl Delinquents in Juvenile Population, 1940-1974

Year	7-15	14/15	16/17	7-17	% of Population
1940	20/2 (11)	42/6 (24)	42/7 (25)	24/3 (14)	------------
1945	30/5 (17)	58/13 (38)	67/11 (40)	37/6 (22)	------------
1955	32/7 (20)	-----------	79/14 (46)	39/8 (24)	------------
1960	25/6 (16)	70/23 (46)	75/16 (45)	33/8 (21)	3.3/.8 (2.1)
1961	26/6 (16)	65/20 (43)	82/17 (50)	35/8 (22)	3.5/.8 (2.1)
1962	29/7 (18)	74/22 (48)	91/18 (54)	38/9 (24)	3.8/.9 (2.4)
1963	25/7 (16)	69/22 (45)	82/17 (50)	35/8 (22)	3.4/.8 (2.1)
1964	33/8 (21)	88/27 (58)	95/18 (57)	44/10 (27)	4.4/1.0 (2.7)
1965	23/6 (15)	66/21 (46)	81/15 (49)	33/8 (21)	3.3/.7 (2.0)
1966	26/7 (17)	68/24 (46)	85/16 (49)	35/8 (22)	3.5/.8 (2.2)
1967	25/7 (16)	65/23 (44)	85/16 (51)	35/8 (22)	3.4/.8 (2.1)
1971	38/8 (23)	104/21 (63)	139/19 (80)	57/10 (33)	5.7/1.0 (3.4)
1972	32/7 (19)	87/19 (53)	113/17 (66)	47/9 (28)	4.7/.9 (2.8)
1973	34/7 (21)	94/21 (57)	128/18 (74)	52/9 (31)	5.2/.9 (3.0)
1974	35/8 (22)	96/22 (59)	144/21 (83)	55/10 (33)	5.5/1.0 (3.3)

Table 28. Number & Percent of Boys' Big 10 Serious Offense Cases & Number of Transfers, 1940—1957, 1959-1985

Year	Burglary	Robbery[i]	Drug Offenses	Indecent Assault/ & Rape	A&B/ Homicide	Carrying Weapon	Arson[v]	Auto Theft	Transfers	Total Number & Percentage
1940	837	158	0	23[iii]	278/3	16	0	286	15	1,538/27.6
1941	795	224	1	21	287/10	27	0	357	3	1,722/30.1
1942	780	192	?	29	255/22	43	0	324	8	1,645/27.1
1943	835	246	3	20/13	344/9	76	0	413	25	1,959/24.8
1944	872	202	1	62/9	442/11	90	0	421	23	2,109/26.5
1945	1,036	212	0	50/6	421/28	154	0	589	38	2,496/30.2
1946	961	167	0	70/10	321/12	108	0	439	21	2,088/29.5
1947	869	138	0	56/16	338/10	116	0	253	24	1,799/30.4
1948	809	137	8	61/17	316/8	74	0	205	20	1,630/26.5
1949	725	145	2	84/16	278/4	130	0	214	57	1,643/27.8
1950	754	122	20	78/30	356/4	149	?	230	30	1,743/33.4
1951	727	182	11	103/23	298/6	134	?	333	36	1,817/34.4
1952	762	180	?	100[iv]	412	210	?	311	41	1,975/34.5
1953	926	323	?	100	540	208	?	422	28	2,029/28.8
1954	1,249	376	5	146/41	578/7	263	?	484	22	3,149/39.4
1955	1,156	408	?	150	705/10	359	?	498	24	3,286/38.7
1956	1,140	292	?	150	876/47	394	?	724	66	3,623/37.5
1957	1,354	415[ii]	4	100/92	673/31	298	?	782	56	3,749/42.8
1959	1,146	450	3	79/75	663/19	296	36	588	33	3,355/43.9
1960	1,234	436	2	111/61	808/39	319	42	654	45	3,706/46.1
1961	1,332	506	1	97/70	810/21	340	34	744	34	3,955/47.1
1962	1,505	616	3	116/103	1,050/44	516	66	904	64	4,923/48.9
1963	1,206	550	4	76/72	1,133/36	343	45	893	71	4,358/47.9
1964	1,878[vi]	700	5	76/185	1,483/45	493	65	1189	113	6,119/52.1
1965	1,416	464	17	77/122	1,254/39	392	78	917	60	4,776/51.2
1966	1,415	532	48	76/88	1,461/44	346	91	1001	66	5,102/50.1
1967	1,634	601	77	79/87	1,398/41	325	122	1093	68	5,457/53.4
1968	2,047	873	199	96/65	1,679/67	503	120	1501	80	7,150/57.5
1969	2,387	1,243	357	113/114	1,818/134	676	113	1758	102	8,713/61.2
1970	2,408	1,431	647	81/103	2,051/136	715	84	1675	129	9,311/62.3
1971	2,906	1,643	656	104/174	2,180/126	805	115	1545	114	10,254/60.6
1972	2,279	1,553	407	66/175	1,613/122	655	94	1000	138	7,923/58.4
1973	2,499	1,807	739	69/253	1,784/77	778	186	1274	162	9,466/63.1
1974	2,828	1,788	1,040	117/286	1,805/18	651	52	1006	34	9,591/62.3
1978	2768	1497	998	112[vii]/96	1596/25	417	38	660	76	8,207/72.1

continued on following page

Table 28. Continued

Year	Burglary	Robbery[i]	Drug Offenses	Indecent Assault/ & Rape	A&B/ Homicide	Carrying Weapon	Arson[v]	Auto Theft	Transfers	Total Number & Percentage
1981	2586	2138	631	69/94	1615/45	382	59	1142	234	8,761/74.1
1983	1842	1670	412	85/94	1455/3	396	50	476	211	6,440/71.0
1985	1719	1990	563	86/89	1269/1	421	52	644	129	6,834/74.1

[i]Robberies and pick pockets were reported separately through 1942. The 1943 JCAR combined robbery and pick pocket charges as did subsequent reports; they were joined under robbery in this Table.

[ii]The 1957 JCAR identifies purse snatching as a separate form of robbery, but the numbers of the two crimes are combined in this Table; this was done in subsequent annual reports as well.

[iii]The number of indecent assaults and rape was not specified in the 1940, 1941 and 1942 JCARs, but other sex-related offenses were. The first 3 numbers in this column are the most of the two crimes that could have occurred those years; they were listed as "others," without explanation, so these are the absolute most that could have happened.

[iv]The 1952, 1953, 1955, and 1956 JCARs were not available so the actual numbers of indecent assaults and rapes were unattainable. These four numbers in those years are rough estimates of the number of indecent assault and rape charges that happened those years. The 1975-1977, 1979-1980, 1982, and 1984 JCARs were also unavailable.

[v]Arson was not identified specifically for years in the annual reports. The columns with a 0 are those years where there were no offenses reported as "other," suggesting that there were zero arsons to report. There were several cases of setting fires reports, but it is unlikely that any of these were arsons. Once arsons were finally identified in 1959, they became frequently identified offenses.

[vi]JCARs from 1964 on identified burglaries from boxcars and vehicles as burglaries. Those offenses were not counted as burglaries in this Table.

[vii]In 1978, involuntary deviate sexual intercourse charges were separated from indecent assaults. The two offenses are joined in this table.

Table 29. Times as Prevalent among Boys' 8 of Big-10 Offenses, 1940-1985,[i] Compared to Boys' 8 of Big-10 Offenses Annual Averages, 1917/1921-1929/1939[ii] & Comparison Big 10 Offenses, 1917-1939 vs. 1940-1985

Times as Prevalent	Burglary, 1917-1939 516.2 ave	Robbery, 1917-1939 104.2 ave.	Indecent Assault[iii] 1917-1929 6.6 ave.	Rape, 1917-1929 11.5 ave.	A&B, 1917-1939 125.6 ave.	Carrying Weapon, 1917-1939 13.0 ave.	Homicide, 1917-1939 3.2 ave.	Auto Theft 1921-1939 135.5 ave.	All Big 10 Offenses 1917-1939 918.9 ave.
2	1945, 54-57, 59-63, 65,66	1945	1943	1950, 51	1940-43, 46-51	1941	1943, 47, 48, 54	1940, 41, 42, 46, 51, 52	1943, 44, 45, 46, 52, 53
3	64,67,68, 83,85	53, 54, 57		54	44, 45	42	41, 44, 46, 55, 83	43, 44, 53, 54, 55	54-56, 59
4	69, 70, 72, 73	59, 60, 61, 65			54		85	45, 59, 60, 78	57, 60, 61, 63
5	71,74, 78, 81	62, 63, 66, 67		60, 68	55, 57, 59	43, 48	59, 74	56, 57, 61	62, 65-67
6		64		59, 61. 63	56, 60, 61	44	42, 61	62, 63, 65	64
7			45	66, 67, 85			78	66, 72, 74	68, 83, 85
8		68	47	57, 62, 70, 78, 81, 83	62	46, 47	45	64, 67, 81	72, 78
9			44, 48	69	63, 65		57	73	69, 81
10			46, 72, 73, 81	65	85	49, 51			70, 73, 74

continued on following page

Table 29. Continued

Times as Prevalent	Burglary, 1917-1939 516.2 ave	Robbery, 1917-1939 104.2 ave.	Indecent Assault[iii] 1917-1929 6.6 ave.	Rape, 1917-1929 11.5 ave.	A&B, 1917-1939 125.6 ave.	Carrying Weapon, 1917-1939 13.0 ave.	Homicide, 1917-1939 3.2 ave.	Auto Theft 1921-1939 135.5 ave.	All Big 10 Offenses 1917-1939 918.9 ave.
11		69	50, 59, 63-67		64, 66, 67, 83	45, 50	63	68, 71	71
12			49, 70, 83		72, 78, 81		60, 65, 67	69, 70	
13		70	85		68		62, 66		
14		72, 78	61, 68		69, 73, 74		56, 64, 81		
15		71	51, 57, 71	71, 72					
16		83	60, 78		70	52, 53			
17		73, 74	62, 69, 74		71				
19		85							
20		81				54	68		
22			54	73		57, 59			
24				74		60	73		
25						67			
26						61, 63, 66			
27						55			
29						81			
30						56, 65, 83			
32						78, 85			
37						64			
38						68	72		
39						62	71		
41							69		
42							70		
50						72, 74			
52						69			
55						70			
59						73			
61						71			

[i]The very few numbers of drug offenses and arsons during the 1917-1939 period make comparisons to the 1940-1985 period pointless. Consequently, only 8 Big 10 offenses are considered in this Table.

[ii]The different ranges of times for the various offenses are due to the non-identification of indecent assaults and rapes during the 1930s, and the absence of autos to steal during the first few years of the 1920s.

[iii]All sex crimes were cumulated and not individually identified during the 1930s. Thus, only the 1917-1929 indecent assault and rape charges are used for comparison purposes in this Table.

[iv]There were no auto thefts by juveniles reported until 1921. Counting the 1917-1920 years for this category of crime would unfairly decrease the average of auto thefts during the 1917-1939 period.

Table 30. Percentage of Recidivist Boys'/Girls' Cases, Overall & Those Resolved by an Adjudicatory Hearing, 1940-1972

Year	% of Overall Cases	% of Adjudicatory Hearings
1940	45/31 (43)	54/38 (52)
1941	45/28 (42)	55/31 (51)
1942	46/25 (43)	54/29 (49)
1943	45/36 (43)	48/37 (46)
1944	47/32 (44)	49/30 (46)
1945	50/37 (46)	53/37 (50)
1946	50/34 (48)	----------[i]
1947	50/35 (48)	----------
1948	46/35 (44)	----------
1949	44/36 (43)	----------
1950	43/35 (41)	----------
1951	43/37 (42)	----------
1952	46/36 (44)	----------
1953	48/40 (47)	----------
1954	48/39 (47)	----------
1955	51/42 (49)	----------
1956	54/39 (52)	----------
1957	58/41 (55)	64/44 (61)
1959	57/40 (54)	62/42 (58)
1960	56/37 (52)	60/40 (56)
1961	56/36 (52)	60/39 (56)
1962	59/35 (55)	63/38 (59)
1963	57/38 (54)	64/42 (60)
1964	56/31 (52)	67/40 (62)
1965	60/35 (56)	67/40 (62)
1966	61/41 (58)	68/45 (64)
1967	61/39 (57)	66/42 (62)
1968	62/36 (58)	----------
1969	63/38 (60)	----------
1970	63/38 (60)	----------
1971	70/50 (68)	86/77 (85)
1972	71/53 (69)	86/83 (86)

[i]All years with ------- in the row were ones in which a recidivist profile for the adjudicatory hearings was not reported.

Table 31. Percentage of Recidivist Boys'/Girls' (Total) Cases, Overall & Those Resolved by an Adjudicatory Hearing, 1920-1939

Year	% of Overall Cases	% of Adjudicatory Hearings
1920	25/20 (24)	42/20 (36)
1921	34/39 (35)	67/60 (65)
1922	34/38 (34)	66/57 (64)
1924	40/22 (37)	39/21 (36)
1925	37/26 (35)	53/34 (50)
1926	38/25 (36)	50/36 (48)
1927	40/23 (38)	52/27 (48)
1928	41/25 (39)	53/29 (50)
1929	38/28 (37)	53/34 (49)
1930	38/25 (36)	54/35 (50)
1931	40/27 (38)	64/40 (58)
1932	39/30 (38)	66/45 (61)
1933	43/29 (41)	65/44 (61)
1934	44/25 (42)	67/39 (61)
1935	42/27 (41)	67/36 (62)
1936	41/25 (39)	61/34 (56)
1937	38/26 (37)	54/34 (51)
1938	41/28 (39)	56/38 (54)
1939[i]	37/30 (37)	50/36 (48)

[i]The percentages reported in 1939 include both juveniles under the age of sixteen and the newly added 16- and 17-year-olds. This resulted in reducing slightly the percentages of both overall cases and those resolved by an adjudicatory hearing. In the first several years in juvenile court, the older youths consistently had lower recidivist numbers than their younger counterparts.

Table 32. Number of Boys'/Girls' Same Year Arrests, Disposed at either Intake (I) or a Court Hearing (CH), 1965-1972

Year	First	Second	Third	Fourth	Fifth	Sixth or (7-10)
1965	717/52 (I) 2,272/324 (CH)	376/57 (I) 1,321/169 (CH)	129/14 (I) 488/25 (CH)	46/6 (I) 160/7 (CH)	19/0 (I) 59/0 (CH)	15/0 (I) 38/0 (CH)
1966	789/82 (I) 2,451/362 (CH)	272/31 (I) 1,615/263 (CH)	85/17 (I) 580/69 (CH)	25/4 (I) 256/21 (CH)	11/3 (I) 102/7 (CH)	8/2 (I) 70/5 (CH)
1967	771/81 (I) 2,294/348 (CH)	342/39 (I) 1,478/209 (CH)	128/11 (I) 607/48 (CH)	50/3 (I) 279/17 (CH)	21/1 (I) 126/6 (CH)	23/0 (I) 95/3 (CH)
1968	3,444/352 (I & CH)	2,272/273 (I & CH)	987/85 (I & CH)	480/24 (I & CH)	237/9 (I & CH)	247/4 (I & CH)
1969	4,129/413 (I & CH)	2,607/306 (I & CH)	1,129/87 (I & CH)	558/32 (I & CH)	293/9 (I & CH)	260/9 (I & CH)
1970	4,494/437 (I & CH)	2,782/313 (I & CH)	1,122/101 (I & CH)	544/30 (I & CH)	275/9 (I & CH)	289/1 (I & CH)
1971	1,949/182 (I) 4,157/572 (CH)	1,073/107 (I) 2,075/195 (CH)	365/28 (I) 984/53 (CH)	142/11 (I) 469/24 (CH)	65/2 (I) 229/13 (CH)	59/0 (I) 354/4 (CH)
1972	5,243/717 (I & CH)	2,419/285 (I & CH)	999/68 (I & CH)	450/25 (I & CH)	229/8 (I & CH)	356/4 (I & CH)

Table 33. Number of Boys'/Girls' Cases: Court Hearings (Pre-Trial/Adjudicatory) vs. Adjusted at Intake, 1965-1991

Year	Pre-Trial[i]	Adjudicatory[ii]	Court Hearings	Adjusted
1965	-------	6479/1327	6479/1327	2857/520
1966	------	7490/1617	7490/1617	2697/490
1967	------	7400/1490	7400/1490	2825/465
1968	3007	7096	8843/1260	3595/812
1969	4888	6214	9744/1258	4502/964
1970	5562	5934	10281/1215	4692/1139
1971	4351	6088	9623/1116	7293/1278
1972	3680	5096	7778/998	5786/1105
1973	4383	6410	9630/1163	5385/1052
1974	4273	6425	9532/1166	5855/1153
1975	4609	7454	10703/1360	5064/1123
1976	4459	6575	9689/1345	4219/808
1977	3838	5710	8453/1095	2344/423
1978	5057	5280	9431/906	1946/285
1979	5766	5200	9970/996	1292/266
1980	4705	5667	9323/1049	1135/258
1981	5403	6543	10756/1100	1060/267
1982	4430	5613	8984/1059	1074/248
1983	4005	5027	8164/868	910/243
1984	3577	5689	9266	987
1985	3939	5605	8593/951	632/142
1986	3051	6598	9649	758
1987	2013	5739	7752	518
1988	1559	7869	8577/851	206/91
1989	1399	7579	8978	154
1990	1250	7192	7678/764	111/83
1991	867	6981	7033/815	132/95

[i]Pre-Trials were introduced in 1968 to alleviate the number of cases headed to an Adjudicatory Hearing, by weeding out cases that could be resolved via plea bargaining or some other informal, non-trial resolution.

[ii]From 1968 on, only the total number of court hearings were tallied; gender was not indicated. Other years in this Table with only a single number are those that did not provide a gender breakdown for the Court Hearings and Adjusted Cases (these 1984, 1986, 1987, and 1989 JCARs were not available to the author).

Table 34. Percentage of <16/16-17 Boys' Big 10 Cases Resolved by Adjudicatory Hearing (AH) & Adjustment (Adj). Percentage of Adjudicatory Hearings & Adjustments Containing Boy's Big 10 Offenses, 1940-1949; 1960-1974

Year	% of Big 10 Cases Resolved by AH	% of Big 10 Cases Resolved by Adj	% of AH with Big 10 Offenses	% of Adj with Big 10 Offenses
1940[i]	65.4/99.1 (79.6)	34.6/.9 (20.4)	20.1/22.1 (42.2)	11.3/.2 (11.6)
1941	64.3/99.1 (77.6)	35.7/.9 (22.4)	23.0/22.0 (45.1)	13.8/.2 (14.0)
1942	69.5/97.6 (80.1)	30.5/2.4 (19.9)	22.8/19.5 (42.3)	10.6/.5 (11.1)
1943	66.4/97.8 (78.9)	33.6/2.2 (21.1)	18.7/18.3 (37.0)	10.6/.5 (11.1)
1944	71.7/97.7 (83.4)	28.3/2.3 (16.6)	18.5/20.5 (39.0)	9.5/.6 (10.2)
1945	69.9/98.1 (82.3)	30.1/1.9 (17.6)	21.0/23.1 (44.1)	11.9/.6 (11.4)
1946	69.0/97.1 (80.5)	31.0/2.9 (19.5)	22.8/22.4 (45.2)	11.4/.7 (12.1)
1947	78.6	21.4	50.1	12.5
1948	81.3	18.7	46.1	9.3
1949	85.2	14.8	46.1	8.5
1960	89.3	10.7	54.4	20.3
1961	89.5	10.5	57.0	18.9
1962	87.4	12.6	58.9	22.5
1963	84.8	15.2	60.1	22.4
1964	90.2	9.8	61.8	21.2
1965	85.2	14.8	62.8	24.7
1966	87.5	12.5	59.6	23.6
1967	83.8	16.2	61.8	31.3
1968	84.6	15.4	68.4	30.6
1969	79.1	20.9	70.8	40.4
1970	81.6	18.4	73.9	36.6
1971	71.6	28.4	76.3	40.0
1972	70.8	29.2	72.2	39.9
1973	76.1	23.9	74.8	42.0
1974	73.8	26.2	74.2	42.9

[i]For the first seven years of the 1940s, boys' cases were divided into those younger than 16 and those 16/17 years old and reported separately. The numbers in parentheses are the combined total for both age groups. The numbers show a significant difference between the two age groups in both case resolution categories. Older youths' Big 10 cases were sent to trial much more often and adjusted much less frequently. Not surprising, the percentage of adjusted cases containing Big 10 offenses was dramatically different for the two age groups; that was not the case, however, for the percentage of trials containing Big 10 offenses. From 1947 on the data on the two age groups were combined.

Table 35. Boys' Delinquent Commitments to Delinquent Facilities, by Offense, 1961-1973

Offense	1961	1962	1963	1964	1965	1966	1967	1968	1969	1971	1972	1973
Larceny[ii]	199	169	183	168	159	127	91	70	87	55	33	40
Burglary	329	451	346	551	465	329	252	199	254	200	159	125[x]
Robbery	138	173	177	246	153	134	99	121	190	181	153	135[xi]
Auto Theft	178	205	255	226	248	222	124	122	118	107	74	95
Homicide	3	10	11	8	14	6	5	6	23	14	8	2
A&B[iii]	192	217	216	282	270	240	164	168	190	189	125	152
Weapons	129	140	89	83	92	58	36	42	63	39	44	52
Resist Officer	2	4	2	8	5	7	3	3	6	8	3	4
Run-Home	34	37	38	57[vii]	49	88	80	30	42	33	27	29
Run-Institution	21	23	3	x	x	x	x	x	x	x	x	x
Incorrigible	97	44	31	51	69	43	18	19	52	17	21	9
Truancy	116	156	141	57	72	76	36	28	48	22	11	3
Malicious Mischief[iv]	40	20	19	50	39	26	2	11	8	11	18	11
Trespassing	5	11	3	4	16	12	7	3	1	1	0	1
Rape by Force	27	46	20	35	52	20	17	13	40	29	26	33
Indecent Assault	15	22	14	13	9	12	10	9	8	x[ix]	x	x
Fornication[v]	29	41	31	29	39	35	5	8	10	x	x	x
Other Sex	3	4	3	5	3	5	3	1	2	7	8	13
Drinking	14	22	9	5	21[viii]	31	20	11	8	2	18	7
Drugs	3	0	6	3	7	13	6	5	4	16	10	3[xii]
Arson	5	8	9	11	17	12	6	12	3	0	2	2
Vandalism	38	15	24	58	40	44	27	11	14	10	4	4
Vagrancy[vi]	6	3	1	1	2	3	2					
Motor Vehicle	1	3	0	3	3	4	2	1	0	0	0	0
Other	4	3	3	4	38	18	8	16	27	14	6	15
Total	1,589	1,827	1,634	1,958	1,882	1,565	1,023	909	1,198	955	751	735

[i]The 1970 JCAR did not identify which offenses resulted in which delinquent commitment. From 1974 on, all annual reports grouped all commitments (i.e., delinquent; other institutions; and, agencies and individuals) into one category.

[ii]Larceny includes parking meter theft, shoplifting, and other stealing.

[iii]Gang fighting was added as a separate offense, but is included here under A&B.

[iv]Malicious mischief includes malicious mischief, acts of carelessness, pulling a fire alarm, creating a disturbance, and disorderly conduct. In 1957, it appears any charges of trespassing, vandalism, and arson were included under other acts of carelessness (which are listed under Malicious Mischief in this table).

[v]Fornication includes fornication, fornication and bastardy, and sodomy.

[vi]In the 1963 JCAR, corner lounging replaced vagrancy as the category title.

[vii]From 1964 on, all runaways were grouped together.

[viii]From 1964 on, glue sniffing was listed as a separate offense but is included with drinking in this Table.

[ix]From 1971 on, all sex offenses other than rape were grouped together as all other sex offense---except rape. Juvenile court also lost jurisdiction over fornication and bastardy charges.

[x]Burglary commitments increased to 316 (1981), 339 (1983), and 413 (1985), but declined after that.

[xi]Robbery commitments experienced an increase to 330 (1981), 339 (1983), and, 465 (1985), but declined after that.

[xii]In the mid-1980s and later, drug offense commitments increased to 58 (1985, 471 (1988), 550 (1990), and, 466 (1991).

Table 36. Number & Percentage of Boys'/Girls' Delinquent Commitments Cases, 1959-1974

Year	Private & Public Agency[i]	Non-Delinquent Inst.[ii]	Delinquent Facility	Mental Treatment Inst[iii]	Parent[iv]	Hospital	Percent Delinquent Facility[v]
1959	55/39	52/21	1,432/320	35/14	13/11	2/11	90.1/76.9
1960	57/25	46/9	1,630/316	42/9	8/6	4/22	91.2/81.7
1961	22/14	33/7	1,589/310	52/19	5/3	5/9	93.1/85.6
1962	9/8	55/14	1,910/275	29/30	10/6	3/17	94.7/78.6
1963	7/5	13/5	1,634/262	34/23	3/7	3/10	96.5/84.0
1964	30/8	24/5	1,958/237	43/25	2/3	2/20	95.1/79.5
1965	17/7	28/1	1,882/213	25/21	1/ 2	2/7	96.3/84.9
1966	27/5	23/0	1,565/171	20/21	1/1	1/17	95.6/79.5
1967	6/3	26/1	1,023/137	26/8	0/0	1/13	94.5/84.6
1968	13/0	39/0	909/77	13/4	----	1/3	93.2/91.7
1969	13/8	20/3	1,198/97	28/5	----	0/4	95.2/82.9
1970	21/18	5/3	1,050/66	38/11	----	1/3	94.2/65.3
1971	30/22	7/2	955/68	?	----	?	96.3/73.9
1972	33/39	13/4	751/68	22/12	----	2/0	91.5/55.3
1973	73/60	66/0	735/63	26/1	----	2/1	81.5/50.4
1974	21/18	?	594/71	44/3	----	?	90.1/77.2

[i]Between 1961 and 1974, Private Agency Commitments ranged from 1-13 for Boys and 0-8 for Girls. In 1959 and 1960, these commitments numbered 41/32 and 26/18, respectively.

[ii]These institutions were identified as either Other Institutions or Institutions for Non-Delinquents from 1960 on.

[iii]These mental treatment institutions were identified as being for mental retards/defectives as well as for emotionally disturbed or mentally ill children in 1960. Although derogatory, the title gives an idea of the scope of children subjected to this disposition. After that time, a less informative Institutions for Mental Treatment was employed as the title.

[iv]For a brief time, "commitments" were directed to parents, relatives or simply individuals. By 1968, these individuals/parents/relatives were grouped with agency commitments.

[v]From 1964 through 1973, the JCARs disregarded mental health and hospital commitments in the official tally of juvenile court commitments; in 1974, these two were included in the official tally. In calculating the percentage of delinquent commitments, mental health, and hospital commitments, if known, were included in*all* years reported in this Table.

Table 37. Number of Facilities Utilized for Delinquent Boys & Girls, 1943-1970

Year	Child-Placing-out	Other/ Dependent	Correctional	Mental Defective	Hospital
1943	9	8	13	7	3
1944	11	11	16	10	9
1945	10	10	17	14	6
1946	12	12	17	7	7
1947	11	13	17	7	7
1948	10	16	19	8	6
1949	11	11	15	10	4
1950	11	13	14	9	5
1951	8	10	16	7	7
1954	11	11	17	9	3
1957	14	15	15	8	2
1959	12	15	18	7	4
1960	9	23	18	11	8
1964	7	9	23	9	5
1965	5	8	21	8	5
1966	4	4	19	9	5
1967	4	4	20	10	4
1968	6	6	22	9[i]	------
1969	6	6	22	9	------
1970	6	6	22	9	------

[i]In the 1968-1970 JCARs, mental and medical hospitals were joined.

Chapter 6
Misidentifying Transfer:
The Terms and Concepts Battle

ABSTRACT

Chapter 6 begins to undo the damage done by the numerous ways in which transfer has been misidentified and mishandled; offense exclusion (OE) is the type of transfer that is most often and extensively mischaracterized. The literature guilty of spreading this disinformation is massive, which the Tables included in this Chapter reveal. The most prevalent misidentification is probably the most understandable, namely, that transfer means juveniles are being tried as adults. The first mission of the Chapter is to lay this notion to rest. Juveniles are not chronically transformed due to being transferred to criminal court (CC). There are actual transformations that do occur, and they are explained fully. The second and more sustained objective is to remedy the many misidentifications of OE; there are at least nine of these. This Chapter also details the two types of mandatory exclusion (ME) and distinguishes them from transfer, which often doesn't happen in both research and literature.

1. CHILDREN ARE BEING PROSECUTED AS ADULTS

The first misidentification is the one found most often in the literature: *children* being transferred *en masse* to CC and being forced to stand trial *as adults*. That sounds inappropriate since children are being treated as adults, which is probably the point. This should not occur.

Before this aspect of the anti-transfer crowd's (ATC's) campaign is examined, we need definitions of child, adolescent, juvenile, and adult; these definitions vary considerably from one source to another. For purposes of this book, a *child* is considered as someone between infancy and the onset of puberty (10-11 for girls and 11-12 for boys); for simplicity and equal treatment, a *child* will be regarded as anyone *younger than 13 years of age*. Those *youths between 13 years of age and 18 years of age* (the most common definition of adulthood) are regarded as *adolescents* herein. Nevertheless, some sources declare that adolescent runs from 12 or 13 until 20 or 21 years of age. The term, *juvenile*, presents its own problem in that it overlaps both child and adolescent identities. Typically, today, any person younger than 18 is a juvenile; three states (GA, TX, WI), however, have adopted 16 years of age as the maximum JC age

DOI: 10.4018/978-1-7998-7923-7.ch006

for criminal prosecution purposes, meaning, in this context, their "adults" start at age 17. A *juvenile* in this text is considered as anyone younger than 18 years of age; typically, and in this book, the age at the time of the offense controls. An *adult* in American society, then, usually is legally defined as 18 years old, the legal voting age. That age, however, is two years beyond driving eligibility in most states (i.e., 16 years old), but still three years too young for the legal consumption of alcohol and the purchase of tobacco products. Since criminal liability is "automatic" for all offenders beyond the age of 18 (except for Vermont that uses 19 for this category), *adult* in this text applies to anyone *18 years of age or older.*

In the literature, *children* are frequently identified as the transferred youth (see Table 38 A). *Oh no*, massive numbers of *children* are headed to CC.

Waiver laws attempt to reconcile the contradictory impulses engendered when the ***child is a criminal and the criminal is a child****... (Feld, 1999a, p. 209, emphasis added).*

****

Are the youngsters transferred to criminal courts ***no longer children*** *in the eyes of the law as a result of that decision?... (Fagan & Zimring, 2000, p.3, emphasis added; see, also, Fagan, 2002, p.9)*

****

The language used to describe the process of transferring defendants to criminal court is itself an invitation to what psychiatrists call "magical thinking," in which it is imagined that changing the location of a case will suddenly remove the characteristics that cause conflict and ambivalence. The physical reality of jurisdictional transfer is rather mundane—to try an accused ***as an adult*** *in a criminal court changes only the location of the hearing; it does not change the characteristics of the defendant... (Zimring, 1998a, p. 132, emphasis added).*

****

Jurisdictions with legislative waiver have effectively created an irrebuttable presumption that ***children*** *of a certain age who are charged with certain crimes are not really* ***children****... (Marrus & Rosenberg, 2005, p. 1178, emphases added).*

Contrary to reports in the literature, children are exceedingly rarely prosecuted in CC. Instead, the vast majority of those transferred are at least 16 years old. These youths are not children.

We do not know the actual nature or number of transfers accomplished via prosecutorial decisions. Offense exclusion (OE) and direct file (DF) provisions, however, overwhelmingly set a minimum age of 15 or 16 as the minimum age qualifying for transfer, unless a capital or life-in-prison earning crime is involved (see Sanborn & Salerno, 2005, pp. 523-526). Percentages are more available for judicial transfer (JT). Many states have a minimum age of 14 for juvenile defendants to qualify for JT, barring a very serious offense (see Sanborn & Salerno, 2005, pp. 519-523). According to the Office of Juvenile Justice and Delinquency Prevention (OJJDP) reports, the percentage of defendants 16 years of age and older transferred by a judge between 1985 and 2018 ranged from 85% (2005) to 94% (1985) (See Table

39). The remaining 6% to 15% are catalogued as 15 years of age or younger, but, certainly, most of this group, probably 95% to 99%, are at least 15 years old. To assert that 90% to 95% of transfers involve youths at least 15 years of age seems reasonable.

The claim that children are being transferred to CC is a distortion, and is likely intended to serve as disinformation, some of which stems from referring to CC as *adult court*. Calling it adult court is a convenient way of separating it from JC, but its official title is *criminal court*. Originally, while most, but certainly not all, juvenile defendants were removed from CCs, the latter lost neither their title nor their jurisdiction over criminal acts, apart from those committed by some juveniles. Criminal Courts remained CCs.

Chronological juveniles' being tried as adults also sounds offensive, which is likely the point. The phrase is so engrained in the vernacular and literature (see Table 38 A) that is it unlikely to stop. The ATC has exploited the propaganda to highlight the purported wrongfulness of the transfer practice in general.

There is no chronological metamorphosis that occurs via transfer. Rather, the juvenile is being prosecuted *as a criminal rather than as a delinquent*. It is not the youth's age that is lost or ignored. It is the defendant's potential status as a delinquent defendant that is being discarded. For those very rare moments when a *true child*, that is, a youth younger than 13, is prosecuted in CC, the common law defense of infancy is available. Not surprising, that common law defense has all but disappeared from modern jurisprudence. Instead, it is immunity from criminal prosecution that is being lost by the youth. Put another way, diversion from CC is being denied.

Prior the introduction of JC, all youth, even younger than 10, prosecuted in CC were not referred to as being tried as adults. Even today, juveniles processed with adults for traffic, boating, hunting, fishing, and violations/summary offenses in "adult-centered" (or age neutral in title) courts are not referred to as being tried as adults. In some states adults will face trial and sentencing in JCs for some minor offenses (such as contributing to the delinquency of a minor). These adult defendants are not referred to as being prosecuted *as juveniles*. It is the jurisdiction of the court, and not the age of the accused, which determines the identity of the defendant. Transfer's meaning a youth will be tried *as a criminal defendant* does not carry the same emotional and prejudicial impact, however.

One ATC source admitted (in a footnote) that the "as adults" claim is inaccurate:

State laws do not change the legal status of a juvenile, who is criminally prosecuted, to an adult. Rather, the transfer mechanisms provide for the prosecution of juveniles as if they were adults, subjecting them to a possible criminal conviction and sentence in a court exercising criminal jurisdiction, in the same manner as an adult offender. However, it is common parlance to refer to a juvenile who is criminally prosecuted as one who is being prosecuted "as an adult" or in "adult court" (Griffin et al., p. 1998: 1, fn 1).[1]

Professor Barry Feld (1999a), a prominent member of the ATC, who originally supported the abolition of JC, frequently acknowledged that the issue is not *child versus adult* but rather *delinquent versus criminal,* by explaining transfer involves

the decision to prosecute a youth as ***a criminal or a delinquent*** *(p. 190, emphasis added).*

****

Each of these statutory (transfer) strategies allocates to a different branch of government… the decision of whether a youth is ***a criminal or a delinquent****… (Podkopacz & Feld, 1995, p. 76, emphasis added).*

Feld (2000) later conceded transfer involves

the decision whether to prosecute a youth as ***a criminal or as a delinquent*** *(p. 84, emphasis added; see, also, Keiter, 1973).*

Also, in direct file (DF) jurisdictions, Feld (2000) asserted prosecutors

have the discretionary authority to charge youths either ***as delinquents or criminals*** *… (p. 117, emphasis added),*

while in Nebraska, prosecutors

have complete discretion to try any youth of any age charged with a felony either as ***a delinquent or criminal****… (Id., emphasis added).*

Feld (2000) also reasserted that the prosecutor's transfer choice as involving the power to

determine a youth's ***delinquent or criminal*** *status (pp. 124-125, emphasis added).*

According to Feld (2001), JT and both forms of prosecutorial transfer (PT)

allocate to different branches of government — judicial, executive, or legislative — the decision whether to prosecute a youth ***as a criminal or as a delinquent****… (p. 4, emphasis added).*

Later in the same article, Feld claimed both OE and DF result in shifting

transfer discretion from juvenile court judges… to prosecutors who determine a youth's ***delinquent or criminal*** *status… (p. 18, emphasis added).*

Feld (2000) also acknowledged:

No per se right exists to be treated as ***a delinquent rather than as a criminal****… (p. 96, emphasis added).*

Nevertheless, by the end of that paragraph, Feld (2000) argued:

If the legislature defines juvenile court jurisdiction to include only those persons below a jurisdictional age and whom prosecutors charge with a nonexcluded offense, then all other persons are ***by definition*** *adults… (Id., emphasis in original; see, also, id., pp. 84, 91, 124-125; Feld, 1999a, p. 219; Feld, 2001, p. 9; Bishop & Feld, 2012, p. 818).*

Similarly, Feld vacillated on whether it actually is a child that is involved in the transfer decision, complaining that OE places "the burden on a young offender to demonstrate that he *really* is a child, an extremely difficult burden… (2000, p.129, emphasis in original)." This complaint is accurate especially since transfer targets are rarely children. An overwhelming majority can legally drive automobiles, so the alleged burden understandably is "extremely difficult." Feld (2000) admits moments later that transfer is not about children "because of differences in rates of offending by race, 'getting tough' on violence (i.e., transfer) meant targeting young black *men*…. (Id, emphasis added)."

Feld's frequent acknowledgements that a child is not actually being prosecuted as an adult has not prevented him from stating that *is* what occurs in virtually all of his writings (see Table 38 A); they far outnumber the previous references of his works.

Professor Franklin Zimring similarly alleged that transfer eradicates childhood by

declaring the defendant to be ***no longer a child****…. (T)he general proclamation that all who are charged with the commission of a particular crime should be regarded* ***as adults*** *removes the ambivalence that is characteristic of reactions to violence by the* ***very young*** *(Zimring, 1998a, p. 14, emphases added; see, also, Conrad, 1981, p. 179; Fagan, 2002, p. 8).*

This observation relies upon an incorrect premise that the *very young* are the typical targets of transfer. Only rarely are the very young subject to transfer; in no way is their transfer typical or common, let alone the majority situation.

Purported Conceptual Violations/Inappropriate Transformations

The ATC has offered a number of alleged conceptual violations and/or inappropriate transformations that are purported to result from transfer to CC:

- conceptual problem of treating a child as an adult (Tanenhaus, 2000, p. 30; see, also, Fagan & Zimring, 2000, p3; Zimring, 1998a, p. 132);
- a violent act does not transform a child into a rational adult (Tanenhaus, 2000, p. 30);
- the question of when a child ceases to be a child (Fagan & Deschenes, 1990, p. 325; Fagan, Piper, & Forst, 1986, p. 4; Tanenhaus, 2000, p. 31);
- transformed children who committed serious offenses into automatic adults (Tanenhaus, 2000, p. 33; see, also, Deitch, Barstow, Lukens, & Reyna, 2009, p.12; Smith, 1995, p. 989);
- irresponsible children one day and responsible adults the next (Feld, 1984b, p. 35; Feld, 1987, p. 500);
- immature delinquent to responsible criminal (Clarke, 2005, p. 676; Feld, 2000, p. 129, citing Feld, 1987, 1995; Torbet, Gable, Hurst, IV, Montgomery, Szymanski, & Thomas, 1996);
- innocent, immature, and dependent children to responsible, autonomous, and mature offenders… (Feld, 2000, p. 129; Feld, 2001, p. 20).

Feld and Bishop (2012) later declared that "the commission of a serious crime does not transform a juvenile into a fully responsible adult (p. 831)," whatever that means. That declaration begs questions, such as: since when does the imposition of punishment or holding one accountable demand "full adult" responsibility?; assuming the accuracy of the statement, how does that disqualify all juveniles from receiving punishment?; again, assuming the accuracy of the statement, how then, contrary to both Feld's and Bishop's transfer policy positions, would *any* juvenile be transferrable to CC?; and, just for kicks and giggles, how many adult criminals are *fully responsible*?

If accurate, these purported transformations, basically from immature child to responsible adult, would seem to be both wrong and cruel. It would appear potentially to strip juveniles of years of their lives. The assertions certainly have ideological impact in making transfer sound wrong, inappropriate, and unreasonable. Many observers must wonder how these transformations can be allowed to occur?

The simple answer (and truth) is that it is not the child that is being transformed. There are a number of things, however, that are transforming, all of them having to do with society's reaction to the chronic, serious, and violent behavior of juveniles.

Actual Appropriate Transformations

Numerous actual and appropriate transformations do occur when juveniles commit chronic and/or serious/violent offenses and face transfer to CC due to those offenses, including:

- *From* behavior that is considered delinquent conduct *to* behavior that is considered criminal conduct due to its being chronic (much like multiple misdemeanors can accumulate to become felonies) and/or severe;
- *From* immunity from criminal prosecution *to* liability for criminal behavior;
- *From* tolerance of young offenders' errant behavior *to* unacceptance and condemnation of young criminals' repeat/violent acts;
- *From* rehabilitation of those considered amenable to treatment *to* punishment of those considered to have ignored or wasted (perhaps several) previous attempts of help/rehabilitation *or* to be beyond the treatment capacity of JC *or* to be worthy of greater punishment than is available via JC;
- *From* seeking mostly the offender's best interests (BI) *to* seeking primarily society's BI;
- *From* looking primarily to protect the youth *to* looking primarily to protect victims and society, and, perhaps, other juveniles;
- *From* commitment to preserve youth's life chances *to* commitment to pursue justice, among other worthy goals;
- *From* disregarding responsibility (or assuming irresponsibility) *to* acknowledging responsibility due to chronic offending and/or the nature of some serious/violent behavior;
- *From* employing a euphemistic vocabulary (e.g., delinquency) designed to suspend reality to protect the youth from debilitating stigma *to* calling and recognizing the behavior for what it really is (i.e., crime);
- *From* diverting the case from CC *to* disqualifying the act/history from the list of diversion eligible cases; and,
- *From* keeping the community unaware of the juvenile's behavior *to* letting everyone know what the youth has done and can do so as to protect the community.

A rare admission by one ATC member acknowledges that transfer is not about children since

calling sixteen- and seventeen-year-olds children is not true to ordinary usage, and, in the context of considering the rights of those convicted of homicide, calling them "children" rings false and strategic (Buss, 2016, p. 759, footnote omitted).

A lengthy but extremely probative and insightful analysis of the child/adult dichotomy by an observer who has advocated the abolition of JC informs much of the debate here:

From our vantage point in the late twentieth century, the Progressives' use of the word "child" to describe the adolescent youth accused of violating the law seems incongruous if not willfully perverse. Just as the turn of the century Progressives reconstructed childhood and adolescence, so too Americans in the last half of the twentieth century have limned a new refiguration of the human life cycle in which childhood and adolescence have been re-imagined. As a result, the Progressives' view of childhood now seems so foreign to our current assumptions that it may be difficult for us to credit that they seriously believed in it.

When adolescence was conceived at the turn of the century, it was assimilated into the familiar category of childhood. Children and adolescents were seen as sub-categories of one larger category, whose members were considered more like infants in their nature and needs than they were like adults. The dichotomy between the essential natures of the child and adult remained intact... (Ainsworth, 1991, p. 1101, citations omitted).

******

Today we are witnessing the breakdown of the binary opposition between child and adult, which provided the conceptual foundation of juvenile court jurisprudence... (Id., p. 1103, citation omitted).

******

(T)he child-adult distinction is a false dichotomy that can no longer support disparate justice systems.... As the socially constituted perception of adolescence and childhood has evolved during the late twentieth century, the premises of the parens patriae juvenile court no longer correspond to our cultural image of the young... (Id., p. 1104, citation omitted).

Ainsworth takes her premise to a logical, but extreme, conclusion: the abolition of JC. Although her observations concerning the child/adult dichotomy are spot on, that does not require the same conclusions. Transfer to CC appears to be a more salient and palatable compromise.

2. OFFENSE EXCLUSION (OE) MISIDENTIFIED AS A LEGISLATIVE OR STATUTORY TRANSFER, WAIVER, OR EXCLUSION

The literature on transfer is inundated with the adjectives, *legislative* or *statutory,* linked with either *transfer, waiver, or exclusion* (see Table 38 B). Indiana refers to this phenomenon as *presumptive transfer* (see Sobol, 2022). These terms are used while talking about what should be called OE. Although evidently not the first to use the term (see Schornhorst, 1967, p. 596), Feld was a pioneer in promoting both the legislative title and OE itself (Feld, 1978, 1981b; see Table 38 B; cf., Stamm, 1973: 139). He considered OE preferable to JT due to the considerable discretion attending the latter type (Feld, 1981b). Feld held JT was marred due to the ambiguity (and potential discrimination) surrounding the amenability to treatment criteria.

Other ATC types have mistakenly reported that OE is a relatively new product and that JT was the only transfer mechanism originally available (see Fagan, Kupchik, & Liberman, 2007). OE's roots can be traced back to the first days of JC, however (see Tanenhaus, 2000, p. 42; Drizin & Tanenhaus, 2002, p. 666).

Using the legislative and statutory titles constitutes a dangerous misrepresentation, moreover. It is even possible that legislative and statutory transfer/exclusion can be presented as two distinct phenomena (see Cooper & Urban, 2012; Jordan & Myers, 2011; Verrecchia, 2003). First, since all exclusion (including transfer) has the legislature as its creator/initiator, and since all forms of exclusion or transfer are captured in statutes, the use of both legislative and statutory is uninformative. More important, it requires an understanding beyond what the words themselves connote. There is no clear communication as to what substantive elements are involved in the legislative/statutory terms. The lack of clarity has resulted in substantial confusion surrounding OE. It has even been identified as presumptive *waiver* (Clarke, 2005, p. 678), a term that should be limited to a form of JT (see Chapter 3).

Although the legislative title is most often used interchangeably with OE, it has even been mistakenly associated with the ME provision of mandatorily removing offenders from JC who have had a previous CC conviction (see Section #12-B, below). Marrus and Rosenberg (2005) claim the so-called Once Adult/Always Adult category "is a true *legislative waiver* statute as there is no room for prosecutorial discretion (p. 1178, emphasis added)."

The legislative title wrongly suggests that the *legislature decides which* cases get transferred:

*In a minority of states it is the **legislature**, not the juvenile court, which determines whether a juvenile will be tried in criminal court... (Sorrentine & Olsen, 1977, p. 503, emphasis added).*

****

*In some states, the **legislature**, not the juvenile court, determines whether the juvenile will be tried in juvenile court or adult criminal court... (Kozich, 1980, p. 174, emphasis added).*

****

*When a judge, prosecutor or **legislature** is considering waiver of juvenile jurisdiction... (Evans, 1992, p. 107, emphasis*

added).

****

*Waiver is used to send juveniles to adult criminal court when the judge, **legislature**, or prosecutor believes that the child needs to face harsher consequences than the juvenile court can provide (Hirase, 1992, p. 164, footnote omitted, emphasis added).*

****

Legislatures *transfer large numbers of young offenders by statutorily excluding them from juvenile court jurisdiction (Sickmund, 1994, p. 3, emphasis added; see, also, Harshbarger & Keshian, 1996).*

****

Each of these statutory strategies allocates to a different branch of government-judicial, ***legislative****, and executive-the decision of whether a youth is a criminal or a delinquent.... (Podkopacz & Feld, 1995, p. 76, emphasis added).*

****

When developing a process for choosing which children to send to the adult court process, states have three alternative decision-makers: ***legislators****, judges, and prosecutors. The choice among these decision-makers... (Glynn, 1997, p. 84, emphasis added; see, also, Gordon, 1999).*

****

Whether the ***legislature makes the forum decision by excluding offenses, or the prosecutor does so on a discretionary basis via concurrent jurisdiction****, these laws reduce or remove both discretionary judicial authority and juvenile courts' clientele (Feld, 1997, p. 80, emphasis added).*

****

Legislatures *and courts transfer youths to criminal court so that they may receive longer sentences as adults than they could in the juvenile system... (Feld, 1998, p. 244, emphasis added; see, also, Rudman, Hartstone, Fagan, & Moore, 1986).*

****

The principal legal devices include judicial waiver, legislative offense exclusion, and prosecutors' choices among concurrent jurisdictions.

Each of these strategies allocates to a different branch of government—judicial, ***legislative****, and executive—the decision to prosecute a youth as a criminal or delinquent... (Feld, 1999a, p. 190, emphasis added; see, also, Feld, 2000, p.108; Feld, 2001, p. 4).*

****

(J)udges, prosecutors, and ***legislatures*** *transfer increasing numbers of younger offenders to criminal courts for prosecution as adults... (Feld, 1999b, p. 358, emphasis added).*

****

*(Transfer law) changes reflect… a transfer of discretion from the judicial to the **legislative** or executive branches… (Id., p. 358, emphasis added).*

****

*There has also been a parallel shift in the method of transfer, with discretion being shifted from the judicial branch to the executive branch and also to the **legislative** branch… (Fagan, 2000, p. 360, emphasis added).*

****

*These (transfer) strategies allocate to different branches of government — judicial, executive, or **legislative** — the decision whether to prosecute a youth as a criminal or as a delinquent… (Feld, 2001, p.4, emphasis added; see, also, Watkins, 1998, p. 154).*

****

***Legislatures** in these (OE) states have essentially predetermined the question of the appropriate forum for prosecution — taking the decision out of both prosecutors' and judges' hands (Griffin, 2003, p. 2, emphasis added; see, also, Griffin et al., 1998).*

****

***Legislatures** "transfer" large numbers of young offenders to criminal court by enacting statutes that exclude certain cases from juvenile court jurisdiction… (Sickmund, 2003, p. 10, emphasis added; see, also, OJJ, 1999, p, 17).*

****

*One form of legislative waiver is a statutory exclusion, whereby a state **legislature essentially predetermines the question of criminal prosecution by taking the decision out of the hands of the prosecutor and the court**, codifying it in state statute… (Cooper & Urban, 2012, p. 45, citation omitted, emphases added).*

****

These (OE) cases eliminate any discretionary choices from both the juvenile court judge and the prosecutor about whether or not to transfer a youth (Samuelson, 2010, p.14, citing Griffin, 2003; Lemmon et al., 2005; McCarthy, 1994; Rainville and Smith, 2003; Sickmund, 2003; Snyder et al., 2000; Torbet and Szymanski, 1998).

****

*The shift in discretion from judges to **legislatures** and prosecutors also raises constitutional issues... (Fagan, 2002, p. 40, emphasis added; see, also, Applegate, Davis, & Cullen, 2008, p. 52).*

****

*Expedited transfer strategies shift the decision-making venue **from the judicial to the legislative arena**... (Clarke, 2005, p. 678, emphasis added).*

****

*There are three mechanisms through which juvenile offenders can be waived: judicial, prosecutorial, and **legislative**... (Burrow, 2005, p. 8, emphasis added).*

****

***Legislatures** "transfer" large numbers of young offenders to criminal court by enacting statutes that exclude certain cases from juvenile court jurisdiction... (Snyder & Sickmund, 2006, p. 113, emphasis added).*

****

***Legislators**, rather than prosecutors or judges, determine the appropriate forum for certain juvenile offenders through statutory exclusion mechanisms (Knox, 2009, p. 1274, emphasis added).*

****

*New "statutory exclusion" and "prosecutorial waiver" statutes had shifted the responsibility for transfer from the judiciary to the **legislative** and executive branches... (Weijers & Grisso, 2009, p. 56, citation omitted, emphasis added).*

****

*(T)he terms "transfer" and "waiver" are used interchangeably to mean the decision to prosecute a juvenile in adult criminal court, whether the decision is made by a judge after a hearing, by a prosecutor pursuant to discretion granted by statute, or by the **legislature** in designating certain offenses for which youth are automatically charged in adult court... (Soler, 2010, p. 17, footnote 1, emphasis added).*

****

*(T)he bulk of transfer decisions are now made by prosecutors or legislatures. A recent multi-jurisdictional study of adult courts in eighteen large urban counties revealed that eighty-five percent of all transfer decisions during a six-month period from January 1, 1998, to June 30, 1998, were made by prosecutors (forty-five percent) or **legislatures** (forty percent) instead of judges (Drizin & Tanenhaus, 2002, p. 667, emphasis added; see, also, Juszkiewicz, 2000, p. 2; Shook, 2005, p.466).*

The reader can rest assured that the *legislatures made and/or engaged* in *zero* percent of these transfers, while they *authorized 100%* of them. In the quotation, above, prosecutors accounted for all 85% of the transfer decisions, not a mere 45% of them.

The legislative title forces observers to guess substantively what is and what is not captured within the concept, and, most important, implies that the transfer is automatic, mandatory, nondiscretionary or is categorical/wholesale (see Butts, Coggeshall, Gouvis, Mears, Travis, Waul, & White, 2002; Butts & Mears, 2001; see Table 38 D & E). One ATC source even identified DF as automatic (see Penney & Moretti, 2005).

The legislature is no more involved in OE determinations than it is in JT rulings or DF choices. In all forms of transfer, the legislature is authorizing either a judge or a prosecutor to make the case-by-case decision as to which youth qualifies to be transferred due to which criteria authorize the transfer. The legislature cannot transfer anyone from the state capitol. This form of transfer does not merit the legislative adjective any more than the other forms of transfer do.

Statutory exclusion usually has been linked with OE and is typically considered and treated as a synonym for legislative transfer/waiver (see Table 38 B). One ATC member, however, has claimed that "prosecutorial discretion (is) *also known as direct file and statutory exclusion* (Thomas, 2016, p. 30, emphasis added)." Another ATC person has drawn a distinction between (1) OE when it is listed as mandatory (judicial) transfer and (2) OE when it is identified as statutory exclusion (Dunn, 2008). They are the same phenomenon, with the single difference that mandatory (judicial) transfer has the preliminary hearing occur in JC while statutory exclusion has the preliminary hearing occur in CC. In both, the offense is excluded, assuming probable cause (PC) exists for the excluded offense. This has been misinterpreted as involving two distinct entities.

There is a discrete difference in mandatory waiver and statutory exclusion. Mandatory waiver cases are initially received by the juvenile court, which will conduct a preliminary hearing to ensure that the mandatory waiver statute has been properly applied and then issues a transfer order to move the case to criminal court. Statutory exclusion, on the other hand, actually removes certain offenses from the jurisdiction of the juvenile court.... (Dunn, 2008, p. 38, citations omitted).

Dunn cites Griffin et al., 1998 for conceptual support of these conclusions. Most important, nevertheless, both types of transfer are examples of OE and involve excluding offenses from JC jurisdiction. One pair of ATC members recognize the identical operation character of the two concepts, but still employ the disparate terminology.

Statutory exclusion and mandatory judicial waiver *are functionally identical: if there is probable cause to believe certain crimes have been committed, jurisdiction lies exclusively in adult court... (Breen & Mills, 2015, p. 299, emphasis added).*

More critical (and confusing), the term, statutory exclusion, has also been associated with both mandatory exclusion (ME) provisions. One false association links statutory exclusion with states that employ a maximum juvenile court age of 16.

One application of this mechanism — lowering the upper age of original juvenile court jurisdiction — excludes the largest number of juveniles from juvenile jurisdiction. Some states have excluded all

17-year-olds... from juvenile court jurisdiction, making them adults for purposes of criminal prosecution... (Torbet et al., 1996, p.3; see also, Arya, 2010; Burrow, 2008a; Cintron, 1995 (via legislative exclusion); Deitch & Arya, 2014; Grundfest et al., 1981; Mulvey & Schubert, 2012; Shook, 2014, p. 395; Sickmund, 1994; Snyder et al., 2000; Thomas & Wilson, 2018, p. 3).

Even worse and more confusing is associating statutory exclusion with *both* the reduced maximum JC age *and* transfer, claiming that in jurisdictions that have adopted statutory exclusion via employing a maximum JC age of 16,

it is possible that more youth younger than 18 are tried in criminal court in this way than by all ***other transfer mechanisms*** *combined...(Sickmund, 2003, p.10, emphasis added).*

Statutory exclusion has also been associated with the second ME provision: the mandatory criminal prosecution of youths previously convicted in CC.

Many states exclude certain serious offenders from juvenile court jurisdiction. Some exclude juveniles who have been previously waived or convicted in criminal court... (Sickmund, 1994, p.3; see, also, Deitch & Arya, 2014; Thomas & Wilson, 2018, p.3).

Using statutory exclusion in these ME contexts takes the confusion in the transfer debate to new heights since it thus has been used to refer to both discretionary *and* mandatory exclusion. That conclusively indicates how confusing and dangerous the statutory exclusion term is. The lack of terminological clarity and conceptual boundaries complicates both an understanding and analysis of transfer to CC.

3. OE MISIDENTIFIED AS HAVING TWO TYPES; INCLUDES AND IGNORES TOO MUCH

OE is simply that, offenses are excluded from JC jurisdiction. There is only one type, not two (see Fritsch & Hemmens, 1995, p.18; Fritsch & Hemmens, 1996, pp. 579-580), depending upon whether an age or prior record is required to trigger OE. Requiring these extra factors just adds to the confusion. Whether a particular age or prior record is required in OE is immaterial. It is the *current charge* that cannot be prosecuted in JC, depending, perhaps, upon the age of the offender and/or the existence of a previous arrest or JC adjudication.

"Legislative" waivers have also been wrongly associated with presumptive and reverse judicial waivers (Rudof, 1998, p. 446). One source identifies three types of *legislative* transfers: discretionary, mandatory, and presumptive (Shelden & Hussong, 2003).

OE as a term includes too much when it is *wrongly extended* to include offenses that are not crimes, such as traffic and fishing/hunting violations (see Fritsch & Hemmens, 1996, p. 580; Wizner, 1984, p. 44). The discussion surrounding OE needs to be limited to felonies (and possibly misdemeanors) excluded from JC jurisdiction and placed within CC jurisdiction, in effect, converting a delinquent to a criminal act. In other words, the offenses can be and have been transferred to CC. Identifying offenses excluded from JC that belong to a third court, such as traffic or a district court, within the reach of OE artificially inflates the behaviors that have been relocated from JC to CC via transfer.

Feld accuses OE of being both over- and under-inclusive:

Legislative offense exclusion that focuses primarily on the seriousness of the present offense rather than on chronic offending fosters an over-and underinclusive response to the problems posed by young career criminals. Such a policy punishes severely one youth's serious, albeit isolated act of violence, while nominally sanctioning less severely a chronic offender's current, less serious property crime (Feld, 2000, p.106).

It is not the content of OE statutes that is deficient. But first, it needs to be noted that OE does not either punish or sanction *any* transfer/offender. That is up to the CCs, and depends upon the states' general sentencing provisions, including whether the JC record can be factored into CC sentences; the CC parties involved (judges, prosecutors, POs, etc.) also play a huge role here. Instead, OE typically promotes the transfer of serious/violent juveniles; some states do place seriously chronic offenders within the reach of OE. But the primary "theory" behind OE is to provide prosecutors the authority to deny "worthy" serious/violent juveniles *immunity from criminal prosecution* by transferring them to CC. Part of this allocation or redirection of power came about because judges refused or were hesitant in transferring those youths, and because legislators concluded that considerations, such as amenability to treatment, should not be relevant, or at least not controlling, in these serious/violent crime situations.

Feld implies that OE must explain the world of juvenile criminality, or, at least, of transfer. His suggestion lacks plausibility and credence. The fact that no state has *only* OE, but rather has adopted OE as a *supplement* to JT, proves that the legislatures never intended their OE policy to capture *all* juveniles who merit transfer to CC. The legislatures have authorized JC judges to transfer the "chronic, less serious property offender" from the first days of JC's existence. To include those offenders within OE provisions likely would be redundant, and would expose legislators to criticisms of having adopted draconian measures for "lesser" criminals, much like the ATC's condemnation of such transfers, in general (see Chapter 7).

4. OE MISIDENTIFIED AS A FORM OF TRANSFER DISTINCT FROM PROSECUTORIAL TRANSFER

OE is also frequently listed as a *third form of transfer* (see Table 38 C), joining JT and DF. Feld was a pioneer in this capacity (1978). For example, critics have complained that both OE *and* "prosecutor-controlled forms of transfer proliferated steadily," and similarly point to the adoption of "prosecutorial discretion *or* statutory exclusion laws (Griffin et al., 2011: 8, 10, emphasis added)."

The implication in this organization of transfer methods is that OE is not prosecutorial in nature. Its independent status makes it much easier to misunderstand and contributes to the three examples of misinterpretation (see #5-7 directly below). OE is simply another type of PT with similarities to DF and one significant difference (see Chapter 3).

Marrus and Rosenberg (2005) first conflate OE with DF. The prosecutor's ability to "directly file" charges in CC via OE seems to have confused them (see, also, Gimbel, 2016). They then claimed that OE represents a third type of transfer that did not "explicitly (give) the district attorney the power to waive (p. 1172)," but later concede "it is often difficult to distinguish it from prosecutorial waiver (or DF) (p. 1177)." That is probably because it is prosecutorial waiver.

5. OE MISIDENTIFIED AS NOT CONSTITUTING PROSECUTORIAL TRANSFER (PT) OR ANY TRANSFER

Many observers combine misidentification numbers 2 and 4, above, which has resulted in misidentification number 5: that someone/something other than a prosecutor decides the OE outcome (see Lehmann & Kobie, 2021). For example, critics have contended that statutory exclusion "automatically places a juvenile in adult court, *regardless of the prosecutor's preference*… (Notes, 2002, p. 1967, citation omitted, emphasis added)." Other critics claim that the exclusion occurs at arrest (Fritsch & Hemmens, 1996, p. 579; Myers, 2003b, p. 79; Singer, 1993, p. 254), ignoring the necessity of prosecutors' charging the excluded offense.

Some observers seem to infer that OE cases simply magically appear in CC without decisions made by any mortal (Tang & Nunez, 2003, p. 38); perhaps the statute itself transfers the juvenile (see Merlo, Benekos, & Cook, 1997b, p. 151; OJJ, 1999, p. 13). Alternatively, this outcome could be related to the "magical thinking" outcome to which Zimring was referencing (1998a, p. 132; see subsection 1, above)).

Under the legislative exclusion model, a state's legislature defines certain offenses that automatically result in initial charges for a juvenile being filed in the adult system… (Marczyk, Heilbrun, Lander, & DeMatteo, 2005, p. 281).

****

(OE) ***does not involve discretion by the judge or prosecutor,*** *but simply excludes juveniles who commit certain offenses from the jurisdiction of juvenile court… (Prochaska, 2018, p. 27, emphasis added; see, also, Guttman, 1995, p. 521).*

****

Statutory exclusion is when the state legislature ***predetermines*** *the question of criminal prosecution; judicial waiver leaves the decision about whether to transfer a juvenile out of juvenile court up to the judge; and prosecutorial discretion gives the prosecutor the power over where to try a juvenile offender (Ward, 2003, p. 259, footnote 20, citation omitted, emphasis added; see, also, Griffin et at., 1998, p. 9; McCurdy-Jackson, 2011, pp. 8-9).*

****

Under statutory exclusion, by contrast, membership in a certain age group or the commission of a certain offense, or both, automatically places a juvenile in adult court, ***regardless of the prosecutor's preference****… (HLRA, 2002, p. 1967, footnote omitted, emphasis added).*

****

Thus, these (OE) cases automatically transfer to criminal court, ***bypassing both judicial and prosecutorial scrutiny****… (Dunn, 2008, p. 38, emphasis added; see, also, Breen & Mills, 2015, p. 299).*

Decades ago, Feld claimed in OE, the *legislature* "places youths charged with those offenses into the adult criminal court (1978, p. 522)." The legislature no more places a youth in CC via OE than it does via JT or DF. Similarly, Feld (1978) commented that OE should not be linked with PT (even though it is a matter of charging) because

it is the legislature and not the prosecutor that makes the policy choice (p. 566; see, also, Noon, 1994, p. 453).

This is a misleading claim. The prosecutor makes the *choice to transfer* a youth as authorized by the *policy that has been adopted by the legislature*; the prosecutor neither establishes nor dictates policy. The legislature, alone, makes two policy choices that are relevant to our discussion, here: first, whether to have a JC and whom to exclude from that forum, and second, whether a judge or a prosecutor is authorized to make the transfer decision. The legislative policy may be compatible with the prosecutor's perspective, but the policy, itself, is not the prosecutor's to choose! The most prosecutors can do in this context is to take advantage of the power granted them by the policy/legislation or to evade that power by choosing not to transfer even when authorized to do so. This choice depends upon personal/political preferences, in addition to views and acceptance/denial of policy options. This reality applies equally to JT or DF; all transfer measures are discretionary. The legislative policy choice effected in OE is no different than the policy choice that lies behind JT and DF. All forms of transfer equally represent the legislature's policy choice and legal conclusion that not all juvenile offenders belong in JC. What typically distinguishes JT from both types of PT are simply the individuals that get to choose to transfer the youth and the criteria that must be followed by those individuals to bring about the transfer.

The most common incorrect assertion in this context is the one mentioned previously, that OE means the legislature makes the transfer call (and not the prosecutor) (see Bishop, 2000, pp. 124-127; Butts & Mears, 2001; Cooper & Urban, 2012; Feld, 2000, pp. 84, 108; Griffin et al., 1998, p.1; Guttman, 1995, pp. 509, 521; Jan, Ball, & Walsh, 2008; Kimbrell, 2015; NDAA, 2002, p. 9; Puzzanchera, Hockenberry, & Sickmund, 2002, p. 98; Sarri & Shook, 2005; Snyder, Sickmund, & Poe-Yamagata, 2000, p. 1; Steinberg & Cauffman, 2001, p. 3; Steiner, 2005, pp. 604, 605; Sulok, 2007, pp. 233-234). Adding to the confusion is the claim that OE is not transfer at all (see Table 38 G).

Legislative transfer is really a misnomer because ***rather than transferring*** *certain children to criminal court jurisdiction, the legislature has merely excluded them from the jurisdiction of the juvenile court... (Stamm, 1973, p. 139, emphasis added).*

Even worse, it has also been asserted that OE is *not waiver but that it is transfer*:

(S)uch cases in fact do not involve a waiver of jurisdiction at all; rather the legislature merely excludes the accused child from the jurisdiction of juvenile court.... Most often this form of transfer is utilized.... (Sorrentino & Olsen, 1977, p. 503).

Feld and Bishop (2012) claim that JT and the two forms of PT

allocate the (transfer) decision to different branches of government: judicial, executive, and ***legislative*** *(p. 802, emphasis added).*

Similarly, Snyder and Hutzler (1981) offer:

*(E)ither the **legislature decides the matter** for a class of offenders, **or it delegates**...the authority to decide on a case by case basis whether a juvenile is to be tried as an adult (p. 5, emphases added).*

Worse is the claim the OE empowers the police to make the transfer call (Fagan, 2008, p. 18; see, also, Myers, 2003) or criminal courts, themselves, make the decision (Vargas, 2014, p. 20).

Similar assertions claim that adopting OE means that the "legislature is essentially predetermining the question of criminal prosecution for itself and taking the decision out of both the prosecutor's and the court's hands (Griffin et al., 1998, p. 1)." Without identifying the recipient of transfer power, one observer states that legislatures adopted OE "rather than leaving that decision to the discretion of the juvenile court or the prosecutor (Slobogin, 2003, p. 103; see also Butts & Harrell, 1998, p. 6; Redding, 2016, p. 944; Snyder et al., 2000, p. xi)." Similarly, OE has been seen as one form of transfer, while *other* forms "allow a prosecutor or judge discretion over selecting youth for transfer... (Kupchik, 2003b, p. 439)." Finally, OE has been characterized as the "most significant and disturbing aspect of the transfer trend" because it results in "bypassing both judicial and prosecutorial scrutiny over the proper forum for the accused... (Brink, 2003-04, p. 1564)." If judges and prosecutors "lack scrutiny over the transfer decision" and legislatures cannot make individual transfer calls, precisely how specific juveniles are actually transferred to CC in the OE context must be a mystery to some ATC members.

OE has also been thought to *expand* the legislature's control over the transfer decision:

Legislative exclusion has appeal...because it permits the legislature to maintain more control over the transfer process... (Bishop & Frazier, 2000, p. 242).

******

*This (OE) method represents attempts by state **legislatures to take control** over transfer decision making by defining ages and offense categories whose members are automatically prosecuted in criminal rather than juvenile court.... (Kupchik, 2006a, p. 16, emphasis added).*

******

*(R)ecent transfer laws that give greater discretion to prosecutors and **legislatures**... (Id., p. 19, emphasis added).*

In OE, the legislature does not grant itself more control over transfer. Nor does the legislature's "control" differ in OE as compared to other methods. In both JT and DF, legislatures define age and offense categories. What these definitions do (in JT, DF, and OE alike) is specify the limits of the judges' and prosecutors' transfer power. In OE (as in DF), it is the *prosecutor* that has been granted *more control* over the transfer process; prosecutors do not have to receive a judge's approval for the transfer. Since OE shares traits with DF (see Chapter 3), the legislature has granted prosecutors similar powers in both forms of PT, contrary to some observations.

*Either **directly** through prosecutorial direct filing or **indirectly** through the charging process in exclusion cases, the prosecutor has emerged with an expanded role in justice system responses to serious and violent juvenile offenders... (Torbet et al., 1996, pp. xv-xvi, emphases added).*

In both OE and DF, prosecutors are authorized to file charges against juvenile offenders directly in CC either originally or following a mere preliminary hearing in JC. OE probably does increase the likelihood of transfer since the power is being extended to prosecutors and not judges, which is probably why so much OE was adopted by legislatures in the 1990s. But that does not increase the legislature's control over the process. For legislatures to garner more control in this area they would have to adopt some ME provision, such as reducing the maximum juvenile court age. That reduction in age would give the legislature direct control over the location of juvenile offenders' prosecution. In transfer, legislatures, lacking direct power to transfer, must grant discretionary power to others; they are accruing neither greater transfer power nor more control over transfer for themselves.

It is possible that the ATC is thinking that OE is "cleaner" than JT because it uses the relatively objective offense/record criteria rather than the more nebulous and amorphous amenability criteria employed in JT. Even still, the legislature does not have more control over transfer via OE than it does via DF or JT. In OE, prosecutors are the ones who can "maintain more control over the transfer process" when they are authorized to transfer as compared to their much lesser authority in JT. Even still, prosecutors can either frustrate or honor the wishes of the legislature every bit as much as judges can. Simply put, in all forms of transfer legislatures must relinquish control to the two court officials they have empowered to act *for them and for the rest of society*!

6. OE MISIDENTIFIED AS MANDATORY/AUTOMATIC/NONDISCRETIONARY

What likely has made reaching an understanding of OE most problematic is the tendency to refer to it as either mandatory, automatic, or nondiscretionary, nearly a universal phenomenon in the literature (see Table 38 D). It is frequently linked with misidentifications #2, 4, and 5 (above). Identifying OE as legislative or statutory transfer/exclusion and listing it separately from DF likely facilitates the misunderstanding of OE as mandatory.[2]

Feld was a pioneer in this categorization (Feld, 1978, 1981a, 1981b, 1983, 1991, 1995). It was the purported mandatory, automatic and nondiscretionary nature of OE that rendered it so preferable to JT, in his eyes. The nature of OE or its account in the literature confused even Professor Francis Allen (2000), who stated in transfer

*the question of the locus of discretionary authority may be of large importance; thus, should the burden of decision in waiver cases be placed wholly or largely with the juvenile court judge, or should a legislative judgment be made to **avoid discretionary decisions altogether** in certain categories of cases and require that they **automatically be removed** from the juvenile to the adult courts?... (p. xiv; emphases added).*

****

*Efforts through legislation, such as modern waiver statutes, **to control discretion by eliminating it** create consequences that are, again, akin to those experienced elsewhere in the penal system... Legislative* *efforts to* ***eliminate discretionary waiver*** *in juvenile courts by* ***mandating automatic transfers*** *to adult courts in certain categories of cases may produce the* ***unforeseen consequence of enlarging prosecutorial authority*** *in transfer cases. Since the prosecutor possesses the authority to select the offense on which the juvenile will be tried, he may charge an offense* ***not included*** *within the automatic transfer statute, thereby gaining final authority over the waiver decision (Id., p. xv; emphases added).*

This statement discloses some serious confusion. OE is discretionary and is not mandatory, automatic, or nondiscretionary, period. In addition, how enlarging the prosecutor's power via OE could have been *unforeseen* is puzzling. The legislature had to have known that someone had to exercise the specific transfer decision in OE and that they, themselves, were not physically able/authorized to do so. Ironically, the potential result in and supposed problem with OE is the opposite of the one mentioned by Allen. If the prosecutor charges an offense that is *not included* in the OE category, the offense clearly remains within JC's jurisdiction. The prosecutor *loses control* over the transfer decision and would have to request a judge's approval to transfer the case. Also noteworthy in Allen's statement is the tendency of some members of the ATC to simultaneously float contradictory propositions that OE is *both discretionary and mandatory*. That can be seen in the claim that OE "eliminates discretionary waiver," while also acknowledging that the prosecutor "possesses the authority to select the offense on which the juvenile will be tried," or in the observation that OE represents "unfettered discretion" (see Marrus & Rosenberg, 2005; Pagnanelli, 2007).

Whether the confusion stems from not understanding the OE phenomenon or from being a victim of the literature is unclear. Allen is not alone in this flip-flopping between claims of OE's being mandatory and acknowledgements of its discretionary character (see also, Sabo., 1996, pp. 2445 and 2451; Zimring, 1998a, p. 120).

It is common for the ATC to claim that OE is mandatory/automatic, only to ultimately acknowledge the truth:

Because it is the district attorney who must make the charging decision, however, to the extent that the prosecutor looks at characteristics of the youth in reaching that determination, he or she may defeat the ***seemingly automatic waiver provisions*** *of the law in individual cases by undercharging. The converse, of course, is also possible. The prosecutor may overcharge to assure that a particular child is tried in criminal court (Rosenberg, 2000, p. 81, footnote 31; emphasis added).*

****

(T)o the extent that the waiver decision depends on the current charges, the prosecutor is ultimately making the determination of whether to waive regardless of the statutory wording that filing in adult court is mandatory.

For even if the legislature mandates the prosecutor to file charges against the child in criminal court, the prosecutor is the official who determines the actual charges. Thus, if a prosecutor decides that a particular child should not be treated in adult court, he or she may simply bring lesser charges...(Marrus & Rosenberg, 2005, p.1177, citations omitted).

****

(E)ven if the legislature mandates a prosecutor file charges against a child in criminal court, a prosecutor can ultimately decide whether to bring adult or juvenile charges (Pagnanelli, 2007, p.182, footnote omitted).

Pagnanelli's treatment (2007) is particularly troubling since he refers to OE as "unfettered discretion" and mandatory is the same article. Evidently, while OE may *seem* to be "automatic," it really is not. And, of course, should the prosecutor overcharge to ensure transfer, the obvious remedy is for the judge to find a lack of PC for the excluded offense case and to keep it in or return it to JC.

One ATC member interpreted the mandatory nature of OE as inviting so many transfers that CCs and prisons would be overwhelmed.

A long period of custodial confinement is the only prudent or tolerable response to some of the violent offenses that teenagers commit. It is precisely the point of the traditional system's waiver hearing to identify such cases by careful examination of the circumstances, and then to direct such cases to criminal court. ***But when blanket policies mandate automatic adult-court prosecution for whole categories of criminal conduct defined broadly in advance, the mandates divert enormous numbers of new cases into the criminal-court system.*** *That step, combined with the strict sentencing policies applicable in adult court, means sweeping large numbers of new inmates into our adult prison system (Schulhofer, 1997, p. 442, emphasis in original; see also Zimring & Fagan, 2000, p. 416).*

Ironically, Schulhofer complained about the inaccurate predictions made in the 1990s about the future explosion of juvenile superpredators, and then made his own wildly inaccurate predictions about the impact of OE. Misunderstanding OE contributed to the inaccuracy of his prediction.

Professor Jeffrey Fagan also has focused on the purported excessive number of transfers that will result from OE:

Returning to discretionary transfer rather than ***"wholesale waiver"*** *would limit the number of youth subjected to criminal court prosecution… (Fagan, 2008, p. 38, emphasis added).*

Similarly, Zimring and Fagan observe:

(T)hings are not equal in the competition between rule and discretion in structuring transfer decisions. The inevitable cost that comes with a rule-based system is overbreadth—the tendency for a formal rule to transfer all cases in a class if some cases require the transfer. Discretionary waiver decisions result in the transfer of a very small fraction of juveniles… (Zimring & Fagan, 2000, p. 416, citation omitted).

The ATC hype the high number of and broad variety in serious/violent crimes committed by juveniles, supposedly making them "mandatory" candidates for OE (see Schulhofer, 1997; Zimring, 1998a, 2000b). They condemn OE, believing prosecutors are either oblivious to the volume and variety or simply do not care about it. The predicted explosion in the numbers of so-called "mandatory" exclusions have not lived up to the estimates (like the superpredator predictions) and have proved the ATC wrong.

7. OE MISIDENTIFIED AS ALLOWING NO INDIVIDUALIZATION; IS: WHOLESALE/CATEGORICAL/OVERINCLUSIVE

Another false ATC claim, closely related to the mandatory misidentification, is that there is no individualization in OE or that OE is either wholesale, categorical or overinclusive. This claim is prevalent in the literature (see Table 38 E). Some observers have made both claims (compare Table 38 D and E). This amounts to a doubling down on the assertion and an endorsement of the nondiscretionary nature of OE.

Exaggeration by the ATC is characteristic of observations in this context, too:

The vice of this type of ***wholesale prescriptive transfer*** *is the same type of overbreadth associated with abolition of the court or reduction in jurisdictional age, though perhaps not to the same degree (Zimring, 2000b, p. 218, emphasis added).*[3]

Unlike OE, reducing the maximum age of JC is, indeed, "wholesale." Tens of thousands of juveniles in many states likely would be removed from JC every year by reducing the age by even just one year. There is no comparison between the potential effects of OE compared to ME via maximum JC age reduction. The former would not have anything like the "same degree" of impact on exclusion as the latter.

Not only has nothing categorical/cataclysmic/wholesale ever happened with OE since its emergence, but also the robberies, etc., that typically qualify for OE are much more limited than the generic title of the offenses within OE (e.g., not all "robberies" qualify for OE) (see Sanborn & Salerno, 2005, pp. 523-526). The ATC tends to focus on broad categories of offensesidentified in OE (such as robbery and assault) and then extrapolates from those crimes that tens of thousands of juvenile robbery and assault defendants will be subject to transfer. Zimring has been among the most prolific critics in this context (see below). However, the typical offense excluded from JC is a serious or violent one (see Sanborn & Salerno, 2005, pp. 523-526). Not all robberies and assaults are equal in seriousness or violence and, most important, will not be viewed or responded to as such by prosecutors; the same applies to other offenses, such as homicide. Like robberies and assaults, homicides are divided into degrees and are not all equal in severity. Less serious homicides, such as manslaughter, are likely to remain outside the reach of OE. Simply put, OE statutes do not cover all potential robbery or assault/homicide charges. Ironically, DF does not seem to experience the same level of criticism as OE, but is more likely to have a wide-open category of offenses for which juveniles are eligible to be transferred (see Id.). Whereas the ATC sees OE as broadening prosecutorial powers, the excluded offenses typically serve as a limitation (compared to DF), reining in the prosecutor's direct transfer authority to include only those crimes or categories of offenses specified in the statute.

Within one page, Zimring twice repeats and then twice backtracks on the "wholesale" characterization and admits prosecutorial discretion can derail OE's supposed categorical potential, which should, but evidently does not, convince him that OE is not categorical.

So prescriptive transfer standards that move entire crime categories into criminal court are unprincipled and overbroad; the best that can befall such systems is prosecutorial discretion being exercised to select only the most serious of within-crime charges to process in the criminal courts... The best we can hope for from categorical transfer edicts is high levels of prosecutorial discretion and very low-visibility decision making (Zimring, 2000b, p. 219).

Of course, prosecutors' selecting the most serious offenders is precisely what legislatures were counting upon when they passed OE statutes and empowered prosecutors to decide transfer.[4]

Otherwise, according to the ATC, similar complaints allege that OE:

- precludes any consideration of an individual's characteristics (Feld, 1987, p. 515);
- (works) in disregard of any mitigating factors (Sabo, 1996, p. 2452);
- (contains) offense categories (that) are necessarily crude and imprecise indicators (Feld, 2000, p. 117); and,
- violate(s) a child's due process right to individualized treatment (Hoeffel, 2013, p. 32).[5]

8. OE MISIDENTIFIED AS TOO DISCRETIONARY

It is ironic that, although Feld originally praised OE due to its perceived "mandatory and nondiscretionary" nature, it is likely now to be condemned due to being too discretionary. What was once OE's strongest feature is now its most critical and fatal liability.

Because offense categories are necessarily crude and imprecise indicators of the "real" seriousness of any particular offense, prosecutors inevitably exercise enormous sentencing discretion when they decide whether to charge a youth with an excluded offense rather than a lesser included offense, or to select the forum in a direct-file jurisdiction. Despite the extensive lists of excluded offenses and the ascendance of get-tough policies, it seems unlikely that state legislators intend prosecutors to charge every theoretically eligible youth in criminal court... (Feld, 2000, pp. 117-118; see, also, Drinan, 2014).

Feld's claim that OE/transfer involves "sentencing" discretion is inaccurate (see Chapter 7). He is very correct, however, in asserting that it is unlikely that legislatures "intend prosecutors to charge every theoretically eligible youth in criminal court." Thus, "wholesale" exclusion has not occurred nor has discretion been excessive or abused. Prosecutors have not taken advantage of their so-called "categorical" powers. Why Feld and others insist on criticizing OE as mandatory or categorical is puzzling. The explanation is probably that since prosecutors surely will transfer more juvenile offenders to CC than judges will, it must be neutralized by the ATC. How OE can be simultaneously mandatory/automatic and too discretionary is also puzzling.

Also ironic is that, contrary to previous assertions (see subsection # 7, above), OE is acknowledged to allow for individualization because previous research

confirms that even within most serious offense categories, prosecutors individualize and differentiate on some basis... (Feld, 2000, p. 119).

According to Feld, both OE and DF statutes

enable prosecutors covertly to manipulate charges to select a juvenile or criminal forum in a low-visibility, discretionary setting with minimal information or record, and without any form of legal accountability or review...." (Id.)

Although Feld's description makes OE and DF appear improper, *all charging* happens in a "low visibility, discretionary setting." The relatively low numbers of transfers via OE and DF contradict the assertion that there is "minimal information or record." And just like with charging adult offenders, there is a review of the prosecutor's transfer decision. It happens when the prosecutor must show PC for the excluded or DF offense.

Feld (2000) vacillates between regarding OE and DF as too rigid *and* too discretionary.

Excluded-offense and direct file laws suffer from the rigidity, inflexibility, political vulnerability and overinclusiveness characteristic of mandatory sentencing statutes. In practice, excluded-offense laws transfer discretion from juvenile court judges in a waiver hearing to prosecutors who determine a youth's delinquent or criminal status by manipulating their charging decisions... (pp. 124-125, citations omitted).

If prosecutors can manipulate charges, one must wonder just how mandatory, rigid and inflexible prosecutorial transfer laws are. One also must wonder about how serious Feld was in objecting to prosecutors' making decisions with minimal information or record.

Because of the diversity of offenses, especially assaults and robberies, prosecutors necessarily will differentiate among offenders ***on some bases*** *when they charge some youths excluded offenses... (Id., p. 125, emphasis added; see, also, Feld, 2001, p. 19).*

And just how anti-transfer Feld is becomes uncertain when he asserts:

But prosecutors can achieve flexibility only by charging youths with a nonexcluded, lesser included offense and, in some instances, deprecating the normative seriousness of a youth's criminal conduct. Allowing prosecutors to manipulate charges to respond to the heterogeneity of offenses vests arbitrary and unreviewable discretion in them rather than in judges... (Id.)

Feld appears to be objecting to keeping juveniles in JC by being charged with offenses less serious than their actual behavior ("deprecating the normative seriousness of a youth's criminal conduct"). That is a strange complaint from someone who purports to be anti-transfer, in general, and who pledges to promote juveniles' best interests. Feld's complaint seems to call for actually expanding OE/DF to make the reduction in charging less severe. More likely his complaint is simply (and maybe only) against prosecutors' being the ones who decide transfer.[6]

OE involves a charge that must survive a preliminary hearing in JC or CC. If the prosecutor is acting arbitrarily, that is more likely to be discovered than a judge's arbitrariness, which was Feld's most poignant complaint against JT, once upon a time (see Feld, 1978). Feld (2000) makes a bad analysis worse by alleging that OE's focus on offenses "requires legal subterfuge to achieve proper results (p. 125)." Where the "legal subterfuge" lies is unclear and unexplained. Feld admits there is a wide range to assault and robbery charges. Somehow, however, it requires manipulation and "legal subterfuge" and an attack on the "normative seriousness of a youth's criminal conduct" for prosecutors to produce a proper charge. Feld provides no allowance for a legitimate adjustment or "manipulation" of charges in situations where the arrest charges exaggerate the actual offense; police officers are not prosecutors, after all. Here, adjustment by the prosecutor in arriving at the correct charge would be both appropriate and legally necessary, and certainly not the product of subterfuge. Of course, the prosecutor could also decide that, although the offense at hand technically qualifies for exclusion, this youth does not merit disqualification from JC for one or more possible legitimate reasons. According to Feld, then, the only way to keep this youth in JC is to manipulate that charge and engage in subterfuge, while inflicting damage on the normative seriousness of the youth's misconduct. Whether Feld would also oppose these exercises in discretion is unclear.

Legislatures cannot subdivide every potential nuance of a robbery or assault charge. They must and do leave discretion in the hands of the prosecutor to make the call (just like what they do with judges in JT). Feld, Zimring and other ATC members have no problem with this discretion provided it is exercised by judges, and not prosecutors (see Chapter 11).

9. OE MISIDENTIFIED AS MANDATORY JUDICIAL TRANSFER (JT)

Legislatures have contributed to the misidentification where OE is called *mandatory JT*. The confusion stems from language in that statute, typically stating that the JC *shall transfer or waive* a case to CC if certain statutory circumstances are met: the defendant's age, the offense, and/or the delinquent record. That language wrongly connotes that the transfer is mandatory, and worse, that it is judicial in nature.[7] It is discretionary, relying upon the prosecutor's decision to charge the required offense(s), just as in OE. Since the court's role is limited to finding probable cause (PC), the power really resides in the prosecutor and not the judge. This transfer is actually OE. The difference between this statute and typical OE provisions is that the latter formally exclude the charge from JC and place it originally in CC. The preliminary hearing in the "mandatory JT" case will occur in JC rather than in CC. One ATC source admitted "in most respects a mandatory waiver law functions more like a statutory exclusion than a traditional judicial waiver law (Griffin, 2008, p. 3)." Calling this transfer mandatory JT results in its being described as something different from OE (see Table 38 F).

(T)he juvenile court has no role other than to confirm that the statutory requirements for mandatory waiver are met. Once it has done so, the juvenile court must send the case to a court of criminal jurisdiction. Mandatory waiver must be distinguished from statutory exclusion. When an offense has been excluded by law from juvenile court jurisdiction, the case against a minor accused of that offense originates in criminal court. Under ordinary circumstances, the juvenile court has no involvement and is entirely bypassed. By contrast, although the juvenile court's involvement in a mandatory waiver case may be minimal, it receives the case initially, conducts some sort of preliminary hearing to ensure that the case is one to which the mandatory waiver statute applies, and issues a transfer order and any other necessary orders, relating to appointment of counsel, interim detention, and so on (Griffin et al., 1998, p. 10).

Using the adjective, mandatory, distorts its discretionary character and confuses critics, who often employ the term only to contradict it soon thereafter.

Unlike legislative exclusion, mandatory waiver is conditional because it is available only if requested by the prosecutor in the exercise of prosecutorial discretion by filing a waiver petition or motion. It is also conditional in the sense that the mandatory provisions apply only if the juvenile court judge finds that the case circumstances (charge, age, history) fall within the scope of the mandatory waiver statute and finds probable cause to believe the juvenile committed an offense covered by the legislation. Even in a mandatory circumstance, the judiciary still retains some limited control over the waiver process. In addition, because a judicial hearing is required before waiver can be ordered under mandatory waiver provisions, the respondent has some leverage to negotiate a hearing-free disposition that may avoid waiver altogether. Such an opportunity is not as easily available in cases of legislative exclusion (Dawson, 2000, p. 65).

******

Legislative exclusions tend to be more absolute in their effects than are mandatory judicial waiver provisions. There is room, but less room, for prosecutorial or judicial control over the process (Id., pp. 66-67).

OE that originates in JC can provide a mighty incentive for the juvenile to plea bargain *to remain in JC*. However, contrary to Dawson's claim, OE that originates in CC provides a an opportunity and perhaps an even more substantial incentive for the defendant to plea bargain *to return to JC*.

Suggesting that there are three types of JT (see Table 38 H) confuses matters. It is important to remember that all JT is discretionary (and never mandatory) whether or not it is presumptive.

10. OE AND DF MISIDENTIFIED AS NOT CONSTITUTING TRANSFER

It is not uncommon for OE and DF to be portrayed as something other than transfer (see Table 38 G). They frequently are contrasted with JT, the only *real* transfer (Dawson, 2000, p. 58; Hoeffel, 2013, p. 50). Remarkably, critical national government publications have identified OE and/or DF as *"nonwaiver transfer mechanisms"* (Adams & Addie, 2009, p. 2, 2010, p. 2, 2011, p. 2, 2012, p. 3; Griffin, Addie, S., Addie, B., & Firestine, 2011, pp. 10, 12; Hockenberry, 2021, p. 3; Hockenberry & Puzzanchera, 2014, p. 3; Puzzanchera & Addie, 2014, p. 3; see, also, Guttman, 1995, p. 521; Lehmann, Pickett, Ryon. & Kosloski, 2019, p. 253). That internally contradictory terminology should suffice to confuse everyone.

One early ATC member had her own contradiction when she described New York's OE law as jurisdictional rather than as transfer particularly because OE does not require a hearing.

Provisions that deny authority over enumerated offenses are jurisdictional rather than waiver statutes since they redefine the jurisdiction of the respective courts and do not involve a certification process... (Flicker, 1983, p. 4).

All transfer provisions potentially "redefine" the jurisdictions of JC and CC. They allow judges and prosecutors to convert otherwise juvenile offenders into defendants eligible for criminal prosecution. There is a certification process when the prosecutor selects a transferrable charge. In addition, there is a hearing involved in OE. The hearing is a preliminary rather than a transfer hearing. That hearing confirms transfer via PC for the excluded or concurrent offense just as JT confirms transfer via nonamenability to treatment.[8]

One feature of PT that evidently has perplexed the critics is that the transfer decision does not occur within the friendly confines of the JC building.

The term "transfer" refers to three general mechanisms. However, only one mechanism (judicial waiver) actually involves the transfer of a juvenile from the juvenile court to the criminal court. Cases that follow the other two paths may never pass through the juvenile court system (Snyder et al., 2000, p. 1, footnote 1).

Even worse is the false claim that in PT the juvenile's relocation to CC occurs prior to charging.

There is no need to determine if a juvenile should be transferred to criminal court, because nonjudicial forms of waiver require criminal justice officials, at the point of arrest, to decide if a juvenile should be charged in criminal court (Singer, Fagan, & Liberman, 2000, p. 354).

Charges selected by police at arrest are subject to interpretation later by prosecutors as well as to processing through a preliminary hearing and/or a grand jury proceeding. To be sure, no charge is set in stone "at the point of arrest."

11. OE MISIDENTIFIED AS RECRIMINALIZING DELINQUENCY

Professor Simon Singer has disparagingly referred to transfer (more specifically, New York's version of OE) as "*recriminalizing delinquency*" (Singer, 1996; see also Benekos & Merlo, 2008, p. 30; Fagan, 1995). To look at OE this way requires considering excluded offenses (such as murder) historically and always as mere acts of delinquency, and regarding JC as allowing all youths to get away with murder (among other excluded crimes). A more complete and accurate description of OE is: Due to the severity of the crime OE represents *recriminalizing criminal behavior*. Since some states had never removed murder from either acrime category or the jurisdiction of CC (see Feld, 1987, 2000, pp. 86, 113) they were not required to *re*introduce it to either the crime category or CC via transfer. It is also puzzling why Singer does not equally regard JT and DF as recriminalizing delinquency since the charging, prosecution, and conviction effects or outcomes in these two transfer situations mirror exactly what happens via OE.

OE has received the most ATC attention. That is probably because it is perceived to constitute the greatest threat to juvenile offenders' remaining in JC. It is also the transfer method that has been most misrepresented in the literature. These misrepresentations of OE make an understanding of PT and transfer, in general, difficult, if not impossible. The inability to understand the phenomenon, in turn, makes relying upon research and analysis of the area next to impossible.

12. MANDATORY EXCLUSION (ME) MISIDENTIFIED AS TRANSFER

A. Reducing the Maximum Age of Jc

Much less prevalent, but perhaps even more problematic than the confusion attending OE, is the declaration that reducing the maximum JC age is an example of transfer rather than ME.

Others (i.e., legislatures) took a far more sweeping approach and lowered the maximum age of the juvenile court jurisdiction, thereby ***transferring*** *entire age categories of young offenders, no matter what* *the offense... (Bishop, 2000, p. 84, emphasis added; see also, Feld & Bishop, 2012, p. 806; Snyder, 2012, p. 27; Table 38 I)*

This ME method used to account for up to two hundred thousand "juvenile" offenders per year being prosecuted in CC. They were not transferred there, however. Including these individuals within a definition of or research study on transfer results in a gross distortion of the results of transfer to CC.

The same effect can be realized by ATC members who simply state that all "juvenile" offenders in CC are transfer cases, whether they are subjects of discretionary transfer or ME.

For purposes of this review, "transfer" refers to placing juveniles under the jurisdiction of the adult criminal justice system, rather than the juvenile justice system.... (McGowan, Hahn, Liberman, Crosby, Fullilove, Johnson, Moscicki, Price, Snyder, Tuma, Lowy, Briss, Cory, & Stone, 2007, p. 57).

******

"(T)ransfer" refers to the various terms used to designate the mechanism(s) available in any State for criminal justice prosecution of alleged juvenile offenders (Torbet et al., 1996, p. 3, footnote 1).

B. Once Adult/Always Adult (Oa/Aa) Provisions

The second type of ME also has been misidentified as transfer: the Once Adult/Always Adult (OA/AA) provision (see Table 38 G). The OA/AA provision refers to youths with previous convictions in CC being regarded as "adults" for all future prosecutions concerning criminal behavior (see Chapter 3). It has been referred to as a "special automatic transfer category (Griffin, 2003, p.11; see, also, Knox, 2009, p. 1274; Mole & White, 2005, p. 10)." OA/AA involves *neither adults* (see subsection #1, above) *nor transfer*. Nevertheless, one observer claimed in the OA/AA situation "*waiver* in future cases becomes mandatory (Szymanski, 2008, p. 1, emphasis added)."

A nationally distributed publication twice made a similar statement.

*A **special transfer category** has been created in 31 States for juveniles who, having once been prosecuted as adults, are subsequently accused of new offenses. Most States with "once an adult/always an adult" provisions simply require criminal prosecution of all such subsequent offenses – by means of either a blanket exclusion or an automatic **waiver** mechanism. Others exclude or require waiver of only a broadly defined subset of these cases – those involving juveniles of a certain age, for instance, or those in which the subsequent offense is sufficiently serious (Griffin et al., 1998, p. 10, emphases added).*

******

*There is a special form of "automatic" **transfer** in 34 states for juveniles who have previously been prosecuted as adults. Most of these "once adult/always adult" laws are comprehensive, mandating criminal handling of all posttransfer offenses... (Griffin et al., 2011, p. 7, emphasis added).*

To assert that the misidentifications of OE and other forms of transfer/exclusion are legion and deleterious is an understatement. Just as numerous and problematic are the misrepresentations concerning their nature and effect (see Chapter 7).

REFERENCES

Adams, B., & Addie, S. (2009). *Delinquency cases waived to criminal court, 2005*. U.S. Department of Justice, Office of Justice Programs, Office of Juvenile Justice and Delinquency Prevention. doi:10.1037/e560412009-001

Adams, B., & Addie, S. (2010). *Delinquency cases waived to criminal court, 2007*. U.S. Department of Justice, Office of Justice Programs, Office of Juvenile Justice and Delinquency Prevention. doi:10.1037/e572932010-001

Adams, B., & Addie, S. (2011). *Delinquency cases waived to criminal court, 2008*. U.S. Department of Justice, Office of Justice Programs, Office of Juvenile Justice and Delinquency Prevention. doi:10.1037/e502532012-001

Adams, B., & Addie, S. (2012). *Delinquency cases waived to criminal court, 2009*. U.S. Department of Justice, Office of Justice Programs, Office of Juvenile Justice and Delinquency Prevention.

Ainsworth, J. E. (1991). Re-imagining childhood and reconstructing the legal order: The case for abolishing the juvenile court. *North Carolina Law Review*, *69*, 1083–1133.

Allen, F. A. (2000). Forward. In J. Fagan & F. E. Zimring (Eds.), *The changing borders of juvenile justice: Transfer of adolescents to the criminal court* (pp. ix–xvi). University of Chicago Press.

Applegate, B. K., Davis, R. K., & Cullen, F. T. (2009). Reconsidering child saving: The extent and correlates of public support for excluding youths from the juvenile court. *Crime and Delinquency*, *55*(1), 51–77. doi:10.1177/0011128707308104

Arya, N. (2010). Using *Graham v. Florida* to challenge juvenile transfer laws. *Louisiana Law Review*, *71*, 99–156.

Benekos, P. J., & Merlo, A. V. (2008). Juvenile justice: The legacy of punitive policy. *Youth Violence and Juvenile Justice*, *6*(1), 28–46. doi:10.1177/1541204007308423

Benekos, P. J., & Merlo, A. V. (2019). A decade of change: *Roper v. Simmons*, defending childhood, and juvenile justice policy. *Criminal Justice Policy Review*, *30*(1), 102–127. doi:10.1177/0887403416648734

Bishop, D. M. (2000). Juvenile offenders in the adult criminal justice system. In M. Tonry (Ed.), *Crime & Justice: A Review of Research, 27, 81-167.* IL University of Chicago Press. doi:10.1086/652199

Bishop, D. M., & Feld, B. C. (2012). Trends in juvenile justice policy and practice. In Feld, B.C., & Bishop, D.M (Eds.). The oxford handbook of juvenile crime and juvenile justice (pp. 898-926). Oxford University Press.

Bishop, D. M., & Frazier, C. E. (2000). Consequences of transfer. In J. Fagan & F. E. Zimring (Eds.), *The changing borders of juvenile justice: Transfer of adolescents to criminal court* (pp. 227–276). University of Chicago Press.

Breen, J. S., & Mills, J. R. (2015). Mandating discretion: Juvenile sentencing schemes after *Miller v. Alabama*. *The American Criminal Law Review*, *52*, 293–319.

Brink, D. O. (2003-2004). Immaturity, normative competence, and juvenile transfer: How (not) to punish minors for major crimes. *Texas Law Review*, *82*, 1555–1585.

Burrow, J. D. (2005). Punishing serious juvenile offenders: A case study of Michigan's prosecutorial waiver statute. *University of California Davis Journal of Juvenile Law & Policy*, *9*, 1–55.

Burrow, J. D. (2008a). Examining the influence of Matza's principles of justice and their impact on reverse waiver decisions: Has Kadi-(In) justice survived? *Youth Violence and Juvenile Justice*, *6*(1), 59–82. doi:10.1177/1541204007308422

Buss, E. (2016). Developmental jurisprudence. *Temple Law Review*, *88*, 741–758.

Butts, J., Coggeshall, M., Gouvis, C., Mears, D., Travis, J., Waul, M., & White, R. (2002). *Youth, guns, and the juvenile justice system. Research report*. Urban Institute. Justice Policy Center.

Butts, J.A., & Harrell, A. V. (1998). *Delinquents or Criminals? Policy Options for Young Offenders*. The Urban Institute, Crime Policy Report.

Butts, J. A., & Mears, D. P. (2001). Reviving juvenile justice in a get-tough era. *Youth & Society*, *33*(2), 169–198. doi:10.1177/0044118X01033002003

Cintron, L. A. (1996). Rehabilitating the juvenile court system: Limiting juvenile transfers to adult criminal court. *Northwestern University Law Review*, *90*, 1254–1282.

Clarke, C. A. (2004). The baby and the bathwater: Adolescent offending and punitive juvenile justice reform. *University of Kansas Law Review. University of Kansas. School of Law*, *53*, 659–725.

Cooper, M. N., & Urban, L. S. (2012). Factors affecting juvenile waiver to adult court in a large Midwestern jurisdiction. *Journal of the Institute of Justice & International Studies*, *12*, 43–59.

Davis, S. M. (2000). The criminalization of juvenile justice: Legislative responses to the phantom menace. *Mississippi Law Journal*, *70*, 1–33.

Dawson, R. O. (2000). Judicial waiver in theory and practice. In J. Fagan & F. E. Zimring (Eds.), *The changing borders of juvenile justice: Transfer of adolescents to the criminal court* (pp. 45–81). University of Chicago Press.

Deitch, M., & Arya, N. (2014). Waivers and transfers of juveniles to adult court. In W. T. Church II, D. W. Springer, & A. R. Roberts (Eds.), *Juvenile justice sourcebook* (2nd ed., pp. 241–263). Oxford University Press.

Deitch, M., Barstow, A., Lukens, L., & Reyna, R. (2009). From time out to hard time: Young children in the adult criminal justice system. Special Project Report. Lyndon B. Johnson School of Public Affairs, University of Texas at Austin.

Drinan, C. H. (2014). Misconstruing *Graham & Miller. Washington University Law Review*, *91*, 785–795.

Drinan, C. H. (2016). The *Miller* Revolution. *Iowa Law Review*, *101*, 1787–1832.

Drizin, S. A., & Tanenhaus, D. S. (2002). Owing to the extreme youth of the accused: The changing legal response to juvenile homicide. *The Journal of Criminal Law & Criminology*, *92*(3/4), 641–705. doi:10.2307/1144240

Dunn, C. (2008). Condemning Our Youth to Lives as Criminals: Incarcerating Children as Adults. *Richmond Journal of Law & Public Interest*, *11*, 30–50.

Evans, K. L. (1992). Trying juveniles as adults: Is the short-term gain of retribution outweighed by the long-term effects on society. *Mississippi Law Journal*, *62*, 95–125.

Fagan, J. (2000). Juvenile justice or injustice? The debate over reform. *St. John's Journal of Legal Commentary*, *14*, 359–369.

Fagan, J. (2002). This will hurt me more than it hurts you: Social and legal consequences of criminalizing delinquency. *Notre Dame Journal of Law, Ethics & Public Policy*, *16*, 1–41. doi:10.2139srn.306531

Fagan, J., & Deschenes, E. P. (1990). Determinants of judicial waiver decisions for violent juvenile offenders. *The Journal of Criminal Law & Criminology*, *81*(2), 314–347. doi:10.2307/1143909

Fagan, J. A. (1995). Separating the men from the boys: The comparative advantage of juvenile versus criminal court sanctions on recidivism among adolescent felony offenders. In J. C. Howell, B. Krisberg, J. D. Hawkins, & J. J. Wilson (Eds.), *Serious, Violent, and Chronic Juvenile Offenders: A Sourcebook* (pp. 238–260). Sage Publications.

Fagan, J. A. (2008). Juvenile crime and criminal justice: Resolving border disputes. 18 *The Future of Children* 81-118 (Pages numbered 1-48 in Columbia Law School Working Paper).

Fagan, J. A., Piper, E., & Forst, M. (1986). *The juvenile court and violent youth: Determinants of the transfer decision*. Center for Law and Social Policy, URSA Institute.

Fagan, J. A., & Zimring, F. E. (2000). Editors' Introduction. In Fagan, J., & Zimring, F.E. (Eds.), The changing borders of juvenile justice: Transfer of adolescents to the criminal court (pp. 1-10). University of Chicago Press.

Feld, B. C. (1978). Reference of juvenile offenders for adult prosecution: The legislative alternative to asking unanswerable questions. *Minnesota Law Review*, *62*, 515–618.

Feld, B. C. (1981a). Juvenile court legislative reform and the serious young offender: Dismantling the "rehabilitative ideal.". *Minnesota Law Review*, *69*, 167–242.

Feld, B. C. (1981b). Legislative policies toward the serious juvenile offender: On the virtue of automatic adulthood. *Crime and Delinquency*, *27*(4), 497–521. doi:10.1177/001112878102700405

Feld, B. C. (1983). Delinquent careers and criminal policy: Just deserts and the waiver decision. *Criminology*, *21*(2), 195–212. doi:10.1111/j.1745-9125.1983.tb00258.x

Feld, B. C. (1984b). The decision to seek criminal charges: Just deserts and the waiver decision. *Criminal Justice Ethics*, *3*(2), 27–41. doi:10.1080/0731129X.1984.9991756

Feld, B. C. (1987). The juvenile court meets the principle of the offense: Legislative changes in juvenile waiver statutes. *The Journal of Criminal Law & Criminology*, *78*(3), 471–533. doi:10.2307/1143567

Feld, B. C. (1995). Violent youth and public policy: A case study of juvenile justice law reform. *Minnesota Law Review*, *79*, 965–1128.

Feld, B. C. (1997). Abolish the juvenile court: Youthfulness, criminal responsibility, and sentencing policy. *The Journal of Criminal Law & Criminology*, *88*(1), 68–136. doi:10.2307/1144075

Feld, B. C. (1998). Juvenile and criminal justice systems' responses to youth violence. *Crime and Justice*, *24*, 189–261. doi:10.1086/449280

Feld, B. C. (1999a). *Bad kids: Race and the transformation of the juvenile court*. Oxford University Press.

Feld, B. C. (1999b). The transformation of the juvenile court—Part II: Race and the crack down on youth crime. *Minnesota Law Review*, *84*, 327–395.

Feld, B. C. (2000). Legislative exclusion of offenses from juvenile court jurisdiction: A history and critique. In J. Fagan & F. E. Zimring (Eds.), *The changing borders of juvenile justice: Transfer of adolescents to the criminal court* (pp. 83–144). University of Chicago Press.

Feld, B. C. (2001). Race, youth violence, and the changing jurisprudence of waiver. *Behavioral Sciences & the Law*, *19*(1), 3–22. doi:10.1002/bsl.427 PMID:11241678

Feld, B. C., & Bishop, D. M. (2012). Transfer of juveniles to criminal court. In Feld, B.C., & Bishop, D.M (Eds.). The oxford handbook of juvenile crime and juvenile justice (pp. 801-842). Oxford University Press.

Flicker, B. (1983). *Transferring juveniles to adult court for trial*. Institute of Judicial Administration.

Fritsch, E., & Hemmens, C. (1995). Juvenile waiver in the United States 1979-1995: A comparison and analysis of state waiver statutes. *Juvenile & Family Court Journal*, *46*(3), 17–35. doi:10.1111/j.1755-6988.1995.tb00820.x

Fritsch, E. J., & Hemmens, C. (1996). An assessment of legislative approaches to the problem of serious juvenile crime: A case study of Texas 1973-1995. *American Journal of Criminal Law*, *23*, 563–609.

Furdella, J., & Puzzanchera, C. (2015). *Delinquency cases in juvenile court, 2013*. Office of Juvenile Justice and Delinquency Prevention.

Gimbel, V. N. (2015). There are no children here: DC youth in the criminal justice system. *The Georgetown Law Journal*, *104*, 1307–1344.

Glynn, G. F. (1997). Arkansas' missed opportunity for rehabilitation: Sending children to adult courts. *University of Arkansas at Little Rock Law Journal*, *20*, 77–127.

Gordon, B. (1999). A criminal's justice or a child's injustice? Trends in the waiver of juvenile court jurisdiction and the flaws in the Arizona response. *Arizona Law Review*, *41*, 193–226.

Griffin, P. (2003). *Trying and sentencing juveniles as adults: An analysis of state transfer and blended sentencing laws*. National Center for Juvenile Justice.

Griffin, P. (2008). *Different from adults: An updated analysis of juvenile transfer and blended sentencing laws, with recommendations for reform*. National Center for Juvenile Justice.

Griffin, P., Addie, S., Addie, B., & Firestine, K. (2011). *Trying juveniles as adults: An analysis of state transfer laws and reporting*. U.S. Department of Justice, Office of Justice Programs, Office of Juvenile Justice and Delinquency Prevention.

Griffin, P., Torbet, P., & Syzmanski, L. (1998). *Trying juveniles in adult court: An analysis of state transfer provisions*. Office of Juvenile Justice and Delinquency Prevention, Office of Justice Programs, U.S. Department of Justice.

Grundfest, A. R., Paskow, A. C., Szabo, H. E., & Williams, R. J. (1981). In Hall, J.C., Hamparian, D.M., Pettibone, John M., & White, Joseph L. (Eds.) Major issues in juvenile justice: Information and Training: Readings in public policy (pp. 321-332). Academy for Contemporary Problems.

Guttman, C. R. (1995). Listen to the children: The decision to transfer juveniles to criminal court. *Harvard Civil Rights-Civil Liberties Law Review*, *30*, 507–542.

Harshbarger, S., & Keshian, C. (1995). The attorney general of Massachusetts' bill relative to the trial and sentencing of serious juvenile offenders. *The Boston University Public Interest Law Journal*, *5*, 135–163.

Hirase, J. (1992). State ex. rel. v. EGT: Waiving childhood goodbye. *Journal of Contemporary Law*, *18*, 159–175.

HLRA. (2002). For the Good of the Child, for the Good of Society: Using Scotland and Jamaica as Models to Reform U. S. Juvenile Justice Policy. *Harvard Law Review*, *115*(7), 1964–1987. doi:10.2307/1342598

Hockenberry, S. (2018). *Delinquency cases in juvenile court, 2015*. Office of Juvenile Justice and Delinquency Prevention.

Hockenberry, S. (2019a). *Delinquency cases in juvenile court, 2016*. Office of Juvenile Justice and Delinquency Prevention.

Hockenberry, S. (2019b). *Delinquency cases in juvenile court, 2017*. Office of Juvenile Justice and Delinquency Prevention.

Hockenberry, S. (2020). Delinquency cases in juvenile court, 2018. U.S. Department of Justice, Office of Justice programs.

Hockenberry, S. (2021). *Delinquency cases waived to criminal court, 2018*. U.S. Department of Justice, Office of Justice Programs.

Hockenberry, S., & Puzzanchera, C. (2014). *Delinquency cases waived to criminal court, 2011*. Office of Juvenile Justice and Delinquency Prevention.

Hoeffel, J. C. (2013). The jurisprudence of death and youth: Now the twain should meet. *Texas Tech Law Review*, *46*, 29–69.

Hyland, N. (2018). *Delinquency cases in juvenile court, 2014*. Office of Juvenile Justice and Delinquency Prevention.

Jan, I. F., Ball, J. D., & Walsh, A. (2008). Predicting public opinion about juvenile waivers. *Criminal Justice Policy Review*, *19*(3), 285–300. doi:10.1177/0887403407307431

Jordan, K. L., & Myers, D. L. (2011). Juvenile transfer and deterrence: Reexamining the effectiveness of a "get-tough" policy. *Crime and Delinquency*, *57*(2), 247–270. doi:10.1177/0011128708319111

Juszkiewicz, J. (2000). *Youth crime/adult time: Is justice served?* Building Blocks for Youth.

Keiter, R. B. (1973). Criminal or delinquent? A study of juvenile cases transferred to the criminal court. *Crime and Delinquency*, *19*(4), 528–538. doi:10.1177/001112877301900408

Kimbrell, M. (2015). It takes a village to waive a child-or at least a jury: Applying *Apprendi* to juvenile waiver hearings in Oregon. *Willamette Law Review*, *52*, 61–98.

Knox, A. (2009). *Blakely* and blended sentencing: A constitutional challenge to sentencing child criminal. *Ohio State Law Journal*, *70*, 1261–1305.

Kozich, S. D. (1980). A model for the transfer of juvenile felony offenders to adult court jurisdiction. *Journal of Juvenile Law*, *4*, 170–185.

Kupchik, A. (2003b). Prosecuting adolescents in criminal courts: Criminal or juvenile justice? *Social Problems*, *50*(3), 439–460. doi:10.1525p.2003.50.3.439

Kupchik, A. (2006a). *Judging juveniles: Prosecuting adolescents in adult and juvenile courts*. New York University Press.

Lehmann, P. S., & Kobie, A. (2021). Effects of Waivers. In S. J. Keenan (Ed.), *The Transferring of America's Youth* (pp. 87–115). Lexington Books.

Lehmann, P. S., Pickett, J. T., Ryon, S. B., & Kosloski, A. E. (2019). Race, juvenile transfer, and sentencing preferences: Findings from a randomized experiment. *Race and Justice*, *9*(3), 251–275. doi:10.1177/2153368717699674

Marczyk, G. R., Heilbrun, K., Lander, T., & DeMatteo, D. (2005). Juvenile decertification: Developing a model for classification and prediction. *Criminal Justice and Behavior*, *32*(3), 278–301. doi:10.1177/0093854804274371

Marrus, E., & Rosenberg, I. M. (2005). After *Roper v. Simmons*: Keeping kids out of adult criminal court. *San Diego L. Rev.*, *42*, 1151-1182.

McCarthy, F. B. (1994). The serious offender and juvenile court reform: The case for prosecutorial waiver of juvenile court jurisdiction. *Saint Louis University Law Journal*, *38*, 629–671.

McCurdy-Jackson, C. A. (2011). *Direct filing/transfer of juvenile cases in Miami-Dade County, Florida*. Eleventh Judicial Circuit of Florida Miami.

McGowan, A., Hahn, R., Liberman, A., Crosby, A., Fullilove, M., Johnson, R., Moscicki, E., Price, L., Snyder, S., Tuma, F., Lowy, J., Briss, P., Cory, S., & Stone, G. (2007). Effects on violence of laws and policies facilitating the transfer of juveniles from the juvenile justice system to the adult justice system: A systematic review. *American Journal of Preventive Medicine*, *32*(4), S7–S28. doi:10.1016/j.amepre.2006.12.003 PMID:17386331

Merlo, A. V., Benekos, P. J., & Cook, W. J. (1997b). Waiver and juvenile justice reform: Widening the punitive net. *Criminal Justice Policy Review*, *8*(2-3), 145–168. doi:10.1177/088740349700800202

Miller v. Alabama. (2012). 567 U.S. 460.

Mole, D., & White, D. (2005). *Transfer and waiver in the juvenile justice system*. Child Welfare League of America.

Mulvey, E. P., & Schubert, C. (2012). *Transfer of juveniles to adult court: Effects of a broad policy in one court. Juvenile Justice Bulletin. December 2012*. U.S. Department of Justice, Office of Justice Programs. Office of Juvenile Justice & Delinquency Prevention.

Myers, D. L. (2003b). The recidivism of violent youths in juvenile and adult court: A consideration of selection bias. *Youth Violence and Juvenile Justice*, *1*(1), 79–101. doi:10.1177/1541204002238365

NDAA. National District Attorney's Association. (2002). *Resource manual and policy positions on juvenile crime issues*. NDAA.

Newman, D. J. (1966). *Conviction: The determination of guilt or innocence without trial*. Little, Brown.

Noon, C. R. (1994). Waiving goodbye to juvenile defendants, getting smart vs. getting tough. *University of Miami Law Review*, *49*, 431–476.

Notes. (2002). For the good of the child, for the good of society: Using Scotland and Jamaica as models to reform U.S. juvenile justice policy. *Harvard Law Review, 115,* 1964-1987.

OJJ. (1999). *Office of Juvenile Justice. Juvenile justice: A century of change*. US Department of Justice, Office of Justice Programs, Office of Juvenile Justice and Delinquency Prevention.

OJJDP. (2018). *Statistical briefing book. Provisions for imposing adult sanctions on juvenile offenders, 2016*. OJJDP. https:/www.ojjdp.gov/ojstagg/structure-process/qa04113.asp?qadate=2016

OJJDP. (2020). *Statistical briefing book. Provisions for imposing adult sanctions on juvenile offenders, 2018*. OJJDP. https:/www.ojjdp.gov/ojstagg/structure-process/qa04113.asp?qadate=2018

Pagnanelli, E. (2007). Children as adults: The transfer of juveniles to adult courts and the potential impact of Roper v. Simmons. *The American Criminal Law Review*, *44*, 175–194.

Penney, S. R., & Moretti, M. M. (2005). The transfer of juveniles to adult court in Canada and the United States: Confused agendas and compromised assessment procedures. *International Journal of Forensic Mental Health*, *4*(1), 19–37. doi:10.1080/14999013.2005.10471210

Podkopacz, M. R., & Feld, B. C. (1995). Judicial waiver policy and practice: Persistence, seriousness, and race. *Minnesota Journal of Law & Inequality*, *14*, 73–178.

Prochaska, B. F. (2018). *Do contextual factors matter in juvenile transfer decisions? A longitudinal multilevel analysis of juvenile waivers to adult court* (Unpublished doctoral dissertation, University of Arkansas at Little Rock].

Puzzanchera, C. M. (2000). *Delinquency cases waived to criminal court, 1988-1997*. U.S. Department of Justice, Office of Justice Programs. Office of Juvenile Justice and Delinquency Prevention. doi:10.1037/e381172004-001

Puzzanchera, C. M. (2001). *Delinquency cases waived to criminal court, 1989-1998*. U.S. Department of Justice, Office of Justice Programs, Office of Juvenile Justice and Delinquency Prevention.

Puzzanchera, C. M. (2003). *Delinquency cases waived to criminal court, 1990-1999*. U.S. Department of Justice, Office of Justice Programs, Office of Juvenile Justice and Delinquency Prevention. doi:10.1037/e377102004-001

Puzzanchera, C. M., & Addie, S. (2014). *Delinquency cases waived to criminal court, 2010*. U.S. Department of Justice, Office of Justice Programs. Office of Juvenile Justice and Delinquency Prevention.

Puzzanchera, C. M., Hockenberry, S., & Sickmund, M. (2022). *Youth and the juvenile justice System:2022 national report*. National Center for Juvenile Justice.

Redding, R. E. (2016). One size does not fit all: The deterrent effect of transferring juveniles to criminal court. *Criminology & Public Policy*, *15*(3), 939–948. doi:10.1111/1745-9133.12239

Rosenberg, I. M. (2000). Teen violence and the juvenile courts: A plea for reflection and restraint. *Houston Law Review*, *37*, 75–96.

Rudman, C., Hartstone, E., Fagan, J., & Moore, M. (1986). Violent youth in adult court: Process and punishment. *Crime and Delinquency*, *32*(1), 75–96. doi:10.1177/0011128786032001005

Rudof, P. R. (1998). Throwing out the baby with the bathwater: Utah's Serious Youth Offender Statute. *Utah Law Review*, 443–464.

Sabo, S. (1996). Rights of passage: An analysis of waiver of juvenile court jurisdiction. *Fordham Law Review*, *64*, 2425–2454.

Samuelson, B. K. (2010). *Mechanisms of juvenile transfer: Variations in incarceration and sentence length in criminal court*. (Unpublished Master's Thesis). University of Maryland, College Park, MD.

Sanborn, J. B., Jr. (1985). *Plea negotiation in juvenile court*. (Unpublished doctoral dissertation). SUNY Albany, Albany, NY., United States.

Sanborn, J. B. Jr. (1993a). Philosophical, legal, and systemic aspects of juvenile court plea bargaining. *Crime and Delinquency*, *39*(4), 509–527. doi:10.1177/0011128793039004006

Sanborn, J. B. Jr, & Salerno, A. W. (2005). *The juvenile justice system: Law and process*. Roxbury Publishing Company. Oxford University Publishing.

Sarri, R., & Shook, J. (2005). Juvenile justice in the United States: Adherence to Human Rights Conventions. In M. Ensalaco & L. C. Majka (Eds.), *Children's human rights: Progress and challenges for children worldwide* (pp. 218–240). Rowman and Littlefield Publishers.

Schornhorst, T. F. (1967). The waiver of juvenile court jurisdiction: Kent revisited. *Indiana Law Review*, *43*, 583–613.

Schulhofer, S. J. (1997). Youth crime—And what not to do about it. *Valparaiso University Law Review. Valparaiso University. School of Law*, *31*, 435–447.

Shelden, R. G., & Hussong, M. (2003). Juvenile crime, adult adjudication, and the death penalty: Draconian policies revisited. *Justice Policy Journal: Analyzing criminal and juvenile justice issues and policies*, 21-40.

Shook, J. J. (2005). Contesting childhood in the US justice system: The transfer of juveniles to adult criminal court. *Childhood*, *12*(4), 461–478. doi:10.1177/0907568205058604

Shook, J. J. (2014). Looking back and thinking forward: Examining the consequences of policies and practices that treat juveniles as adults. *Journal of Evidence-Based Social Work*, *11*(4), 392–403. doi:10.1080/10911359.2014.897112 PMID:25105333

Sickmund, M. (1994). How juveniles get to criminal court. U.S. Department of Justice, OJP, OJJDP.

Sickmund, M. (2003). *Juveniles in court*. U.S. Department of Justice, Office of Justice Programs, Office of Juvenile Justice and Delinquency Prevention.

Singer, S. I. (1993). The automatic waiver of juveniles and substantive justice. *Crime and Delinquency*, *39*(2), 253–261. doi:10.1177/0011128793039002009

Singer, S. I. (1996). *Recriminalizing delinquency: Violent juvenile crimes and juvenile justice reform*. Cambridge University Press. doi:10.1017/CBO9780511527562

Singer, S. I., Fagan, J., & Liberman, A. (2000). The reproduction of juvenile justice in criminal court: A case study of New York's juvenile offender law. In J. Fagan & F. E. Zimring (Eds.), *The changing borders of juvenile justice: Transfer of adolescents to the criminal court* (pp. 353–375). University of Chicago Press.

Slobogin, C. (2013). Treating juveniles like juveniles: Getting rid of transfer and expanded adult court jurisdiction. *Texas Tech Law Review*, *46*, 103–132.

Smith, A. (1994). They dream of growing older: On kids and crime. *Boston College Law Review. Boston College. Law School*, *36*, 953–1024.

Snyder, H. N. (2012). Juvenile delinquents and juvenile justice clientele: Trends and patterns in crime and justice system responses. In Feld, B.C., & Bishop, D.M (Eds.). The oxford handbook of juvenile crime and juvenile justice (pp. 3-30). Oxford University Press.

Snyder, H. N., & Hutzler, J. L. (1981). *The serious juvenile offender: The scope of the problem and the response of juvenile courts*. National Center for Juvenile Justice.

Snyder, H. N., & Sickmund, M. (2006). Juvenile offenders and victims: 2006 national report. *Office of juvenile justice and delinquency prevention*.

Snyder, H. N., Sickmund, M., & Poe-Yamagata, E. (2000). *Juvenile transfers to criminal court in the 1990s: Lessons learned from four studies*. U.S. Department of Justice, Office of Justice Programs, Office of Juvenile Justice and Delinquency Prevention.

Sobol, S. (2022). Rethinking juvenile rehabilitation: Presumptive waiver and alternative sentencing in Indiana. *Indiana Law Journal (Indianapolis, Ind.)*, *97*, 365–391.

Soler, M. (2010). Missed opportunity: Waiver, race, data, and policy reform. *Louisiana Law Review*, *71*, 17–33.

Sorrentino, J. N., & Olsen, G. K. (1977). Certification of juveniles to adult court. *Pepperdine Law Review*, *4*, 497–522.

Stamm, M. J. (1973). Transfer of jurisdiction in juvenile court: An A\analysis of the proceeding, its role in the administration of justice, and A proposal for the reform of Kentucky law. *Kentucky Law Journal (Lexington, Ky.)*, *62*, 122–199.

Steinberg, L., & Cauffman, E. (2001). Adolescents as adults in court: A developmental perspective on the transfer of juveniles to criminal court. *Social Policy Report*, *15*(4), 1–16. doi:10.1002/j.2379-3988.2001.tb00016.x

Steiner, B. (2005). Predicting sentencing outcomes and time served for juveniles transferred to criminal court in a rural northwestern state. *Journal of Criminal Justice*, *33*(6), 601–610. doi:10.1016/j.jcrimjus.2005.08.008

Sulok, M. M. (2007). Extended jurisdiction juvenile prosecutions: To revoke or not to revoke. *Loyola University of Chicago Law Journal. Loyola University of Chicago. School of Law*, *39*, 215–284.

Szymanski, L. A. (2007). *"Once an adult/always an adult" (2007 update). NCJJ Snapshot 12(4)*. National Center for Juvenile Justice.

Szymanski, L. A. (2008). *Once an adult/always an adult (2008 update). NCJJ Snapshot 13(4)*. National Center for Juvenile Justice.

Szymanski, L. A. (2009). *Once an adult/always an adult (2009 update). NCJJ Snapshot 14(5)*. National Center for Juvenile Justice.

Szymanski, L. A. (2010a). *Can juveniles transferred for criminal prosecution be held for pre-trial detention in adult jails? NCJJ Snapshot 15(8)*. National Center for Juvenile Justice.

Tanenhaus, D. S. (2000). The evolution of transfer out of the juvenile court. In J. Fagan & F. E. Zimring (Eds.), *The changing borders of juvenile justice: Transfer of adolescents to the criminal court* (pp. 13–43). University of Chicago Press.

Tang, C. M., & Nunez, N. (2003). Effects of defendant age and juror bias on judgment of culpability: What happens when a juvenile is tried as an adult? *American Journal of Criminal Justice*, *28*(1), 37–52. doi:10.1007/BF02885751

Thomas, J. M. (2017). *Raising the bar: State trends in keeping youth out of adult courts (2015-2017)*. Campaign for Youth Justice.

Thomas, J. M., & Wilson, M. (2018). *The color of youth transferred to the adult criminal justice system: Policy & practice recommendations*. National Association of Social Workers.

Torbet, P. M., Gable, R., Hurst, I. V. H., Montgomery, I., Szymanski, L. A., & Thomas, D. (1996). *State responses to serious and violent juvenile crime*. Office of Juvenile Justice and Delinquency Prevention.

Vargas, J. H. (2014). *Juvenile Court Judges and their Concerns about Vulnerability, Experienced Uncertainty and the Law: Extralegal Factors, Legal Considerations and Judicial Transfer Decision-making*. (Unpublished doctoral dissertation). University of Nevada, Reno, NV.

Verrecchia, P. J. (2003). The effect of transfer mechanism from juvenile court on the likelihood of incarceration in criminal court. *Free Inquiry in Creative Sociology*, *31*, 15–24.

Ward, J. M. (2003). Deterrence's difficulty magnified: The importance of adolescent development in assessing the deterrence value of transferring juveniles to adult court. *University of California Davis Journal of Juvenile Law & Policy*, *7*, 253–284.

Watkins, J. C. Jr. (1998). *The juvenile justice century: A sociological commentary on American juvenile courts*. Carolina Academic Press.

Wizner, S. (1984). Discretionary waiver of juvenile court jurisdiction: An invitation to procedural arbitrariness. *Criminal Justice Ethics*, *3*(2), 41–50. doi:10.1080/0731129X.1984.9991757

Zimring, F. E. (1998a). *American youth violence*. Oxford University Press.

Zimring, F. E. (2000b). The punitive necessity of waiver. In J. Fagan & F. E. Zimring (Eds.), *The Changing Borders of Juvenile Justice: Transfer of adolescents to the criminal court* (pp. 207–224). University of Chicago Press.

ENDNOTES

1 The Office of Juvenile Justice and Delinquency Prevention (OJJDP) started reporting national data on transfer numbers in the mid- to late-1980s. Until the end of the Twentieth Century, the wording used to describe the phenomena was that juveniles were tried "*as if they were adults* (see Puzzanchera, 2000, p. 1, 2001, p. 1, 2003, p. 1)." Beginning in 2005 (Adams & Addie, 2009, p. 1), and since the wording was changed to "as adults (see Adams & Addie, 2010, p. 1, 2011, p. 1, 2012, p. 1; Furdella & Puzzanchera, 2015, p, 3; Hockenberry, 2018, p. 3, 2019a, p. 3, 2019b, p. 3, 2020, p. 3, 2021, p.1; Hockenberry & Puzzanchera, 2014, p. 1; Hyland, 2018, p. 3; Puzzanchera & Addie, 2014, p. 1)." It is possible that the authors deleted the three intermediate words to save on printing costs, but somehow that seems doubtful.

2 One pair of ATC members (Breen & Mills, 2015) hopes that the U.S. Supreme Court's *Miller v. Alabama* decision (2012) requiring individual consideration of "life without parole" sentences (and negating mandatory sentences of this nature) for juveniles convicted in CC can be used to negate OE statutes because the critics infer that the latter are mandatory and disallow individual analysis of

the juvenile's status or situation (see, also, Benekos & Merlo, 2019, p. 119; Drinan, 2016). Besides the critical fact that OE is neither mandatory nor wholesale/categorical in nature, the individual examination required for sentencing to avoid outcomes that violate the Eighth Amendment does not apply to charging youths and to transferring them to CC to stand trial.

3 The "perhaps not to the same degree" is an understatement. That is similar to an explosives expert who, after comparing two forms of weapons, argues that while a hand grenade, like a nuclear bomb, is an explosive, the grenade neither causes as much damage nor kills as many people, and can fit in one's pocket.

4 The ATC's saying OE/transfer is wrong for one reason or another and then *unsaying the very same thing* is common: [T]*hese legislative seriousness decisions are categorical and absolute. They lack,* **in theory,** *any elements of individualization of the sorting decision. In reality, individualization is permissible, but only in factually limited circumstances. A prosecutor might exercise discretion in a case in which conduct might or might not be excluded from juvenile court jurisdiction to charge the conduct as a juvenile jurisdiction offense rather than a criminal jurisdiction offense. Such a prosecutor might do so by bringing charges for a lesser included offense or a less serious offense related to an excluded offense* (Dawson, 2000, p. 48, emphasis added). Evidently, OE is categorical and absolute until it is not.

5 Rarely, some ATC folks acknowledge OE does not lack individualization: *First, legislative exclusion does not end the influence of elements of juvenile justice either in jurisprudence or procedure. Individualization, treatment concerns, changeability, and discretion influence both the initial decision to charge a teenager in criminal court and also the allocation of punishment once transferred...* (Singer, Fagan & Liberman, 2000, p. 370).
Prosecutorial charging discretion ensures that OE is not mandatory, nondiscretionary, or categorical.

6 Feld's objection is unclear. "Deprecating the normative seriousness" of criminal conduct occurs *daily, if not hourly,* in CC. Selecting lesser charges is the "normative" conduct of prosecutors. Prosecutors routinely reduce felonies to misdemeanors to steer the case from a trial court of general jurisdiction to a trial court of limited jurisdiction. Prosecutors also reduce charges routinely to negotiate a plea bargain in both JC and CC (see Newman, 1966; Sanborn 1985, 1993a).

7 Calling it mandatory JT underreports the number of states with OE (see Griffin et al., 1998; Griffin, et al., 2011; OJJDP, 2018, 2020; Szymanski, 2007, 2008, 2009, 2010a; Torbet et al., 1996). It also misrepresents the control legislatures supposedly enjoy over *judges* in this context.

8 Flicker (1983) went on to wrongly allege that the reverse waiver provision, whereby a juvenile offender can be returned to JC from CC, is the only true waiver element in the statute (p. 4). She then offered another internally contradictory and incorrect assertion: *If the findings based on which the court must transfer are limited to immutable facts: the age of the juvenile, the specific offense, prior adjudications, time elapsed between offenses, the age of the victim, etc., the decision to waive should be deemed mandatory* (Id., p. 5). All of the items mentioned here are indeed immutable, except, of course, for the most important factor: the specific offense.
Confusion surrounding transfer seems to be unavoidable. Even straightforward concurrent jurisdiction has been identified as something separate and apart from prosecutorial discretion (see Davis, 2000, pp. 10-12).

CHAPTER 6 TABLES

Sources Making Misidentifications of Transfer Terms & Concepts

Table 38a. The Children/Kids Tried "as Adults"

Abrams, (2013)
Acton, (1996)
Adams & Addie, (2009), (2010), (2011), (2012)
Ainsworth, (1991), (1995)
Allard & Young, (2002)
Allen, D.C., (2002) (T)
Allen, K.L., (2012) (T)
Allen, Trzcinski, & Kubiak, (2012)
Alliance, (2003)
Angell, (2004) (T)*
Annino, (2000)
Applegate & Davis, (2006)
Applegate, Davis & Cullen, (2009)
Arteaga, (2002)
Arthur & Schwartz, (1993)
Arya, (2010), (2011)
Augustyn & Loughran, (2017)
Augustyn & McGloin, (2018)
Backstrom & Walker, (2006)
Baird & Samuels, (1996) (T)
Baquedano, (2015)
Barnes & Franz, (1989) (T)
Baruwa, (2013)
Beale, (2009)
Beaudry-Cyr, Leiber, Brubaker, & Jaynes, (2020)
Benekos & Merlo, (2008), (2019)
Beresford, (2000)
Bishop, (2000), (2009)
Bishop & Frazier, (1991)
Bishop, Frazier, Lanza-Kaduce, & Winner, (1996)
Bishop, Lanza-Kaduce & Frazier, (1998)
Blumhardt, (2000)
Bortner, (1986)

Bove, (1991)
Braithwaite & Shore, (1981)
Brandau, (2004)
Brannen, Salekin, R.T., Zapf, Salekin, K. L., Kubak, & DeCoster, (2006)
Breen & Mills, (2015)
Brink, (2003-04)
Brinkerhoff, (1984) (T)
Brown & Sorensen, (2013)
Browne, (1977)
Buckingham, (1993)
Burgess-Proctor, Holtrop, & Villarruel, (2008)
Burns, (1990) (T)
Burrow, (2005), (2008a), (2008b)
Burrow & Lowery, (2015)
Butts, (1997)
Butts & Harrell, (1998)
Butts & Mitchell, (2000)
Carroll, (2009)
Carter, (2006)
Caselli, (2011)
Cassady, (2017)
Cauffman, (2012)
Cauffman, Fine, Mahler, & Simmons, (2018)
Cellucci, Swift, Governor, Perlov, & O'Toole, (2001)
CFYJ, (2014)
Chamberlin, (2000) (T)
Cintron, (1996)
Clarke, C.A., (2005)
Clarke & Kooy, (n.d.) (T)
Cohen et al., (2016) (T)
Cohn & Mialson, (2008)
Conrad, (1981)
Cornish, (1982) (T)

continued on following page

Table 38a. Continued

Coupet, (2000)
Cross, (1998) (T)
CYJ, (2007) (T)
Dale, (2004)
D'Ambra, (1997)
D'Angelo, (2007)
Davis, (2000)
Davis & Ziedenberg, (2014)
Dawson, (1990)
DeFrances & Strom, (1997)
Deitch & Arya, (2014)
Deitch, Barstow, Lukens, & Reyna, (2009) (T)
DeJong & Merrill, (2001)
Dempsey, (2020)
Dodge, (2000)
Drinan, (2014), (2016)
Drizin & Tanenhaus, (2002)
Dugan, (1998)
Dunn, (2008) (T)
Ensalaco, & Majka, (2005).
Evans, 1992 (T)
Fagan, (1991), (2002), (2008)
Fagan & Deschenes, (1990)
Fagan, Forst, & Vivona, (1987a), (1987b) (T)
Fagan & Hartstone, (1984) (T)
Fagan, Piper, & Forst, (1986)
Fagan, Kupchik, & Liberman, (2007)
Fagan & Zimring, (2000)
Farrington, Loeber, & Howell, (2012)
Federle, (1996), (1999), (2016)
Feiler & Sheley, (1999)
Feld, (1978) (T), (1980), (1981) (T), (1983), (1984a), (1984b), (1987), (1988), (1989), (1991),
(1993a), (1993b), (1995), (1997), (1998), (1999a), (1999b), (2000), (2001), (2003a),
(2003b), (2004), (2007a), (2007b), (2008), (2013a), (2017a), (2017b)
Feld & Bishop, (2012)
Flesch, (2004)
Flicker, (1981) (T), (1983)
Flynn, (2008)
Forst & Blomquist, (1991)
Fowler & Kurlychek, (2018)
Frazier, Bishop, Lanza-Kaduce, & Marvasti, (1998)
Fritsch & Hemmens, (1995), (1996)
Frost Clausel & Bonnie, (2000)
Furdella & Puzzanchera, (2015)
Gallini, (2008)
Garberg & Libkuman, (2009)
Gardner & Lanza-Kaduce, (2015)
Garner, (1973)
Gasper & Katkin, (1980)
Geraghty, D., (2016)
Geraghty, T., (1997) (T)
Geraghty & Drizin, (1998)
Geraghty & Rhee, (1998) (T)
Giardino, (1996)
Gibson & Krohn, (2012)
Gimbel, (2016)
Glynn, (1997) (T)
Gordon, (1999) (T)
Gowen, Thurau, & Wood, (2011)
Gray, (2007)
Greathouse, Sothmann, Levett, & Kovera, (2011)
Green, (2005)
Greene, Duke, & Woody, (2017)
Greene, (2010) (T)
Griffin, 2003 (T), (2008), (2012)
Griffin, Torbet, & Szymanski, (1998) (T)
Griffin et al., (2011) (T)
Grisso, (1996)
Grundfest, Paskow, Szabo, & Williams, (1981)
Guggenheim, (2017)
Gulstad, (2016)
Guttman, (1995) (T)
Hager, (1995)
Hamilton, Moak, & Golden, (2007)
Hamparian, (1981)

continued on following page

Table 38a. Continued

Hamparian, Estep, Muntean, Priestino, Swisher, Wallace, & White, (1982)
Hannan, (2008)
Harris & Allen, (2003)
Harshbarger, & Keshian, (1995)
Hart, (1998)
Hartney, (2006)
Hays & Solway, (1972) (T)
Henderson, (2000)
Henning, (2013)
Herkal, (1999)
Hess, (2014) (T)
Hess, Furr, Armstrong, Francis, & White, (2010) (T)
Hirase, (1992) (T)
HLRA, (2002) (T)
Hockenberry, (2018), (2019a), (2019b), (2020), (2021)
Hockenberry & Puzzanchera, (2014a), (2014b)
Hoeffel, (2013)
Hofacket, (2002) (T)
Hogan, (1974)
Holstein, (1982) (T)
Holtzman, (2004)
Hornback, (2021)
Horowitz, (2000)
Houghtalin & Mays, (1992)
House, (2013) (T)
Howell, Feld, Mears, Farrington, Loeber, & Petechuk, (2013)
Howell, J. C., Wilson, Sickmund, Hodges, & Howell, M. Q., (2017)
Hunt, (1998)
Hurst, III, (1999)
Hyland, (2018)
Jackson & Pabon, (2000) (T)
Jan, Ball, & Walsh, (2008)
Johnson & Kurlychek, (2012)
Johnson, K.D., (2001)
Jordan, (2005), (2013)
Jordan & Freiburger, (2010)
Juszkiewicz, (2000)

Kaasa, Tatar, II, Dezember, & Cauffman, (2018)
Kellar, (2006)
Keenan, Rush, & Cheeseman, (2015)
Kimbrell, (2015) (T)
Kinder, Veneziano, Fichter, & Azuma, (1995) (T)
King, C., (2018)
King, R., (2006)
Kirkish, Screenivasan, Welsh, Van Gorp, Spencer, Shoptaw, & Ling, (2000) (T)
Klein, (1998)
Knipps, (1993)
Knox, (2009) (T)
Kokrda, (2005)
Kolbe, (2006)
Kole, (2001)
Kozich, (1980)
Kruh & Brodsky, (1997)
Kukino, (2014)
Kumli, (2002)
Kupchik, (2003a) (T), (2003b), (2006a), (2006b)
Kupchik, Fagan & Liberman, (2003)
Kurlychek, (2010)
Kurlychek & Johnson, (2010)
Lahey, (2016)
Lambie & Randell, (2013)
Langemo, (2004)
Lanza-Kaduce, Bishop, Frazier & Winner, (1996)
Lanza-Kaduce, Frazier & Bishop, (1999)
Lanza-Kaduce, Frazier, Lane & Bishop, (2002)
Law, Harrington, Niekus, & Cao, (2019)
Lehmann & Kobie, (2021)
Leistico & Salekin, (2003)
Lemmon, Sontheimer, & Saylor, (1991)
Lin, Bussiere, Matthews, & Wilber, (1994)
Linares & Bunton, (2010)
Liwanga & Ibe, (2021) (T)
Lockwood, (2020) (T)
Loeffler & Grunwald, (2015) (T)
Logan, (1998)

continued on following page

Table 38a. Continued

Loken & Rosettenstein, (1998) (T)
Lynn-Whaley & Russi, (2011)
Lyons, (2011)
Males & Macallair, (2000)
Mahoney, (1991)
Mallett, (2007)
Marczyk, Heilbrun, Lander, & DeMatteo, (2005)
Maroney, (2009), (2011)
Marrus & Rosenberg, (2005) (T)
Massey, (2005)
May, (1998)
Mays & Gregware, (1996)
Mays & Houghtalin, (1992) (T)
McCurdy-Jackson, (2011)
McLatchey, (1999)
Means, Heller, & Janofsky, (2012)
Mears, (2001) (T), (2003)
Mears, Hay, Gertz & Mancini, (2007)
Merlo & Benekos, (2003), (2010)
Merlo, Benekos, & Cook, (1997a), (1997b), (1999)
Miller, N.G., (1984)
Miller & Applegate, (2015)
Miner-Romanoff, (2014) (T)
Mole & White, (2005)
Monahan, Steinberg, & Piquero, (2015)
Moore, (2007)
Mulvey & Schubert, (2012)
Myers, (2003a), (2003b), (2005) (T), (2016)
Myers & Kiehl, (2001)
Myers et al., (2011)
Nagin, Piquero, Scott, & Steinberg, (2006)
NASEM, (2019)
NeMoyer, (2017)
Nguyen, (2016)
Noon, (1994)
Notes, (2002)
NRC, (2013)
Nunez, Dahl, Tang, & Jensen, (2007)
OJJ, (1999)
Oliver, (2006) (T)
Olson, (2004)
Osbun & Rode, (1984) (T)
Pagnanelli, (2007) (T)
Park, (2007)
Pegg, (2015) (T)
Penney & Moretti, (2005)
PHR, (2007) (T)
Pine, (1996)
Podkopacz & Feld, (1995), (1996), (2001)
Pollitt, (2004)
Prochaska, (2018)
Puzzanchera & Addie, (2014)
Puzzanchera, Hockenberry, & Sickmund, (2022)
Quinn, (2015)
Redding, (1997), (1999), (2003) (T), (2005), (2008), (2010), (2016)
Redding & Fuller, (2004) (T)
Redding & Mrozoski, (2005)
Reidy, Sorensen, & Cihan, (2018)
Riggs Romaine, Goldstein, Hunt, & DeMatteo, (2011).
Risler, Sweatman, & Nackerud, (1998)
Romaine, (2010)
Rosenberg, (2000)
Rossiter, (2006) (T)
Rovner, (2016) (T)
Rowley, Ewing, & Singer, (1987)
Roysher & Edelman, (1981) (T)
Rubin, (2006)
Ruddell & Mays, (2012)
Ruddell, Mays, & Giever, (1998)
Rudman, Hartstone, Fagan, & Moore, (1986)
Ryan, (2012)
Sabo, (1996)
Salazar, (1982)
Salekin, (2002)
Salekin, Rogers, & Ustad, (2001)
Salekin, Yff, Neumann, Leistico, & Zalot, (2002)
Sanborn, (2004a) (T)

continued on following page

Table 38a. Continued

Sargent & Gordon, (1963)
Sarri & Shook, (2005)
Schetky, (2003)
Schiraldi & Soler, (1998)
Schiraldi & Ziedenberg, (1999) (T)
Schornhorst, (1968)
Schubert, Mulvey, Loughran, Fagan, Chassin, Piquero, Losoya, Steinberg, & Cauffman, (2010)
Schulhofer, (1997)
Schwartz Alers, (1973)
Scialabba, (2016)
Scism, (2019)
Scott, (2000), (2013) (T), (2013b)
Scott & Grisso, (1997), (2005)
Scott, Grisso, Levick, & Steinberg, (2016)
Scott & Steinberg, (2003), (2008), (2010)
Sellers & Arrigo, (2009)
Semple & Woody, (2011) (T)
Sewell, (2009)
Sewell, (2019)
Sharlein, (2018)
Sheffer, (1995)
Shefi, (2003)
Shelden & Hussong, (2003)
Shiller, (2006)
Shook, (2004) (T), (2005) (T), (2013) (T), (2014) (T)
Sickmund, (1994), (2003)
Singer, (1994), (1996a), (2003)
Singer & McDowall, (1988)
Slaten, (2003)
Slobogin, (2013)
Smallheer, (1999)
Smith, A., (1994) (T)
Smith, C. K., (2013)
Smith, & Yarussi, (2012)
Snyder, (2012)
Snyder & Hutzler, (1981)
Snyder & Sickmund, (2006)
Snyder, Sickmund, & Poe-Yamagata, (2000)

Sobol, (2022)
Soler, (2010)
Solway, Hays, Schreiner, & Cansler, (1980) (T)
Sorrentino & Olsen, (1977)
Soung, (2011)
Spring, (1998)
Sridharan, Greenfield, & Blakley, (2004)
Stafford, (2013)
Stalans & Henry, (1994)
Stamm, (1973)
Steinberg, (2000) (T), (2009)
Steinberg & Cauffman, (1999) (T), (2001) (T)
Steinberg et al., (2003) (T)
Steinberg & Piquero, 2010 (T)
Steiner & Hemmens, (2003)
Stevens, (2014) (T)
Steward-Lindsey, (2006)
Suffredini, (1994)
Sulok, (2007)
Sullivan, (2001)
Swanson, (2018)
Szymanski, (1996), (1998), (2002), (2007), (2008), (2009), (2010b), (2011)
Tanenhaus, (2000), (2013)
Tanenhaus & Drizin, (2002)
Tang & Nunez, (2003) (T)
Tanner, (2000)
Tashea & Passarella, (2014) (T)
Taylor-Thompson, (2014)
Teji & Males, (2011)
Teitelbaum, (1991)
Thomas & Bilchik, (1985)
Thomas & Wilson, (2018)
Torbet, Gable, Hurst IV, Montgomery, Szymanski & Thomas, (1996).
Torbet, Griffin, Hurst & MacKenzie, (2000).
Torbet & Szymanski, (1998)
Traver, (2000)
Troilo, (2018)

continued on following page

Table 38a. Continued

Trulson, Caudill, Belshaw & DeLisi, (2011)	White, Frazier, & Lanza-Kaduce, (1999)
Ullman, (2000)	Wilbourn, (1996)
Urbina, (2005)	Williams, E.J., (2022)
Urbina & White, (2009)	Williams, J. (2015)
Vandervort & Ladd, (2001)	Winner, Lanza-Kaduce, Bishop & Frazier, (1997)
Vannella, (2006)	Witt, (2003)
Van Vleet, (1999)	Wizner, (1984), (1995)
Vargas, (2014)	Woolard, Fondacaro, & Slobogin, (2001)
Verrecchia, (2011)	Wright, Muddle, Rountree, & Rich, (2019) (T)
Vladimer, (1982)	Wu, (2000)
Walker, (2021)	Yellen, (1996)
Ward, (2003)	Young, (1981)
Washburn, Teplin, Voss, Simon, Abram, & McClelland, (2008)	Young, (2000) (T)
Watkins, (1998)	Young, & Gainsborough, (2000)
Weijers, & Grisso, (2009)	Zane, Welsh, & Drakulich, (2016)
Welch et al., (2019)	Ziedenberg, (T), (2011)
	Zimring, (1981), (1998a), (1999)

(T)* Indicates Child/Kid/Adult appears as the title of the work.

*Table 38b. Legislative or Statutory Exclusion or Transfer or Waiver (or Mandatory/Automatic Transfer) **

Abeyratne, & Sizemore, (1999)
Abrams, (2013)
Acton, (1996)
Adams & Addie, (2009), (2010), (2011), (2012)
Allard & Young, (2002)
Allen, K.L., (2012)
Alliance, (2003)
Angell, (2004)
Applegate & Davis, (2006)
Arteaga, (2002)
Arya, (2011)
Augustyn & Loughran, (2017)
Augustyn & McGloin, (2018)
Backstrom & Walker, (2006)
Baquedano, (2015)
Baruwa, (2013)
Beale, (2009)
Beatty, (1995)
Benekos, & Merlo, (2008), (2019)
Beresford, (2000)
Bishop, (2000), (2009)
Bishop & Feld, (2012)
Bishop, Frazier, Lanza-Kaduce, & Winner, (1996)
Bishop & Frazier, (1991), (2000)
Bishop, & Frazier, Lanza-Kaduce, Winner, (1996)
Bishop, Lanza-Kaduce & Frazier, (1998)
Blumhardt, (2000)
Bove, (1991)
Brandau, (2004)
Brannen et al., (2006)
Breen & Mills, (2015)
Bryson & Peck, (2020)
Burgess-Proctor et al., (2008)
Burrow, (2005), (2008a), (2008b)
Burrow & Lowery, (2015)
Butts, (2000)
Butts, Coggeshall, Gouvis, Mears, Travis, Waul, & White, (2002)
Butts & Harrell, (1998)
Butts & Mears, (2001)
Butts & Mitchell, (2000)
Carroll, (2009)
Carter, (2006)
Cassady, (2017)
Cauffman & Steinberg, (2000)
Cellucci et al., (2001)
CFYJ, (2014)
Chamberlin, (2000)
Champion & Mays, (1991)
Cintron, (1996)
Clarke, C.A., (2005)
Clarke, E. E., (1996)
Clement, (1997)
Cloherty, (1992)
Cohn & Mialson, (2008)
Cooper & Urban, (2012)
Coupet, (2000)
Cross, (1998)
D'Ambra, (1997)
Danziger, (2003)
Davis, Irvine, & Ziedenberg, (2014)
Dawson, (2000)
DeFrances, (2002)
DeFrances & Strom, (1997)
Deitch & Arya, (2014)
Deitch et al., (2009)
DeJong & Merrill, (2001)
Dodge, (2000)
Dugan, (1998)
Drake, (2014)
Drinan, (2014)
Drizin & Tanenhaus, (2002)
Dunn, (2008)
Evans, (1992)
Fagan, (1990), (1991), (2008), (2010)
Fagan, Forst, & Vivona, (1987b)
Fagan, Kupchik, & Liberman, (2007)
Fagan & Zimring, (2000)

continued on following page

Table 38b. Continued

Federle, (1996), (1999), (2016)
Feld, (1978), (1983), (1980), (1981), (1983), (1984b), (1987), (1989), (1991), (1993a), (1993b), (1995), (1997), (1998), (1999a), (2000), (2001), (2003a), (2003b), (2004), (2007a), (2007b), (2008), (2013a), (2017a), (2017b)
Feld & Bishop, (2012)
Flesch, (2004)
Flynn, (2008)
Forst & Blomquist, (1991)
Fowler & Kurlychek, (2018)
Fritsch & Hemmens, (1995), (1996)
Frost Clausel & Bonnie, (2000)
Gallini, (2008)
Garberg & Libkuman, (2009)
Gardner & Lanza-Kaduce, (2015)
Gasper & Katkin, (1980)
Geraghty, D., (2016)
Gimbel, (2015)
Glynn, (1997)
Gordon, (1999)
Gray, (2007)
Greathouse et al., (2011)
Green, (2005)
Griffin, (2003), 2008), (2012)
Griffin et al., (1998), (2011)
Grisso, (1997), (2010)
Grundfest et al., (1981)
Gulstad, (2016)
Guttman, (1995)
Hager, (1995)
Hahn et al., (2007)
Hamack, (2014)
Hamilton et al., (2007)
Hannan, (2008)
Harris & Allen, (2003)
Harshbarger, & Keshian, (1995)
Hartney, (2006)
Heilbrun, Leheny, Thomas, & Huneycutt, (1997)
Henderson, (2000)

Henning, (2013)
Hirase, (1992)
HLRA, (2002)
Hockenberry, (2021)
Hockenberry & Puzzanchera, (2014a), (2014b)
Hoeffel, (2013)
Hofacket, (2002)
Hogan, (1974)
Holtzman, (2004)
Horowitz, (2000)
Howell, (1996)
Howell et al., (2013)
Hughes, (2017)
Hunt, (1998)
Hurst, III, (1999)
Jackson & Pabon, (2000)
Jan, Ball, & Walsh, (2008)
Jensen, (1994)
Jensen & Metsger, (1994)
Johnson, Banister, & Alm, (2004)
Johnson, Lanza-Kaduce, & Woolard, (2011)
Johnson & Kurlychek, (2012)
Jordan, (2005), (2006)
Jordan & Freiburger, (2010)
Jordan & Maroun, (2016)
Jordan & Myers, (2007), (2011)
Jordan & McNeal, (2016)
Juszkiewicz, (2000)
Kaasa et al., (2018)
Kimbrell, (2015)
King, C., (2018)
King, R., (2006)
Klein, (1998)
Knox, (2009)
Kozich, (1980)
Kruh & Brodsky, (1997)
Kukino, (2014)
Kumli, (2002)
Kupchik, (2003a), (2003b), (2006a), (2006b)

continued on following page

Table 38b. Continued

Kupchik, Fagan & Liberman, (2003)
Kurlychek, (2010), (2016)
Kurlychek & Johnson, (2004)
Kurlychek & Johnson, (2010)
Lane, Lanza-Kaduce, Frazier, & Bishop, (2002)
Langemo, (2004)
Lanza-Kaduce, Bishop, Frazier & Winner, (1996)
Lanza-Kaduce, Frazier & Bishop, (1999)
Lanza-Kaduce, Frazier, Lane & Bishop, (2002)
Law et al., (2019)
Leeper, (1991)
Lehmann, Chiricos, & Bales, (2017)
Lehmann & Kobie, (2021)
Lehmann, Pickett, Ryon, & Kosloski, (2019)
Leistico & Salekin, (2003)
Lemmon, Austin, Verrecchia, & Fetzer, (2005)
Lemmon, Sontheimer, & Saylor, (1991)
Linares & Bunton, (2010)
Liwanga & Ibe, (2021)
Lockwood, (2020)
Logan, (1998)
Loughran et al., (2010)
Lynn-Whaley & Russi, (2011)
Mahoney, (1991)
Mallett, (2007)
Marczyk et al., (2005)
Maroney, (2009)
Marrus & Rosenberg (2005)
Martin, (1992)
Massey, (2005)
May, (1998)
Mays & Gregware, (1996)
McCarthy, (1994)
McCurdy-Jackson, (2011)
McGowan et al., (2007)
McLatchey, (1999)
McNulty, (1996)
Means, Heller, & Janofsky, (2012)
Mears, (2003)

Mears & Field, (2000)
Mears, Hay, Gertz & Mancini, (2007)
Merlo & Benekos, (2010)
Merlo, Benekos, & Cook, (1997a), (1997b), (1999)
Miller, N., (1995)
Miner-Romanoff, (2014)
Mlyniec, (1976)
Mole & White, (2005)
Mulvey & Schubert, (2012)
Myers, (2001), (2003a), (2003b), (2005)
Myers & Kiehl, (2001)
NASEM, (2019)
NDAA, (2002)
NeMoyer, (2017)
Nguyen, (2016)
Noon, (1994)
Notes, (2002)
NRC, (2013)
OJJ, (1999)
OJJDP, (2018), (2020)
Olson, (2004)
Otto & Borum, (2004)
Paganelli, (2007)
Park, (2007)
Pegg, (2015)
Penney & Moretti, (2005)
Perry, (2006)
PHR, (2007)
Pine, (1996)
Podkopacz & Feld, (1995), (1996), (2001)
Polachek, (2008)
Pollitt, (2004)
Prescott, (2000)
Prochaska, (2018)
Puzzanchera, Hockenberry, & Sickmund, (2022)
Quinn, (2015)
Rainville, (2008)
Rainville & Smith, (2003)
Redding, (1997), (1999), (2003), (2008), (2010), (2016)

continued on following page

Table 38b. Continued

Redding & Howell, (2000)	Shook, (2004), (2005), (2014)
Redding & Mrozoski, (2005)	Shook & Sarri, (2008) (T)
Reidy et al., (2018)	Sickmund, (1994), (2003)
Riggs Romaine, Goldstein, Hunt, & DeMatteo, (2011)	Singer, (1993), (1994), (1996a), (1996b), (2003)
Risler et al, (1998)	Singer, Fagan & Liberman, (2000)
Robertson, Gardner, Haynes, & Gresham, (2019)	Singer & McDowall, (1988)
Rodriguez, (2003)	Slaten, (2003)
Romaine, (2010)	Slobogin, (1999)
Rose, (2002)	Smith, C. K., (2013)
Rosenberg, (2000)	Snyder & Hutzler, (1981)
Rossum, (1995)	Snyder & Sickmund, (1995), (1999), (2006)
Rubin, (2006)	Snyder et al., (2000)
Ruddell & Mays, (2012)	Sobol, (2022)
Ruddell et al., (1998)	Soler, (2010)
Rudman, Hartstone, Fagan, & Moore, (1986)	Sorrentino & Olsen, (1977)
Rudof, (1998)	Soung, (2011)
Ryan, (2012)	Spring, (1998)
Sabo, (1996)	Sridharan, Greenfield, & Blakley, (2004)
Salekin, (2002)	Stafford, (2013)
Salekin et al., (2001)	Stalans & Henry, (1994)
Salekin et al., (2002)	Stamm, (1973)
Samuelson, (2010)	Steinberg, (2000), (2009)
Sarri & Shook, (2005)	Steinberg & Cauffman, (2000), (2001)
Schaefer & Uggen, (2016)	Steiner, (2005), (2009)
Schetky, (2003)	Steiner & Hemmens, (2003)
Schiraldi & Ziedenberg, (1999)	Steiner, Hemmens, & Bell (2006)
Schornhorst, (1968)	Steiner & Wright, (2006)
Schubert et al., (2010)	Stevens, (2014)
Scialabba, (2016)	Sullivan, (2001)
Scism, (2019)	Sulok, (2007)
Scott, (2000), (2013a), (2013b)	Swanson, (2018)
Scott & Grisso, (1997), (2005)	Tanenhaus & Drizin, (2002)
Scott & Steinberg, (2003), (2008), (2010)	Tang & Nunez, (2003)
Sellers & Arrigo, (2009)	Taylor, (2015)
Sewell, (2009)	Teigen, (2021)
Sharlein, (2018)	Thomas, (2016)
Sheffer, (1995)	Thomas & Wilson, (2018)
Shelden & Hussong, (2003)	Torbet et al., (1996)
Shiller, (2006)	Torbet et al., (2000)

continued on following page

Table 38b. Continued

Torbet & Szymanski, (1998)	Weijers & Grisso, (2009)
Traver, (2000)	Weston, (2016)
Ullman, (2000)	White, Frazier, & Lanza-Kaduce, (1999)
Urbina, (2005)	Whitebread & Batey, (1977)
Urbina & White, (2009)	Wilbourn, (1996)
Valliere, (1986)	Williams, E.J., (2022)
Vannella, (2006)	Witt, (2003)
Van Vleet, (1999)	Wizner, (1984)
Vargas, (2014)	Woolard, Fondacaro, & Slobogin, (2001)
Verrecchia, (2003), (2011)	Wright et al., (2019)
Visser, (2011)	Yellen, (1996)
Vladimer, (1982)	Young, (1981)
Walker, (2021)	Young, & Gainsborough, (2000)
Wallance, (1975)	Zane, (2017), (2018)
Ward, (2003)	Zane, Welsh, & Drakulich, (2016)
Washburn et al., (2008)	Zane, Welsh, & Mears, (2016)
Watkins, (1998)	Zimring, (1981), (2014)

*A few of the sources cited in section (B), above, are not included in section (C), below. They deserve honorary membership in section (C), nevertheless. The reason they are omitted from mention in section (C) is that only 2 forms of transfer (JT and OE) were reviewed in the article (ignoring DF) and were thus not placed in the category of identifying three sources of transfer.

Table 38c. Offense Exclusion is a Form of Transfer Separate from Prosecutorial

Abeyratne, & Sizemore, (1999)
Abrams, (2013)
Acton, (1996)
Adams & Addie, (2009), (2010), (2011), (2012)
Ainsworth, (1995)
Allard & Young, (2002)
Allen, K.L., (2012)
Alliance, (2003)
Angell, (2004)
Arteaga, (2002)
Arthur & Schwartz, (1993)
Arya, (2010), (2011)
Augustyn & Loughran, (2017)
Augustyn & McGloin, (2018)
Backstrom & Walker, (2006)
Baquedano, (2015)
Baruwa, (2013)
Beale, (2009)
Benekos & Merlo, (2008), (2019)
Beresford, (2000)
Bishop, (2000), (2009)
Bishop & Feld, (2012)
Bishop & Frazier, (1991), (2000)
Bishop, & Frazier, Lanza-Kaduce, Winner, (1996)
Bishop, Lanza-Kaduce & Frazier, (1998)
Blumhardt, (2000)
Bove, (1991)
Brandau, (2004)
Brannen et al., (2006)
Breen & Mills, (2015)
Brink, (2003-04)
Bryson & Peck, (2020)
Burgess-Proctor et al., (2008)
Burrow, (2005), (2008a), (2008b)
Butts, (1997), (2000)
Butts et al., (2002)
Butts & Harrell, (1998)
Butts & Mears, (2001)
Butts & Mitchell, (2000)

Carroll, (2009)
Carter, (2006)
Cassady, (2017)
Cauffman & Steinberg, (2000)
Cellucci et al., (2001)
CFYJ, (2014)
Chamberlin, (2000)
Cintron, (1996)
Clarke, C.A., (2005)
Clement, (1997)
Cloherty, (1992)
Cohn & Mialson, (2008)
Cooper & Urban, (2012)
Coupet, (2000)
Dale, (2004)
D'Ambra, (1997)
Davis, (2000)
Davis & Ziedenberg, (2014)
Dawson, (2000)
DeFrances, (2002)
DeFrances & Strom, (1997)
Deitch & Arya, (2014)
Deitch et al., (2009)
Drake, (2014)
Drinan, (2016)
Drizin & Tanenhaus, (2002)
Dugan, (1998)
Dunn, (2008)
Evans, (1992)
Fagan, (1990), (1991), (2008), (2010)
Fagan & Deschenes, (1990)
Fagan, Forst, & Vivona, (1987b)
Fagan & Hartstone, (1984)
Fagan, Kupchik, & Liberman, (2007)
Fagan & Zimring, (2000)
Federle, (1996), (1999), (2016)
Feiler & Sheley, (1999)

continued on following page

Table 38c. Continued

Feld, (1978), (1980), (1981), (1983), (1987), (1989), (1993a), (1995), (1997), (1998), (1999a), (2000), (2001), (2003a), (2003b), (2004), (2007a), (2007b), (2008), (2013a), (2017a),
(2017b)
Feld & Bishop, (2012)
Flesch, (2004)
Flynn, (2008)
Forst & Blomquist, (1991)
Fowler & Kurlychek, (2018)
Fritsch & Hemmens, (1995), (1996)
Frost Clausel & Bonnie, (2000)
Gallini, (2008)
Garberg & Libkuman, (2009)
Gardner & Lanza-Kaduce, (2015)
Garner, (1973)
Gasper & Katkin, (1980)
Gimbel, (2015)
Glynn, (1997)
Gordon, (1999)
Gray, (2007)
Greathouse et al., (2011)
Green, (2005)
Griffin, (2003), (2008), (2012)
Griffin et al., (1998), (2011)
Grisso, (1997)
Grundfest et al., (1981)
Gulstad, (2016)
Guttman, (1995)
Hager, (1995)
Hamack, (2014)
Hamilton et al., (2007)
Hamparian et al., (1982)
Hannan, (2008)
Harris & Allen, (2003)
Harshbarger, & Keshian, (1995)
Hartney, (2006)
Heilbrun, Leheny, Thomas, & Huneycutt, (1997)
Henderson, (2000)
Henning, (2013)

Hess et al., (2010)
Hirase, (1992)
HLRA, (2002)
Hockenberry, (2021)
Hockenberry & Puzzanchera, (2014a), (2014b), (2019)
Hoeffel, (2013)
Hofacket, (2002)
Hogan, (1974)
Holtzman, (2004)
Hornback, (2021)
Horowitz, (2000)
Howell, (1996)
Howell et al., (2013)
Hughes, (2017)
Hurst, III, (1999)
Jackson & Pabon, (2000)
Jan, Ball, & Walsh, (2008)
Jensen, (1994)
Johnson, Banister, & Alm, (2004)
Johnson & Kurlychek, (2012)
Johnson, Lanza-Kaduce, & Woolard, (2011)
Jordan, (2005), (2006)
Jordan & Freiburger, (2010)
Jordan & Maroun, (2016)
Jordan & McNeal, (2016)
Jordan & Myers, (2007)
Juszkiewicz, (2000)
Kaasa et al., (2018)
Kimbrell, (2015)
King, C., (2018)
King, R., (2006)
Klein, (1998)
Knox, (2009)
Kruh & Brodsky, (1997)
Kukino, (2014)
Kumli, (2002)
Kupchik, (2003b), (2006a)
Kupchik, Fagan & Liberman, (2003)
Kurlychek, (2016)

continued on following page

Table 38c. Continued

Kurlychek & Johnson, (2004)
Kurlychek & Johnson, (2010)
Lane et al., (2002)
Langemo, (2004)
Lanza-Kaduce, Bishop, Frazier & Winner, (1996)
Lanza-Kaduce, Frazier & Bishop, (1999)
Lanza-Kaduce, Frazier, Lane & Bishop, (2002)
Law et al., (2019)
Leeper, (1991)
Lehmann, Chiricos, & Bales, (2017)
Lehmann & Kobie, (2021)
Lehmann, Pickett, Ryon & Kosloski, (2019)
Leistico & Salekin, (2003)
Lemmon, Austin, Verrecchia, & Fetzer, (2005)
Lemmon, Sontheimer, & Saylor, (1991)
Linares & Bunton, (2010)
Liwanga & Ibe, (2021)
Lockwood, (2020)
Loeffler & Grunwald, (2015)
Logan, (1998)
Loughran et al., (2010)
Lynn-Whaley & Russi, (2011)
Lyons, (2011)
Mallett, (2007)
Marczyk et al., (2005)
Maroney, (2009)
Marrus & Rosenberg (2005)
Martin, (1992)
Massey, (2005)
Mathias, DeMuro, & Allison, (1984)
McCarthy, (1994)
McCurdy-Jackson, (2011)
McGowan et al., (2007)
McLatchey, (1999)
McNulty, (1996)
Means, Heller, & Janofsky, (2012)
Mears, (2003)
Mears & Field, (2000)
Mears, Hay, Gertz, & Mancini, (2007)

Merlo & Benekos, (2010)
Merlo, Benekos, & Cook, (1997a), (1997b), (1999)
Miller, N., (1995)
Mole & White, (2005)
Mulvey & Schubert, (2012)
Myers, (2003a), (2003b)
Myers & Kiehl, (2001)
Myers et al., (2005), (2011)
NASEM, (2019)
NDAA, (2002)
NeMoyer, (2017)
Nguyen, (2016)
Noon, (1994)
Notes, (2002)
NRC. (2013)
OJJ, (1999)
OJJDP, (2018), (2020)
Oliver, (2006)
Olson, (2004)
Otto & Borum, (2004)
Parent, Dunworth, McDonald & Rhodes, (1997)
Park, (2007)
Pegg, (2015)
Penney & Moretti, (2005)
Perry, (2006)
PHR, (2007)
Pine, (1996)
Podkopacz & Feld, (1995), (1996), (2001)
Polachek, (2008)
Pollitt, (2004)
Poulos & Orchowsky, (1994)
Prescott, (2000)
Prochaska, (2018)
Puzzanchera & Addie, (2014)
Puzzanchera, Hockenberry, & Sickmund, (2022)
Rainville, (2008)
Rainville & Smith, (2003)
Redding, (1997), (1999), (2003), (2005), (2008), (2010), (2016)

continued on following page

Table 38c. Continued

Redding & Fuller, (2004)
Redding & Howell, (2000)
Redding & Mrozoski, (2005)
Reidy et al., (2018)
Riggs Romaine, Goldstein, Hunt, & DeMatteo, (2011).
Robertson et al., (2019)
Romaine, (2010)
Rose, (2002)
Rossum, (1995)
Rovner, (2016)
Rubin, (2006)
Ruddell & Mays, (2012)
Ruddell et al., (1998)
Rudman, Hartstone, Fagan, & Moore, (1986)
Rudof, (1998)
Ryan, (2012)
Sabo, (1996)
Salekin, (2002)
Salekin et al., (2001)
Salekin et al., (2002)
Samuelson, (2010)
Sarri & Shook, (2005)
Schaefer & Uggen, (2016)
Schetky, (2003)
Schiraldi & Soler, (1998)
Schiraldi & Ziedenberg, (1999)
Schornhorst, (1968)
Schubert et al., (2010)
Scialabba, (2016)
Scism, (2019)
Scott, (2000), (2013a)
Sewell, (2009)
Shiller, (2006)
Shook, (2004), (2005), (2013), (2014)
Sickmund, (1994), (2003)
Singer, (1996a), (1996b), (2003)
Singer & McDowall, (1988)
Slaten, (2003)
Slobogin, (1999)
Slobogin, (2013)
Smith, A., (1995)
Smith, C. K., (2013)
Snyder, (2012)
Snyder & Hutzler, (1981)
Snyder & Sickmund, (1995), (1999), (2006)
Snyder et al., (2000)
Soler, (2010)
Sorrentino & Olsen, (1977)
Soung, (2011)
Spring, (1998)
Sridharan, Greenfield, & Blakley, (2004)
Stafford, (2013)
Stahl, (1999)
Stamm, (1973)
Steinberg, (2000), (2009)
Steinberg & Cauffman, (2000), (2001)
Steiner, (2009)
Steiner & Hemmens, (2003)
Steiner, Hemmens, & Bell (2006)
Steiner & Wright, (2006).
Stolzenberg & D'Alessio, (2009)
Sullivan, (2001)
Sulok, (2007)
Swanson, (2018)
Tanenhaus & Drizin, (2002)
Tang & Nunez, (2003)
Taylor, (2015)
Teigen, (2021)
Thomas, (2016)
Thomas & Wilson, (2018)
Torbet et al., (1996)
Torbet et al., (2000)
Torbet & Szymanski, (1998)
Traver, (2000)
Troilo, (2018)
Ullman, (2000)
Urbina, (2005)
Urbina & White, (2009)

continued on following page

Table 38c. Continued

Valliere, (1986)
Vannella, (2006)
Vargas, (2014)
Visser, (2011)
Vladimer, (1982)
Walker, (2021)
Wallance, (1975)
Ward, (2003)
Washburn et al., (2008)
Watkins, (1998)
Weijers & Grisso, (2009)
Weston, (2016)
White, Frazier, & Lanza-Kaduce, (1999)
Whitebread & Batey, (1977)
Whitehead & Lab, (1996)

Wilbourn, (1996)
Williams, E.J., (2022)
Witt, (2003)
Wizner, (1984)
Wright et al., (2019)
Yellen, (1996)
Young, (1981)
Young, (2000)
Young, & Gainsborough, (2000)
Zane, (2017), (2018)
Zane, Welsh, & Drakulich, (2016)
Zane, Welsh, & Mears, (2016)
Ziedenberg, (2011)
Zimring, (2000b), (2010), (2014)

*Table 38d. Offense Exclusion (OE) is Mandatory/Automatic/Nondiscretionary**

Abeyratne, & Sizemore, (1999)
Abrams, (2013)
Acton, (1996)
Adams & Addie, (2009), (2010), (2011), (2012)
Ainsworth, (1991), (1995)
Allard & Young, (2002)
Allen, F.A., (2000)
Allen, K.L. (2012)
Alliance, (2003)
Angell, (2004)
Applegate & Davis, (2006)
Applegate et al., (2009)
Arteaga, (2002)
Arya, (2010), (2011)
Augustyn & Loughran, (2017)
Augustyn & McGloin, (2018)
Backstrom & Walker, (2006)
Baird & Samuels, (1996)
Baquedano, (2015)
Beale, (2009)
Beatty, (1995)
Benekos & Merlo, (2008), (2019)
Beresford, (2000)
Beschle, (1999)
Bishop, (2000), (2009)
Blumhardt, (2000)
Bove, (1991)
Braithwaite & Shore, (1981)
Brandau, (2004)
Brannen et al., (2006)
Breen & Mills, (2015)
Brink, (2003-04)
Bryson & Peck, (2020)
Burgess-Proctor et al., (2008)
Burrow, (2005), (2008a)
Burrow & Lowery (2015)
Butts, (1997), (2000)
Butts et al., (2002)
Butts & Harrell, (1998)
Butts & Mears, (2001)
Butts & Mitchell, (2000)
Carter, (2006)
Cassady, (2017)
Cauffman, (2012)
Cauffman et al., (2018)
Cellucci et al., (2001)
CFYJ, (2014)
Chamberlin, (2000)
Champion, (1989)
Cintron, (1996)
Clarke, C.A., (2005)
Clarke, E. E., (1996)
Clarke & Kooy, (n.d.)
Clement, (1997)
Cohen et al., (2016)
Cohn & Mialson, (2008)
Cooper & Urban, (2012)
Coupet, (2000)
Cross, (1998)
D'Ambra, (1997)
Davis, (2000)
Davis & Ziedenberg, (2014)
Dawson, (2000)
Deitch & Arya, (2014)
Deitch et al., (2009)
DeJong & Merrill, (2001)
Dodge, (2000)
Dugan, (1998)
Drake, (2014)
Drinan, (2014), (2016)
Drizin & Tanenhaus, (2002)
Dunn, (2008)
Evans, (1992)
Fagan, (2008), (2010)
Fagan & Deschenes, (1990)
Fagan, Forst, & Vivona, (1987b)
Fagan, Piper, & Forst, (1986)
Federle, (2016)

continued on following page

Table 38d. Continued

Feiler & Sheley, (1999)
Feld, (1978), (1980), (1981), (1983), (1984b), (1987), (1989), (1991), (1993a), (1993b), (1995), (1997), (1998), (1999b), (2000), (2003a), (2003b), (2004), (2007b), (2013a)
Feld & Bishop, (2012)
Flesch, (2004)
Flynn, (2008)
Frost Clausel & Bonnie, (2000)
Fritsch & Hemmens, (1995), (1996)
Gallini, (2008)
Garberg & Libkuman, (2009)
Gardner & Lanza-Kaduce, (2015)
Gasper & Katkin, (1980)
Geraghty, D., (2016)
Geraghty, T., (1997)
Geraghty & Drizin, (1998)
Giardino, (1996)
Gimbel, (2015)
Glynn, (1997)
Gordon, (1999)
Gourdie, (2021)
Gray, (2007)
Greathouse et al., (2011)
Green, (2005)
Greene, Duke, & Woody, (2017)
Griffin, (2003), (2008), (2012)
Griffin et al., (1998), (2011)
Grisso, (1996), (1997), (2010)
Grundfest et al., (1981)
Gulstad, (2016)
Guttman, (1995)
Hahn et al., (2007)
Hamack, (2014)
Hamilton et al., (2007)
Hannan, (2008)
Harris & Allen, (2003)
Harshbarger, & Keshian, (1995)
Hartinger-Saunders, (2008)
Hartney, (2006)

Heilbrun, Leheny, Thomas, & Huneycutt, (1997)
Henning, (2013)
Herkal, (1999)
Hess et al., (2010)
Hirase, (1992)
HLRA, (2002)
Hockenberry, (2021)
Hockenberry & Puzzanchera, (2014a)
Hoeffel, (2013)
Hofacket, (2002)
Hogan, (1974)
Holtzman, (2004)
Hornback, (2021)
Horowitz, (2000)
Howell, (1996)
Howell et al., (2017)
Hughes, (2017)
Hunt, (1998)
Hurst, III, (1999)
Jackson & Pabon, (2000)
Jensen, (1994)
Jensen & Metsger, (1994)
Jenson, Potter, & Howard, (2001)
Johnson & Kurlychek, (2012)
Jordan, (2005), (2006)
Jordan & Freiburger, (2010)
Jordan & McNeal, (2016)
Jordan & Myers, (2007), (2011)
Juszkiewicz, (2000)
Kaasa et al., (2018)
Keenan et al., (2015)
Kimbrell, (2015)
King, C., (2018)
King, R., (2006)
Klein, (1998)
Knox, (2009)
Kozich, (1980)
Kruh & Brodsky, (1997)
Kukino, (2014)

continued on following page

Table 38d. Continued

Kumli, (2002)
Kupchik, (2003a), (2003b), (2006a)
Kupchik, Fagan & Liberman, (2003)
Kurlychek & Johnson, (2010)
Lane et al., (2002)
Langemo, (2004)
Lanza-Kaduce, Bishop, Frazier, & Winner, (1996)
Lanza-Kaduce, Frazier, Lane & Bishop, (2002)
Law et al., (2019)
Leeper, (1999)
Lehmann, Chiricos, & Bales, (2017)
Lehmann, Pickett, Ryon & Kosloski, (2019)
Leistico & Salekin, (2003)
Lemmon, Austin, Verrecchia, & Fetzer, (2005)
Lin et al., (1994)
Linares & Bunton, (2010)
Liwanga & Ibe, (2021)
Loeffler & Grunwald, (2015)
Logan, (1998)
Loughran et al., (2010)
Lynn-Whaley & Russi, (2011)
Lyons, (2011)
Mallett, (2007)
Marczyk et al., (2005)
Maroney, (2009), (2011)
Marrus & Rosenberg (2005)
Massey, (2005)
May, (1998)
McCurdy-Jackson, (2011)
McGowan et al., (2007)
McLatchey, (1999)
McNulty, (1996)
Means, Heller, & Janofsky, (2012)
Mears & Field, (2000)
Merlo & Benekos, (2010)
Merlo, Benekos, & Cook, (1997a), (1997b), (1999)
Miller, N., (1995)
Miner-Romanoff, (2014)
Mole & White, (2005)
Moore, (2007)
Mulvey & Schubert, (2012)
Myers, (2003b)
Myers & Kiehl, (2001)
NASEM, (2019)
NDAA, (2002)
Nguyen, (2016)
Noon, (1994)
Notes, (2002)
NRC, (2013)
Nunez et al., (2007)
OJJ, (1999)
OJJDP, (2018), (2020)
Oliver, (2006)
Olson, (2004)
Osbun & Rode, (1984)
Otto & Borum, (2004)
Paganelli (2007)
Parent, Dunworth, McDonald & Rhodes, (1997)
Park, (2007)
Penney & Moretti, (2005)
PHR, (2007)
Pine, (1996)
Polachek, (2008)
Pollitt, (2004)
Prescott, (2000)
Prochaska, (2018)
Puzzanchera, (2000), (2001), (2003)
Puzzanchera & Addie, (2014)
Puzzanchera, Hockenberry, & Sickmund, (2022)
Rainville, (2008)
Rainville & Smith, (2003)
Redding, (1997), (1999), (2003), (2005), (2008), (2010), (2016)
Redding, & Fuller, (2004)
Redding & Howell, (2000)
Redding & Mrozoski, (2005)
Reidy et al., (2018)
Risler et al., (1998)

continued on following page

Table 38d. Continued

Robertson et al., (2019)	Singer, (1993), (1994), (2003)
Rodriguez, (2003)	Singer, Fagan & Liberman, (2000)
Romaine, (2010)	Singer & McDowall, (1988)
Rose, (2002)	Slaten, (2003)
Rosenberg, (2000)	Slobogin, (1999)
Rossum, (1995)	Slobogin, (2013)
Rovner, (2016)	Smallheer, (1999)
Roysher & Edelman, (1981)	Smith, A., (1995)
Rubin, (2006)	Smith, C.K., (2013)
Ruddell & Mays, (2012)	Snyder, (2012)
Ruddell et al., (1998)	Snyder et al., (2000)
Rudman, Hartstone, Fagan, & Moore, (1996)	Snyder & Sickmund, (2006)
Ryan, (2012)	Sobol, (2022)
Sabo, (1996)	Soler, (2010)
Salekin, (2002)	Sorrentino & Olsen, (1997)
Salekin et al., (2001)	Soung, (2011)
Salekin et al., (2002)	Spring, (1998)
Samuelson, (2010)	Springer, (1991)
Sarri & Shook, (2005)	Sridharan, Greenfield, & Blakley, (2004)
Schaefer & Uggen, (2016)	Stafford, (2013)
Schetky, (2003)	Stahl, (1999)
Schiraldi & Soler, (1998)	Stalans & Henry, (1994)
Schiraldi & Ziedenberg, (1999)	Stamm, (1973)
Schubert et al., (2010)	Steinberg, (2000), (2009)
Schulhofer, (1997)	Steinberg & Cauffman, (2001)
Scialabba, (2016)	Steiner, (2009)
Scism, (2019)	Steiner & Hemmens, (2003)
Scott, (2000), (2013a), (2013b)	Steiner, Hemmens, & Bell (2006)
Scott & Grisso, (1997), (2005)	Steiner & Wright, (2006)
Scott, Grisso, Levick, & Steinberg, (2016)	Sullivan, (2001)
Scott, Reppucci, & Woolard, (1995)	Sulok, (2007)
Scott & Steinberg, (2003), (2008), (2010)	Swanson, (2018)
Sellers & Arrigo, (2009)	Tanenhaus & Drizin, (2002)
Sewell, (2009)	Tang & Nunez, (2003)
Sheffer, (1995)	Tashea & Passarella, (2014)
Shelden & Hussong, (2003)	Tate, Reppucci, & Mulvey, (1995)
Shiller, (2006)	Taylor-Thompson, (2014)
Shook, (2004), (2005)	Teigen, (2021)
Sickmund, (2003)	Thomas, (2016)

continued on following page

Table 38d. Continued

Thomas & Wilson, (2018)
Torbet et al, (1996)
Torbet et al., (2000)
Torbet & Szymanski, (1998)
Traver, (2000)
Troilo, (2018)
Ullman, (2000)
Urbina, (2005)
Urbina & White, (2009)
Vandervort & Ladd, (2001)
Vannella, (2006)
Van Vleet, (1999)
Verrecchia, (2003), (2011)
Visser, (2011)
Vitiello, (1976)
Walker, (2021)

Ward, (2003)
Washburn et al., (2008)
White, Frazier, & Lanza-Kaduce, (1999)
Whitebread & Batey, (1977), (1981)
Wilbourn, (1996)
Williams, E.J., (2022)
Witt, (2003)
Wizner, (1984)
Wright et al., (2019)
Young, (1981)
Young, (2000)
Young, & Gainsborough, (2000)
Zane, (2017), (2018)
Zane, Welsh, & Drakulich, (2016)
Zane, Welsh, & Mears, (2016)
Zimring, (1991), (1998a), (1998b), (2000b), (2010)

*All sources cited in Section (D), above, likely believe OE is *both* categorical, etc., *and* not a matter of transfer/PT, and likely deserve to be included in Sections (E) and (G), respectively, below. Those not included did not explicitly mention categorical and/or did not touch upon how OE juveniles arrived in CC.

Table 38e. Offense Exclusion = no Individualization; is: Categorical/ "Wholesale"/ Overinclusive

Adams & Addie, (2009), (2010), (2011), (2012)	Frost Clausel & Bonnie, (2000)
Acton, (1996)	Glynn, (1997)
Allen, K.L., (2012)	Gordon, (1999)
Alliance, (2003)	Gray, (2007)
Angell, (2004)	Griffin et al., (1998), (2011)
Arya, (2010)	Grundfest et al., (1981)
Baquedano, (2015)	Guttman, (1995)
Baruwa, (2013)	Hamilton et al., (2007)
Benekos & Merlo, (2019)	Hannan, (2008)
Beresford, (2000)	Harshbarger, & Keshian, (1995)
Bishop, (2000)	Hirase, (1992)
Bishop & Frazier, (2000)	HLRA, (2002)
Blumhardt, (2000)	Hockenberry & Puzzanchera, (2014a)
Brandau, (2004)	Hoeffel, (2013)
Brannen et al., (2006)	Hogan, (1974)
Breen & Mills, (2015)	Hornback, (2021)
Burgess-Proctor et al., (2008)	Horowitz, (2000)
Burrow, (2005), (2008a)	Hurst, III, (1999)
Cassady, (2017)	Jordan, (2005)
Cintron, (1996)	Kaasa et al., (2018)
Clarke, C.A., (2005)	Klein, (1998)
Clarke & Kooy, (n.d.)	Kukino, (2014)
Cohen et al., (2016)	Kupchik, (2003b), (2006a)
D'Ambra, (1997)	Langemo, (2004)
Danziger, (2003)	Lin et al., (1994)
Davis, (2000)	Linares & Bunton, (2010)
Dawson, (2000)	Maroney, (2009), (2011)
Deitch & Arya, (2014)	Marrus & Rosenberg (2005)
Deitch et al., (2009)	McLatchey, (1999)
DeJong & Merrill, (2001)	Merlo & Benekos, (2003)
Drinan, (2016)	Merlo, Benekos, & Cook, (1997a), (1997b)
Drizin & Tanenhaus, (2002)	Mulvey & Schubert, (2012)
Dunn, (2008)	Myers, (2003b)
Evans, (1992)	NASEM, (2019)
Fagan, (2008), (2010)	Nguyen, (2016)
Fagan, Kupchik, & Liberman, (2007)	Notes, (2002)
Federle, (1996), (2016)	NRC, (2013)
Feld, (1981), (1983), (1984b), (1987), (1989), (1991), (1998), (1999a), (2000)	Park, (2007)
	Penney & Moretti, (2005)

continued on following page

Table 38e. Continued

Puzzanchera & Addie, (2014)	Sewell, (2009)
Redding, (2016)	Slaten, (2003)
Redding & Mrozoski, (2005)	Spring, (1998)
Romaine, (2010)	Springer, (1991)
Rosenberg, (2000)	Stafford, (2013)
Sabo, (1996)	Steiner & Hemmens, (2003)
Salekin, (2002)	Sulok, (2007)
Salekin et al., (2001)	Tanenhaus & Drizin, (2002)
Salekin et al., (2002)	Thomas, (2016)
Samuelson, (2010)	Thugpen et al., (2010)
Sarri & Shook, (2005)	Torbet, (2000)
Schiraldi & Ziedenberg, (1999)	Torbet et al., (1996)
Schubert et al., (2010)	Traver, (2000)
Schulhofer, (1997)	Urbina, (2005)
Scism, (2019)	Verrecchia, (2003)
Scott, (2000), (2013)	Young, (1981)
Scott, Grisso, Levick, & Steinberg, (2016)	Zane, (2017)
Scott, Reppucci, & Woolard, (1995)	Zane, Welsh, & Mears, (2016)
Scott & Steinberg, (2008), (2010)	Zane, Welsh, & Drakulich, (2016)
Sellers & Arrigo, (2009)	Ziedenberg, (2011)
	Zimring, (1981), (1991), (1998a), (1998b), (2000b)

Table 38f. Offense Exclusion = Mandatory Judicial Transfer/Direct File

Adams & Addie, (2009), (2010), (2011), (2012)	McLatchey, (1999)
Alliance, (2003)	Means, Heller, & Janofsky, (2012)
Arya, (2010)	Merlo, Benekos, & Cook, (1999)
Baquedano, (2015)	Miller, N., (1995)
Beschle, (1999)	Mole & White, (2005)
Bishop, (2000), (2009)	OJJ, (1999)
Breen & Mills, (2015)	OJJDP, (2018), (2020)
Brink, (2003-04)	Olson, (2004)
Butts, (2000)	Park, (2007)
Butts et al., (2002)	PHR, (2007)
Butts & Mitchell, (2000)	Pollitt, (2004)
Cellucci et al., (2001)	Puzzanchera, Hockenberry, & Sickmund, (2022)
Cohn & Mialson, (2008)	Robertson et al., (2019)
Cooper & Urban, (2012)	Rosenberg, (2000)
Dawson, (2000)	Rubin, (2006)
Deitch & Arya, (2014)	Rudman, Hartstone, Fagan, & Moore, (1986)
Dunn, (2008)	Sabo, (1996)
Fagan, (2008)	Schetky, (2003)
Federle, (2016)	Scialabba, (2016)
Gardner & Lanza-Kaduce, (2015)	Scott, (2013b)
Griffin, (2003), (2008), (2012)	Shelden & Hussong, (2003)
Griffin et al., (1998), (2011)	Shiller, (2006)
Hamack, (2014)	Shook, (2014)
Hartney, (2006)	Sickmund, (2003)
Hockenberry, (2021)	Slaten, (2003)
Hoeffel, (2013)	Snyder et al., (2000)
Holtzman, (2004)	Snyder & Sichmund, (2006)
Hornback, (2021)	Spring, (1998)
Jordan, (2006)	Sridharan, Greenfield, & Blakley, (2004)
Keenan et al., (2015)	Steinberg, (2000)
King, R., (2006)	Steiner & Hemmens, (2003)
Kukino, (2014)	Szymanski, (2007), (2008), (2009), (2010a)
Lanza-Kaduce, Bishop, Frazier & Winner, (1996)	Teigen, (2021)
Lanza-Kaduce, Frazier, Lane & Bishop, (2002)	Thomas, (2016)
Law et al., (2019)	Thomas & Wilson, (2018)
Lemmon, Austin, Verrecchia, & Fetzer, (2005)	Torbet & Szymanski, (1998)
Mallett, (2007)	White, Frazier, & Lanza-Kaduce, (1999)
Marrus & Rosenberg (2005)	Young, & Gainsborough, (2000)
McCurdy-Jackson, (2011)	

Table 38g. Offense Exclusion (OE) is not Prosecutorial Transfer (PT)

Abrams, (2013)	Juszkiewicz, (2000)
Adams & Addie, (2009), (2010), (2011), (2012)	Kimbrell, (2015)
Allen, K.L., (2012)	King, C., (2018)
Baquedano, (2015)	King, R., (2006)
Baruwa, (2013)	Knox, (2009)
Brandau, (2004)	Kupchik, (2003b), (2006a)
Breen & Mills, (2015)	Lehmann, Pickett, Ryon. & Kosloski, (2019)
Burrow, (2005), (2008b)	Martin, (1992)
Butts et al., (2002)	McLatchey, (1999)
Cellucci et al., (2001)	Means, Heller, & Janofsky, (2012)
Cintron, (1996)	Merlo, Benekos, & Cook, (1997b)
Cohn & Mialson, (2008)	Myers, (2003b)
Cooper & Urban, (2012)	NDAA, (2002)
Dawson, (2000)	Notes, (2002)
Deitch & Arya, (2014)	OJJ, (1999)
Deitch et al., (2009)	Oliver, (2006)
Drinan, (2016)	Parent, Dunworth, McDonald & Rhodes, (1997)
Drizin & Tanenhaus, (2002)	Park, (2007)
Dugan, (1998)	Perry, (2006)
Dunn, (2008)	Prochaska, (2018)
Evans, (1992)	Puzzanchera & Addie, (2014)
Fagan, (2000), (2008)	Puzzanchera, Hockenberry, & Sickmund, (2022)
Federle, (2016)	Redding, (2016)
Flicker, (1983)	Rubin, (2006)
Gardner & Lanza-Kaduce, (2015)	Salekin, (2002)
Glynn, (1997)	Sarri & Shook, (2005)
Gordon, (1999)	Schiraldi & Soler, (1998)
Griffin et al., (2011)	Scott, (2013a)
Grundfest et al., (1981)	Shook, (2014)
Guttman, (1995)	Sickmund, (1994), (2003)
Harshbarger, & Keshian, (1995)	Singer, Fagan & Liberman, (2000)
HLRA, (2002)	Snyder et al., (2000)
Hockenberry, (2021)	Soler, (2010)
Hockenberry & Puzzanchera, (2014a), (2019)	Sorrentino & Olsen, (1977)
Hoeffel, (2013)	Springer, (1991)
Hughes, (2017)	Stafford, (2013)
Hurst, III (1999)	Stamm, (1973)
Jackson & Pabon, (2000)	Steinberg & Cauffman, (2001)
Jordan, (2005)	Steiner, (2005)

continued on following page

Table 38g. Continued

Swanson, (2018)	Williams, E.J., (2022)
Thomaas, (2016)	Zane, (2018)
Thomas & Wilson, (2018)	Zane, Welsh, & Mears, (2016)
Vargas, (2014)	Zane, Welsh, & Drakulich, (2016)

Table 38h. Three Types of Judicial Transfer: Discretionary; Presumptive; Mandatory

Adams & Addie, (2009), (2010), (2011), (2012)
Alliance, (2003)
Baquedano, (2015)
Bishop, (2000), (2009)
Bishop & Feld, (2012)
Breen & Mills, (2015)
Butts et al., (2002)
Butts & Mitchell, (2000)
Cellucci et al., (2001)
Clarke, C.A., (2005)
Cohn & Mialson, (2008)
Cooper & Urban, (2012)
Deitch & Arya, (2014)
Fagan, (2008)
Feld, (1987)
Gardner & Lanza-Kaduce, (2015)
Griffin, (2003), (2008), (2012)
Griffin et al., (1998), (2011)
Hartney, (2006)
Hockenberry, (2021)
Hockenberry & Puzzanchera, (2014a)
Hoeffel, (2013)
Holtzman, (2004)
Jordan, (2006)
Keenan et al., (2015)
King, R., (2006)
Kukino, (2014)
Lanza-Kaduce, Frazier, Lane & Bishop, (2002)
Lyons, (2011)

Mallett, (2007)
McCurdy-Jackson, (2011)
Means, Heller, & Janofsky, (2012)
Mears, Hay, Gertz, & Mancini, (2007)
Merlo, Benekos, & Cook (1999)
Miller, N., (1995)
Mole & White, (2005)
OJJ, (1999)
OJJDP, (2018), (2020)
Olson, (2004)
Park, (2007)
Puzzanchera & Addie, (2014)
Puzzanchera, Hockenberry, & Sickmund, (2022)
Robertson et al., (2019)
Rubin, (2006)
Schetky, (2003)
Shelden & Hussong, (2003)
Shook, (2014)
Sickmund, (2003)
Slaten, (2003)
Snyder & Sickmund, (2006)
Snyder et al., (2000)
Spring, (1998)
Steinberg, (2000)
Thomas, (2016)
Thomas & Wilson, (2018)
Washburn et al., (2008)
Wright et al., (2019)
Young, & Gainsborough, (2000)

Table 38i. Mandatory Exclusion (Reduced Max JC Age) = Transfer

Allard & Young, (2002)
Arya, (2010)
Augustyn & Loughran, (2017)
Augustyn & McGloin, (2018)
Bishop, (2000), (2009)
Browne, (1977)
Butts & Mitchell, (2000)
Cassady, (2017)
Clarke, C.A., (2005)
Deitch & Arya, (2014)
Evans, (1992)
Fagan, (2008)
Federle, (1996)
Forst & Blomquist, (1991)
Gordon, (1999)
Griffin et al., (2011)
Hahn et al., (2007)
Hamparian et al., (1982)
Harshbarger, & Keshian, (1995)
Lahey, (2016)
Lehmann & Kobie, (2021)
Lehmann, Pickett, Ryon & Kosloski, (2019)
Lin et al., (1994)

McGowan et al., (2007)
Mulvey & Schubert, (2012)
Myers et al., (2011)
Myers, (2016)
Noon, (1994)
Pegg, (2015)
Redding, (2003)
Sabo, (1996)
Schetky, (2003)
Schornhorst, (1968)
Scott & Steinberg, (2008)
Sellers & Arrigo, (2009)
Sickmund, (2003)
Slobogin, (2013)
Smith, (2013)
Snyder et al., (2000)
Steinberg, (2009)
Thomas & Wilson, (2018)
Whitebread & Batey, (1977)
Wizner, (1984)
Zane, Welsh, & Mears, (2016)
Zimring, (1981)

*Table 39. Percentage of Transfers to Criminal Court by Age, 1985-2018 <16 & 16/older**

Year	% < 16	%16/older
1985	6/7[i]	93/94
1988	7	93
1989	11	89
1990	10	90
1994	12/13/15	85/87/88
1997	13	87
1998	13	87
1999	14	86
2005	15	85
2007	12	88
2008	13	87
2009	11	89
2010	11	89
2011	8	92
2017	13	87
2018	11	89

*Derived from Furdella & Puzzanchera, 2015; Hockenberry & Puzzanchera, 2014a; Puzzanchera, 2000, 2001, 2003; Puzzanchera & Addie, 2014; Sickmund et al., 2019.

[i]The years with multiple percentages noted reflect differences in reporting in subsequent years.

Table 38 References

Abeyratne, S., & Sizemore, B. (1999). *Juveniles waived to criminal courts in Ohio 1995-1997: Adjudication and disposition*. Ohio Department of Youth Services.

Abrams, L. S. (2013). Juvenile justice at a crossroads: Science, evidence, and twenty-first century reform. *The Social Service Review*, *87*, 725–752.

Acton, R. B. (1996). Gubernatorial initiatives and rhetoric of juvenile justice reform. *Journal of Law and Policy*, *5*, 277–338.

Adams, B., & Addie, S. (2009). *Delinquency cases waived to criminal court, 2005*. U.S. Department of Justice, Office of Justice Programs, Office of Juvenile Justice and Delinquency Prevention.

Adams, B., & Addie, S. (2010). *Delinquency cases waived to criminal court, 2007*. U.S. Department of Justice, Office of Justice Programs, Office of Juvenile Justice and Delinquency Prevention.

Adams, B., & Addie, S. (2011). *Delinquency cases waived to criminal court, 2008*. U.S. Department of Justice, Office of Justice Programs, Office of Juvenile Justice and Delinquency Prevention.

Adams, B., & Addie, S. (2012). *Delinquency cases waived to criminal court, 2009*. U.S. Department of Justice, Office of Justice Programs, Office of Juvenile Justice and Delinquency Prevention.

Ainsworth, J. E. (1991). Re-imagining childhood and reconstructing the legal order: The case for abolishing the juvenile court. *North Carolina Law Review*, *69*, 1083–1133.

Ainsworth, J. E. (1995). Youth justice in a unified court: Response to critics of juvenile court abolition. *Boston College Law Review. Boston College. Law School*, *36*, 927–951.

Allard, P., & Young, M. C. (2002). Prosecuting juveniles in adult court: The practitioner's perspective. *Journal of Forensic Psychology Practice*, *2*(2), 65–77.

Allen, D. C. (2002). Trying children as adults. *Jones Law Review*, *6*, 27.

Allen, F. A. (2000). Forward. In J. Fagan & F. E. Zimring (Eds.), *The changing borders of juvenile justice: Transfer of adolescents to the criminal court* (pp. ix–xvi). University of Chicago Press.

Allen, K. L. (2012). An analysis of juvenile transfer laws and the appropriateness of prosecuting juveniles as adults. [Unpublished Master's Thesis, University of Wisconsin-Platteville].

Allen, T. T., Trzcinski, E., & Kubiak, S. P. (2012). Public attitudes toward juveniles who commit crimes: The relationship between assessments of adolescent development and attitudes toward severity of punishment. *Crime and Delinquency*, *58*, 78–102.

Alliance, C. A. (2003). *Prosecuting juveniles in the adult criminal justice system: Key issues and recommendations for Arizona*. Children's Action Alliance.

Angell, K. M. (2004). The regressive movement: When juvenile offenders are treated as adults, nobody wins. *Southern California Interdisciplinary Law Journal*, *14*, 125–149.

Annino, P. G. (2000). Children in Florida adult prisons: A call for a moratorium. *Florida State University Law Review. Florida State University. College of Law*, *28*, 471–490.

Applegate, B. K., & Davis, R. K. (2006). Public views on sentencing juvenile murderers: The impact of offender, offense, and perceived maturity. *Youth Violence and Juvenile Justice*, *4*, 55–74.

Applegate, B. K., Davis, R. K., & Cullen, F. T. (2009). Reconsidering child saving: The extent and correlates of public support for excluding youths from the juvenile court. *Crime and Delinquency*, *55*, 51–77.

Arteaga, J. A. (2002). Juvenile (in) justice: Congressional attempts to abrogate the procedural rights of juvenile defendants. *Columbia Law Review*, *102*, 1051–1088.

Arthur, L. G., & Schwartz, L. J. (1993). Certification–An Overview. *Juvenile & Family Court Journal*, *44*(3), 61–71.

Arya, N. (2010). Using *Graham v. Florida* to challenge juvenile transfer laws. *Louisiana Law Review*, *71*, 99–156.

Arya, N. (2011). *State trends: Legislative victories from 2005 to 2010: Removing youth from the adult criminal justice system*. Campaign for Youth Justice.

Augustyn, M. B., & Loughran, T. A. (2017). Juvenile waiver as a mechanism of social stratification: A focus on human capital. *Criminology*, *55*, 405–437.

Augustyn, M. B., & McGloin, J. M. (2018). Revisiting juvenile waiver: Integrating the incapacitation experience. *Criminology*, *56*, 154–190.

Backstrom, J. C., & Walker, G. L. (2006). The role of the prosecutor in juvenile justice: Advocacy in the courtroom and leadership in the community. *William Mitchell Law Review*, *32*, 963–988.

Baird, M. I., & Samuels, M. B. (1996). Policy review: Justice for youth: The betrayal of childhood in the United States. *Journal of Law and Policy*, *5*, 177–202.

Baquedano, M. J. (2015). Taking the direct file statute to criminal court: Immigration consequences for juveniles. *University of Miami Race & Social Justice Law Review*, *6*, 169–191.

Barnes, C., & Franz, R. (1989). Questionably adult: Determinants and effects of the juvenile waiver decision. *Justice Quarterly*, *6*, 117–135.

Baruwa, B. (2013). Should juveniles be transferred to adult criminal court in the criminal justice system. *Tennessee Journal of Race Gender & Social Justice*, *2*, 101–127.

Beale, S. S. (2009). You've come a long way, baby: Two waves of juvenile justice reforms as seen from Jena, Louisiana. *Harvard Civil Rights-Civil Liberties Law Review*, *44*, 511–545.

Beatty, H. (1995). Is the trend to expand juvenile transfer statutes just an easy answer to a complex problem. *University of Toledo Law Review. University of Toledo. College of Law*, *26*, 979–1025.

Beaudry-Cyr, M., Leiber, M., Brubaker, S. J., & Jaynes, C. (2020). The liberation hypothesis perspective and juvenile court outcomes: Implications for an understanding of the interplay between offender and offense characteristics. *Crime and Delinquency*, *66*(6-7), 806–836.

Benekos, P. J., & Merlo, A. V. (2008). Juvenile justice: The legacy of punitive policy. *Youth Violence and Juvenile Justice*, *6*, 28–46.

Benekos, P. J., & Merlo, A. V. (2019). A decade of change: *Roper v. Simmons*, defending childhood, and juvenile justice policy. *Criminal Justice Policy Review*, *30*, 102–127.

Beresford, L. S. (2000). Is lowering the age at which juveniles can be transferred to adult criminal court the answer to juvenile crime? A state-by-state assessment. *The San Diego Law Review*, *37*, 783–851.

Beschle, D. L. (1999). The juvenile justice counterrevolution: Responding to cognitive dissonance in the law's view of the decision-making capacity of minors. *Emory Law Journal*, *48*, 65–105.

Bishop, D. M. (2000). Juvenile offenders in the adult criminal justice system. In M. Tonry (Ed.), *Crime & Justice: A Review of Research, 27* (pp. 81–167). University of Chicago Press.

Bishop, D. M. (2009). Juvenile transfer in the United States. In Junger-Tas & Dunkel, F. (Eds.), Reforming juvenile justice (pp. 85-104). Springer.

Bishop, D. M., & Feld, B. C. (2012). Trends in juvenile justice policy and practice. In Feld, B.C., & Bishop, D.M (Eds.). The oxford handbook of juvenile crime and juvenile justice (pp. 898-926). Oxford University Press.

Bishop, D. M., & Frazier, C. E. (1991). Transfer of juveniles to criminal court: A case study and analysis of prosecutorial waiver. *Notre Dame Journal of Law, Ethics & Public Policy*, *5*, 281–302.

Bishop, D. M., & Frazier, C. E. (2000). Consequences of transfer. In J. Fagan & F. E. Zimring (Eds.), *The changing borders of juvenile justice: Transfer of adolescents to criminal court* (pp. 227–276). University of Chicago Press.

Bishop, D. M., Frazier, C. E., Lanza-Kaduce, L., & Winner, L. (1996). The transfer of juveniles to criminal court: Does it make a difference? *Crime and Delinquency*, *42*, 171–191.

Bishop, D. M., Lanza-Kaduce, L., & Frazier, C. E. (1998). Juvenile justice under attack: An analysis of the causes and impact of recent reforms. *University of Florida Journal of Law and Public Policy*, *10*, 129–155.

Blumhardt, L. (2000). In the best interests of the child: Juvenile justice or adult retribution. *University of Hawaii Law Review*, *23*, 341–362.

Bortner, M. A. (1986). Traditional rhetoric, organizational realities: Remand of juveniles to adult court. *Crime and Delinquency*, *32*, 53–73.

Bove, C. M. (1991). The child-adult: Michigan waiver law. *Detroit College of Law Review*, *1991*, 1071–1096.

Braithwaite, L., & Shore, A. (1981). Treatment rhetoric versus waiver decisions. *The Journal of Criminal Law & Criminology*, *72*, 1867–1891.

Brandau, T. J. (2004). Transfer of juvenile offenders to adult court in Delaware. Delaware Criminal Justice Council. Campaign for Youth Justice.

Brannen, D. N., Salekin, R. T., Zapf, P. A., Salekin, K. L., Kubak, F. A., & DeCoster, J. (2006). Transfer to adult court: A national study of how juvenile court judges weigh pertinent *Kent* criteria. *Psychology, Public Policy, and Law*, *12*, 332–355.

Breen, J. S., & Mills, J. R. (2015). Mandating discretion: Juvenile sentencing schemes after *Miller v. Alabama*. *The American Criminal Law Review*, *52*, 293–319.

Brink, D. O. (2003-2004). Immaturity, normative competence, and juvenile transfer: How (not) to punish minors for major crimes. *Texas Law Review*, *82*, 1555–1585.

Brinkerhoff, J. C. (1984). Prosecution as a juvenile or an adult-is the discretion vested in the district attorney by section 14-6-203 (c) of the Wyoming statutes unconstitutional and violation of the proper role of a prosecutor? *Land and Water Law Review*, *19*, 187–205.

Brown, J. M., & Sorensen, J. R. (2013). Race, ethnicity, gender, and waiver to adult court. *Journal of Ethnicity in Criminal Justice*, *11*(3), 181–195.

Browne, E. W. (1977). Guidelines for statutes for transfer of juveniles to criminal court. *Pepperdine Law Review*, *4*, 479–495.

Bryson, S. L., & Peck, J. H. (2020). Understanding the subgroup complexities of transfer: The impact of juvenile race and gender on waiver decisions. *Youth Violence and Juvenile Justice*, *18*(2), 135–155.

Buckingham, R. S. (1993). The Erosion of Juvenile Court Judge Discretion in the Transfer Decision Nationwide and in Oregon. *Willamette Law Review*, *29*, 689–510.

Burgess-Proctor, A., Holtrop, K., & Villarruel, F. A. (2008). *Youth transferred to adult court: Racial disparities*. Campaign for Youth Justice.

Burns, B. J. (1990). Prosecutor's wild card: Certifying juveniles for trial as adults under the indictment provision of the Florida Juvenile Justice Act. *St. Thomas Legal Forum, 2,* 49.

Burrow, J. D. (2005). Punishing serious juvenile offenders: A case study of Michigan's prosecutorial waiver statute. *University of California Davis Journal of Juvenile Law & Policy, 9,* 1–55.

Burrow, J. D. (2008a). Examining the influence of Matza's principles of justice and their impact on reverse waiver decisions: Has Kadi-(In) justice survived? *Youth Violence and Juvenile Justice, 6,* 59–82.

Burrow, J. D. (2008b). Reverse waiver and the effects of legal, statutory, and secondary legal factors on sentencing outcomes for juvenile offenders. *Crime and Delinquency, 54,* 34–64.

Burrow, J. D., & Lowery, P. G. (2015). A preliminary assessment of the impact of plea bargaining among a sample of waiver-eligible offenders. *Youth Violence and Juvenile Justice, 13,* 211–227.

Butts, J. A. (1997). *Delinquency cases waived to criminal court, 1985-1994*. US Department of Justice, Office of Justice Programs, Office of Juvenile Justice and Delinquency Prevention.

Butts, J. A. (2000). *Can we do without juvenile justice?* Urban Institute.

Butts, J. A., Coggeshall, M., Gouvis, C., Mears, D., Travis, J., Waul, M., & White, R. (2002). *Youth, guns, and the juvenile justice system. Research report*. Urban Institute. Justice Policy Center.

Butts, J.A., & Harrell, A. V. (1998). *Delinquents or Criminals? Policy Options for Young Offenders*. The Urban Institute, Crime Policy Report.

Butts, J. A., & Mears, D. P. (2001). Reviving juvenile justice in a get-tough era. *Youth & Society, 33,* 169–198.

Butts, J. A., & Mitchell, O. (2000). Brick by brick: Dismantling the border between juvenile and adult justice. *Criminal Justice 2000: Boundary changes in criminal justice organizations, Volume 2,* pp. 167-213.

Carroll, J. E. (2009). Rethinking the constitutional criminal procedure of juvenile transfer hearings: *Apprendi*, adult punishment, and adult process. *The Hastings Law Journal, 61,* 101–153.

Carter, A. M. (2006). Age matters: The case for a constitutionalized infancy defense. *University of Kansas Law Review. University of Kansas. School of Law, 54,* 687–749.

Caselli, L. P. (2011). Criminal law-one small step for juveniles, one giant leap for juvenile justice; Graham v. Florida, 130 S. Ct. 2011 (2010). *Wyoming Law Review, 11,* 269-293.

Cassady, A. (2017). The juvenile ultimatum: Reframing blended sentencing laws to ensure juveniles receive a genuine one last chance at success. *Minnesota Law Review, 102,* 391–425.

Cauffman, E. (2012). Aligning justice system processing with developmental science. *Criminology & Public Policy, 11,* 751–758.

Cauffman, E., Fine, A., Mahler, A., & Simmons, C. (2018). How developmental science influences juvenile justice reform. *University of California Irvine Law Review, 8,* 21–40.

Cauffman, E., & Steinberg, L. (2000). (Im) maturity of judgment in adolescence: Why adolescents may be less culpable than adults. *Behavioral Sciences & the Law*, *18*, 741–760.

Cellucci, P., Swift, J., Governor, G. L., Perlov, J., & O'Toole, M. J. (2001). *Implementation of the Juvenile Justice Reform Act: Youthful offenders in Massachusetts*. Massachusetts Statistical Analysis Center.

CFYJ. (2014). *State trends legislative victories from 2011-2013: Removing youth from the adult criminal justice system*. Campaign for Youth Justice.

Chamberlin, C. (2000). Not kids anymore: A need for punishment and deterrence in the juvenile justice system. *Boston College Law Review. Boston College. Law School*, *42*, 391–419.

Champion, D. J. (1989). Teenage felons and waiver hearings: Some recent trends, 1980-1988. *Crime and Delinquency*, *35*, 577–585.

Champion, D. J., & Mays, G. L. (1991). *Transferring juveniles to criminal courts: Trends and implications for criminal justice*. Praeger.

Cintron, L. A. (1996). Rehabilitating the juvenile court system: Limiting juvenile transfers to adult criminal court. *Northwestern University Law Review*, *90*, 1254–1282.

Clarke, C. A. (2005). The baby and the bathwater: Adolescent offending and punitive juvenile justice reform. *University of Kansas Law Review. University of Kansas. School of Law*, *53*, 659–725.

Clarke, E., & Kooy, L. (n.d.). Illinois law gives judges more discretion over youth charged as adults. *Juvenile Justice Initiative.*

Clarke, E. E. (1996). A case for reinventing juvenile transfer: The record of transfer of juvenile offenders to criminal court in Cook County, Illinois. *Juvenile & Family Court Journal*, *47*(4), 3–22.

Clement, M. J. (1997). A five-year study of juvenile waiver and adult sentences: Implications for policy. *Criminal Justice Policy Review*, *8*, 201–219.

Cloherty, J. J. III. (1992). The serious juvenile offender in the adult criminal system: The jurisprudence of Rhode Island's waiver and certification procedures. *Suffolk University Law Review*, *26*, 407–441.

Cohen, A. O., Bonnie, R. J., Taylor-Thompson, K., & Casey, B. J. (2016). When does a juvenile become an adult: Implications for law and policy. *Temple Law Review*, *88*, 769–788.

Cohn, J.M., & Mialson, H.M., (2008). The relationship between tougher juvenile transfer laws and juvenile crime rates. *Paper delivered by Emory University*, pp. 33. SSRN 1289963.

Conrad, J. P. (1981). Crime and the Child. In J. C. Hall, D. M. Hamparian, J. M. Pettibone, & J. L. White (Eds.), *Major Issues in Juvenile Justice Information and Training: Readings in Public Policy* (pp. 179–192). Academy for Contemporary Problems.

Cooper, M. N., & Urban, L. S. (2012). Factors affecting juvenile waiver to adult court in a large Midwestern jurisdiction. *Journal of the Institute of Justice & International Studies*, *12*, 43–59.

Cornish, T. R. (1982). Where have all the children gone—reverse certification. *Oklahoma Law Review*, *35*, 373.

Coupet, S. M. (2000). What to do with sheep in wolf's clothing: The role of rhetoric and reality about youth offenders in the constructive dismantling policy of the juvenile justice system. *University of Pennsylvania Law Review, 148*, 1303–1346.

Cross, K. S. (1998). When juvenile delinquents are treated as adults: The constitutionality of Alabama's automatic transfer statute. *Alabama Law Review, 50*, 155.

CYJ. Campaign for Youth Justice. (2007). *The consequences aren't minor: The impact of trying youth as adults and strategies for reform.* Campaign for Youth Justice.

D'Ambra, L. (1997). A legal response to juvenile crime: Why waiver of juvenile offenders is not a panacea. *Roger Williams University Law Review, 2*, 277–303.

D'Angelo, J. M. (2007). The complex nature of juvenile court judges' transfer decisions: A study of judicial attitudes. *The Social Science Journal, 44*(1), 147–159.

Dale, M. J. (2004). Making sense of the Lionel Tate case. *Nova Law Review, 28*, 467–478.

Danziger, G. (2003). Delinquency jurisdiction in a unified family court: Balancing intervention, prevention, and adjudication. [e]. *Family Law Quarterly*, 37, 381–401.

Davis, A., Irvine, A., & Ziedenberg, J. (2014). *Stakeholders' views on the movement to reduce youth incarceration.* National Council on Crime and Delinquency.

Davis, S. M. (2000). The criminalization of juvenile justice: Legislative responses to the phantom menace. *Mississippi Law Journal, 70*, 1–33.

Dawson, R. O. (1990). The violent juvenile offender: An empirical study of juvenile determinate sentencing proceedings as an alternative to criminal prosecution. *Texas Tech Law Review, 21*, 1897–1939.

Dawson, R. O. (2000). Judicial waiver in theory and practice. In J. Fagan & F. E. Zimring (Eds.), *The changing borders of juvenile justice: Transfer of adolescents to the criminal court* (pp. 45–81). University of Chicago Press.

DeFrances, C. J. (2002). *Prosecutors in state courts, 2001. BJS Bulletin.* U.S. Department of Justice, Office of Justice Programs.

DeFrances, C. J., & Strom, K. J. (1997). *Juveniles prosecuted in state criminal courts, 1994. BJS Bulletin.* U.S. Department of Justice, Office of Justice Programs.

Deitch, M., & Arya, N. (2014). Waivers and transfers of juveniles to adult court. In W. T. Church II, D. W. Springer, & A. R. Roberts (Eds.), *Juvenile justice sourcebook* (2nd ed., pp. 241–263). Oxford University Press.

Deitch, M., Barstow, A., Lukens, L., & Reyna, R. (2009). *From time out to hard time: Young children in the adult criminal justice system. Special Project Report. Lyndon B.* Johnson School of Public Affairs, University of Texas at Austin.

DeJong, C., & Merrill, E. S. (2000). Getting tough on crime: Juvenile waiver and the criminal court. *Ohio Northern University Law Review, 27*, 175–196.

Dempsey, A. (2020). Transfer law and today's youth: Rehabilitating or creating lifetime criminals? A comparative analysis of juvenile transfer law in Kentucky, Florida, and New York. *University of Louisville Law Review, 59*, 519.

Dodge, L. M. (2000). Our juvenile court has become more like a criminal court": A century of reform at the Cook County (Chicago) juvenile court. *The Michigan Historical Review*, 51–89.

Drake, E. (2013). *The effectiveness of declining juvenile court jurisdiction of youth*. Washington State Institute for Public Policy.

Drinan, C. H. (2014). Misconstruing *Graham & Miller. Washington University Law Review, 91*, 785–795.

Drinan, C. H. (2016). The *Miller* Revolution. *Iowa Law Review, 101*, 1787–1832.

Drizin, S. A., & Tanenhaus, D. S. (2002). Owing to the extreme youth of the accused: The changing legal response to juvenile homicide. *The Journal of Criminal Law & Criminology, 92*, 641–705.

Dugan, B. (1998). Juveniles in adult jails: More kids in jail. *American Jails, 12*(4), 79–85.

Dunn, C. (2008). Condemning Our Youth to Lives as Criminals: Incarcerating Children as Adults. *Richmond Journal of Law & Public Interest, 11*, 30–50.

Ensalaco, M., & Majka, L. C. (Eds.). (2005). *Children's human rights: Progress and challenges for children worldwide*. Rowman & Littlefield Publishers.

Evans, K. L. (1992). Trying juveniles as adults: Is the short-term gain of retribution outweighed by the long-term effects on society. *Mississippi Law Journal, 62*, 95–125.

Fagan, J. (1990). Social and legal policy dimensions of violent juvenile crime. *Criminal Justice and Behavior, 17*, 93–133.

Fagan, J. (1991). *The comparative impacts of juvenile and criminal court sanctions on adolescent offenders. Final Report*. US Department of Justice, Office of Justice Programs, National Institute of Justice.

Fagan, J. (2000). Juvenile justice or injustice? The debate over reform. *St. John's Journal of Legal Commentary, 14*, 359–369.

Fagan, J. (2002). This will hurt me more than it hurts you: Social and legal consequences of criminalizing delinquency. *Notre Dame Journal of Law, Ethics & Public Policy, 16*, 1–41.

Fagan, J. (2010). The contradictions of juvenile crime & punishment. *Daedalus, 139*(3), 43–61.

Fagan, J., & Deschenes, E. P. (1990). Determinants of judicial waiver decisions for violent juvenile offenders. *The Journal of Criminal Law & Criminology, 81*, 314–347.

Fagan, J., Forst, M., & Vivona, T. S. (1987a). Racial determinants of the judicial transfer decision: Prosecuting violent youth in criminal court. *Crime and Delinquency, 33*, 259–286.

Fagan, J., Forst, M. L., & Vivona, T. S. (1987b). *Separating the men from the boys: The criminalization of youth violence through judicial waiver*. Ursa Institute.

Fagan, J., Kupchik, A., & Liberman, A. (2007). Be careful what you wish for: Legal sanctions and public safety among adolescent offenders in juvenile and criminal court. *Columbia Law School, Public Law Research Paper* 03-61.

Fagan, J., & Zimring, F. E. (2000). Editors' Introduction. In Fagan, J., & Zimring, F.E. (Eds.), The changing borders of juvenile justice: Transfer of adolescents to the criminal court (pp. 1-10). University of Chicago Press.

Fagan, J. A. (2008). Juvenile crime and criminal justice: Resolving border disputes. 18 *The Future of Children* 81-118 (Pages numbered 1-48 in Columbia Law School Working Paper).

Fagan, J. A., & Hartstone, E. (1984). Strategic planning in juvenile justice — defining the toughest kids. In R. A. Mathias, P. DeMuro, & R. S. Allison (Eds.), *Violent juvenile offenders: An anthology* (pp. 31–51). NCCD.

Fagan, J. A., Piper, E., & Forst, M. (1986). *The juvenile court and violent youth: Determinants of the transfer decision*. Center for Law and Social Policy, URSA Institute.

Farrington, D. P., Loeber, R., & Howell, J. C. (2012). Young adult offenders: The need for more effective legislative options and justice processing. *Criminology & Public Policy, 11*, 729–750.

Federle, K. H. (1996). Emancipation and execution: Transferring children to criminal court in capital cases. *Wisconsin Law Review*, 447–494.

Federle, K. H. (1999). Is there a jurisprudential future for the juvenile court? *The Annals of the American Academy of Political and Social Science, 564*(1), 28–36.

Federle, K. H. (2016). The right to redemption: Juvenile dispositions and sentences. *Louisiana Law Review, 77*, 47–73.

Feiler, S., & Sheley, J. (1999). Legal and racial elements of public willingness to transfer juvenile offenders to adult court. *Journal of Criminal Justice, 27*, 55–64.

Feld, B. C. (1978). Reference of juvenile offenders for adult prosecution: The legislative alternative to asking unanswerable questions. *Minnesota Law Review, 62*, 515–618.

Feld, B. C. (1980). Juvenile court legislative reform and the serious young offender: Dismantling the "rehabilitative ideal.". *Minnesota Law Review, 65*, 167–242.

Feld, B. C. (1981). Legislative policies toward the serious juvenile offender: On the virtue of automatic adulthood. *Crime and Delinquency, 27*, 497–521.

Feld, B. C. (1983). Delinquent careers and criminal policy: Just deserts and the waiver decision. *Criminology, 21*, 195–212.

Feld, B. C. (1984a). Criminalizing juvenile justice: Rules of procedure for the juvenile court. *Minnesota Law Review, 69*, 141–276.

Feld, B. C. (1984b). The decision to seek criminal charges: Just deserts and the waiver decision. *Criminal Justice Ethics, 3*(2), 27–41.

Feld, B. C. (1987). The juvenile court meets the principle of the offense: Legislative changes in juvenile waiver statutes. *The Journal of Criminal Law & Criminology*, *78*, 471–533.

Feld, B. C. (1989). Bad law makes hard cases: Reflections on teen-aged axe-murderers, judicial activism, and legislative default. *Law & Inequality*, *8*, 1–101.

Feld, B. C. (1991). The transformation of the juvenile court. *Minnesota Law Review*, *75*, 691–725.

Feld, B. C. (1993a). Criminalizing the American juvenile court. In Tonry, M. (Ed.), Crime & Justice: A Review, 17, 197-280.

Feld, B. C. (1993b). Juvenile (in) justice and the criminal court alternative. *Crime and Delinquency*, *39*, 403–424.

Feld, B. C. (1995). Violent youth and public policy: A case study of juvenile justice law reform. *Minnesota Law Review*, *79*, 965–1128.

Feld, B. C. (1997). Abolish the juvenile court: Youthfulness, criminal responsibility, and sentencing policy. *The Journal of Criminal Law & Criminology*, *88*, 68–136.

Feld, B. C. (1998). Juvenile and criminal justice systems' responses to youth violence. *Crime and Justice*, *24*, 189–261.

Feld, B. C. (1999a). *Bad kids: Race and the transformation of the juvenile court*. Oxford University Press.

Feld, B. C. (1999b). The transformation of the juvenile court—Part II: Race and the crack down on youth crime. *Minnesota Law Review*, *84*, 327–395.

Feld, B. C. (2000). Legislative exclusion of offenses from juvenile court jurisdiction: A history and critique. In J. Fagan & F. E. Zimring (Eds.), *The changing borders of juvenile justice: Transfer of adolescents to the criminal court* (pp. 83–144). University of Chicago Press.

Feld, B. C. (2001). Race, youth violence, and the changing jurisprudence of waiver. *Behavioral Sciences & the Law*, *19*, 3–22.

Feld, B. C. (2003a). Competence, culpability, and punishment: Implications of Atkins for executing and sentencing adolescents. *Hofstra Law Review*, *32*, 463–553.

Feld, B. C. (2003b). Race, politics, and juvenile justice: The Warren court and the conservative backlash. *Minnesota Law Review*, *87*, 1447–1577.

Feld, B. C. (2004). Juvenile transfer. *Criminology & Public Policy*, *3*, 599–604.

Feld, B. C. (2007a). A century of juvenile justice: A work in progress or a revolution that failed. *Northern Kentucky Law Review*, *34*, 189–256.

Feld, B. C. (2007b). Unmitigated punishment: Adolescent criminal responsibility and LWOP sentences. *Journal of Law & Family Studies*, *10*, 11–82.

Feld, B. C. (2008). A slower form of death: Implications of Roper v. Simmons for juveniles sentenced to life without parole. *Notre Dame Journal of Law, Ethics & Public Policy*, 22, 9–65.

Feld, B. C. (2013a). Adolescent criminal responsibility, proportionality, and sentencing policy: Roper, Graham, Miller/Jackson, and the youth discount. *Law & Inequality*, *31*, 263–330.

Feld, B. C. (2017a). Competence and culpability: Delinquents in juvenile courts, youths in criminal courts. *Minnesota Law Review*, *102*, 473–576.

Feld, B. C. (2017b). My life in crime: An intellectual history of the juvenile court. *Nevada Law Journal*, *17*, 299–329.

Feld, B. C., & Bishop, D. M. (2012). Transfer of juveniles to criminal court. In Feld, B.C., & Bishop, D.M (Eds.). The oxford handbook of juvenile crime and juvenile justice (pp. 801-842). Oxford University Press.

Flesch, L. M. (2004). Juvenile crime and why waiver is not the answer. *Family Court Review*, *42*(3), 583–596.

Flexen, J. L., Stolzenberg, L., & D'Alessio, S. J. (2009). Cheating the hangman: The effect of Roper v. Simmons decision on homicides committed by juveniles. *Crime and Delinquency*, *56*, 928–948.

Flicker, B. (1981). Prosecuting juveniles as adults: A symptom of a crisis in the juvenile courts. In J. C. Hall, D. M. Hamparian, J. M. Pettibone, & J. L. White (Eds.), *Major issues in juvenile justice information and training: Readings in public policy* (pp. 351–377). Academy for Contemporary Problems.

Flicker, B. (1983). *Transferring juveniles to adult court for trial*. Institute of Judicial Administration.

Flynn, E. H. (2008). Dismantling the felony-murder rule: Juvenile deterrence and retribution post-" *Roper v. Simmons*. *University of Pennsylvania Law Review*, *156*(4), 1049–1076.

Forst, M., & Blomquist, M. E. (1991). Cracking down on juveniles: The changing ideology of youth corrections. *Notre Dame Journal of Law, Ethics & Public Policy*, *5*, 323–375.

Fowler, E., & Kurlychek, M. C. (2018). Drawing the line: Empirical recidivism results from a natural experiment raising the age of criminal responsibility. *Youth Violence and Juvenile Justice*, *16*, 263–278.

Frazier, C. E., Bishop, D. M., Lanza-Kaduce, L., & Marvasti, A. (1998). Juveniles in criminal court: Past and current research from Florida. *Quinnipiac Law Review*, *18*, 573–596.

Fritsch, E., & Hemmens, C. (1995). Juvenile waiver in the United States 1979-1995: A comparison and analysis of state waiver statutes. *Juvenile & Family Court Journal*, *46*(3), 17–35.

Fritsch, E. J., & Hemmens, C. (1996). An assessment of legislative approaches to the problem of serious juvenile crime: A case study of Texas 1973-1995. *American Journal of Criminal Law*, *23*, 563–609.

Frost Clausel, L. E., & Bonnie, R. J. (2000). Juvenile justice on appeal. *The changing borders of juvenile justice: Transfer of adolescents to the criminal court*, 181-206.

Furdella, J., & Puzzanchera, C. (2015). *Delinquency cases in juvenile court, 2013*. Office of Juvenile Justice and Delinquency Prevention.

Gallini, B. R. (2008). Equal sentences for unequal participation: Should the Eighth Amendment allow all juvenile murder accomplices to receive life without parole? *Oregon Law Review*, *87*, 29–92.

Garberg, N. M., & Libkuman, T. M. (2009). Community sentiment and the juvenile offender: Should juveniles charged with felony murder be waived into the Adult Criminal Justice System? *Behavioral Sciences & the Law*, *27*, 553–575.

Gardner, K., & Lanza-Kaduce, L. (2015). Putting the processing of juvenile offenders into context. In Welsh, W.N., Harding, C., Krohn, M.D., & Lane, J. (Eds.), The handbook of juvenile delinquency and juvenile justice (pp. 85-100). John Wiley & Sons.

Garner, M. C. Jr. (1973). Due process and waiver of juvenile court jurisdiction. *Washington and Lee Law Review*, *30*, 591–613.

Gasper, J., & Katkin, D. (1980). A rationale for the abolition of the juvenile court's power to waive jurisdiction. *Pepperdine Law Review*, *7*, 937–951.

Geraghty, D. (2016). Bending the curve: Reflections on a decade of Illinois juvenile justice reform. *Children's Legal Rights Journal*, *36*, 71–89.

Geraghty, T. F. (1997). Justice for children: How do we get there? *The Journal of Criminal Law & Criminology*, *88*, 190–241.

Geraghty, T. F., & Drizin, S. A. (1997). The debate over the future of juvenile courts: Can we reach consensus? *The Journal of Criminal Law & Criminology*, *88*, 1–13.

Geraghty, T. F., & Rhee, W. (1998). Learning from tragedy: Representing children in discretionary transfer hearings. *Wake Forest Law Review*, *33*, 595–650.

Giardino, L. F. (1996). Statutory rhetoric: The reality behind juvenile justice policies in America. *Journal of Policy & Law*, *5*, 223–276.

Gibson, C. L., & Krohn, M. D. (2012). Raising the age: Issues in emerging adulthood and adult court referral of youthful offenders. *Criminology & Public Policy*, *11*, 759–768.

Gillespie, L. K., & Norman, M. D. (1984). Does certification mean prison: Some preliminary findings from Utah. *Juvenile & Family Court Journal*, *35*, 23–34.

Gimbel, V. N. (2015). There are no children here: DC youth in the criminal justice system. *The Georgetown Law Journal*, *104*, 1307–1344.

Glynn, G. F. (1997). Arkansas' missed opportunity for rehabilitation: Sending children to adult courts. *University of Arkansas at Little Rock Law Journal*, *20*, 77–127.

Gordon, B. (1999). A criminal's justice or a child's injustice? Trends in the waiver of juvenile court jurisdiction and the flaws in the Arizona response. *Arizona Law Review*, *41*, 193–226.

Gourdie, H. R. (2021). The guiding hand of counsel, for a price: Juvenile public defender fees and their effects. *William and Mary Law Review*, *62*, 999–1040.

Gowen, C., Thurau, L., & Wood, M. (2011). ABA's approach to juvenile justice reform: Education, eviction, and employment: The collateral consequences of juvenile adjudication. *Duke Forum for Law & Social Change*, *3*, 187–203.

Gray, A. (2007). Another day in the life of the juvenile justice system: The fight against the abolishment of the system. *Richmond Journal of Law & Public Interest*, *11*, 71–88.

Greathouse, S. M., Sothmann, F. C., Levett, L. M., & Kovera, M. B. (2011). The potentially biasing effects of voir dire in juvenile waiver cases. *Law and Human Behavior*, *35*(6), 427–439.

Green, S. T. (2005). Prosecutorial waiver into adult criminal court: A conflict of interests violation amounting to the states' legislative abrogation of juveniles' due process right. *Penn State Law Review*, *110*, 233–282.

Greene, E., Duke, L., & Woody, W. D. (2017). Stereotypes influence beliefs about transfer and sentencing of juvenile offenders. *Psychology, Crime & Law*, *23*(9), 841–858.

Greene, T. (2010). *Treating juveniles as adults: sending America's children to adult courts*. Grimes County Sheriff's Office Anderson.

Griffin, P. (2003). *Trying and sentencing juveniles as adults: An analysis of state transfer and blended sentencing laws*. National Center for Juvenile Justice.

Griffin, P. (2008). *Different from adults: An updated analysis of juvenile transfer and blended sentencing laws, with recommendations for reform*. National Center for Juvenile Justice.

Griffin, P. (2012). Legal boundaries between the juvenile and criminal justice systems in the United States. In R. Loeber & D. P. Farrington (Eds.), *From Juvenile Delinquency to Adult Crime: Criminal Careers, Justice Policy, and Prevention* (pp. 184–199). Oxford University Press.

Griffin, P., Addie, S., Addie, B., & Firestine, K. (2011). *Trying juveniles as adults: An analysis of state transfer laws and reporting*. U.S. Department of Justice, Office of Justice Programs, Office of Juvenile Justice and Delinquency Prevention.

Griffin, P., Torbet, P., & Syzmanski, L. (1998). *Trying juveniles in adult court: An analysis of state transfer provisions*. Office of Juvenile Justice and Delinquency Prevention, Office of Justice Programs, U.S. Department of Justice.

Grisso, T. (1996). Society's retributive response to juvenile violence: A developmental perspective. *Law and Human Behavior*, *20*, 229–247.

Grisso, T. (1997). The competence of adolescents as trial defendants. *Psychology, Public Policy, and Law*, *3*, 3–32.

Grisso, T. (2010). Clinicians' transfer evaluations: How well can they assist judicial discretion. *Louisiana Law Review*, *71*, 157–189.

Grundfest, A. R., Paskow, A. C., Szabo, H. E., & Williams, R. J. (1981). In Hall, J.C., Hamparian, D.M., Pettibone, John M., & White, Joseph L. (Eds.) Major issues in juvenile justice: Information and Training: Readings in public policy (pp. 321-332). Academy for Contemporary Problems.

Guggenheim, M. (2017). Barry Feld: An Intellectual History of a Juvenile Court Reformer. *Nevada Law Journal*, *17*, 371–391.

Gulstad, R. (2016). *Juveniles in adult court repercussions and benefits for juveniles and communities.* [M.S.W. Clinical Research Paper. St. Catherine University and the University of St. Thomas St. Paul].

Guttman, C. R. (1995). Listen to the children: The decision to transfer juveniles to criminal court. *Harvard Civil Rights-Civil Liberties Law Review, 30*, 507–542.

Hager, D. A. (1995). Does the Texas juvenile waiver statute comport with the requirements of due process? *Texas Tech Law Review, 26*, 813–856.

Hahn, R., McGowan, A., Liberman, A., Crosby, A., Fullilove, M., Johnson, R., Moscicki, E., Price, L., Snyder, S., Tuma, F., Lowy, J., Briss, P., Cory, S., & Stone, G. (2007). Effects on violence of laws and policies facilitating the transfer of youth from the juvenile to the adult justice system: A report on recommendations of the Task Force on Community Preventive Services. *Morbidity and Mortality Weekly Report: Recommendations and Reports, 56*(9), 1–11.

Hamack, B. (2014). Go directly to jail, do not pass juvenile court, do not collect due process: Why waiving juveniles into adult court without a fitness hearing is a denial of their basic due process rights. *Wyoming Law Review, 14*, 775–828.

Hamilton, L., Moak, S. C., & Golden, J. W. (2007). Arkansas Legislative Reforms Provide Framework for Change While Supporting *Parens Patriae* Philosophy of Juvenile Court. *Juvenile & Family Court Journal, 58*(1), 37–47.

Hamparian, D. M. (1981). Introduction. In Hall, J.C., Hamparian, D.M., Pettibone, John M., & White, Joseph L. (Eds.) Major issues in juvenile justice: Information and Training: Readings in public policy (pp. 169-177). Academy for Contemporary Problems.

Hamparian, D. M., Estep, L. K., Muntean, S. M., Priestino, R. R., Swisher, R. G., Wallace, P. L., & White, J. L. (1982). *Major issues in juvenile justice information and training: Youth in adult courts: Between two worlds: Southeast Region*. Academy for Contemporary Problems.

Hannan, W. (2008). Judicial waiver as the only equitable method to transfer juvenile offenders to criminal court. *Notre Dame Journal of Law, Ethics & Public Policy, 22*, 193–223.

Harris, A., & Allen, W. (2003). Lest we forget thee…: The under-and over-representation of Black and Latino youth in California higher education and juvenile justice institutions. *Race and Society, 6*(2), 99–123.

Harshbarger, S., & Keshian, C. (1995). The attorney general of Massachusetts' bill relative to the trial and sentencing of serious juvenile offenders. *The Boston University Public Interest Law Journal, 5*, 135–163.

Hart, T. C. (1998). Causes and consequences of juvenile crime and violence: Public attitudes and question-order effect. *American Journal of Criminal Justice, 23*, 129–143.

Hartinger-Saunders, R. (2008). The history of defining youth: Current implications for identifying and treating delinquent youth. *The New York Sociologist, 3*, 88-106. http://newyorksociologist.org/08/Hartinger-08.pdf

Hartney, C. (2006). *Youth under age 18 in the adult criminal justice system*. National Council on Crime and Delinquency.

Hays, J., & Solway, K. S. (1972). The role of psychological evaluation in certification of juveniles for trial as adults. *Houston Law Review*, *9*, 709–715.

Heilbrun, K., Leheny, C., Thomas, L., & Huneycutt, D. (1997). A national survey of US statutes on juvenile transfer: Implications for policy and practice. *Behavioral Sciences & the Law*, *15*, 125–149.

Henderson, R. E. (2000). Blended sentencing in Montana: A new way to look at an old problem. *Montana Law Review*, *61*, 337–369.

Henning, K. (2013). Criminalizing normal adolescent behavior in communities of color: The role of prosecutors in juvenile justice reform. *Cornell Law Review*, *98*, 383–461.

Herkal, C. J. (1998). You live, you learn: A comment on Oklahoma's Youthful Offender Act. *Tulsa Law Journal*, *34*, 599–624.

Hess, W., Furr, L., Armstrong, K., Francis, S., & White, A. (2010). *Just kids: Baltimore's youth in the adult criminal justice system. A report of the just kids partnership to end the automatic prosecution of youth as adults*. Just Kids Partnership.

Hess, W. N. (2014). Kids can change: Reforming South Dakota's juvenile transfer law to rehabilitate children and protect public safety. *South Dakota Law Review*, *59*, 312.

Hirase, J. (1992). State ex. rel. v. EGT: Waiving childhood goodbye. *Journal of Contemporary Law*, *18*, 159–175.

HLRA. Harvard Law Review Association. (2002). For the Good of the Child, for the Good of Society: Using Scotland and Jamaica as Models to Reform U. S. Juvenile Justice Policy. *Harvard Law Review*, *115*, 1964–1987.

Hockenberry, S. (2018). *Delinquency cases in juvenile court, 2015*. Office of Juvenile Justice and Delinquency Prevention.

Hockenberry, S. (2019a). *Delinquency cases in juvenile court, 2016*. Office of Juvenile Justice and Delinquency Prevention.

Hockenberry, S. (2019b). *Delinquency cases in juvenile court, 2017*. Office of Juvenile Justice and Delinquency Prevention.

Hockenberry, S. (2020). Delinquency cases in juvenile court, 2018. U.S. Department of Justice, Office of Justice programs.

Hockenberry, S. (2021). *Delinquency cases waived to criminal court, 2018*. U.S. Department of Justice, Office of Justice Programs.

Hockenberry, S., & Puzzanchera, C. (2014a). *Delinquency cases waived to criminal court, 2011*. Office of Juvenile Justice and Delinquency Prevention.

Hockenberry, S., & Puzzanchera, C. (2014b). *Juvenile court statistics, 2011*. National Center for Juvenile Justice.

Hockenberry, S., & Puzzanchera, C. (2019). *Juvenile court statistics, 2017*. National Center for Juvenile Justice.

Hoeffel, J. C. (2013). The jurisprudence of death and youth: Now the twain should meet. *Texas Tech Law Review*, *46*, 29–69.

Hofacket, J. K. (2002). Justice or vengeance: How young is too young for a child to be tried and punished as an adult? *Texas Tech Law Review*, *34*, 159.

Hogan, C. (1974). Waiver of juvenile jurisdiction and the hard-core youth. *North Dakota Law Review*, *51*, 655–677.

Holstein, S. B. (1982). Slamming the door on prodigals: Changing conceptions of childhood and the demise of juvenile justice. *Northern Kentucky Law Review*, *9*, 517.

Holtzman, A. R. (2004). Juvenile justice-The increased propensity for juvenile transfer to the criminal court system in Pennsylvania and the need for a revised approach to juvenile offenders. *Penn State Law Review*, *109*, 657–682.

Hornback, T. (2021). A Tale of two systems: A comparative analysis of Scotland's community-based juvenile justice and America's prosecutorial discretion laws. *University of Miami International & Comparative Law Review*, *28*, 437–461.

Horowitz, M. A. (2000). Kids who kill: A critique of how the American legal system deals with juveniles who commit homicide. *Law and Contemporary Problems*, *63*, 133–177.

Houghtalin, M., & Mays, G. L. (1991). Criminal dispositions of New Mexico juveniles transferred to adult court. *Crime and Delinquency*, *37*, 393–407.

House, R. (2013). Seen but not heard: Using judicial waiver to save the juvenile justice system and our kids. *University of Toledo Law Review. University of Toledo. College of Law*, *45*, 149.

Howell, J. C. (1996). Juvenile transfers to the criminal justice system: State of the art. *Law & Policy*, *18*, 17–60.

Howell, J. C., Feld, B. C., Mears, D. P., Farrington, D. P., Loeber, R., & Petechuk, D. (2013). [*Young offenders and an effective response in the juvenile and adult justice systems: What happens, what should happen, and what we need to know*] [Study Group on the Transitions Between Juvenile Delinquency and Adult Crime] [. NCJRS.]. *Bulletin*, 5.

Howell, J. C., Wilson, J. J., Sickmund, M. H., Hodges, N. J., & Howell, M. Q. (2017). Caught in the act: States doing some things right in juvenile justice. *Juvenile & Family Court Journal*, *68*(4), 25–42.

Hughes, C. S. (2017). *Legislative waiver. The Encyclopedia of Juvenile Delinquency and Justice*. Wiley.

Hunt, C. J. (1998). Juvenile sentencing: Effects of recent punitive sentencing legislation on juvenile offenders and a proposal for sentencing in the juvenile court. *Boston College Third World Law Journal*, *19*, 621–681.

Hurst, H. III. (1999). Juvenile court–As we enter the millennium. *Juvenile & Family Court Journal*, *50*(4), 21–27.

Hyland, N. (2018). *Delinquency cases in juvenile court, 2014*. Office of Juvenile Justice and Delinquency Prevention.

Jackson, R., & Pabon, E. (2000). Race and treating other people's children as adults. *Journal of Criminal Justice, 28*(6), 507–515.

Jan, I. F., Ball, J. D., & Walsh, A. (2008). Predicting public opinion about juvenile waivers. *Criminal Justice Policy Review, 19*, 285–300.

Jensen, E. L. (1994). The waiver of juveniles to criminal court: Policy goals, empirical realities, and suggestions for change. *Idaho Law Review, 31*, 173–204.

Jensen, E. L., & Metsger, L. K. (1994). A test of the deterrent effect of legislative waiver on violent juvenile crime. *Crime and Delinquency, 40*, 96–104.

Jenson, J. M., Potter, C. C., & Howard, M. O. (2001). American juvenile justice: Recent trends and issues in youth offending. *Social Policy and Administration, 35*(1), 48–68.

Johnson, B. D., & Kurlychek, M. C. (2012). Transferred juveniles in the era of sentencing guidelines: Examining judicial departures for juvenile offenders in adult criminal court. *Criminology, 50*, 525–564.

Johnson, D. L., Banister, D. E., & Alm, M. L. (2004). The violent youth offender and juvenile transfer to the adult criminal court. *Journal of the Institute of Justice & International Studies, 4*, 84.

Johnson, K., Lanza-Kaduce, L., & Woolard, J. (2011). Disregarding graduated treatment: Why transfer aggravates recidivism. *Crime and Delinquency, 57*, 756–777.

Johnson, K. D. (2001). *The Miami-Dade Public Defender's Office Juvenile Sentencing Advocacy Project. Miami-Dade Public Defender's Office*. Bureau of Justice Assistance Bulletin.

Jordan, K. J. (2005). *Violent youth in adult court: A comprehensive examination of legislative waiver and decertification*. [Doctoral dissertation, Indiana University of Pennsylvania, Indiana, Pennsylvania].

Jordan, K. L. (2006). *Violent youth in adult court: The decertification of transferred youth*. LFB Scholarly.

Jordan, K. L. (2014). Juvenile status and criminal sentencing: Does it matter in the adult system? *Youth Violence and Juvenile Justice, 12*, 315–331.

Jordan, K. L., & Freiburger, T. L. (2010). Examining the impact of race and ethnicity on the sentencing of juveniles in the adult court. *Criminal Justice Policy Review, 21*, 185–201.

Jordan, K. L., & Maroun, R. (2016). Minority threat and criminal sentencing: Examining juveniles in the adult criminal justice system. *Journal of Criminal Justice, 39*, 41–54.

Jordan, K. L., & McNeal, B. A. (2016). Juvenile penalty or leniency: Sentencing of juveniles in the criminal justice system. *Law and Human Behavior, 40*, 387–400.

Jordan, K. L., & Myers, D. L. (2007). The decertification of transferred youth: Examining the determinants of reverse waiver. *Youth Violence and Juvenile Justice, 5*, 188–206.

Jordan, K. L., & Myers, D. L. (2011). Juvenile transfer and deterrence: Reexamining the effectiveness of a "get-tough" policy. *Crime and Delinquency, 57*, 247–270.

Juszkiewicz, J. (2000). *Youth crime/adult time: Is justice served?* Building Blocks for Youth.

Kaasa, S. O. II, J. R. T., Dezember, A., & Cauffman, E. (2018). The impact of waiver to adult court on youths' perceptions of procedural justice. *Psychology, Public Policy, and Law*, *24*(4), 418–429.

Keenan, S. J., Rush, J. P., & Cheeseman, K. A. (2015). Judicial waiver decisions in two southern states: A study of judicial perceptions. *American Journal of Criminal Justice*, *40*, 100–115.

Kellar, A. M. (2006). They're just kids: Does incarcerating juveniles with adults violate the Eighth Amendment? *Suffolk University Law Review*, *40*, 155.

Kimbrell, M. (2015). It takes a village to waive a child-or at least a jury: Applying *Apprendi* to juvenile waiver hearings in Oregon. *Willamette Law Review*, *52*, 61–98.

Kinder, K., Veneziano, C., Fichter, M., & Azuma, H. (1995). A comparison of the dispositions of juvenile offenders certified as adults with juvenile offenders not certified. *Juvenile & Family Court Journal*, *46*, 37–42.

King, C. M. (2018). The psycholegal factors for juvenile transfer and reverse transfer evaluations. *Behavioral Sciences & the Law*, *36*(1), 46–64.

King, R. (2006). *Transferring juveniles to the adult court: A factorial survey of Florida prosecutors.* [Unpublished doctoral dissertation, University of Central Florida, Orlando, Florida].

Kirkish, P., Sreenivasan, S., Welsh, R., Van Gorp, W., Eth, S., Shoptaw, S., & Ling, W. (2000). The future of criminal violence: Juveniles tried as adults. *The Journal of the American Academy of Psychiatry and the Law*, *28*(1), 38–46.

Klein, E. K. (1997). Dennis the Menace or Billy the Kid: An analysis of the role of transfer to criminal court in juvenile justice. *The American Criminal Law Review*, *35*, 371–410.

Knipps, S. K. (1992). What is a fair response to juvenile crime? *The Fordham Urban Law Journal*, *20*, 455–466.

Knox, A. (2009). *Blakely* and blended sentencing: A constitutional challenge to sentencing child criminal. *Ohio State Law Journal*, *70*, 1261–1305.

Kokrda, J. M. (2005). Juvenile sex offenders and the Virginia transfer statute: Let treatment fit the crime. *Developments in Mental Health Law*, *24*, 1–4.

Kolbe, V. L. (2006). Proposed bar to transferring juveniles with mental disorders to criminal court: Let the punishment fit the culpability. *Virginia Journal of Social Policy & the Law*, *14*, 418.

Kole, T. (2001). Juvenile offenders. *Harvard Journal on Legislation*, *38*, 231–247.

Kozich, S. D. (1980). A model for the transfer of juvenile felony offenders to adult court jurisdiction. *Journal of Juvenile Law*, *4*, 170–185.

Kruh, I. P., & Brodsky, S. L. (1997). Clinical evaluations for transfer of juveniles to criminal court: Current practices and future research. *Behavioral Sciences & the Law*, *15*(2), 151–165.

Kukino, S. E. (2014). Juvenile transfer to adult criminal court: Why transfer is not the best method in addressing juvenile delinquency. [Senior Thesis, Claremont McKenna College, Claremont, CA].

Kumli, K. E. (2002). California's judicial transfer process: From antiquated to complicated. *Corrections Today*, *64*(6), 98–100.

Kupchik, A. (2006a). *Judging juveniles: Prosecuting adolescents in adult and juvenile courts*. New York University Press.

Kupchik, A. (2006b). The decision to incarcerate in juvenile and criminal courts. *Criminal Justice Review*, *31*, 309–336.

Kupchik, A., Fagan, J., & Liberman, A. (2003). Punishment, proportionality, and jurisdictional transfer of adolescent offenders: A test of the leniency gap hypothesis. *Stanford Law & Policy Review*, *14*, 57–83.

Kupchik, A. C. (2003a). *Children in an adult world: Prosecuting adolescents in criminal and juvenile jurisdictions*. [Unpublished doctoral dissertation, New York University, New York, N.Y.].

Kupchik, A. C. (2003b). Prosecuting adolescents in criminal courts: Criminal or juvenile justice? *Social Problems*, *50*, 439–460.

Kurlychek, M. C. (2010). Pathways to adult court: Does the road traveled impact the final destination? *Justice Research and Policy*, *12*(2), 1–24.

Kurlychek, M. C. (2016). Effectiveness of juvenile transfer to adult court: Implications from current research and directions for future study. *Criminology & Public Policy*, *15*, 897–900.

Kurlychek, M. C., & Johnson, B. D. (2004). The juvenile penalty: A comparison of juvenile and young adult sentencing outcomes in criminal court. *Criminology*, *42*, 485–515.

Kurlychek, M. C., & Johnson, B. D. (2010). Juvenility and punishment: Sentencing juveniles in adult criminal court. *Criminology*, *48*, 725–758.

Lahey, J. (2016, January 8). The steep cost of keeping juveniles in adult prisons. *Atlantic (Boston, Mass.)*, 21.

Lambie, I., & Randell, I. (2013). The impact of incarceration on juvenile offenders. *Clinical Psychology Review*, *33*, 448–459.

Lane, J., Lanza-Kaduce, L., Frazier, C. E., & Bishop, D. M. (2002). Adult versus juvenile sanctions: Voices of incarcerated youths. *Crime and Delinquency*, *48*, 431–455.

Langemo, B. (2004). Serious consequences for serious juvenile offenders: Do juveniles belong in adult court? *Ohio Northern University Law Review*, *30*, 141–165.

Lanza-Kaduce, L., Bishop, D. M., Frazier, C. E., & Winner, L. (1996). Changes in juvenile waiver and transfer provisions: Projecting the impact in Florida. *Law & Policy*, *18*, 137–150.

Lanza-Kaduce, L., Frazier, C. E., & Bishop, D. M. (1999). Juvenile transfers in Florida: The worst of the worst? *University of Florida Journal of Law and Public Policy*, *10*, 277–312.

Lanza-Kaduce, L., Frazier, C. E., Lane, J., & Bishop, D. M. (2002). Juvenile transfer to criminal court study: Final report. Florida Department of Juvenile Justice.

Law, S. P., Harrington, J., Niekus, M., & Cao, J. (2019). *An economic and fiscal analysis of direct file reform proposals*. Southern Poverty Law Center.

Leeper, J. L. (1991). Recent issues in juvenile jurisdictional waiver hearings. *Journal of Juvenile Law, 12*, 35–46.

Lehmann, P. S., Chiricos, T., & Bales, W. D. (2017). Sentencing transferred juveniles in the adult criminal court: The direct and interactive effects of race and ethnicity. *Youth Violence and Juvenile Justice, 15*, 172–190.

Lehmann, P. S., & Kobie, A. (2021). Effects of waivers. In S. J. Keenan (Ed.), *The transferring of America's youth* (pp. 87–115). Lexington Books.

Lehmann, P. S., Pickett, J. T., Ryon, S. B., & Kosloski, A. E. (2019). Race, juvenile transfer, and sentencing preferences: Findings from a randomized experiment. *Race and Justice, 9*, 251–275.

Leistico, A. M. R., & Salekin, R. T. (2003). Testing the reliability and validity of the Risk, Sophistication-Maturity, and Treatment Amenability Instrument (RST-i): An assessment tool for juvenile offenders. *International Journal of Forensic Mental Health, 2*(2), 101–117.

Lemmon, J. H., Austin, T. L., Verrecchia, P. J., & Fetzer, M. (2005). The effect of legal and extralegal factors on statutory exclusion of juvenile offenders. *Youth Violence and Juvenile Justice, 3*, 214–234.

Lemmon, J. H., Sontheimer, H., & Saylor, K. A. (1991). *A study of Pennsylvania juveniles transferred to criminal court in 1986*. The Pennsylvania Juvenile Court Judges' Commission.

Lin, J. C., Bussiere, A., Matthews, M. A., & Wilber, S. L. (1994). Youth violence: Redefining the problem, rethinking the solutions. *Clearinghouse Review, 28*, 357–369.

Linares, H., & Bunton, D. (2010). An open door to the criminal courts: Analyzing the evolution of Louisiana's system for juvenile waiver. *Louisiana Law Review, 71*, 191–230.

Liwanga, R. C., & Ibe, P. (2021). Transfer of child offenders to adult criminal courts in the USA: An unnecessary exercise, unconstitutional practice, international law violation, or all of the above? *Georgia Journal of International & Comparative Law, 49*, 99–128.

Lockwood, M. (2020). Challenging moral and policy rationales for charging youth as adults. [Unpublished undergraduate senior thesis, Pitzer College, Claremont, California].

Loeffler, C. E., & Grunwald, B. (2015). Processed as an adult: A regression discontinuity estimate of the crime effects of charging non-transfer juveniles as adults. *Journal of Research in Crime and Delinquency, 52*, 890–922.

Logan, W. A. (1998). Proportionality and punishment: Imposing life without parole on juveniles. *Wake Forest Law Review, 33*, 681–725.

Loken, G. A., & Rosettenstein, D. (1998). The juvenile justice counter-reformation: Children and adolescents as adult criminals: Introduction. *Quinnipiac Law Review, 18*, 351.

Loughran, T. A., Mulvey, E.P., Schubert, C.A., Chassin, L.A., Steinberg, L., Piquero, A.R., Cota-Robles, S., & Cauffman, E., & Losoya. (2010). Differential effects of adult court transfer on juvenile offender recidivism. *Law and Human Behavior, 24*, 476–488.

Lynn-Whaley, J., & Russi, A. (2011). *Improving juvenile justice policy in California: A closer look at transfer laws impact on young men and boys of color. The Chief Justice Earl Warren Institute on Law & Social Policy*. University of California, Berkeley Law School.

Lyons, S. T. (2011). Risk, treatment amenability, and the nature of weapon: Influences on juvenile judges' transfer decisions. [Unpublished doctoral dissertation, Drexel University, Philadelphia, PA, United States].

Mahoney, A. R. (1990). Man, I'm already dead: Serious juvenile offenders in context. *Notre Dame Journal of Law, Ethics & Public Policy, 5*, 443–465.

Males, M., & Macallair, D. (2000). *The color of justice: An analysis of juvenile adult court transfers in California*. Justice Policy Institute, Building Blocks for Youth Initiative.

Mallett, C. A. (2007). Death is not different: The transfer of juvenile offenders to adult criminal courts. *Criminal Law Bulletin, 43*(4), 1–18.

Marczyk, G. R., Heilbrun, K., Lander, T., & DeMatteo, D. (2005). Juvenile decertification: Developing a model for classification and prediction. *Criminal Justice and Behavior, 32*, 278–301.

Maroney, T. A. (2009). The False promise of adolescent brain science in juvenile justice. *The Notre Dame Law Review, 85*, 89–176.

Maroney, T. A. (2011). Adolescent brain science after Graham v. Florida. *The Notre Dame Law Review, 86*, 765–794.

Marrus, E., & Rosenberg, I. M. (2005). After *Roper v. Simmons*: Keeping kids out of adult criminal court. *San Diego L. Rev., 42*, 1151-1182.

Martin, G. A. Jr. (1992). The delinquent and the juvenile court: Is there still a place for rehabilitation? *Connecticut Law Review, 25*, 57–93.

Massey, H. J. (2005). Disposing of children: The Eighth Amendment and juvenile life without parole after Roper. *Boston College Law Review. Boston College. Law School, 47*, 1083–1118.

Mathias, R. A., DeMuro, P., & Allison, R. S. (1984). Introduction. In R. A. Mathias, P. DeMuro, & R. S. Allison (Eds.), *Violent juvenile offenders: An anthology* (pp. xv–xx). NCCD.

May, K. S. (1998). Shifting away from rehabilitation: State v. Ladd's equal protection challenge to Alaska's automatic waiver law. *Alaska Law Review, 15*, 367-402.

Mays, G. L., & Gregware, P. R. (1996). The children's code reform movement in New Mexico: The politics of expediency. *Law & Policy, 18*, 179–193.

Mays, G. L., & Houghtalin, M. (1992). Trying juveniles as adults: A note on New Mexico's recent experience. *Justice System Journal, 15*, 814–823.

McCarthy, F. B. (1994). The serious offender and juvenile court reform: The case for prosecutorial waiver of juvenile court jurisdiction. *Saint Louis University Law Journal, 38*, 629–671.

McCurdy-Jackson, C. A. (2011). *Direct filing/transfer of juvenile cases in Miami-Dade County, Florida*. Eleventh Judicial Circuit of Florida Miami.

McGowan, A., Hahn, R., Liberman, A., Crosby, A., Fullilove, M., Johnson, R., Moscicki, E., Price, L., Snyder, S., Tuma, F., Lowy, J., Briss, P., Cory, S., & Stone, G. (2007). Effects on violence of laws and policies facilitating the transfer of juveniles from the juvenile justice system to the adult justice system: A systematic review. *American Journal of Preventive Medicine*, *32*, S7–S28.

McLatchey, S. F. (1999). Juvenile crime and punishment: An analysis of the "get tough" approach. *University of Florida Journal of Law and Public Policy*, *10*, 401–422.

McNulty, E. W. (1996). The transfer of juvenile offenders to adult court: Panacea or problem? *Law & Policy*, *18*, 61–75.

Means, R. F., Heller, L. D., & Janofsky, J. S. (2012). Transferring juvenile defendants from adult to juvenile court: How Maryland forensic evaluators and judges reach their decisions. *The Journal of the American Academy of Psychiatry and the Law*, *40*(3), 333–340.

Mears, D. P. (2001). Getting tough with juvenile offenders: Explaining support for sanctioning youths as adults. *Criminal Justice and Behavior*, *28*, 206–226.

Mears, D. P. (2003). A critique of waiver research: Critical next steps in assessing the impacts of laws for transferring juveniles to the criminal justice system. *Youth Violence and Juvenile Justice*, *1*, 156–172.

Mears, D. P., & Field, S. H. (2000). Theorizing sanctioning in a criminalized juvenile court. *Criminology*, *38*, 983–1020.

Mears, D. P., Hay, C., Gertz, M., & Mancini, C. (2007). Public opinion and the foundation of the juvenile court. *Criminology*, *45*, 223–257.

Merlo, A. V., & Benekos, P. J. (2003). Defining juvenile justice in the 21st century. *Youth Violence and Juvenile Justice*, *1*, 276–288.

Merlo, A. V., & Benekos, P. J. (2010). Is punitive juvenile justice policy declining in the United States? A critique of emergent initiatives. *Youth Justice*, *10*, 3–24.

Merlo, A. V., Benekos, P. J., & Cook, W. J. (1997a). 'Getting tough' with youth: Legislative waiver as crime control. *Juvenile & Family Court Journal*, *48*(3), 1–15.

Merlo, A. V., Benekos, P. J., & Cook, W. J. (1997b). Waiver and juvenile justice reform: Widening the punitive net. *Criminal Justice Policy Review*, *8*(2-3), 145–168.

Merlo, A. V., Benekos, P. J., & Cook, W. J. (1999). The juvenile court at 100 years: Celebration or wake. *Juvenile & Family Court Journal*, *50*, 1–10.

Miller, J. G. (1984). Epilogue: The issue of violent juvenile crime. In R. A. Mathias, P. DeMuro, & R. S. Allison (Eds.), *Violent juvenile offenders: An anthology* (pp. 379–383). NCCD.

Miller, N. (1995). *State Laws on Prosecutors' and Judges' Use of Juvenile Records*. US Department of Justice, Office of Justice Programs, National Institute of Justice.

Miller, R. N., & Applegate, B. K. (2015). Adult crime, adult time? Benchmarking public views on punishing serious juvenile felons. *Criminal Justice Review*, *40*, 151–168.

Miner-Romanoff, K. (2014). Juvenile offenders tried as adults: What they know and implications for practitioners. *Northern Kentucky Law Review*, *41*, 205–224.

Mlyniec, W. J. (1976). Juvenile delinquent or adult convict—The prosecutor's choice. *The American Criminal Law Review*, *14*, 29–57.

Mole, D., & White, D. (2005). *Transfer and waiver in the juvenile justice system*. Child Welfare League of America.

Monahan, K., Steinberg, L., & Piquero, A. R. (2015). Juvenile justice policy and practice: A developmental perspective. *Crime and Justice*, *44*(1), 577–619.

Moore, E. A. (2007). Juvenile justice: The Nathaniel Abraham murder case. *University of Michigan Journal of Law Reform. University of Michigan. Law School*, *41*, 215–241.

Mulvey, E. P., & Schubert, C. (2012). *Transfer of juveniles to adult court: Effects of a broad policy in one court. Juvenile Justice Bulletin. December 2012*. U.S. Department of Justice, Office of Justice Programs. Office of Juvenile Justice & Delinquency Prevention.

Myers, D. L. (2001). *Excluding violent youths from juvenile court: The effectiveness of legislative waiver*. LFB Scholarly Publications.

Myers, D. L. (2003a). Adult crime, adult time: Punishing violent youth in the adult criminal justice system. *Youth Violence and Juvenile Justice*, *1*, 173–197.

Myers, D. L. (2003b). The recidivism of violent youths in juvenile and adult court: A consideration of selection bias. *Youth Violence and Juvenile Justice*, *1*, 79–101.

Myers, D. L. (2005). *Boys among men: Trying and sentencing juveniles as adults*. Praeger Publishers.

Myers, D. L. (2016). Juvenile transfer to adult court: Ongoing search for scientific support. *Criminology & Public Policy*, *15*, 927–938.

Myers, D. L., & Kiehl, K. (2001). The predispositional status of violent youthful offenders: Is there a "custody gap" in adult criminal court? *Justice Research and Policy*, *3*, 115–143.

Myers, D. L., Lee, D., Giever, D., & Gilliam, J. (2011). Practitioner perceptions of juvenile transfer in Pennsylvania. *Youth Violence and Juvenile Justice*, *9*, 222–240.

Nagin, D. S., Piquero, A. R., Scott, E. S., & Steinberg, L. (2006). Public preferences for rehabilitation versus incarceration of juvenile offenders: Evidence from a contingent valuation survey. *Criminology & Public Policy*, *5*, 627–651.

NASEM. National Academies of Sciences, Engineering, and Medicine. (2019). The promise of adolescence: Realizing opportunity for all youth. The National Academies Press.

NDAA. National District Attorney's Association. (2002). *Resource manual and policy positions on juvenile crime issues*. NDAA.

NeMoyer, A. (2017). *Kent* revisited: Aligning judicial waiver criteria with more than fifty years of social science research. *Vermont Law Review*, *42*, 441–528.

Nguyen, T. V. H. (2016). Juvenile justice: Searching for a flexible alternative to the strict and over-inclusive transfer system for serious juvenile offenders. *Southern California Law Review*, *90*, 343–382.

Noon, C. R. (1994). Waiving goodbye to juvenile defendants, getting smart vs. getting tough. *University of Miami Law Review*, *49*, 431–476.

Notes. (2002). For the good of the child, for the good of society: Using Scotland and Jamaica as models to reform U.S. juvenile justice policy. *Harvard Law Review, 115,* 1964-1987.

NRC. National Research Council. (2013). Reforming juvenile justice: A developmental approach. The National Academies Press.

Nunez, N., Dahl, M. J., Tang, C. M., & Jensen, B. L. (2007). Trial venue decisions in juvenile cases: Mitigating and extralegal factors matter. *Legal and Criminological Psychology*, *12*(1), 21–39.

OJJ. (1999). *Office of Juvenile Justice. Juvenile justice: A century of change*. US Department of Justice, Office of Justice Programs, Office of Juvenile Justice and Delinquency Prevention.

OJJDP. (2018). *Statistical briefing book. Provisions for imposing adult sanctions on juvenile offenders, 2016*. https:/www.ojjdp.gov/ojstagg/structure-process/qa04113.asp?qadate=2016

OJJDP. (2020). *Statistical briefing book. Provisions for imposing adult sanctions on juvenile offenders, 2018*. https:/www.ojjdp.gov/ojstagg/structure-process/qa04113.asp?qadate=2018

Oliver, B. E. (2006). *Does trying juveniles as adults work? An analysis*. The Juvenile Justice Foundation of North Carolina.

Olson, J. K. (2004). *Waiver of juveniles to criminal court: Judicial discretion and racial disparity* [Unpublished graduate course paper, University of Nevada-Las Vegas. Las Vegas, Nevada].

Osbun, L. A., & Rode, P. A. (1984). Prosecuting juveniles as adults: The quest for "objective" decisions. *Criminology*, *22*, 187–202.

Otto, R., & Borum, R. (2004). Evaluation of youth in the juvenile justice system. In *Handbook of forensic psychology* (pp. 873–895). Academic Press.

Pagnanelli, E. (2007). Children as adults: The transfer of juveniles to adult courts and the potential impact of Roper v. Simmons. *The American Criminal Law Review*, *44*, 175–194.

Parent, D. G., Dunworth, T., McDonald, D., & Rhodes, W. (1997). *Transferring serious juvenile offenders to adult courts*. U.S. Department of Justice, Office of Justice Programs, National Institute of Justice.

Park, J. (2007). Balancing rehabilitation and punishment: A legislative solution for unconstitutional juvenile waiver policies. *The George Washington Law Review*, *76*, 786–818.

Pegg, K. (2015). The" once an adult, always an adult" doctrine: More harm than good. *Indiana Journal of Law and Social Equality*, *3*(1), 144–160.

Penney, S. R., & Moretti, M. M. (2005). The transfer of juveniles to adult court in Canada and the United States: Confused agendas and compromised assessment procedures. *International Journal of Forensic Mental Health*, *4*(1), 19–37.

Perry, S. W. (2006). *Prosecutors in state courts, 2005. BJS Bulletin*. U.S. Department of Justice, Office of Justice Programs.

PHR. Physicians for Human Rights. (2007). *Kids in the adult criminal system*. Fact Sheet. http: physiciansforhumanrights.org/juvenile-justice/kids-in-the-adult-system.html

Pine, J. B. (1996). Juvenile waiver in Rhode Island. *Roger Williams University Law Review*, *2*, 257–276.

Podkopacz, M. R., & Feld, B. C. (1996). The end of the line: An empirical study of judicial waiver. *The Journal of Criminal Law & Criminology*, *86*, 449–492.

Podkopacz, M. R., & Feld, B. C. (2001). The back-door to prison: Waiver reform, blended sentencing, and the law of unintended consequences. *The Journal of Criminal Law & Criminology*, *91*, 997–1071.

Polachek, E. A. (2008). Juvenile transfer: From get better to get tough and where we go from here. *William Mitchell Law Review*, *35*, 1162.

Pollitt, B. (2004). Buying justice on credit instead of investing in long-term solutions: Foreclosing on trying juveniles in criminal court. *Journal of Law & Family Studies*, *6*, 281–300.

Poulos, T. M., & Orchowsky, S. (1994). Serious juvenile offenders: Predicting the probability of transfer to criminal court. *Crime and Delinquency*, *40*, 3–17.

Prescott, M. M. (1999). Another option for older, nonviolent juveniles: Statutory retention of juvenile court jurisdiction past the age of majority. *Iowa Law Review*, *85*, 997–1033.

Prochaska, B. F. (2018). *Do contextual factors matter in juvenile transfer decisions? A longitudinal multilevel analysis of juvenile waivers to adult court* [Unpublished doctoral dissertation, University of Arkansas at Little Rock, Little Rock, AR].

Puzzanchera, C. M. (2000). *Delinquency cases waived to criminal court, 1988-1997*. U.S. Department of Justice, Office of Justice Programs. Office of Juvenile Justice and Delinquency Prevention.

Puzzanchera, C. M. (2001). *Delinquency cases waived to criminal court, 1989-1998*. U.S. Department of Justice, Office of Justice Programs, Office of Juvenile Justice and Delinquency Prevention.

Puzzanchera, C. M. (2003). *Delinquency cases waived to criminal court, 1990-1999*. U.S. Department of Justice, Office of Justice Programs, Office of Juvenile Justice and Delinquency Prevention.

Puzzanchera, C. M., & Addie, S. (2014). *Delinquency cases waived to criminal court, 2010*. U.S. Department of Justice, Office of Justice Programs. Office of Juvenile Justice and Delinquency Prevention.

Puzzanchera, C. M., Hockenberry, S., & Sickmund, M. (2022). *Youth and the juvenile justice System:2022 national report*. National Center for Juvenile Justice.

Quinn, M. C. (2015). In loco juvenile justice: Minors in munis, cash from kids, and adolescent pro se advocacy-Ferguson and beyond. *Brigham Young University Law Review*, 1247–1308.

Rainville, G. (2008). Juveniles transferred to criminal courts: Is their criminal sentence dependent on how they got there? *Criminal Justice Policy Review*, *19*, 301–313.

Rainville, G., & Smith, S. (2003). *Juvenile felony defendants in criminal courts: Survey of 40 counties, 1998. Bureau of Justice Statistics Special Report*. US Department of Justice, Office of Justice Programs.

Redding, R. E. (1997). Juveniles transferred to criminal court: Legal reform proposals based on social science research. *Utah Law Review*, *1997*, 709–763.

Redding, R. E. (1999). Legal, psychological, and behavioral outcomes. *Juvenile & Family Court Journal*, *50*(1), 1–20.

Redding, R. E. (2003). The effects of adjudicating and sentencing juveniles as adults: Research and policy implications. *Youth Violence and Juvenile Justice*, *1*, 128–155.

Redding, R. E. (2005). Adult punishment for juvenile offenders: Does it reduce crime? In Dowd, N. Singer, D., & Wilson, R. (Eds.), Handbook of children, culture, and violence (Chapter 19). Sage Publications.

Redding, R. E. (2008). Juvenile transfer laws: An effective deterrent to delinquency? *Juvenile Justice Bulletin*.

Redding, R. E. (2010). *Juvenile transfer laws: An effective deterrent to delinquency?* U.S. Department of Justice, Office of Juvenile Justice & Delinquency Prevention.

Redding, R. E. (2016). One size does not fit all: The deterrent effect of transferring juveniles to criminal court. *Criminology & Public Policy*, *15*, 939–948.

Redding, R. E., & Fuller, E. J. (2004). What do juvenile offenders know about being tried as adults? Implications for deterrence. *Juvenile & Family Court Journal*, *55*(3), 35–44.

Redding, R. E., & Howell, J. C. (2000). Blended sentencing in American juvenile courts. In J. Fagan & F. E. Zimring (Eds.), *The changing borders of juvenile justice: Transfer of adolescents to the criminal court* (pp. 145–180). University of Chicago Press.

Redding, R. E., & Mrozoski, B. (2005). Adjudicatory and Dispositional Decision Making. In K. Heilbrun, N. Goldstein, & R. Redding (Eds.), *Juvenile delinquency: Prevention, assessment, and intervention* (pp. 232–256). Oxford University Press.

Reidy, T. J., Sorensen, J. R., & Cihan, A. (2018). Institutional misconduct among juvenile offenders serving a blended sentence. *Journal of Criminal Justice*, *57*, 99–105.

Riggs Romaine, C. L., Goldstein, N. E. S., Hunt, E., & DeMatteo, D. (2011). Traumatic experiences and juvenile amenability: The role of trauma in forensic evaluations and judicial decision making. *Child and Youth Care Forum*, *40*(5), 363–380.

Risler, E. A., Sweatman, T., & Nackerud, L. (1998). Evaluating the Georgia legislative waiver's effectiveness in deterring juvenile crime. *Research on Social Work Practice*, *8*, 657–667.

Robertson, A., Gardner, S., Haynes, S., & Gresham, K. (2019). *A comprehensive model for effective juvenile justice: Recommendations for improving the Mississippi juvenile justice system*. Researchgate.net.

Robinson, G. E. (1971). Certification of Minors to the Juvenile Court: An Empirical Study. *The San Diego Law Review*, *8*, 404.

Rodriguez, N. (2003). Youth transfer decisions: Exploring county variations. *Juvenile & Family Court Journal*, *54*(1), 33–46.

Romaine, C. L. R. (2010). *Juvenile decertification in Philadelphia County: A model for jurisdiction-specific research* [Unpublished doctoral dissertation, Drexel University, Philadelphia, PA].

Rose, J. T. (2002). Innocence lost: The detrimental effect of automatic waiver statutes on juvenile justice. *Brandeis Law Journal*, *41*, 977.

Rosenberg, I. M. (2000). Teen violence and the juvenile courts: A plea for reflection and restraint. *Houston Law Review*, *37*, 75–96.

Rossiter, M. J. (2006). Transferring children to adult criminal court: How to best protect our children and society. *Journal of Juvenile Law*, *27*, 123.

Rossum, R. A. (1995). Holding juveniles accountable: Reforming America's "juvenile injustice system.". *Pepperdine Law Review*, *22*, 907–931.

Rovner, J. (2016). *How tough on crime became tough on kids: Prosecuting teenage drug charges in adult courts*. The Sentencing Project.

Rowley, J. C., Ewing, C. P., & Singer, S. I. (1987). Juvenile homicide: The need for an interdisciplinary approach. *Behavioral Sciences & the Law*, *5*, 3–10.

Roysher, M., & Edelman, P. (1981). Treating juveniles as adults in New York: What does it mean and how is it working? In J. C. Hall, D. M. Hamparian, J. M. Pettibone, & J. L. White (Eds.), *Major Issues in Juvenile Justice Information and Training: Readings in Public Policy* (pp. 265–293). Academy for Contemporary Problems.

Rubin, H. T. (2006). *Return them to juvenile court. Policy brief. Adultification series* (Vol. 1). Campaign for Youth Justice.

Ruddell, R., & Mays, G. L. (2012). Transferring pre-teens to adult criminal courts: Searching for a justification. *Juvenile & Family Court Journal*, *63*(4), 22–36.

Ruddell, R., Mays, G. L., & Giever, D. M. (1998). Transferring juveniles to adult courts. Recent trends and issues in Canada and the United States. *Juvenile & Family Court Journal*, *49*(3), 1–15.

Rudman, C., Hartstone, E., Fagan, J., & Moore, M. (1986). Violent youth in adult court: Process and punishment. *Crime and Delinquency*, *32*, 75–96.

Rudof, P. R. (1998). Throwing out the baby with the bathwater: Utah's Serious Youth Offender Statute. *Utah Law Review*, 443–464.

Ryan, L. (2012). *Youth in the adult criminal justice system*. Campaign for Youth Justice.

Sabo, S. (1996). Rights of passage: An analysis of waiver of juvenile court jurisdiction. *Fordham Law Review*, *64*, 2425–2454.

Salazar, A. B. (1982). The expanding scope of prosecutorial discretion in charging juveniles as adults: A critical look at People v. Thorpe. *University of Colorado Law Review*, *54*, 617.

Salekin, R. T. (2002). How can developmental and child psychology inform policy decision making? In B. L. Bottoms, M. B. Kovera, & B. D. McAuliff (Eds.), *Children, social science, and the law* (pp. 203–232). Cambridge University Press.

Salekin, R. T., Rogers, R., & Ustad, K. L. (2001). Juvenile waiver to adult criminal courts: Prototypes for dangerousness, sophistication–maturity, and amenability to treatment. *Psychology, Public Policy, and Law*, *7*, 381–408.

Salekin, R. T., Yff, R., Neumann, C. S., Leistico, A. M. R., & Zalot, A. A. (2002). Juvenile transfer to adult courts: A look at the prototypes for dangerousness sophistication-maturity and amenability to treatment through a legal lens. *Psychology, Public Policy, and Law*, *8*, 373–410.

Samuelson, B. K. (2010). *Mechanisms of juvenile transfer: Variations in incarceration and sentence length in criminal court.* [Unpublished Master's Thesis, University of Maryland, College Park, MD].

Sanborn, J. B. Jr. (2004a). The "adultification" of youth. In P. J. Benekos & A. V. Merlo (Eds.), *Controversies in juvenile justice and delinquency* (pp. 143–164). Anderson Publishing Company.

Sargent, D. A., & Gordon, D. H. (1963). Waiver of jurisdiction: An evaluation of the process in the juvenile court. *Crime and Delinquency*, *9*, 121–128.

Sarri, R., & Shook, J. (2005). Juvenile justice in the United States: Adherence to Human Rights Conventions. In M. Ensalaco & L. C. Majka (Eds.), *Children's human rights: Progress and challenges for children worldwide* (pp. 218–240). Rowman and Littlefield Publishers.

Schaefer, S. S., & Uggen, C. (2016). Blended sentencing laws and the punitive turn in juvenile justice. *Law & Social Inquiry*, *41*, 435–463.

Schetky, D. H. (2003). Juveniles standing trial: Waiver to adult court. *Journal of Psychiatric Practice*, *9*(6), 465–468.

Schiraldi, V., & Soler, M. (1998). The will of the people? The public's opinion of the Violent and Repeat Juvenile Offender Act of 1997. *Crime and Delinquency*, *44*, 590–601.

Schiraldi, V., & Ziedenberg, J. (1999). *The Florida experiment: An analysis of the impact of granting prosecutors discretion to try juveniles as adults*. Justice Policy Institute.

Schornhorst, T. F. (1968). The waiver of juvenile court jurisdiction: Kent revisited. *Indiana Law Review*, *43*, 583–613.

Schubert, C. A., Mulvey, E. P., Loughran, T. A., Fagan, J., Chassin, L. A., Piquero, A. R., Losoya, S. H., Steinberg, L., & Cauffman, E. (2010). Predicting outcomes for youth transferred to adult court. *Law and Human Behavior*, *34*(6), 460–475.

Schulhofer, S. J. (1997). Youth crime—and what not to do about it. *Valparaiso University Law Review. Valparaiso University. School of Law*, *31*, 435–447.

Schwartz Alers, M. (1973). Transfer of jurisdiction from juvenile to criminal court. *Crime and Delinquency, 19*, 519–527.

Scialabba, N. (2016). Should juveniles be charged as adults in the criminal justice system? *American Bar Association, 3*.

Scism, M. R. (2019). Children are different: The need for reform of Virginia's juvenile transfer laws. *Richmond Public Interest Law Review, 22*, 445–464.

Scott, E., Grisso, T., Levick, M., & Steinberg, L. (2016). Juvenile sentencing reform in a constitutional framework. *Temple Law Review, 88*, 675–716.

Scott, E. S. (2000). The legal construction of adolescence. *Hofstra Law Review, 29*, 547–598.

Scott, E. S. (2013a). Children are different: Constitutional values and justice policy. *Ohio State Journal of Criminal Law, 11*, 71–105.

Scott, E. S. (2013b). *Miller v. Alabama* and the (past and) future of juvenile crime regulation. *Law & Inequality, 31*, 535–558.

Scott, E. S., & Grisso, T. (1997). The evolution of adolescence: A developmental perspective on juvenile justice reform. *The Journal of Criminal Law & Criminology, 88*, 137–189.

Scott, E. S., & Grisso, T. (2004). Developmental incompetence, due process, and juvenile justice policy. *North Carolina Law Review, 83*, 793–845.

Scott, E. S., Reppucci, D., & Woolard, J. L. (1995). Evaluating adolescent decision making in legal contexts. *Law and Human Behavior, 19*, 221–244.

Scott, E. S., & Steinberg, L. (2002). Blaming youth. *Texas Law Review, 81*, 799–840.

Scott, E. S., & Steinberg, L. (2008). Adolescent development and the regulation of youth crime. *The Future of Children, 18*(2), 15–33.

Scott, E. S., & Steinberg, L. (2010). Social welfare and fairness in juvenile crime regulation. *Louisiana Law Review, 71*, 35–97.

Sellers, B. G., & Arrigo, B. A. (2009). Adolescent transfer, developmental maturity and adjudicative competence: An ethical and justice policy inquiry. *Criminology, 29*, 435–488.

Semple, J. K., & Woody, W. D. (2011). Juveniles tried as adults: The age of the juvenile matters. *Psychological Reports, 109*(1), 301–308.

Sewell, R. J. (2019). It's time to have an adult discussion about Alabama's juvenile transfer laws. *Cumberland Law Review, 50*, 5.

Sewell, S. M. (2009). *A policy recommendation for the juvenile waiver. (Unpublished Master's in Public Administration policy position paper)*. California State University.

Sharlein, J. (2018). Beyond recidivism: Investigating comparative educational and employment outcomes for adolescents in the juvenile and criminal justice systems. *Crime and Delinquency, 64*, 26–52.

Sheffer, J. P. (1995). Serious and habitual juvenile offender statutes: Reconciling punishment and rehabilitation within the juvenile justice system. *Vanderbilt Law Review*, *48*, 479–512.

Shefi, E. D. (2002). Waiving goodbye: Incarcerating waived juveniles in adult correctional facilities will not reduce crime. *University of Michigan Journal of Law Reform. University of Michigan. Law School*, *36*, 653–689.

Shelden, R. G., & Hussong, M. (2003). Juvenile crime, adult adjudication, and the death penalty: Draconian policies revisited. *Justice Policy Journal: Analyzing criminal and juvenile justice issues and policies*, 21-40.

Shiller, R. (2006). Fundamental unfairness of the discretionary direct file process in Florida: The need for a return to juvenile court waiver hearings. *Whittier Journal of Child & Family Advocacy*, *6*, 13–52.

Shook, J. J. (2004). *Treating juveniles as adults in the justice system: A case study of decision making and case processing*. (Unpublished doctoral dissertation). University of Michigan, Ann Arbor, MI.

Shook, J. J. (2005). Contesting childhood in the US justice system: The transfer of juveniles to adult criminal court. *Childhood*, *12*, 461–478.

Shook, J. J. (2013). Juvenile or adult? Negotiating and contesting childhood in the courtroom. *Children and Youth Services Review*, *35*(8), 1236–1244.

Shook, J. J. (2014). Looking back and thinking forward: Examining the consequences of policies and practices that treat juveniles as adults. *Journal of Evidence-Based Social Work*, *11*(4), 392–403.

Shook, J. J., & Sarri, R. C. (2008). Trends in the committee of juveniles to adult prisons: Toward an increased willingness to treat juveniles as adults. *Wayne Law Review*, *54*, 1725.

Sickmund, M. (1994). How juveniles get to criminal court. U.S. Department of Justice, OJP, OJJDP.

Sickmund, M. (2003). *Juveniles in court*. U.S. Department of Justice, Office of Justice Programs, Office of Juvenile Justice and Delinquency Prevention.

Singer, S. I. (1993). The automatic waiver of juveniles and substantive justice. *Crime and Delinquency*, *39*, 253–261.

Singer, S. I. (1994). *The case processing of juvenile offenders in criminal court and legislative waiver in New York State. Office of Juvenile Justice and Delinquency Prevention. Office of Justice Programs.* U.S. Department of Justice.

Singer, S. I. (1996a). Merging and emerging systems of juvenile and criminal justice. *Law & Policy*, *18*, 1–15.

Singer, S. I. (1996b). *Recriminalizing delinquency: Violent juvenile crimes and juvenile justice reform*. Cambridge University Press.

Singer, S. I. (2003). Incarcerating juveniles into adulthood: Organizational fields of knowledge and the back end of waiver. *Youth Violence and Juvenile Justice*, *1*(2), 115–127.

Singer, S. I., Fagan, J., & Liberman, A. (2000). The reproduction of juvenile justice in criminal court: A case study of New York's juvenile offender law. In J. Fagan & F. E. Zimring (Eds.), *The changing borders of juvenile justice: Transfer of adolescents to the criminal court* (pp. 353–375). University of Chicago Press.

Singer, S. I., & McDowall, D. (1988). Criminalizing delinquency: The deterrent effects of the New York juvenile offender law. *Law & Society Review*, 521–535.

Slaten, M. (2002). Juvenile transfers to criminal court: Whose right is it anyway? *Rutgers Law Review*, *55*, 821–853.

Slobogin, C. (1999). Treating kids right: Deconstructing and reconstructing the amenability to treatment concept. *Journal of Contemporary Legal Issues*, *10*, 299–333.

Slobogin, C. (2013). Treating juveniles like juveniles: Getting rid of transfer and expanded adult court jurisdiction. *Texas Tech Law Review*, *46*, 103–132.

Smallheer, R. L. (1999). Sentence blending and the promise of rehabilitation: Bringing the juvenile justice system full circle. *Hofstra Law Review*, *28*, 259–289.

Smith, A. (1994). They dream of growing older: On kids and crime. *Boston College Law Review. Boston College. Law School*, *36*, 953–1024.

Smith, B. V., & Yarussi, J. (2012). *Juveniles convicted as adults: An annotated bibliography of current research*. National Institute of Corrections.

Smith, C. K. (2013). Nothing About Us Without Us! The failure of the modern juvenile justice system and a call for community-based justice. *Journal of Applied Research on Children: Informing Policy for Children at Risk*, *4*(1), 11.

Snyder, H. N. (2012). Juvenile delinquents and juvenile justice clientele: Trends and patterns in crime and justice system responses. In Feld, B.C., & Bishop, D.M (Eds.). The oxford handbook of juvenile crime and juvenile justice (pp. 3-30). Oxford University Press.

Snyder, H. N., & Hutzler, J. L. (1981). *The serious juvenile offender: The scope of the problem and the response of juvenile courts*. National Center for Juvenile Justice.

Snyder, H. N., & Sickmund, M. (1995). *Juvenile offenders and victims: A national report*. National Center for Juvenile Justice. Office of Justice Programs, Office of Juvenile Justice and Delinquency Prevention.

Snyder, H. N., & Sickmund, M. (1999). *Juvenile offenders and victims: National report*. National Center for Juvenile Justice. Office of Justice Programs. Office of Juvenile Justice and Delinquency Prevention.

Snyder, H. N., & Sickmund, M. (2006). *Juvenile offenders and victims: 2006 national report*. National Center for Juvenile Justice. Office of Justice Programs. Office of Juvenile Justice and Delinquency Prevention.

Snyder, H. N., Sickmund, M., & Poe-Yamagata, E. (2000). *Juvenile transfers to criminal court in the 1990s: Lessons learned from four studies*. U.S. Department of Justice, Office of Justice Programs, Office of Juvenile Justice and Delinquency Prevention.

Sobol, S. (2022). Rethinking juvenile rehabilitation: Presumptive waiver and alternative sentencing in Indiana. *Indiana Law Journal (Indianapolis, Ind.)*, *97*, 365–391.

Soler, M. (2010). Missed opportunity: Waiver, race, data, and policy reform. *Louisiana Law Review*, *71*, 17–33.

Solway, K. S., Hays, J. R., Schreiner, D., & Cansler, D. (1980). Clinical study of youths petitioned for certification as adults. *Psychological Reports*, *46*, 1067–1073.

Sorrentino, J. N., & Olsen, G. K. (1977). Certification of juveniles to adult court. *Pepperdine Law Review*, *4*, 497–522.

Soung, P. (2011). Social and biological constructions of youth: Implications for juvenile justice and racial equity. *Northwestern Journal of Law and Social Policy*, *6*, 428–444.

Spring, M. E. (1998). Extended jurisdiction juvenile prosecution: A new approach to the problem of juvenile delinquency in Illinois. *Marshall Law Review*, *31*, 1351–1384.

Springer, C. E. (1991). Rehabilitating the juvenile court. *Notre Dame Journal of Ethics & Public Policy*, *5*, 397–420.

Sridharan, S., Greenfield, L., & Blakley, B. (2004). A study of prosecutorial certification practice in Virginia. *Criminology & Public Policy*, *3*, 605–632.

Stafford, D. W. (2013). *Predictive factors effecting outcomes for juvenile delinquent cases in Tennessee* (Unpublished doctoral dissertation). Tennessee State University. Nashville, Tennessee.

Stahl, A. L. (1999). *Delinquency cases waived to criminal court, 1987-1996*. US Department of Justice, Office of Justice Programs, Office of Juvenile Justice and Delinquency Prevention.

Stalans, L. J., & Henry, G. T. (1994). Societal views of justice for adolescents accused of murder: Inconsistency between community sentiment and automatic legislative transfers. *Law and Human Behavior*, *18*, 675–696.

Stamm, M. J. (1973). Transfer of jurisdiction in juvenile court: An analysis of the proceeding, its role in the administration of justice, and A proposal for the reform of Kentucky law. *Kentucky Law Journal (Lexington, Ky.)*, *62*, 122–199.

Steinberg, L. (2000). *Should juvenile offenders be tried as adults? A developmental perspective on changing legal policies* (No. 147). Northwestern University/University of Chicago Joint Center for Poverty Research.

Steinberg, L. (2009). Adolescent development and juvenile justice. *Annual Review of Clinical Psychology*, *5*, 459–485.

Steinberg, L., & Cauffman, E. (1999). A developmental perspective on serious juvenile crime: When should juveniles be treated as adults. *Federal Probation*, *63*, 52–57.

Steinberg, L., & Cauffman, E. (2000). A developmental perspective on jurisprudential boundary. In Fagan. J., & Zimring, F.E. (Eds.), The Changing Borders of Juvenile Justice: Transfer of Adolescents to the Criminal Court (pp. 379-406). University of Chicago Press.

Steinberg, L., & Cauffman, E. (2001). Adolescents as adults in court: A developmental perspective on the transfer of juveniles to criminal court. *Social Policy Report, 15*(4), 1–16.

Steinberg, L., Grisso, T., Woolard, J., Cauffman, E., Scott, E. S., Graham, S., Lexcen, F., Reppucci, N. D., & Schwartz, R. (2003). Juveniles' competence to stand trial as adults. *Social Policy Report, 17*(4), 1–16.

Steinberg, L., & Piquero, A. R. (2010). Manipulating public opinion about trying juveniles as adults: An experimental study. *Crime and Delinquency, 56*, 487–506.

Steiner, B. (2005). Predicting sentencing outcomes and time served for juveniles transferred to criminal court in a rural northwestern state. *Journal of Criminal Justice, 33*, 601–610.

Steiner, B. (2009). The effects of juvenile transfer to criminal court on incarceration decisions. *Justice Quarterly, 26*, 77–106.

Steiner, B., & Hemmens, C. (2003). Juvenile waiver 2003: Where are we now? *Juvenile & Family Court Journal, 54*(2), 1–24.

Steiner, B., Hemmens, C., & Bell, V. (2006). Legislative waiver reconsidered: General deterrent effects of statutory exclusion laws enacted post-1979. *Justice Quarterly, 23*, 34–59.

Steiner, B., & Wright, E. (2006). Assessing the relative effects of state direct file waiver laws on violent juvenile crime: Deterrence or irrelevance? *The Journal of Criminal Law & Criminology, 96*, 1451–1477.

Stevens, J. (2014). The unreviewable irredeemable child: Why the District of Columbia needs reverse waiver. *University of the District of Columbia Law Review, 17*, 220–243.

Steward-Lindsey, S. (2006). Fulfilling the promise of *Kent:* Fixing the Texas juvenile waiver statute. *American Journal of Criminal Law, 34*, 109–126.

Stolzenberg, L., & D'Alessio, S. J. (2009). Cheating the hangman: The effect of Roper v. Simmons decision on homicides committed by juveniles. *Crime and Delinquency, 56*, 928–948.

Strom, K. J., Smith, S. K., & Snyder, H. N. (1998). Juvenile felony defendants in criminal courts. State court processing statistics, 1990-94. U.S. Department of Justice. Bureau of Justice Statistics Special Report.

Suffredini, B. R. (1994). Juvenile gunslingers: A place for punitive philosophy in rehabilitative juvenile justice. *Boston College Law Review. Boston College. Law School, 35*, 885–925.

Sullivan, C. (2001). Juvenile delinquency in the Twenty-First Century: Is blended sentencing the middle-road solution for violent kids? *Northern Illinois University Law Review, 21*, 483–514.

Sulok, M. M. (2007). Extended jurisdiction juvenile prosecutions: To revoke or not to revoke. *Loyola University of Chicago Law Journal. Loyola University of Chicago. School of Law, 39*, 215–284.

Swanson, H. L. (2018). *An empirical analysis of the effects of juvenile offender placement in adult facilities on recidivism rates* (Unpublished master's thesis). Iowa State University, Ames Iowa.

Szymanski, L. A. (1996). *Specialized waiver provisions: Reverse waiver and once an adult/always an adult. NCJJ Snapshot, 1(3)*. National Center for Juvenile Justice.

Szymanski, L. A. (1998). *"Once an adult/always an adult." NCJJ Snapshot 3 (7).* National Center for Juvenile Justice.

Szymanski, L. A. (2002). *"Once an adult/always an adult" (2001 update), and juvenile can request transfer to criminal court. NCJJ Snapshot 7(7).* National Center for Juvenile Justice.

Szymanski, L. A. (2007). *"Once an adult/always an adult" (2007 update). NCJJ Snapshot 12(4).* National Center for Juvenile Justice.

Szymanski, L. A. (2008). *Once an adult/always an adult (2008 update). NCJJ Snapshot 13(4).* National Center for Juvenile Justice.

Szymanski, L. A. (2009). *Once an adult/always an adult (2009 update). NCJJ Snapshot 14(5).* National Center for Juvenile Justice.

Szymanski, L. A. (2010a). *Can juveniles transferred for criminal prosecution be held for pre-trial detention in adult jails? NCJJ Snapshot 15(8).* National Center for Juvenile Justice.

Szymanski, L. A. (2010b). *Once a juvenile is transferred to criminal court must they be tried as adults for all future offenses? NCJJ Snapshot, 15(6).* National Center for Juvenile Justice.

Szymanski, L. A. (2011). *Once a Juvenile is Transferred to Criminal Court Must They be Tried as Adults For all Future Offenses? NCJJ Snapshot, 16(9).* National Center for Juvenile Justice.

Tanenhaus, D. S. (2000). The evolution of transfer out of the juvenile court. In J. Fagan & F. E. Zimring (Eds.), *The changing borders of juvenile justice: Transfer of adolescents to the criminal court* (pp. 13–43). University of Chicago Press.

Tanenhaus, D. S. (2013). First things first: Juvenile justice reform in historical context. *Texas Tech Law Review*, *46*, 281–290.

Tanenhaus, D. S., & Drizin, S. A. (2002). Owing to the extreme youth of the accused: The changing legal response to juvenile homicide. *The Journal of Criminal Law & Criminology*, *92*, 641–705.

Tang, C. M., & Nunez, N. (2003). Effects of defendant age and juror bias on judgment of culpability: What happens when a juvenile is tried as an adult? *American Journal of Criminal Justice*, *28*, 37–52.

Tanner, C. H. (1999). Arkansas's Extended Juvenile Jurisdiction Act: The Balance of Offender Rehabilitation and Accountability. *University of Arkansas Little Rock Law Review*, *22*, 647–657.

Tashea, J. R., & Passarella, A. (2015). Youth charged as adults: The use and outcomes of transfer in Baltimore City. *University of Maryland Law Journal of Race, Religion. Race, Gender, & Class*, *14*, 273–302.

Tate, D. C., Reppucci, N. D., & Mulvey, E. P. (1995). Violent juvenile delinquents: Treatment effectiveness and implications for future action. *The American Psychologist*, *50*(9), 777–781.

Taylor, M. (2015). Juvenile transfers to adult court: An examination of the long-term outcomes of transferred and non-transferred juveniles. *Juvenile & Family Court Journal*, *66*(4), 29–47.

Taylor-Thompson, K. (2014). Minority rule: Redefining the age of criminality. *New York University Review of Law & Social Change*, *38*, 101–158.

Teigen, A. (2021). *Juvenile age of jurisdiction and transfer to adult court laws*. NCSL.

www.ncsl.org/research/civil-and-criminal-justice/juvenile-ag
e-of-jurisdiction-and-transfer-to-adult-court-laws.aspx

Teitelbaum, L. E. (1991). Youth crime and the choice between rules and standards. *Brigham Young University Law Review*, 351–402.

Teji, S., & Males, M. (2011). *An analysis of direct adult criminal court filing 2003-2009: What has been the effect of Proposition 21?* Center on Juvenile and Criminal Justice.

Thomas, C. W., & Bilchik, S. (1985). Prosecuting juveniles in criminal courts: A legal and empirical analysis. *The Journal of Criminal Law & Criminology*, *76*, 439–479.

Thomas, J. M. (2017). *Raising the bar: State trends in keeping youth out of adult courts (2015-2017)*. Campaign for Youth Justice.

Thomas, J. M., & Wilson, M. (2018). *The color of youth transferred to the adult criminal justice system: Policy & practice recommendations*. National Association of Social Workers.

Torbet, P., Griffin, P., Hurst, H., & MacKenzie, L. (2000). *Juveniles facing criminal sanctions: Three states that changed the rules*. US Department of Justice, Office of Justice Programs, Office of Juvenile Justice and Delinquency Prevention.

Torbet, P. M., Gable, R., Hurst, I. V. H., Montgomery, I., Szymanski, L. A., & Thomas, D. (1996). *State responses to serious and violent juvenile crime*. National Center for Juvenile Justice.

Torbet, P. M., & Szymanski, L. (1998). *State legislative responses to violent juvenile crime: 1996-97 update*. US Department of Justice, Office of Justice Programs, Office of Juvenile Justice and Delinquency Prevention.

Traver, D. P. (2000). The wrong answer to a serious problem: A story of school shootings, politics and automatic transfer. *Loyola University of Chicago Law Journal. Loyola University of Chicago. School of Law*, *31*, 281–315.

Troilo, M. (2018). Locking up youth with adults: An Update. *Prison policy initiative*. www.prisonpolicy.org/blog

Trulson, C. R., Caudill, J. W., Belshaw, S. H., & DeLisi, M. (2011). A problem of fit: Extreme delinquents, blended sentencing, and the determinants of continued adult sanctions. *Criminal Justice Policy Review*, *22*, 263–284.

Ullman, R. P. (1999). Federal juvenile waiver practices: A contextual approach to the consideration of prior delinquency records. *Fordham Law Review*, *68*, 1329–1369.

Urbina, M. G. (2005). Transferring juveniles to adult court in Wisconsin: Practitioners voice their views. *Criminal Justice Studies*, *18*(2), 147–172.

Urbina, M. G., & White, W. S. (2009). Waiving juveniles to criminal court: Court officials express their thoughts. *Social Justice (San Francisco, Calif.)*, *36*, 122–139.

Valliere, B. J. (1986). The transfer of juvenile offenders to adult courts in Massachusetts: Reevaluating the rehabilitative ideal. *Suffolk University Law Review*, *20*, 989–1028.

Van Vleet, R. K. (1999). The attack on juvenile justice. *The Annals of the American Academy of Political and Social Science*, *564*(1), 203–214.

Vandervort, F. E., & Ladd, W. E. (2000). The worst of all possible worlds: Michigan's juvenile justice system and international standards for the treatment of children. *University of Detroit Mercy Law Review*, *78*, 203–258.

Vannella, D. M. (2006). Let the jury do the waive: How *Apprendi v. New Jersey* applies to juvenile transfer proceedings. *William and Mary Law Review*, *48*, 723–770.

Vargas, J. H. (2014). *Juvenile Court Judges and their Concerns about Vulnerability, Experienced Uncertainty and the Law: Extralegal Factors, Legal Considerations and Judicial Transfer Decision-making*. (Unpublished doctoral dissertation). University of Nevada, Reno, NV.

Verrecchia, P. J. (2003). The effect of transfer mechanism from juvenile court on the likelihood of incarceration in criminal court. *Free Inquiry in Creative Sociology*, *31*, 15–24.

Verrecchia, P. J. (2011). The effect of transfer mechanism from juvenile court on conviction on a target offense in criminal court. *Contemporary Justice Review*, *14*(2), 189–201.

Visser, S. (2011). Utah's automatic waiver statute and discretion to deprive teens of life and liberty. *Journal of Law & Family Studies*, *13*, 363.

Vitiello, M. (1976). Constitutional safeguards for juvenile transfer procedure: The ten years since Kent v. United States. *De Paul Law Review*, *26*, 23–53.

Vladimer, R. J. (1982). Massachusetts juvenile transfer statute-Justice for juvenile offenders? *New England Journal on Prison Law*, *8*, 483–527.

Walker, H. (2021). School-to-prison pipeline. *Marquette Benefits& Social Welfare Law Review*, *22*(2), 147–179.

Wallance, G. J. (1975). Sending the accused juvenile to adult criminal court: A due process analysis. *Brooklyn Law Review*, *42*, 309.

Ward, J. M. (2003). Deterrence's difficulty magnified: The importance of adolescent development in assessing the deterrence value of transferring juveniles to adult court. *University of California Davis Journal of Juvenile Law & Policy*, *7*, 253–284.

Washburn, J. J., Teplin, L. A., Voss, L. S., Simon, C. D., Abram, K. M., & McClelland, G. M. (2008). Psychiatric disorders among detained youths: A comparison of youths processed in juvenile court and adult criminal court. *Psychiatric Services (Washington, D.C.)*, *59*(9), 965–973.

Watkins, J. C. Jr. (1998). *The juvenile justice century: A sociological commentary on American juvenile courts*. Carolina Academic Press.

Weijers, I., & Grisso, T. (2009). Criminal responsibility of adolescents: Youth as junior citizenship. In J. Junger-Tas & F. Dünkel (Eds.), *Reforming juvenile justice* (pp. 45–67). Springer.

Welch, K., Butler, L. F., & Gertz, M. (2019). Saving children, damning adults? An examination of public support for juvenile rehabilitation and adult punishment. *Criminal Justice Review*, *44*, 470–491.

Weston, B. (2016). Balancing rehabilitation and punishment: Combing juvenile court waiver mechanisms to create a balanced justice system. *The American Criminal Law Review*, *53*, 235–254.

White, H. G., Frazier, C. E., & Lanza-Kaduce, L. (1998). A socio-legal history of Florida's juvenile transfer reforms. *University of Florida Journal of Law and Public Policy*, *10*, 249–275.

Whitebread, C. H., & Batey, R. (1977). Transfer between courts: Proposals of the juvenile justice standards project. *Virginia Law Review*, *63*, 221–243.

Whitebread, C. H., & Batey, R. (1981). The role of waiver in the juvenile court: Questions of philosophy and function. In J. C. Hall, D. M. Hamparian, J. M. Pettibone, & J. L. White (Eds.), *Major Issues in Juvenile Justice Information and Training: Readings in Public Policy* (pp. 207–226). Academy for Contemporary Problems.

Whitehead, J. T., & Lab, S. B. (1989). A meta-analysis of juvenile correctional treatment. *Journal of Research in Crime and Delinquency*, *26*, 276–295.

Wilbourn, B. (1995). Waiver of juvenile court jurisdiction: National trends and the inadequacy of the Texas response. *American Journal of Criminal Law*, *23*, 633–649.

Williams, E. J. (2022). *"Is the criminal justice system failing our youth": An analysis of juvenile jurisdiction transfer laws for youth charged with serious crimes and effective alternatives.* (Unpublished graduate paper). University of Wisconsin-Platteville, Platteville, Wisconsin.

Williams, J. (2015). The Consequences of Florida's Discretionary Direct File Law and Its Particular Impact on Young African American Males. *Social Justice Policy & Justice*, *9*, 57.

Winner, L., Lanza-Kaduce, L., Bishop, D. M., & Frazier, C. E. (1997). The transfer of juveniles to criminal court: Reexamining recidivism over the long term. *Crime and Delinquency*, *43*, 548–563.

Witt, P. H. (2003). Transfer of juveniles to adult court: The case of H. H. *Psychology, Public Policy, and Law*, *9*(3-4), 361–380.

Wizner, S. (1984). Discretionary waiver of juvenile court jurisdiction: An invitation to procedural arbitrariness. *Criminal Justice Ethics*, *3*, 41–50.

Wizner, S. (1995). On youth crime and the juvenile court. *Boston College Law Review. Boston College. Law School*, *36*, 1025–1035.

Woolard, J. L., Fondacaro, M. R., & Slobogin, C. (2001). Informing juvenile justice policy: Directions for behavioral science research. *Law and Human Behavior*, *25*, 13–24.

Wright, K., Muddle, A., Rountree, M., & Rich, E. 2019. *Balancing punitive and rehabilitative approaches to juvenile justice: An investigation into the common mechanisms used by countries to prosecute young offenders as adults*. Macquarie University & HAQ: Centre for child rights.

Wu, B. (2000). Determinants of public opinion toward juvenile waiver decisions. *Juvenile & Family Court Journal*, *51*(1), 9–20.

Yellen, D. (1996). What juvenile court abolitionists can learn from the failures of sentencing reform. *Wisconsin Law Review*, 577–602.

Young, M. (1981). Waiver from a judge's standpoint. In Hall, J.C., Hamparian, D.M., Pettibone, John M., & White, Joseph L. (Eds.) Major issues in juvenile justice: Information and Training: Readings in public policy (pp. 309-320). Academy for Contemporary Problems.

Young, M. C. (2000). *Providing effective representation for youth prosecuted as adults*. US Department of Justice, Office of Justice Programs, Bureau of Justice Assistance.

Young, M. C., & Gainsborough, J. (2000). *Prosecuting juveniles in adult court: An assessment of trends and consequences*. The Sentencing Project.

Zane, S. N. (2017). Do criminal court outcomes vary by juvenile transfer mechanism? A multi-jurisdictional, multilevel analysis. *Justice Quarterly*, *34*, 542–569.

Zane, S. N. (2018). Exploring the minority threat hypothesis for juveniles in criminal court: Static versus dynamic threat and diffuse versus targeted effects. *Youth Violence and Juvenile Justice*, *16*(4), 418–441.

Zane, S. N., Welsh, B. C., & Drakulich, K. M. (2016). Assessing the impact of race on the juvenile waiver decision: A systematic review and meta-analysis. *Journal of Criminal Justice*, *46*, 106–117.

Zane, S. N., Welsh, B. C., & Mears, D. P. (2016). Juvenile transfer and the specific deterrence hypothesis: Systematic review and meta-analysis. *Criminology & Public Policy*, *15*, 901–925.

Ziedenberg, J. (2011). *You're an adult now: Youth in adult criminal justice systems*. National Institute of Corrections.

Zimring, F. E. (1981). Notes toward a jurisprudence of waiver. In J. C. Hall, D. M. Hamparian, J. M. Pettibone, & J. L. White (Eds.), *Major issues in juvenile justice information and training: Readings in public policy* (pp. 193–205). Academy for Contemporary Problems.

Zimring, F. E. (1991). The treatment of hard cases in American juvenile justice: In defense of discretionary waiver. *Notre Dame Journal of Law, Ethics & Public Policy*, *5*, 267–280.

Zimring, F. E. (1998a). *American youth violence*. Oxford University Press.

Zimring, F. E. (1998b). Toward a jurisprudence of youth violence. *Crime and Justice*, *24*, 477–501.

Zimring, F. E. (1999). The hardest of the hard cases: Adolescent homicide in juvenile and criminal courts. *Virginia Journal of Social Policy & the Law*, *6*, 437–469.

Zimring, F. E. (2000b). The punitive necessity of waiver. In J. Fagan & F. E. Zimring (Eds.), *The Changing Borders of Juvenile Justice: Transfer of adolescents to the criminal court* (pp. 207–224). University of Chicago Press.

Zimring, F. E. (2010). The power politics of juvenile court transfer: A mildly revisionist history of the 1990s. *Louisiana Law Review*, *71*, 1–15.

Zimring, F. E. (2014). The power politics of juvenile court transfer in the 1990s. In F. E. Zimring & D. S. Tanenhaus (Eds.), *Choosing the Future for American Juvenile Justice* (pp. 37–52). New York University Press.

Zimring, F. E., & Fagan, J. (2000). Transfer policy and law reform. In J. Fagan & F. E. Zimring (Eds.), *The changing borders of juvenile justice: Transfer of adolescents to the criminal court* (pp. 407–424). University of Chicago Press.

Table 39 References

Furdella, J., & Puzzanchera, C. (2015). *Delinquency cases in juvenile court, 2013*. Office of Juvenile Justice and Delinquency Prevention.

Hockenberry, S., & Puzzanchera, C. (2014a). *Delinquency cases waived to criminal court, 2011*. Office of Juvenile Justice and Delinquency Prevention.

Puzzanchera, C. M. (2000). *Delinquency cases waived to criminal court, 1988-1997*. U.S. Department of Justice, Office of Justice Programs. Office of Juvenile Justice and Delinquency Prevention.

Puzzanchera, C. M. (2001). *Delinquency cases waived to criminal court, 1989-1998*. U.S. Department of Justice, Office of Justice Programs, Office of Juvenile Justice and Delinquency Prevention.

Puzzanchera, C. M. (2003). *Delinquency cases waived to criminal court, 1990-1999*. U.S. Department of Justice, Office of Justice Programs, Office of Juvenile Justice and Delinquency Prevention.

Puzzanchera, C. M., & Addie, S. (2014). *Delinquency cases waived to criminal court, 2010*. U.S. Department of Justice, Office of Justice Programs. Office of Juvenile Justice and Delinquency Prevention.

Sickmund, M., Sladky, A., & Kang, W. (2019). *Easy access to juvenile court statistics: 1985-2017. Online*. National Center for Juvenile Justice. https://www.ojjdp.gov/ojstatbb/ezajcs/

Chapter 7
Mischaracterizing the Nature and Effect of Transfer

ABSTRACT

Chapter 7 continues unraveling the confusion in the transfer literature. This anti-transfer crowd (ATC) misinformation deals with misrepresenting the effect of transfer, exaggerating its reach, and distorting its operation. Chapter 7 shows prosecutors' transfer powers are never unreviewable beyond the charging itself; excessiveness on the prosecutor's part is subject to nullification by a judge and/or jury at trial. The Chapter explains how, contrary to ATC assertions, transfer is not sentencing; it is charging. Similarly, granting prosecutors transfer authority is not a violation of the separation of powers; actually, granting judges this authority arguably is. Although prosecutorial transfer (PT) certainly means the offenders' best interests are not paramount, that does not mean they are irrelevant. Even still, PT is not a rejection of JC, nor does it contribute to the criminalization of JC. Finally, Chapter 7 explains why transfer is neither inextricably tied to a crime rate nor acts primarily like a safety valve.

INTRODUCTION

The explosion in transfer laws due to the explosion in violent juvenile crime in the mid-1990s has been under continuous attack by the ATC since those provisions were adopted. Most of the anger has been directed at PT, especially at offense exclusion (OE), primarily because it appears to provide the greatest potential to transfer juvenile offenders to CC. Critics began their attack mostly on the illogical or nefarious motivations behind that expansion in transfer law. For example, Zimring (1998a) argued:

"The current concern with juvenile violence has produced a flood of legislative activity designed to increase the number of violent offenses by juveniles that qualify for transfer to criminal court."

(This is very true).

DOI: 10.4018/978-1-7998-7923-7.ch007

"In large part, this stance is a specific type of get-tough strategy that is more focused on increasing the punishment for such offenses…"

(This also is very true)

"than in fine tuning the niceties of court jurisdiction."

(Cherry-picking-transfer of chronic/violent offenders is the very essence of fine tuning, however).

"But something more than the wish for greater punishment is at work…."

(This alleged "something more" was never disclosed or explained).

"If the strategic mission was to get tough on as many juvenile offenders as possible,"

(It never was)

"a downward shift in jurisdiction maximum age would have vastly more impact on adolescent offenders than relaxing the standards for transfer to criminal court for specific offenses (p. 108)."

(True, but, again, this was never the objective of the pro-transfer legislation).

Zimring set up a false premise (i.e., the so-called, never identified "strategic mission"), guaranteed to reach a nasty but irrelevant conclusion (the alleged legislative mistake in not reducing JC maximum age). Beginning with false premises about and attributing negative motivations to pro-transfer measures are common ATC tactics.

A. THE SPECIAL PROBLEM OF PROSECUTORIAL TRANSFER (PT)

Why PT Is Purportedly Wrong and Amounts to A Betrayal of Justice, Society And/Or JC

(1) The Supposedly Unreviewed/Unreviewable Prosecutorial Powers in Offense Exclusion (OE)

Numerous ATC critics have complained about OE's supposed nonreviewability:

[T]ransfer is possible…at the discretion of a prosecutor, who might choose whether to file for the most serious charge ***without a judge's final authority*** *(Zimring, 1998a, pp. 13-14, cite omitted, emphasis added).*

******

[A]utomatic transfer, in which the prosecutorial power to choose the forum operates ***without judicial review...*** *(Id., p. 125, emphasis added, see also id., pp. 74, 121, 122; see, also, Benekos & Merlo, 2019).*

******

The accretion of authority to prosecutors in this (anti-judicial discretion) regime is clear: the prosecutor has the ***unreviewable discretion*** *to select charges and, in turn, to select jurisdiction (Fagan, 2008, p. 37, emphasis added).*

****

[U]nlike judicial waiver/sentencing discretion, which is subject to appellate review, the prosecutor's charging decision is ***not subject to any type of judicial review*** *(Feld, 1987, p. 514, emphasis added, footnote omitted).*

Earlier, Feld (1978), originally an OE advocate, had acknowledged the PT decision is not unreviewable:

The only factual issues involved in the charging decision relate to probable cause and legal guilt, and the prosecutor's determinations in this regard are subjected to judicial review at trial... (p. 560).

These ATC accusations are not valid or justified. Prosecutors regularly *select* charges *without a judge's final authority*. Charging belongs to the executive branch, not to the judicial branch. What the ATC promotes is a violation of the separation of powers. This absence of judicial approval in charging occurs *within both* JC and CC. Since there is no "judge's final authority" for charging *within* each court, it is puzzling why there must be "a judge's final authority" for prosecutorial transfer that is *a charging decision that is between or bridges* the two courts. More important, perhaps, contrary to these assertions, filing the most serious or any OE charge does not constitute unreviewed or unreviewable discretion; the same applies to direct file (DF) (see Steiner & Wright, 2006). OE charging effects a transfer that will nearly immediately require a judge's sanctioning that transfer by finding probable cause (PC) for the excluded offense. That means for the charges to "stick" or for an OE (or DF) transfer to be upheld, "a judge's final authority" is required in either JC or CC. Prosecutors who overcharge juvenile offenders to transfer them risk judges' exercising their *actual final authority* by reversing the transfer via a finding the charge lacks PC.

Similarly, the ATC complains that OE:

- involves decisions made unilaterally;
- occurs without a hearing; Feld (2000) calls it "adulthood" without a hearing (p. 91);
- occurs without defense attorney/PO input;
- occurs without a written account of the decision; and,
- involves a decision outside the adversarial process (see Coupet, 2000, p. 1319; Hoeffel, 2013, p. 50; Sabo, 1996, p. 2426).

These complaints ring hollow. They also apply equally to DF. *All* initial prosecutorial charging decisions (apart from the grand jury indictment) are *unilateral* and are made *without a hearing, without a defense attorney's* (or anyone else's) *input,* and *without a written account*, all occurring *outside the adversarial process.* There is a hearing following the charging/transfer decision. It is a preliminary hearing that serves as a check on the prosecutor's transfer power. It is the same check that applies to charging adults. At the preliminary hearing, a defense attorney can appear and represent the defendant with an abundance of adversariness. There also will be a written decision, delivered by a judge, too; it will address the presence or absence of PC for the excluded/concurrent offense, which determines the transfer outcome. All of these characteristics constitute the design of OE (and all charging). The legislatures knew and must have desired these outcomes when adopting OE. These elements of the ATC wish list and potential obstacles to transfer are trademarks of judicial transfer and are precisely what the legislatures knew prosecutors would be able to avoid in OE. These features also are why the ATC prefers JT to any form of PT.

(2) OE Supposedly Disserves Justice and Constitutes Moral Panic

Another supposed affront to justice in OE is its having no transparency and its being ripe for abuse (Bishop, 2000: 89-92). Some members of the ATC perceive DF as less problematic than OE.

Although direct file provisions offer some degree of transparency, exclusion statutes (which account for a large number of transfers) offer none (Fagan, 2008, p. 37; see also Feld, 2000, p. 125).

******

Unlike legislative offense exclusion, in which the actual offense alleged determines juvenile or criminal jurisdiction, direct-file laws allow the prosecutor to select the forum without engaging in any charging subterfuges… (Feld, 2000, pp. 98-99).

For this assertion to be accurate, the DF statute would have to be limited to identifying only age and record requirements since these are the only relevant immutable items, not subject to prosecutorial manipulations. Most important, this assertion is incorrect wherever DF requires a certain level of offense for the case to be eligible for concurrent jurisdiction. For example, if DF is possible for felonies only (and especially if a certain class/degree of felony is needed), prosecutors can indeed engage in at least an overcharging subterfuge in the hope of achieving (an otherwise illegitimate) transfer. Undercharging subterfuge, on the other hand, would seem to make little, if any, sense in DF, to be sure.

Actually, DF and OE involve the same lack of transparency, as does all charging! Ironically, OE forces prosecutors to be more careful in selecting an excluded or non-excluded offense compared to DF where much broader categories of offenses typically are present. This means prosecutors need to be careful in selecting the triggering charge via OE. It can be argued that limiting transfer eligibility to the most serious and identified offenses (a la OE) binds the prosecutor more than occurs via DF.

Legislators have also been accused of disserving society due to their adoption of both PT and broader JT provisions. Those ATC folks who have focused on PT exclusively (and especially OE) have accused legislators of capitulating to political pressures or promoting merely symbolic gestures (Feld, 2000, p. 125; see, also, Butts & Mears, 2001; Lehmann & Kobie, 2021; Zimring, 1999), and have questioned legislators' integrity.

Legislative offense exclusion suffers from rigidity, overinclusiveness, and the ***demagogic tendency*** *of get-tough politicians to adopt ever-expansive lists (Feld, 1999a, p. 243, emphasis added).*

******

It remains to be seen whether legislators can resist ***demagogic impulses*** *and enact responsible youth crime policies (Feld, 2000, p. 129, emphasis added; see, also, Feld, 1999a, p. 242).*

These accusations are, indeed, ironic since Feld was one of the first and most avid supporters of OE. Perhaps many state legislatures were simply following his lead/advocacy.

That legislators responded to perceived holes or gaps in transfer policies with measures designed to prevent miscarriages of justice by inappropriately allowing for immunity from criminal prosecution in some chronic/violent juvenile offender situations hardly makes them demagogic. Supposedly, legislatures have achieved nothing by adopting PT.

(O)ffense exclusion and prosecutors' choice do not provide either a jurisprudentially satisfactory or politically practical solution (Feld, 1999a, p. 219).

That may be Feld's opinion, but he offered no support for that position, beyond merely claiming it as his point of view. PT provisions have been neither rescinded by legislatures nor reversed by appellate courts; both are politically practical and jurisprudentially satisfactory solutions.

There are limits on OE. Specifying the offense/record limits the prosecutor's power. A first-time simple assault is not going to be excluded, but it could make its way onto the DF list *and* to a finding of nonamenability via JT. It is also possible to track charging decisions to ensure there is no "subterfuge." It is next to impossible to pin down nonamenability rulings, which is why Feld originally opposed them. Nevertheless, the ATC's trust in judges (and distrust of prosecutors) encourages them to accept JT and to reject PT.

Also ridiculed is the sanity of legislators. Legislatures reacted to the explosion of juvenile violence during the 1990s by expanding the types of juvenile offenders who were eligible for transfer to CC (see Sanborn, 1996b). The ATC accuses legislators of launching an expansion that

has features of what sociologists describe as a ***moral panic****, in which the media, politicians, and the public reinforce each other in an escalating pattern of alarmed reaction to a perceived social threat (Scott & Steinberg, 2003, p. 807, emphasis added; see, also, NRC, 2013; Scott, 2013, pp. 537-541).*

****

Moral panics*, driven by media and politicians, have created a lucrative market for punitive policies, regardless of the crime rate… (Slobogin, 2013, p. 105, emphasis added).*

******

A drive to punish young offenders for their supposed increasingly violent behavior.... The general public's concern about perceived increases in youth criminal activity...continues to fuel the ***public's hysteria****.... (Politicians continue) to* ***pander to people's fears****... (Coupet, 2000, pp. 1306-07, emphases added, footnotes omitted).*

The very real hysteria/moral panic that marked the original JC's operation was of much greater scope, intensity, and duration (see Chapter 4). The violent juvenile crime epidemic of the 1990s was not a "supposed" increase in violent juvenile behavior. Those actual violent crimes warranted a proportionate reaction from the legislatures, by expanding transfer capabilities, especially when judges refused or were reluctant to transfer these juvenile offenders.

Irony abounds in the ATC support for a no-transfer policy in the alleged nature of today's juvenile offender. That nature contains a profile of violent juvenile offenders as: impulsive, pressured by peers, not thinking of short- or long-term consequences, having an undeveloped moral compass, and being immature and reckless (see Chapter 9). If this profile is anywhere close to being accurate, these purported character traits constitute grounds for a legitimate, gigantic moral panic after all![1]

(3) The Purportedly Excessive Outcomes and Provisions of OE

A gross exaggeration by the ATC is that PT via OE has replaced JT.

The movement of adolescents to adult court was no longer the product of a juvenile court judge exercising his or her discretion... (Mulvey & Schubert, 2012, pp. 2-3).

Both types of PT complement and have not replaced JT. In some states, PT does not even exist. It can be said that PT represents a distrust and rejection of JT:

Exclusion also represents an expression of legislative distrust of juvenile court judges' discretionary decision-making... (Feld, 1987, p. 520).

Judges' frequent refusal to transfer "deserving" cases certainly played a part in the adoption of OE and the expansion of DF as well (McCarthy, 1994; Sanborn, 1996b).

Another objection is that, as a result of OE, transfer is targeting virtually all offenders. Flicker insisted that offense-based pro-transfer measures reflect a belief

that all juvenile crimes except minor offenses belong in adult court... (Flicker, 1983, p. i).

Flicker's assessment today would have to be even harsher. Others have argued that OE includes "thoughtless and draconian transfer provisions," and that OE has gone too far by

(a)llowing transfer at such young ages and for such minor offenses means it is practically certain that transfer is not being authorized for the worst of the worst... (Hoeffel, 2013, pp. 31, 40).

******

(S)everal states now allow children of any age to be transferred for most crimes... Redding, 2003, p. 129).

******

The position of these critics is that the traditional juvenile court is the wrong place to adjudicate ***any serious crime*** *committed by teenagers. This is a critique of American juvenile justice rather than an argument based on the particularity of violent crimes or the adolescents who commit them. (Zimring, 1998a, p. 161, emphasis added).*

First, where low or no minimum ages are required, only murder tends to be eligible for OE. Additionally, contrary to ATC accounts, the offenses specified in OE (and in some DF statutes) are reserved for the most serious/violent crimes, mostly restricted to older juvenile offenders, who sometimes need to have a previous adjudication as well to be transfer material (see Sanborn & Salerno, 2005, pp. 523-526). Amazingly and apparently lost on the ATC, the vast majority of serious crimes committed by juvenile offenders are still prosecuted in JC.

At the other end of the spectrum, OE has been accused of not going far enough:

Legislative offense exclusion suffers from rigidity and inflexibility and fails to respond to young career offenders whose present offense is nonviolent... (Feld, 1999a, p. 231).

Had OE statutes included the nonserious offenders legislators would have been criticized, if not condemned, for that. More important, the criticism is specious. "Young career offenders whose present offense is nonviolent" are well covered and transferrable via JT or DF (and even some OE laws). To reach the target population Feld seeks, OE statutes would need to develop compound matrices of prior record and current offense, well beyond what most, if not all, current OE statutes do now.

(4) OE Purportedly is a Rejection of JC

Perhaps one of the ATC's gravest criticisms of OE is that it is inconsistent with the JC's mission and constitutes a rejection of JC such that one cannot believe in JC rehabilitation *and* transfer (see, e.g., Angell, 2004, p.130; Beatty, 1995; Cohen, Bonnie, Taylor-Thompson, & Casey, 2016, pp.772-773; Feld, 1980, 1984b; Giardino, 1996; Hogan, 1974; Redding and Howell, 2000, p. 167; Sargent & Gordon, 1963; Schornhorst, 1968; Stamm, 1973; Traver, 2000; Valliere, 1986; Vitiello, 1976; Whitebread & Batey, 1981, p. 218; Wilbourn, 1996; Zimring, 1981).[2] This is another possible example of the "magical thinking" that Zimring had accused pro-transfer types of harboring. This contention would be the same as asserting that *expelling disruptive students from school means the principal is rejecting school and education.*

ATC members have offered that OE and broader DF/JT capabilities amount to a "loss of faith in juvenile court (Tanenhaus, 2000, p. 33)," and question the need for a separate JC:

(T)he trend to try juveniles as adults ignores the corrective rationale for a system of juvenile justice.... The trend to try juveniles as adults is inconsistent... with...rationales for having a separate system of juvenile justice... (Brink, 2003-04, pp. 1558, 1585).

****

The proliferation of promiscuous transfer regimes over the past three decades calls into question the very rational for a juvenile court... (Fagan, 2008, p. 36; see, also, Flicker, 1983, pp. i, ii).

****

Automatic waiver statutes represent a total repudiation of the philosophy of the parens patriae juvenile court, which stemmed from the belief that juveniles were so different in nature from adults as to justify a separate justice system for them... (Ainsworth, 1991, p. 1112, citation omitted).

****

Moreover, exclusion on the basis of offenses represents legislative repudiation of the court's philosophical premise that it can aid those appearing before it by denying the courts the opportunity to try, without even an inquiry into the characteristics of the offending youth... (Feld, 1987, p. 519; see, also, Mulvey & Schubert, 2012, p.2).

According to the ATC, to support JC, one must oppose transfer to CC (Zimring and Fagan, 2000: 408). Zimring (2000b) saw transfer as "a universal exception to a universal rule" (of JC's jurisdiction), and questioned: "If juvenile court is a good place to process and sanction most young offenders, why not all young offenders? (p. 207)." His answer is only *some murders* are transferrable, but even that narrow policy contradicts his *come one — come all* demand for JCs.

The ATC has engaged in revisionist history by suggesting that transfer breaks a JC tradition of transferring only chronic offenders (Fagan, 2008, p. 12). That statement disregards that, even during the initial years of JC, prosecutors in Illinois, Pennsylvania and elsewhere could criminally prosecute some juveniles older than 10 years of age and offenders who committed crimes while on probation via DF and/or OE (see Tanenhaus, 2000, p. 20). Moreover, the maximum age of JC jurisdiction was a young 15 during the early years of the court. In addition, relatively few major crimes (as little as 10%) were committed by juveniles during the beginning years (see Chapter 4). Moreover, many jurisdictions excluded the most serious offenses and transferred many that were initially referred to JC. Tanenhaus admitted:

The first state juvenile laws also shielded juvenile courts from at least some potentially volatile cases. Jurisdictional upper age limits, excluded offenses, and transfer mechanisms reduced the likelihood of juvenile court judges hearing cases involving adolescents charged with serious crimes (Tanenhaus, 2000, p. 21).

Finally, the ATC ignores that had legislatures been disgusted with the overall performance of JC, it would have reduced the maximum age of JC rather than allowing prosecutors and judges to cherry pick the worst chronic, serious, and violent juvenile offenders for criminal prosecution.

The chronic offenders targeted in OE contradict Feld's assertion that the offender's characteristics are irrelevant to OE. Those with previous records have not been denied "an opportunity to try" to receive JC help. What they have been denied is *unlimited* opportunities for help. Those prior offenses and failed rehabilitation efforts will help inform OE decisions. Simply because OE concentrates on offense/record does not mean they categorically ignore "the characteristics of the offending youth." Prosecutors will look beyond the offense (see Griffin et al., 1998, p. 14). Most important, perhaps, Feld suggested that JC's "philosophical premise" is that the rehabilitation of *all* juvenile offenders has been and should continue to be the exclusive consideration in retaining juvenile offenders in JC. That philosophical premise was never a part of JC operation from its very first days, and, has no role or place in the contemporary JC.[3]

B. Why PT is Fundamentally Wrong; JT is the only Appropriate/Acceptable Method

(1) OE Supposedly Ignores the Juveniles' Amenability to Treatment and/or Best Interests (BI)

Many ATC members feel OE includes juveniles who are amenable to JC intervention (see Frost Clausel & Bonnie, 2000, p. 188; Hirase, 1992, p. 166; Slobogin, 1999), and that it ignores the juveniles' best interests (BI) (Sabo, 1996, pp. 2428, 2452; Zimring & Fagan, 2000, p. 408).

Legislative waiver systematically places these juveniles in criminal courts, regardless of circumstances that might indicate some juveniles would be amenable to the rehabilitative treatment available in the juvenile justice system (Sabo, 1996, p. 2428; see, also, Sargent & Gordon, 1963; Stamm, 1973).

****

(Judicial transfer) is the only waiver mechanism that provides a hearing before a juvenile is sent to criminal court jurisdiction, thereby serving the best interests of the juvenile and society (Id., p. 2452).

The second assertion is accurate to the extent that a *transfer hearing* will not occur in JC under OE, but it is also inaccurate since OE in some states has a *preliminary hearing* (PH) occur in JC to establish PC, thereupon which the case is sent to CC (other states have the PH occur in CC). The first assertion is also accurate. The mischaracterization lies in suggesting PT is supposed to serve either of these ends. PT represents a repudiation of JT and its focus on amenability to treatment. As Feld, Zimring and other ATC members have complained, PT focuses too much on the offense and record, meaning amenability is not officially a factor and certainly is not an obstacle to PT. That does not mean prosecutors will disregard treatment history and amenability. It does mean that prosecutors are *not obligated* to consider them. PT is constituted to serve society's (and perhaps the victim's) BI. The chronicity of and/or violence in the offense/record trumps the youth's BI *and* amenability to treatment. Even still, this disregard (of best interests) also happens in JT whenever a judge decides to transfer, a point seemingly lost or ignored by the ATC. Taken to its logical extreme, if juvenile offenders' BI rule, there can be no forcible transfer. There are situations in which the offender's BI will be better served by being transferred (see Chapter 14), but in the vast majority of cases, defendants' BI are better served by remaining in JC. If the former situation exists, the juvenile will either self-transfer or not fight the state's pursuit of transfer. If the latter situation exists, there should be a serious contesting of the transfer by the defense. Regardless, the juvenile offender's BI are potentially secondary when PT is permitted; that potential depends upon the perspective of the prosecutor(s) in charge.

The ATC also alleges that transfer undermines JC's developing treatment options or that JC has been at fault in not developing more treatment options (see, e.g., Bortner, 1986; Feld, 1978; Flicker, 1981; Schornhorst, 1968; Sorrentino & Olsen, 1977; Stamm, 1973).

If transfer were eliminated, courts would have to confront the problems caused by the current paucity of treatment programs and might become more willing to force legislatures to (treat) them.... (Transfer) undermines efforts to pressure courts and legislatures into making treatment options in the juvenile system even better... (Slobogin, 2013, pp. 80, 124).

Of course, this position necessarily assumes that the JC has sufficient time within which to offer the offender rehabilitation programs. Older offenders, the typical subject of transfer decisions, are most likely going to be too old to profit sufficiently from whatever juvenile justice (JJ) has to offer. More important, retaining all juvenile offenders could overwhelm and corrupt treatment programs that do exist and/or implode JJ altogether (see Chapter 13). There is nothing stopping JCs from developing treatment programs for more chronic/violent juvenile offenders without the physical presence of these offenders in JC. The major treatment limitations of JC involve money, time, and space. By design, there are limited beds in juvenile facilities, making the accommodation of all "worthy" juvenile offenders a problem, exacerbated by the high cost of each bed. As mentioned previously, there is also limited time (i.e., the JC's retention age) to work with many juvenile offenders, especially, but not only, the older ones. Private groups and agencies develop programs for juvenile offenders all the time. Total inclusion could make the juvenile justice system worse and keeping all juvenile delinquents would jeopardize others' gaining access to treatment programs. Keeping all could force facilities to accept some offenders that pose a danger to others (see Chapter 13).

(2) PT Supposedly Constitutes a Violation of Separation of Powers

One of the most ironic/outrageous claims is that PT constitutes a violation of separation of powers (see Shiller, 2006). This claim is made (together with the one, below) to further the JT-only cause.

Prosecutorial juvenile transfers are shocking in the broad relinquishment of judicial power to the executive.... (In PT), a unilateral juvenile transfer power gives the prosecutor a quasi-judicial power to decide eligibility based on statutory criteria and then to decide whether to proceed with a transfer hearing. This is a direct usurpation of a judicial function and a side step around a juvenile's due process rights. The consequences of ending the childhood status of a juvenile offender are dire. The decision to do so is not a charging decision — ***the charge remains the same*** *in both jurisdictions — but a qualitative decision... (Hoeffel, 2013, pp. 64, 65, emphasis added; see, also, Green, 2003).*

What is truly "shocking" is this allegation. First, it needs to be noted that in OE the charge does not remain the same in both jurisdictions (it legally cannot be the same since the offense has been *excluded* from JC). While the *elements* of the crime may be the same in both jurisdictions, JC jurisdiction involves *delinquency,* while CC jurisdiction is *criminal.* This description applies to CC charging, too, so the absence of an ATC complaint regarding prosecutorial charging in CC is a mystery. JT also involves a prosecutor's deciding "whether to proceed with a transfer hearing."

There is irony in the ATC claim that adopting PT violates separation of powers or intrudes upon proper judicial authority. Exactly what judicial authority is impinged upon is unclear. It cannot be charging power, right? If the impingement involves transfer authority, that is laughable since the legislature has historically had the authority to grant either judges or prosecutors the authority to transfer. To claim that only judges can be authorized to transfer juvenile offenders to CC is simply without any historical or legal foundation. Only tradition can account for *any* validity in the practice of judicial transfer.

There is an actual separation of powers violation and that involves JT; this is where the irony manifests. Charging is constitutionally restricted to the executive branch of government (i.e., prosecutors). Judges are not constitutionally permitted to criminally charge offenders; it exists nowhere in the criminal justice (CJ) system. To extend charging power to judges in the CJ system would be viewed automatically as a violation of separation of powers. Interestingly, granting JC judges (or CC judges) the authority to charge juvenile offenders as criminal defendants (via allowing transfer) or as juvenile defendants (via denying transfer or via what's called reverse transfer) is a clear-cut violation of separation of powers, but on the judge's and not the prosecutor's part. It has been tolerated, justifiably perhaps, due to the founders' notions of who should work in JC (i.e., judges), and, more important, who should *not work* in juvenile court (i.e., prosecutors). That old fashioned notion of valid JC membership, among dozens of other ideas (compare Chapters 4 and 5), has been deservedly discarded. The ATC cherry-picks and promotes what they like about the original court, ignoring what was wrong from back in the day, provided they like it. Regardless, the ATC will not likely abandon its anti-PT argument as long as prosecutors exercise their transfer authority.

Green (2003) contended there is *not only* a violation of the separation of powers, *but also* a *conflict of interests* in PT since she believes the prosecutor is supposed to act solely in a *parens patriae* manner (and always pursue juveniles' best interests), which supposedly cannot occur if the prosecutor is charged with transfer responsibility at the same time. Ironically, the judge is considered *the* primary *parens patriae* agent in JC (see Sanborn, 2001a), while defense attorneys can operate in a similar parallel capacity (see Sanborn, 1994c; Sanborn & Salerno, 2005). If prosecutors were to operate as Green considers appropriate, there would be *no* court official promoting society's interests. Moreover, since judges are truly the personification of *parens patriae*, JT also would seem to present an even greater conflict of interests (how can they serve as *parens patriae* agents and transfer, too?), leaving no one available to transfer offenders to CC, which likely underlies Green's erroneous views.

(3) Transfer is Purportedly Sentencing (So PT Supposedly Violates Separation of Powers, While JT Does Not)

Asserting that transfer amounts to sentencing seeks to establish that JT is the only acceptable form of transfer (see Arya, 2010, pp. 138, 146). One ATC supporter has taken the sentencing analogy to heart and has contended that since juries are constitutionally required to determine the facts critical to a CC sentence (see *Apprendi v. New Jersey*, 2000), only a jurycan determine the facts that make transfer to CC appropriate and legal (Carroll, 2009; Kimbrell, 2015; Vannella, 2006).

Another ATC advocate has gone further and has claimed that transfer decisions parallel the imposition of death penalty and life without parole sentences.

If children deserve individualized consideration from a judicial actor in the decision to impose life without parole, then they deserve the same individualized judicial consideration in the transfer decision (Hoeffel, 2013, p. 65; see, also, Green, 2003).

This author also suggested that transfer violates the proportionality requirement of the 8th Amendment (see Hoeffel, 2013, p. 30). The absence of a conviction that is required to trigger any Eighth Amendment claim renders this argument invalid (see Maroney, 2011, pp. 786-7).

Zimring and Feld have led the charge in trying to equate transfer with sentencing.

*(T)he nature of the decision is **sufficiently similar to criminal sentencing** so that judges are better suited to the task than prosecutors (Zimring, 1998a, p. 109, emphasis added; see, also, Dawson, 2000, p. 55).*

****

*(I)f waiver seems **more like a sentencing** than a charging decision, then maintaining judicial authority seems preferable to the concentration of all power in the prosecutor.... (Zimring, 2000b, pp. 218-19, emphasis added).*

Of course, the prosecutor's lack of direct authority to convict and sentence any defendant (apart from influencing plea bargaining outcomes) completely refutes Zimring's "concentration of all power" argument.

Feld's most pertinent observations are among his most recent:

*Prosecutors dominate these waiver processes either by charging youths with excluded offenses or by directly selecting the juvenile or criminal forum. These strategies reflect a fundamental shift of **sentencing discretion** from the judicial to the executive branch (Feld, 2000, p. 112, emphasis added).*

****

*State laws that exclude long lists of offenses from juvenile courts or that give prosecutors greater authority to direct file charges in either juvenile or criminal court simply shift **sentencing discretion** from judges in a waiver hearing to prosecutors in their offices... (Id., p. 117, emphasis added).*[4]

****

*Transfer of jurisdiction constitutes a type of **sentencing decision**... (Feld & Bishop, 2012, p. 801, emphasis in original; see. also, p. 821).*

Interesting, Feld has much more frequently acknowledged that OE indeed involves charging (see Table 40).

A legitimate reply to the Zimring/Feld contentions would be to analogize as follows:

Indictment involves a finding of guilt by the (grand) jury after a hearing in which evidence of the defendant's criminal behavior has been presented by a prosecutor and reviewed by that jury.

Conviction involves a finding of guilt by the (trial) jury after a hearing in which evidence of the defendant's criminal behavior has been presented by a prosecutor and reviewed by that jury.

Indictment, then, is sufficiently similar to conviction (indictment even sounds worse). When there has been an indictment, we can dispense with a trial since guilt has already been found.

If a trial is necessary, since it is so similar to a grand jury proceeding, prosecutors should control its operation the same way they do the grand jury hearing; accordingly, defense attorneys and judges do not get to participate at trial, just like they do not in the grand jury proceeding.

Hopefully, the superficial logic in this absurd proposition would be as easily refuted as is the claim that transfer to CC amounts to sentencing.

Feld (2000) embraced JT over PT. He made an interesting acknowledgement/slip that he preferred JT even though "waiver hearings are less administratively 'efficient' than prosecutors' *charging decision...* (p. 128, emphasis added)." Seems that transfer is really charging, after all. Table 40 discloses just how frequently Feld has made this "slip."

Taking Zimring's own words and perspective into account, JCs today constitute an institutional diversionary outlet for CCs. Transfer to CC, then, amounts to an *exception to and individual reversal of that institutional diversionary decision* via an election to prosecute a selected case in CC. Like transfer, diversionary decisions are individually made and, more important, squarely belong to the province of the prosecutor because it is a charging decision.

The bottom line is that both JT and PT involve charging and not sentencing. Transfer decides which court will be authorized to *hear* the case, in which court the *charges* will be filed and *prosecuted.* That is charging, just as much as it is when prosecutors make the call in CC. Most important, at the transfer stage *there has not been a conviction, and there may never be one.* Without a conviction there can be no sentencing. Transfer, then, cannot be equated with what at most is a speculative sentencing occurrence. Calling transfer sentencing is simply a misguided ATC attempt to establish what it hopes will be the disqualification of PT.[5]

C. Transfer's Basic/Generic Problems (including, but beyond PT)

(1) Transfer Supposedly Inappropriately Includes Minor Property Offenders, Too

JT, more than PT, has historically been aimed mostly at chronic offenders who commit relatively nonserious offenses, typically property crimes. The qualification, relatively, is important. Burglary is a property offense, but should not be considered nonserious, especially, but not only, if it is residential in nature, occurs at an occupied dwelling and/or at night (not to mention if committed by an armed offender and is still called a burglary). Similarly, victims of auto theft are probably not willing to call that offense, nonserious. These two offenses historically have been among the most likely to involve recidivists and have accounted for a sizable proportion of property-oriented transfers.

Most often what is happening here is that while criticizing PT, and especially OE, the ATC intimates that PT is supposed to be aimed at prosecuting only violent offenders in CC, but overwhelmingly the numbers show a majority of (all) transfers are "mere" property offenders. This would appear to violate the reason(s) OE statutes were adopted, at least according to ATC accounts. The ATC had pulled off an ingenious, if not disingenuous, tactic here by conflating JT and PT transfers. While JT surely could account for the transfer of numerous (and predominantly) property crime offenders, at least if they are chronic in nature, chances are OE cannot be blamed due to the limits placed on the severity of offenses that OE statutes include. "Mere" property offenses tend not to be included within OE statutes, unless older and chronic offenders are involved. Chances are the ATC has access to only the nature of judicial transfers since numbers for OE are traditionally unknown/unavailable. What seems to be at hand here, then, is that the ATC consults known (or judicial) transfer numbers and find a dominance of property offenders. Those numbers are then turned around as examples of the misuse of OE.

Meanwhile, DF statutes could produce results similar to JT, if legislatures have given prosecutors that much latitude in charging property offenses in either JC or CC. Again, it is likely that these property offenders sent to CC via DF are older and/or chronic offenders. Those statistics are neither acknowledged nor addressed by the ATC, however. Also, it is ironic that JT is the overwhelmingly ATC preferred transfer method (assuming there must be one), but, again, assuming amenability to treatment is still the major JT factor, JT is the method most likely to transfer the highest concentration of "mere" property offenders.

Most important, perhaps, the ATC crowd has ignored and/or opposed the idea that transfer has targeted property offenders for decades, if not a century.[6] Even though these offenders are likely to be both older and chronic, and many would have exhausted JJ resources (failing to be rehabilitated by what the JJ system has to offer), the ATC does not regard them as appropriate candidates for transfer.

Transfer research in the 1970's and 1980's found that, contrary to conventional wisdom, transfers (1) were not necessarily violent offenders, (2) did not necessarily receive harsher sanctions in criminal court than they would have received in juvenile court, (3) were not necessarily incarcerated, and (4) if incarcerated, did not necessarily receive longer sentences than their juvenile court counterparts... (Snyder et al., 2000, p. xii).

****

Studies found that although transfer to criminal court was intended for the most serious juvenile offenders, many transferred were not violent offenders, but repeat property offenders... (Id., p. 5).[7]

****

The underlying assumption is that transfer is reserved for the most serious cases...(O)ne would expect cases handled in criminal court to be more serious than those remaining in juvenile court. However, with numerous studies finding large proportions of relatively less serious cases (e.g., property cases) among the transferred cases, it remains uncertain what case characteristics trigger a decision to transfer (Id., p. 6).

****

(S)upporters of transfer ought at least to acknowledge that transferring so many juvenile offenders for property and other nonviolent crimes is not adequately connected to the purported goal of transfer (Notes, 2002, p. 1972, fn. 50; see, also, Quinn, 2015).

That research from the 1970s/1980s would have found anything different would have been the surprise. Ignoring historical reality, the ATC thinks transfer has always been about violent offenders only.

It would be intriguing to discover the source of that so-called "conventional wisdom." For decades, the ATC criticized transfer for targeting nonserious/nonviolent offenders (see Ruddell, Mays, & Giever,

1998). These criticisms occurred even though nonserious repeat offenders purposely had been the primary transfer targets and were legitimate transfer candidates due to establishing nonamenability via a history of treatment failures. Violent offenders were not the primary, and never the exclusive, focus of transfer until the mid-1990s explosion of violent crime and the expansion of transfer provisions made in response to that violent crime.[8]

(2) Transfer Supposedly Amounts to the Criminalization of JC

Transfer to CC has been identified by the ATC as contributing to the *criminalization* of JC. Another way of phrasing this is to allege that policymakers are "beginning to dismantle the legal and procedural border between juvenile justice and criminal justice (Butts & Mitchell, 2000, p. 178; see, also, Herkal, 1999; Rudof, 1998)." While blended sentences certainly can be accused of literally merging the two systems and obliterating some of this border, transfer operates to reinforce the border and boundaries by disqualifying from JC treatment and returning to CC (or denying immunity from criminal prosecution to) the most serious, violent and chronic juvenile offenders.

Criminalization refers to the ways in which JC has become a clone of CC. It is unclear whether *all* examples of criminalization, such as granting defendants constitutional rights at the adjudicatory hearing (AH), are decried by the ATC. But examples of "getting tough" with juvenile offenders, such as more punitive JC sentencing and transfer to CC, are consistently met with serious pushback from the ATC. Transfer witnesses the most vehement complaints likely due to the undeniably serious consequences attending it.

What is most important to remember is that JCs remain committed primarily to the rehabilitation of juvenile offenders and to their best interests (BI) (see Sanborn, 2004b). JC purpose clauses overwhelmingly still reflect the original notions of JC operation (see Id.).

Regardless of whether the ATC complaints are accurate or consistent, their concern is real. The more JC functions similarly to CC, the greater, legitimate worry there is that JC is abandoning its critical features, such as rehabilitation and operating in the juveniles' BI.[9] There could also be a procedural price to pay, such that JC could be forced to adopt all CC procedural characteristics. A comparable situation existed in pre-*Gault* days, and the U.S. Supreme Court responded by making procedural adjustments, seriously altering the atmosphere in JC. Any more procedural modification could bring about a "domino theory" cited and feared by the Court in *McKeiver v. Pennsylvania* (1970). The Court believed complete parity between the two courts, which would occur if the right to jury trial were granted to defendants in JC, could lead to a refutation of JC and the abandonment of the experiment started in 1899. There would seem to be no reason to preserve two courts that operated identically in procedure.

There have been many changes in JC's operation and offender population that have played a key role in criminalizing JC (see Chapter 5). Ironically, transfer actually contributes to the *prevention* of greater criminalization in JC. By siphoning off the worst juvenile offenders, in terms of chronic and/or serious/violent offenses, transfer helps JC to avoid pressures to adopt true indicators of criminalization, such as even more severe/harsh sentencing. The ATC insists, however:

(T)he waiver of serious offenders into the adult system... (has) contributed to the ***criminalization*** *of the juvenile court... (Feld, 1984a, p. 163, emphasis added; see, also, Boyd, Huss, & Myers, 2008, p. 196; Rubin, 2008, p. 9).*

****

The waiver of a serious offender into the adult system on the basis of his offense rather than an individualized evaluation of the youth's "amenability to treatment" or "dangerousness" is both an indicator of and a contributor to the substantive as well as procedural ***criminalization*** *of the juvenile court (Feld, 1987, pp. 472-73, emphasis added, 1989, p. 4, fn.10, Podkopacz & Feld, 1995, p. 75, fn. 3; See, also Feld, 1991, p. 696).*[10]

(3) Transfer/Criminalization Supposedly Means JC is Abandoning Treatment

Similarly, transfer has been alleged to constitute a rejection of JC and its commitment to rehabilitation.

To those committed to rehabilitation as a goal of the justice system, waiver of juvenile court jurisdiction over any offender seemsnonsensical... (Whitebread & Batey, 1981, p. 218).

Transfer has been credited with creating an identity crisis for JC. Some critics have gone as far as to claim that transfer, among other developments, has forced a shift in juvenile justice policy from rehabilitation to punishment, or worse, to the complete abandonment or dismantling of rehabilitation (see Table 41 (A); NRC, 2013; cf., Sabo, 1996, p. 2434).

Probably the most extreme, and outrageous, claim is that transfer amounts to warfare against children (Acton, 1996; Arteaga, 2002; Baird & Samuels, 1996; Giardino, 1996; Guttman, 1995; Sherman & Talley, 1995).

Critics of waiver argue that transferring juveniles to the criminal court is in conflict with the juvenile court's treatment philosophy... (Krisberg & Austin, 1993, p. 70).

******

(I)s there any reason to maintain a separate punitive juvenile court whose only distinction is its persisting procedural deficiencies (Feld, 1993b, p. 403)?

****

(J)uvenile courts have changed their focus from rehabilitation of youngsters to retribution for the offenses they have committed... (Soler, 1994, p. 297).

****

(T)he rehabilitative juvenile justice system has disappeared (Noon, 1994, p. 433).

****

(T)he juvenile system has virtually thrown away the rehabilitative ideal in favor of a system governed by procedural formality and punitive-oriented sanctions... Now, the courts focus on punishing the juvenile offender instead of looking at what is in the best interests of the child... (Beatty, 1995, pp. 989-990, citations omitted).

****

(T)he philosophical shift from rehabilitation to punishment that had taken hold in the criminal justice system filtered down to the juvenile justice system... (Redding & Howell, 2000, p. 145, citation omitted).

******

These recent changes (in transfer laws) signal a fundamental inversion in juvenile court jurisprudence from treatment to punishment, from rehabilitation to retribution... (Feld, 1997, p. 79; see, also, Cintron, 1996, p. 1275).

******

Changes (in transfer laws) reflect fundamental... policy shifts — from rehabilitation to retribution... (Feld, 1999b, p. 358).

****

(Adopting OE provisions) symbolize a fundamental change in juvenile justice jurisprudence from rehabilitation to retribution...(Feld, 2000, p. 128).

There has been an increase in JC's punitiveness during the last few decades, especially in terms of sentencing. The increase in the amount/severity of juvenile crime has brought about that increase in punitiveness. That punitiveness has been aimed primarily at the very chronic/violent juveniles who arguably should have been transferred to CC; retaining them in JC has profound consequences.

The ATC's decrying and criticizing the abandonment of rehabilitation, together with the increase in retribution in JC, makes it puzzling that, according to the ATC, transfer represents a sharp contrast in prosecution between the all-rehabilitation JC and the all-punishment CC.

Waiver of juvenile court jurisdiction presents the stark choice between treating a youth in the juvenile system and punishing him in the criminal justice system... (Feld, 2007b, p. 38, footnote omitted).

Both representations are extreme. The JC is neither 100% treatment, nor is CC 100% punishment. It is also puzzling how JC can be so enamored of and representative of retribution and yet so "starkly" different from CC at the same time.

The JC has remained primarily rehabilitative in its approach to offenders (see Sanborn and Salerno, 2005; see, also, Levesque & Tomkins, 1995; Suffredini, 1994). This approach applies to the vast majority of juvenile offenders who are the younger, non-chronic and/or non-violent, the same ones who are not transfer targets. They are the same ones who dominated the original JC population back in the day. This majority continues to experience benevolently motivated dispositions and opportunities for youthful offenders to turn their lives around (and to not ruin their life chances), thanks, in part, to the presence of transfer.

Transfer has helped JC remain faithful to its rehabilitative mission by removing from its responsibility the older, chronic, and violent offenders who would undermine rehabilitation and threaten the success of treatment for those juvenile offenders who can benefit from it. More important, perhaps, the ATC claims of doom and gloom can damage the image of JC.

The only virtue of the contemporary juvenile court is that juveniles convicted of serious crimes receive shorter sentences than do adults (Feld, 1991, p. 724).

****

(Transfer law) changes have transformed the juvenile court from a nominally rehabilitative social welfare agency into a scaled-down, ***second-class criminal court*** *for young offenders that provides neither therapy nor justice.... (Feld, 1999b, p.328, emphasis added, footnote omitted).*

****

(Transfer law) changes have converted the juvenile court into a ***second-class criminal court*** *for young offenders that provides neither therapy nor justice (Feld, 2003b, p. 1573, emphasis added).*

If JC and CC are mostly indistinguishable, if JC truly is only “a second-class” or “a deficient criminal court (Feld, 1997, p.69),” then it is puzzling that the ATC perceives not only a need to preserve JC but to subject virtually every juvenile offender to its second-class, deficient operation. Shorter sentences certainly do not require JC to exist. It is more than just a little ironic that the ATC, the very ones who are supposedly so enamored of JC that they want no juvenile-aged offender to be excluded from it, believe that JJ has no rehabilitation and only punishment to offer, and is now simply and completely an inadequate clone of CC. Fortunately, they are incorrect. The ATC needs to be saved from their own rhetoric.

Finally, transfer does not necessarily mean that “the principles of retribution, isolation and deterrence are elevated above rehabilitation (Ruddell, et al., 1998, p.3).” It is possible that due to the age of offenders or the complexity of their problems that there is not sufficient time remaining within the JC’s authority to address those problems, which is a rehabilitation-oriented concern.

(4) The Need for Transfer Provisions Supposedly is Inextricably Tied to the Crime Rate

It is a common trait among the ATC to argue that the burgeoning juvenile crime rate from the mid-1980s to mid-1990s that gave rise to the explosion in transfer provisions has subsided. Of course, neither a significant increase in the number of transfers nor the rise in juvenile confinement within JJ that resulted from the crime wave is given any credit for the decline in violent juvenile crime. Ignoring that, the ATC insists that it is time to reverse or dismantle the transfer apparatus (Arya, 2011; D’Ambra, 1997; Greene, 2010; Hoeffel, 2013; Griffin, Addie, Adams, & Firestine, 2011; Kurlychek, 2016; Pagnanelli, 2007; Scialabba, 2016; Vandervort & Ladd, 2011; Zane et al., 2016; see, also, Miller & Applegate, 2015).

Violent crime rates and juvenile crime have been in a steady decline over the past 20 years; however, reforms to restore the juvenile court system to its original version have not been as swift... (Scialabba, 2016, unpaginated, cite omitted).[11]

Besides dismissing any influence of the get-tough movement, this argument ignores the fact that most transfers are aimed at nonviolent criminals. Most important, it misses the point that *transfer provisions* are not related to the crime rate. Instead, the *number* of transfers, themselves, are steered by the crime rate. If the crime rate drops, the *number of*, not the *need for*, transfers should decline as well. That result is exactly what the numbers have shown.

The explosion of violent/serious juvenile crime that brought about the corresponding explosion in transfer capability did not *create* the need for more transfer, it simply made the need *more acute*. The need for transfer was more acute due to either the lack of provisions that addressed the specific crimes being committed and/or that judges who already had the authority to transfer were not exercising that authority. That made the vast expansion of PT necessary. Legislatures had left tradition mostly alone for decades and let JT be the major source of transfer. PT was perceived as necessary due to the failure of JT. More important, the crime explosion did not make transfer more legitimate. The authority to send juvenile murderers to CC for trial is legitimate whether one or one hundred murders per year are committed by juveniles.[12]

Why dismantle and then have to reassemble (too late for worthy crimes in the interim) for even the occasional violent offense? Better to have a transfer mechanism in place and not need it than to not have a transfer mechanism in place and desperately need it.

(5) Transfer is Supposedly Nothing More Than a Safety Valve for JC/Legislators

The ATC portrays juvenile rapists, murderers, and chronic burglars, among others, as the "victims" of transfer. Supposedly, even when chronic/violent juvenile offenders are not fully mature *and* are amenable to JC treatment, "(t)he community will not tolerate mild responses to heinous offenses (Bishop, 2000, p. 82)." These offenders just must go to CC so JC can survive.

The availability of a mechanism for prosecuting the hard-core youthful offender as an adult is thus an important ***safety valve****, permitting the* ***expiatory sacrifice*** *of some youths to quiet political and community clamor... (Feld, 1978, p. 518, footnote omitted, emphases added; see, also, Hager, 1995; Martin, 1992).*

****

Mechanisms to prosecute some youths as adults provide an important ***safety valve****, permit the* ***expiatory sacrifice*** *of some youths to quiet political and public clamor, and enable legislators to avoid otherwise irresistible pressures to lower the maximum age of juvenile court jurisdiction (Feld, 1999a, p. 209, emphases added; see, also, Feld, 2000, p. 83; Feld, 2001, p. 4; Noon, 1994, p. 451; Tanenhaus, 2013, p. 286; Valliere, 1986, pp. 990-992).*

****

(S)uch (OE and DF) laws prescribe a simplistic, politically attractive "sound-bite" solution for a complex problem, curtail judicial discretion and juvenile courts' clientele, and obscure the bases and processes of "adulthood" decisions (Feld, 2001, p. 18).

Transfer thus supposedly operates as a safety valve, sparring JC and legislators (and judges and prosecutors) from the political hazards of retaining chronic/violent offenders in JC (see, also, Fagan, Kupchik, & Liberman, 2007; Table 41 B).[13] It is difficult to square this ATC contention with the ever-numerous ATC one that alleges that mere property offenders are the bulk of transfer cases.

The vast majority of transfers occur off the radar and do not involve the super serious or violent cases. Even most of the latter escape media scrutiny and are handled behind closed doors. Ironically, one ATC member suggested that transfer helps JC

(b)y providing a mechanism to eliminate such dangerous children from the juvenile system, waiver also assuages community concern that the system is too lenient for the protection of the public (Flicker, 1983, p. ii).

The irony stems from the fact that were the community really aware of the dispositions handed down to even some chronic/serious/violent juvenile offenders in some urban JCs, much of the public would be apoplectic. It is fortunate for JC that the community/public does not have a clue about what really happens in JC.[14]

Most transfers are from the beyond-rehabilitation group, involving non-serious crimes. "The number of juvenile offenders who attract the community's attention, let alone hostility, is rather small, and many of them are prosecuted in juvenile court (Sanborn, 1994a, p. 268)."

Having said all that, transfer does serve a valuable role as a safety valve, even if this applies to so *very few* high-profile cases (see Hamilton, Moak, & Golden, 2007). Transferring the notorious, vicious juvenile-centered crimes, as few as they may be, *can serve* as a safety valve for JC. Some cases simply do not belong in JC and were not prosecuted there back in the day. Even still, "safety valve" hardly explains transfer.

To the extent that transfer is a safety valve, it has the potential for numerous, ominous leaks.

REFERENCES

Acton, R. B. (1996). Gubernatorial initiatives and rhetoric of juvenile justice reform. *Journal of Law and Policy*, *5*, 277–338.

Ainsworth, J. E. (1991). Re-imagining childhood and reconstructing the legal order: The case for abolishing the juvenile court. *North Carolina Law Review*, *69*, 1083–1133.

Angell, K. M. (2004). The regressive movement: When juvenile offenders are treated as adults, nobody wins. *Southern California Interdisciplinary Law Journal*, *14*, 125–144.

Apprendi v. New Jersey. (2000). 530 U.S 466.

Arteaga, J. A. (2002). Juvenile (in) justice: Congressional attempts to abrogate the procedural rights of juvenile defendants. *Columbia Law Review*, *102*(4), 1051–1088. doi:10.2307/1123650

Arya, N. (2010). Using *Graham v. Florida* to challenge juvenile transfer laws. *Louisiana Law Review*, *71*, 99–156.

Arya, N. (2011). *State trends: Legislative victories from 2005 to 2010: Removing youth from the adult criminal justice system*. Campaign for Youth Justice.

Baird, M. I., and Mina B. Samuels. (1996). Policy review: Justice for youth: The betrayal of childhood in the United States. *Journal of Law & Policy,* 5 *(1),* 177-202.

Beatty, H. (1994). Is the trend to expand juvenile transfer statutes just an easy answer to a complex problem. *University of Toledo Law Review. University of Toledo. College of Law*, *26*, 979–1025.

Beresford, L. S. (2000). Is lowering the age at which juveniles can be transferred to adult criminal court the answer to juvenile crime? A state-by-state assessment. *The San Diego Law Review*, *37*, 783–851.

Bishop, D. M. (2000). Juvenile offenders in the adult criminal justice system. In M. Tonry (Ed.), *Crime & Justice: A Review of Research, 27, 81-167.* IL University of Chicago Press. doi:10.1086/652199

Bishop, D. M., & Frazier, C. E. (1991). Transfer of juveniles to criminal court: A case study and analysis of prosecutorial waiver. *Notre Dame Journal of Law, Ethics & Public Policy*, *5*, 281–302.

Bishop, D. M., Frazier, C. E., & Henretta, J. C. (1989). Prosecutorial waiver: A case study of questionable reform. *Crime and Delinquency*, *35*(2), 179–201. doi:10.1177/0011128789035002001

Bortner, M. A. (1986). Traditional rhetoric, organizational realities: Remand of juveniles to adult court. *Crime and Delinquency*, *32*(1), 53–73. doi:10.1177/0011128786032001004

Boyd, R. J., Huss, S. M., & Myers, D. L. (2008). Antecedents and consequences of juvenile case processing: Where are we now, and where do we go from here? *Youth Violence and Juvenile Justice*, *6*(2), 195–220. doi:10.1177/1541204007305529

Brink, D. O. (2003-2004). Immaturity, normative competence, and juvenile transfer: How (not) to punish minors for major crimes. *Texas Law Review*, *82*, 1555–1585.

Butts, J. A., & Mears, D. P. (2001). Reviving juvenile justice in a get-tough era. *Youth & Society*, *33*(2), 169–198. doi:10.1177/0044118X01033002003

Butts, J. A., & Mitchell, O. (2000). Brick by brick: Dismantling the border between juvenile and adult justice. *Criminal Justice 2000: Boundary changes in criminal justice organizations, 2*, pp. 167-213.

Carroll, J. E. (2009). Rethinking the constitutional criminal procedure of juvenile transfer hearings: *Apprendi*, adult punishment, and adult process. *The Hastings Law Journal*, *61*, 101–153.

Champion, D. J. (1989). Teenage felons and waiver hearings: Some recent trends, 1980-1988. *Crime and Delinquency*, *35*(4), 577–585. doi:10.1177/0011128789035004005

Champion, D. J., & Mays, G. L. (1991). *Transferring juveniles to criminal courts: Trends and implications for criminal justice*. Praeger Publishers.

Cintron, L. A. (1996). Rehabilitating the juvenile court system: Limiting juvenile transfers to adult criminal court. *Northwestern University Law Review, 90*, 1254–1282.

Cohen, A. O., Bonnie, R. J., Taylor-Thompson, K., & Casey, B. J. (2016). When does a juvenile become an adult: Implications for law and policy. *Temple Law Review, 88*, 769–788.

Coupet, S. M. (2000). What to do with sheep in wolf's clothing: The role of rhetoric and reality about youth offenders in the constructive dismantling policy of the juvenile justice system. *University of Pennsylvania Law Review, 148*(4), 1303–1346. doi:10.2307/3312844

CYJ. Campaign for Youth Justice. (2007). *The consequences aren't minor: The impact of trying youth as adults and strategies for reform.* Campaign for Youth Justice.

D'Ambra, L. (1997). A legal response to juvenile crime: Why waiver of juvenile offenders is not a panacea. *Roger Williams University Law Review, 2*, 277–303.

Dawson, R. O. (2000). Judicial waiver in theory and practice. In J. Fagan & F. E. Zimring (Eds.), *The changing borders of juvenile justice: Transfer of adolescents to the criminal court* (pp. 45–81). University of Chicago Press.

Deitch, M., Barstow, A., Lukens, L., & Reyna, R. (2009). From time out to hard time: Young children in the adult criminal justice system. [Special Project Report, Lyndon B. Johnson School of Public Affairs, University of Texas at Austin].

Fagan, J. (2002). This will hurt me more than it hurts you: Social and legal consequences of criminalizing delinquency. *Notre Dame Journal of Law, Ethics & Public Policy, 16*, 1–41. doi:10.2139srn.306531

Fagan, J. (2008). Juvenile crime and criminal justice: Resolving border disputes. 18 *The Future of Children* 81-118 (Pages numbered 1-48 in Columbia Law School Working Paper).

Fagan, J., & Deschenes, E. P. (1990). Determinants of judicial waiver decisions for violent juvenile offenders. *The Journal of Criminal Law & Criminology, 81*(2), 314–347. doi:10.2307/1143909

Fagan, J., Forst, M., & Vivona, T. S. (1987). Racial determinants of the judicial transfer decision: Prosecuting violent youth in criminal court. *Crime and Delinquency, 33*(2), 259–286. doi:10.1177/0011128787033002004

Fagan, J., Kupchik, A., & Liberman, A. (2007). Be careful what you wish for: Legal sanctions and public safety among adolescent offenders in juvenile and criminal court. *Columbia Law School, Public Law Research Paper* 03-61.

Feld, B. C. (1978). Reference of juvenile offenders for adult prosecution: The legislative alternative to asking unanswerable questions. *Minnesota Law Review, 62*, 515–618.

Feld, B. C. (1980). Juvenile court legislative reform and the serious young offender: Dismantling the "rehabilitative ideal.". *Minnesota Law Review, 69*, 167–242.

Feld, B. C. (1981). Legislative policies toward the serious juvenile offender: On the virtue of automatic adulthood. *Crime and Delinquency, 27*(4), 497–521. doi:10.1177/001112878102700405

Feld, B. C. (1984a). Criminalizing juvenile justice: Rules of procedure for the juvenile court. *Minnesota Law Review, 69*, 141–276.

Feld, B. C. (1984b). The decision to seek criminal charges: Just deserts and the waiver decision. *Criminal Justice Ethics*, *3*(2), 27–41. doi:10.1080/0731129X.1984.9991756

Feld, B. C. (1987). The juvenile court meets the principle of the offense: Legislative changes in juvenile waiver statutes. *The Journal of Criminal Law & Criminology*, *78*(3), 471–533. doi:10.2307/1143567

Feld, B. C. (1989). Bad law makes hard cases: Reflections on teen-aged axe-murderers, judicial activism, and legislative default. *Minnesota Journal of Law & Inequality*, *8*, 1–101.

Feld, B. C. (1991). The transformation of the juvenile court. *Minnesota Law Review*, *75*, 691–725.

Feld, B. C. (1993b). Juvenile (in) justice and the criminal court alternative. *Crime and Delinquency*, *39*(4), 403–424. doi:10.1177/0011128793039004001

Feld, B. C. (1995). Violent youth and public policy: A case study of juvenile justice law reform. *Minnesota Law Review*, *79*, 965–1128.

Feld, B. C. (1997). Abolish the juvenile court: Youthfulness, criminal responsibility, and sentencing. *The Journal of Criminal Law & Criminology*, *88*(1), 68–136. doi:10.2307/1144075

Feld, B. C. (1998). Juvenile and criminal justice systems' responses to youth violence. *Crime and Justice*, *24*, 189–261. doi:10.1086/449280

Feld, B. C. (1999a). *Bad kids: Race and the transformation of the juvenile court*. Oxford University Press.

Feld, B. C. (1999b). The Transformation of the juvenile court—Part II: Race and the crack down on youth crime. *Minnesota Law Review*, *84*, 327–395.

Feld, B. C. (2000). Legislative exclusion of offenses from juvenile court jurisdiction: A history and critique. In J. Fagan & F. E. Zimring (Eds.), *The changing borders of juvenile justice: Transfer of adolescents to the criminal court* (pp. 83–144). University of Chicago Press.

Feld, B. C. (2001). Race, youth violence, and the changing jurisprudence of waiver. *Behavioral Sciences & the Law*, *19*(1), 3–22. doi:10.1002/bsl.427 PMID:11241678

Feld, B. C. (2003b). Race, politics, and juvenile justice: The Warren court and the conservative backlash. *Minnesota Law Review*, *87*, 1447–1577.

Feld, B. C. (2007b). Unmitigated punishment: Adolescent criminal responsibility and LWOP sentences. *Journal of Law & Family Studies*, *10*, 11–82.

Feld, B. C. (2013a). Adolescent criminal responsibility, proportionality, and sentencing policy: Roper, Graham, Miller/Jackson, and the youth discount. *Law & Inequality*, *31*, 263–330.

Feld, B. C., & Bishop, D. M. (2012). Transfer of juveniles to criminal court. In Feld, B.C., & Bishop, D.M (Eds.). The oxford handbook of juvenile crime and juvenile justice (pp. 801-842). Oxford University Press.

Flesch, L. M. (2004). Juvenile crime and why waiver is not the answer. *Family Court Review*, *42*(3), 583–596. doi:10.1177/1531244504042200314

Flicker, B. (1981). Prosecuting juveniles as adults: A symptom of a crisis in the juvenile courts. In J. C. Hall, D. M. Hamparian, J. M. Pettibone, & J. L. White (Eds.), *Major issues in juvenile justice information and training: Readings in public policy* (pp. 351–377). Academy for Contemporary Problems.

Flicker, B. (1983). *Transferring juveniles to adult court for trial.* Institute of Judicial Administration.

Fritsch, E. J., Caeti, T. J., & Hemmens, C. (1996). Spare the needle but not the punishment: The incarceration of waived youth in Texas prisons. *Crime and Delinquency, 42*(4), 593–609. doi:10.1177/0011128796042004006

Frost Clausel, L. E., & Bonnie, R. J. (2000). Juvenile justice on appeal. In J. Fagan & F. E. Zimring (Eds.), *The changing borders of juvenile justice: Transfer of adolescents to the criminal court* (pp. 181–206). University of Chicago Press.

Giardino, L. F. (1996). Statutory rhetoric: The reality behind juvenile justice policies in America. *Journal of Policy & Law, 5*, 223–276.

Green, S. T. (2005). Prosecutorial waiver into adult criminal court: A conflict of interests violation amounting to the states' legislative abrogation of juveniles' due process right. *Penn State Law Review, 110*, 233–282.

Greene, T. (2010). *Treating juveniles as adults: sending America's children to adult courts.* Grimes County Sheriff's Office Anderson.

Gilbert, J., Grimm, R., & Parnham, J. (2000). Applying therapeutic principles to a family-focused juvenile justice model (delinquency). *Alabama Law Review, 52*, 1153–1212.

Gillespie, L. K., & Norman, M. D. (1984). Does certification mean prison: Some preliminary findings from Utah. *Juvenile & Family Court Journal, 35*(3), 23–34. doi:10.1111/j.1755-6988.1984.tb00541.x

Griffin, P., Addie, S., Addie, B., & Firestine, K. (2011). *Trying juveniles as adults: An analysis of state transfer laws and reporting.* U.S. Department of Justice, Office of Justice Programs, Office of Juvenile Justice and Delinquency Prevention.

Griffin, P., Torbet, P., & Syzmanski, L. (1998). *Trying juveniles in adult court: An analysis of state transfer provisions.* Office of Juvenile Justice and Delinquency Prevention, Office of Justice Programs, U.S. Department of Justice.

Guttman, C. R. (1995). Listen to the children: The decision to transfer juveniles to criminal court. *Harvard Civil Rights-Civil Liberties Law Review, 30*, 507–542.

Hager, D. A. (1995). Does the Texas juvenile waiver statute comport with the requirements of due process? *Texas Tech Law Review, 26*, 813–856.

Hamparian, D. M., Eastep, L. K., Muntean, S. M., Priestino, R. R., Swisher, R. G., Wallace, P. L., & White, J. L. (1982). *Major issues in juvenile justice information and training: Youth in adult courts: Between two worlds.* Academy for Contemporary Problems.

Hamilton, L., Moak, S. C., & Golden, J. W. (2007). Arkansas legislative reforms provide framework for change while supporting *parens patriae* philosophy of juvenile court. *Juvenile & Family Court Journal, 58*(1), 37–47. doi:10.1111/j.1755-6988.2007.tb00134.x

Herkal, C. J. (1998). You live, you learn: A comment on Oklahoma's Youthful Offender Act. *Tulsa Law Journal, 34*, 599–624.

Hirase, J. (1992). State ex. rel. v. EGT: Waiving childhood goodbye. *Journal of Contemporary Law, 18*, 159–175.

Hoeffel, J. C. (2013). The jurisprudence of death and youth: Now the twain should meet. *Texas Tech Law Review, 46*, 29–69.

Hogan, C. (1974). Waiver of juvenile jurisdiction and the hard-core youth. *North Dakota Law Review, 51*, 655–677.

Houghtalin, M., & Mays, G. L. (1991). Criminal dispositions of New Mexico juveniles transferred to adult court. *Crime and Delinquency, 37*(3), 393–407. doi:10.1177/0011128791037003006

Howell, J. C. (1996). Juvenile transfers to the criminal justice system: State of the art. *Law & Policy, 18*(1-2), 17–60. doi:10.1111/j.1467-9930.1996.tb00163.x

In re Gault. (1967). 387 U.S. 1.

In re Winship. (1970). 397 U.S. 358.

Jensen, E. L. (1994). The waiver of juveniles to criminal court: Policy goals, empirical realities, and suggestions for change. *Idaho Law Review, 31*, 173–204.

Kent v. United States. (1966). 383 U.S. 541.

Kimbrell, M. (2015). It takes a village to waive a child-or at least a jury: Applying *Apprendi* to juvenile waiver hearings in Oregon. *Willamette Law Review, 52*, 61–98.

Krisberg, B., & Austin, J. (1993). *Reinventing juvenile justice*. Sage Publications. doi:10.4135/9781483326450

Kurlychek, M. C. (2016). Effectiveness of juvenile transfer to adult court: Implications from current research and directions for future study. *Criminology & Public Policy, 15*(3), 897–900. doi:10.1111/1745-9133.12240

Lehmann, P. S., & Kobie, A. (2021). Effects of waivers. In S. J. Keenan (Ed.), *The transferring of America's youth* (pp. 87–115).

Levesque, R. J., & Tomkins, A. J. (1995). Revisioning juvenile justice: Implications of the new child protection movement. *Washington University Journal of Urban and Contemporary Law, 48*, 87–116.

Maroney, T. A. (2011). Adolescent brain science after Graham. *The Notre Dame Law Review, 86*, 765–794.

Martin, G. A. Jr. (1992). The delinquent and the juvenile court: Is there still a place for rehabilitation? *Connecticut Law Review, 25*, 57–93.

McCarthy, F. B. (1994). The serious offender and juvenile court reform: The case for prosecutorial waiver of juvenile court jurisdiction. *Saint Louis University Law Journal, 38*, 629–671.

McNulty, E. W. (1996). The transfer of juvenile offenders to adult court: Panacea or problem? *Law & Policy, 18*(1-2), 61–75. doi:10.1111/j.1467-9930.1996.tb00164.x

Miller, R. N., & Applegate, B. K. (2015). Adult crime, adult time? Benchmarking public views on punishing serious juvenile felons. *Criminal Justice Review, 40*(2), 151–168. doi:10.1177/0734016814546039

Mulvey, E. P., & Schubert, C. (2012). *Transfer of juveniles to adult court: Effects of a broad policy in one court. Juvenile Justice Bulletin. December 2012*. U.S. Department of Justice, Office of Justice Programs. Office of Juvenile Justice & Delinquency Prevention.

Nimick, E., Szymanski, L., & Snyder, H. (1986). *Juvenile court waiver: A study of juvenile court cases transferred to criminal court*. National Center for Juvenile Justice.

Noon, C. R. (1994). Waiving goodbye to juvenile defendants, getting smart vs. getting tough. *University of Miami Law Review, 49*, 431–476.

Norman, M., & Gillespie, L. K. (1986). Changing horses: Utah's shift in adjudicating serious juvenile offenders. *Journal of Contemporary Law, 12*, 85–98.

NRC. National Research Council. (2013). Reforming juvenile justice: A developmental approach. The National Academies Press.

Osbun, L. A., & Rode, P. A. (1984). Prosecuting juveniles as adults: The quest for "objective" decisions. *Criminology, 22*(2), 187–202. doi:10.1111/j.1745-9125.1984.tb00296.x

Pagnanelli, E. (2007). Children as adults: The transfer of juveniles to adult courts and the potential impact of Roper v. Simmons. *The American Criminal Law Review, 44*, 175–194.

Podkopacz, M. R., & Feld, B. C. (1995). Judicial waiver policy and practice: Persistence, seriousness, and race. *Minnesota Journal of Law & Inequality, 14*, 73–178.

Quinn, M. C. (2015). In loco juvenile justice: Minors in munis, cash from kids, and adolescent pro se advocacy-Ferguson and beyond. *Brigham Young University Law Review*, •••, 1247–1308. doi:10.2139srn.2614552

Redding, R. E. (1997). Juveniles transferred to criminal court: Legal reform proposals based on social science research. *Utah Law Review, 1997*, 709–763.

Redding, R. E. (2003). The effects of adjudicating and sentencing juveniles as adults: Research and policy implications. *Youth Violence and Juvenile Justice, 1*(2), 128–155. doi:10.1177/1541204002250875

Redding, R. E., & Howell, J. C. (2000). Blended sentencing in American juvenile courts. In J. Fagan & F. E. Zimring (Eds.), *The changing borders of juvenile justice: Transfer of adolescents to the criminal court* (pp. 145–180). University of Chicago Press.

Rubin, H. T. (2006). *Return them to juvenile court.* Policy brief. Adultification series, volume 1. Campaign for Youth Justice.

Ruddell, R., Mays, G. L., & Giever, D. M. (1998). Transferring juveniles to adult courts. Recent trends and issues in Canada and the United States. *Juvenile & Family Court Journal, 49*(3), 1–15. doi:10.1111/j.1755-6988.1998.tb01481.x

Rudman, C., Hartstone, E., Fagan, J., & Moore, M. (1986). Violent youth in adult court: Process and punishment. *Crime and Delinquency, 32*(1), 75–96. doi:10.1177/0011128786032001005

Rudof, P. R. (1998). Throwing out the baby with the bathwater: Utah's Serious Youth Offender Statute. *Utah Law Review*, 443–464.

Sabo, S. (1996). Rights of passage: An analysis of waiver of juvenile court jurisdiction. *Fordham Law Review, 64*, 2425–2454.

Sagatun, I., McCollum, L. L., & Edwards, L. P. (1985). The effects of transfers from juvenile to criminal courts: A loglinear analysis. *Crime and Justice, 8*(1), 65–92. doi:10.1080/0735648X.1985.9721310

Sanborn, J. B. Jr. (1994a). Certification to criminal court: The important policy questions of how, when, and why. *Crime and Delinquency, 40*(2), 262–281. doi:10.1177/0011128794040002007

Sanborn, J. B. Jr. (1994c). Remnants of *parens patriae* in the adjudicatory hearing: Is a fair trial possible in juvenile court. *Crime and Delinquency, 40*(4), 599–615. doi:10.1177/0011128794040004008

Sanborn, J. B. Jr. (1996b). Policies regarding the prosecution of juvenile murderers: Which system and who should decide? *Law & Policy, 18*(1-2), 151–178. doi:10.1111/j.1467-9930.1996.tb00168.x

Sanborn, J. B. Jr. (2001a). A *parens patriae* figure or impartial fact finder: Policy questions and conflicts for the juvenile court judge. *Criminal Justice Policy Review, 12*(4), 311–332. doi:10.1177/0887403401012004004

Sanborn, J. B., Jr. (2004b). *The criminalization of juvenile court: Hyperbole in search of policy.* Paper presented at the annual conference of the Academy of Criminal Justice Sciences. Las Vegas, NV, March 9-13, 2004.

Sanborn, J. B. Jr, & Salerno, A. W. (2005). *The juvenile justice system: Law and process.* Roxbury Publishing Company. Oxford University Publishing.

Sargent, D. A., & Gordon, D. H. (1963). Waiver of jurisdiction: An evaluation of the process in the juvenile court. *Crime and Delinquency, 9*(2), 121–128. doi:10.1177/001112876300900202

Schornhorst, T. F. (1968). The waiver of juvenile court jurisdiction: Kent revisited. *Indiana Law Review, 43*, 583–613.

Scialabba, N. (2016). Should juveniles be charged as adults in the criminal justice system? *American Bar Association. Volume 3,* October 3, 2016.

Schiraldi, V., & Ziedenberg, J. (1999). *The Florida experiment: An analysis of the impact of granting prosecutors discretion to try juveniles as adults.* Justice Policy Institute.

Scott, E. S. (2013). Miller v. Alabama and the (past and) future of juvenile crime regulation. *Law & Inequality, 31*, 535–558.

Scott, E. S., & Steinberg, L. (2003). Less guilty by reason of adolescence: Developmental immaturity, diminished responsibility, and the juvenile death penalty. *The American Psychologist, 58*(12), 1009–1018. doi:10.1037/0003-066X.58.12.1009 PMID:14664689

Sherman, F. T., & Talley, W. Jr. (1995). Struggling for a future: Juvenile violence, juvenile justice. *Boston College Law Review. Boston College. Law School, 36*, 889–892.

Shiller, R. (2006). Fundamental unfairness of the discretionary direct file process in Florida: The need for a return to juvenile court waiver hearings. *Whittier Journal of Child & Family Advocacy, 6*, 13–52.

Singer, S. I. (1993). The automatic waiver of juveniles and substantive justice. *Crime and Delinquency, 39*(2), 253–261. doi:10.1177/0011128793039002009

Slobogin, C. (1999). Treating kids right: Deconstructing and reconstructing the amenability to treatment concept. *Journal of Contemporary Legal Issues, 10*, 299–333.

Slobogin, C. (2013). Treating juveniles like juveniles: Getting rid of transfer and expanded adult court jurisdiction. *Texas Tech Law Review, 46*, 103–132.

Snyder, H. N., & Sickmund, M. (1995). *Juvenile offenders and victims: A national report*. U.S. Department of Justice, Office of Justice Programs, Office of Juvenile Justice and Delinquency Prevention.

Snyder, H. N., Sickmund, M., & Poe-Yamagata, E. (2000). *Juvenile transfers to criminal court in the 1990s: Lessons learned from four studies*. U.S. Department of Justice, Office of Justice Programs, Office of Juvenile Justice and Delinquency Prevention.

Soler, M. (1994). Re-imagining the juvenile court. In Humm, S. R., Ort, B.A., Anbari, M.M., Lader, W.S., & Biel, W.S. (Eds.). Child, parent and state: Law and policy reader (pp. 596-610). Temple University Press.

Sorrentino, J. N., & Olsen, G. K. (1977). Certification of juveniles to adult court. *Pepperdine Law Review, 4*, 497–522.

Stamm, M. J. (1973). Transfer of jurisdiction in juvenile court: An A\analysis of the proceeding, its role in the administration of justice, and A proposal for the reform of Kentucky law. *Kentucky Law Journal (Lexington, Ky.), 62*, 122–199.

Steinberg, L. (2000). *Should juvenile offenders be tried as adults? A developmental perspective on changing legal policies* (No. 147). Northwestern University/University of Chicago Joint Center for Poverty Research.

Steiner, B., & Wright, E. (2006). Assessing the relative effects of state direct file waiver laws on violent juvenile crime: Deterrence or irrelevance? *The Journal of Criminal Law & Criminology, 96*, 1451–1477.

Suffredini, B. R. (1994). Juvenile gunslingers: A place for punitive philosophy in rehabilitative juvenile justice. *Boston College Law Review. Boston College. Law School, 35*, 885–925.

Tanenhaus, D. S. (2000). The evolution of transfer out of the juvenile court. In J. Fagan & F. E. Zimring (Eds.), *The changing borders of juvenile justice: Transfer of adolescents to the criminal court* (pp. 13–43). University of Chicago Press.

Tanenhaus, D. S. (2013). First things first: Juvenile justice reform in historical context. *Texas Tech Law Review*, *46*, 281–290.

Thomas, C. W., & Bilchik, S. (1985). Prosecuting juveniles in criminal courts: A legal and empirical analysis. *The Journal of Criminal Law & Criminology*, *76*(2), 439–479. doi:10.2307/1143613

Traver, D. P. (2000). The wrong answer to a serious problem: A story of school shootings, politics and automatic transfer. *Loyola University of Chicago Law Journal. Loyola University of Chicago. School of Law*, *31*, 281–315.

Valliere, B. J. (1986). The transfer of juvenile offenders to adult courts in Massachusetts: Reevaluating the rehabilitative ideal. *Suffolk University Law Review*, *20*, 989–1028.

Vandervort, F. E., & Ladd, W. E. (2000). The worst of all possible worlds: Michigan's juvenile justice system and international standards for the treatment of children. *University of Detroit Mercy Law Review*, *78*, 203–258.

Vannella, D. M. (2006). Let the jury do the waive: How *Apprendi v. New Jersey* applies to juvenile transfer proceedings. *William and Mary Law Review*, *48*, 723–770.

Vitiello, M. (1976). Constitutional safeguards for juvenile transfer procedure: The ten years since Kent v. United States. *De Paul Law Review*, *26*, 23–53.

Whitebread, C. H., & Batey, R. (1981). The role of waiver in the juvenile court: Questions of philosophy and function. In J. C. Hall, D. M. Hamparian, J. M. Pettibone, & J. L. White (Eds.), *Major Issues in Juvenile Justice Information and Training: Readings in Public Policy* (pp. 207–226). Academy for Contemporary Problems.

Wilbourn, B. (1995). Waiver of juvenile court jurisdiction: National trends and the inadequacy of the Texas response. *American Journal of Criminal Law*, *23*, 633–649.

Wizner, S. (1984). Discretionary waiver of juvenile court jurisdiction: An invitation to procedural arbitrariness. *Criminal Justice Ethics*, *3*(2), 41–50. doi:10.1080/0731129X.1984.9991757

Young, M. C. (2000). *Providing effective representation for youth prosecuted as adults*. US Department of Justice, Office of Justice Programs, Bureau of Justice Assistance. doi:10.1037/e527162006-001

Zane, S. N., Welsh, B. C., & Mears, D. P. (2016). Juvenile transfer and the specific deterrence hypothesis: Systematic review and meta-analysis. *Criminology & Public Policy*, *15*(3), 901–925. doi:10.1111/1745-9133.12222

Zimring, F. E. (1981). Notes on the jurisprudence of waiver. In J. C. Hall, D. M. Hamparian, J. M. Pettibone, & J. L. White (Eds.), *Major issues in juvenile justice information and training: Readings in public policy* (pp. 193–205). Academy for Contemporary Problems.

Zimring, F. E. (1991). The treatment of hard cases in American juvenile justice: In defense of discretionary waiver. *Notre Dame Journal of Law, Ethics & Public Policy*, *5*, 267–280.

Zimring, F. E. (1998a). *American youth violence*. Oxford University Press.

Zimring, F. (1999). The New Politics of Criminal Justice: Of Three Strikes, Truth-in-Sentencing, and Megan's Laws. *Perspectives on Crime & Justice*, *4*, 1–22.

Zimring, F. E. (2000b). The punitive necessity of waiver. In J. Fagan & F. E. Zimring (Eds.), *The Changing Borders of Juvenile Justice: Transfer of adolescents to the criminal court* (pp. 207–224). University of Chicago Press.

Zimring, F. E., & Fagan, J. (2000). Transfer policy and law reform. In J. Fagan & F. E. Zimring (Eds.), *The changing borders of juvenile justice: Transfer of adolescents to the criminal court* (pp. 407–424). University of Chicago Press.

ENDNOTES

1 There is also a claim of extreme cruelty in legislatures' enacting transfer laws:
Of course, youths who violate laws should be treated differently than adults; should we imprison 6-year-olds (Zimring, 1998a, p. 75)?
****
Juvenile transfer is not as dire or as final as death, but to place a developmentally immature child in a criminal court situation is to send his childhood off to a slow, but certain, death... (Hoeffel, 2013, p. 69).

2 From an ahistorical viewpoint, Angell (2004) has argued: *Any juvenile justice policy that emphasizes punishment over treatment lies far afield of the system's original aim of addressing the special needs of young offenders. The "get tough" mantra and its progeny represent the antithesis of the Progressive goal on individualized treatment and rehabilitation of juvenile delinquents* (p. 130). OE and DF (as well as JT) can be reasonably perceived as a reaffirmation of JC and its focus on rehabilitation as well as support for its population of (retained) juvenile offenders.

3 There are numerous counter arguments to the purported anti-JC rhetoric of transfer:
• First, the traditional JC did not have jurisdiction over most transfer-eligible offenders! Only when JC extended its jurisdiction did transfer become more relevant and necessary.
• Second, not just *any serious crime* is transferred — indeed the vast, overwhelming majority of serious (and even chronic) juvenile criminal offenders are retained in JC.
• Third, JC originally and continually has had serious limits in the maximum retention age. There is limited time to address the serious/chronic crimes of offenders, especially older ones. Even Zimring does not want to expand the JC's retention/sentencing capacity. You cannot have it both ways — keep JCs mostly treatment-oriented, with limited sentencing capacity, together with an unlimited jurisdiction over chronic/violent/serious crime.
• Fourth, insisting that a select/relatively few juvenile offenders should be excluded from JC is as much (or more) about reaffirming JC and rehabilitation as it is undermining same (see Chapter 13). Asserts that not all offenders belong in JC does not equate into not believing in rehabilitation, or in JC. It reasonably can be asserted that these transfer targets do not deserve the JC, its amenities, and immunity from criminal prosecution.
• Fifth, it reasonably can be argued that JC has never had a foundation of justice sufficient to sustain a murder conviction (or for a brutal rape or chronic violence). It can be argued that these

youths belong in CC and still support the traditional JC for the vast majority of rank-and-file juvenile offenders; arguably it is the only way to preserve a JC.

Consider the plethora of situations where an all-or-nothing proposition would fail miserably:

- If a country puts a ceiling on the economic status that qualifies for welfare, that does not equate with that country's being anti-welfare or anti-human.
- If a country places a minimum age restriction on voting/driving/drinking/gambling rights, that does not equate with that country's being anti-voting/driving/drinking/gambling or anti-adolescent.
- If an insurance company refuses to insure a driver due to a horrible driving record, that does not equate with that insurance company's being anti-driver or anti-insurance.
- If an elementary or secondary school principal determines that a frequently-suspended student has finally earned an expulsion due to the latest infraction, that does not equate with that principal's being anti-education or anti-student.
- If a restaurant refuses service to all of those who will not pay for their meals, that does not equate with that restaurant's being anti-eating, anti-patron or anti-human.
- If a country refuses to retain immigrants who have gained entry illegally, that does not equate with that country's being anti-immigration or anti-human.
- If a country denies voting privileges to non-citizens, that does not equate to that country's being anti-non-citizen or anti-voting.
- If country/swim clubs refuse golf/swimming privileges to non-members, that does not equate to those country/swim clubs' being anti-golfing/swimming or anti-human.
- If a homeowners' association denies community voting privileges to non-residents, that does not equate to that HOA's being anti-voting or anti-human.

The above is about who qualifies for inclusion in the "club." Arguing *some* offenders *do not belong* in the JC club does not equate with being anti-JC, anti-rehabilitation, or anti-juvenile offender.

4 The *Kent v. U.S.* (1960) decision on *JT and findings of amenability to treatment* cited many offense-related criteria that are embraced by many from the ATC. Thus, it is questionable how much of a shift from *offender to offense* there was in adopting OE as Feld alleges (2000, p. 106). The actual shift was taking power away from judges who would not exercise it (via JT) and extending it to prosecutors (via PT) who would. Feld has spent a good part of his career arguing that transfer is sentencing (see Table 40). His initial analysis of OE involved regarding it as JC's being invaded by "just deserts" or retribution. OE's focus on offense and record, and its empowerment of a prosecutor were welcomed by Feld as a departure from and preferable alternative to JT. Feld portrayed OE as a rebuke of JC's rehabilitation platform; rehabilitation was soon alleged by him to be only "nominal" in JC. As years and publications evolved, Feld's focus on OE transitioned from support for its use of objective transfer criteria to reconceptualizing PT (and JT) as sentencing to challenging PT as an impermissible reallocation of sentencing power from the judiciary to the executive branch of government. This evolution is interesting since it involves an eminent juvenile justice scholar. The evolution in Feld's transfer views parallel his transformation from total exclusion (abolition of JC) to selective exclusion (OE) to near nearly zero exclusion (JT in limited circumstances).

5 Prosecutors act judicial-like (i.e., in a sentencing-like capacity) when they gauge what they want from a case before deciding upon a charge and whether to pursue a plea bargain. Prosecutors in the

CJ system also select a forum (like in DF) when thy address lower-level felonies, deciding whether to charge that felony in a trial court of general jurisdiction or to downgrade it (i.e., "undercharge" as they may do in OE) to a misdemeanor and file that charge in a trial court of limited jurisdiction. In most major CC cases a plea bargain will determine the outcome. Prosecutors regularly make case worth estimates (desired sentences) in deciding the charge and the best deal. Sentence bargaining is prevalent in CC, meaning prosecutors who arrange the sentence arrangements are deciding the appropriate/acceptable sentence, not judges. The latter mostly simply ratify what prosecutors have arranged with defense counsel.

6 See Angell, 2004; Bishop & Frazier, 1991; Bishop, Frazier, & Henretta, 1989; Bortner, 1986; Champion, 1989; Champion & Mays, 1991; D'Ambra, 1997; Feld, 1981a, 1981b, 1987, 1989; Hamilton, Moak, & Golden, 2007; Hamparian, Eastep, Muntean, Priestino, Swisher, Wallace, & White, 1982; Howell, 1996; Nimick, Szymanski, & Snyder, 1986; Snyder & Sickmund, 1995; Zimring, 1991.

7 See, also, Beresford, 2000; Bortner, 1986; Butts & Mears, 2001; Champion, 1989; Cintron, 1996; CYJ, 2007; Deitch, Barstow, Lukens, & Reyna, 2009; Fagan, 2002; Fagan & Deschenes, 1990; Fagan, Forst, & Vivona, 1987; Feld, 1987, 1989, 1995, 1997, 1998; Flesch, 2004; Fritsch, Caeti, & Hemmens, 1996; Gilespie & Norman, 1984; Green, 2003; Greene, 2010; Houghtalin & Mays, 1992; Jensen, 1994; McNulty, 1996; Nimick, Szymanski, & Snyder, 1986; Norman & Gilespie, 1986; NRC, 2013; Osbun & Rodes, 1984; Rudman et al., 1986; Sagatun, McCollum, & Edwards, 1985; Schiraldi & Ziedenberg, 1999; Singer, 1993; Steinberg, 2000; Thomas & Bilchik, 1985; Wizner, 1984; Young, 2000.

8 Recently adopted transfer measures have been criticized for ignoring nonserious recidivists: (W)*hile transfer laws often target first-time serious offenders, repeat offenders are more likely to recidivate and probably are less amenable to rehabilitation in the juvenile justice system…* (Redding, 1997, p. 709). The continuous, in fact, never-ending transfer focus on recidivist offenders (or, to borrow Zimring's phraseology, *the grist for the theoretical JT mill*) makes it strange that legislators could be accused of ignoring this traditional transfer target.

9 Some blame *In re Gault* (1967) and *In re Winship* (1970) for the abandonment of treatment. "(A) dversarial proceedings replaced informal conferences in which judges attempted to do what is in the best interests of the juvenile… (Gilbert, Grimm, & Parnham, 2000, p. 1166)."

10 There were at least major three phases of criminalization; the timetable and extent vary by location:

Phase 1)

Original JC changes its population/character:

Older defendants (not only adding 16/17 but also an increase in average age);

Serious/violent crimes increase;

Decrease in number of child-placing/serving institutions and the rise of delinquent correctional facilities;

More regular crimes; fewer status offenses; and,

End of the vestiges of clinic-like operation.

Phase 2)

Original JC changes its operation

Academics begin analysis and criticism of JC;

President's Crime Commission severely criticizes JC;

U.S. Supreme Court intervention *(In re Gault* and its progeny);
Adoption of more rights for juvenile defendants;
Defense attorneys and prosecutors regularly appear in JC; and, Preliminary hearings, trials and separate disposition stages occur.
Phase 3)
Original JC experiences real criminalization:
Explosion in drug, rape, indecent assault, homicide, robbery, carrying weapons, and, arson charges;
Removal of RIT (runaway, incorrigibility, and truancy) offenses;
(ICs) Informal complaints dry up as do adjustments;
Rise in number of adjudicatory hearings (AHs) and more formal proceedings;
Increase in # of recidivists headed to JC and AH;
Increase in ratio of delinquents per 1000 juveniles;
Increase in % of population as criminal — 1983: 3% of JC age kids referred to JC but 10% of boys 15-17, and 13% of boys 16;
Minimum JC age adopted/raised (e.g., to 10 in Pennsylvania);
Fundamental change in characteristics of JDs put away (older/more serious/more chronic/more violent);
Expansion of prosecutorial powers: intake/charging/diversion/transfer;
Even older defendants; 16/17 becomes majority age group;
Adopt numerous get-tough measures, especially in detention and sentencing; and Correctional facilities become virtually only placement outlet for offenders.

11 Restoring JC's original version would require reinventing juvenile crime, returning the maximum JC age of 15 (if not younger), reopening child-care facilities, and, ignoring Supreme Court decisions, among other renovations.

12 Serious and violent crime has been declining; there are examples of violent offenses still occurring, however. If there is a reduction in the serious/violent crime among juveniles, there should be a corresponding reduction in the number of transfers for these youths, which the data bear out. That does not suggest a reduction/elimination of transfer capability. If a jurisdiction witnesses no murders during a five-year stretch, that is no reason to no longer exclude murder from JC. It means no juvenile murder defendants will appear in CC during that time. A juvenile murder charge that occurs in the sixth year should be transferred. Simply because crime rates decline does not mean the appropriateness of this behavior's being prosecuted in CC has ended. The decline might be due to the availability or threat of transfer. The ATC exaggerate a decline but cannot claim an absence of chronic/violent/serious juvenile crime, behaviors which should be eliminated before transfer is. In a comparable scenario, the ATC would argue that since hijacking planes has virtually disappeared, there is no longer a need for laws prohibiting it, airport security screening measures to detect it, and air marshals to deter and prevent it. It is a different situation/phenomenon to have a surplus of hospitals and to keep all operating; keeping them open costs funds. Recent history may have proven the lack of wisdom in shuttering hospitals when pandemics are possible. But transfer laws differ markedly from maintaining hospitals, nevertheless; there is no cost to maintaining transfer provisions that remain unused, for the moment.

13 Chapters 13 to 15 show that the *safety valve* reason is not a major justification for or reason behind transfer. The ATC criticizes transfer's operating as a safety valve and then appears determined to

guarantee that result by eliminating transfer or in limiting transfer to the most serious offenses (where transfer probably would have to operate like a safety valve).

14 In the rare sensational case, transfer can operate this way. One study found the safety valve and societal retribution ideas were validated by only a minority of JC workers (25% and 34%, respectively), and they worked in an urban area with a high rate of serious/violent juvenile crime (see Sanborn, 1994a). JC workers were two or three times more likely to cite a lack of resources (78%) or youths' irresolvable problems (81%) as reasons to transfer (Id., p. 272). *The workers considered transfer as simply the inability of juvenile court to service all youths, rather than acting like a safety valve or a form of societal retribution...* (Id., p. 275).

CHAPTER 7 TABLES

Table 40. Professor Feld's Stance on Transfer as Sentencing vs. Charging

As this Table discloses, Professor Feld frequently characterized transfer as *both* charging and sentencing in one reference, indeed, sometimes in the same sentence (Cf., Sections ***A*** & ***B***, below). If sheer number of references reflects confidence in and commitment to a position, Feld appears much more equipped to acknowledge fact and concede that transfer or waiver is a matter of *charging* and *selecting the proper forum or court for trial*. At the very least, this Table should reveal and explain, in part, the abundant confusion in the transfer literature. And, charging and sentencing are neither synonyms nor interchangeable concepts.
A. Transfer as Sentencing
It is important to note that such a waiver decision is also a *sentencing* decision that represents a choice between the punitive disposition of adult criminal court and the "rehabilitative" disposition of the juvenile court (Feld, 1984a, p. 269, footnote omitted, emphasis in original). * * * * * * * *
Commentators concerned about excessive judicial discretion have emphasized that "waiver of juvenile court jurisdiction requires a central guiding principle." The catalogue of miscellaneous factors promulgated by the Minnesota Supreme Court provides neither a "central guiding principle" nor much practical guidance to juvenile court judges struggling with this difficult *sentencing* decision. Instead, Rule 32's emphasis on vague, discretionary, and ultimately unquantifiable factors simply compounds all the preexisting problems of the process and submits the most important *dispositional* decision in the juvenile court to the subjective reaction of each individual juvenile court judge… (Id., p. 272, footnote omitted, emphases added; see, also, Feld, 1989, p. 49,footnote 130). * * * * * * * *
Waiver for adult prosecution is the most significant *dispositional* decision of the juvenile court… (Feld, 1984b, p. 29, emphasis added). * * * * * * * *
A waiver decision is also a *sentencing* decision which represents a choice between the punitive dispositions of adult criminal courts and the nominally rehabilitative dispositions of the juvenile court. Increasingly, the principle of offense dominates this *sentencing* decision, as "just deserts" based on the offense, rather than the real needs of the offender, prescribe the appropriate disposition. The waiver of a serious offender into the adult system on the (Feld, 1987, p. 472, emphases added). * * * * * * * *
The waiver decision is a form of *sentencing* decision that represents a choice between the explicitly punitive dispositions of adult criminal courts and the nominally rehabilitative dispositions of juvenile courts… (Id., p. 487, citation omitted, emphasis added). * * * * * * * *
The analysis of waiver as a *sentencing decision* addresses two interrelated policy issues… (Id., p. 489, emphasis added). * * * * * * * *
(J)udicial waiver statutes that are couched in terms of amenability to treatment or dangerousness are simply broad, standardless grants of *sentencing* discretion characteristic of the individualized, offender-oriented dispositional statutes of the juvenile court… (Id., p. 491, emphasis added). * * * * * * * *
Since 1970, twenty-six have amended their (transfer) statutes to add either minimum offense limitations or present offense/prior offense criteria to structure judicial *sentencing discretion*… (Id., p. 504, emphasis added). * * * * * * * *
Regardless of the statutory details, the thrust of these (PT) laws is to remove *sentencing discretion* from judges with respect to the juvenile or adult disposition and to base the *sentencing decision* explicitly on some aspects of the offenses charged… (Id. p. 517, emphases added). * * * * * * * *
The addition of presumptive or mandatory waiver requirements for youths meeting offense criteria removes a significant element of judicial *sentencing discretion*… (Id., p. 519, emphasis added). * * * * * * * *
Once waiver is analyzed as a *sentencing* decision… (Id., p. 531; see, also, id., p 517, emphasis added). * * * * * * * *
In *Kent v. United States*, the Supreme Court mandated that procedural due process must be observed in judicial waiver determinations, thereby formalizing this *sentencing* decision…. (Id., p. 489, citation omitted, emphasis added). * * * * * * * *

continued on following page

Table 40. Continued

A waiver decision is a *sentencing* choice between the punitive dispositions of adult criminal court and the nominally rehabilitative dispositions of juvenile court. The theoretical differences between juvenile and criminal courts' sentencing philosophies become most visible in juvenile waiver proceedings. (Feld, 1989, p. 3, emphasis in original). * * * * * * * *
Although judicial waiver reflected individualized *sentencing* practices from its inception, the decision-making process has been substantially revised. In *Kent v. United States*, the United States Supreme Court held that some procedural due process protections must be accorded juveniles in judicial waiver determinations, thereby formalizing this special *sentencing* decision (Id., p. 12, citations omitted, emphases added). * * * * * * * *
(W)aiver is the most significant *sentencing* decision that juvenile court judges make… (Id., p, 41, emphasis added). * * * * * * * *
Judicial waiver practices pose two primary and interrelated problems--the highly discretionary, idiosyncratic nature of this individualized *sentencing* decision, and the lack of integration between the criteria for (transfer)…and the *sentencing* practices in adult criminal courts. The source of both problems is individualized judicial *sentencing* discretion (Id., p. 46, emphases added). * * * * * * * *
Once waiver is viewed as a *sentencing* decision, the lack of objective substantive guidelines remits the transfer decision to every judge in every county in the state with highly variable and unpredictable outcomes…. This "justice by geography" emerges under a law of general applicability and raises very troubling questions about the even-handed administration of justice with respect to the most important *sentencing* decision made by juvenile courts. (Id., p. 94, emphases added). * * * * * * * *
(One problem) posed by judicial waiver practices: the highly discretionary idiosyncratic nature of this individualized *sentencing* decision… (Id. p.95, emphasis added). * * * * * * * *
Offense exclusion, a form of mandatory *sentencing,* provides a rational, nondiscretionary, and easily administered method for deciding which youths should be prosecuted as adults (Id., p. 96, emphasis added). * * * * * * * *
(I)t is abundantly clear that Minnesota's judicial waiver legislation is fundamentally flawed… and leave(s) unresolved the most important *sentencing* policy issue in juvenile justice… (Id., p. 101, emphasis added). * * * * * * * * * *
Two types of statutes, judicial waiver and legislative offense exclusion, highlight the differences between juvenile and criminal courts' *sentencing* philosophies… (Feld, 1991, p. 701, emphasis added). * * * * * * * * * *
A waiver decision entails a *sentencing* policy choice between punishment in adult criminal court and rehabilitation in juvenile court (Podkopacz & Feld, 1995, p. 74, emphasis added). * * * * * * * *
Whether to waive a juvenile to criminal court for prosecution as an adult is the single most important *sentencing* decision that juvenile court judges can make… (Feld, 1995, p. 1006, emphasis added). * * * * * * * *
Because a certification hearing is a type of *sentencing* proceeding…(Id., p. 1037, emphasis added). * * * * * * * *
The legislative change from "amenability to treatment" to "public safety" significantly alters the framework of the most important *sentencing* decision in juvenile court… (Id., pp. 1121-1122, emphasis added). * * * * * * * *
Jurisdictional waiver represents a type of *sentencing* decision (Feld, 1998, p. 195, emphasis added). * * * * * * * * * *
Analyzing waiver as a *sentencing* decision… (Id., p. 197, emphasis added). * * * * * * * * * *
States that use a concurrent-jurisdiction prosecutor-choice strategy simply make the allocation of power and *sentencing authority* explicit (Id., p. 201, emphasis added). * * * * * * * * * * *

continued on following page

Table 40. Continued

In *Kent v. United States*, the Court held that states must provide juveniles with some procedural due process protections in judicial waiver hearings, thereby "formalizing" this special *sentencing* decision… Podkopacz & Feld, 1996, pp. 451-452, citation/footnote omitted, emphasis added). * * * * * * * * * *
This finding is consistent with our contention that judicial waiver is a highly individualized, discretionary *sentencing* decision in which the outcomes depend significantly upon who is the judge (Id., p. 479, emphasis added). * * * * * * * * * *
Jurisdictional waiver represents a type of *sentencing* decision… (Feld, 1999a, p. 209, emphasis in original). * * * * * * * *
Jurisdictional waiver represents a type of *sentencing* decision… (Feld, 2000, p. 83, emphasis in original). * * * * * * * *
Prosecutors dominate these waiver processes either by charging youths with excluded offenses or by directly selecting the juvenile or criminal forum. These strategies reflect a fundamental shift of *sentencing* discretion from the judicial to the executive branch (Id., p. 112, emphasis added). * * * * * * * *
State laws that exclude long lists of offenses from juvenile courts or that give prosecutors greater authority to direct file charges in either juvenile or criminal court simply shift *sentencing* discretion from judges in a waiver hearing to prosecutors in their offices… (Id., p. 117, emphasis added). * * * * * * * *
Because offense categories are necessarily crude and imprecise indicators of the "real" seriousness of any particular offense, prosecutors inevitably exercise enormous *sentencing* discretion when they decide whether to charge a youth with an excluded offense rather than a lesser included offense, or to select the forum in a direct-file jurisdiction… (Id., pp. 117-118, emphasis added). * * * * * * * *
As a matter of *sentencing* policy, the question recurs whether prosecutors will make better-informed and more appropriate decisions under such circumstances than would judges in an adversarial waiver hearing guided by appropriate waiver criteria (Id., p. 119, emphasis added). * * * * * * * *
The concurrent jurisdiction direct-file strategy simply makes the allocation of power and *sentencing* authority from the judicial to the executive branch… (Id., p. 125, emphasis added). * * * * * * * * * *
Jurisdictional waiver represents a type of *sentencing* decision… (Feld, 2001, p. 4, emphasis in original). * * * * * * * * * *
The jurisprudential shift (from JT to PT) in *sentencing* emphases from considerations of the offender to characteristics of the offense relocated *waiver and sentencing* discretion from judges to prosecutors… (Id., p.5. emphases added). * * * * * * * * * *
These strategies (DF and OE) reflect a fundamental shift of *sentencing* discretion from the judicial to the executive branch (Id., p. 17, emphasis added). * * * * * * * * * *
The concurrent jurisdiction "direct file" strategy simply makes explicit the allocation of power and *sentencing* authority from the judicial to the executive branch… (Id., p. 19, emphasis added). * * * * * * * * * *
Transfer of jurisdiction constitutes a type of *sentencing* decision… (Feld & Bishop, 2012, p. 801, emphasis in original). * * * * * * * * * *
Because offense categories are necessarily crude and imprecise indicators of the seriousness of any offense, prosecutors exercise enormous *sentencing* discretion when they decide to *charge* a youth (in CC) …. (Id., p. 821, emphases added). * * * * * * * * * * *
Cumulatively, these changes reflect fundamental *sentencing* policy shifts from rehabilitation to retribution… (Feld, 1999b, p. 358, emphasis added). * * * * * * * * * * *

continued on following page

Table 40. Continued

Jurisdictional waiver represents a type of *sentencing* decision...(Feld, 2001, p. 4, emphasis added). * * * * * * * * * * *
Jurisdictional waiver represents a type of *sentencing* decision... (Feld, 2004, p. 599, emphasis added). The shift of sentencing discretion from the judicial branch to the executive branch via "direct-file" legislation raises a host of *sentencing* policy questions... (Id., p. 600, emphasis added). * * * * * * * * * * *
Judicial waiver reflects juvenile courts' individualized *sentencing* processes...(Feld, 2007b, p. 38, footnote omitted, emphasis added). * * * * * * * * * *
The shift of *de facto sentencing* discretion from judges to prosecutors has had a major impact on the numbers and characteristics of youths tried in criminal court... (Id., p. 40, emphasis added).
B. Transfer as Charging
Although legislative waiver, which mandates adult prosecution of juveniles *charged* with certain offenses, is sometimes referred to as prosecutorial waiver, "pure" prosecutorial waiver vests the prosecutor's office with discretion in making the transfer decision... (Feld, 1978, p. 521, citations omitted, emphasis added). * * * * * * * * * *
By excluding certain categories of offenses, the legislature automatically places youths *charged* with those offenses into the adult criminal courts...(Id., p. 522, emphasis added). * * * * * * * * * *
The principal alternative to judicial waiver simply excludes certain categories of offenses from juvenile court jurisdiction by legislative definition. If *charged* with one of these offenses, youths above a statutory minimum age are treated as adults... (Id., p. 556, footnote omitted, emphasis added). * * * * * * * * * *
Statutes mandating adult prosecution on the basis of offense *charged* rather than the characteristics of the offender have been criticized extensively as inconsistent with the rehabilitative philosophy of the juvenile court.... The due process claim is directed at the unreviewability of the *charging decision* and the prosecutor's exercise of discretion in removing youths from the juvenile court. The equal protection claim attacks the rationality of the legislative decision to treat youths *charged* with certain offenses as adults rather than juveniles... (Id., p. 557, emphases added). * * * * * * * * * *
(The appellate court in *Bland*) declined to impose procedural requirements on the prosecutor's *charging decision* under the offense exclusion legislation (Id. p. 558, emphasis added). * * * * * * * * * *
The issue whether to impose judicial review on a prosecutor's *charging decision* cannot turn alone, as Judge Wright suggested, on the seriousness of the consequences to the defendant of being tried as an adult rather than a juvenile (Id., p. 559, emphasis added). * * * * * * * * * *
Judge Wright's real concern in *Bland* seems to have been not simply that the prosecutor's *charging decision* may have serious consequences for a youthful offender but, more specifically, that in deciding what *charge* to bring, the prosecutor may foreclose any subsequent consideration of a youth's amenability to juvenile treatment... Wright suggested that the factual determinations at issue in a judicial waiver decision are also at issue when the prosecutor makes his *charging decision*... (Id., p. 560, emphases added). * * * * * * * * * *
The only factual issues involved in the *charging decision* relate to probable cause and legal guilt, and the prosecutor's determinations in this regard are subjected to judicial review at trial (Id., emphasis added). * * * * * * * * * *
In addition to challenges based on the absence of procedural safeguards in connection with the prosecutor's *charging decision*, legislative waiver statutes have been challenged as violations of equal protection by youths claiming that the statutory distinction between those committing serious and minor offenses is arbitrary... (Id., p. 562, emphasis added, footnote omitted). * * * * * * * * * *
(T)he policy reasons that militate against subjecting the prosecutor's *charging decision* to prior judicial review do not preclude examining it after the fact. Finally, in the absence of a transfer-back provision, legislative waiver statutes lend themselves to prosecutorial abuse via *overcharging* (Id., p. 564, emphases added, footnote omitted; see, also, Feld, 1987, pp. 499-500, footnote 121). * * * * * * * * * *

continued on following page

Table 40. Continued

The proposed matrix (OE statute requirement of age, offense and record) has both direct and indirect effects on the exercise of discretion within the juvenile justice system. First, and most obviously, the matrix eliminates all discretion with respect to the *decision to refer for adult prosecution*. Once the decision to proceed against the offender has been made and the appropriate *charge* determined, the decision whether to proceed in the juvenile court or the district court is made mechanically by reference to the matrix… (Id. p.588, emphases added). * * * * * * * * * *
(T)he proposed legislation may foster more consistent *charging decisions* by juvenile and adult prosecutors and, in so doing, may ultimately contribute to a greater equality of result in juvenile and adult proceedings… (Id., p. 614, emphasis added). * * * * * * * * * *
The prosecutor's *charging decision* would initially determine whether a case is subject to juvenile or adult court jurisdiction… (Id., p. 581, emphasis added). * * * * * * * * * *
(In) legislative waiver-the legislature redefines juvenile court jurisdiction to exclude from juvenile courts those youths *charged* with certain offenses (Feld, 1980, p. 174, citation omitted, emphasis added). * * * * * * * * * *
Legislative waiver, the principal alternative to judicial waiver, excludes from juvenile court jurisdiction offenders who are *charged* with certain offenses or who have particular records of prior adjudications in conjunction with a present offense (Id., p. 185, emphasis added). * * * * * * * * * *
(T)here was a substantial and dramatic increase in the number of youths who were tried as adults after having been *charged* with one of the enumerated offenses (Id., pp. 216-217, emphasis added). * * * * * * * * * *
(I)n the absence of a transfer-back provision keyed to the ultimate offense of conviction, legislative waiver statutes lend themselves to prosecutorial abuse via *overcharging*. Finally, to the extent that youths *charged* with major person-excluded offenses do not fit the "worst case" envisioned by the legislature, that fact can be taken into account through the exercise of *prosecutorial discretion in charging*… (Feld, 1984b, p. 38, citing Feld, 1978, p, 564, emphases added). * * * * * * * * * *
In concurrent jurisdiction states… the prosecutor's *charging decision* determines whether a case will be heard in the juvenile or adult forum… To the extent that the prosecutor's decision to *charge* certain offenses in criminal courts divests the juvenile court of jurisdiction… (Feld, 1987, p. 488, footnote 75, emphases added). * * * * * * * * * *
The other transfer mechanism, in which the legislative definition of juvenile court jurisdiction excludes youths *charged* with certain offenses from juvenile courts, is termed legislative waiver or offense exclusion…(Id., p. 488, emphasis added). * * * * * * * * * *
Legislative waiver, the principal alternative to judicial waiver, excludes from juvenile court jurisdiction youths who are *charged* with specified offenses or who have particular records of prior adjudications in conjunction with a present offense… Statutes mandating the prosecution of a youth as an adult on the basis of the offense *charged* or offense history are inconsistent with the individualized rehabilitative philosophy of juvenile courts… (Id., p. 494, emphases added). * * * * * * * * * *
Offense categories are necessarily crude and imprecise classifications, and many youths *charged* and tried as adults will ultimately plead or be found guilty of lesser, nonexcluded offenses... (Id., p. 499, emphasis added). * * * * * * * * * *
(T)here was a dramatic increase in the number of youths who were tried as adults after having been *charged* with one of the enumerated offenses… (Id., p. 509, citation omitted, emphasis added). * * * * * * * * * *
Minnesota legislation provides that if the prosecution *charges* certain types of present offenses or various combinations of present offenses and prior records, a prima facie case, for waiver is established… (Id., p. 510, citation omitted, emphasis added). * * * * * * * * * *

continued on following page

Table 40. Continued

States have accomplished this goal by legislatively narrowing the scope of juvenile court jurisdiction to exclude youths *charged* with certain serious offenses. In many states, the excluded offenses… have been supplemented by judicial waiver statutes that also allow for the discretionary transfer of juveniles *charged* with other nonexcluded offenses. Some states exclude only youths *charged* with offenses punishable by capital punishment or life imprisonment. In addition to excluding youths *charged* with murder, some jurisdictions also exclude youths *charged* with other serious offenses, such as criminal sexual conduct, armed robbery, and kidnapping. Still other jurisdictions exclude youths *charged* with repeat offenses…. In three states… juvenile and criminal courts have concurrent jurisdiction over all offenses, and the prosecutor's charging decision determines the forum in which the case is heard. Because jurisdiction is determined by the *prosecutor's filing of criminal charges* rather than by a judicial waiver/ sentencing hearing, these concurrent jurisdiction statutes are tabulated with excluded offense legislation… (Id., p. 511, emphases added). * * * * * * * * * *
Concurrent jurisdiction statutes grant prosecutors nonreviewable discretion to *file charges* against chronological minors in either juvenile or adult courts. The jurisdictions of juvenile and criminal courts overlap on certain categories of offenses, and the *charging decision* determines the forum in which the case is heard. See *supra* text footnote 75… (Id., p. 513, Table 2, emphases added). * * * * * * * * * *
(Ohio law) excludes from juvenile court jurisdiction any youth who was previously wavied (sic) for adult *prosecution, tried and convicted* of murder or aggravated murder or an aggravated felony of the first or second degree or a felony of the first or second degree, who is *charged* with any of those offense (sic) on a subsequent occasion (Id., p, 514, footnote 7, emphases added). * * * * * * * * * *
(Utah law) gives concurrent jurisdiction to juvenile and criminal courts over youths aged 16 or older who are *charged* with any degree of murder or attempted murder, and six (6) other major offenses against the person, including aggravated robbery, burglary, arson, kidnapping, or rape. *Indicting or criminally charging* a youth with one of those offenses divests the juvenile court or jurisdiction (Id., footnote 9, emphases added). * * * * * * * * * *
(U)nlike judicial waiver/sentencing discretion, which is subject to appellate review, the prosecutor's *charging decision* is not subject to any type of judicial review (Id., footnote omitted, emphasis added). * * * * * * * * * *
(With direct file) prosecutors are more likely than juvenile court judges to be responsive to political pressures and the visibility of serious offenses, more likely to emphasize retributive considerations over rehabilitative ones, and, as adversaries, less likely to consider the welfare of the accused, their *charging decisions* will more frequently emphasize considerations of the offense, such as probable cause and provable legal guilt, than considerations of the offender… (Id., footnote omitted, emphasis added). * * * * * * * * * *
The principal conceptual alternative to judicial waiver is legislation which simply excludes certain categories of serious offenses and/ or prior records from juvenile court jurisdiction. If *charged* with one of these offenses, youths above a statutory minimum age are tried as adults. While such statutes are sometimes characterized as prosecutorial waivers because the decision as to the *offense charged* determines the forum, it is the legislature, not the prosecutor, which makes the policy choice… (Id., pp. 514-515, emphases added). * * * * * * * * * *
(Illinois legislature decided) to exclude entirely from its jurisdiction any youth aged fifteen or older who was *charged* with murder, armed robbery, or rape…. (NY law) excludes thirteen-year-olds charged with murder, and fourteen-year-olds *charged* with kidnapping, arson, rape, and the like…. (Id., p. 515, footnotes omitted, emphases added). * * * * * * * * * *
Connecticut excludes youths charged with a Class A felony who have a prior Class A felony conviction. For youths *charged* with Class B offenses, however, two prior convictions of Class A or B offenses are required. Kansas and Rhode Island exclude youths *charged* with any felony who have two prior felony convictions… (Id., pp. 516-517, emphases added). * * * * * * * * * *
Regardless of the statutory details, the thrust of these (PT) laws is to remove sentencing discretion from judges with respect to the juvenile or adult disposition and to base the sentencing decision explicitly on some aspects of the offenses *charged*… (Id. p. 517, emphasis added). * * * * * * * * * *
In concurrent jurisdiction states… the prosecutor's *charging decision* determines whether a case will be heard in a juvenile or adult forum…. To the extent that the prosecutor's decision to *charge* certain offenses in criminal courts divests the juvenile court of jurisdiction, however, this waiver mechanism will be treated as a sub-category of offense-based decision-making (Feld, 1989, p. 4, footnote 12, references omitted, emphases added). * * * * * * * * * *

continued on following page

Table 40. Continued

The other transfer mechanism may be termed legislative waiver, or offense exclusion, in which the legislative definition of juvenile court jurisdiction excludes youths *charged* with certain offenses… (Id., p. 5, emphasis added). * * * * * * * * * *
Legislative waiver, the principal alternative to judicial waiver, excludes from juvenile court jurisdiction youths who are *charged* with specified offenses or who have records of prior adjudications in addition to the present offense…. (Id., p. 17, citation omitted, emphasis added). * * * * * * * * * *
Statutes mandating the prosecution of a youth as an adult on the basis of the offense *charged* or the offense history, however, are inconsistent with the individualized rehabilitative philosophy of juvenile courts… (Id., emphasis added). * * * * * * * * * *
Many youths *charged* and tried as adults will ultimately plead to or be found guilty of lesser, nonexcluded offenses… (Id., p. 21, emphasis added). * * * * * * * * * *
(T)he policy reasons that militate against subjecting the prosecutor's *charging decision* to prior judicial review do not preclude examining it after the fact. Finally, in the absence of a transfer-back provision, legislative waiver statutes lend themselves to prosecutorial abuse via *overcharging* (Id., footnote 72, citation omitted, emphases added). * * * * * * * * * *
(T)he prosecution can prove a prima facie case for certification by *charging* a sixteen-year-old, who possesses a specified prior record, with certain types of serious offenses… (Id., p. 52, emphasis added). * * * * * * * * * *
Although *J.L.B.* presents a seemingly straightforward waiver case—an older juvenile *charged* with a very serious offense… (Id., p. 88, emphasis added). * * * * * * * * * *
(F)ar more juveniles *charged* with similar offenses and with similar prior records are retained as juveniles than are waived as adults… (Id., p. 94, emphasis added). * * * * * * * * * *
Whether those young juveniles *charged* with the most serious crimes should be tried as adults requires the legislature to make an explicit value choice between an emphasis on the offender and on the offense… (Id., pp. 99-100, emphasis added). * * * * * * * * * *
During the 1989 Minnesota legislative session, several bills excluding from juvenile court jurisdiction any youth aged 14 or older *charged* with murder or manslaughter were introduced… (Id., p. 100, footnote 297, citation omitted, emphasis added). * * * * * * * * * *
In contrast to judicial waiver, legislative waiver simply excludes from juvenile court jurisdiction youths *charged* with certain offenses (Feld, 1991, p.706, footnote omitted, emphasis added). * * * * * * * * * *
(A)bout half of the states have… emphasized policies of retribution or incapacitation, and excluded youths *charged* with serious offenses from juvenile court jurisdiction (Id., p. 708, footnote omitted, emphasis added). * * * * * * * * * *
(W)here general juvenile court jurisdiction extends until eighteen years of age, some states may automatically place younger youths *charged* with serious offenses in adult criminal court (Feld 1987). In a few states, juvenile and criminal courts exercise concurrent jurisdiction over young offenders, which means that the prosecutor's decision to *charge* a youth as a juvenile delinquent or as an adult criminal determines the forum in which the case will be heard (Feld 1978, 1987; Hamparian et al. 1982) … (Feld, 1993a, p. 208, emphases added). * * * * * * * * * *
With legislative offense exclusion, by statutory definition youths *charged* with certain offenses, typically capital crimes or the most serious felonies- such as murder, rape, or armed robbery-simply are not within juvenile court jurisdiction (Feld 1987) … (Id., p. 233, emphasis added). * * * * * * * * * *
Some jurisdictions exclude only capital crimes or murder while others may place youths *charged* with rape, armed robbery, and other offenses automatically in adult criminal court (Hamparian et al. 1982; Feld 1987). While most prescribe some minimum age for "automatic adulthood," typically sixteen years of age, youths as young as thirteen *charged* with murder in New York are *prosecuted* as adults (Feld 1987) … (Id., p. 239, emphases added). * * * * * * * * *

continued on following page

Table 40. Continued

(T)here was a dramatic increase in the numbers of youths who were *tried* as adults after being *charged* with one of the enumerated offenses … (Id., p. 241, emphases added). * * * * * * * * * *
Nearly half of the states have excluded some offenses and offenders from juvenile court jurisdiction. While some states exclude only youths *charged* with capital crimes, murder, or offenses punishable by life imprisonment, others exclude longer lists of offenses or youths *charged* with repeat offenses (Feld 1987) … (Id., p. 242, emphases added). * * * * * * * * * *
(One) study of waived youths' dispositions in Florida, where prosecutors can *charge* juveniles directly in adult court … (Id., emphasis added). * * * * * * * * * *
(Minnesota law excludes) youths sixteen years or older and *charged* with first degree murder from the jurisdiction of the juvenile court and plac(es) them automatically in adult criminal court (Feld, 1995, p. 968, emphasis added). * * * * * * * * * *
In 1980 the Minnesota Legislature created a rebuttable presumption-a prima facie case-that youths *charged* with certain offenses and previous records should be *tried* as adults… (Id., p. 989, footnote omitted, emphasis added). * * * * * * * * * *
By excluding offenders sixteen years or older and *charged* with first degree murder, the new statute clearly defines the limits of legislative tolerance …(Id., p. 1122, emphasis added). * * * * * * * * * *
(A) prosecutor could establish a prima facie case for certification by *charging* a sixteen-year-old, who possesses a specified prior record, with certain types of serious offenses… (Podkopacz & Feld, 1995, p. 94, footnote omitted, emphasis added). * * * * * * * * * *
The county attorney decides against which offenders to *file motions for reference for adult prosecution*. We do not have information about the other youths against whom the prosecutor did not file a reference motion or what factors influenced that *charging decision*… (Id., p.84, footnote 78, emphases added). * * * * * * * * * *
Although the "prima facie" case waiver statute provides a type of legal definition to guide the selection of juveniles to *refer for adult certification*, prosecutors are neither required to select all youths whose delinquencies fit the definition nor precluded from filing motions against those who do not. Thus, the prosecutors' unrestricted *charging discretion* necessarily defines the characteristics of the youths included in the study, because they decide against whom to *file reference motions*… (Id., p. 116, emphases added). * * * * * * * * * *
Although prima facie case statutory definitions attempt to guide prosecutors' selection of which juveniles to *file motions against for adult reference*, prosecutors are neither expected to *charge* all youths whose delinquency background fits the criteria, nor precluded from *charging* other youths who do not meet the criteria… (Podkopacz & Feld, 1996, p. 462, emphases added). * * * * * * * * * *
Juveniles can be motioned for certification more than once if additional serious offenses are *charged* while they are chronologically still juveniles….Because we lack information about the other youths against whom the prosecutor did not *file reference motions*, we cannot determine what factors influenced their *charging decision*… (Id., footnote 60, emphases added). * * * * * * * * * *
The seriousness of youth crime, County Attorney *charging* policies, defense attorney plea negotiation strategies, and juvenile placement options all affect transfer rates… (Id., p. 472, emphasis added). * * * * * * * * * *
By contrast, when judicial waiver decisions, legislatively excluded offenses, or *prosecutorial charging decision* focus on violent young offenders… (Feld, 1997, p. 78, emphasis added). * * * * * * * * * *
Under concurrent-jurisdiction statutes, legislatures grant prosecutors more authority to *charge* youths directly in criminal courts…. As states continue to … expand the lists of excluded offenses, and grant to prosecutors authority to *"direct file"* more cases in criminal court….(Id., p. 80, footnote 23, emphases added). * * * * * * * * * *
(Legislative) efforts to "crack down" and to "get tough" repudiate rehabilitation and judicial discretion, narrow juvenile courts' jurisdiction, base youths' "adult" status increasingly on the offense *charged,* and reflect a shift toward more retributive sentencing policies (Id., p. 80, emphasis added). * * * * * * * * * *

continued on following page

Table 40. Continued

A graduated age-culpability sentencing scheme in an integrated criminal justice system avoids the inconsistencies and injustices associated with the binary either-juvenile-or-adult drama currently played out in judicial waiver proceedings and in prosecutorial *charging decisions*...(Id., p. 127, emphasis added). * * * * * * * * * *
To the extent that a prosecutor's decision to *charge* a case in criminal courts divests the juvenile court of jurisdiction, prosecutorial waiver constitutes a form of offense-based decision making, like legislative offense exclusion... (Feld, 1998, p. 197, citation omitted, emphasis added). * * * * * * * * * *
If they define juvenile court jurisdiction to include only those persons below a jurisdictional age and whom prosecutors *charge* with a non-excluded offense... (Id., p 201, emphasis added). * * * * * * * * * *
In practice, offense exclusion transfers discretion from judges to prosecutors who determine delinquent or criminal status by manipulating their *charging decisions* (Id., emphasis added). * * * * * * * * * *
(A)s legislators expand lists of excluded offenses to encompass less serious crimes or lesser included offenses and lower the ages at which prosecutors may *charge* youths as adults, they also reduce... (Id., p. 207, emphasis added). * * * * * * * * * *
Under concurrent-jurisdiction statutes, legislatures also grant prosecutors more authority to *charge* youths directly in criminal courts... (Id., pp. 207-208, emphasis added). * * * * * * * * * *
(There are) estimates that prosecutors in some jurisdictions may *charge* as many as 10 percent of chronological juveniles in adult court. Indeed, by some calculations, prosecutors in Florida alone may *direct file* as many juveniles into criminal courts in that state as judges waive judicially nationwide... (Id., p. 208, citations omitted, emphasis added). * * * * * * * * * *
The recent changes in waiver laws increase the number of chronological juveniles *charged, tried,* detained, and sentenced in criminal courts...(Id., p. 212, emphases added). * * * * * * * * * *
Because of the constitutional doctrine of separation of powers, courts ordinarily do not review discretionary executive decisions, and most judicial opinions characterize prosecutorial transfer as an *ordinary charging decision* (Feld 1978). To the extent that a prosecutor's *decision to charge a case in criminal court* divests the juvenile court of jurisdiction, prosecutorial waiver constitutes a form of offense-based decision making like legislative offense exclusion (Feld, 1999a, p.210, emphases added, citation omitted). * * * * * * * * *
Invoking the doctrine of separation of powers, the judiciary generally declines to review prosecutors' *charging decisions* (when OE and DF cases are challenged) ... (Id., p. 218, emphasis added). * * * * * * * * * *
For example, (in DF) prosecutors may exercise their discretion to *select juvenile or criminal processing* for youths sixteen or older and charged with murder.... To the extent that a prosecutor's decision to *charge* a case in criminal court rather than in juvenile court determines the jurisdiction, prosecutorial waiver constitutes a form of offense-based decision making like legislative offense exclusion (Feld, 2000, p. 85, emphases added, citations omitted). * * * * * * * * * *
Some of these initiatives simplify transfer of young offenders to criminal courts by excluding categories of offenses from juvenile court jurisdiction or by allowing prosecutors to *"direct file"* and *charge* youths as adults. Both (OE and DF) ... base a youth's adult criminal status on various combinations of age, the seriousness of the present offense and prior record, and prosecutor's *charging decisions* (Id., emphases added). * * * * * * * * * *
Concurrent jurisdiction direct-file laws grant to prosecutors the power to choose whether to *charge* a youth in juvenile or criminal court ... (Id., p. 91, emphasis added, citations omitted). * * * * * * * * * *
(In challenges to PT) youths direct their due-process claims at the lack of judicial review of prosecutors' *discretionary charging decisions* that result in their *removal to criminal court.* Their equal protection claims question the rationality of the legislative decision to classify youths *charged* with certain offenses as adults rather than as juveniles (Id., emphases added). * * * * * * * * * *

continued on following page

Table 40. Continued

In *U. S. v. Bland* … the prosecutor *charged* the sixteen-year-old Bland with armed robbery, an "excluded offense" that mandated his prosecution as an adult in criminal court…. Bland claimed he deserved a hearing because the ultimate result is the same whether a judge waives jurisdiction or a legislature excludes and a prosecutor *charges* a youth in criminal court (Id., p. 92, emphases added, citation omitted). * * * * * * * * * *
(Bland) urged the court to subject prosecutors' *charging-waiver* decisions to the same fitness hearing that it required of judges. Judge Wright's argument (in dissent) … did not persuade the majority of the *Bland* court to impose procedural requirements or to review prosecutors' *charging decisions* … (Id., p. 92, emphases added). * * * * * * * * * *
(Judge Wright) misconceived the basic legal issue. The question whether or not judges should review prosecutors' *charging decisions* does not turn on the seriousness of the consequences to the defendant of being *tried* as an adult rather than as a juvenile. Many prosecutorial decisions have great consequences for defendants — the decision not to charge, the decision to charge conduct as a misdemeanor rather than a felony, the decision to invoke any one of several applicable statutes. As the *Bland* majority noted, due process never has required "an adversary hearing before the prosecutor can exercise his age-old function of deciding what *charge* to bring against whom." Judge Wright's *Bland* dissent objected that a prosecutor's *charging decision* foreclosed any subsequent consideration of a youth's amenability to juvenile treatment … Judge Wright insisted that the same amenability issues should arise when a prosecutor *charges* a youth as an adult or when a judge decides whether to waive jurisdiction. According to Judge Wright, "a 'guilty' child may, under certain circumstances, have a right to be *charged* as a juvenile" … Judge Wright's desire to extend *Kent* procedural requirements to *prosecutors' charging decisions* stemmed from his misconstruing what prosecutors decide under an offense exclusion statute. The only factual issues involved in a *charging decision* relate to the nature of the offense, probable cause, and provable legal guilt…. The issue of amenability to treatment that Judge Wright sought to resolve in *an adversary proceeding prior to trial* simply is not a factor in the factual accuracy of a prosecutor's *charging decision* …. Offense exclusion legislation accords conclusive primacy to the offense *charged* rather than to aspects of the offender (Id., pp. 95-96, emphases added, citations omitted). * * * * * * * * * *
(Under DF statutes) (a) prosecutor can choose to *charge* a youth with the same offense in either justice system…. Essentially, the prosecutor makes two types of decisions: whether probable cause exists to believe that the youth committed a particular offense and, if that offense is one for which concurrent jurisdiction exists, whether to *charge* the youth in juvenile or criminal court…. About ten states have adopted some version of prosecutorial waiver statutes and allow prosecutors to *charge* youths of certain ages and offenses in either justice systems… Unlike legislative offense exclusion, in which the actual offense alleged determines juvenile or criminal jurisdiction, direct-file laws allow the prosecutor to *select the forum* without engaging in any *charging* subterfuges…. (Id., pp. 98-99, emphases added, citations omitted). * * * * * * * * * *
(Prosecutors' philosophies) had very little impact on their *charging* or waiver practices…. (Id., p. 99, emphasis added). * * * * * * * * * *
The prosecutor *charged* Mohi as an adult in criminal court with intentional or reckless homicide with a firearm… Mohi argued that the direct-file provision created a statutory scheme that treated one class of persons *charged* with a particular crime differently than another class of persons *charged* with the same crime. The Utah direct-file statute, like those in every other "concurrent" jurisdiction, allowed prosecutors to *charge* some youths with serious offenses in juvenile court while prosecuting other youths charged with identical offenses in criminal court…. Because the statute contained no criteria or rationale, however, the court could discern no reasons to justify why prosecutors *charged* some youths as adults in criminal court while other youths of the same age and *charged* with the same offenses remained in juvenile court… (Id., p. 100, emphases added). * * * * * * * * * *
Although *Bland* declined to review a prosecutor's *charging decision before a trial*… In the absence of some "transfer back" provision, offense-based waiver criteria lend themselves to prosecutorial abuse via *overcharging*… (Id., p. 112, emphases added). * * * * * * * * * *
Prosecutors dominate these waiver processes either by *charging* youths with excluded offenses or by directly *selecting the juvenile or criminal forum*. These strategies reflect a fundamental shift of sentencing discretion from the judicial to the executive branch (Id, emphases added). * * * * * * * * *
Louisiana statutorily excludes from juvenile court jurisdiction youths fifteen years of age or older *charged* with murder, rape, or kidnapping, and gave prosecutors authority to *charge and try* other offenses… Amendments in 1995 added aggravated burglary, oral sex battery, and battery with a firearm to the list of offenses that prosecutors could elect to *charge* in criminal court… (Id., pp 114-115, emphases added). * * * * * * * * * *

continued on following page

Table 40. Continued

The "Willie Bosket Law" excluded "juvenile offenders" (JOs) as young as thirteen years of age *charged* with murder and those fourteen years of age *charged* with rape, robbery, assault, and violent burglaries... (Id., p. 115, emphases added) * * * * * * * * * *
Thirty-four of the states and the District of Columbia exclude youths *charged* with murder.... Several states impose no minimum age restrictions or exclude juveniles as young as ten or thirteen years of age whom prosecutors *charge* with murder from the jurisdiction of their juvenile courts. Half of the states also exclude from juvenile court jurisdiction youths *charged* with rape or other sexual offenses. More than one-third of states exclude youths *charged* with kidnapping or aggravated robbery.... A somewhat smaller number of states also exclude youths *charged* with gang offenses, drug offenses, carjacking, or other categories of felonies...(Id., p. 116, emphases added). * * * * * * * * * *
Prosecutors in virtually every direct-file jurisdiction have discretionary authority to *charge* youths either as delinquents or criminals for murder... Prosecutors in half or more of the concurrent jurisdiction states enjoy complete discretion to *direct file* into criminal court youths *charged* with aggravated burglary or assault and battery. Finally, prosecutors in Nebraska have complete discretion *to try* any youth of any age *charged* with a felony... (Id., p. 117, emphases added). * * * * * * * * * *
State laws that exclude long lists of offenses from juvenile courts or that give prosecutors greater authority to *direct file charges* in either juvenile or criminal court simply shift sentencing discretion from judges in a waiver hearing to prosecutors in their offices. Because offense categories are necessarily crude and imprecise indicators of the "real" seriousness of any particular offense, prosecutors inevitably exercise enormous sentencing discretion when they decide whether to *charge* a youth with an excluded offense rather than a lesser included offense, or to *select the forum* in a direct-file jurisdiction. Despite the extensive lists of excluded offenses and the ascendance of get-tough policies, it seems unlikely that state legislators intend prosecutors to *charge* every theoretically eligible youth in criminal court... (Id., pp. 117-118, emphases added). * * * * * * * * * *
A study of prosecutorial *charging practices* in filing waiver motions in Texas ... (Id., p.118, emphasis added). * * * * * * * * * *
Such statutes enable prosecutors covertly to *manipulate charges* or to *select a juvenile or criminal forum* ... (Id. p. 119, emphases added). * * * * * * * * * *
In practice, excluded-offense laws transfer discretion from juvenile court judges in a waiver hearing to prosecutors who determine a youth's delinquent or criminal status by manipulating their *charging decisions* ... (Id., pp. 124-125, emphasis added). * * * * * * * * * *
Because of the diversity of offenses... prosecutors necessarily will differentiate among offenders on some bases when they *charge* some youths with excluded offenses. But prosecutors can achieve flexibility only by *charging* youths with a nonexcluded, lesser included offense.... Allowing prosecutors to *manipulate charges* to respond to the heterogeneity of offenses... (Id., p. 125, emphases added). * * * * * * * * * *
However, as legislators zealously expand lists of excluded offenses to encompass less serious crimes and lower the ages at which prosecutors may *charge* youths as adults... (Id., p. 126, emphasis added). * * * * * * * * * *
The number of states that endorse the direct-file strategy and authorize prosecutors to *charge* youths directly in criminal courts has more than doubled within the past decade... (E)ven if prosecutors were inclined to "individualize" their *forum-charging decisions*... As with excluded-offense legislation, we lack extensive data on the numbers or characteristics of youths against whom prosecutors *directly filed* in criminal court. Research in some states indicates that they may *charge* as many as 10 percent of chronological juveniles in criminal court... (Id., p. 127, emphases added, citations omitted) .... * * * * * * * * * *
In transfer back proceedings, however, the prosecutor's *charge* or the excluded offense may create a presumption of unfitness ... (Id., emphasis added). * * * * * * * * * *
(W)aiver hearings are less administratively "efficient" than prosecutors' *charging decision* (sic)... (Id., p. 128, emphasis added). * * * * * * * * * *
So which chronological juveniles should a state *prosecute* as adults...(Id., emphasis added). * * * * * * * * * *
(Transfer mechanisms) allocate to different branches of government — judicial, executive, or legislative — the decision whether to *prosecute* a youth as a criminal or as a delinquent... (Feld, 2001, p. 4, emphasis added). * * * * * * * * * *

continued on following page

Table 40. Continued

"(G)et tough" legislators greatly augmented the lists of excluded offenses, lowered the ages at which states could *prosecute* youths as adults, and expanded prosecutors' *"direct file"* discretion... (Id., p. 5, emphases added). * * * * * * * * * *
Legislative offense exclusion simply removes from juvenile court jurisdiction youths *charged* with certain offenses.... Concurrent jurisdiction "direct file" laws grant to prosecutors the power to *charge* a youth in juvenile or criminal court... (Id., p. 9, emphases added). * * * * * * * * * *
Bland asserted that he should receive *Kent's* procedural safeguards because the ultimate result is the same whether a judge waives jurisdiction or a legislature excludes and a prosecutor *charges* a youth in criminal court (Id., emphasis added). * * * * * * * * * *
Judge Wright's *Bland* dissent objected that a prosecutor's *charging decision* foreclosed any consideration of a youth's amenability to treatment. However, the only factual issues involved in a *charging decision* relate to the nature of the offense, probable cause, and provable legal guilt... Offense exclusion legislation accords primacy to the offense *charged* rather than to aspects of the offender. In addition to challenges based on the absence of procedural safeguards associated with prosecutors' *charging decisions*, youths have argued that offense-exclusion laws violate equal protection... (Id., p. 10, emphases added). * * * * * * * * *
"Pure" prosecutorial waiver statutes create concurrent jurisdiction to *"direct file" or charge* youths of certain ages with the same offense in either forum. Unlike offense exclusion where *charges* only for certain offenses can result in criminal prosecution, *"direct file"* laws give prosecutors greater discretionary authority to *choose the forum*. Juvenile and criminal courts share concurrent jurisdiction over youths of certain ages who commit any felony or other enumerated crime and a prosecutor can choose to *charge* a youth with the same offense in either justice system... Essentially, the prosecutor makes two decisions: whether probable cause exists to believe that the youth committed a particular offense and, if that offense is one for which concurrent jurisdiction exists, in which court to *charge* the youth... (Id. p. 11, citations omitted, emphases added). * * * * * * * * *
Prosecutors dominated these waiver processes either by *charging* youths with excluded offenses or by *directly selecting the juvenile or criminal forum*. These strategies reflect a fundamental shift of sentencing discretion from the judicial to the executive branch. (Id., p. 17, emphases added). * * * * * * * * *
(T)hese laws (OE and DF) transfer discretion from juvenile court judges in a waiver hearing to prosecutors who determine a youth's delinquent or criminal status by manipulating their *charging decisions*... (Id., p. 18, emphasis added). * * * * * * * * *
Because of the diversity of offenses, especially assaults and robberies, prosecutors necessarily will differentiate among offenders on some bases when they *charge* youths with excluded offenses. But prosecutors can achieve flexibility only by *charging* youths with a non-excluded, lesser included offense and, in some instances, deprecating the normative seriousness of a youth's criminal conduct. Allowing prosecutors to *manipulate charges* to respond to the heterogeneity of offenses vests arbitrary and unreviewable discretion in them rather than in judges... (Id., p. 19, emphases added). * * * * * * * * *
The number of states that endorse the "direct file" strategy and authorize prosecutors to *charge* youths directly in criminal courts has more than doubled within the past two decades... (Id., citations omitted, emphasis added). * * * * * * * * *
(OE) shifted waiver discretion from the judicial branch-judges in a waiver hearing-to the executive branch-prosecutors who make *charging decisions* (Feld, 2007b, p. 40, emphasis added, footnote omitted). * * * * * * * * *
(OE) shifted waiver discretion from the judicial branch - judges in a waiver hearing - to the executive branch - prosecutors who make unreviewable *charging decisions* (Feld, 2007a, p. 237, emphasis added, footnote omitted). * * * * * * * * * *
Legislatures may exclude serious offenses from juvenile court jurisdiction and youths *charged* with those crimes are tried in criminal court without any hearing. A dozen states give prosecutors discretion to *direct file or charge* some youths in either juvenile or criminal court without any review of their forum-selection decision... (Feld, 2013a, p. 266, footnote omitted, emphases added). * * * * * * * * * *
(OE) shifted discretion from a judge in a waiver hearing to a prosecutor making a *charging* decision... (P)rosecutors' *charging* decisions determine the adult status of most youths without any hearing. By some estimates, prosecutors rather than judges determined the adult status of eighty-five percent of youths based on age and offense. As a consequence, juvenile court judges do not assess the culpability or competence of most juveniles whom states *prosecute* as adults (Id., pp. 267-268, citations omitted, emphases added). * * * * * * * * * *
In many jurisdictions, transfer is automatic for youths *charged* with murder Feld, 2013b, p. 134, footnote 127, emphasis added).

Table 41a. Sources for Transfer (especially Offense Exclusion): Rejection of JC; JC Abandonment of Rehabilitation; JC Shift from Rehabilitation to Punishment

Acton, (1996)
Ainsworth, (1991), (1995)
Angell, (2004)
Baird & Samuels, (1996)
Baruwa, (2013)
Beatty, (1995)
Blomquist & Forst, (1992)
Bortner, (1986)
Butts & Harrell, (1998)
Cintron, (1996)
Clarke, C.A., (2005)
Cohen, Bonnie, Taylor-Thompson & Casey, (2016)
Coupet, (2000)
Fagan, (1990)
Fagan, Forst, & Vivona, (1987a), (1987b)
Feld, (1980), (1981a), (1984b), (1987), (1988), (1989), (1991), (1993b), (1997), (1999a),
(1999b), (2000)
Flicker, (1981)
Fritsch & Hemmens, (1995), (1996)
Gardner, (1987)
Giardino, (1996)
Gilbert, Grimm, & Parnham, (2001)
Guttman, (1995)
Hirase, (1992)
Hoeffel, (2013)
Hogan, (1974)
Houghtalin & Mays, (1991)
Klein, (1998)

Krisberg & Austin, (1993)
Krisberg, Schwartz, Litsky, & Austin, (1986)
Martin, (1992)
May, (1998)
Merlo & Benekos, (2003)
Merlo, Benekos, & Cook (1997b), (1999)
Mylniec, (1976)
Noon, (1994)
NRC, (2013)
Redding & Howell, (2000)
Ruddell, Mays, & Giever, (1998)
Rudman, Hartstone, Fagan, & Moore, (1986)
Sabo, (1996)
Sargent & Gordon, (1963)
Schornhorst, (1968)
Schwartz, J.S, (1982)
Scialabba, (2016)
Sherman & Talley, (1995)
Soler, (1994)
Steiner & Hemmens, (2003)
Thomas & Bilchik, (1985)
Traver, (2000)
Valliere, (1986)
Vitiello, (1976)
Walkover, (1984)
Whitebread & Batey, (1981)
Wilbourne, (1996)
Zane, Welsh, & Mears., (2016)
Zimring, (1981), (1991), (1998a)

Table 41b. Transfer Serves as a Safety Valve for JC/Legislators/Judges/Prosecutors and/or as Societal Retribution

Baruwa, (2013)	Keith, (1969)
Beatty, (1995)	Martin, (1992)
Bortner, (1986)	Mears et al., (2014)
Braithwaite & Shore, (1981)	Merz, (1968)
Buss, (1968)	Noon, (1994)
Champion, (1989)	Notes, (1966)
Coupet, (2000)	Notes & Comments, (1967)
Dawson, (1992), (2000)	Parker, (1976)
Dunn, (2008)	Penney & Moretti, (2005)
Fagan, (2002)	Pierce, (1981)
Fagan, Kupchik, & Liberman, (2007)	Sargent & Gordon, (1963)
Feld, (1978), (1984b), (1999a), (1999b), (2000), (2001)	Schornhorst, (1968)
Flicker, (1983)	Schwartz, (1982)
Gasper & Katkin, (1980)	Slobogin, (2013)
Glynn, (1997)	Stamm, (1973)
Grundfest et al., (1981)	Tanenhaus, (2000), (2013)
Hagar, (1995)	Valliere, (1986)
Hamilton, Moak, & Golden, (2007)	Vitiello, (1976)
Hogan, (1974)	Wizner, (1984)
Jensen, (1994)	Zimring, (1991), (2000a), (2000b)
Keiter, (1973)	Zimring & Fagan, (2000)

Table 40 References

Feld, B. C. (1978). Reference of juvenile offenders for adult prosecution: The legislative alternative to asking unanswerable questions. *Minnesota Law Review*, *62*, 515–618.

Feld, B. C. (1980). Juvenile court legislative reform and the serious young offender: Dismantling the "rehabilitative ideal.". *Minnesota Law Review*, *65*, 167–242.

Feld, B. C. (1984a). Criminalizing juvenile justice: Rules of procedure for the juvenile court. *Minnesota Law Review*, *69*, 141–276.

Feld, B. C. (1984b). The decision to seek criminal charges: Just deserts and the waiver decision. *Criminal Justice Ethics*, *3*(2), 27–41.

Feld, B. C. (1987). The juvenile court meets the principle of the offense: Legislative changes in juvenile waiver statutes. *The Journal of Criminal Law & Criminology*, *78*, 471–533.

Feld, B. C. (1989). Bad law makes hard cases: Reflections on teen-aged axe-murderers, judicial activism, and legislative default. *Law & Inequality*, *8*, 1–101.

Feld, B. C. (1991). The transformation of the juvenile court. *Minnesota Law Review, 75*, 691–725.

Feld, B. C. (1993a). Criminalizing the American juvenile court. In Tonry, M. (Ed.), Crime & Justice: A Review, 17, 197-280.

Feld, B. C. (1995). Violent youth and public policy: A case study of juvenile justice law reform. *Minnesota Law Review, 79*, 965–1128.

Feld, B. C. (1997). Abolish the juvenile court: Youthfulness, criminal responsibility, and sentencing policy. *The Journal of Criminal Law & Criminology, 88*, 68–136.

Feld, B. C. (1998). Juvenile and criminal justice systems' responses to youth violence. *Crime and Justice, 24*, 189–261.

Feld, B. C. (1999a). *Bad kids: Race and the transformation of the juvenile court*. Oxford University Press.

Feld, B. C. (1999b). The transformation of the juvenile court—Part II: Race and the crack down on youth crime. *Minnesota Law Review, 84*, 327–395.

Feld, B. C. (2000). Legislative exclusion of offenses from juvenile court jurisdiction: A history and critique. In J. Fagan & F. E. Zimring (Eds.), *The changing borders of juvenile justice: Transfer of adolescents to the criminal court* (pp. 83–144). University of Chicago Press.

Feld, B. C. (2001). Race, youth violence, and the changing jurisprudence of waiver. *Behavioral Sciences & the Law, 19*, 3–22.

Feld, B. C. (2004). Juvenile transfer. *Criminology & Public Policy, 3*, 599–604.

Feld, B. C. (2007a). A century of juvenile justice: A work in progress or a revolution that failed. *Northern Kentucky Law Review, 34*, 189–256.

Feld, B. C. (2007b). Unmitigated punishment: Adolescent criminal responsibility and LWOP sentences. *Journal of Law & Family Studies, 10*, 11–82.

Feld, B. C. (2013a). Adolescent criminal responsibility, proportionality, and sentencing policy: Roper, Graham, Miller/Jackson, and the youth discount. *Law & Inequality, 31*, 263–330.

Feld, B. C. (2013b). The youth discount: Old enough to do the crime, too young to do the time. *Ohio State Journal of Criminal Law, 11*, 1–148.

Feld, B. C., & Bishop, D. M. (2012). Transfer of juveniles to criminal court. In Feld, B.C., & Bishop, D.M (Eds.). The oxford handbook of juvenile crime and juvenile justice (pp. 801-842). Oxford University Press.

Podkopacz, M. R., & Feld, B. C. (1995). Judicial waiver policy and practice: Persistence, seriousness, and race. *Law & Inequality, 14*, 73–178.

Podkopacz, M. R., & Feld, B. C. (1996). The end of the line: An empirical study of judicial waiver. *The Journal of Criminal Law & Criminology, 86*, 449–492.

Table 41 References

Acton, R. B. (1996). Gubernatorial initiatives and rhetoric of juvenile justice reform. *Journal of Law and Policy, 5*, 277–338.

Ainsworth, J. E. (1991). Re-imagining childhood and reconstructing the legal order: The case for abolishing the juvenile court. *North Carolina Law Review, 69*, 1083–1133.

Ainsworth, J. E. (1995). Youth justice in a unified court: Response to critics of juvenile court abolition. *Boston College Law Review. Boston College. Law School, 36*, 927–951.

Angell, K. M. (2004). The regressive movement: When juvenile offenders are treated as adults, nobody wins. *Southern California Interdisciplinary Law Journal, 14*, 125–144.

Baird, M. I., and Mina B. Samuels. (1996). Policy review: Justice for youth: The betrayal of childhood in the United States. *Journal of Law & Policy,* 5 *(1),* 177-202.

Baruwa, B. (2013). Should juveniles be transferred to adult criminal court in the criminal justice system. *Tennessee Journal of Race Gender & Social Justice, 2*, 101–127.

Beatty, H. (1995). Is the trend to expand juvenile transfer statutes just an easy answer to a complex problem. *University of Toledo Law Review. University of Toledo. College of Law, 26*, 979–1025.

Blomquist, M. E., & Forst, M. L. (1992). Punishment, accountability, and the new juvenile justice. *Juvenile & Family Court Journal, 43*(1), 1–10.

Bortner, M. A. (1986). Traditional rhetoric, organizational realities: Remand of juveniles to adult court. *Crime and Delinquency, 32*, 53–73.

Braithwaite, L., & Shore, A. (1981). Treatment rhetoric versus waiver decisions. *The Journal of Criminal Law & Criminology, 72*, 1867–1891.

Buss, C. A. (1968). Waiver of jurisdiction in Wisconsin juvenile courts. *Wisconsin Law Review, 1968*, 551–555.

Butts, J. A., & Harrell, A. (1998). *Delinquents or criminals: Policy options for young offenders. Crime & Policy Report, June 1998*. The Urban Institute.

Champion, D. J. (1989). Teenage felons and waiver hearings: Some recent trends, 1980-1988. *Crime and Delinquency, 35*, 577–585.

Cintron, L. A. (1996). Rehabilitating the juvenile court system: Limiting juvenile transfers to adult criminal court. *Northwestern University Law Review, 90*, 1254–1282.

Clarke, C. A. (2005). The baby and the bathwater: Adolescent offending and punitive juvenile justice reform. *University of Kansas Law Review. University of Kansas. School of Law, 53*, 659–725.

Cohen, A. O., Bonnie, R. J., Taylor-Thompson, K., & Casey, B. J. (2016). When does a juvenile become an adult: Implications for law and policy. *Temple Law Review, 88*, 769–788.

Coupet, S. M. (2000). What to do with sheep in wolf's clothing: The role of rhetoric and reality about youth offenders in the constructive dismantling policy of the juvenile justice system. *University of Pennsylvania Law Review, 148*, 1303–1346.

Dawson, R. O. (1992). An empirical study of *Kent* style juvenile transfers to criminal court. *St. Mary's Law Journal, 23*, 975–1054.

Dawson, R. O. (2000). Judicial waiver in theory and practice. In J. Fagan & F. E. Zimring (Eds.), *The changing borders of juvenile justice: Transfer of adolescents to the criminal court* (pp. 45–81). University of Chicago Press.

Dunn, C. (2008). Condemning Our Youth to Lives as Criminals: Incarcerating Children as Adults. *Richmond Journal of Law & Public Interest, 11*, 30–50.

Fagan, J. (1990). Social and legal policy dimensions of violent juvenile crime. *Criminal Justice and Behavior, 17*, 93–133.

Fagan, J. (2002). This will hurt me more than it hurts you: Social and legal consequences of criminalizing delinquency. *Notre Dame Journal of Law, Ethics & Public Policy, 16*, 1–41.

Fagan, J., Forst, M., & Vivona, T. S. (1987a). Racial determinants of the judicial transfer decision: Prosecuting violent youth in criminal court. *Crime and Delinquency, 33*, 259–286.

Fagan, J., Forst, M. L., & Vivona, T. S. (1987). *Separating the men from the boys: The criminalization of youth violence through judicial waiver*. Ursa Institute.

Fagan, J., Kupchik, A., & Liberman, A. (2007). Be careful what you wish for: Legal sanctions and public safety among adolescent offenders in juvenile and criminal court. *Columbia Law School, Public Law Research Paper* 03-61.

Feld, B. C. (1978). Reference of juvenile offenders for adult prosecution: The legislative alternative to asking unanswerable questions. *Minnesota Law Review, 62*, 515–618.

Feld, B. C. (1980). Juvenile court legislative reform and the serious young offender: Dismantling the "rehabilitative ideal.". *Minnesota Law Review, 69*, 167–242.

Feld, B. C. (1981a). Juvenile court legislative reform and the serious young offender: Dismantling the "rehabilitative ideal.". *Minnesota Law Review, 69*, 167–242.

Feld, B. C. (1984b). The decision to seek criminal charges: Just deserts and the waiver decision. *Criminal Justice Ethics, 3*(2), 27–41.

Feld, B. C. (1987). The juvenile court meets the principle of the offense: Legislative changes in juvenile waiver statutes. *The Journal of Criminal Law & Criminology, 78*, 471–533.

Feld, B. C. (1988). The juvenile court meets the principle of offense: Punishment, treatment, and the difference it makes. *Boston University Law Review. Boston University. School of Law, 68*, 821–915.

Feld, B. C. (1989). Bad law makes hard cases: Reflections on teen-aged axe-murderers, judicial activism, and legislative default. *Law & Inequality, 8*, 1–101.

Feld, B. C. (1991). The transformation of the juvenile court. *Minnesota Law Review, 75*, 691–725.

Feld, B. C. (1993b). Juvenile (in) justice and the criminal court alternative. *Crime and Delinquency, 39*, 403–424.

Feld, B. C. (1997). Abolish the juvenile court: Youthfulness, criminal responsibility, and sentencing. *The Journal of Criminal Law & Criminology, 88*, 68–136.

Feld, B. C. (1999a). *Bad kids: Race and the transformation of the juvenile court*. Oxford University Press.

Feld, B. C. (1999b). The transformation of the juvenile court—Part II: Race and the crack down on youth crime. *Minnesota Law Review, 84*, 327–395.

Feld, B. C. (2000). Legislative exclusion of offenses from juvenile court jurisdiction: A history and critique. In J. Fagan & F. E. Zimring (Eds.), *The changing borders of juvenile justice: Transfer of adolescents to the criminal court* (pp. 83–144). University of Chicago Press.

Feld, B. C. (2001). Race, youth violence, and the changing jurisprudence of waiver. *Behavioral Sciences & the Law, 19*, 3–22.

Flicker, B. (1981). Prosecuting juveniles as adults: A symptom of a crisis in the juvenile courts. In J. C. Hall, D. M. Hamparian, J. M. Pettibone, & J. L. White (Eds.), *Major issues in juvenile justice information and training: Readings in public policy* (pp. 351–377). Academy for Contemporary Problems.

Flicker, B. (1983). *Transferring juveniles to adult court for trial*. Institute of Judicial Administration.

Fritsch, E., & Hemmens, C. (1995). Juvenile waiver in the United States 1979-1995: A comparison and analysis of state waiver statutes. *Juvenile & Family Court Journal, 46*(3), 17–35.

Fritsch, E. J., & Hemmens, C. (1996). An assessment of legislative approaches to the problem of serious juvenile crime: A case study of Texas 1973-1995. *American Journal of Criminal Law, 23*, 563–609.

Gardner, M. R. (1987). Punitive juvenile justice: Some observations on a recent trend. *International Journal of Law and Psychiatry, 10*, 129–151.

Gasper, J., & Katkin, D. (1980). A rationale for the abolition of the juvenile court's power to waive jurisdiction. *Pepperdine Law Review, 7*, 937–951.

Giardino, L. F. (1996). Statutory rhetoric: The reality behind juvenile justice policies in America. *Journal of Policy & Law, 5*, 223–276.

Gilbert, J., Grimm, R., & Parnham, J. (2000). Applying therapeutic principles to a family-focused juvenile justice model (delinquency). *Alabama Law Review, 52*, 1153–1212.

Glynn, G. F. (1997). Arkansas' missed opportunity for rehabilitation: Sending children to adult courts. *University of Arkansas at Little Rock Law Journal, 20*, 77–127.

Grundfest, A. R., Paskow, A. C., Szabo, H. E., & Williams, R. J. (1981). In Hall, J.C., Hamparian, D.M., Pettibone, John M., & White, Joseph L. (Eds.) Major issues in juvenile justice: Information and Training: Readings in public policy (pp. 321-332). Academy for Contemporary Problems.

Guttman, C. R. (1995). Listen to the children: The decision to transfer juveniles to criminal court. *Harvard Civil Rights-Civil Liberties Law Review, 30*, 507–542.

Hager, D. A. (1995). Does the Texas juvenile waiver statute comport with the requirements of due process? *Texas Tech Law Review*, *26*, 813–856.

Hamilton, L., Moak, S. C., & Golden, J. W. (2007). Arkansas legislative reforms provide framework for change while supporting *parens patriae* philosophy of juvenile court. *Juvenile & Family Court Journal*, *58*(1), 37–47.

Hirase, J. (1992). State ex. rel. v. EGT: Waiving childhood goodbye. *Journal of Contemporary Law*, *18*, 159–175.

Hoeffel, J. C. (2013). The jurisprudence of death and youth: Now the twain should meet. *Texas Tech Law Review*, *46*, 29–69.

Hogan, C. (1974). Waiver of juvenile jurisdiction and the hard-core youth. *North Dakota Law Review*, *51*, 655–677.

Houghtalin, M., & Mays, G. L. (1991). Criminal dispositions of New Mexico juveniles transferred to adult court. *Crime and Delinquency*, *37*, 393–407.

Jensen, E. L. (1994). The waiver of juveniles to criminal court: Policy goals, empirical realities, and suggestions for change. *Idaho Law Review*, *31*, 173–204.

Keiter, R. B. (1973). Criminal or delinquency? A study of juvenile cases transferred to the criminal court. *Crime and Delinquency*, *19*, 528–538.

Keith, H. B. (1969). Waiver of jurisdiction in juvenile courts. *Ohio State Law Journal*, *30*, 132–143.

Klein, E. K. (1998). Dennis the menace or Billy the Kid: An analysis of the role of transfer to criminal court in juvenile justice. *The American Criminal Law Review*, *35*, 371–410.

Krisberg, B., & Austin, J. (1993). *Reinventing juvenile justice*. Sage Publications.

Krisberg, B., Schwartz, I. M., Litsky, P., & Austin, J. (1986). The watershed of juvenile justice Reform. *Crime and Delinquency*, *32*, 5–38.

Martin, G. A. Jr. (1992). The delinquent and the juvenile court: Is there still a place for rehabilitation? *Connecticut Law Review*, *25*, 57–63.

May, K. S. (1998). Shifting away from rehabilitation: State v. Ladd's equal protection challenge to Alaska's automatic waiver law. *Alaska Law Review, 15*, 367-402.

Mears, D. P., Cochran, J. C., Stults, B. J., Greenman, S. J., Bhati, A. S., & Greenwald, M. A. (2014). The "true" juvenile offender: Age effects and juvenile court sanctioning. *Criminology*, *52*, 169–194.

Merlo, A. V., & Benekos, P. J. (2003). Defining juvenile justice in the 21st century. *Youth Violence and Juvenile Justice*, *1*, 276–288.

Merlo, A. V., Benekos, P. J., & Cook, W. J. (1997b). Waiver and juvenile justice reform: Widening the punitive net. *Criminal Justice Policy Review*, *8*(2-3), 145–168.

Merlo, A. V., Benekos, P. J., & Cook, W. J. (1999). The juvenile court at 100 years: Celebration or wake. *Juvenile & Family Court Journal*, *50*, 1–10.

Merz, C. L. (1967). Representing the juvenile defendant in waiver proceedings. *Saint Louis University Law Journal*, *12*, 424–465.

Mylniec, W. J. (1976). Juvenile delinquent or adult convict: Prosecutor's choice. *The American Criminal Law Review*, *14*, 29–57.

Noon, C. R. (1994). Waiving goodbye to juvenile defendants, getting smart vs. getting tough. *University of Miami Law Review*, *49*, 431–476.

Notes. (1966). Juvenile delinquents: The police, state courts, and individualized justice. *Harvard Law Review, 79*, 775-810.

Notes & Comments. (1967). Separating the criminal from the delinquent: Due process in certification procedure. *Southern California Law Review*, *40*, 158–164.

NRC. National Research Council. (2013). Reforming juvenile justice: A developmental approach. The National Academies Press.

Parker, D. B. (1976). Juveniles in the criminal courts: A substantive view of the fitness decision. *UCLA Law Review. University of California, Los Angeles. School of Law*, *23*, 988–1016.

Penney, S. R., & Moretti, M. M. (2005). The transfer of juveniles to adult court in Canada and the United States: Confused agendas and compromised assessment procedures. *International Journal of Forensic Mental Health*, *4*(1), 19–37.

Pierce, J. R. (1981). Relinquishment of jurisdiction for purposes of criminal prosecution of juveniles. *Northern Kentucky Law Review*, *8*, 377–393.

Redding, R. E., & Howell, J. C. (2000). Blended sentencing in American juvenile courts. In J. Fagan & F. E. Zimring (Eds.), *The changing borders of juvenile justice: Transfer of adolescents to the criminal court* (pp. 145–180). University of Chicago Press.

Ruddell, R., Mays, G. L., & Giever, D. M. (1998). Transferring juveniles to adult courts. Recent trends and issues in Canada and the United States. *Juvenile & Family Court Journal*, *49*(3), 1–15.

Rudman, C., Hartstone, E., Fagan, J., & Moore, M. (1986). Violent youth in adult court: Process and punishment. *Crime and Delinquency*, *32*, 75–96.

Sabo, S. (1996). Rights of passage: An analysis of waiver of juvenile court jurisdiction. *Fordham Law Review*, *64*, 2425–2454.

Sargent, D., & Gordon, D. H. (1963). Waiver of jurisdiction: An evaluation of the process in the juvenile court. *Crime and Delinquency*, *9*, 121–128.

Schornhorst, T. F. (1968). The waiver of juvenile court jurisdiction: Kent revisited. *Indiana Law Review*, *43*, 583–613.

Scialabba, N. (2016). Should juveniles be charged as adults in the criminal justice system? *American Bar Association. Volume 3,* October 3, 2016.

Schwartz, J. S. (1982). The youth offender: Transfer to the adult court and subsequent sentencing. *Criminal Justice Journal*, *6*, 281–313.

Sherman, F. T., & Talley, W. Jr. (1995). Struggling for a future: Juvenile violence, juvenile justice. *Boston College Law Review. Boston College. Law School, 36*, 889–892.

Slobogin, C. (2013). Treating juveniles like juveniles: Getting rid of transfer and expanded adult court jurisdiction. *Texas Tech Law Review, 46*, 103–132.

Soler, M. (1994). Re-imagining the juvenile court. In Humm, S. R., Ort, B.A., Anbari, M.M., Lader, W.S., & Biel, W.S. (Eds.). Child, parent and state: Law and policy reader (pp. 596-610). Temple University Press.

Stamm, M. J. (1973). Transfer of jurisdiction in juvenile court: An A\analysis of the proceeding, its role in the administration of justice, and A proposal for the reform of Kentucky law. *Kentucky Law Journal (Lexington, Ky.), 62*, 122–199.

Steiner, B., & Hemmens, C. (2003). Juvenile waiver 2003: Where are we now? *Juvenile & Family Court Journal, 54*(2), 1–24.

Tanenhaus, D. S. (2000). The evolution of transfer out of the juvenile court. In J. Fagan & F. E. Zimring (Eds.), *The changing borders of juvenile justice: Transfer of adolescents to the criminal court* (pp. 13–43). University of Chicago Press.

Thomas, C. W., & Bilchik, S. (1985). Prosecuting juveniles in criminal court: A legal and empirical analysis. *The Journal of Criminal Law & Criminology, 76*, 439–479.

Traver, D. P. (2000). The wrong answer to a serious problem: A story of school shootings, politics and automatic transfer. *Loyola University of Chicago Law Journal. Loyola University of Chicago. School of Law, 31*, 281–315.

Valliere, B. J. (1986). The transfer of juvenile offenders to adult courts in Massachusetts: Reevaluating the rehabilitative ideal. *Suffolk University Law Review, 20*, 989–1028.

Vitiello, M. (1976). Constitutional safeguards for juvenile transfer procedure: The ten years since Kent v. United States. *De Paul Law Review, 26*, 23–53.

Walkover, A. (1984). The infancy defense in the new juvenile court. *UCLA Law Review. University of California, Los Angeles. School of Law, 31*, 503–562.

Whitebread, C. H., & Batey, R. (1981). The role of waiver in the juvenile court: Questions of philosophy and function. In J. C. Hall, D. M. Hamparian, J. M. Pettibone, & J. L. White (Eds.), *Major Issues in Juvenile Justice Information and Training: Readings in Public Policy* (pp. 207–226). Academy for Contemporary Problems.

Wilbourn, B. (1995). Waiver of juvenile court jurisdiction: National trends and the inadequacy of the Texas response. *American Journal of Criminal Law, 23*, 633–649.

Wizner, S. (1984). Discretionary waiver of juvenile court jurisdiction: An invitation to procedural arbitrariness. *Criminal Justice Ethics, 3*, 41–50.

Zane, S. N., Welsh, B. C., & Mears, D. P. (2016). Juvenile transfer and the specific deterrence hypothesis: Systematic review and meta-analysis. *Criminology & Public Policy, 15*, 901–925.

Zimring, F. E. (1981). Notes toward a jurisprudence of waiver. In J. C. Hall, D. M. Hamparian, J. M. Pettibone, & J. L. White (Eds.), *Major issues in juvenile justice information and training: Readings in public policy* (pp. 193–205). Academy for Contemporary Problems.

Zimring, F. E. (1991). The treatment of hard cases in American juvenile justice: In defense of discretionary waiver. *Notre Dame Journal of Law, Ethics & Public Policy*, *5*, 267–280.

Zimring, F. E. (1998a). *American youth violence*. Oxford University Press.

Zimring, F. E. (2000b). The punitive necessity of waiver. In J. Fagan & F. E. Zimring (Eds.), *The Changing Borders of Juvenile Justice: Transfer of adolescents to the criminal court* (pp. 207–224). University of Chicago Press.

Zimring, F. E., & Fagan, J. (2000). Transfer policy and law reform. In J. Fagan & F. E. Zimring (Eds.), *The changing borders of juvenile justice: Transfer of adolescents to the criminal court* (pp. 407–424). University of Chicago Press.

Chapter 8
The Elimination Argument, Part 1:
Juvenile Offenders Should Not Go to CC

ABSTRACT

Chapter 8 addresses a popular anti-transfer crowd (ATC) tactic in arguing for the elimination of transfer. The ATC has employed a couple of maneuvers, here. The first move is contending that a singular case that suggests or shows the possible inappropriateness of transfer is sufficient to claim that all transfers are wrong. Specifically, the ATC says that since juveniles are generally (more) amenable to treatment, and are less mature (i.e., culpable) and less deterrable than adults, they should not see CC. This Chapter exposes the corrupt use of converting the singular and relative cases to establish a false categorical. The ATC also moves in the opposite direction in claiming that a categorical (e.g., OE) establishes the wrongfulness of transfer applied to a particular juvenile. Since violent behavior is supposedly normal juvenile behavior, this normal juvenile behavior should not qualify for transfer. This Chapter debunks both false conversions.

INTRODUCTION

The ATC has employed a tactic that involves two conversions. First, the ATC converts a singular case/relative condition to a categorical level. The ATC vehemently opposes categoricals when they wrongly see them in OE. The ATC does not hesitate, however, in constructing categoricals when their mission is served by them, even when their categoricals are wrong. The ATC opposes categoricals that do not exist but is willing to create ones that are inappropriate. The second conversion deals with transporting an alleged categorical trait to an individual level.

DOI: 10.4018/978-1-7998-7923-7.ch008

A. The Tactic of Converting the Singular Case or a Relative Status to a Categorical

1. If One Transfer Can/Might Be Bad, All Transfers Are Bad[1]

ATC members conjure up an *arguably* bad transfer case and highlight it as the reason transfer should not exist (see Maroney, 2009, p. 131).[1] That transfer in their selected cases is unreasonable is debatable. Even if this transfer was inappropriate, that the entire transfer system should be condemned/abandoned is what is unreasonable in this situation. Zimring (1998a) questioned the wisdom of imprisoning a 6-year-old (p. 75). The prospects of imprisoning 6-year-olds may have propaganda impact but lacks a basis in reality. Zimring also suggests that "if the defendant is 15 years old and of slightly subnormal intelligence, to try and punish him as if he were adult in all respects is a dangerously counterfactual enterprise (Id., p. 132)." Zimring's example does not represent the typical transfer candidate. It is even possible that Zimring's case example could/would not be transferred in the first place. Ironically, the handicap from which Zimring's offender suffers might receive a more sympathetic response in CC. In CC, there's a possibility this offender would not be convicted due to mental impairment or could be sentenced leniently due to his condition. Meanwhile, in JC, this condition could be the basis for a JC judge's determining the youth needs to be (inappropriately) adjudicated delinquent to receive the JC's help. At the same time, that 15-year-olds of "slightly subnormal intelligence" should always/automatically be granted immunity from CC prosecution, regardless of offense and record, is what constitutes a very dangerous counterfactual enterprise.

2. If Juveniles are More Amenable to Treatment, All Juveniles are Amenable to Treatment

According to the ATC, JC was founded on the premise that juveniles are, by and large, *more* salvageable/amenable to treatment. The ATC translates this truth into a contention that JC should treat *all* juvenile offenders (see Bishop, 2000; Bonnie & Grisso, 2000; Brink, 2003-2004; DeJong & Merrill, 2001; Gasper & Katkin, 1980; Hogan, 1974; Kirkish et al., 2000; Steinberg & Cauffman, 2000; Steinberg & Schwartz, 2000; Vitiello, 1976). Feld endorsed this proposal.

Although "rehabilitative" juvenile courts assume that all offenders differ and no direct relationship exists between their offenses and their "real needs," legislators appear to presume and courts to accept without further elaboration that youths who commit serious crimes differ from minor offenders... (Feld, 2000, p. 97, quotation marks in original).

Feld questions the existence of a true rehabilitative state of JCs but then fights to ensure that virtually all juvenile offenders are prosecuted there, presumably, to receive treatment. More important, why are legislators incorrect in presuming that violent (or chronic) offenders differ significantly from minor, one-time offenders? Assuming Feld is correct that JCs are not about rehabilitation, serious juvenile offenders *certainly* should be differentiated from minor ones. Even in treatment terms, those willing to stab someone to death or brutally rape are fundamentally different from shoplifters and burglars, and certainly qualify for different reactions from JCs. While the violent/chronic offender is somewhat of an outlier, the relatively minor offender is the criminal norm for juveniles. The extremely violent or chronic criminal juvenile offender can certainly have "real needs" that differ from those of minor offenders, and require handling that JC cannot satisfy, and that goes far beyond JC treatment. The ATC insists juvenile offenders differ dramatically from adults. Why, then, can't chronic/violent offending serve as a point of differentiation among juvenile offenders?

Some ATC members simply assert that all juveniles *can* change so that even the most violent offenders should be kept in JC, which, like society, should be satisfied in the *potential* for a turnaround in criminality, *at some point.*

Our experiences tell us that even children who commit the most heinous offense, such as joining a group of "friends" to stomp an elderly defense-less person to death, are ultimately capable of understanding what they had really done… (Marrus & Rosenberg, 2005, p. 1182).

These ATC representatives appear satisfied that these murderers are capable of possibly "understanding" what they have done in committing this wanton murder "ultimately" (whatever that means). If these as-of-yet nonunderstanding murderers cannot appreciate the effect or meaning of joining their homies to stomp an elderly person to death at the time of the murder, waiting for a possible transformation to an understanding/appreciation of that murder within the friendly confines of JC asks too much of society and the victim's family (not to mention justice, accountability, punishment, etc.). The possibility that these murderers will never gain or adopt the implications of such an understanding does not seem to impress these ATC members. Finally, the idea that a simple "understanding" of the stomping-to-death behavior (whatever that really means) would suffice to grant these youths immunity from criminal prosecution is simply outrageous and unacceptable.

Others see transfer as JCs' being nasty and stingy with their rehabilitation services.

[W]aiver of juvenile court jurisdiction is a compromise of principle dictated by the ***unwillingness of society to pay the price*** *necessary to find out whether our theories of justice for the juvenile are at all valid… (Schornhorst, 1968, p. 602, emphasis added).*

******

[S]ince the inception of the juvenile court, there has also been a seemingly contradictory belief that some youth are ***not worthy*** *of the benevolent nature of the juvenile justice system… (Kurlychek, 2016, p. 897, emphasis added; see, also, Sargent & Gordon, 1963; Schornhorst, 1968. P. 602; Stamm, 1973, p. 148).*

****

Any transfer of jurisdiction strikes at the most basic philosophical elements of the juvenile court system, for it is an admission that the system cannot or does not want to try to rehabilitate one member of the class of individuals for whom it was created. The very existence of juvenile court is predicated upon recognition of the fact that a child is capable of rehabilitation no matter what he may have done and that he has a right to expect no less than that society, through the special establishment of juvenile court, will seek to identify and treat the root causes of the trouble in which he is involved rather than seek retribution against him (Stamm, 1973, p. 145).

These observations are inaccurate and unfair. Almost all states have pretty limited retention ages (invading adulthood as it is) within which JCs must work. Typically, older juvenile offenders can remain under JC control and help for only three or four years. It is unfair to expect JCs to deal with *all* youths, including chronic, older, severely troubled, and dangerous juvenile criminals.

This reasoning...forces juvenile court to make an untenable choice: either accept the referrals of all juvenile offenders or acknowledge the inability to help all young criminals, which is translatable, then, as not being equipped to rehabilitate any juvenile delinquents (Sanborn, 1994a, pp. 267-68).[2]

Retaining all juvenile offenders is both extreme and unreasonable.

It is also implausible to conceive of a juvenile system that provides solutions to all young criminals. It is naïve, as well, to assume that juvenile court will not experience failures, and does not have to answer to the community for the crimes committed by youths... (Id., p. 276).

****

What should distinguish the juvenile from the criminal courts is their greater emphasis on rehabilitation, not their exclusive preoccupation with it (Schornhorst, 1968, p. 593).

3. If Juveniles are Less Mature than Adults, All Juveniles are Not Mature; and are Not Culpable (or Transferrable); Retribution Fails

The most prevalent ATC conversion maneuver insists that juveniles' tendency to be less mature than adults translates into no juvenile offender is mature. This means juvenile offenders are not culpable or able to be punished in CC. "Tendency" and "less" are words in constant use in these arguments. The outcome of this *tendency*, the ATC claims, is that all juveniles bear *less* responsibility for their crimes compared to adults, and, thus, can never be punished equally as an adult (see Brink, 2003-04; Buss, 2016; Cohen et al., 2016; Fagan, 2008; Hoeffel, 2013; McGowan et al., 2007).

Their lesser capacities for reasoning and moral judgment diminish their culpability and render them undeserving of the full burden of retributive punishments...(Bishop, 2000, p. 82).[3]

Developmental Psychologists (DPs) create *P*eer pressure, lack of *R*isk aversion, lack of *I*mpulse control, no ability to consider long-term *C*onsequences (or *PRIC*) formula as foundation for juveniles' lesser culpability

Developmental psychologists (DPs) have led the charge in declaring juvenile offenders too immature to be culpable/transferable. Their "research" has "discovered" that delinquents suffer from a condition known as *PRIC,* which stands for: *P*eer pressure; lack of *R*isk aversion; lack of *I*mpulse control; and, no ability to consider long-term *C*onsequences [4] DPs insist that

any evaluation of an individual's culpability ought to depend upon the degree of maturity of the process through which his or her decision was made (Cauffman & Steinberg, 2000b, p. 328).

Understandably, the DPs object to CC punishment being imposed upon

a child who did not understand the consequences of his or her actions or who was unable to exert control over his or her behavior.... (And upon) a defendant whose understanding of the law is limited by intellectual immaturity or whose judgment is impaired by emotional immaturity... (Steinberg & Cauffman, 2000, p. 381).[5]

Steinberg and Cauffman (2000) focused on *psychosocial maturity*, containing 3 factors:

responsibility *(the capacity to make a decision in an independent, self-reliant fashion),* ***perspective*** *(the capacity to place a decision within a broader temporal and interpersonal context, and* ***temperance*** *(the capacity to exercise self-restraint and control one's impulses) ... (p. 396, emphases in original, citations omitted).*

Based on these elements, Steinberg and Cauffman (2000) concluded:

Compared with adults...adolescents scored lower on measures on self-restraint, consideration of future consequences, and self-reliance, three widely cited components of psychosocial maturity... (Those with higher scores) were more likely to make socially responsible decisions in the hypothetical situations than those who were less psychosocially mature... On average, then, adolescents make poorer (more antisocial) decisions than adults because they are more psychosocially immature (p. 397).[6]

Not all youths are lost souls. Citing other research, Steinberg and Cauffman (2000) admitted:

Research on psychosocial development makes it quite clear that children as young as nine have the capacity for intentional behavior and know the difference between right and wrong... (p. 398, citation omitted).

The DPs admit there is inadequate research and that they are unable to draw age-related bright lines that would distinguish levels of immaturity among adolescents. These deficiencies have not prevented them from asserting that all juveniles are less mature than adults and that factor should lead to question, if not eliminate, transfer to CC. Unanswered are three questions:

- how many adult offenders suffer from a "juvenile"-level of immaturity?
- assuming all juveniles suffer from relative immaturity, why do so few of them end up becoming chronic, serious, and violent offenders and transfer material?
- assuming these traits are common among chronic, serious, and violent juvenile offenders only (and perhaps adult offenders as well), perhaps the traits (and not age) are steering the bus, here?

Others from the ATC insist delinquents be *philosopher kings* to be criminally liable.

(R)esponsible agents must be able to distinguish between the intensity and authority of their values, deliberate about the value or authority of their desires, and regulate their actions in accordance with their deliberations. One must possess this sort of normative competence to qualify in law and morals as a responsible agent or person. Agents who possess this normative competence but do not exercise it properly are responsible for their wrongdoing. (Brink, 2003-04, p. 1569).

Brink raised the bar to ensure few, if any, juveniles qualify as "responsible" agents. Does any adult offender possess this level of introspection/understanding? Juveniles are the victims of *PRIC*.

Older adolescents may have many of the cognitive abilities that adults have, but they lack the wealth of experience and factual information that adults typically possess. And even when older adolescents share cognitive abilities with adults, they typically lack familiar forms of emotional and social maturity and control — they are less able to represent the future adequately, with the result that they are more impulsive and less risk—averse. Moreover, adolescents are also less able to represent the interests of others adequately, with the result that their sense of empathy, which is crucial in inhibiting harmful behavior, is less strong. They also tend to be more susceptible to the influence of peers, with the result that they lack autonomy, which is a key ingredient in normative competence and control...(Id., p. 1571).[7]

One is left wondering whether any juvenile (or adult) would qualify for accountability, according to Brink's formula. More interesting, the sociopathic gang member seemingly would enjoy immunity from criminal prosecution forever.

Brink wants moral responsibility (MR) before there is criminal liability, but MR is subjective and varies by each individual, according to that person's moral compass. Brink created "sky is the limit" criteria before he will acknowledge MR exists. MR is best reserved for relationships with one's creator/some universal moral code.[8] Legal responsibility (LR) is what one owes others via a social contract/criminal law; it is negotiable. LR demands cognitive awareness of behavior before *mens rea* and criminal liability exist. Being impulsive, prone to peer influence, not averse to risks, and short sightedness, without a clear and committed focus upon the future, does not render one incapable of forming intent or possessing and demonstrating *mens rea*.

The maturity and development DPs demand can easily result in juveniles' never being considered culpable for their crimes, including multiple homicides. One DP described a juvenile who murdered two and wounded another thirteen at Santana High School in Santee, California:

Williams made a subjectively rational decision, yet had he exercised the requisite responsibility, autonomy, perspective and temperance, he would have demonstrated a more reasonable, mature sense of judgment. Therefore, adolescent choice to participate in criminal activity reflects immaturity of judgment despite the display of a seemingly cognitive decision-making processes (Wong, 2002, pp. 175-176, citations omitted).

Evidently, all criminal activities in which juveniles are engaged are the products of an immature sense of judgment, meaning there can never be criminal responsibility for the conduct. Were juveniles to act mature, like adults, there would be no crime (due to a mature sense of judgment).

Every offender portrayed by the DPs is a victim of something; juveniles are less culpable or completely non-culpable because they make bad decisions and make them badly. But the "bad" decisions are according to the DPs' beliefs, while "badly" makes them incompetent offenders, not non-culpable ones. DPs constantly employ qualifying verbs to not be pinned down, such as *could, should, might, may not,* or qualifying adverbs, such as *less, possibly, most/mostly, as much, more,* and *partly*. Nevertheless, the qualifying words do not prevent the DPs from reaching absolute or categorical conclusions/positions. They also offer the most innocuous situations as examples of juvenile offenses and the inappropriateness of transfer.

Developmental factors could affect choices about participating in crime. Consider the following example. A youth hangs out with his buddies on the street. Someone suggests holding up a nearby convenience store. The boy has mixed feelings about the proposal, but cannot think of ways to extricate himself — although perhaps a more mature person might develop a strategy. The possibility that one of his friends has a gun, and the consequences of that fact, may not occur to him. He goes along with the plan partly because he fears rejection by his friends — and that carries substantial weight in his calculus. Also, the excitement of the holdup and the possibility of getting some money are attractive. These considerations weigh more heavily in his decision than the cost of possible apprehension by the police, or the long-term costs to his future life of conviction of a serious crime (Scott, 2000, p. 306, citing Scott, Reppucci, & Woolard, 1995).

At least this youth was not portrayed as seeking money to pay for his mother's cancer treatment.

It appears the inability (or unwillingness, perhaps) to conduct (an accurate) cost benefit analysis constitutes a defense to criminal prosecution, according to the DPs. Perhaps it was the juvenile offender's simply reaching a cost benefit conclusion that *differed* from the DPs' calculation rather than an *inability* on the offender's part to engage in such an analysis.

The DPs' "example" lacks credibility. The innocent boy here has no idea a member of the gang has a gun or the possible consequences? Does he have the mind and experience of a four-year-old? Is this his first day with the gang? What is truly interesting is that in none of the "examples" cited by the DPs does any victim get raped or murdered. So, of what value are their examples? Ironically, if this were an accurate description of an actual case, it could lead a prosecutor to not transfer this youth, while choosing to transfer one or more of the other youths involved. DPs establish (age-related) hard core categoricals prohibiting all transfers derived from cases that *would very likely not result in transfer in the first place.* Meanwhile, all those committed to violence, etc. (such as the youth(s) who originated the crime) get a free ride on this youth's coattails.

Several more realistic changes would completely alter the DPs' scenario.

"Our" 17-year-old youth starts it all — wanting money to help purchase an abortion for his 13-year-old girlfriend and to buy into a cache of drugs soon to arrive in his area, from which he seeks profits. He insists upon bringing a gun he knows was used in several previous robberies by him and his fellow gang members. He then entices several others in his gang to join him in the escapade — from which he is convinced he will also earn serious street cred and advance his position in the gang (his first armed robbery satisfied his initiation requirements)—to rob the corner store that his gang is eager to hit because they do not like the proprietor, especially her Asian background (plus she always insists they pay for merchandise). Then he and 6 others rob the store during which he gratuitously shoots and kills the store owner (the benefit of leaving one less witness, which he learned from Dateline) and pistol whips a customer (mistakenly thinking/hoping he killed her).

Of course, all of this represents reasoned and preferable choices for this "innocent" youth since his plan B was to kill the pregnant girlfriend.

The DPs' mission seems to be to promote a proferred academically-sound theory (*PRIC*) as a foundation from which to negate culpability among juvenile offenders. In the end, simple immaturity, without any necessary connection to *PRIC*, will suffice. Even when a juvenile offender checks off each of the *PRIC* boxes, there is still no culpability because DPs *would argue that a young teen who robs a liquor store with his friends exhibits poor judgment regardless of whether he does so because he is unaware of the risks or because he feared the disapproval of his friends... (Cauffman & Steinberg, 2000b, p. 328).*

Why does the robbery automatically represent poor judgment? What if our liquor store robber

- gets away with it repeatedly at various locations and purchases things he wants with the proceeds;
- was fully aware of the risks and calculated more gain than pain;
- led the initiative to rob this store;
- would have done it alone;
- was not impulsive since he had cased the store for days (as he always does); and,
- had no panic or fears in executing the robbery since he knew the proprietor of the store would be unarmed (as are *all* the stores he robs, ensured via casing them)?[9]

To prove injustice, DPs present transfers as victims of circumstances, as errant lads unjustly caught in transfer's web. They write of adolescents trapped in a state of chaotic development, surprised by their actions and circumstances, "victimized" via accidents, irrational thinking, instinctive reactions, and complete surprise, caught so off-guard that thinking was impossible (a horrible upbringing is common, too). The stories are constructed to suggest that transferring these offenders is immoral, but inevitable. A one-sided account is presented, the offender's. Noticeably absent are the perspectives of the alleged victim (who has caused the offender's predicament, of course) and any witnesses. If the events are as described (likely self-defense is a recurrent theme), the offender has a better chance of prevailing in CC with a jury than before a *parens patriae* judge who sees an errant youth who should not have been carrying a knife/gun.

The highlighted crime invariably involves a younger youth's reacting to the event rather than planning a scenario that had no surprises/unanticipated consequences. Burglaries involve youths who suddenly find themselves inside a house that is not theirs. Arsons involve youths who either did not or do not remember setting the fire. This is favorable to the ATC's argument, but it has no bearing or relationship to the violent/chronic offenders who are transferred.

The DPs acknowledge they do not know how each of the characteristics required for maturity and juvenile culpability develop or their interrelationship and cumulative impact upon decision-making. They do know *these* characteristics are *more predictive* of judgment than *age*!

(A)lthough adults tended to make more socially responsible decisions than adolescents, this difference in decision-making was due to differences in psychosocial maturity. On average, adolescents make poorer (more antisocial) decisions than adults because they are more psychosocially immature (Cauffman & Steinberg, 2000b, p. 333).

Making matters and policy development worse:

The relative importance of cognitive versus psychosocial characteristics in evaluating culpability is not clear, nor is it certain if particular psychosocial factors ought to be weighed more heavily than others... (Id., p. 332).

These DPs work a faulty premise to develop a self-fulfilling, equally faulty syllogism:

Mature decisions are legal ones; Legal decisions are mature;

Illegal decisions are poor ones and result from immature/poor judgment;

Juvenile offenders must be immature to exercise poor judgment and commit crime.

Aside from making bold assertions, the DPs never explain how or why crime is linked to immaturity and poor judgment. Perhaps the DPs think crime is self-defeating or immoral or that committing crime is simply a product of being immature. There are plenty of seasoned and mature adult criminals that prove them wrong. What if immaturity is a life-style choice? DPs say that *possible* desistance of this offender from future crime due to *possible development of maturity* and an *ability to just say no* is sufficient to construct a prohibition against transfer.

The DPs are also hard pressed to explain how mitigating factors possessed by *one/ a few* juvenile offenders translate into mitigation for *all* juvenile offenders. The DPs are not just moving the goalposts in the football game of transfer. They are changing the game altogether to badminton!

Criminologists Utilize DPs' PRIC Formula as Foundation for Diminished Responsibility (DR)

The DPs provided the "anti-categorical" Zimring (when it comes to OE) a foundation from which to construct a categorical prohibition against transfer. Zimring's categorical involves diminished responsibility (DR) based mostly upon the previously described *PRIC* formula. DR acts as an insurmountable barrier to transfer.[10] Surmounting DR, Zimring stated, is a substantial task. For starters, sufficient cognition did not suffice in Zimring's (1998a) account:

But persons who, for reasons not their own fault, lack the ability observed in the common citizen either to appreciate the difference between wrong and allowable conduct or to conform their conduct to the law's requirements may be blameless because of their incapacity. Even where the offender has sufficient cognitive skill and emotional control to pass the threshold of criminal capacity, a significant deficit in the ability to appreciate or control behavior would mean that the forbidden conduct is not ***as much*** *the offender's fault, and the quantum of appropriate punishment is less (pp. 76-77, emphasis in original).*

One is left wondering how typical offenders were able to refrain from committing crimes until their teenage years. One might think that their being law abiding (or at least not being caught) until the typical first offense age of 12 or 13 would have provided enough time to learn both rights and wrongs, and the ability to conform behavior. By the age of first offense, juveniles have had an abundance of exposure to and experience in society to have learned both illegal behavior and restraint. Even accepting Zimring's perspective, his qualifiers of "as much" and "less" do not mean criminal prosecution is inappropriate. At most, and after a lot of stretching, these deficit-ladened juvenile offenders perhaps should not be punished *as severely as* non-deficit adult offenders (assuming they exist). There is no necessity for that sentencing to occur in JC, however. Feld has been active as well in promoting the diminished responsibility cause (see Feld, 1997, 1998, 1999a, 1999b, 2007a, 2007b, 2013a, 2017a).

Zimring (1998a) continued to construct requirements for his concept of responsibility:

*(O)lder children and younger adolescents **may lack** fully developed cognitive abilities to comprehend the moral content of commands and to apply legal and moral rules to social situations. The lack of this kind of capacity is at the **heart of infancy as an absolute defense** to criminal liability... (p. 77, emphases added).*

This is simply a false claim. Comprehending "the moral content of commands" and applying "legal and moral rules to social situations" have *never* been factored into the defense of infancy. Most college graduates (and their instructors) probably would fail this requirement. The infancy defense, which is restricted to *mens rea* considerations, starts to dissipate at age seven and completely disappears by age fourteen. Between those ages if prosecutors can demonstrate the defendant had sufficient cognitive capacity to be held criminally liable, they are able to be convicted in CC; this Zimring-created "capacity" has never been among the prosecutor's obligations.

Zimring (1998a) expanded his requirements for the concept of responsibility:

A second skill that is required to transform understanding into the capacity to obey the law is the ability to control impulses.... Long after a child knows that taking property is wrong, the capacity to resist temptation may not be fully operational. To an important extent, self-control is a habit of behavior developed over a period of time, a habit of behavior developed over a period of time, a habit dependant (sic) on the experience of successfully exercising it. This particular type of maturity, like so many others, takes practice... (p.77).

The objective and fair thing to do, Zimring asserted, is to not assign or allow the imposition of criminal responsibility "until adult levels of behavioral control are achieved (Id.)," whatever that means. One is left wondering whether the term, *adult*, is simply a proxy for *legal*.

Refusing to exercise self-control is a permanent defense to being charged with any crime in JC or AC; defendants lacking it are "blameless," according to Zimring. Lacking self-control may sound non-threatening when "mere" stealing is at stake. If the defense has legitimacy, however, it would have to apply to *all* crimes. Juveniles committed to never developing self-control can offend *ad infinitum* without criminal liability. JC would also seem to necessarily lack jurisdiction over this chronic, violent juvenile offender since responsibility is required there, too.

Zimring (1998a), then constructed the final component for his responsibility concept:

The ability to resist peer pressure is the third social skill that is not fully developed in many adolescents. A teen may know right from wrong and may even have developed the capacity to control his or her impulses if left alone to do so, but resisting temptation while alone is a different task from resisting the pressure to commit an offense when among adolescent peers who wish to misbehave. Most adolescent decisions to break the law or not take place on a social stage, where the immediate pressure of peers is the real motive for most teenage crime. A necessary condition for an adolescent to stay law-abiding is the ability to deflect or resist peer pressure. Many youths lack this crucial social skill for a long time. (p. 78).

"Adolescent peers," "social stage" and "immediate pressure of peers" seem to be code words for gang-related crime/activity. If Zimring's DR formula gains traction, an extra layer of immunity lies in joining a gang. Zimring's DR provides juveniles multiple layers of insularity from prosecution for any crime until at least adulthood, and perhaps beyond, since adults also join gangs.

Zimring (1998a) claimed being propelled into gang violence is due to a lack of "group management skills." He minimizes the true potential of gang crime/violence when he proclaims:

Fear of being ***called chicken*** *is almost certainly the major cause of death and injury from youth violence in the United States… (p. 80, emphasis added).*

To suggest that fear of being labelled a chicken would/should suffice to serve as a defense of duress to rape or murder (and as immunity from criminal prosecution) strains believability. Moreover, a betting person would wager that one (or more) of the following exclamations likely explain(s) more juvenile violence utterances than "come on chicken," such as: "let's do it," let's get it on," "we gonna fuck them up," "motherfuckers gonna die," "grab the guns," "aim for their heads;" gang rape victims are more likely to hear "I want some," "hold her down," "she still conscious?" "I like it when they fight back," "who's next?" "where should we leave her?" or "I'm next" than "I/we had no choice but to shoot/stab/rape you or I/we might be called chickens, sorry!"

Zimring's perspective on gang crime could easily end up being seen in the hood as:

Get one or two to help with this crime and we'll end up doing half the time!!

This is not to completely discount or rule out gang pressure and its effect on some members. But to insist that *all* participation in gang crime/violence is due to pressure, let alone under pressure, is an exaggeration.

Not resisting peer pressure does not necessarily mean *an inability* to resist peer pressure. It could mean agreeing with and voluntarily committing the crime. What if the crime was the independent goal of more than one of the group? Why should we automatically assume group crime is a result of peer pressure? Wouldn't at least one of this group be the party responsible for initiating the crime? Moreover, most single-person crimes likely lack peer pressure.[11]

In the culpability arena there aren't two legal standards for JCs or CCs. The ATC version of culpability (i.e., its alleged inextricable tie to *PRIC*) means juveniles lack criminal liability, which means across-the-board immunity; they would never be able to be prosecuted in either JC or CC and would not be answerable to the state for "criminal" behavior until adulthood, if then. Zimring explained, if cognition were sufficient, juveniles would acquire criminal liability at age 16. If self-control and resistance to peer pressure are added to the formula, however,

expecting the experienced-based ability to be fully formed before the age of 18 or 19 would seem to be wishful thinking. ***Becoming an adult*** *is a gradual process in modern industrial societies… (Id., p. 81, emphasis added).*

But the pressing question is: since when (and why) does *becoming an adult* serve as a prerequisite for being held criminally responsible and punishable for criminal behavior? Arguably there are adult offenders who do not act *like adults*.

Zimring concluded with a DR categorical:

There is no logical basis for limiting the scope of a mitigating principle because the harm caused by the criminal act is great.... Diminished responsibility is either ***generally applicable*** *or* ***generally unpersuasive*** *as a mitigating principle (Id., p. 84, emphasis added).*

Zimring's version of DR is so expansive that *his* premise is *generally unpersuasive.* DR *is generally applicable.* Ironically, it is called juvenile court. The entire JJ system can be and should be perceived as mitigation for juvenile criminal behavior. At most, DR mitigates, not exculpates. While true DR would appropriately *reduce* the level of culpability and punishment, it does not *erase* culpability or punishment. Zimring wants us to accept his application of mitigation to perhaps all chronic/violent juvenile offenders. That is simply unreasonable and inappropriate. If a legitimate and non-extreme instance of DR exists (rather than his extreme version of DR), the mitigation can occur within the confines of CC. There is no necessary or apparent need to jump to full immunity from criminal prosecution via a JC prosecution.[12]

Zimring (1998a) concluded:

Young offenders do not become any ***less young*** *because they pull the trigger that ends a human life, and the victim is* ***just as dead*** *as if shot by an adult. (p. 84, emphases added).*

The young do not become less young due to violence, but they do become *less worthy* of immunity. The severity of the offense and outcome certainly can lead reasonably to refuse this young offender the benefit of JC prosecution precisely because the victim is *just as dead.*[13]

While mitigation can be appropriate and principled, DR, as defined by Zimring/ATC, is neither. Lacking cognition, such as represented in the defense of infancy/insanity, is categorical, meaning conviction is not legally possible if the offender lacks *mens rea.* This is appropriate. But the ATC wants to include impulse control, moral awareness/awakening, and the ability to resist peer pressure within the concept of responsibility. The intent to harm becomes relevant when these ingredients are added to the responsibility mix. It is one thing when the offender says, "I did not realize setting that fire would burn down the building and might kill people," (mitigation might be appropriate). It is quite another when the offender says, "I knew people would be hurt or killed due to my act of arson, but it just gives me a rush to watch buildings burn," or "I would not have gained gang membership unless I torched the place and people died," or "I fully understood those 3 families would die due to my act of arson, but I do not consider those people to be fully moral/legitimate human beings because they are gay or Asian or Mormons or illegals or transgendered" (pick one) (mitigation can be logically, reasonably, and morally denied).[14]

The ATC Hoists JC Founders on Their Own Petard

Fagan joined Zimring in calling out JC founders. Evidently, the founders' hyperbole regarding juvenile offenders paved the way for accusations of hypocrisy due to their ultimate but still early awareness and understanding of what some juvenile offenders were capable of doing.

Now here is the problem. If some youths under the maximum jurisdictional age were to be pushed out of the juvenile court and into the jurisdiction of the disfavored criminal courts, what could justify the rejection? If fault was irrelevant to the definition and treatment of delinquency, how could fault be an important distinguishing characteristic for waiver? And if juveniles are never at fault, why should they ever be subject to transfer to criminal courts (Fagan & Zimring, 2000, p. 4)?

To be sure, the founders were naïve and guilty of excessive optimism. In hindsight, it seems the promises of psychology and sociology to stem or reverse the tide of crime just did not pan out. Juvenile offenses at the founding of JC were truly innocuous (see Chapter 4); this lasted about until the 1950s/1960s. The original JC low maximum age and exclusion of serious offenses disprove that *all* "juvenile" offenders were seen by the JC founders as blameless.[15]

Fagan and Zimring labelled the founders' support of transfer as "a huge gap between theory and practice within the juvenile court." The founders learned their mistakes concerning some juvenile offenders. Judge Tuthill observed within a decade of the court's founding:

All right-minded people are willing to have boys and girls have chances to do the right thing, but after they persistently throw chances away the same people would have a right to insist that these young people be really controlled, even if it takes the criminal court process to do it. (Fagan & Zimring, 2000, pp. 4-5, quoting Judge Tuthill, Report of the Cook County Juvenile Court, Chicago, IL. 1907)

Fagan and Zimring saw this statement as "doublespeak." Tuthill's statement, however, could be simply a recognition very early that the founders recognized the overreach of their rhetoric. The founders can be criticized for their excessive optimism, but had they reacted with a "guess we'll just have to bite the bullet" in addressing chronic/violent juvenile crime, rather than with a transfer response, they would have been making a bad situation worse by compounding their initial optimism, and threatening JC's survival.

Fagan and Zimring (2000) continued:

If the ideology of the juvenile court was treatment, the lack of amenability to that single tool was the sole theoretically justified ground for expulsion from the system dedicated to treat delinquent youth (p. 5).

The founders had serious limits on both the crimes/ages of juvenile offenders who were eligible for JC intervention. The vast majority of transfer targets today were not JC subjects "back in the day." Not only was JC *not mostly about* kids' committing crimes, but it was also *barely about* kids' committing crimes. Besides serious age/crime limits, transfer was always an option, from the very first days, so founders' hypocrisy and inconsistency cannot be as extreme as some in the ATC would let on. The JC was never about processing 100% of the crimes

The founders took off their blinders and saw some juveniles for what they were: chronic and violent criminals. The founders did not anticipate these juveniles as JCs were set in motion. Soon, however, they encountered these offenders. They decided JC was not the proper forum to address their behavior. Fagan and Zimring (2000) shamed Judge Tuthill for his comment:

This is one of the earliest documents in the administration of American juvenile justice, and the vocabulary of blame is already a major element in the operational rhetoric of the court in waiver cases (p. 5).[16]

The founders likely found fault in the behavior of some, perhaps many, juvenile clients, even some of those who had committed mere infractions and status offenses. They simply chose to deny/repress that reality of fault in favor of promoting juveniles' irresponsibility and youthful status. The latter promotion was critical (and *mostly* correct). The founders needed to pitch to legislatures (and ultimately to the public) a benevolent rehabilitation program that promised to be nice to juvenile miscreants/offenders, some of whom had committed serious crimes. This was not only new, but it was also completely radical.

Emphasizing the fault of the kids, rather than their "innocence" would not likely have helped produce the authorization they sought to create a new court. Maybe even more pertinent is why or how 100% of juvenile offenders would lack any blame for their conduct? This would be especially relevant to chronic offending. If juveniles cannot ever accrue blame, then perhaps the existence of JC and not transfer to CC should be the focus of Fagan's and Zimring's inquiry and disdain.[17]

Fagan and Zimring have been critical of the founders' views towards juvenile offenders and transfer but can offer very little real guidance themselves. They have embraced the lesser culpability theory, which has emotional appeal, but provides no clear demarcations that indicate levels of responsibility or the proper age for transfer. Fagan and Zimring (2000) admitted:

(T)here is no single cognitive, social, or behavioral boundary in the developmental findings on criminal responsibility of adolescent offenders, the incremental differences between ascending age groups do not easily translate into binary distinctions like juvenile or adult, full versus partial culpability... (Another) limit of the developmental data on adolescence as a direct measure of penal responsibility is that assessments of responsibility are essentially moral judgments that can be informed by but not decided (by) behavioral data.... (L)egal policy can very rarely be derived from behavioral data... (pp. 419-420).

Zimring (1998a) also conceded there is no way yet to measure the extent of DR (p. 80).

Zimring insisted that juveniles need to learn pro-social, law-abiding values (Sellers & Arrigo, 2009; Zimring, 1998a), which, evidently, chronic juvenile offenders have failed to grasp on repeated occasions. Apparently, transfer targets just have not finished the lesson. Retorts to this are:

- *most juveniles do learn*, challenging the idea that chronic and violent juvenile should get a break and avoid criminal prosecution forever;
- *most juvenile delinquents also have learned* or they would have been arrested at ages 5, 6, 7, 8 and not for the first time at 13, 14, 15, let alone 16 or 17;
- rather than impulsiveness, perhaps just *a lack of self-control and discipline* and *not believing in or willing to abide by deferred gratification* are what lead to criminal behavior;
- why is there a failure in our chronic offenders to learn and understand consequences? Perhaps *their experiences in JC do not instruct/deter*; and,
- what exactly are they supposed to learn? Is it, how to commit crime more successfully or how to conform to the law? If it is the latter, most should have learned it (albeit without serious consequences in JC) and either forgot it or chose to ignore it.

What juveniles lack in culpability, society has more than its share, according to Feld:

Moreover, the crimes of juveniles are seldom their fault alone; society shares at least some of the blame for their offenses as a result of juveniles' limited opportunities to learn to make correct choices. Indeed, even though the ability to make responsible choices is learned behavior, the dependent status of juveniles systematically deprives them of opportunities to learn to be responsible. Finally, even if a youth is aware of the abstract criminal prohibition, juveniles are more susceptible to peer group influences and group process dynamics than are their older counterparts (Feld, 1987, p. 526, citations omitted).

It is hard to believe that there is *any* adolescent who has not had opportunities to "learn to make correct choices." Not being in JC constantly, if at all, testifies to the vast majority of youths' having learned to obey the law or at least how to evade it. Adolescents' awareness of the wrong or illegality attending hitting someone or ripping them off does not require an intricate understanding of criminal law; we are not talking about calculus, here. Certainly, adolescents are "aware of the abstract criminal prohibition" connected to assault/theft offenses/behaviors.

Interesting, not all ATC folks endorse the "DR means no transfer to CC policy." One serious card-carrying member of the ATC noted DR can be accommodated very well in CC.

The diminished culpability rationale facilitates discounted sentences, but it also justifies carrying out those sentences in adult court, where culpability is king. Moreover, because the scientific evidence indicates that, from mid-adolescence onward, juveniles are not significantly different from adults in terms of traditional culpability doctrine, the diminished culpability rationale does not require or justify sentences that are significantly shorter sentences. In light of the inordinate length of today's adult dispositional practices, juvenile dispositions can justifiably still be quite long even if the diminished culpability model ultimately wins the day.... (D)esert-based punishment — even discounted punishment — requires adult-style sentences for the more serious crimes... (Slobogin, 2013, pp. 106-107).

Slobogin (2013) went as far as to challenge the extreme conclusions of the DPs' research:

(I)n describing the lesser culpability of juveniles, the (diminished culpability) model stretches the implications of developmental research beyond what it will bear. Juveniles are less culpable than adults, but they are not as impaired in their judgment as advocates of the diminished retributive model seem to think (p. 110).[18]

Finally, Slobogin (2013) feared that the DPs' focus on culpability actually

undermines the argument for a separate juvenile justice system and...facilitates maintenance of a wide-ranging, but counterproductive transfer mechanism (p. 110, citations omitted).

The great disconnect is that, assuming all juveniles share these traits of immaturity (or even if all juvenile offenders share these traits), why do *so few* among them evolve into the violent and chronic offenders that are transfer targets?

What this all means, according to the ATC, is that transfer should not happen because retributive goals cannot be served when relatively non-culpable offenders are being exposed to CC punishments (see Brink, 2003-04; Slobogin, 2013).[19]

A problem with the Zimring/DP/ATC position is that pushing for categorical mitigation, besides encompassing many/most offenders who do not deserve the mitigation, reinforces in adolescents that risks of serious offending are indeed few. This can certainly encourage many would-be offenders to go out and commit even more crime. It also could easily lead to older gang members pressuring younger ones (i.e., JC-only material) to commit crimes for the gang's benefit. For many, their history in juvenile justice (JJ) has already convinced them there is nothing to fear in a JC adjudication.

To the extent that people need encouragements to do the right thing and discouragements to refrain from doing the wrong thing, Zimring/DPs are encouraging adolescents to not refrain from doing the wrong thing. If adopted as a policy, the state has committed to keep all juvenile offenders in JC, regardless of offense and record, which is a dangerous get-out-of-jail card (literally) to would-be offenders.

4. If Juveniles are Less Deterrable, All Juveniles are Not Deterrable

The ATC says juvenile offenders are also less deterrable, rendering transfer less effective or completely ineffective. Those who oppose transfer do not believe that chronic and violent juvenile offenders can be deterred by any threat implicit (or explicit) represented in the CJ system. Since chronic juvenile offenders dominate their research, the ATC uses a biased sample; these offenders already were not deterred from their start in JC — perhaps multiple times.

Part of this lesser deterrability is due to the same alleged traits that render juvenile offenders less mature and culpable (see Slobogin, 2013).[20]

Moreover, from a purely utilitarian perspective, their limited ability to anticipate and weigh long term consequences makes it unlikely that threats of criminal sanctions will deter them (Bishop, 2000, p. 82, citation omitted).

****

(T)he deterrent effect of sanctions crucially depends on potential criminals being rational calculators of expected utility. Immaturity compromises this assumption. Adolescents are not rational calculators of utility. Not only do they lack the cognitive capacities of adults, but also, and more importantly, they lack the ability to vividly represent the future and are prone to discount the significance of future benefits and harms out of proportion to their actual magnitude. But this means that sanctions that might, in principle, work for adults just won't have the same deterrent value for juveniles... (Brink, 2003-04, pp. 1573-74).[21]

One of the factors that could contribute to a lack of deterrence for juvenile offenders is the relative, and, at times, extreme, leniency of JC dispositions, compared to possible sentences in CC. The ATC never mentions this factor. This factor could/would be especially relevant to chronic offenders who have experienced JC and have found that they are no worse off via a JC disposition than if they had never been caught in the first place. Those who have never been arrested/adjudicated can learn from peers that remaining in JC is mostly nothing to fear.[22]

B. The Tactic of Converting the Categorical to the Individual/Group

Zimring ushered conversions in another direction when he took an (incorrect) categorical claim and extended it to individual instances. Zimring (1998a) endorsed the assumption that criminal offenses are "a more or less normal adolescent phenomena (p. 82) (see also, Kupchik, 2003b; Scott, 2000; Zimring, 1978)." Zimring (1998a) then made a bold statement such that

violent crime ***is*** *kid stuff...Just under half of all male adolescents report being responsible for an assault at some time during their teen years. So a very large proportion of the male population crosses the border into violence at least once in adolescence... (p. 84, emphasis in original).*

Zimring based his *naturally violent juvenile* conclusion completely on the findings of self-report studies that ask school aged youth to admit their previous wrongs. The findings contradict Zimring's conclusion. What these reports disclose is that nearly all youths commit a criminal offense while growing up. Fortunately for society, the vast majority of these miscreants do not report being either chronic or violent in their offending. The reported offenses rarely involve knifings, shootings, or muggings (let alone homicides or rapes). Most kids get into scrapes, schoolyard, or neighborhood fights or personally steal items from other kids during teenage years, smoke cigarettes/dope or drink alcohol, but only very few commit chronic and violent acts that would be targeted for transfer. This is corroborated by the small percentage of juveniles who are transferred. To conclude from these self-reports that widespread numbers of juveniles are naturally (let alone repeatedly) violent requires more than just a quantum leap.

More important, one page later, moreover, Zimring (1998a) critically admitted,

Assaults and robberies vary tremendously in seriousness and, these two offenses account for 94 percent of all youth violence arrests (p. 85).

Zimring wants it both ways. He posited that violence is supposedly natural behavior for juveniles, implying that kids are just being kids when they act violently. But Zimring also conceded that his identified "violent" crimes (assaults and robberies) "vary tremendously in seriousness." Zimring's term of violent crime has incredible elasticity, here. More critical, Zimring's second statement undermines his first. It is precisely the tremendous variability in seriousness of assaults and robberies that demands caution in contending that juveniles are naturally violent. Assaults run the gamut from attempted murder by stabbing or shooting someone to pushing another kid in the school yard. The same variation in violence/seriousness applies to robberies. Zimring is aware of that. But then he used those offenses as a basis for claiming juveniles are *naturally* violent. Only a small fraction of assaults and robberies are transferred, meaning most are not of such a violent nature that transfer was pursued or imposed. In fact, Zimring is ever critical of the necessary discretion utilized by prosecutors to decide which acts of "violence" merit a pursuit of transfer.[23]

Within the topic of the typicality of juvenile misbehavior, Zimring also tried to establish an equivalency between teenage drivers and violent offenders. Zimring implied that teenage drivers should be seen as dangerous and threatening to society as are violent offenders. So, since we permit teenagers to learn how to drive through sometimes serious miscues (i.e., not without dangerous potential consequences) without seeking to permanently shut them down or to adopt other drastic measures, we should be equally tolerant of violent offenders and not transfer them.

Why, then, are there few serious proposals to radically redefine youth traffic regulations, to defer driver's licenses until age 21, or to revoke them permanently when youths have accidents (Id., p. 86)?

This analogy does not work, however. One little irony is that in many states juvenile traffic offenders go to traffic court and not to JC. Answering Zimring, we do not let them drive without serious restrictions until at least 16, which just happens to be the age ripe for transfer, too. Second, it is not the learning to drive that constitutes the threat; many, if not most, teenagers learn how to drive and do not act recklessly while learning. It is acting recklessly after learning how to drive that is the real danger and the criminal act, depending upon the behavior. Third, learning to drive is already heavily regulated. Fourth, we do punish teenage drivers who drive recklessly. Their misconduct is not ignored, depending upon the nature of the recklessness and its outcome. A traffic fatality, such as vehicular manslaughter could indeed be transferred to CC. Fifth, it is not fair to deprive the overwhelming majority of responsible teenagers their opportunity to drive due to the irresponsibility of the minority. This would be like confining all juveniles in their homes after school hours due to the criminal activity of a minority of teenagers.

Most would-be drivers do not need to worry about Draconian driving restrictions, much like most juvenile offenders (not to mention the law-abiding youths) do not need to worry about expansive transfer laws. Sixth, as Zimring noted elsewhere, the *intention to harm* is critical. While that intent is absent from the vast majority of irresponsible traffic violations, it is a prerequisite to be charged with a violent crime that merits transfer. Seventh, as Zimring later noted: "I do not mean to argue that the American public should regard the two problems (highway deaths and homicide) as equivalent… (Id.)." Why he initially suggested an equivalency does exist, then, is puzzling. Finally, even a reckless fatal auto *accident* that is just an accident qualifies as a mistake. If it is not, then it is a crime that easily could end up being transferred. Unlike most traffic offenses, homicides and rapes are not mistakes or accidents or simple errors in judgment. Zimring (1998a) disagreed, nevertheless, seeing most, perhaps nearly all, violent juvenile crime as mistakes:

(T)he outcome in such cases will be a disservice to socially important interests by not allowing young people to fully recover from their adolescent mistakes… (p. 143).

Morse (1998) provides a comprehensive rebuttal to Zimring's risk/mistake proposition.

Adolescent criminal conduct for the most part involves the intentional infliction of harm: the offender intentionally killed, inflicted grievous bodily harm, raped, stole, destroyed, or burned. That is, it is the adolescent's conscious objective to cause in the immediate future precisely the harm the law prohibits. Unless serious adolescent offenders are especially unlucky or unskillful, they are practically certain to produce the harm that is their conscious objective, and they know it. The intentional harmdoer knows that the conduct invades the interests of others; those interests may be given little value or otherwise ignored or rationalized away, but they must be present to the adolescent agent's mind. Adolescents can surely commit crimes of risk creation, such as reckless homicide, but primarily serious crimes of intention raise the issues that concern us. And for crimes of serious risk creation, the risk is immediate and, once again, the risked result will at least be present to the adolescent's mind (pp. 53-54).

****

If risky conduct is statistically normal for adolescents, treating adolescents as criminals or proto-criminals may appear to be criminalizing "normality," but this is not the case. Again the law does not criminalize or seriously criminalize much risk-creating conduct. More important, no matter how much adolescents may prefer risk, it can scarcely be claimed that serious crime is the statistically normal mode that adolescents use to express their preference for risk. To treat an adolescent murderer, rapist, arsonist, and the like as simply a kid in search of risk and to suggest that we should consider decriminalizing such conduct among kids is neither justified by the data nor morally warranted (Id., p. 55).

To be sure, there should be no cases (and likely are not any cases) where transfer targets *mere mistakes*. Rape and murder are not mistakes or they would not be charged as such crimes. Chronic burglaries, robberies, arsons, and auto thefts, the most likely targets of transfer, also do not qualify as mistakes. If all of these behaviors are categorized as mere mistakes, there is no such thing as crime.

REFERENCES

Arya, N. (2010). Using *Graham v. Florida* to challenge juvenile transfer laws. *Louisiana Law Review, 71*, 99–156.

Bishop, D. M. (2000). Juvenile offenders in the adult criminal justice system. In M. Tonry (Ed.), *Crime & Justice: A Review of Research, 27, 81-167.* IL University of Chicago Press. doi:10.1086/652199

Bonnie, R. J., & Grisso, T. (2000). Adjudicative competence and youthful offenders. In T. Grisso & R. G. Schwartz (Eds.), *Youth on trial: A developmental perspective on juvenile justice* (pp. 73–103). University of Chicago Press.

Brink, D. O. (2003-2004). Immaturity, normative competence, and juvenile transfer: How (not) to punish minors for major crimes. *Texas Law Review, 82*, 1555–1585.

Buss, E. (2016). Developmental jurisprudence. *Temple Law Review, 88*, 741–758.

Cauffman, E. E. (1996). *Maturity of judgment: Psychosocial factors in adolescent decision-making.* Temple University.

Cauffman, E. E., & Steinberg, L. (2000a). (Im)maturity of judgment in adolescence: Why adolescents may be less culpable than adults. *Behavioral Sciences & the Law, 18*(6), 741–760. doi:10.1002/bsl.416 PMID:11180420

Cauffman, E. E., & Steinberg, L. (2000b). Researching adolescents' judgment and culpability. In T. Grisso & R. G. Schwartz (Eds.), *Youth on trial: A developmental perspective on juvenile justice* (pp. 325–343). University of Chicago Press.

Cohen, A. O., Bonnie, R. J., Taylor-Thompson, K., & Casey, B. J. (2016). When does a juvenile become an adult: Implications for law and policy. *Temple Law Review, 88*, 769–788.

DeJong, C., & Merrill, E. S. (2000). Getting tough on crime: Juvenile waiver and the criminal court. *Ohio Northern University Law Review, 27*, 175–196.

Fagan, J. (2008). Juvenile crime and criminal justice: Resolving border disputes. 18 *The Future of Children* 81-118 (Pages numbered 1-48 in Columbia Law School Working Paper).

Fagan, J., & Zimring, F. E. (2000). Editors' Introduction. In Fagan, J., & Zimring, F.E. (Eds.), The changing borders of juvenile justice: Transfer of adolescents to the criminal court (pp. 1-10). University of Chicago Press.

Feld, B. C. (1987). The juvenile court meets the principle of the offense: Legislative changes in juvenile waiver statutes. *The Journal of Criminal Law & Criminology, 78*(3), 471–533. doi:10.2307/1143567

Feld, B. C. (1997). Abolish the juvenile court: Youthfulness, criminal responsibility, and sentencing. *The Journal of Criminal Law & Criminology, 88*(1), 68–136. doi:10.2307/1144075

Feld, B. C. (1998). Juvenile and criminal justice systems' responses to youth violence. *Crime and Justice, 24*, 189–261. doi:10.1086/449280

Feld, B. C. (1999a). *Bad kids: Race and the transformation of the juvenile court.* Oxford University Press.

Feld, B. C. (1999b). The Transformation of the juvenile court—Part II: Race and the crack down on youth crime. *Minnesota Law Review*, *84*, 327–395.

Feld, B. C. (2000). Legislative exclusion of offenses from juvenile court jurisdiction: A history and critique. In J. Fagan & F. E. Zimring (Eds.), *The changing borders of juvenile justice: Transfer of adolescents to the criminal court* (pp. 83–144). University of Chicago Press.

Feld, B. C. (2007a). A century of juvenile justice: A work in progress or a revolution that failed. *Northern Kentucky Law Review*, *34*, 189–256.

Feld, B. C. (2007b). Unmitigated punishment: Adolescent criminal responsibility and LWOP sentences. *Journal of Law & Family Studies*, *10*, 11–82.

Feld, B. C. (2013a). Adolescent criminal responsibility, proportionality, and sentencing policy: Roper, Graham, Miller/Jackson, and the youth discount. *Law & Inequality*, *31*, 263–330.

Feld, B. C. (2017a). Competence and culpability: Delinquents in juvenile courts, youths in criminal courts. *Minnesota Law Review*, *102*, 473–576.

Forst, M., & Blomquist, M. E. (1991). Cracking down on juveniles: The changing ideology of youth corrections. *Notre Dame Journal of Law, Ethics & Public Policy*, *5*, 323–375.

Gasper, J., & Katkin, D. (1980). A rationale for the abolition of the juvenile court's power to waive jurisdiction. *Pepperdine Law Review*, *7*, 937–951.

Graham v. Florida. (2010). 560 U.S 48, 2010.

Hoeffel, J. C. (2013). The jurisprudence of death and youth: Now the twain should meet. *Texas Tech Law Review*, *46*, 29–69.

Hogan, C. (1974). Waiver of juvenile jurisdiction and the hard-core youth. *North Dakota Law Review*, *51*, 655–677.

Kirkish, P., Sreenivasan, S., Welsh, R., Van Gorp, W., Eth, S., Shoptaw, S., & Ling, W. (2000). The future of criminal violence: Juveniles tried as adults. *The Journal of the American Academy of Psychiatry and the Law*, *28*(1), 38–46. PMID:10774840

Kupchik, A. (2003b). Prosecuting adolescents in criminal courts: Criminal or juvenile justice? *Social Problems*, *50*(3), 439–460. doi:10.1525p.2003.50.3.439

Kurlychek, M. C. (2016). Effectiveness of juvenile transfer to adult court: Implications from current research and directions for future study. *Criminology & Public Policy*, *15*(3), 897–900. doi:10.1111/1745-9133.12240

Maroney, T. A. (2009). The False promise of adolescent brain science in juvenile justice. *The Notre Dame Law Review*, *85*, 89–176.

Marrus, E., & Rosenberg, I. M. (2005). After *Roper v. Simmons*: Keeping kids out of adult criminal court. *San Diego L. Rev.*, *42*, 1151-1182.

McGowan, A., Hahn, R., Liberman, A., Crosby, A., Fullilove, M., Johnson, R., Moscicki, E., Price, L., Snyder, S., Tuma, F., Lowy, J., Briss, P., Cory, S., & Stone, G. (2007). Effects on violence of laws and policies facilitating the transfer of juveniles from the juvenile justice system to the adult justice system: A systematic review. *American Journal of Preventive Medicine*, *32*(4), S7–S28. doi:10.1016/j.amepre.2006.12.003 PMID:17386331

Miller v. Alabama. (2012). 132 S Ct. 2455.

Monahan, K. C., Steinberg, L., Cauffman, E., & Mulvey, E. P. (2009). Trajectories of antisocial behavior and psychosocial maturity from adolescence to young adulthood. *Developmental Psychology*, *45*(6), 1654–1668. doi:10.1037/a0015862 PMID:19899922

Morse, S. J. (1998). Immaturity and irresponsibility. *The Journal of Criminal Law & Criminology*, *88*(1), 15–67. doi:10.2307/1144074

Pegg, K. (2015). The" once an adult, always an adult" doctrine: More harm than good. *Indiana Journal of Law and Social Equality*, *3*(1), 144–160.

Roper v. Simmons. (2005). 543 U.S. 551.

Sanborn, J. B., Jr. (1985). *Plea negotiation in juvenile court*. [Unpublished doctoral dissertation, SUNY Albany, Albany, NY., United States].

Sanborn, J. B. Jr. (1994a). Certification to criminal court: The important policy questions of how, when, and why. *Crime and Delinquency*, *40*(2), 262–281. doi:10.1177/0011128794040002007

Sargent, D. A., & Gordon, D. H. (1963). Waiver of jurisdiction: An evaluation of the process in the juvenile court. *Crime and Delinquency*, *9*(2), 121–128. doi:10.1177/001112876300900202

Schornhorst, T. F. (1968). The waiver of juvenile court jurisdiction: Kent revisited. *Indiana Law Review*, *43*, 583–613.

Scott, E. S. (2000). Criminal responsibility in adolescence: Lessons from developmental psychology. In T. Grisso & R. G. Schwartz (Eds.), *Youth on Trial: A Developmental Perspective on Juvenile Justice* (pp. 291–324). University of Chicago Press.

Scott, E. S. (2013). Miller v. Alabama and the (past and) future of juvenile crime regulation. *Law & Inequality*, *31*, 535–558.

Scott, E. S., & Grisso, T. (1997). The evolution of adolescence: A developmental perspective on juvenile justice reform. *The Journal of Criminal Law & Criminology*, *88*(1), 137–189. doi:10.2307/1144076

Scott, E. S., Reppucci, N. D., & Woolard, J. L. (1995). Evaluating adolescent decision making in legal contexts. *Law and Human Behavior*, *19*(3), 221–244. doi:10.1007/BF01501658

Sellers, B. G., & Arrigo, B. A. (2009). Adolescent transfer, developmental maturity and adjudicative competence: An ethical and justice policy inquiry. *Criminology*, *29*, 435–488.

Slobogin, C. (2013). Treating juveniles like juveniles: Getting rid of transfer and expanded adult court jurisdiction. *Texas Tech Law Review*, *46*, 103–132.

Stamm, M. J. (1973). Transfer of jurisdiction in juvenile court: An A\analysis of the proceeding, its role in the administration of justice, and A proposal for the reform of Kentucky law. *Kentucky Law Journal (Lexington, Ky.)*, *62*, 122–199.

Steinberg, L. (2009). Adolescent development and juvenile justice. *Annual Review of Clinical Psychology*, *5*(1), 459–485. doi:10.1146/annurev.clinpsy.032408.153603 PMID:19327037

Steinberg, L., & Cauffman, E. (2000). A developmental perspective on jurisprudential boundary. In Fagan. J., & Zimring, F.E. (Eds.), The Changing Borders of Juvenile Justice: Transfer of Adolescents to the Criminal Court (pp. 379-406). University of Chicago Press.

Steinberg, L., & Schwartz, R. G. (2000). Developmental psychology goes to court. In T. Grisso & R. G. Schwartz (Eds.), *Youth on Trial: A Developmental Perspective in Juvenile Justice* (pp. 9–31). University of Chicago Press.

Vitiello, M. (1976). Constitutional safeguards for juvenile transfer procedure: The ten years since Kent v. United States. *De Paul Law Review*, *26*, 23–53.

Wong, T. (2002). Adolescent minds, adult crimes: Assessing a juvenile's mental health and capacity to stand trial. *University of California Davis Journal of Juvenile Law & Policy*, *6*, 163–188.

Zimring, F. E. (1978). *Confronting youth crime: report of the Twentieth Century Fund Task Force on Sentencing Policy Toward Young Offenders; background paper*. Holmes & Meier.

Zimring, F. E. (1981). Notes on the jurisprudence of waiver. In J. C. Hall, D. M. Hamparian, J. M. Pettibone, & J. L. White (Eds.), *Major issues in juvenile justice information and training: Readings in public policy* (pp. 193–205). Academy for Contemporary Problems.

Zimring, F. E. (1991). The treatment of hard cases in American juvenile justice: In defense of discretionary waiver. *Notre Dame Journal of Law, Ethics & Public Policy*, *5*, 267–280.

Zimring, F. E. (1998a). *American youth violence*. Oxford University Press.

Zimring, F. E. (1998b). Toward a jurisprudence of youth violence. *Crime and Justice*, *24*, 477–501. doi:10.1086/449285

Zimring, F. E. (2000a). Penal proportionality for the young offender: Notes on immaturity, capacity, and diminished responsibility. In T. Grisso & R. G. Schwartz (Eds.), *Youth on Trial: A Developmental Perspective on Juvenile Justice* (pp. 271–289). University of Chicago Press.

Zimring, F. E. (2000b). The punitive necessity of waiver. In J. Fagan & F. E. Zimring (Eds.), *The Changing Borders of Juvenile Justice: Transfer of adolescents to the criminal court* (pp. 207–224). University of Chicago Press.

ENDNOTES

1 The ATC similarly claims that transfer is a safety valve to relieve pressure off legislatures and JC officials when no more than *one or two cases a year* per city would apply such pressure.
In a similar vein, it is common for the ATC to cite a "bad" hypothetical case to solicit condemnation of the entire transfer/exclusion concept:
Consider this scenario: on the same day, two sixteen-year-olds are apprehended after shoplifting DVDs from the same local superstore. One child's case is processed by the juvenile court, and he or she receives an extremely lenient disposition consisting of a verbal warning from the judge accompanied by no mark on his or her criminal record. However, the other child's case is transferred to the adult criminal court system. This child faces the possibility of much harsher punishment and an additional mark on his or her criminal record that will hinder his or her ability to successfully apply to school programs and jobs. How can such disparate treatment occur? The second youth had been previously transferred to adult court for a minor charge two years prior, at the whim of a prosecutor who chose to directly file the case in adult court. In light of the widely enacted "once an adult, always an adult" doctrine that requires transfer of all previously transferred juveniles to adult court for subsequent crimes, a scenario similar to the one described above can occur in over half of the states, regardless of the severity of the crime (Pegg, 2015, p. 144).
First off, the poor lad headed to CC was not transferred there (see Chapter 6)! Like many of her ATC compatriots, this anti-ME proponent provided a slanted and fact-deprived account. She neglected to mention in *her* scenario that the poor lad who fell victim to this nasty, unforgiving ME provision had had 9 prior JC adjudications, including several armed robberies and residential burglaries, had failed in 5 previous placements and intensive treatment programs (following four failed probation efforts that engaged expensive and highly regarded community services), and was finally transferred for a relatively minor commercial burglary because there was honestly no JC disposition that would make any sense and not be a complete waste of resources. Meanwhile, the conviction for the commercial burglary in CC netted another unwise probation sentence, encouraging him yet again to not stop committing crimes. Perhaps he believed (correctly) that the relatively minor shoplifting charge would net yet another lenient probation sentence in CC. Making matters worse (fabricated and embellished scenarios work both ways, in case you're wondering), this career delinquent/criminal lad was the one who convinced the "novice" to also steal a DVD, promising nothing "bad" would happen to *him*, which proved accurate since the JC disposition was non-reporting probation. Perhaps it is not the ME provision that is the problem in this scenario, but rather JC's waiting too long to transfer the criminal wannabe in the first place and/or CC's imposing anther lenient sentence on a career delinquent/criminal when he finally secured a conviction in CC (after experiencing a history of relative (if not absolute) and repeated leniency for criminal behavior in JC).

2 There would have to be either total inclusion or total exclusion. Considering jails and prisons and mental health facilities would require their closure should one former inmate offend. JC workers do not regard transfer as a failure in JC philosophy (Sanborn, 1994a, p. 272).

3 Bishop cited Forst & Blomquist, 1991; Scott & Grisso, 1997; Zimring, 1981, 1991, 1998a in support of her statement.

4 See Cauffman, 1996; Cauffman & Steinberg, 2000a; Cauffman & Steinberg, 2000b; Cohen et al., 2016; Feld, 1987; Monahan, Steinberg, Cauffman, & Mulvey, 2009; Steinberg & Schwartz, 2000; Scott, 2000, 2013; Scott, Reppucci & Woolard, 1995; Steinberg, 2009; Steinberg & Cauffman, 2000; Zimring, 1998a, 2000a, 2000b.
There are numerous characteristics, apart from *PRIC*, that could explain most juveniles and comprise elements of (im)maturity, while also distinguishing some chronic and violent juvenile offenders from some non-chronic/violent offenders (or at least to distinguish *as well as* the *PRIC* maturity elements do):

- lack of respect for others' property (refusal to accept other peoples' ownership);
- lack of pro-social values;
- lack of proper socialization;
- never taking/acknowledging responsibility or admitting being wrong;
- wrongfully blaming others;
- feeling a rush in defying authority and the law;
- perceiving more benefits than detriments in committing crime;
- general sense of entitlement;
- disdain for hard, lawful work and earnings;
- feelings of invincibility;
- dismissing the feelings of others;
- lack of commitment to not hurt others;
- self-centered, narcissism;
- disregard for an effect on others;
- being a sore loser;
- feeling entitled to the affections of others;
- eager (not pushed) to engage in fights;
- perceive JC as an insignificant threat, minimal risk (maybe reasonably see themselves as not taking on any risk via crime, considering the nature of JC);
- committed to thrill-seeking through burglary, robbery, rape, homicide, etc.;
- denial of an afterlife, (grab all you can now from whomever or be a sucker);
- enjoy calling others names;
- enjoying aggravating, insulting, bothering others;
- feeling disrespected by the slightest affront;
- being "raised" by family/peers who consider stealing and assaulting others as a rush/an entitlement/not problematic; and,
- finding the only true friendship/familial relationships among members of a gang or criminal associates dedicated to violence/crime.

Perhaps chronic/serious/violent juvenile offenders have these traits as well as the immaturity ones, while the non-chronic/serious/violent crowd does not, which distinguishes the two groups. Perhaps DPs need to expand their inquiry into the characteristics of juvenile offenders.

5 Agreeing which juveniles cannot understand the consequences of these actions (for which reasons) or are unable to control their behavior (for which reasons) becomes the issue. It is accepting the contents of intellectual/emotional immaturity that is problematic. Is that intellectual and emotional immaturity based on moral/street/criminal conduct or thug life maturity?

6 Interesting, DPs routinely admit that they are not able to draw age-related bright lines that would distinguish levels of immaturity among adolescents. (A)*dolescence does not lend itself to such a precise partitioning on the basis of chronological age...* (It is) *difficult to draw generalizations about the psychological capabilities of individuals who share the same chrono-logical age....* (F)*rom early adolescence on, chronological age is a very poor marker for developmental maturity....* (D)*ifferences* **within** *a given age group — differences among fourteen-year-olds, for example — are likely to be greater than differences* **between** *this age group and the adjacent ones...* (Steinberg & Cauffman, 2000, p. 384, emphases in original).
****

Further research is required, however, to determine the degree to which these developmental factors directly affect the decisions of youths participating in delinquent activity (Scott, 2000, p. 307). This uncertainty has not prevented the DPs from prescribing anti-transfer policy, however, involving age cutoffs in the eligibility for transfer to CC.

7 But even possessing empathy *and* passing the *PRIC* test are not enough:

(I)*t is possible to engage in means-end reasoning in the formation of plans and to display resoluteness in the execution of such plans without being suitably competent to deliberate about one's ends and to put one's emotions and desires into proper perspective. Children often engage in elaborate planning in the service of whims or other ends for which they are not accountable. A version of this can be found among adolescents as well. They may commit crimes that reflect elaborate and temporally extended planning, but they may nonetheless be unable to appreciate fully the normative significance of the ends for the sake of which they have planned. Their ends may reflect steep temporal discounting of long-term benefits and harms, an inadequate ability to empathize with the interests of others whom their actions affect, or an exaggerated concern with approval of their peers expressed in the inflation of petty jealousies, resentment and rivalries. Such failings correspond to different dimensions of normative competence — capacities for temporal neutrality, empathy, and autonomy. Because premeditation does not guarantee these other aspects of normative competence and these aspects of normative competence tend to be immature and developing in juveniles, premeditation does not rebut the case for reduced juvenile culpability* (Brink, 2003-04, p. 1578).

8 Decisions, such as unnecessarily ending the life of a fetus, belong here.

9 DPs say juveniles need to display maturity of judgment that comes with maturation and experience before they can be criminally liable. Is an eighth robbery, a ninth burglary or a fifteenth auto theft sufficient experience? How can we know when that occurs? Consider this: Does a 15-year-old who has been living on his own for months in abandoned urban buildings and has succeeded in breaking the connection with his family and in learning survival skills quite adequately (*responsibility*), who is quite aware of the ups and downs of robbing the check-cashing service by having witnessed a previous successful robbery and having received tips from a previous robber and fellow gang member (especially the downside of leaving a live witness), has secured a gun in order to better effect the robbery and likely murder (he has been constantly practicing with the gun) and covets what the income will do for his diet and next three months of survival generally (*perspective*) and has cased the service for weeks, knowing Tuesday nights are the best times to strike (*temperance*) have sufficient *maturity of judgment* to be held criminally liable for the armed robbery that resulted in the purposeful homicide of the store proprietor?

10 Recently, the U.S. Supreme Court has used categoricals in deciding the sentencing of some juveniles in CC. This trend began with *Roper v. Simmons* (2005), where the Court eliminated the

death penalty for juvenile murderers. The Court imposed prohibitions of mandatory life sentences for juvenile murderers (*Graham v. Florida,* 2010) and, life without parole sentences for non-murderers (*Miller v. Alabama*, 2012). These prohibitions are categorical, which the ATC is exploiting.

For example, Arya (2010) asserts that *Graham*

may be used to reform the juvenile and criminal justice systems by eliminating the ability to prosecute youth as adults in the first place (p. 100, footnote omitted).

******

(L)*awyers* (should) *consider using* Graham *to ensure that every child under the age of eighteen...is entitled to a chance to atone for his crimes and learn from his mistakes...* (Id., p. 102).

****

(*Graham* establishes) *the possibility of removing retribution as a valid goal of the criminal justice system as applied to youth, and firmly establishing a constitutional right to rehabilitation...* (Id.).

Arya (2010) wants the Supreme Court to "declare all transfer statutes... unconstitutional (Id., p. 103)."

The Supreme Court is all-powerful and can create all the categoricals it wants, even when history and constitutional law suggest otherwise. There is nothing stopping the Supreme Court from adopting the extreme policy position of eradicating transfer to CC. The dominant hold that ATC has had on transfer literature has produced biased/one-sided accounts of transfer that could lead the Court to make a regrettable decision. That potential development inspired this book.

11 It is one thing to insist you were pressured to drink beer or to smoke marijuana, it is quite another to argue you were pressured to rape or murder someone or even to burglarize a house or to rob at gunpoint. Zimring and the DPs insist that we must mitigate due to pressures of peer influence. The question, then, is when (if ever) does submission to gang influence run its course: one year, three years? Similarly, how many crimes (3, 7, 12) are required? If a 12-year-old joins a gang, is he/she under the same clock/offense consideration as a 15/16/17-year-old initial joiner? Does the resilience of gang affiliation count as mitigation (peer influence) or as aggravation (likely lack of desistence)? Is it a one-time mitigation or a perpetual one during juvenility? One or more of the group could be real followers. If the evidence supports that, the prosecutor might not transfer this/these defendant(s), and/or make a plea bargain to get this youth to roll on others. This could explain two youths charged with the same offense could end up with one in CC and the other in JC, having implications for research that relies upon "matched" pairs.

12 The DPs and Zimring ignore how much of a criminal nature and commitment to committing crime it takes to progress through or leapfrog levels of learning/attitudes/behaviors.

Just about all kids have done:

- does not take too much to talk back to parents/teachers;
- does not take much more to skip school, break curfew, smoke cigarettes, drink alcohol;
- does not take much more to shoplift, engage in minor vandalism/graffiti, trespass;

Fewer kids have done:

- it takes a little more to experiment with controlled substances;
- it takes a little more to break into a commercial building;
- it takes a decent bit to steal a car;
- it takes a lot more to burglarize a residence;

- it takes a lot more to burglarize an occupied residence;
- it takes a lot more to burglarize that occupied residence at night;

Even fewer kids have done:

- it takes a significant amount to rob/carjack someone;
- it takes a significant amount to rob/carjack someone at gunpoint;

Very few kids have done:

- it takes a tremendous amount to engage in sex/drug trafficking;
- it takes a hell of a lot to stab or shoot someone; and,
- it takes more than an incredible amount to purposely rape or murder someone.

The offenders along this continuum are not equal in their nature or behavior:

- in the reprehensibility of their actions;
- in the level of tolerance society should extend them; and
- in the level of court and punishment that should respond to them.

What needs to be examined and explained includes:

- do all juveniles share the same traits, suggesting it is the particular juvenile (i.e., offender) and not the traits of being a juvenile that are the problem;
- do only the offenders have the traits, meaning only the offenders clearly are at fault;
- if all juveniles do share the traits, then what is the explanation for youths to subdivide along the above continuum:

1. act out, but in non-criminal ways (talk back to teachers/parents);
2. commit only status offenses and do not cross the delinquency boundary;
3. commit only non-serious offenses and do not cross the chronic, serious, or violent boundary; and
4. simply elect not to commit any offenses.

13 Zimring's diminished responsibility (DR)-oriented cases might have to be removed from JC as well. A major branch of the ATC insists that juveniles are incompetent to stand trial (IST) (see Chapter 9), meaning there would be nowhere to prosecute the offenders. This IST situation would result in "a case without a courthouse." This topic typically is ignored by competency to stand trial (CST)-oriented ATC people and DR folks as well.

14 There is a world of difference between a 17-year-old first-offender who stole a car because friends were relentless in pushing him to do so versus the 17-year-old fourth-time recidivist who was the sixth in line to rape the young girl because he could not be the only one not to do so and save face. The former reasonably can be granted leniency and be retained in JC. The latter merits "no mercy" or immunity and should face full prosecution in CC, regardless of any lack of impulse control, deficits in moral recognition, or inability to withstand peer pressure.

15 Fagan, Zimring and the ATC take JC out of context. The common traits of JC in the early years were a population younger than 14 (55.2% between 1920 and 1939) who rarely committed serious (or violent) offenses. It is easy to understand the founders' naivete/optimism. Some offenders' potential depravity and intransigence must have shocked early JC workers. They concluded some of these offenders were beyond the JC's help and belonged "back" in CC. Even still, for decades, 99% or more of juvenile offenders were retained by JC, which is not good enough for Fagan and Zimring who appear committed to hang the founders for their original hyperbole or for not adhering to an extreme policy of permanent total inclusion.

16 It is uncertain whether Fagan and Zimring are critical of the founder's naivete or of the refusal of the founders to remain naïve and optimistic after seeing serious/repetitive behaviors by juveniles.

17 Public schools were specifically designed to educate. Does that mean that 100% of juveniles must be educated by public schools or the design has been corrupted/violated? Many juveniles and their parents elect to bypass those public schools and enroll in private schools. Juveniles can be disqualified from attending public school by virtue of misbehavior or schoolrule violations. These two groups account for considerable numbers of youths who do not attend public school. Nevertheless, public schools are not accused of failing in their mission due to the choices or behaviors of these youths/parents. Public schools are not mandated to educate 100% of youths or stand to be accused of failing their education mission.

18 Slobogin (2013) admited that the DPs' research can support transfer for most juveniles. *Even if the courts were to take a more explicitly empirical perspective, they are unlikely to conclude that deep mitigation is justified on the basis of youth. Research measuring youthful capacities indicates that mid and late adolescents, the juveniles who commit the bulk of the offending, possess a fairly high degree of cognitive maturity. Laurence Steinberg and Elizabeth Cauffman, the preeminent researchers in this area, state that under most circumstances the "vast majority of individuals below the age of thirteen lack certain intellectual and psychosocial capabilities that need to be present in order to hold someone fully accountable for his or her actions." But their research also indicates that, while fourteen through sixteen-year-olds are more impulsive, less risk-averse, more prone to peer influence, and less formed characterologically than adults, their judgments regarding antisocial conduct are not significantly different (in absolute terms) from those of young adults. Furthermore, Steinberg and Cauffman found that seventeen-year-olds generally "possess the intellectual and psychosocial capacities that permit the exercise of good judgment, even under difficult circumstances.... They also suggest, however, that even pre-teens might have full capacity for accountability when the consequences of their actions are clear and peer pressure is not involved* (p. 112, footnote 66, citations omitted).

19 There are numerous responses to the lesser mature/culpable ATC argument. That most juveniles do not commit chronic or violent transferable offenses questions the relevance of the traits that are supposed to make juveniles less mature/culpable. While *some juvenile offenders are more culpable than others, not all juvenile offenders are less culpable than adults.* Most critical, even where lesser culpability exists in a particular juvenile offender that does not necessarily mean that this offender merits to remain in the juvenile justice (JJ) system (this offender may still deserve a disposition more than the maximum available to JC) or that this offender deserves to be punished or sentenced below the CC threshold. The lesser maturity and culpability potential does not merit categorical inclusionary application (i.e., all juvenile offenders remain in JC). If we derive these *PRIC*/DR features from the lowest common denominator (delinquents) are not we just taking characteristics of these offenders and transforming them into defenses, excuses or arguments for reduced punishment? Are these characteristics representative of juveniles or just young offenders? Are older offenders devoid of these characteristics? What rules: age or character? Ironically, inasmuch as research has found some juveniles sentenced less harshly in CC than they potentially would have experienced in JC, should not the DPs/ATC welcome some transfers to CC?

20 Slobogin (2013) claimed the mentally ill are not processed in CC because they are not deterrable. *The lesser deterrability rationale has long sanctioned separate justice systems for people with mental*

disabilities on the theory that the prospect of criminal punishment is less likely to inhibit crimes by those types of individuals and that an alternative, prevention-oriented commitment regime is, therefore, necessary. The same rationale can easily justify a juvenile justice system, because juveniles as a group are demonstrably less risk-averse and more impulsive that adults… (p. 106, citations omitted). Important, the two groups are separated because the mentally ill lack responsibility, not deterrability.

21 Brink admited many adults will fail in this calculation and are not deterrable.

22 JC dispositions are purposely designed to improve juveniles' lives. Unless offenders climb to the highest JJ facility (a level 10 or prison; see Sanborn, 1985) it is possible they are better off after an adjudication in JC. That was the original JC plan and it still is. JCs may not always live up to their mandate, but, overall, juveniles have relatively little to fear in being adjudicated in JC. Expecting much in the way of deterrence for juvenile offenders is mostly pure folly. One implication of *no transfer due to no deterrence* is to increase the severity of JC dispositions to see if JC can get the attention and respect of juveniles. That potential is never addressed by the ATC.

23 Morse (1998) continueed with a critical explanation:
Risky conduct in general is different in important ways from conduct intended to cause immediate harm: risky conduct often is not criminal or seriously so; it often affects primarily the risktaker; often the probability of the harm risked may not be high; and finally, often the risked result is a long-term, rather than an immediate, consequence. For example, an adolescent may intentionally drive too fast and engage in other forms of bravado, but much conduct of this sort is not criminal. Much of the risk is to themselves, and the probability of a serious harm, such as death, is not high. Adolescents may also intentionally experiment with drugs, but they face only the longer term and low probability risks of endangering their ultimate social success and health. Similarly, adolescents may intentionally engage in unprotected sex, but such behavior is not criminal and creates again the longer term, low probability risk of disease and pregnancy, and so on. The harms risked are serious, but the risky conduct does not demonstrate substantial antisocial potential, and in none of these cases is the result practically certain. When an adolescent (or anyone else) decides whether to engage in risky conduct, the potential harm does not weigh as heavily as the adolescent's gratification. The latter is certain; the former is not. Moreover, driven by a desire for gratification, it is easier to fail to weigh sufficiently the interests of others that one does not desire to harm and to underestimate the longer term risk one's conduct produces (p. 54).
****
In sum, the relevance of the research on adolescent immaturity and poor judgment to intentional criminal behavior is unclear. The desire for immediate gratification is likely to exert more influence when the potential harm is uncertain (and not criminal) than when it is intended (and criminal). What is more, the moral reason not to engage in conduct is in general vastly stronger and more immediate when the harm is intended rather than risked, 64 which explains why we consider intentional harmdoing more culpable than risky harmdoing. Although poor judgment may be characteristic of adolescent risk-taking, there is no evidence that such judgment also infects intentional criminal behavior. Adolescents have stronger reason to avoid poor judgment when intentional criminal behavior is contemplated. If the primary variable adolescent offenders underestimate is the risk of getting caught for their wrongdoing, this is hardly reason to think that they are less responsible. More-over, recent research suggests that adolescents respond to the incentive structure of the juvenile and criminal law much like adults (Id., p. 55).

Chapter 9
The Elimination Argument, Part 2:
Juvenile Offenders Cannot Go to CC

ABSTRACT

Chapter 9 deals with the part of the anti-transfer crowd (ATC) campaign that argues juvenile offenders cannot go to criminal court (CC) for two reasons. The first is the ATC claim that the best interests (BI) of juvenile offenders must always prevail, which, impliedly, means transfer can never occur. This Chapter reveals how both segments of the sentence are incorrect. Nowhere in JC history has any reasonable authority asserted that the juveniles' BI were sacrosanct and that all offenders must be prosecuted in JC. Also ironic is that there are occasions in which the juveniles' BI would be served by transfer. The second alleged obstacle is that juveniles, en masse, are incompetent to stand trial (IST) due to the same characteristics we saw in Chapter 8 that were engineered to establish their lesser culpability. Chapter 9 debunks this contention, including a thorough critique of the concepts and research relied upon by the ATC to make their claim.

INTRODUCTION

The ATC has constructed two categoricals to ensure that juvenile offenders *cannot go to CC*. The ATC condemned categoricals when they mistakenly perceived them to be present in offense exclusion (OE). Seemingly, categoricals are acceptable to the ATC, however, provided they work in favor of their ideology.

A. Juveniles' Best Interests (BI) Must Always Prevail; Transfer is Illegitimate/Wrong

Although it is typically not the main or sole argument, the ATC frequently offers the primacy of juveniles' BI as an insurmountable obstacle to transfer (see Sabo, 1996, pp. 2446-53).

DOI: 10.4018/978-1-7998-7923-7.ch009

The scope of the prosecutor's virtually unfettered discretion makes her an inappropriate party to make the waiver decision. Prosecutorial waiver ignores the best interests of the juvenile ... and may place the prosecutor in the double bind of trying to ascertain the juvenile's best interests while simultaneously attempting to represent the community's best interests. Furthermore, prosecutorial waiver is not procedurally fair because it does not provide a hearing or written finding from which a juvenile can meaningfully appeal (Id., p. 2446).

If "prosecutorial waiver ignores the best interests of the juvenile," why there would be a double (or any) bind for the prosecutor? Moreover, if there is a conflict between the defendant's BI and society's BI, why are not prosecutors permitted to make the call since they are charged to represent society's interests. Moreover, judges make the same transfer decision. Unlike the prosecutor, however, the judge is charged with acting and serving as the embodiment of *parens patriae* in JC. *Parens patriae* is supposedly the doctrine establishing the state as the ultimate parent for errant children. Considering the judge's assigned and recognized role, wouldn't that make putting the transfer decision in the judge's hands also constitute a conflict of interests. The conflict would seem even greater with judges, leaving no one, then, who could make the transfer call without an alleged conflict, which some ATC members would cite as a reason for abolishing transfer.

The point of prosecutorial transfer (PT) is to give the juvenile offenders' BI much less, if any, weight. There is a hearing with PT; it just does not involve the amenability consideration. Instead, the sufficiency of the charge serves as the focus of the hearing. And there is an appeal for being charged or transferred, it is called trial in CC.

Similarly, Zimring and Fagan contended:

The best interests of serious delinquents might be better served by ***not allowing transfer at all...*** *(Zimring & Fagan, 2000, p. 412, emphasis added; see, also, Liwanga & Ibe, 2021; Notes, 2002; Rudman, Hartstone, Fagan, & Moore, 1986; Skibinski & Koszuth, 1986).*

The ATC claims JC was founded on that exclusive commitment to juveniles' BI (i.e., rehabilitate *all* offenders).

The Progressives who created the juvenile court envisioned a benevolent treatment agency staffed by expert judges and assisted by social services personnel. They emphasized informality, flexibility, and discretionary dispositions in the "best interests of the child... (Feld, 1987, pp. 482-83)."

****

The juvenile court's "rehabilitative ideal" envisioned a specialized judge trained in social science and child development whose empathic qualities and insight would enable her to make individualized therapeutic dispositions in the "best interests" of the child... (Feld, 1997, p. 71).

Transfer supposedly betrays this commitment to juveniles' BI; juveniles' BI must prevent transfer.

The first incorrect assertion, here, is that remaining in JC is always in the juvenile's BI. Some juvenile offenders would be better off in CC. The BI of retained juveniles are better served through the transfer of chronic/violent offenders (see Chapter 14). That translates into 90-95% of juvenile offenders (i.e., retained) are benefitted by transfer, which the ATC chooses to ignore.

Second, JC was not founded to promote the BI of *all* juvenile offenders. There are some ATC members that acknowledge this fact:

(S)imply because a juvenile system was created separate from the adult system ***did not mean that all youth would be tried and sentenced in the juvenile system.*** *In fact, juveniles were, and still are, often transferred to adult court... (Cauffman, Fine, Mahler & Simmons, 2018, p. 33, emphasis added).*

Offenders most likely to be transferred today involve juveniles who had not been permitted in JC originally. The framers' beliefs were formed while addressing mostly non-criminal behavior of youths younger than 14 (see Chapter 4). Moreover, even the *original JC Act* reflected concern for the community's interests and protection of the public. JC was founded

to secure for each minor subject hereto such care and guidance, preferably in his own home, as will serve the moral, emotional, mental, and physical welfare of the minor and the ***best interests of the community;*** *to preserve and strengthen the minor's family ties whenever possible, removing him from the custody of his parents only when his welfare or* ***safety or the protection of the public*** *cannot be adequately safeguarded without removal... (Illinois Juvenile Court Act, 1899, p. 131, emphases added).*

Older offenders and more serious crimes arriving in JC during the mid-Twentieth Century decades and later required reconceptualizing juveniles' BI in JC as well adopting broader opportunities to transfer those offenders whose BI did not merit priority.

Third, the progressive founders likely oversold their program. They created JC to be more of a social agency than a court of law. JCs' focus was mostly on status offenses and obnoxious "offenses." The founders perceived these juveniles as mostly blameless, whose BI could be promoted without serious and detrimental repercussions. It was safe to preserve the life chances of youths who merely misbehaved (much like parents are trusted to do) and to also preserve those life chances by preventing an evolution from youths' misbehaviors to crimes. Very few violent offenders found themselves in JC; society's interests could be mostly ignored, even assuming they differed from those of the youth's. More important, even the original JCs never gave offenders *carte blanche*. Moreover, assuming there ever was a completely blind and naïve commitment to an unassailable BI of all juvenile offenders, any such original commitment would have to have been adjusted before long, as the founders and their heirs learned the true capacity and tenacity of juvenile offenders.

Fourth, even assuming that furthering juvenile offenders' BI was the be-all and end-all of JCs back in the day,[1] since at least the 1960s and the U.S. Supreme Court's intervention into JC operations, JCs have been instructed by their legislatures to promote other interests that conflict with those of juvenile offenders. The older ages of defendants and the more serious offenses committed by juvenile offenders changed the atmosphere inside JCs, and encouraged legislatures to officially recognize JCs *should not be only about kids*. Society and victims also have interests at stake that are not always compatible with those of juvenile offenders. Those interests were finally and officially recognized in changes made to the Purpose Clauses of JC Acts following the 1960s (see Sanborn, 1994d). Although the BI of juveniles were still prominent and primary, they were no longer the sole interests to be officially respected and furthered in JCs. Society's BI and those of juveniles were no longer perceived as singular.[2]

B. *PRIC* Means Juveniles are Incompetent to Stand Trial (IST)[3]

The primary argument why juvenile offenders *cannot be* transferred to CC is that they are not competent to stand trial (CST). According to development psychologists (DPs), even when juvenile offenders are culpable and also are not amenable to JC treatment, juveniles, as a class, are purportedly incompetent to stand trial (IST), which serves as an insurmountable barrier to facing prosecution in CC. Transfer to CC cannot be allowed.

In the DPs' research and policy recommendations, the *PRIC* formula (***P***eer pressure, lack of both ***R***isk aversion and ***I***mpulse control and no long-term ***C***onsequences appreciation) that explains the lack of culpability when it comes to youth's committing crimes does double duty in establishing youths' being IST in CC, and possibly in JC, too.

To be CST, however, very little is required of a defendant as the U.S. Supreme Court held in *Dusky v. United States* in 1960.

To be competent to stand trial, defendants must have a rational and factual understanding of the nature of the proceedings against them, and an ability to consult with a lawyer with a reasonable degree of rational understanding. Thus, if defendants are basically aware that they are on trial for committing crimes and could be headed to probation, jail, or prison and can communicate with their attorneys about those offenses, they are likely to be found competent. Typically, a serious mental illness or an advanced stage of mental retardation would have to exist for a defendant to be incompetent to stand trial (Sanborn, 2009a, pp. 137-138, citations omitted).

All appellate courts have held that juvenile defendants must be CST because:[4]

- CST ensures the right to counsel, which requires CST (to cooperate/communicate);
- CST ensures that the juvenile understands the nature of the charges;
- CST is needed to prepare and present a defense (to increase accuracy of the proceedings);
- CST is needed to confront and cross-examine witnesses;
- CST is needed to be able to testify; and,
- CST ensures the right to be present at a hearing (for case law citations and current law, see Sanborn, 2009a, pp. 139-140; Larson & Grisso, 2011; O'Donnell & Gross, 2012; Panza, Deutsch, & Hermann, 2020).[5]

The DPs have developed two tests for determining juvenile IST. They involve maturity-of- judgment models that identify three psychosocial factors that share common elements.

The first model, proposed by Cauffman and Steinberg, contains the factors of "responsibility, temperance, and perspective." Responsibility pertains to the ability to be self-reliant, and to enjoy clarity of identity and healthy autonomy. Temperance involves one's ability to limit impulsivity, to avoid extremes, and to evaluate situations before acting. Perspective relates to one's ability to understand the complexity of a situation and place it in a broader context. Scott, Reppucci, and Woolard developed the second model, which addresses the factors of "conformity, risk perception, and temporal perspective." Conformity pertains to one's susceptibility to influence or tendency to comply with peers and parents. Risk perception involves just that, in addition to attitudes toward risk and a tendency to focus more on the possibility of gains than losses. Temporal perspective relates to the ability to consider both long- and short-term implications of behaviors, and to make decisions without being influenced by external pressures (Sanborn, 2009a, pp. 150-151, citing Cauffman & Steinberg, 1995, pp. 1773-1887; and Scott & Reppucci and Woolard, 1995, p. 229).[6]

Before maturity-focused juvenile CST research became vogue, Thomas Grisso, a leading scholar in the juvenile mental comprehension arena, summarized his and related research on juveniles' CST in 2000. This analysis preceded the infamous 2003 Grisso-led MacArthur Study.

(1) By age thirteen, most juveniles accurately identify trial participants and their roles, as well as the purposes of trial and that as defendants they are charged with offenses and are facing punitive consequences;
(2) By age fourteen, there are few differences vis-a-vis adults in understanding trial-related matters, and some will have the same abilities related to competency to stand trial as adults; and,
(3) By age fifteen, juveniles are as capable as adults in providing information to attorneys from their experiences, they can track the trial process as it unfolds and can relate one event to another later one (as in contradictory testimony), and they begin to develop the ability to think in terms of hypothetical conditions (Sanborn, 2009a, p. 154; see id. for citations).

According to these numbers, nearly all offenders that would be candidates for transfer are CST. Nevertheless, the DPs insist there is widespread juvenile IST that prevents legitimate transfer to CC.

C. DPs' Problematic Competency to Stand Trial (CST) Research Methodology

There was a burst of juvenile CST research conducted after the explosion in both juvenile violent crime and transfer provisions of the mid-1990s (see Table 42).[7] Most of the research had a small number of respondents and a suspect quality of tests used to gauge CST. Both limitations reduce the validity and reliability of the findings.[8] The results of the DPs' research mission to find juvenile defendants IST were far from being either consistent or supportive of the cause.

Sample Problems

The number of juveniles selected to participate in the CST research ranged from a low of 18 (Redlich, Silverman & Steiner, 2003) to 27 (Fanniff, 2009) to a robust 927 in the MacArthur Study (Grisso, Steinberg, Woolard, Scott, Graham, Lexcen, Reppucci, & Schwartz, 2003). Most samples were not representative of lawful or even delinquent juveniles; they were either:

- completely from the ranks of arrested or adjudicated delinquents (Baerger, Griffin, Lyons, & Simmons, 2003; Boyd, 1999; Cooper, 1995; Fanniff, 2009);
- completely from detention centers (Boyd, 1999; Fanniff, 2009; Ficke, Hart, & Deardorff, 2006; Krause, 1998; Poythress, Lexcen, Grisso, & Steinberg, 2006; Schmidt, Reppucci, & Woolard, 2003; Viljoen, 2004; Viljoen, Klaver, & Roesch, 2005; Viljoen & Roesch, 2005; Woolard, 1998); or long-term facilities (Schnyder, 1998);
- disproportionately from detention centers (Burnett, 1999; Grisso et al., 2003);

- completely male (Boyd, 1999; Krause, 1998; Lexcen, 2000; Lyle, 2003; Poythress et al., 2006; Schmidt, Reppucci, & Woolard, 2003; Schnyder, 1998; Warren, Aaron, Ryan, Chauhan, & DuVal, 2003; Woolard, 1998);
- completely from juveniles referred for a competency evaluation (Cowden & McGee, 1995; McGee, 1998; McKee & Shea, 1999); or,
- completely from juveniles already detained in psychiatric facilities (Lexcen, 2000; Warren et al., 2003).

Although delinquency is a common trait among all juveniles (Scott, 2000; Scott & Grisso 1997; Taylor-Thompson, 2003), DPs tend to examine *only* those youths who have been arrested and/or adjudicated, or worse, detained and institutionalized (some for CST evaluations). The general juvenile population has been ignored in most of the DP research.

The prevalent detention-only approach is particularly problematic. Only a minority of juvenile defendants experience detention (Sanborn & Salerno, 2005). "Unlike jail, detention is known as a holding ground for offenders with problems (Sanborn, 2009a, p. 210, citation omitted)." Not surprising, the DP studies consistently found the detained population had numerous emotional problems, substance abuse issues, and intellectual deficiencies, and presented considerably worse in these areas compared to the general juvenile population. Needless to say, "the test scores of (many) samples in the DPs' research on competency to stand trial cannot be said to reflect the competency of juvenile defendants in general (Id., p. 202)."[9] The tests scores are even furthered removed from reflecting the competency of the general juvenile population.

Testing Problems

Invariably, the respondents were given a pencil and paper survey that supposedly ascertained their CST via their knowledge of police- and court-related issues/situations. Some of the questions were exceedingly vague and subject to multiple legitimate answers. For example:

1. When a prosecutor offers a plea bargain, does that mean the prosecutor is "for" or "against" the defendant?
2. When the defense attorney reveals that the youth will probably be committed to a juvenile facility, does this mean the attorney is "for" or "against" the defendant?
3. When you have to go to court, does the judge know if you have ever been in trouble before?
4. Does the judge think about whether you have ever been in trouble before when s/he decides what is going to happen to you? (Cooper, 1995, pp. 42-44).

Offenders with a JC history would likely find themselves perplexed as to how to answer these questions, especially considering the viewpoint/bias of the DPs as to what were "correct" answers. In all the tests, there are no meaningful instructions provided and there is

no way to ascertain whether the test-taker is ignorant of court-related facts or cannot comprehend what a criminal trial is all about even after an explanation… (Sanborn, 2009a, p. 154).

The youths' knowledge of the dynamics of criminal procedure at test time does not indicate their CST. The examinations also ignored the fact that most youths will have counsel to assist them, particularly if they are potential candidates for placement in a juvenile facility.

While the first studies employed either the Competency Screening Test (CSTest; see Savitsky and Karras, 1984), the Georgia Court Competency Test (GCCT; see Cooper, 1995; Schnyder, 1998), or the Fitness Interview Test-Revised Edition (FIT-R; see Viljoen, 2004), most research has utilized the more advanced MacArthur Competence Assessment Tool — Criminal Adjudication (MacCAT-CA) developed primarily for the MacArthur Study. The MacCAT-CA

ascertains the individual's abilities in three contexts: ***Understanding*** *(the roles of opposing counsel, judge, jury);* ***Reasoning*** *(distinguishing more from less legally relevant information); and* ***Appreciation*** *(perception of being treated fairly). The MacCAT-CA has twenty-two items and involves the reading of a vignette (Sanborn, 2009a, p. 160, citations omitted, emphases in original).*

Although more advanced and specially developed, the MacCAT-CA shares a common deficiency with the other tests: they are not valid assessments of CST (Sanborn, 2009a, p. 197).[10] The MacCAT-CA has problems of its own, which was acknowledged by its developers such

that it cannot be the sole basis for a competency assessment and that it is not intended as a test of competency. Similar to other research-oriented tests, it measures knowledge rather than capacity to understand rights and the process as explained to the youth. It also forces the youth to focus on someone else's case via a vignette (Id., p. 199, citation omitted).[11]

In the MacArthur Study, Grisso et al. (2003) used vignettes to examine respondents' abilities to identify risks, their consideration of short- versus long-term consequences, and the degree of peer influence in response to three legal vignettes (e.g., cooperation during a police interrogation, disclosing information to an attorney and responding to a plea deal). Cooperation during police interrogation is not related to trial competence, and responding to a plea deal is incredibly subjective, as we have seen before. In addition, the focus of the survey questions is a problem, too:

A defendant's understanding of the trial process should not involve receiving points for offering "plausible" reasons for choosing between a bench and a jury trial. Many youths may have experienced or may have been told by defense attorneys that juvenile court judges will adjudicate regardless of the strength of evidence. Perhaps this would help explain why defendants with previous juvenile court experience perform "poorly" on these competency to stand trial tests (Sanborn, 2009a, p. 200).

Findings/Results Problem (i.e., Despite the Lack of a CST Problem)

Some of the most intriguing results from the DPs' research emanated from the sample referred for a competency evaluation. Despite the bias in that sample only the very youngest youths were found IST (81.8% of 11-year-olds and 72.7% of 12-year-olds). The population most likely to be subjected to transfer fared much better. The age-based CST rates were: 13 (55.6%) 14 (67.7%) 15 (84.4%) and 16 y/o (72%) (Cowden & McKee: 1995). With a larger sample, McKee (1998) found an 85.2% CST rate. Moreover, the juveniles outperformed the adults on knowing and defining charges, court officers and adversarial nature of court, appropriate court behavior, testifying and challenging witnesses, and disclosing facts to an attorney. Again, in the same category of offenders, McKee and Shea (1999) disclosed an 85.7% CST rate. Among two samples of psychiatric inpatients, age was neither a significant predictor of CST (Lexcen, 2000) nor accounted for significant age differences in MacCAT-CA scores (Warren et al., 2003).

The first implementation of the MacCAT-CA with juveniles (Krause, 1998) found no age differences in the CST-related results of the test. Juveniles did as well or better than adults:

[T]he results... indicate that juveniles do not, by nature of their develop-mental status alone, possess deficits in adjudicative competence relative to similarly functioning adults. Indeed, the juveniles included in this study demonstrated a level of understanding, reasoning, and appreciation that was no different from that of the adult comparison group .... [T]heir youth alone is not a bar to their ability to possess "a reasonable degree of rational understanding as well as a factual understanding of the proceedings" or to "assist in preparing" a defense (Krause, 1998, p. 78).

Equally interesting is the age-based equivalency went beyond mere cognitive elements:

Krause also found no significant difference by age on sensation seeking, suppression of aggression, impulse control, responsibility, or time perspective/future orientation. Krause explained "age did not appear to contribute significantly to differences in... decisional temperance or risk perception/sensation seeking."' No significant correlations existed between MacCAT-CA scores for any age and emotional distress, decisional temperance, risk perception, and perspective. The only significant correlation was between perspective and reasoning for adults only. This correlation supports the developmental theory that reasoning abilities improve the more one has the ability to consider others' feelings and reactions. However, younger adolescents nearly equaled, while older adolescents actually outscored, adults on the reasoning subscale (Sanborn, 2009a: 161, citing Krause, 1998, pp. 34, 45, 62, 65, 67, 75).

Woolard discovered *adolescent competence* that rivaled adults in Krause's sample.

[T]he stereotypes and research describing greater impulsivity and risk preferences in adolescents as compared to adults were not supported by these data .... The theory that adolescents focus more on losses than gains, and short term rather than long term consequences is not fully supported by the data (Woolard, 1998, p. 58,66).

Probably the most pertinent findings came from two studies that examined juveniles who were prosecuted in CC. In one study, juveniles were either forced into CC via mandatory exclusion (ME) (maximum JC age of 15) or were transferred there (Boyd, 1999). The second study compared transferred juveniles to adults and to juveniles who had been retained in JC (Poythress et al., 2006).

Boyd found juveniles between the ages of 13 and 17 to be equal to adults in CST terms:

Age was not associated with understanding and reasoning, but was associated with Appreciation. The author conceded that the correlation between age and appreciation "is probably not meaningful given the poor internal consistency of the Appreciation measure in this study."' All juvenile groups outscored the adults on understanding, while youths fifteen and younger tied the adults on reasoning, and sixteen- and seventeen-year-olds nearly accomplished this feat. Boyd concluded that, based on her findings, "the juveniles prosecuted as adults have similar competence-related abilities to those of adults.'' Boyd's study shows that qualified defendants are being chosen for criminal prosecution in North Carolina (Sanborn, 2009a: 164, citing Boyd, 1999, pp. 55, 57, 70-71).

Poythress et al. (2006) had similar results for transferred 16- and 17-year-olds compared to both adults and retained juveniles, some of whom fared better than adults.[12] They explained:

This examination of 16-17-year-old defendants transferred to criminal court by direct file found few differences between them and 18-24-year-old criminal defendants in competence-related abilities and developmental characteristics with potential significance for decision making in the legal process. Where differences existed, they suggested somewhat better performance for the Direct File sample than for the Adult Defendant sample. The results of this study, therefore, provide no basis for concern that direct-file mechanisms in the transfer to criminal court of 16-17-year-old male adolescents, who, as a result of immaturity, have impaired competence-related abilities relative to those of adults (p. 88)

In the end, the DPs' research yielded conflicting results along the lines of age:

- Mean scores improved with age: (Baerger et al., 2003; Burnett, 1999; Fanniff, 2009; Ficke et al., 2006; Grisso et al., 2003; Savitsky & Karras, 1984; Schnyder, 1998);
- Age mostly or simply not related: (Boyd, 1999; Krause, 1998; Lexcen, 2000; Lyle, 2003; Viljoen et al., 2005; Warren et al., 2003);
- Age in some areas was related/others not: (Fanniff, 2009; Redlich, Silverman, & Steiner 2003; Viljoen, 2004); and,
- Some/all juveniles beat adults in some/all areas: (Boyd, 1999; Burnett, 1999; Grisso et al. 2003; Krause, 1998; Poythress et al., 2006; Woolard, 1998).

By far, the variable that has been most consistently found to be most strongly and significantly related to performance on the CST tests is IQ.[13] Krause (1998) argued:

[I]ntelligence alone, and not age or the interaction between age and intelligence, appears to be contributing to differences in MacCAT-CA performance, especially on the Understanding and Reasoning Subscales .... [Krause noted that her] results suggest that differences in MacCAT-CA Understanding and Reasoning scores can be attributed to differences in intelligence, regardless of the impact of age or race. (p. 41)

The critical MacArthur Study found most juveniles to be CST. The Study divided their groupings of impairment (to CST) into minimal/no, mild, and significant levels. Using their criteria, the

MacArthur group identified 30% of the eleven- to thirteen-year-olds, 19% of the fourteen- to fifteen-year-olds, and 12% of the sixteen- to seventeen-year-olds and adults as "significantly impaired" due to scores on the Understanding and Reasoning subscales. Overall, adults performed slightly worse than the sixteen- to seventeen-year-olds. The study found no variation in gender, ethnicity, SES, and geography, but lower IQ scores were correlated with worse performances on the MacCAT-CA. In the end, age was related to risk recognition and long-term consequence identification, in addition to performance on the MacCAT-CA.

The MacArthur group admitted that they did not find large numbers of actual incompetent to stand trial adolescents since even "[a] score in the 'clinically significant impairment' range does not represent 'incompetence to stand trial.'" This admission was necessary because the MacCAT-CA "assesses capacities that are relevant for the competence question, but not legal competence itself (Sanborn, 2009a, p. 172, citing Grisso, et al., 2003, pp. 344, 347-48, 353-57)."

Employing the FIT-R, Viljoen (2004) used an adolescent norm formula to gauge CST. Only 16.2% of those between 11-14, and only 2.8% of those between 15-17 were impaired.

Reporting DP Research in A Disingenuous, If Not Purposely Misleading, Way

One might think that the DP research results were devastating to anyone supporting transfer to CC. However, most juvenile offenders are CST, according to the DPs. As Sanborn (2009a) reported:

Although the MacArthur group admitted that the study results had to be carefully interpreted, they emphasized that their study found that eleven to thirteen-year-olds were "more than three times" (actually 2.5 times-- 30% vs. 12%) "as likely as young adults to be 'seriously impaired' on the evaluation of competence-relevant abilities," while those fourteen to fifteen years old "were twice" (actually 1.6 times-19% vs. 12%) "as likely as young adults to be 'seriously impaired.' Success rates of 70% and 81%, respectively, for the eleven- to thirteen-year-olds and fourteen- to fifteen-year-olds were not sufficient to let them escape a suggestion from the MacArthur Study authors that they were presumptively incompetent: "Our results indicate that juveniles aged fifteen and younger are significantly more likely than older adolescents and young adults to be impaired in ways that compromise their ability to serve as competent defendants in a criminal proceeding. (pp. 172-3, citing Grisso et al., 2003, pp. 356-357)."

There is a serious problem with this reporting. At best, it is disingenuous, as Sanborn (2009a) noted:

While technically accurate, this reporting style is very misleading. Imagine the report that would have been written by the MacArthur group had 90% of the eleven- to thirteen-year-olds, 95% of the fourteen- to fifteen-year-olds, and 99% of the sixteen- to seventeen-year-olds and adults passed the MacCAT-CA. All of these imagined defendants would have performed better than those in the MacArthur Study (and probably close to actual numbers). The DPs would report, however, that among the imagined defendants, eleven- to thirteen-year-olds were ten times as likely, while fourteen- to fifteen-year-olds were five times as likely as sixteen- to seventeen-year-olds and adults to be incompetent to stand trial (p. 173, emphasis in original).[14]

Subsequent Misreporting of The DP Research

Despite their findings, the DPs assert that their research has discovered a CST problem among juvenile defendants.[15] Typically, the issue is phrased as juveniles' being *less* CST than adults (Chien, Coker, Parke, Tejani, Sirken, Sanchez-Jaquez, Rausch, & Azeem, 2015; Kivisto, Moore, Fite, & Seidner, 2011;

Larson & Grisso, 2011). Citing Grisso et al. (2003), McGowan et al. (2007) asserted that the MacArthur study "indicates that at less than 16 years of age, juveniles on average lack cognitive competence to understand and participate in the judicial process… (p. S8)." Similarly, Kivisto et al. (2011) claimed that "age has consistently been found to be related to trial competence…. (p. 317)." Chien et al. (2016) announced that "(s)everal studies have shown that age is related to a juvenile's competency to stand trial (p. 452)." They then cited only one study in support of that claim. Ironically, that cited study (Warren, DuVal, Komarovskaya, Chauhan, Bluffington-Vollum, & Ryan, 2009) emphasized the large proportion (72%) of juveniles who had been referred for clinical help due to being initially diagnosed as IST were eventually restored to competency. O'Donnell and Gross (2012) cited only 2 studies after having stated *several* studies have associated age with IST, but then they honestly asserted:

The notion that most juveniles are incompetent to stand trial in juvenile courts under prevailing legal standards, as suggested by some authors… does not seem well supported by research.

It is reasonable to conclude that developmental incompetence is likely to affect only a small proportion of juvenile cases for several reasons. First, as noted above, a relatively low proportion of juveniles score in the impaired range on criminal competency instruments. Second, arrest statistics indicate that a majority of juvenile defendants are over age 15 and thus fall outside of the age range where developmental immaturity is likely to be a concern… (pp. 990-91, citations omitted).

D. DP Research/Policy Recommendations based on Critical Faulty Premises

The findings of the DP research are questionable and exaggerated by the DPs and the ATC. Several critical premises adopted by the DPs in reaching their "conclusions" and in formulating their "recommendations" are seriously flawed and compromise what they propose. They are:

1. That CST is Relative or That There are Degrees of Competence

Defendants who are legally able to be tried should probably never have been called competent to stand trial (CST). Competent can easily be interpreted as having levels. Levels of competency in parenting and student performance are examples. However, CST does not have levels of relativity as the U.S. Supreme Court noted decades ago in *Godinez v. Moran* (1993):

Requiring that a criminal defendant be competent has a modest aim: It seeks to ensure that he has the capacity to understand the proceedings and to assist counsel. While psychiatrists and scholars may find it useful to classify the various kinds and degrees of competence… the Due Process Clause does not impose these additional requirements (p. 402).

Identifying trial-qualified defendants as certified or eligible to stand trial would have been wiser, less confusing, and not as likely subject to manipulation.

Defendants would not likely be considered more or less certified or eligible to stand trial. Some defendants are more competent than others in performing certain tasks, such as remembering the incident or communicating with counsel. To that extent, some defendants are "better" or more effective than others;

defendants have not been created equal in abilities. Once defendants have passed the necessary--that is, Dusky--threshold they are competent to stand trial; none is "more competent to stand trial" than others. Similarly, defendants must waive rights voluntarily with an understanding of the consequences of the waiver. While some defendants feel less pressure, are more intelligent, and possess a better understanding of the implications behind a waiver than others, surrender of rights by the better equipped is not "more valid" than when made by the lesser equipped (Sanborn, 2009a, p. 183).[16]

The DPs' cause depends on the relativity claim that juveniles are *less competent* than adults to stand trial. That is simply incorrect and amounts to a misrepresentation of the legal concept. At most, perhaps fewer juveniles will be found CST compared to adults.

In the end, defendants have a right to equal justice, but, contrary to the DPs' suggestions, there is no right to be as equally capable as others in performing as an accused at trial (Id., p. 184).

2. That All Juveniles are IST Because Juveniles on Average are "Less" CST Than Adults

Again, relying upon relativity, DPs argue that since *some* juveniles in their studies register *lower* scores on *some* competency tests, juveniles *as a group* are "less" CST than adults.

The scores that were earned by juveniles on the MacCAT-CA were not equal to those of adults which indicates that juveniles do not adequately understand all of the issues that are involved in competence to stand trial (Id., citing Burnett 1999, p. 88).[17]

The DPs are using the relativity focus/claim to cash in on the door they think was left open for this in *Roper v. Simmons* (2005) that categorically outlawed the death penalty for juvenile murderers due to their lesser culpability than adult murderers. The Supreme Court's reliance upon relativity in reaching the *Roper* decision does not transfer to CST standards, however.[18]

CST is not a categorical/group phenomenon; it is individual in nature. That juveniles may be less capable generally than adults does not render juveniles IST. That *more* juveniles could be found IST does not mean *all* juveniles are IST. Applying the DPs' logic/standards to adult groups could lead to declaring men IST because, compared to women, they are less capable of organized thinking. If "average" adults scored better on competency tests than those with any mental illness or slight retardation, the latter two groups could be claimed to be IST. The list of comparison groups is endless. Younger adults could be found "less" competent that older folks, who may also be superior in performances on tests than geriatrics. On the other hand,

(a)ssuming a fairly bright group of retirees can be located and tested as a comparison group, as long as their scores were better than younger adults, it might be impossible to prosecute anyone younger than sixty years old (Sanborn, 2009a, p. 186).[19]

The constitutional right to be CST is individual and personal, as is being declared IST. It is not enough to be the member of a group that has more incompetent members than other groups. CST is about thresholds. CST is not about relative standings or abilities.[20]

3. That All Juveniles of a Designated Age are IST Because Some or Most Juveniles of an Age are IST

The DPs again promote categoricals when arguing that when some members of a juvenile group are determined to be IST all members of that age group are IST. The MacArthur Study found 30% of the 11-to-13 years old IST. Despite those numbers, the DPs concluded that no one from this age group should ever be transferred to criminal court (Grisso et al., 2003, p. 344). According to this logic, if at least 30% (or maybe less) of any and all groups is found IST, that would call for/justify never criminally prosecuting any member of such group.

4. That CST is About Maturity of Judgment and Perfect Defendants

Previous research has demonstrated that teenagers are competent in cognitive ability. The Supreme Court has employed cognitive ability to develop the constitutional requirements of CST (*Dusky v. U.S.*, 1960). Since that focus results in the majority of even very young people being CST, the DPs expanded the scope of the CST inquiry to include maturity of judgment.[21]

There are no limits to what maturity of judgment can include: self-reliance or healthy autonomy, the ability to understand the complexity of a situation and to place it in a broader context, temperance or the ability to limit impulsivity, the ability to resist peer pressure, an appropriate attitude toward and perception of risk, or a balance of short-term and long-term perspectives. Moreover, juveniles' judgment can be slightly less developed or immature as compared to adults in any of these areas, and they can qualify as incompetent to stand trial (Sanborn, 2009a, p. 188, citations omitted).

The DPs' formula requires a perfect defendant and dictates that only that defendant is CST.[22]

Once upon a time, DPs recognized the difference between *effectiveness of participation* (EP) and *adjudicative competence* (AC) or CST, which was accepted as binary or non-relative.

Adjudicative competence directs us to examine the degree to which defendants are at risk of having deficits that seriously jeopardize their defense in ways that have constitutional implications, and the decision regarding this question is binary: the individual either is or is not competent to proceed to trial. In contrast, effectiveness of participation focuses on a continuum of lesser to greater capacities for contributing to one's defense, and it provides a foundation for seeking ways to maximize defendants' effectiveness (Sanborn, 2009a, p. 190, citing Grisso, 2000, p. 141, emphases added).[23]

Despite this recognition, the DPs have merged AC with EP, wanting the latter to be used to determine CST for juveniles. They have abandoned the binary, non-relative character of AC and have demanded that the relative character of EP become the actual measure of CST.[24]

It might be impossible for a juvenile to display sufficient effectiveness so that DPs agree there is CST. For example, they offer a scenario in which a boy was charged with felony murder and faced a 25-year minimum sentence. Although offered a plea bargain of 17 years, and despite the presence of strong evidence, the youth rejected the plea. The DPs perceived him to be IST.

Discussion with the examinee indicated that his decision making regarding the plea agreement and his insistence to go forward with a trial was significantly affected by his consideration of the 17-year sentence in light of his own age, and he specifically stated that the sentence was for a period of time longer than he had lived. Thus, although this 16-year-old "knew" that he faced a minimum of 25 years in prison if he was convicted, and he understood that a conviction was highly likely, his decision making was affected by his age and appreciation of time and was likely quite different than the decision making and appreciation of a 32-year-old male who might find himself in the same predicament (Otto & Goldstein, 2005, pp. 182-183).[25]

An alternative interpretation of this defendant's capacities can be constructed: he saw OJ Simpson and Casey Anthony walk away from "certain" convictions (all the pundits had predicted convictions and were wrong so why cannot the DPs' estimates be wrong in his case, also); he believed eight years is simply not enough of a discount for which to exchange a guilty plea (the reward should be greater); he calculated perhaps the jury and/or judge will engage in some partial or complete nullification and either convict on a lesser included offense (that would result in a "mere" 10-year-sentence) or acquit entirely. This juvenile would be savvy (and maybe or maybe not a risk taker) and certainly not IST.

In short, the DPs insist that juvenile defendants share the DPs' values and perspectives.

The DPs describe the need for defendants to understand the gravity of potential consequences of a criminal conviction in order to be competent. The critical question becomes, then, gravity according to whom? Competency demands a defendant's awareness that a conviction will potentially result in a ten-year prison sentence. But the DPs demand more; they want defendants to share their opinions on the gravity of the consequences. Thus, whereas that ten-year sentence could surely impress a DP accustomed to the good life, the failure of that same sentence to equally impress a juvenile offender supposedly constitutes incompetency. Repeat offenders' experiences with a juvenile justice system known for humane and possibly beneficial, rehabilitation-oriented dispositions (some youths end up in a facility that is an improvement over where they have lived) could also render them unimpressed with threatened sanctions for criminal behavior. The point is that neither juveniles nor adults need to have the same reactions to punishment as the DPs in order to be competent to stand trial (Sanborn, 2009a, p. 196, citation omitted, emphasis added).

5. That CST Involves Performances of Complex Activities

Steinberg and Cauffman (2000) have listed supposed *intricate competencies* for one to be found CST that would seem to require a college diploma, if not a law degree. The five competencies sound daunting, but are not:

- engage in *hypothetical and logical decision making* (in order to weigh the costs and benefits of different pleas or the likely outcome of guilty pleas/plea bargains versus pleas of not guilty; the strength of evidence against the accused; the likelihood of conviction and the possible sentence following one; the nature of prison, if applicable);
- demonstrate *reliable episodic memory* (in order to provide accurate information about the offense in question: can the youth recount the alleged offense?);

- *extend thinking into the future* (in order to envision the consequences of different pleas—see the first entry, above);
- engage in *advanced social perspective taking* (in order to understand the roles of prosecutors, judges, and defense attorneys as well as the motives of different participants in the adversarial process); and,
- understand and *articulate one's own motives and psychological state* (in order to assist counsel in mounting a defense; what does the youth want the defense attorney to do and why?) (p. 391)

Not one of these alleged competencies is statutorily or constitutionally required of adults to be CST. Moreover, when they are reduced to non-disciplinary jargon, they require nothing more than awareness of what is transpiring before them and ability to communicate with counsel. The DPs think 12 is the youngest we can expect defendants to be able to perform these tasks. Of course, that age (and above) would account for 98-99% of all transfers. Perhaps the most difficult task for those with previous JC experience is understanding that CC differs considerably from JC.

6. That CST Requires Belief in/Endorsement of the Ideals of the Adversary Process

Besides being perfect defendants, juveniles must endorse the DPs' ideal version of adversariness. An IST finding can result from failing to embrace any one of these ideals, including:

- there is a true adversarial contest in court;
- anything said to defense counsel will remain confidential;
- defense attorneys are advocates who will fight vehemently for the legal interests of the defendant;
- defendants must tell the defense attorney everything and be truthful; and,
- failure to trust and develop a meaningful relationship with counsel is wrong (see Sanborn, 2009a, p. 195).[26]

Studies suggests a very different picture of JC adversariness than that contemplated by the DPs.[27] Many juvenile defendants will have had vastly different personal experiences if they have been prosecuted previously in JC, especially as to the veracity of the first three ideals and the potential counterproductiveness of the fourth ideal.

7. That CST Matters Less in JC Than in CC; JCs Punish Less Than CCs

The DPs realize that their CST formula could potentially result in declaring nearly every juvenile offender IST. Categoricals tend to work that way. To avoid panic in the streets, perhaps, and as consolation for the radical competency standards they propose, the DPs assure us that juvenile offenders will be held accountable for their crimes. That accountability simply will have to occur in JC, instead of in CC. The ATC posits that juvenile offenders declared IST in CC can simply be returned to JC (Scott & Grisso, 2005, pp. 826-27). This needs to happen to avoid an "institutional crisis" that would occur if juvenile offenders could not be prosecuted in either court (Id., p. 827).

As a purely conceptual matter, the adoption of dual standards is quite feasible because competence, unlike many procedural protections is largely ***a continuous rather than a binary*** *construct (Id., p. 834, emphasis added).*

Five years earlier, Grisso had acknowledged the true binary nature of CST. The DPs warn that not accepting their compromise position will be a calamity for JC, and that CST is not very important there, anyway (see Grisso et al., 2003; Sellers & Arrigo, 2009; Steinberg & Cauffman, 2000)

(F)ailure to adopt their "relaxed" competency standard in juvenile court will lead to "serious disruption" in the prosecution of delinquency cases because forcing a "uniform competence standard" (i.e., Dusky) upon juvenile court will produce "a flood of petitions for competence evaluations and hearings, resulting in a major diversion of financial and human resources to a process that most would agree should have ***limited importance*** *in this legal setting (Sanborn, 2009a, p. 206, citing Scott & Grisso, 2005, pp. 835-836, emphasis added)."* [28]

There are numerous problems with what the DPs propose, perhaps foremost of which is their inability to develop an actual default standard for CST in JC. DPs talk of a "relaxed" or "tailored" JC standard, which is incomprehensible and impossible to implement.[29] JCs do not currently operate with a "lesser" standard of CST. The U.S. Supreme Court made it clear, in *Breed v. Jones* (1975), that JC adjudicatory hearings are equivalent to CC criminal prosecutions, at least in terms of the jeopardy that attaches in both proceedings. That such an equivalency exists between two hearings, but that they could operate with different CST standards, is impossible to believe.

Whenever one is charged with a crime the accused must be CST, regardless of the forum. That requirement is independent of the potential punishment. CST is not like the right to counsel or jury trial where potential sentence matters. CST is like the privilege against self-incrimination and the right to be convicted only upon proof beyond a reasonable doubt, which must be upheld regardless of the severity of the outcome. Also puzzling is what would be done with the many defendants who face more punishment in JC than they would in CC. Moreover, JCs today punish significantly (for serious crimes). Even minor offenses can result in lengthy dispositions since, in many JCs, it is still the youth's problem and not the offense that steers the sentence. Most important, JC adjudications can be factored into subsequent CC sentencing in most states (Sanborn, 1998, 2000). Adopting the DPs' stance minimally would require reversing both of those trends, as well as requiring the Supreme Court agree with officially holding that a first-class, jeopardy-related prosecution in JC allows a second-class level of CST for defendants.[30]

With little doubt, the DP ideology is not to ensure only CST juveniles are prosecuted for crimes, but rather to ensure there is no transfer to CC.[31] The DPs start juvenile CST dialogue insisting how important CST is to the integrity and dignity of proceedings; they claim neither can exist if the defendant is IST. By the end of the conversation, it is all about the preferred forum and not youths' CST. Evidently, JC proceedings require neither integrity nor dignity.[32]

8. That an IST Designation is Final and Fatal

The DPs did not discover an abundance of juveniles even in suspect locations, such as detention, to be IST. Multiple studies found majorities of juveniles who had been referred for a competency examination were CST (Cowden & McKee, 1995; McKee, 1998; McKee & Shea, 1999) as were juveniles who were housed in psychiatric facilities (Lexcen, 2000; Warren et al., 2003). Perhaps the most important fact is that research into the restoration process is impressive and positive. Research has found most juveniles initially determined to be IST were eventually restored to CST.

Our study examines the experiences of 563 youth ordered into restoration services after a judicial finding of adjudicative incompetence. Among this group, 72% were determined to be restored to competence usually within 90 to 120 days of services provided in the least restrictive environment allowed by the courts (Warren et al., 2009, p. 245).

****

These data indicate that 76% of (the 1,913) youth ordered into remediation services can attain competency, a percentage that is equal to that found among adult defendants determined by the court to be incompetent to stand trial.... However, age does matter to the remediation process with 66% of youth aged eight to 10 years being remediated all compared to 80% of those aged 11 to 13 and 76% of those 14 to 16 years of age... (Warren, Jackson, Skowysz, Kiefner, Reed, Leviton, Nacu, Jiggets, & Walls, 2019, p. 66, citations omitted).

****

In this study, subjects included all juveniles who were admitted to the Albert J. Solnit Children's Center for inpatient competency restoration in the period spanning January 1, 2005, through December 31, 2012. Sixty-one juveniles were referred during this period, and 58 were included in the final analyses (and 40 were restored). Several demographic and clinical variables were tested to identify which factors were associated with successful competency restoration. There was a high rate of psychiatric comorbidity in the sample, with 54 of 58 juveniles (93%), having more than one Axis I disorder. IQ was the only significant predictor of successful competency restoration...(Chien et al., 2016, p. 451).

So, there is really no juvenile CST problem, and in the few cases where a CST problem actually exists, a solution (restoration) is readily available.

E. The Takeaways from DPs' Juvenile CST "Research"

The "research" is seriously flawed for many reasons. This research has not even examined the extent of CST. It has ascertained the extent of juveniles' legal knowledge upon entering the system at most, as well as whether they share DPs' values and beliefs in the adversary process. DPs believe a youth's prediction of performance at a police interrogation is relevant to CST status. It is not.

Even still most juveniles have been found CST — at every age group examined (even the MacArthur study found a 70% CST rate among the 11- to 13-year-olds) — *with the expanded CST criteria they invented, and the law does not recognize*. In short, there is no juvenile CST problem. All of the "research" was conducted without any assistance or guidance provided to the youths, a situation dramatically unlike any courtroom experience. Even the numbers of alleged IST juveniles are grossly inflated/exaggerated due to seriously flawed DP methodology and reporting standards. Meanwhile, most youths originally designated or merely believed to be IST can be and are eventually restored.

The lack of a juvenile CST problem has not deterred the DPs/ATC from arguing that the legally non-existent "lesser" juvenile CST is an insurmountable barrier to transfer, with the identified relevant age varying only by the aggressiveness of the commentator.

There may be numerous juveniles who are actually IST, but it is not due solely, or even primarily, to age. Rather than age, deficiencies in IQ, psychiatric comorbidity and other mental impediments are what is going to render juvenile (and adults) IST (see Bath, Reba-Harrelson, Peace, Shen, & Liu, 2015; Chien et al., 2016). The only thing that is about age is the ATC's/DPs' policies that attempt to exploit age to prevent transfer.

Research has shown juvenile competency in so many other critical decision-making areas, such as abortion (see Ambuel & Rappaport, 1992; Foster & Sprinthall, 1992; Grisso, 1996; Weithorn & Campbell, 1982). It is simply incomprehensible, and more than merely counter-intuitive, for them to become alleged raging incompetents when it comes to comprehending the supposed complications of a criminal trial.

Inasmuch as CST is an individual trait and not a group phenomenon, CST and matters such as transfer to CC should be made on an individual and not categorical basis. Beschle (1999) noted that competencies are individually based and should be gauged/judged that way:

Perhaps this leads to the conclusion that categorical rules are therefore inappropriate, and that the degree to which adolescents' decisions are entitled to respect must be assessed and on an individual basis. This would support case-by-case determinations of whether a juvenile offender should be referred to the adult system, and at the same time, case-by-case consideration of whether an adolescent's reproductive decisions should be respected. Of course, this is precisely the system that now exists on these issues in many jurisdictions... (p. 104).

The most we get out of and can say about juvenile CST research is that *some, very young* juveniles *may be unaware* of *certain legal facts* (due to never having been taught legal facts?) or are skeptical of the justice they will receive in CC (based on JC experiences?) *suggesting* that perhaps these *few* are *unprepared* to face CC *alone at the time they enter* the system.

We saw previously that, in 1905, the PA Supreme Court manufactured a distorted version of *parens patriae* as authority for PA JCs to prosecute offenders without any rights, and that this decision, lacking a legitimate foundation, became the foundation for every other state to hold the same for their youths. It remains to be seen whether a DP/ATC policy based upon research that has no legitimate foundation will experience a similar history in becoming the foundation for the prohibition of transfer to CC due to a purported IST condition among a few juvenile offenders.

In the end, to conclude that there is no IST problem, large scale or otherwise, among juveniles seems more than reasonable.[33]

REFERENCES

Ambuel, B., & Rappaport, J. (1992). Developmental trends in adolescents' psychological and legal competence to consent to abortion. *Law and Human Behavior*, *16*(2), 129–154. doi:10.1007/BF01044794 PMID:11659675

Baerger, D. R., Griffin, E. F., Lyons, J. S., & Simmons, R. (2003). Competency to stand trial in preadjudicated and petitioned juvenile defendants. *The Journal of the American Academy of Psychiatry and the Law*, *31*, 314–320. PMID:14584530

Bath, E., Reba-Harrelson, L., Peace, R., Shen, J., & Liu, H. (2015). Correlates of competency to stand trial among youths admitted to a juvenile mental health court. *The Journal of the American Academy of Psychiatry and the Law*, *43*, 329–339. PMID:26438811

Beschle, D. L. (1999). The juvenile justice counterrevolution: Responding to cognitive dissonance in the law's view of the decision-making capacity of minors. *Emory Law Journal*, *48*, 65–105.

Beyth-Marom, R., Austin, L., Fischhoff, B., Palmgren, C., & Jacobs-Quadrel, M. (1993). Perceived consequences of risky behaviors: Adults and adolescents. *Developmental Psychology*, *29*(3), 549–563. doi:10.1037/0012-1649.29.3.549

Bonnie, R. J., & Grisso, T. (2000). Adjudicative competence and youthful offenders. In T. Grisso & R. G. Schwartz (Eds.), *Youth on trial: A developmental perspective on juvenile justice* (pp. 73–103). University of Chicago Press.

Boyd, J. C. (1999). *The competence-related abilities of juveniles prosecuted in criminal court* [Unpublished doctoral dissertation, University of South Florida, Tampa, FL, United States].

Breed v. Jones. (1975). 421 U.S. 519.

Burnett, M. R. 1999. *Evaluation of competency to stand trial in a juvenile population* [Unpublished doctoral dissertation, University of Southern Mississippi, Hattiesburg, MS., United States].

Buss, E. (2000). The role of lawyers in promoting juveniles' competence as defendants. In T. Grisso & R. G. Schwartz (Eds.), *Youth on trial: A developmental perspective on juvenile justice* (pp. 243–265). University of Chicago Press.

Cauffman, E., Fine, A., Mahler, A., & Simmons, C. (2018). How developmental science influences juvenile justice reform. *University of California Irvine Law Review*, *8*, 21–40.

Cauffman, E. E., & Steinberg, L. (1995). The cognitive and affective influences on adolescent decision-making. *Temple Law Review*, *68*, 1763–1789.

Cauffman, E. E., Woolard, J., & Reppucci, N. D. (1999). Justice for juveniles: New perspectives on adolescents' competence and culpability. *Quinnipiac Law Review*, *18*, 403–419.

Chien, J., Coker, K. L., Parke, S., Tejani, N., Sirken, R. A., Sanchez-Jaquez, C., Rausch, F., & Azeem, M. W. (2016). Predictors of competency to stand trial in Connecticut's inpatient juvenile competency restoration program. *The Journal of the American Academy of Psychiatry and the Law*, *44*, 451–456. PMID:28003389

Cooper, D. K. (1995). *Juvenile competency to stand trial: The effects of age and presentation of factual information in the attainment of competency in juveniles* [Unpublished doctoral dissertation, University of Georgia, Athens, GA, United States].

Cowden, V. L., & McKee, G. R. (1995). Competency to stand trial in juvenile delinquency proceedings: Cognitive maturity and the attorney-client relationship. *Journal of Family Law, 33*, 629–661.

Dusky v. United States. (1960). 362 U.S. 402.

Ex parte Daniecki. (1935). 117 N.J. Eq. 527, 177 Atl. 91. N. J. Court of Errors and Appeals.

Ex parte Mei. (1937). 122 N.J. Eq. 125, 192 Atl. 81. N.J. Court of Errors and Appeals.

Fanniff, A. M. (2009). *The measurement ofjuveniles' competence related abilities*. [Unpublished doctoral dissertation, The University of Arizona. Tucson, AZ, United States].

Feld, B. C. (1987). The juvenile court meets the principle of the offense: Legislative changes in juvenile waiver statutes. *The Journal of Criminal Law & Criminology, 78*(3), 471–533. doi:10.2307/1143567

Feld, B. C. (1997). Abolish the juvenile court: Youthfulness, criminal responsibility, and sentencing. *The Journal of Criminal Law & Criminology, 88*(1), 68–136. doi:10.2307/1144075

Ficke, S. L., Hart, K. J., & Deardorff, P. A. (2006). The performance of incarcerated juveniles on the MacArthur Competence Assessment Tool — Criminal Adjudication (MacCAT-CA). *The Journal of the American Academy of Psychiatry and the Law, 34*, 360–373. PMID:17032960

Foster, V., & Sprinthall, N. A. (1992). Developmental profiles of adolescents and young adults choosing abortion: Stage sequence, decalage, and implications for policy. *Adolescence, 27*(107), 655–673. PMID:1414576

Furby, L., & Beyth-Marom, R. (1992). Risk taking in adolescence: A decision-making perspective. *Developmental Review, 12*(1), 1–44. doi:10.1016/0273-2297(92)90002-J

Garrison, E. G. (1991). Children's competence to participate in divorce custody decisionmaking. *Journal of Clinical Child and Adolescent Psychology, 20*(1), 78–87. doi:10.120715374424jccp2001_10

G.J.I. v. State (1989). 778 P.2d 485, 487. Oklahoma Court of Criminal Appeal.

Godinez v. Moran. (1993). 509 U.S. 389.

Grisso, T. (1986). *Evaluating competencies: Forensic assessments and instruments*. Plenum Press. doi:10.1007/978-1-4899-5046-8

Grisso, T. (1996). Society's retributive response to juvenile violence: A developmental perspective. *Law and Human Behavior, 20*(3), 229–247. doi:10.1007/BF01499022

Grisso, T. (1997). Juveniles' competence to stand trial: New questions for an era of punitive juvenile justice reform. In Puritz, P., Capozello, A., & Shang, W. (Eds.), More than meets the eye: rethinking assessment competency and sentencing for a harsher era of juvenile justice (pp. 23-32). American Bar Association Juvenile Justice Center

Grisso, T. (1998). *Instruments for assessing understanding & appreciation of Miranda rights*. Professional Resource Press/Professional Resource Exchange.

Grisso, T. (2000). What we know about youths' capacities as trial defendants. In T. Grisso & R. G. Schwartz (Eds.), *Youth on Trial: A Developmental Perspective on Juvenile Justice* (pp. 139–171). University of Chicago Press.

Grisso, T., Miller, M. O., & Sales, B. (1987). Competency to stand trial in juvenile court. *International Journal of Law and Psychiatry, 10*(1), 1–20. doi:10.1016/0160-2527(87)90009-4 PMID:3610428

Grisso, T., Steinberg, L., Woolard, J., Cauffman, E. E., Scott, E. S., Graham, S., Lexcen, F., Reppucci, N. D., & Schwartz, R. (2003). Juveniles' competence to stand trial: A comparison of adolescents' and adults' capacities as trial defendants. *Law and Human Behavior, 27*(4), 333–363. doi:10.1023/A:1024065015717 PMID:12916225

Grisso, T., & Vierling, L. (1978). Minors' consent to treatment: A developmental perspective. *Professional Psychology, 9*(3), 412–427. doi:10.1037/0735-7028.9.3.412 PMID:11662545

Heilbrun, K., Hawk, G., & Tate, D. C. (1996). Juvenile competence to stand trial: Research issues in practice. *Law and Human Behavior, 20*(5), 573–578. doi:10.1007/BF01499043

Illinois Juvenile Court Act. (1899). An act to regulate the treatment and control of dependent, neglected and delinquent children. *Illinois Laws*, 133-137.

Kivisto, A. J., Moore, T. M., Fite, P. A., & Seidner, B. G. (2011). Future orientation and competency to stand trial: The fragility of competence. *The Journal of the American Academy of Psychiatry and the Law, 39*, 316–326. PMID:21908747

Krause, M. S. (1998). *Methodological and developmental issues in the assessment of adjudicative competence*. [Unpublished doctoral dissertation, University of Virginia, Charlottesville, VA, United States].

Larson, K. A., & Grisso, T. (2011). *Developing statutes for competency to stand trial in juvenile delinquency proceedings: A guide for lawmakers*. National Youth Screening and Assessment Project. Models for Change, System Reform in Juvenile Justice.

Lewis, C. C. (1980). A comparison of minors' and adults' pregnancy decisions. *The American Journal of Orthopsychiatry, 50*(3), 446–453. doi:10.1111/j.1939-0025.1980.tb03304.x PMID:7406029

Lexcen, F. J. 2000. *Factors Associated with Juvenile Competence to Stand Trial: Neuropsychological, Psychopathological, and Psychosocial Variables*. [Unpublished doctoral dissertation, University of Virginia, Charlottesville, VA, United States].

Liwanga, R. C., & Ibe, P. (2021). Transfer of child offenders to adult criminal courts in the USA: An unnecessary exercise, unconstitutional practice, international law violation, or all of the above? *Georgia Journal of International & Comparative Law, 49*, 99–128.

Lyle, V. K. (2003). *Emotional maturity and trial competence in urban male adolescents.* [Unpublished doctoral dissertation, Walden University. (Online)].

Mann, L., Harmoni, R., & Power, C. (1989). Adolescent decision-making: The development of competence. *Journal of Adolescence, 12*(3), 265–278. doi:10.1016/0140-1971(89)90077-8 PMID:2687339

McKee, G. R. (1998). Competency to stand trial in preadjudicatory juveniles and adults. *The Journal of the American Academy of Psychiatry and the Law*, *26*, 89–99. PMID:9554713

McKee, G. R., & Shea, S. J. (1999). Competency to stand trial in family court: Characteristics of competent and incompetent juveniles. *The Journal of the American Academy of Psychiatry and the Law*, *27*, 65–73. PMID:10212027

Melton, G. B., Petrila, J., Poythress, N. G., Slobogin, C., Otto, R. K., Mossman, D., & Condie, L. (1997). *Psychological evaluations for the courts: A handbook for mental health professionals and lawyers* (2nd ed.). Guilford Publications.

Morris v. Slappy. (1983). 461 U.S. 1.

Notes. (2002). For the good of the child, for the good of society: Using Scotland and Jamaica as models to reform U.S. juvenile justice policy. *Harvard Law Review, 115,* 1964-1987.

O'Donnel, P. C., & Gross, B. (2012). Developmental incompetence to stand trial in juvenile courts. *Journal of Forensic Sciences*, *57*(4), 989–996. doi:10.1111/j.1556-4029.2012.02093.x PMID:22384998

Otto, R. K., & Goldstein, A. M. (2005). Juveniles' Competence to Confess and Competence to Participate in the Juvenile Justice Process. In K. Heilbrun, N. E. S. Goldstein, & R. E. Redding (Eds.), *Juvenile delinquency: Prevention, Assessment, and Intervention* (pp. 179–208). Oxford University Press. doi:10.1093/med:psych/9780195160079.003.0009

Panza, N. R., Deutsch, E., & Hamann, K. (2020). Statutes governing juvenile competency to stand trial proceedings: An analysis of consistency with best practice recommendations. *Psychology, Public Policy, and Law*, *26*(3), 274–285. doi:10.1037/law0000237

People v. Bruno. (1931). 346 Ill. 449. Illinois Supreme Court.

People v. Fitzgerald. (1926). 322 Ill. 54. Illinois Supreme Court.

People v. Lattimore. (1935). 362 Ill. 206, 199 N.E. 275. Illinois Supreme Court.

Peterson-Badali, M., & Abramovitch, R. (1992). Children's knowledge of the legal system: Are they competent to instruct legal counsel? *Canadian Journal of Criminology*, *34*(2), 139–160. doi:10.3138/cjcrim.34.2.139

Poythress, N. G., Lexcen, F. J., Grisso, T., & Steinberg, L. (2006). The competence-related abilities of adolescent defendants in criminal court. *Law and Human Behavior*, *30*(1), 75–92. doi:10.100710979-006-9005-4 PMID:16729209

Redding, R. E. (2000). *Adjudicative competence in juveniles: Legal and clinical issues*. Juvenile Justice Fact Sheet.

Redlich, A. D., Silverman, M., & Steiner, H. (2003). Pre-adjudicative and adjudicative competence in juveniles and young adults. *Behavioral Sciences & the Law*, *21*(3), 393–410. doi:10.1002/bsl.543 PMID:12808697

Roper v. Simmons. (2005). 543 U.S. 551.

Rudman, C., Hartstone, E., Fagan, J., & Moore, M. (1986). Violent youth in adult court: Process and punishment. *Crime and Delinquency*, *32*(1), 75–96. doi:10.1177/0011128786032001005

Sabo, S. (1996). Rights of passage: An analysis of waiver of juvenile court jurisdiction. *Fordham Law Review*, *64*, 2425–2454.

Sanborn, J. B. Jr. (1993a). Philosophical, legal, and systemic aspects of juvenile court plea bargaining. *Crime and Delinquency*, *39*(4), 509–527. doi:10.1177/0011128793039004006

Sanborn, J. B. Jr. (1994c). Remnants of *parens patriae* in the adjudicatory hearing: Is a fair trial possible in juvenile court. *Crime and Delinquency*, *40*(4), 599–615. doi:10.1177/0011128794040004008

Sanborn, J. B. Jr. (1994d). The juvenile, the court, or the community: Whose best interests are currently being promoted in juvenile court? *Justice System Journal*, *17*(2), 249–266. doi:10.1080/23277556.1994.10871207

Sanborn, J. B. Jr. (1995b). How parents can affect the processing of delinquents in juvenile court. *Criminal Justice Policy Review*, *7*(1), 1–26. doi:10.1177/088740349500700101

Sanborn, J. B. Jr. (1998). Second-class justice and first-class punishment: The use of juvenile records in sentencing adults. *Judicature*, *81*, 206–213.

Sanborn, J. B. Jr. (2000). Striking out on the first pitch in criminal court. *Barry Law Review*, *1*, 7–61.

Sanborn, J. B. Jr. (2009a). Juveniles' competency to stand trial: Wading through the rhetoric and the evidence. *The Journal of Criminal Law & Criminology*, *99*, 135–214.

Sanborn, J. B. Jr, & Salerno, A. W. (2005). *The juvenile justice system: Law and process*. Roxbury Publishing Company. Oxford University Publishing.

Savitsky, J. C., & Karras, D. (1984). Competency to stand trial among adolescents. *Adolescence*, *19*, 349–358. PMID:6464817

Scherer, D. G. (1991). The capacities of minors to exercise voluntariness in medical treatment decisions. *Law and Human Behavior*, *15*(4), 431–449. doi:10.1007/BF02074080 PMID:11660093

Schmidt, M. G., Reppucci, N. D., & Woolard, J. L. (2003). Effectiveness of participation as a defendant: The attorney-juvenile client relationship. *Behavioral Sciences & the Law*, *21*(2), 175–198. doi:10.1002/bsl.532 PMID:12645044

Schnyder, C. (1998). *The competence of juveniles to assist in their own defense: An investigation of trust and understanding in the attorney relationship*. [Unpublished doctoral dissertation, University of Alabama, Tuscaloosa, Alabama, United States].

Scott, E. S. (2000). Criminal responsibility in adolescence: Lessons from developmental psychology. In T. Grisso & R. G. Schwartz (Eds.), *Youth on Trial: A Developmental Perspective on Juvenile Justice* (pp. 291–324). University of Chicago Press.

Scott, E. S., & Grisso, T. (1997). The evolution of adolescence: A developmental perspective on juvenile justice reform. *The Journal of Criminal Law & Criminology*, *88*(1), 137–189. doi:10.2307/1144076

Scott, E. S., & Grisso, T. (2005). Developmental incompetence, due process, and juvenile justice policy. *North Carolina Law Review, 83*, 793–845.

Scott, E. S., Reppucci, N. D., & Woolard, J. L. (1995). Evaluating adolescent decision making in legal contexts. *Law and Human Behavior, 19*(3), 221–244. doi:10.1007/BF01501658

Sellers, B. G., & Arrigo, B. A. (2009). Adolescent transfer, developmental maturity and adjudicative competence: An ethical and justice policy inquiry. *Criminology, 29*, 435–488.

Skibinski, G. J., & Koszuth, A. M. (1986). Getting tough with juvenile offenders: Ignoring the best interests of the child. *Juvenile & Family Court Journal, 37*(5), 43–50. doi:10.1111/j.1755-6988.1986.tb00854.x

Steinberg, L., & Cauffman, E. (2000). A developmental perspective on jurisprudential boundary. In Fagan. J., & Zimring, F.E. (Eds.), The Changing Borders of Juvenile Justice: Transfer of Adolescents to the Criminal Court (pp. 379-406). University of Chicago Press.

Steinberg, L., & Schwartz, R. G. (2000). Developmental psychology goes to court. In T. Grisso & R. G. Schwartz (Eds.), *Youth on Trial: A Developmental Perspective in Juvenile Justice* (pp. 9–31). University of Chicago Press.

Tanenhaus, D. S. (2000). The evolution of transfer out of the juvenile court. In J. Fagan & F. E. Zimring (Eds.), *The changing borders of juvenile justice: Transfer of adolescents to the criminal court* (pp. 13–43). University of Chicago Press.

Taylor-Thompson, K. (2003). States of mind/states of development. *Stanford Law & Policy Review, 14*, 143–156.

Viljoen, J. L. 2004. *Police interrogation and criminal adjudication of child and adolescent defendants: Legal abilities, decisions, and standards*. [Unpublished doctoral dissertation, Simon Fraser University, British Columbia, Canada].

Viljoen, J. L., Klaver, J., & Roesch, R. (2005). Legal decisions of preadolescent and adolescent defendants: Predictors of confessions, pleas, communication with attorneys, and appeals. *Law and Human Behavior, 29*(3), 253–277. doi:10.100710979-005-3613-2 PMID:15965628

Viljoen, J. L., & Roesch, R. (2005). Competence to waive interrogation rights and adjudicative competence in adolescent defendants: Cognitive development, attorney contact. and psychological symptoms. *Law and Human Behavior, 29*(6), 723–742. doi:10.100710979-005-7978-y PMID:16382358

Warren, J. I., Aaron, J., Ryan, E., Chauhan, P., & DuVal, J. (2003). Correlates of adjudicative competence among psychiatrically impaired juveniles. *The Journal of the American Academy of Psychiatry and the Law, 31*, 299–309. PMID:14584528

Warren, J. I., DuVal, J., Komarovskaya, I., Chauhan, P., Buffington-Vollum, J., & Ryan, E. (2009). Developing a forensic service delivery system for juveniles adjudicated incompetent to stand trial. *International Journal of Forensic Mental Health, 8*(4), 245–262. doi:10.1080/14999011003635670

Warren, J. I., Jackson, S. L., Skowysz, B. E., Kiefner, S. E., Reed, J., Leviton, A. C. R., Nacu, M. N., Jiggetts, C. J., & Walls, G. G. (2019). The competency attainment outcomes of 1913 juveniles found incompetent to stand trial. *Journal of Applied Juvenile Justice Services, 18*, 47–74. doi:10.52935/19.23118.1

Weithorn, L. A. (1983). Involving children in decisions affecting their own welfare: Guidelines for Professionals. In G. B. Melton, G. P. Koocher, & M. J. Saks (Eds.), *Children's competence to consent* (pp. 235–260). Springer. doi:10.1007/978-1-4684-4289-2_12

Weithorn, L. A., & Campbell, S. B. (1982). The competency of children and adolescents to make informed treatment decisions. *Child Development, 53*(6), 1589–1598. doi:10.2307/1130087 PMID:7172783

Wong, T. (2002). Adolescent minds, adult crimes: Assessing a juvenile's mental health and capacity to stand trial. *University of California Davis Journal of Juvenile Law & Policy, 6*, 163–188.

Woolard, J. L. (1998). *Developmental aspects of judgment and competence in legally relevant contexts.* [Unpublished doctoral dissertation, University of Virginia, Charlottesville, VA, United States].

Woolard, J. L. (2001). *Understanding violence from a developmental perspective*. University of Florida Studies in Criminology & Law, Position Paper.

Zapf, P. A., & Roesch, R. (2005). An investigation of the construct of competence: A comparison of the FIT, the MacCAT-CA, and the MacCAT-T. *Law and Human Behavior, 29*(2), 309–320. doi:10.100710979-005-2194-4 PMID:15912726

Zimring, F. E. (2000b). The punitive necessity of waiver. In J. Fagan & F. E. Zimring (Eds.), *The Changing Borders of Juvenile Justice: Transfer of adolescents to the criminal court* (pp. 207–224). University of Chicago Press.

Zimring, F. E., & Fagan, J. (2000). Transfer policy and law reform. In J. Fagan & F. E. Zimring (Eds.), *The changing borders of juvenile justice: Transfer of adolescents to the criminal court* (pp. 407–424). University of Chicago Press.

ENDNOTES

1 Even in the early days of the JC, appellate courts recognized that JC was not meant to either service all offenders or to put their BI first and only. The Illinois Supreme Court upheld direct file, evidencing that not all juvenile offenders were headed to JC, and that society had an interest, perhaps equal or superior to the juveniles,' to be represented in the prosecution of some juvenile offenders (see *People v. Fitzgerald*, 1926; and, *People v. Bruno*, 1931). Other appellate decisions revealed much of the same attitude/perspective, one from the Illinois Supreme Court and two from the New Jersey Court of Errors and Appeals (from Tanenhaus, 2000, pp. 27-29):
It was not intended by the legislature that the juvenile court should be made a haven of refuge where a delinquent child of the age recognized by law as capable of committing a crime should be immune from punishment for violation of the criminal laws of the state committed by such child subsequent to his or her being declared a delinquent child (People v. Lattimore, 1935, p. 275).
****

[I]*t is inconceivable that the Legislature intended to make the juvenile court a sanctuary for juvenile felons* (*Ex parte* Daniecki, 1935, p. 92).
****

[T]*hat a charge which is in effect that of murder cuts so deeply into human emotions, collides so violently with life's experiences and fair expectations, and is so horrible in fact and in contemplation of society, that it remains a crime within the purview of the Constitution, whatever name and whatever treatment may be appended to it by the Legislature* (*Ex parte* Mei, 1937, p. 83).

2 The *Gault* decision also made it clear that the contest in JC was adversarial. If only the BI of offenders must be advanced by JCs, purpose clauses in nearly every state would have to be amended to reflect the following: *Regardless of the number and severity of crimes committed by those younger than 18, the defendants' BI must prevail. The state's response to criminal offenses must always be only about and for juvenile offenders. Public protection, the interests of society, justice for the victim, and the BI of JC and retained defendants must yield to would-be transfers' BI.*

3 Most of this Chapter relies heavily upon and is borrowed from Sanborn, 2009a.

4 The Oklahoma Court of Criminal Appeals held CST is not required because JC proceedings are rehabilitative (see *G.J.I. v. State*, 1989).

5 As Sanborn (2009a) explained: *Recently, several states have adopted formal positions regarding competency to stand trial in juvenile court. Nevertheless, twenty states continue to process defendants in juvenile court without a clearly and broadly applicable competency standard. Thirteen states have mostly or completely transported Dusky or their criminal court provision on competency to stand trial to juvenile court. Finally, eighteen jurisdictions have adopted specific standards on competency to stand trial in juvenile court, via either juvenile court statutes or court rules* (p. 140, citations omitted; see id. for citations). Appellate courts have found even mentally challenged juveniles CST in JC/CC (see Id., pp. 143-149).

6 The DPs theorize juvenile defendants suffer numerous deficits, and, compared to adults, will be defendants less effective in many ways (see Sanborn, 2009a, pp. 151-152).

7 Most of the research involved PhD dissertations (see Boyd, 1999; Burnett, 1999; Cooper, 1995; Fanniff, 2009; Krause, 1998; Kyle, 2003; Lexcen, 2000; Schnyder, 1998; Woolard, 1998; Viljoen, 2004).

8 While measuring the responses of remarkably small samples of respondents may be (in Zimring's words) the *grist mill of DP dissertations/research*, those numbers do not provide a sufficient foundation from which either to extrapolate to CST conditions among age groups or juveniles in general, or to develop broad policy recommendations regarding juvenile CST or transfer to CC.

9 The reliability and validity of these findings are suspect. If delinquency theories were derived from similar samples, the research would be summarily dismissed.

10 As Sanborn (2009a) noted: *While research can tell us what to look for in terms of a defendant's deficiencies and what can be done to improve competence, it cannot tell us if any group of juveniles is competent. The research tests yield high rates of false positives, which probably explains why they are not typically employed by evaluators who actually determine a defendant's competency* (p. 198, footnotes and citations omitted)." All the CST "tests" used on juveniles have serious methodological problems (see Id.).

11 The MacCAT-CA has serious methodological problems (Sanborn, 2009a, pp. 199- 200).

12 The MACCAT-CA study did not prove juveniles' IST. On some measures juveniles outperformed adults (see Sanborn, 2009a, pp. 179-80).

13 See Boyd, 1999; Burnett, 1999; Ficke et al., 2006; Grisso et al., 2003; Lyle, 2003; Schnyder, 1998; Warren et al., 2003.

14 After an analysis of CST studies, Sanborn (2009a) summarized the findings: *Thus far, the DPs' research has not supported their claim that juveniles are incompetent to stand trial in criminal court. Examination of arguably the most salient and significant variable in this inquiry, scores on various competency tests, has produced divided results. Age has been found related and not related to these scores. The relationship between age and various factors has also produced conflicting results. Thus, factors such as peer attachment or influence, accepting a plea bargain, risk perception, risk appraisal, risk recognition, risk preference, and future orientation or temporal perspective have and have not been associated with age. Otherwise, age has been found related but not significantly to understanding the defense attorney's role, and to responsibility and consideration of others, but not in a linear fashion and with no adverse effects on performance in the MacCAT-CA. Age was associated with not agreeing with counsel and with not seeking an appeal.* (pp. 181-82). Sanborn also offered a comprehensive list of factors found to be supposedly related and not related to juvenile CST (see Id.).

15 See Bonnie & Grisso, 2000; Heilbrun, Hawk, & Tate, 1996; Oberlander, Goldstein, & Ho, 2001; Sellers & Arrigo, 2009; Scott, 2000; Steinberg & Cauffman, 2000; Steinberg & Schwartz, 2000; Wong, 2002; Zimring, 2000b.

16 Sanborn (2009a) continued: *A parallel situation can be seen in licensed automobile drivers. Some drivers are better than others at performing certain driving-related tasks, and there are some incompetent drivers, but that does not mean that some are "more licensed to drive" than others. Once all drivers pass the necessary minimum threshold, they occupy the same legal status as a licensed driver. There would have been much confusion if authorized drivers were identified as competent to drive instead of licensed to do so* (p. 183).

17 In similar fashion, Grisso asserted: *The question for policy and judicial decisions about juvenile competence, therefore, is not whether they have deficits in these areas, but whether their deficits are sufficiently great to render them less capable of participating in their defense than is the average adult defendant. Do adolescents' capacities relevant for trial competence differ on average from those of adults* (Sanborn, 2009a, p. 184, citing Grisso, 1997, p. 29)?

18 Sanborn (2009a) distinguished culpability from competency: (U)*nlike competency, culpability has long been recognized as relative, such that aggravating and mitigating circumstances, such as youth, should affect sentencing. Inasmuch as there needs to be proportionality between culpability and punishment (and offense), especially in capital cases, it is hardly astonishing that the Supreme Court would find that juveniles are generally less culpable than adults and less deserving of the ultimate punishment. The lesser culpability of juveniles was (a) cornerstone of the founding of juvenile court. Competency to stand trial is not a matter of proportionality, however; it is equally necessary for the prosecution of crime in juvenile and criminal court. Moreover, whereas most (if not all) fourteen- and fifteen- year-old murderers could demonstrate lesser culpability vis-a-vis adult murderers (everything's being relative in culpability), most (if not all) fourteen- and fifteen-year-old juvenile murderers would be competent (unless the elements of competency are radically redefined)* (pp. 184-185). For more distinguishing characteristics, see Id.

19 As Sanborn (2009a) explained: *Another problem with this premise is that juveniles of the same age are not necessarily on the same developmental page. There will be considerable variation in the capabilities of all fifteen-year-olds, some of whom will be more capable than some adults. As Grisso notes, they will differ markedly in their ability-and inclination-to:*

- *take an active role in decision making and monitoring the trial process;*

• *consider both short-range and long-range consequences when making decisions;*
• *respond to assistance offered by parents and attorneys; and*
• *manage their behavior both inside and outside the courtroom ....*
Thus, there could be sub-groups of juveniles less competent than other juvenile groups (who, in turn, could be more competent than some groups of adults). Perhaps public school-educated adolescents, overall, would not fare as well as private school students. Or perhaps delinquents would score lower, on average, than non-delinquents on competency tests; if so, then no delinquent would ever be able to stand trial (p. 186, citing Grisso, 2000, p. 143).

20 In other words: **all** *defendants who fulfill the* Dusky *requirements are competent to stand trial, regardless of whether one group of these defendants is better equipped than another generally in terms of satisfying the* Dusky *criteria. Otherwise, all juveniles would escape from criminal liability simply because some of them-and not necessarily the ones who are facing trial-fall below the average adult's capability or score. The adults who fall below the average juvenile and adult scores, perhaps significantly, but who are above the* Dusky *threshold are competent to stand trial, so why would juveniles, en masse, be incompetent to stand trial and collectively receive a walk* (Sanborn, 2009a, pp. 186-187, emphasis in original). See Id., for more detailed problems with the DPs' way of thinking here.

21 See Cauffman & Steinberg, 1995; Cauffman, Woolard & Repucci, 1999; Scott, Reppucci & Woolard, 1995; Taylor-Thompson, 2003; Wong, 2002.

22 See Bonnie & Grisso, 2000; Grisso, 1986, 2000; Melton, Petrila, Poythress, Slobogin, Otto, Mossman, & Condie,1997; Oberlander, Goldstein & Ho, 2001; Redding, 2000; Woolard, 2001; Zapf & Roesch, 2005.There may be no limit to the potential IST factors, including a *lack of empathy and an inability to take another's perspective or an inability to tolerate the stress of trial or to behave appropriately in court, including having "some capacity to tolerate shame, humiliation, loss of respect, disapproval, and guilt." Moreover, defendants must be motivated to self-defense (for example, questioning the permissibility of guilty pleas), and must be able to appraise the likely outcome of the proceedings. It is also not enough that juveniles simply appreciate the prospect of conviction and punishment, they must be able to gauge whether the judge will treat them more or less fairly than other defendants charged with the same crime. Other factors include a youth's suggestibility, parental influence, and the defense attorney's personality characteristics. In effect, the DPs want an idealized defendant, a veritable Philosopher King, in order to be competent to stand trial. More than just adult-like maturity, juveniles must also possess wisdom and emotional stability. Thus, juveniles would have to be both competent and extremely effective in order to stand trial in criminal court* (Sanborn, 2009a, p. 189, citations omitted).

23 Grisso was not alone in this acknowledgment, as Woolard and Reppucci admitted: *Effective participation goes beyond the consideration of constitutionally required capacities to include those capacities that might affect the nature and quality of a defendant's participation but* **do not cross the threshold of incompetence to stand trial**.... (Sanborn, 2009a, p. 190, citing Woolard & Reppucci, 2000, p. 173, emphasis added). DPs Schmidt and colleagues also acknowledged the difference between AC and EP: *(A)n interesting distinction between the concept of* adjudicative competence *as it is legally defined and the notion of* effective participation *as a defendant. Whereas the legal definition of adjudicative competence establishes a minimum standard of required capacities for a defendant's case to go forward, effective participation encompasses abilities beyond those that are constitutionally required that may influence the quality and nature of a defendant's participation in the trial process*

without crossing the threshold for legal competence .... In particular, youths who have the cognitive capacities required to meet the formal legal criteria for competence to stand trial under the Dusky standard may nevertheless possess certain developmental characteristics that impair their effective participation as trial defendants.... (Sanborn, 2009a, p. 190, citing Schmidt, Repucci & Woolard, 2003, citations omitted).

24 While these maneuvers have done little to advance an understanding of juvenile CST, they have promoted the DPs' objectives to militate against transfer to CC. *The DPs have created the perfect criterion for keeping juvenile defendants from ever being found competent to stand trial in the maturity of judgment theory. First, the maturity requirement is immeasurable. Adolescents mature at different rates and times, and can even experience periods of regression. In short, they are all over the "maturity map." Not only are youths ever shifting within the maturity spectrum, but the inventors of the maturity of judgment theory admit that the maturity elements are variable as well and are dependent upon context.... Moreover, there is no agreement as to what constitutes maturity or how maturity is best measured. Thus, gauging maturity is a very subjective analysis that will vary considerably among evaluators. Using such a requirement as the basis for a competency determination would create serious equal protection problems in that the determination of competency would depend upon the particular examiner involved* (2009a, pp. 191-192, citations omitted). For more problems in this context, see Sanborn, 2009a, p. 192.

25 Evidently, the thinking of 32-year-olds is the latest criterion by which to gauge the CST of 16-year-olds. What if this youth were acquitted? There is no way to determine whether the thinking of juveniles and 32-year-olds would have differed; the latter could have made the same decision. The DPs simply did not like/agree with this defendant's choice, so the youth is IST in their eyes.

Moreover, a "different" decision does not equate to an incompetent decision. Conviction and a twenty-five-year minimum sentence were highly likely, but not guaranteed. A clearly thinking sixteen-year-old could have thought that an eight-year reduction was not a sufficient discount for his guilty plea. Rejection of this offer surely does not automatically constitute an absence of logic, let alone render the defendant incompetent to stand trial (Sanborn, 2009a, p. 193).

The 16-year-old could have been convinced the jury would be sympathetic due to his youth or he knew that a necessary witness would not appear at trial or would recant a damaging statement that incriminated him (perhaps his fellow gang members helped the witness disappear). It may have been that "since I guarantee myself 17 years inside with a guilty plea, I might as well roll the die and see if I can walk away." The DPs' facts do not make a case that this defendant is IST.

Sanborn (2009a) pointed out: *Calling for youth or immaturity alone to be the basis for incompetency to stand trial would be like allowing mental illness or retardation alone to qualify as incompetent. A better case can be made for mental illness or retardation automatically to be grounds for incompetency, since these individuals are likely to have impaired thinking capabilities, and not simply underdeveloped or developing capabilities. Compared to the general population, those with mental disorders could have:*

- *less clarity in their thinking and analysis abilities;*
- *less ability to appraise the likely outcome of the proceedings;*
- *less overall understanding of the proceedings;*
- *less ability to empathize with others;*

- *less ability to tolerate the stress of trial;*
- *less ability to behave properly in court;*
- *less memory about events;*
- *less ability to think long-term;*
- *less ability to defer gratification;*
- *less ability to relate to defense counsel;*
- *less inclination to disclose information to counsel;*
- *less ability to discuss strategy with counsel;*
- *more susceptibility to the suggestions and urgings of others;*
- *more impaired communication skills;*
- *more paranoia and distrust of counsel and judges; and,*
- *more problems in experiencing psychotic delusions.* (p. 194).

26 See Grisso, 1998; Grisso, Miller & Sales, 1987; Lyle, 2003; Peterson-Baldi & Abramovitch, 1992; Redding, 2000; Redlich, Silverman & Steiner, 2003; Schmidt, Reppucci & Woolard, 2003; Schnyder, 1998. Grisso also demanded meaningful collaboration with defense counsel, but the Supreme Court explicitly rejected this in *Morris v. Slappy* (1983).

27 JC research has found numerous features that challenge the plausibility of the DPs' ideal notion of the adversary contest. Prosecutors and defense attorneys regularly plea bargain, suggesting there is more cooperation than adversariness (Sanborn, 1985, 1993a). Private defense attorneys reveal defendants' confidences to parents because the latter are the paying customer; confidentiality is not guaranteed (Sanborn, 1995b). Guardian defense attorneys promote the youths' treatment interests rather than their legal interests, and fight for an adjudication/plea deal rather than an acquittal (Sanborn, 1994c), making the attorney appear as an enemy. Youths could know any disclosure of guilt to the attorney means they cannot take the stand and lie. The DPs have examined many juveniles with prior JC experience who might not believe in "adversarial contests," "confidential disclosures," "advocate defense attorneys," "full and honest disclosures to counsel," or in developing a "meaningful relationship with counsel." These stances make them more perceptive than cynical/distrustful and means they are truly qualified defendants, not IST.

28 As Sanborn (2009a) pointed out: *This proposition is puzzling. Statutes and case law have applied* Dusky *to juvenile courts for years. Yet, there has been barely a trickle (let alone a flood) of appellate case law in this area and no widespread reports of disruption in juvenile court. By far, however, the most puzzling aspect of the DPs' proposal is their description of the "tailored juvenile court standard." "Under the competence criteria that [the DPs] endorse, a youth facing a delinquency proceeding must have a basic understanding of the charges and proceeding and of her position as defendant in that proceeding, and the capacity to communicate with her attorney." Of course, this "relaxed," "tailored" standard is indistinguishable from that established by* Dusky (p. 206, citing Scott & Grisso, 2005, pp. 836, 838, footnote omitted).

29 Sanborn (2009a) has demonstrated the implausibility of the DPs' proposal: *The DPs explain that the juvenile court standard means the youth could have a "lesser ability to foresee remote consequences" of a conviction and still be competent. But a greater or lesser ability to foresee remote consequences not only defies measurement, it also is not related to or required by competency criteria. The DPs also assert that youths would "need not understand how advocacy is translated into practice in a way that would be required of an adult," whatever that means; but this, too, is not measurable and is not related to or required for competency to stand trial. Finally, the DPs*

contend that youths "need not have the ability to weigh the value of defense strategies, or to advise counsel accordingly," which also is not a part of competency to stand trial and thus also not required of adult defendants. The DPs have not created a "relaxed" standard of competency for juvenile court. Instead, the DPs are attempting to rewrite constitutional law to guarantee no juveniles are prosecuted in adult court (p. 207, quoting Scott & Grisso, 2005, p. 838).

30 The prosecution-in-JC-as-consolation-prize for imposing the DPs' CST standards is illogical and implausible. The DPs' "research" used tests that used watered-down CST factors and standards, considerably below those employed in CC. Although only a minority of juveniles "failed" those tests, the DPs claimed entire groups were IST for criminal prosecution. Assuming failures by only a minority of juveniles continue to drive the DP policy, how can anyone from an age group that had some members who failed the CST tests be considered CST even in JC?

31 As Sanborn (2009a) previously observed: *It does tend to support a theory, however, that the DPs' research and policy pursuits have been more concerned with ensuring that juvenile defendants do not see criminal court rather than ensuring that only truly competent juvenile defendants stand trial in either system. As one defense attorney in the DP camp offered: "If a finding of incompetence could secure the minor's adjudication in juvenile court, a lawyer should think twice about engaging in efforts to enhance her client's trial competence in adult court* (p. 197, quoting Buss, 2000, p. 252)."

32 Sanborn (2009a) pointed out: *If competency to stand trial were the real concern, DPs should welcome prosecution in criminal court. The very things that purportedly offend the DPs, such as lesser advocacy by defense counsel and violation of confidentiality between counsel and defendant, are trademarks of juvenile court. First, the DPs denigrate juvenile defendants (and accuse them of being incompetent) for their believing, perhaps after directly experiencing, that, among other things, defense attorneys will not work diligently for their acquittal. Then, the DPs insist that the solution for this alleged incompetency is holding trial in juvenile court where juvenile defendants are likely to (re)encounter that very same lack of vigorous representation. And, the DPs are willing to reduce the supposed competencies associated with competency to stand trial so as to allow this prosecution to occur in juvenile court. Actually, taking the DPs' logic to its natural extreme, if juvenile court is to become the haven for juvenile defendants who are theoretically incompetent to stand trial, then competent juveniles should be prosecuted in criminal court, particularly all sixteen- and seventeen-year-olds who regularly outperform adults on the competency tests employed in DP research* (p. 212).

33 Numerous studies have found few differences between adolescents and adults in formal decision-making abilities (see Ambuel & Rappaport, 1992; Garrison, 1991; Lewis, 1980; Scherer, 1991; Weithorn & Campbell, 1982). The conclusions reached in several studies are that by age fourteen or fifteen, little distinguishes adolescents from adults in the cognitive capacity aspect of decision-making (see Beyth-Marom, Austin, Fischhoff, Palmgren, & Jacobs-Quadrel, 1993; Furby & Beyth-Marom, 1992; Grisso & Vierling, 1978; Mann, Harmoni & Power, 1989; Weithorn, 1983.

CHAPTER 9 TABLES

Table 42. Research on Juveniles' Competency to Stand Trial (CST)

Baerger, Griffin, Lyons, & Simmons, (2003)
Boyd, (1999)
Burnett, (1999)
Cooper, (1995)
Cowden & McKee, (1995)
Fanniff, (2009)
Ficke, Hart & Deardorff, (2006)
Grisso et al., (2003)
Krause, (1998)
Lexcen, (2000)
Lyle, (2003)
McKee, (1998)
McKee & Shea, (1999)
Otto, Poythress, Nicholson, & Edens, (1998)
Poythress, Lexcen, Grisso, & Steinberg, (2006)
Redlich, Silverman & Steiner, (2003)
Savitsky & Karras, (1984)
Schmidt, Repucci, & Woolard, (2003)
Schnyder, (1998)
Viljoen, (2004)
Viljoen, Klaver, & Roesch, (2005)
Viljoen & Roesch, (2005)
Warren, Aaron, Ryan, Chauhan, & DuVal, (2003)
Woolard, (1998)

Table 42 References

Baerger, D. R., Griffin, E. F., Lyons, J. S., & Simmons, R. (2003). Competency to stand trial in preadjudicated and petitioned juvenile defendants. *The Journal of the American Academy of Psychiatry and the Law*, *31*, 314–320.

Boyd, J. C. (1999). *The competence-related abilities of juveniles prosecuted in criminal court* [Unpublished doctoral dissertation, University of South Florida, Tampa, FL, United States].

Burnett, M. R. 1999. *Evaluation of competency to stand trial in a juvenile population* [Unpublished doctoral dissertation, University of Southern Mississippi, Hattiesburg, MS., United States].

Cooper, D. K. (1995). *Juvenile competency to stand trial: The effects of age and presentation of factual information in the attainment of competency in juveniles* [Unpublished doctoral dissertation, University of Georgia, Athens, GA, United States].

Cowden, V. L., & McKee, G. R. (1995). Competency to stand trial in juvenile delinquency proceedings: Cognitive maturity and the attorney-client relationship. *Journal of Family Law, 33*, 629–661.

Fanniff, A. M. (2009). *The measurement of juveniles' competence related abilities*. [Unpublished doctoral dissertation, The University of Arizona. Tucson, AZ, United States].

Ficke, S. L., Hart, K. J., & Deardorff, P. A. (2006). The performance of incarcerated juveniles on the MacArthur Competence Assessment Tool — Criminal Adjudication (MacCAT-CA). *The Journal of the American Academy of Psychiatry and the Law, 34*, 360–373.

Grisso, T., Steinberg, L., Woolard, J., Cauffman, E. E., Scott, E. S., Graham, S., Lexcen, F., Reppucci, N. D., & Schwartz, R. (2003). Juveniles' competence to stand trial: A comparison of adolescents' and adults' capacities as trial defendants. *Law and Human Behavior, 27*, 333–363.

Krause, M. S. (1998). *Methodological and developmental issues in the assessment of adjudicative competence*. [Unpublished doctoral dissertation, University of Virginia, Charlottesville, VA, United States].

Lexcen, F. J. 2000. *Factors Associated with Juvenile Competence to Stand Trial: Neuropsychological, Psychopathological, and Psychosocial Variables*. [Unpublished doctoral dissertation, University of Virginia, Charlottesville, VA, United States].

Lyle, V. K. (2003). *Emotional maturity and trial competence in urban male adolescents*. [Unpublished doctoral dissertation, Walden University. (Online university)].

McKee, G. R. (1998). Competency to stand trial in preadjudicatory juveniles and adults. *The Journal of the American Academy of Psychiatry and the Law, 26*, 89–99.

McKee, G. R., & Shea, S. J. (1999). Competency to stand trial in family court: Characteristics of competent and incompetent juveniles. *The Journal of the American Academy of Psychiatry and the Law, 27*, 65–73.

Otto, R. K., Poythress, N., Nicholson, R. A., & Edens, J. F. (1998). Psychometric properties of the MacArthur Competence Assessment Tool — Criminal Adjudication. *Psychological Assessment, 10*, 435–443.

Poythress, N. G., Lexcen, F. J., Grisso, T., & Steinberg, L. (2006). The competence-related abilities of adolescent defendants in criminal court. *Law and Human Behavior, 30*, 75–92.

Redlich, A. D., Silverman, M., & Steiner, H. (2003). Pre-adjudicative and adjudicative competence in juveniles and young adults. *Behavioral Sciences & the Law, 21*, 393–410.

Savitsky, J. C., & Karras, D. (1984). Competency to stand trial among adolescents. *Adolescence, 19*, 349–358.

Schmidt, M. G., Reppucci, N. D., & Woolard, J. L. (2003). Effectiveness of participation as a defendant: The attorney-juvenile client relationship. *Behavioral Sciences & the Law, 21*, 175–198.

Schnyder, C. (1998). *The competence of juveniles to assist in their own defense: An investigation of trust and understanding in the attorney relationship*. [Unpublished doctoral dissertation, University of Alabama, Tuscaloosa, Alabama, United States].

Viljoen, J. L. 2004. *Police interrogation and criminal adjudication of child and adolescent defendants: Legal abilities, decisions, and standards*. [Unpublished doctoral dissertation, Simon Fraser University, British Columbia, Canada].

Viljoen, J. L., Klaver, J., & Roesch, R. (2005). Legal decisions of preadolescent and adolescent defendants: Predictors of confessions, pleas, communication with attorneys, and appeals. *Law and Human Behavior*, *29*, 253–277.

Viljoen, J. L., & Roesch, R. (2005). Competence to waive interrogation rights and adjudicative competence in adolescent defendants: Cognitive development, attorney contact. and psychological symptoms. *Law and Human Behavior*, *29*, 723–742.

Warren, J. I., Aaron, J., Ryan, E., Chauhan, P., & DuVal, J. (2003). Correlates of adjudicative competence among psychiatrically impaired juveniles. *The Journal of the American Academy of Psychiatry and the Law*, *31*, 299–309.

Woolard, J. L. (1998). *Developmental aspects of judgment and competence in legally relevant contexts*. [Unpublished doctoral dissertation, University of Virginia, Charlottesville, VA, United States].

Chapter 10
The Limitation Argument, Part 1:
Minimizing the Transfer Target

ABSTRACT

Chapter 10 deals with the anti-transfer crowd (ATC) tactic of limiting the reach of transfer to criminal court (CC), assuming its elimination proves unattainable. The ATC mission, here, is to limit the target of transfer, especially in terms of age, offense, and disposition. A common claim is that only older (typically 16 and 17) delinquents should be transfer eligible. Inasmuch as the vast majority of transfers involves youths of this age the claim is mostly moot. Another argument is that only violent and person-related crimes should be transferred. This Chapter emphasizes that the chronic offender, the most prevalent subject of transfer, would very likely be beyond transfer's reach under this formula, which was probably the ATC's goal. Finally, the ATC demands that transfer be limited to youths who "require" a sentence longer than that available to JC. Although this is a critical reason for transfer, it is far from the only/primary reason to transfer.

INTRODUCTION

While some ATC members are *no-transfer* types, *some* concede *some* transfer is needed.

No scholar or practitioner or advocate denies that it is sometimes necessary to transfer adolescents to criminal court. The public must be protected from dangerous youth who are not likely to be helped by treatment-oriented or supervisory sanctions... (Fagan, 2008, pp. 37-38).

It would appear, then, that total inclusion types are neither scholars nor practitioners. In the alternative, perhaps Fagan has simply not encountered these folks or read their works.

DOI: 10.4018/978-1-7998-7923-7.ch010

The Age Focus

The claimed necessary circumstances for transfer vary. Sometimes it is a matter of a minimum age. Some ATC representatives simply emphasize that transfers should be "older" (NRC, 2013). Other ATC members concentrate on an age below which transfer is unacceptable, such as 12 due to ramifications of incarcerating these youths with adults, (Deitch, Barstow, Lukens, & Reyna, 2009), or 13 due to CST concerns (Steinberg, 2000; Steinberg & Cauffman, 2000), or 14 due to culpability limits (Hoeffel, 2013), or 15 due to fairness requirements (see Drizin & Tanenhaus, 2002, p. 690), or 16/17 due to a desire to preserve "life chances" (Zimring, 2000a, 2000b; see, also, IJA/ABA, 1980, pp. 15-16; NAC, 1980, p. 303). Feld (2000) identified the choices as among 14, 15 or 16 years of age (p. 112). More recently, Feld chose a minimum age of 16 (2017a). The ABA originally recommended 16, but later reduced it to 15 (Flicker, 1983, p. 11). DPs admit that youths "as young as 9 have the capacity for intentional behavior and know the difference between right and wrong (Steinberg, 2000, p. 6)." More important, perhaps, nearly all transfers are at least 15, and the vast majority are either 16 or 17; ATC age-related limitations, then, are mostly irrelevant, if not unnecessary.

The Offense Focus

The Never Nonserious Offense Policy

The ATC has reached a consensus in drawing a red line around nonserious offenses. These transfers are simply improper and unacceptable to the ATC. Feld (1987) observed:

To the extent that organizational or political considerations result in youths being waived for less serious offenses, the inconsistency between juvenile and adult criminal sentencing practices is further aggravated (p. 504).

Similarly, Zimring (2000b) complained that nonserious offenses have unnecessarily been transferred:

Of course, not all of the cases transferred out of juvenile court are super-serious. In this regard, it is necessary to distinguish between the type of case that makes transfer necessary and the much wider variety of cases that get transferred. Once transfer out of juvenile court is institutionalized, the practice is often not restricted to the superserious cases that rendered it necessary. All manner of older, recidivist, and recalcitrant juveniles are pushed into criminal courts once the channel between the two institutions has been opened…. (p. 211, citations omitted; see, also, Cintron, 1995; Juszkiewicz, 2000; Shook, 2005).

Zimring implied here that the transfer of nonserious cases is both unnecessary and a violation of transfer laws. It is neither. Never have "super serious" cases been the *only* ones either subjected to transfer or considered necessary to be transferred. This policy completely ignores a major focus of transfer policy: chronic offenders who are beyond JC treatment capabilities. This offender may have committed a serious offense, which alone may have qualified for transfer, but typically, it is the chronic offending and persistent treatment failures that merit transfer in these cases. In some jurisdictions, these beyond-treatment transfers far outnumber the "super serious" group.

Some ATC members place transfer policies in a no-win crossfire, suggesting that supposedly overbroad transfer provisions today include

a broad range of offenders who are neither particularly serious nor particularly chronic… (Bishop & Frazier, 2000, p. 265; Bishop &Feld, 2012, p. 906; Fritsch & Hemmens, 1996).

The exact parameters of the adverb, *particularly*, in this reference are not defined and are worthy of suspicion. More important, perhaps, an older defendant, without a significant record, who has committed a relatively non-serious offense could easily qualify for transfer due to the age factor, alone. Although possibly (the most) prevalent among transfers, this offender would be "neither particularly serious nor particularly chronic." To the extent that this category of offender dominates the statistics consulted by ATC members, these criticisms about transfer populations are pointless, possibly disingenuous. Moreover, a residential burglary, thought by many academics to be "not particularly serious," could be very much so, especially to the victims and JC. The same applies to many auto thefts. Many serious juvenile offenders, such as the ones mentioned here, will be transferred after only one or two offenses (making them appear to be non-chronic), while many chronic offenders will be transferred even when their most recent crime is not serious.

A single JC adjudication can result in multiple "dispositions" but still be officially counted and recorded as one. A failure to respond to treatment at a lower level of rehabilitation can result in promotion to another higher level of treatment on a single adjudication without a subsequent arrest/adjudication (see Sanborn, 1985). This offender could be transfer material on what would appear to be a non-chronic history. Having a previous diversion experience, while not amounting to an adjudication and postponing a chronic label, could seriously impact a subsequent disposition, including transfer, due to the youth's failure to appreciate and take advantage of JC's largesse and perhaps intensive treatment effort via diversion.

It is About Violent and Person-Related Offenses Only

Closely related to the nonserious offense prohibition is the ATC contention that only violent and person-oriented offenses should qualify for transfer (Champion, 1989; Fagan & Deschenes, 1990; Feld, (1989). For example, Bishop complained:

Expansive transfer policies send many minor and nonthreatening offenders to the adult system… (Bishop, 2000, p. 81; see, also, Greene, 2010; Mahoney, 1991).

Similarly, Singer, Fagan and Liberman (2000) suggested:

(Legislatures need) to restrict eligibility for automatic waiver to a narrow list of violent offenses. Murder is the one offense for which there is considerable jurisprudential and organizational support for letting criminal justice officials decide if criminal punishment is warranted. By restricting the discretionary decision making of criminal justice officials to capital crimes, the opportunity they currently have to introduce disparities among juveniles charged with a wide range of offenses would be eliminated… (p. 372, citation omitted).

Hoeffel (2013) suggested that even if transfer is warranted to promote incapacitation and victim vindication, that

does not explain the transfer of cases where the offense is non-violent and not against the person. Statistics of transfer to adult court demonstrate that, in 2007, half of the cases transferred were not offenses against the person (p. 61, citation omitted).[1]

Some ATC followers go as far as to misrepresent history by claiming only violent offenders were transferred traditionally (Grisso, 1996; NRC, 2013).

No jurisdiction limits transfer to violent/person offenses only. It is unwise and inaccurate to assume that *all* person offenses are the "worst" or that all property offenses are nonserious. Victims of nighttime residential burglaries might argue they experienced extremely serious and traumatic offenses. A robbery involving a shove before stealing a bike might yield the opposite reaction. Moreover, property offenders are usually chronic before they experience transfer. This ATC branch takes exception to nonamenability-based transfers; every jurisdiction permits them, nevertheless.

Assuming *greater* emphasis should be given to person offenses does not translate to giving *no* emphasis to property offenses (e.g., residential burglary) or perhaps some other crimes, such as arson and some drug offenses, especially if committed by chronic and/or older offenders.

It is About Serious Crimes (and/or Records) and/or Public Safety (and Retribution)

Other ATC members demand that only certain serious offenses, such as murder (Zimring, 1998b), should be transferrable, and usually only when they constitute a threat to public safety (Guttman, 1995; Myers, 2016; NASEM, 2019; NRC, 2013).

The ABA initially developed standards that limited transfer to class 1 offenses, which were punishable in CC by a sentence of 20 years to life. Also, a "prior record of adjudicated delinquency involving the infliction or threat of serious bodily harm" was required, as was a demonstration that JC dispositions were likely ineffective, while CC services/sentences had to be both appropriate and available. In the final draft, the Class 1 offense did not require a previous adjudication, while Class 2 offenses (5–20-year sentence) were added as well (Flicker, 1983, p.11).

Redding endorsed some of the ABA view, but emphasized offense history rather than offense seriousness. He saw waiver as the next step in graduated sanctions so the youth must be a chronic offender who has failed at previous sanctions (see, also, Johnson, Lanza-Kaduce, & Woolard, 2011). Transfer

should be predicated on the juvenile's treatment needs, offense history, and community protection needs rather than on the violent nature of the charged offense... (Redding, 2016, p. 944).

Redding saw offense history as a better predictor of recidivism than the seriousness of the current offense (see Redding, 2008); he evidently did not associate a violent crime with community protection, however.

Bishop shared Redding's views of offense record, coupled with treatment history and public safety considerations (see Steinberg & Cauffman, 2000).

The other class traditionally targeted for removal consists of chronic offenders who have been afforded all appropriate interventions at the juvenile court's disposal and have not responded to them. The court reasonably concludes that they are so intractable that further efforts to reform them would be futile. As a last resort, they are transferred to criminal courts that are better equipped to incapacitate those who present a continuing threat to the public welfare (Bishop, 2000, p. 82).

Snyder et al. (2000) similarly endorsed the serious offense limit on transfer:

The underlying assumption is that transfer is reserved for the most serious cases...(O)ne would expect cases handled in criminal court to be more serious than those remaining in juvenile court. However, with numerous studies finding large proportions of relatively less serious cases (e.g., property cases) among the transferred cases, it remains uncertain what case characteristics trigger a decision to transfer (p. 6).

Feld (2000) maintained transfer is all and only about serious crimes, prior record, and public safety.

Because the question of waiver arises primarily in the context of a concern for public safety, transfer criteria should focus directly on the present offense and record of recidivism rather than on amorphous factors like amenability to treatment or dangerousness... (p. 111).

Feld restricted transfer primarily to a "concern for public safety." He summarily dismissed and eliminated the traditionally most prevalent reason to transfer (nonamenability). Also, Feld (2000) added further qualifiers (or, for him, disqualifiers), including his version of what retribution permits, compounded by what he claimed prevention and incapacitation supposedly demand:

Retributive criteria would identify older youths who commit very serious offenses, such as intentional homicide, rape, armed robbery, or assault with a firearm or with substantial injury to the victim. Preventive or incapacitative waiver criteria would focus on an extensive record of offending rather than an isolated serious offense. The trade-off between seriousness and persistence requires an explicit policy choice... (pp. 111-112).

Feld is incorrect in implying that retribution is limited to serious offenses (or to older offenders). Feld stacked "legitimate" reasons for transfer and, by doing so, aimed to progressively limit the scope of valid transfers. He claimed each sentencing rationale works at cross purposes with each other, which results in each's limiting the other. Feld refused to consider their being additive. Preventive and incapacitative concerns *do not subtract* criteria from valid retributive transfer criteria. Rather, they are *additive, expanding* legitimate reasons for transfer. Only Feld perceived a need to "trade-off between seriousness and persistence." Both qualify for transfer and both account for transfer availability in every state. Contrary to Feld's portrait, each sentencing rationale provides a separate justification for transferring a case.

Similarly, Zimring (1998a) married three limits — age (16/17), longer sentences (see below), and protection of public — so as to emerge with a murder-only (and not always) transfer policy.

The intentional taking of life without justification requires a punitive response in most circumstances in which the offender has even a minimal appreciation of the nature of his or her act. Thus punishment must be one of the appropriate responses of any legal authority responsible for addressing adolescent homicide (p. 132).

****

(T)he great majority of cases close to the waiver border will be homicide charges, but not all homicide charges will be strong candidates for waiver. In my view, even murder charges are better thought of as a necessary but not a sufficient condition for transfer of juvenile defendants to criminal courts... (Zimring, 2000b, p. 211).[2]

Zimring circled his wagon around a murder-only policy. He believes, appropriately, that juveniles' "life chances" need to be preserved and that JC can and should be analogized to a "learner's permit" (Zimring, 1977) where juvenile offenders can learn from mistakes without witnessing CC. Navigating JC experiences and treatment programs can be compared to learning to drive. Failing a driver's test should not, in and of itself, be fatal. This is how JC approaches the vast majority of juvenile offenders. Barring an initial violent crime, they are allowed multiple JC attempts to learn/improve. Only a small number fail frequently or seriously enough to ever experience CC. Respecting the "learner's permit" through JC policy does not translate into either granting passes in *all* driver's tests, *regardless of performance*, or giving continued chances to earning a license to those who have *failed the test repeatedly* or have purposely run over and killed pedestrians during the test. It is one thing to not obliterate one's "life chances" frivolously. It is quite another thing to give older/chronic/violent offenders a perpetual "get out of jail" card.

Preserving life chances is appropriate policy but ceases to be reasonable, however, when:

- violent crimes are at hand, which, also, are not mistakes (especially acts intended to harm);
- offense history is so sustained that not having learned from multiple attempts to teach becomes unreasonable/unforgivable/intolerable; or,
- the offender is so old that it is not feasible to encourage or force the offender to partake in "driving" lessons.

In other words, the three major candidates for transfer today — the old, the chronic and the serious/violent offenders have abused their learner's permit and do not deserve to drive the car at this time.

The Sentence/Disposition Focus

The Lengthier Sentence Requirement

The most popular ATC limit on transfer targets is the argument that the sole justification for transfer is when the necessary punishment for the offense exceeds the maximum sentence available to JC.[3] Thus, transfer is legitimate/necessary only when CC is needed to impose that longer/harsher sentence. This serves as a proxy for the serious/violent offenses transfer policy.[4]

Zimring (1981) appears to have been among the first to advocate the *longer-sentence* rationale.

(T)he justification for waiver is ***singular****: transfer to criminal court is necessary when the* ***maximum punishment available in juvenile court is clearly inadequate…*** *(T)he standard for making a waiver decision is a determination that the maximum social control available in juvenile court falls* ***far short*** *of the minimum social control necessary if a particular offender is guilty of the serious crime he is charged with (p. 201, emphases added).*

Just *how far* must *far short* be is not explained by Zimring. More important, Zimring's limiting transfer to murder violates his standard of the longer sentence justification. There are many brutal rapes and attempted murders and armed robberies, etc. that justify *much* longer sentences than those available in JC, but evidently would still not satisfy Zimring's criterion.

Before long, Feld (1984b) offered the same opinion regarding longer sentences:

The ***primary*** *justification for waiver is the need for minimum lengths of confinement that are* ***substantially in excess*** *of the maximum sanctions available within the juvenile court… (p. 33, citing Zimring, 1981, p. 201, emphases added).*

******

There is a certain anomaly when youths are waived from juvenile court because they ***presumably require longer sentences*** *than the juvenile system can provide and then are placed on probation as adults… (Id., p, 36, emphasis added).*

****

(L)egislative exclusion is appropriate only when a juvenile offender's record of persistence and the seriousness of his present offense warrant confinement for ***substantially longer*** *terms than could be imposed on him as a juvenile (Id., p. 37, emphasis added).*

****

If ***the*** *rationale for adult prosecution is the need for minimum lengths of confinement* ***substantially in excess*** *of the juvenile court's maximum age jurisdiction… (Feld, 1987, p. 495, emphases added).*

******

The ***primary*** *justification for waiver is the need for minimum confinement periods* ***longer than*** *the maximum sanctions typically available to juvenile court, i.e., a sixteen-year-old could not be confined "for long enough" if juvenile court retained jurisdiction...* ***If*** *the rationale for adult prosecution is the need for minimum lengths of confinement* ***in excess*** *of the juvenile court's maximum remaining jurisdiction… (Feld, 1989, p. 18, citations omitted, emphases added).*[5]

More recently, Feld also added:

Legislatures and courts transfer youths to criminal court so that they may receive ***longer sentences*** *as adults than they could in the juvenile system. However, chronic property offenders constitute the bulk of juveniles judicially waived in most states; they may receive shorter sentences as adults than as property offenders retained in juvenile court (Feld, 1998, p. 244, emphasis added)*

******

Legislators, prosecutors, and judges transfer youths to criminal court so that they may receive ***longer sentences*** *than they could have received in the juvenile justice system... (Feld, 1999, p. 243, emphasis added).*

****

Several commentators *contend that the* ***primary*** *occasion to waive youths is when their serious or persistent offenses require minimum lengths of confinement in excess of the maximum sanctions available in juvenile courts... (Feld, 2000, p. 110, citing Zimring, 1991 and Feld, 1995, emphases added).*

****

If minimum sentences ***substantially in excess*** *of juvenile courts' maximum sanctions provide the jurisprudential justification for adult prosecution, then retribution and incapacitation provide the rationale to define waiver criteria.... Most offenders do not require incarceration, and waiver policies should focus only on the most serious offenses and prior records that justify confinement for* ***much longer*** *term (sic) than juvenile courts can impose (Feld, 2000, p. 111, emphases added).*

******

A state should waive only those youths whose serious and persistent offenses require minimum lengths of confinement that ***greatly exceed*** *the maximum sanctions available in juvenile court (Feld, 2017a, p. 548, emphasis added).*

In these declarations, Feld vacillated between mere *longer* sentences and *substantially* longer sentences. Which one controls policy, then, remains somewhat a mystery. His most recent "greatly exceed" position seems to reflect his current perspective. Nevertheless, like Zimring, Feld provided no clue as to how this "standard" translates into actual policy or practice. Is there a minimum of a one-year difference or is it a matter of years; if so, how many? It would seem as though (even many) months of difference would not suffice. Is gauging the difference geared by simply subtracting the JC's maximum retention age from the offender's current age (or expected age at the time of sentencing)? Considering how critical (sometimes all-determining) the age variable would be under this scheme, would there be equal protection problems surfacing between two offenders "identical" in terms of offense, delinquent record, and even treatment history who differ only in one or two (or more) years in age? Do the attitudinal leanings or disposition history of the involved JC judge play a part; if so, would that lead to significant variations in transfer outcomes within and between JCs in a jurisdiction?

Like Zimring (who employs the adjective, *singular)*, Feld claimed to have identified the *primary* justification for transfer (which before long evolved from primary into the *only* acceptable justification for transfer, in his eyes). Also interesting is how the limited-transfer-rationale for these experts evolved from something of an observation/recommendation to a done deal in their views. Neither Zimring's nor Feld's position enjoys *any authority*, however, beyond the ideology/desires of the observers.

By the beginning of the 21st Century, Zimring made transfer policy recommendations based on that assumption that the longer sentences rationale was controlling: "If waiver is restricted to cases where sanctions available in juvenile court are clearly inadequate… (Zimring, 2000b, p. 211)," then only some murders can be transferred. According to Zimring, the problem was identified "as the limited punishment powers of juvenile court… (2000b, p. 214)." Zimring (2000b) added:

The best outcome is to transfer only those cases where ***high-magnitude punishments*** *are required over to criminal courts through a process that minimizes the transfer of juvenile court cases where a transfer is not necessary. The optimal outcome is a system that produces selective transfer only of cases where there is a direct conflict between the upper bounds of juvenile court punishment and the minimum punishment deserved by an offender if guilty of the charged offense…. (Transfer policy should) place heavy emphasis on a single criterion: the gap between available juvenile sanctions and the minimum deserved punishment if defendant is guilty… (pp. 216-17, 221, emphasis added).*[6]

Others from the ATC have joined ranks with Zimring and Feld:

The most pervasive rationale for the remand of juveniles to adult court is that such action provides greater protection to the public than does juvenile justice processing. This is an assumption for which there is little empirical validation (Bortner, 1986, p. 56; see, also, Houghtalin & Mays, 1991).

****

If the primary objective of transfers is to subject juvenile offenders to more stringent penalties in criminal courts, for committing more serious crime, then the wrong population is being targeted for waivers here (Champion, 1989, p. 583).

****

The underlying assumption is that transfer is reserved for the most serious cases. Because the very rationale for transfer is to allow courts to impose potentially harsher penalties on the most serious juvenile offenders, one would expect cases handled in criminal court to be more serious than those remaining in juvenile court. However, with numerous studies finding large proportions of relatively less serious cases (e.g., property cases) among transferred cases, it remains uncertain what case characteristics trigger a decision to transfer. If, in fact, transferred cases are more serious than cases remaining in juvenile court, one would expect the sanctions imposed in criminal court to be harsher than those imposed in apparently similar cases in juvenile court… (Snyder et al., 2000, p. 6).

****

Transfer statutes and policy typically are designed to increase the certainty, length, and severity of punishment… (Fagan, 2008, p. 29).

****

(T)he primary thrust of transfer laws was to increase the length and severity of punishment. A serious assessment of transfer as a policy must engage its retributive component…. (Id., p. 30).

****

Only the belief that juvenile dispositions do not give serious juvenile offenders what they deserve, combined with a desire to make sure they receive the punishment regardless of cost, can support the continued existence of transfer (Slobogin, 2013, p. 121).

The Zimring/Feld tactic is to create a self-serving, imaginary premise, restate it often enough that it becomes established as undisputed reality and truth, and from there demand policy adherence. The strategy behind the only-longer-sentence transfer policy is two-fold. First, it is intended to severely limit the number of juveniles that can be subjected to transfer; many, if not most, in the beyond-treatment category would not be transferrable. The second motive is to delegitimize transfers, both those cases that did not fit the criteria, of course, as well as those cases that did meet the criteria but resulted in a sentence in CC that was not lengthier than what could have been imposed in JC. Of course, this argument assumes that the JC judge would follow through and impose the maximum available JC disposition. Considering how few juveniles are committed to a juvenile facility, (Mears, Cochran, Greenman, Bhati, & Greenwald, 2011), relying on JCs to institutionalize any particular offender may be a fool's errand.

Not surprising, the ATC has exploited the longer sentence rationale to claim (perhaps all) transfers to CC are unnecessary and therefore are illegitimate.[7] Transfers have been claimed to be cosmetic/devoid of substance (Champion and Mays, 1991).

The moderate rate of incarceration (in CC) is important because it demonstrates the discrepancy between the popular rationale for remand and the actual consequences of such actions (Bortner, 1986, pp. 57-58).

****

If waivers are not resulting in more severe penalties for juveniles, what are they accomplishing? These findings suggest that their use in the present jurisdictions is primarily cosmetic (Champion, 1989, p. 584).

****

It is fundamentally contradictory for juvenile court judges to send youths to adult court because they require longer sentences, and then have those criminal court judges sentence those same youths to probation (Feld, 1995, p. 1013, footnote omitted).

****

Although legislatures and courts transfer youths to criminal court so that they may receive longer sentences as adults than they could in the juvenile system, chronic property offenders constitute the bulk of juveniles judicially waived in most states, and they often receive shorter sentences as adults than do property offenders retained in juvenile court (Feld, 1997, pp. 80-81, citation omitted).

****

(A) number of studies consistently report a punishment gap and question whether criminal court judges actually impose more-severe sanctions than juvenile courts would if they had retained jurisdiction... (Feld, 1999, p. 243).[8]

Obviously, this *one* justification, *if* it were indeed the *only* justification, would eliminate substantial numbers of otherwise meritorious transfer cases. This is likely why the ATC has circled the wagons and has offered it as a sacrificial lamb for their otherwise no-transfer initiative. There is *no justification* for this *stand-alone justification*, however. It does not even satisfy Feld's potential candidate list. Persistent offenders are frequently the target of transfer, to be sure, and Feld seems to have conceded that point. The problem, here, is that many persistent offenders are not also serious offenders, such as the commercial burglars or auto thieves who have racked up a dozen of these offenses in the JJ system. JCs could very reasonably want to cut ties with these offenders who have exhausted treatment services and not have a significant CC sentence in mind or one that would exceed the maximum disposition in JC.

It is having to use ***any JC disposition at all***, rather than attempting ***to exceed the maximum one***, that motivates *many*, and, in some locations, *most* transfers to CC.

Pursuing a longer sentence available in CC is certainly one very valid reason for transfer. In fact, it is *sometimes* the controlling one. It just as certainly is *not the only one*. Suffice it to say there are numerous reasons/benefits attending transfer (see Chapters 13-16). Nor is the validity of the transfer called into question due to a lack of a lengthy or lengthier (or any) sentence in CC (even if that had been the motive for transfer).

(I)t is not the fault of juvenile court or the waiver process that adult courts do not give harsh sentences to all youths who are convicted there. Criminal court leniency does not indicate that transfer was unnecessary (Sanborn, 1994a, p. 276).

Those arguing for complete or nearly complete inclusion (i.e., no or few transfers) ignore that judicial transfer (JT) has been considered appropriate and even necessary for those youths who have been chronic offenders and who have not benefitted from rehabilitation efforts within the JJ system. Keeping these youths in JC is a waste of resources, creates a bad image for JC, and potentially undermines the rehabilitation of other delinquents. This individual may not be destined for a lengthy sentence in CC and may not be stopped from committing crime until incarcerated in prison. That does not mean this youth belongs in JC.

Moreover, prosecutors realize that the criminal prosecution of some chronic/violent youths will not guarantee either longer sentences or a desistance from criminal behavior. For one thing, in CC many youths can secure release via bail, whereas they likely would have been detained without access to bail in JC. Obviously, this opens the door (or cell) for some of these youths to commit crimes prior to trial that would not have been possible absent transfer. There can exist a kind of "custody gap" between the two systems.

ATC people are quick to pounce on this prospect as proof that transfer does not protect society. It is ironic and anomalous (not to mention very illiberal) for this group to rely upon the lack of due process in JC as a hallmark for protecting society. The same can be said when the ATC criticizes and argues against transfer because of the more due process-oriented trial defendants receive in CC compared to the adjudicatory hearing. CC provides greater opportunities to "beat a conviction." Not beating convictions is one reason JCs were created in the first place (see Chapter 2), and why some juvenile offenders will self-transfer or not oppose a forcible transfer attempt. Obviously, prosecutors must weigh the prospect that the greater due process available in CC could mean acquittal for a youth who would be adjudicated guilty in JC. Thus, transfer cannot be pigeonholed into being only about longer sentences.

When Even Longer Sentences are Not Enough

Feld (2000) added a further limit on transfer beyond the "longer sentence" criterion. Not only must there be a need for lengthier CC sentences,

substantive waiver criteria should identify only those combinations of serious present offenses, offense histories, offender culpability and criminal participation, and other aggravating and mitigating factors that deserve "real time" sentences of substantially longer duration than those available in juvenile court ... (p. 128, citation omitted).

This limitation poses a serious challenge for chronic property offenders.

Feld admitted that while violent offenders typically get longer sentences in CC, chronic property offenders are most likely to get lesser sentences. It is the former for whom longer sentences are more likely desired, not the property offenders. Feld's (2000) longer sentence rationale applies to chronic property offenders, too, however:

The small group of chronic offenders also may deserve or require longer minimum sentences than the maximum sanctions available in juvenile court because of persistent offending... (p. 111).

But Feld (1999) also perceived illegitimacy when this group does not receive lengthier sentences while only violent offenders do. He saw these differential sentencing outcomes as

***anomalous** patterns in which waived violent offenders receive much harsher sentences and transferred property offenders receive more lenient sentences as adults than either would if sentenced as a juvenile.... (p. 244, emphasis added).*

This is a very possible scenario that is not an anomaly. This group of chronic offenders is likely to be the largest group threatened with and experiencing transfer. Feld is limiting these transfers to occur only when a lengthier CC sentence is desired. That criterion would exclude most of these offenders. Many, if not most, chronic offenders' offenses are likely to be more obnoxious than particularly serious; they are crimes that do not call for lengthy prison terms, let alone those exceeding JC's potential.[9]

Feld was correct in criticizing the main reason chronic offenders often are sentenced relatively leniently in CC, despite a possible extensive JC record. Until recently, JC records have not been factored into CC sentencing (Sanborn, 1998, 2000). That means chronic juvenile offenders traditionally have been seen and necessarily considered to be virgins on their first appearance in CC. This "anomaly" was purposely designed and created for many reasons: the young age of the juvenile offender, the traditional, relative lack of due process in JC, especially in adjudicatory hearings, and the desire to not have JC records permanently stigmatize and disadvantage the offender. This so-called "punishment gap" allows many chronic offenders to avoid harsh sentences in CC, assuming a current nonserious offense:

The punishment gap, which represents the system's failure to intervene most strongly in the lives of chronic and active criminal offenders, occurs both because of qualitative differences in the nature of juveniles' offenses and because of the failure to integrate juvenile and adult criminal records for sentencing purposes. Adult criminal courts tend to rely on the seriousness of the present offense and the prior adult criminal history in making sentencing decisions. Their failure to include the juvenile component of the offender's criminal history stems from the confidential nature of juvenile court records, the functional and physical separation of the respective court services staffs, and the sheer bureaucratic ineptitude that makes the maintenance of an integrated system for tracking offenders and compiling complete criminal histories extremely difficult (Feld, 1987, pp. 502-03, citations omitted).

Although Feld was correct in identifying this "glitch" or gap between the two systems, this problem has been eliminated in many jurisdictions since his article was published. The remedy in narrowing the gap has been to factor JC adjudications into CC sentencing. In some jurisdictions the gap has been nearly completely erased. Reducing the gap has created constitutional problems, not yet recognized by the U.S. Supreme Court (see Sanborn, 1998, 2000).

When lengthier sentences must link with a particular sentencing rationale

Feld (1987) claimed that because the longer-sentencing rationale rules transfer, this self-imposed limit, in turn, limits the appropriate CC sentencing philosophies, such that

the appropriate theories of punishment to structure the choice of waiver criteria are retribution and selective incapacitation... (p. 495).

According to Feld (2000), all of transfer's legitimate eggs are located in the baskets of these two sentencing philosophies. Once that link had been established, Feld (2000) claimed that retribution

*limits severe sanctions to the **most culpable and blameworthy**, imposes a degree of proportionality and determinacy on decisions, and **restricts eligibility for waiver only to the most serious crimes...** (p. 111, emphases added).*

****

A retributive policy would limit severe sanctions (and transfer) to youths charged with homicide, rape, robbery or assault with a firearm or substantial injury (Feld, 2017a, p. 548).

We have yet another false premise leading to yet another false conclusion. According to Feld, not only must the desired CC sentence be *lengthier* than JC dispositions, but they must also be *severe,* evidently. More important, Feld falsely portrayed retribution. Retribution is *not linked with or limited to* lengthy or severe sanctions. Feld is stacking again and has purposely invented this limit to expand his limit on the types of transfer cases. Contrary to Feld's declaration, juvenile offenders whose behavioral profiles lack quality (i.e., committing the most serious crimes), can very adequately compensate for that deficit with a quantity of behavior (e.g., the chronic armed robbers, burglars and auto thieves). Given an adequate foundation of seriousness (robbery/burglary/auto theft, etc.), a retributionist would be very amenable to imposing severe sanctions on the chronic offenders due to that's being proportionate to a record of chronic offending. In fact, due to the continuous offending, a retributionist might be more insistent upon and confident in imposing a severe sanction, convinced that these offenders have earned such a response, considering the several previous warnings/punishments that were constantly ignored by them. Feld's proposal would insist that *quality* (only most serious crimes) *replace quantity* as the justification for transfer.

Feld (2000) was not sure that satisfying retribution suffices to establish legitimate transfer policies:

[A] retributive rationale alone may be overly inclusive and inflict penal harm without any offsetting utilitarian gain, because violent offenders desist at about the same rate as do older youths (p. 111; see, also, Feld, 1984b, p. 34).

****

[S]everely punishing all youths who commit serious crimes would be counterproductive because youths arrested for an initial violent offense desist at similar rates to other delinquents (Feld, 2017a, p. 548).

Feld again stacked anti-transfer arguments to make it much more difficult, if not impossible, for transfer to ever appear legitimate/appropriate. The false premises and conclusions promoted by the ATC cumulate. He is also guilty of seriously misrepresenting retribution once again.

Retributionists will be very upset to see that their sentencing rationale has been hijacked by Feld's declaration such that it must achieve utilitarian gains or account for possible future desistance. A true retributionist will be satisfied by imposing a sentence that reflects the import of the current offense and the prior record. Retribution stands by itself and neither wants to nor aims to satisfy utilitarian objectives. Only utilitarian types, disguising themselves as something else, would force feed utilitarian goals on retribution. For retributionists, any gain apart from achieving an appropriate proportionate punishment (such as deterrence and incapacitation) is pure bonus and not part of the proper retribution formula. And relying upon desistance in any particular offender is irrelevant to retribution. Retribution's focus is on the behavior that has already occurred. Projecting desistance is speculation and is ripe for discrimination (e.g., not profiling well) and an ugly backfire; the offender who is projected to but does not desist is that much freer to commit another offense.

Besides the fact that there are multiple rationales that support transfer, there are also multiple appropriate theories of punishment that support transfer, too (see Chapters 13-16). Simply put, not all of transfer's eggs are confined to retribution's basket; nor does transfer rely upon particular offenses or longer sentences rationales.

Should the total inclusion/no transfer policy prove implausible, the ideal Plan B for the ATC would be to marry all of the above limitations, such that *only* violent, person-related crimes (and perhaps only some murders), committed by older, persistent offenders who require a sentence beyond that which is possible in JC would be vulnerable to transfer orders. This policy would likely address solely those juvenile offenders who were originally excluded from JCs in the first place. The outcome of this position would be that JC would be forced to retain countless juvenile offenders who will receive either no disposition in JC or will receive one that will simply be a waste of valuable juvenile justice resources.

REFERENCES

Bishop, D. M. (2000). Juvenile offenders in the adult criminal justice system. In M. Tonry (Ed.), *Crime & Justice: A Review of Research, 27, 81-167*. IL University of Chicago Press. doi:10.1086/652199

Bishop, D. M., & Feld, B. C. (2012). Trends in juvenile justice policy and practice. In Feld, B.C., & Bishop, D.M (Eds.). The oxford handbook of juvenile crime and juvenile justice (pp. 898-926). Oxford University Press.

Bishop, D. M., & Frazier, C. E. (2000). Consequences of transfer. In J. Fagan & F. E. Zimring (Eds.), *The changing borders of juvenile justice: Transfer of adolescents to criminal court* (pp. 227–276). University of Chicago Press.

Bortner, M. A. (1986). Traditional rhetoric, organizational realities: Remand of juveniles to adult court. *Crime and Delinquency*, *32*(1), 53–73. doi:10.1177/0011128786032001004

Champion, D. J. (1989). Teenage felons and waiver hearings: Some recent trends, 1980-1988. *Crime and Delinquency*, *35*(4), 577–585. doi:10.1177/0011128789035004005

Champion, D. J., & Mays, G. L. (1991). *Transferring juveniles to criminal courts: Trends and implications for criminal justice*. Praeger Publishers.

Cintron, L. A. (1996). Rehabilitating the juvenile court system: Limiting juvenile transfers to adult criminal court. *Northwestern University Law Review*, *90*, 1254–1282.

Deitch, M., Barstow, A., Lukens, L., & Reyna, R. (2009). From time out to hard time: Young children in the adult criminal justice system. Special Project Report. Lyndon B. Johnson School of Public Affairs, University of Texas at Austin.

Drizin, S. A., & Tanenhaus, D. S. (2002). Owing to the extreme youth of the accused: The changing legal response to juvenile homicide. *The Journal of Criminal Law & Criminology*, *92*(3/4), 641–705. doi:10.2307/1144240

Edwards, L. (1977). The case for abolishing fitness hearings in juvenile court. *Santa Clara Law Review*, *17*, 595–630.

Fagan, J. (1990). Social and legal policy dimensions of violent juvenile crime. *Criminal Justice and Behavior*, *17*(1), 93–133. doi:10.1177/0093854890017001007

Fagan, J. (2008). Juvenile crime and criminal justice: Resolving border disputes. 18 *The Future of Children* 81-118 (Pages numbered 1-48 in Columbia Law School Working Paper).

Fagan, J., & Deschenes, E. P. (1990). Determinants of juvenile waiver decisions for violent juvenile offenders. *The Journal of Criminal Law & Criminology*, *81*(2), 314–347. doi:10.2307/1143909

Feld, B. C. (1983). Delinquent careers and criminal policy: Just deserts and the waiver decision. *Criminology*, *21*(2), 195–212. doi:10.1111/j.1745-9125.1983.tb00258.x

Feld, B. C. (1984a). Criminalizing juvenile justice: Rules of procedure for the juvenile court. *Minnesota Law Review*, *69*, 141–276.

Feld, B. C. (1984b). The decision to seek criminal charges: Just deserts and the waiver decision. *Criminal Justice Ethics*, *3*(2), 27–41. doi:10.1080/0731129X.1984.9991756

Feld, B. C. (1987). The juvenile court meets the principle of the offense: Legislative changes in juvenile waiver statutes. *The Journal of Criminal Law & Criminology*, *78*(3), 471–533. doi:10.2307/1143567

Feld, B. C. (1988). The juvenile court meets the principle of offense: Punishment, treatment, and the difference it makes. *Boston University Law Review. Boston University. School of Law*, *68*, 821–915.

Feld, B. C. (1989). Bad law makes hard cases: Reflections on teen-aged axe-murderers, judicial activism, and legislative default. *Minnesota Journal of Law & Inequality*, *8*, 1–101.

Feld, B. C. (1995). Violent youth and public policy: A case study of juvenile justice law reform. *Minnesota Law Review*, *79*, 965–1128.

Feld, B. C. (1997). Abolish the juvenile court: Youthfulness, criminal responsibility, and sentencing. *The Journal of Criminal Law & Criminology*, *88*(1), 68–136. doi:10.2307/1144075

Feld, B. C. (1998). Juvenile and criminal justice systems' responses to youth violence. *Crime and Justice*, *24*, 189–261. doi:10.1086/449280

Feld, B. C. (1999). *Bad kids: Race and the transformation of the juvenile court*. Oxford University Press.

Feld, B. C. (2000). Legislative exclusion of offenses from juvenile court jurisdiction: A history and critique. In J. Fagan & F. E. Zimring (Eds.), *The changing borders of juvenile justice: Transfer of adolescents to the criminal court* (pp. 83–144). University of Chicago Press.

Feld, B. C. (2017a). Competence and culpability: Delinquents in juvenile courts, youths in criminal courts. *Minnesota Law Review*, *102*, 473–576.

Flicker, B. (1981). Prosecuting juveniles as adults: A symptom of a crisis in the juvenile courts. In J. C. Hall, D. M. Hamparian, J. M. Pettibone, & J. L. White (Eds.), *Major issues in juvenile justice information and training: Readings in public policy* (pp. 351–377). Academy for Contemporary Problems.

Flicker, B. (1983). *Transferring juveniles to adult court for trial*. Institute of Judicial Administration.

Fritsch, E. J., Caeti, T. J., & Hemmens, C. (1996). Spare the needle but not the punishment: The incarceration of waived youth in Texas prisons. *Crime and Delinquency*, *42*(4), 593–609. doi:10.1177/0011128796042004006

Fritsch, E. J., & Hemmens, C. (1996). An assessment of legislative approaches to the problem of serious juvenile crime: A case study of Texas 1973-1995. *American Journal of Criminal Law*, *23*, 563–609.

Fritsch, E. J., Hemmens, C., & Caeti, T. J. (1996). Violent youth in juvenile and adult Court: An Assessment of Sentencing Strategies in Texas. *Law & Policy*, *18*(1-2), 115–136. doi:10.1111/j.1467-9930.1996.tb00166.x

Gasper, J., & Katkin, D. (1980). A rationale for the abolition of the juvenile court's power to waive jurisdiction. *Pepperdine Law Review*, *7*, 937–951.

Gillespie, L. K., & Norman, M. D. (1984). Does certification mean prison: Some preliminary findings from Utah. *Juvenile & Family Court Journal*, *35*(3), 23–34. doi:10.1111/j.1755-6988.1984.tb00541.x

Greenwood, P. W., Petersilia, J., & Zimring, F. E. (1980). *Age, Crime, and Sanctions: The Transition from Juvenile to Adult Court*. Rand Corporation.

Grisso, T. (1996). Society's retributive response to juvenile violence: A developmental perspective. *Law and Human Behavior*, *20*(3), 229–247. doi:10.1007/BF01499022

Guttman, C. R. (1995). Listen to the children: The decision to transfer juveniles to criminal court. *Harvard Civil Rights-Civil Liberties Law Review*, *30*, 507–542.

Houghtalin, M., & Mays, G. L. (1991). Criminal dispositions of New Mexico juveniles transferred to adult court. *Crime and Delinquency*, *37*(3), 393–407. doi:10.1177/0011128791037003006

IJA/ABA. (1980). Institute of Judicial Administration/American Bar Association. *Standards relating to transfer between courts*. Ballinger Publishing Company. Juvenile Justice Standards Project.

Johnson, K., Lanza-Kaduce, L., & Woolard, J. L. (2011). Disregarding graduated treatment. *Crime and Delinquency*, *57*(5), 756–777. doi:10.1177/0011128708328867

Juszkiewicz, J. (2000). *Youth crime/adult time: Is justice served?* Building Blocks for Youth.

Krisberg, B., & Austin, J. (1993). *Reinventing juvenile justice*. Sage Publications. doi:10.4135/9781483326450

Loughran, T. A., Mulvey, E. P., Schubert, C. A., Chassin, L. A., Steinberg, L., Piquero, A. R., Cota-Robles, S., & Cauffman, E. (2010). Differential effects of adult court transfer on juvenile offender recidivism. *Law and Human Behavior*, *24*(6), 476–488. doi:10.100710979-009-9210-z PMID:20195895

Mahoney, A. R. (1990). Man, I'm already dead: Serious juvenile offenders in context. *Notre Dame Journal of Law, Ethics & Public Policy*, *5*, 443–465.

Mays, G. L., & Houghtalin, M. (1992). Trying juveniles as adults: A note on New Mexico's recent experience. *Justice System Journal*, *15*(3), 814–823. doi:10.1080/23277556.1993.10871163

Mears, D. P., Cochran, J. C., Greenman, S. J., Bhati, A. S., & Greenwald, M. A. (2011). Evidence on the effectiveness of juvenile court sanctions. *Journal of Criminal Justice*, *39*(6), 509–520. doi:10.1016/j.jcrimjus.2011.09.006

Myers, D. L. (2016). Juvenile transfer to adult court: Ongoing search for scientific support. *Criminology & Public Policy*, *15*(3), 927–938. doi:10.1111/1745-9133.12232

NAC. (1980). *National Advisory Committee. Report of the task force on juvenile justice & delinquency prevention*. National Advisory Committee on Criminal Justice Standards and Goals.

NASEM. National Academies of Sciences, Engineering, and Medicine. (2019). The promise of adolescence: Realizing opportunity for all youth. The National Academies Press.

NRC. National Research Council. (2013). Reforming juvenile justice: A developmental approach. The National Academies Press.

Redding, R. E. (2003). The effects of adjudicating and sentencing juveniles as adults: Research and policy implications. *Youth Violence and Juvenile Justice*, *1*(2), 128–155. doi:10.1177/1541204002250875

Redding, R. E. (2008). *Juvenile transfer laws: An effective deterrent to delinquency? Juvenile Justice Bulletin, August*. Office of Juvenile Justice and Delinquency Prevention.

Redding, R. E. (2016). One size does not fit all: The deterrent effect of transferring juveniles to criminal court. *Criminology & Public Policy*, *15*(3), 939–948. doi:10.1111/1745-9133.12239

Rudman, C., Hartstone, E. C., Fagan, J., & Moore, M. (1986). Violent youth in adult court: Process and punishment. *Crime and Delinquency*, *32*(1), 75–96. doi:10.1177/0011128786032001005

Sagatun, I., McCollum, L. L., & Edwards, L. P. (1985). The effects of transfers from juvenile to criminal courts: A loglinear analysis. *Crime and Justice*, *8*(1), 65–92. doi:10.1080/0735648X.1985.9721310

Salekin, R. T., Rogers, R., & Ustad, K. L. (2001). Juvenile waiver to adult criminal courts: Prototypes for dangerousness, sophistication–maturity, and amenability to treatment. *Psychology, Public Policy, and Law*, *7*(2), 381–408. doi:10.1037/1076-8971.7.2.381

Sanborn, J. B. Jr. (1993c). Review of the book, *Transferring juveniles to criminal courts: Trend and implications for criminal justice*, by Champion, D.J., & Mays, D.G. Praeger Publishers, 1991. *Criminal Justice Review*, *18*, 118–120. doi:10.1177/073401689301800128

Sanborn, J. B. Jr. (1994a). Certification to criminal court: The important policy questions of how, when, and why. *Crime and Delinquency*, *40*(2), 262–281. doi:10.1177/0011128794040002007

Sanborn, J. B. Jr. (1998). Second-class justice and first-class punishment: The use of juvenile records in sentencing adults. *Judicature*, *81*, 206–213.

Sanborn, J. B. Jr. (2000). Striking out on the first pitch in criminal court. *Barry Law Review*, *1*, 7–61.

Shook, J. J. (2005). Contesting childhood in the US justice system: The transfer of juveniles to adult criminal court. *Childhood*, *12*(4), 461–478. doi:10.1177/0907568205058604

Singer, S. I. (1996). *Recriminalizing delinquency: Violent juvenile crimes and juvenile justice reform*. Cambridge University Press. doi:10.1017/CBO9780511527562

Singer, S. I., Fagan, J., & Liberman, A. (2000). The reproduction of juvenile justice in criminal court: A case study of New York's juvenile offender law. In J. Fagan & F. E. Zimring (Eds.), *The changing borders of juvenile justice: Transfer of adolescents to the criminal court* (pp. 353–375). University of Chicago Press.

Slobogin, C. (2013). Treating juveniles like juveniles: Getting rid of transfer and expanded adult court jurisdiction. *Texas Tech Law Review*, *46*, 103–132.

Snyder, H. N., Sickmund, M., & Poe-Yamagata, E. (2000). *Juvenile transfers to criminal court in the 1990s: Lessons learned from four studies*. U.S. Department of Justice, Office of Justice Programs, Office of Juvenile Justice and Delinquency Prevention.

Stamm, M. J. (1973). Transfer of jurisdiction in juvenile court: An A\analysis of the proceeding, its role in the administration of justice, and A proposal for the reform of Kentucky law. *Kentucky Law Journal (Lexington, Ky.)*, *62*, 122–199.

Steinberg, L. (2000). *Should juvenile offenders be tried as adults? A developmental perspective on changing legal policies* (No. 147). Northwestern University/University of Chicago Joint Center for Poverty Research.

Steinberg, L., & Cauffman, E. (2000). A developmental perspective on jurisprudential boundary. In Fagan. J., & Zimring, F.E. (Eds.), The Changing Borders of Juvenile Justice: Transfer of Adolescents to the Criminal Court (pp. 379-406). University of Chicago Press.

Whitebread, C. H., & Batey, R. (1981). The role of waiver in the juvenile court: Questions of philosophy and function. In J. C. Hall, D. M. Hamparian, J. M. Pettibone, & J. L. White (Eds.), *Major Issues in Juvenile Justice Information and Training: Readings in Public Policy* (pp. 207–226). Academy for Contemporary Problems.

Zimring, F. E. (1977). Pursuing juvenile justice: Comments on some recent reform proposals. *University of Detroit Journal of Urban Law*, *55*, 631–648.

Zimring, F. E. (1981). Notes on the jurisprudence of waiver. In J. C. Hall, D. M. Hamparian, J. M. Pettibone, & J. L. White (Eds.), *Major issues in juvenile justice information and training: Readings in public policy* (pp. 193–205). Academy for Contemporary Problems.

Zimring, F. E. (1991). The treatment of hard cases in American juvenile justice: In defense of discretionary waiver. *Notre Dame Journal of Law, Ethics & Public Policy*, *5*, 267–280.

Zimring, F. E. (1998a). *American youth violence*. Oxford University Press.

Zimring, F. E. (2000a). Penal proportionality for the young offender: Notes on immaturity, capacity, and diminished responsibility. In T. Grisso & R. G. Schwartz (Eds.), *Youth on Trial: A Developmental Perspective on Juvenile Justice* (pp. 271–289). University of Chicago Press.

Zimring, F. E. (2000b). The punitive necessity of waiver. In J. Fagan & F. E. Zimring (Eds.), *The Changing Borders of Juvenile Justice: Transfer of adolescents to the criminal court* (pp. 207–224). University of Chicago Press.

ENDNOTES

1 Hoeffel (2013) cited 2008 data that showed the types of cases transferred as: 44.7% person; 31% property; and, 11% drug. To Hoeffel that meant:
The sheer breadth of offenses should demonstrate that those being transferred were not the worst of the worst. In addition, in 23% of the cases, the transferred youths were first offenders who had not had any opportunity to benefit from juvenile programming... (p. 41, cite omitted).
Hoeffel takes exception to nonamenability-oriented transfers, permitted in every state. Hoeffel conflates what were almost definitely violent offenses (the 23% first offenders who were transferred) with nonviolent ones to further bolster his objection against nonviolent transfers.

2 Given Zimring's support for the intentional harm criterion, why would transfer not be an appropriate response for defendants who shoot numerous people who fortunately do not die, or one who rapes (for the third time or more). If intent to harm is critical, why is it limited to a successful homicide?

3 See Bishop, 2000; Bortner, 1986; Champion, 1989; Champion & Mays, 1991; Fagan, 1990; Fagan & Deschenes, 1990; Feld, 1983, 1984a, 1984b, 1987, 1998; Flicker, 1981; Fritsch, Caeti, & Hemmens, 1996; Fritsch, Hemmons & Caeti, 1996; Gasper & Katkin, 1980; Greenwood, Petersilia, & Zimring, 1980; Houghtalin & Mays, 1991; Krisberg & Austin, 1993; Loughran et al., 2010; Mays & Houghtalin, 1992; Redding, 2003; Rudman, Hartstone, Fagan, & Moore, 1986; Salekin, Rogers, & Ustad, 2001; Singer, 1996; Stamm, 1993; Whitebread & Batey, 1981; Zimring, 1981, 1991.

4 Some chronic nonserious offenses also qualify for transfer, according to this rationale.

5 Feld (1987, p. 495) repeated the above quote from Zimring a few times (see, also 1989, p. 18, fn. 59;1991, p. 707, fn. 76; 2000, p. 110), while Zimring (1991) did the same as well (p. 276).

6 Although this rationale is a relatively recent creation, it is perhaps the most popular today.

7 See Bortner, 1986; Champion, 1989; Champion & Mays, 1991; Edwards, 1977; Fagan, 1990; Fagan & Deschenes, 1990; Feld, 1984b; Fritsch, Caeti, & Hemmens, 1996; Gasper & Katkin, 1980; Gillespie & Norman, 1984; Houghtalin & Mays, 1991; Rudman et al., 1986; Sagatun, McCollum, & Edwards, 1985.

8 These critics offer these comments with the full realization that "nonserious," but chronic, property offenders are often among (and perhaps dominate) the transfer population.

9 Some ATC members admit the beyond-rehabilitation group are viable candidates for transfer but later resort to challenging the transfer if it did not result in a lengthier CC sentence. Regardless, the lesser CC sentence does not retroactively invalidate the transfer:
Many of these young offenders will not appear serious to criminal court officials because, in fact, many have not committed serious crimes. Moreover, if everything is relative, even some of the worst offenders in juvenile court will seem comparatively innocuous to criminal court personnel (Sanborn, 1993c, p. 119)

Chapter 11
The Limitation Argument, Part 2:
Minimizing the Transfer Method

ABSTRACT

Chapter 11's focus is also on the anti-transfer crowd's (ATC's) transfer-limitation-mission, this time addressing the claim that judicial transfer (JT) is only the permissible method. To establish this position, the ATC falsely floats the idea that JT is a constitutional requirement. Chapter 11 establishes that since there is no constitutional right to prosecution in JC, there is no constitutional right to JT prior to prosecution in CC. Some ATC members strongly object to the amenability-to-treatment considerations inherent in JT, however, this is due to the nebulous and ambiguous criteria employed and the potential discriminatory outcomes invited. Although all ATC folks prefer JT to PT, then, only some are willing to embrace traditional JT. Stripping amenability from JT, nevertheless, leaves judges with the solitary chore of gauging offenses, which prosecutors can do well and better. The bottom line is that the ATC demands JT because they know certainly that judges are less inclined than prosecutors to transfer.

INTRODUCTION

Although ATC folks disagree on how to construct the narrowest scope of possible transfer targets, there is unanimity that the only permissible method is JT. The explanation is that judges are less likely to transfer than are prosecutors. The one divide is how JT should operate.

Judicial Transfer (JT) Means There Is a Less Likely Prospect Of Transfer's Occurring

Fearing prosecutors will transfer vast numbers of juveniles to CC, the ATC has gone to great lengths to portray prosecutorial transfer (PT) as illegitimate or evil (see Deitch, Barstow, Lukens, & Reyna, 2009; Feld, 1995, 2000, p. 125; Zimring, 1991). The ATC is upset that appellate courts have continuously up-

DOI: 10.4018/978-1-7998-7923-7.ch011

held the validity of PT. These rulings have held it does not amount to an unconstitutional grant of power to these officials by the legislature (see Frost & Bonnie, 2000, pp. 183-4). These courts have ruled that there is no constitutional right to be prosecuted in JC, and that charging power rightfully belongs to the executive branch of government, not to the judicial branch. The ATC resents these appellate decisions as one observer claimed:

*This interpretation created a **perverse** incentive for state legislatures to **rewrite** judicial waiver laws altogether by instituting more statutory exclusion and prosecutorial discretion laws (Arya, 2010, p. 145, footnote omitted, emphases added).*

There is nothing perverse about PT, although the ATC disdain is perhaps understandable since prosecutors are indeed more likely to transfer. A good deal of the expansion of PT in the mid- to late-1990s was due to both a sharp rise in violent juvenile crime and an unwillingness of JC judges to transfer many of those offenders to CC (see McCarthy, 1994; Sanborn, 1996b).

Prosecutors are the chief law enforcers of the community. They are the victim's and society's representatives. Typically, prosecutors' transfer authorization needs only a qualified offense, and possibly a certain age and record. On the other hand, judges are less inclined to see wrongdoing only, and their only client is justice. Judges also usually have to rely upon a PO's assessment (and possibly treatment providers' analyses), and have more criteria to consider and satisfy before being authorized to transfer juvenile offenders. That judges transfer fewer offenders is easy to understand, then, as is the ATC's endorsement of this transfer method.

JT Is Allegedly a Constitutional Right

Many of the ATC insist that their JT-only policy has constitutional roots, likely coupled with a claim there is a constitutional right to treatment (Comment, 1973; Flicker, 1981; Hirase, 1992; Kimbrell, 2015; Linares & Bunton, 2010; Manning, 2020; Mlyniec, 1976; Park, 2007; Vitiello, 1976). Some ATC members have gone as far as to declare that only a jury is authorized to transfer a juvenile offender to CC (Carroll, 2009; Kimbrell, 2015; Vannella, 2006).

The first U.S. Supreme Court case dealing with juvenile justice (JJ) was *Kent v. U.S.* in 1966. A juvenile offender from Washington, D.C., was transferred to CC without a hearing and the assistance of counsel. The Court ruled the transfer violated the statute that required a "full investigation" before transfer. Kent's appellate counsel challenged the transfer on statutory grounds. The Court ultimately heard the appeal because it is the highest appellate court in D.C. The decision was statutory-based, but ATC types have held on to an illusory take on the holding as being constitutional in nature. In *Kent*, the Supreme Court declared the statute required four rights be granted to youths facing transfer in the jurisdiction: counsel, a hearing, counsel's being granted access to the JC's records regarding the youth, and a requirement that the judge write supporting reasons for the transfer, should that be the decision.

The Supreme Court effectively proved *Kent* was not constitutional, nevertheless, when several years later, in *U.S. v Bland* (1972), the Court denied *certiorari* to a D.C. Circuit Court case that had upheld an offense exclusion (OE) statute that was passed reputedly as retaliation against the *Kent* decision. Supposedly, Congress did not agree with the Supreme Court that the transfer statute it had written was intended to require the rights the Court had granted. In response, Congress authorized prosecutors to transfer via an OE provision that eliminated all that the *Kent* holding had demanded, including a hearing and a judge's input on the transfer decision itself. No court since has found OE (or DF) unconstitutional due to being a violation of *Kent*. In short, if OE and DF are constitutional, *Kent* cannot be and there is no constitutional right to either prosecution in JC or a right to a JT.

One ATC member who claimed *Kent*'s constitutionality was Feld (2000). He explained that while the holding was actually statutorily-based, there were nevertheless constitutional overtones.

Although Kent was decided in the context of a District of Columbia statute, its language, especially when read in conjunction with such subsequent decisions as In re Gault, suggests an underlying constitutional basis for requiring that any judicial waiver decision be accompanied by procedural due process (p. 524; see, also, Artega, 2002; Cross, 1998; Flesch, 2004; Gimbel, 2016; Hamack, 2014; Jacobs, 2012; Notes, 2002; Quinn, 2015).

What Feld claimed is accurate.[1] The Warren Court never saw an issue (such as transfer) it was not ready to categorize as constitutional. Some ATC members agree with Feld (see Schornhorst, 1968).

[Kent] ruled that juveniles are constitutionally entitled to a formal hearing and a determination of their suitability for transfer in accordance with explicit criteria—(Bishop, 2000, p. 88, citing Kent v. U.S.,1966).

****

These prosecutorial and statutory waiver laws effectively circumvent the due process protections governing judicial waiver hearings, as mandated by Kent v. United States... (Rosenberg, 2000, p. 82; see also Garner, 1973; Sabo, 1996, pp. 2446-47; Green, 2003).

Schulhofer (1997) first claimed *Kent* is constitutional (p. 437), but then admitted it is not.

In Kent v. United States, the Supreme Court indicated that there is a constitutionally protected right to a hearing on the decision whether to waive the juvenile into adult court (Id.).

****

Technically, Kent held only that such a right should be read into a provision of District of Columbia law, as a matter of statutory interpretation, but the Court's reasoning rested heavily on constitutional principles of procedural due process (Id., footnote 8).

Zimring's *Kent* claim (1998a) was somewhat bolder:

It is no accident that the first successful challenge to judicial power in the juvenile court on constitutional grounds concerned a hearing to decide about the waiver of an accused in which the juvenile was not represented by counsel (p. 110, citing Kent v US).

Actually, *Kent was* mostly an accident since the Court was ruling on an appeal from a lower D.C. appellate court; it had to review the case since it dealt with the interpretation of a D.C. statute. It is highly unlikely the Court would have accepted an appeal of this nature from one of the states; that would have *required* the Court to adopt a constitutional stance regarding transfer. At the time of *Kent*, defendants did not enjoy the right to counsel (among other rights) in most JCs. It would have been difficult, then, for the Court to extend this right to juveniles exiting the JC system. Moreover, juvenile offenders prosecuted in CC would have had a right to counsel, assuming adult defendants already enjoyed that right. What caused the confusion in interpreting *Kent* was that the Supreme Court granted several constitutional rights, including the right to counsel, to defendants prosecuted in JC the year after *Kent,* in *In re Gault* (1967). *Kent* paved the way for the *Gault* decision; the paving did not involve constitutional tiles, however.

Fagan (2008) criticized offense exclusion (OE) statutes because they "moot *Kent* by rendering a legislative judgment about the future behavior and malleability of excluded youth… (p. 18)." It is puzzling that Fagan did not argue that DF statutes also "moot" *Kent* since they also authorize transfer to CC without securing a judge's approval first. Legislatures do not require "a judgment about the future behavior and malleability" of offenders via OE (or DF); JT engages in that speculation. OE/DF statutes address present crime and past behavior and both moot *Kent*. JC judges do not make the decision and there is no requirement to write reasons for the transfer. If the past behavior is relevant to OE/DF, counsel would have access to the JC records, as required by *Kent*; that review would have to occur in CC, however. The other two *Kent* rights: the rights to counsel and a hearing are not violated by PT. Both rights are respected prior to trial in CC. The hearing is simply a preliminary hearing (PH) to find probable cause (PC) for the crime rather than a transfer hearing that examines the youth's amenability to treatment.

If *Kent* were constitutional, OE certainly would be unconstitutional. Some claim the unconstitutionality stems from not giving juvenile offenders individualized consideration that would occur via a JT or *Kent* hearing (Frost Clausel & Bonnie, 2000, p. 192). OE does provide for individualized consideration, but the consideration is rendered by the prosecutor instead of by the judge, and the focus is on crime/record rather than on amenability. Misunderstanding the actual non-categorical nature of OE leads to an incorrect conclusion about OE (see Chapter 6). Of course, DF would be equally unconstitutional, but that transfer method is mostly ignored by the ATC.

Again, if *Kent* were constitutional, there would also have to be a constitutional right to prosecution in JC. Juveniles' having a constitutional right to JC would mean that right can be lost only through a youth's decision to self-transfer (waiving the right to JC) or through a JT where there would be a proceeding, complete with due process, sanctioning the forced waiver of the right. The ATC forgets there is no such constitutional right to JC; only rarely is this acknowledged:

It is well-established law that a juvenile has neither a constitutional right nor a common law right nor a fundamental right to adjudication in juvenile court. Treatment as a juvenile is not an inherent right but one granted by the state legislature and, therefore, the legislature may restrict or qualify that right as it sees fit, as long as no arbitrary or discriminatory classification is involved (Szymanski, 2007, p. 1).[2]

The ATC also insists that there must be a *Kent*-like due process before transfer to CC because of serious differences in JC and CC outcomes (see Arya, 2010, p. 151). But juvenile defendants receive due process via a PH in either JC or CC before prosecution occurs in CC, the same due process adult defendants enjoy. An interesting question is why not demand a *Kent*-like charging hearing before prosecution in JC, considering the serious outcomes there?

Another reason behind the *only-JT stand* is the contention the youths' BI must prevail:

A juvenile's best interests are not served by a system in which a prosecutor does not have to consider those best interests... (Sabo, 1996, p. 2446).

If the youth's BI must prevail, it is difficult to see when transfer would *ever be allowed*, unless it were a self-transfer. In JT, the judge is authorized to promote interests other than only the juvenile offender's BI.

Amenability to Treatment Considerations Mean JT Is Allegedly Improper

While the ATC endorses JT, some of its most prominent members are also critical of it. Feld and Zimring have been very vocal in criticizing JT; Zimring has been slightly more prolific. Feld saw JT as problematic due to the alleged inability either to diagnose nonamenability to treatment or to predict dangerousness, two essential elements of JT. Moreover, Feld (1978) thought there was too much: vagueness in relevant JT concepts, discretion, and, potential for discrimination, all exacerbated by treatment modalities and programs that are ineffective (see pp. 523-556).

In short, judicial waiver statutes require juvenile court judges to determine a youth's amenability to treatment even though there is little evidence indicating that serious delinquents or criminals respond to coercive intervention, there are no distinct behavioral categories of those who are or are not responsive to intervention, and there are no validated objective indicators that permit individual diagnostic classification of amenable and nonamenable serious offenders (Id., p. 535).

Zimring (1998a) objected to the impact the *seriousness of the offense* criterion has had on JT:

It should come as no surprise that a considerable gap opened up between the doctrinal characteristics that were supposed to govern waiver decisions and the actual circumstances that did so. ***Age, maturity, and demonstrated nonamenability to treatment*** *were the sort of characteristics that might comfortably explain a decision to push a subject out of juvenile court in a regime where treatment was the dominant rationale of a court for children. But the* ***seriousness of the offense*** *was probably a much more powerful predictor of waiver than a solely rehabilitative orientation would ever allow... (p. 110, emphases added).*

Although the exact import of offense seriousness was not disclosed, it constituted a surprise to Zimring. All we know is that offense seriousness "was *probably* a much more powerful predictor of waiver...." That claim would seem to depend upon just how powerful a predictor one would expect it to be, in the first place. Other observers, from a different perspective, could view the same data with surprise that offense seriousness had a less significant impact than they expected.

Why this would surprise Zimring is itself a surprise for several reasons. First, precisely *why* seriousness of offense would *not* be a proper and perhaps the most powerful predictor in an amenability-oriented JT decision is unclear. The revered and supposedly constitutional-based *Kent* decision (1966) included an Appendix to the ruling that listed the criteria contained in the D.C. judicial transfer statute that demanded a "full investigation" prior to transfer. Of the eight waiver critèria not only is *seriousness of the offense* the very *first* criterion, the second and third also are offense-related, the fourth and fifth relate to other aspects of a criminal case, while the seventh relates to prior record (pp. 566-567).

Second, seriousness of offense could be a proxy for factors Zimring conceded would be expected: "age, maturity, and demonstrated nonamenability to treatment." Third, many violent crimes may involve deep seated problems that cannot be remedied by JC, at least not with the time allowed within the retention age of JC. Facilities that lack certain therapeutic interventions (such as fire starter programs for arsonists) can mean there is nowhere to send an offender within the juvenile justice (JJ) system. Finally, judges and JC staff could reasonably regard the seriousness of an offense as requiring an intervention that will require a sustained period of control and treatment well beyond what JC has available.

The *age* factor that originally could "comfortably explain a (JT) decision" (see Zimring, 1998a, p. 110, above) eventually became bothersome to Zimring:

Two elements of cases that have no direct bearing on amenability to specialized treatment have been important in predicting transfer — the ***advanced age*** *of the juvenile and the seriousness of the offense... (Zimring, 2010, p. 2, citation omitted, emphasis added).*

Zimring saw age as having "no direct bearing on amenability" despite previous findings that states with a lower retention age than other states were about twice as likely to transfer youths,

suggesting that ***availability of or for treatment*** *may be a crucial element of* ***amenability*** *to treatment (Snyder and Hutzler, 1981, p. 8, emphases in original).*

Waiver was also a more frequent outcome for those with more than two prior referrals to JC (Id., at 9). If juvenile offenders wait until later years in juvenility to commit the most serious offenses, and have also compiled a significant record by then, it would not be surprising for seriousness of offense to have the most significant association with transfer among older youths.

Like Feld, Zimring (1998a) was unhappy with the extent of discretion granted to judges in JT.

The ad hoc and discretionary nature of judicial waiver decisions was neither a secret nor an accident. Judicial discretion unfettered by rules or principles more concrete than "the best interests of the child" was supposed to govern all the decisions of juvenile court judges... Yet the serious consequences of waivers and the fact that discretion was linked to a rejection of the juvenile, rather than treatment or protection, made judicial discretion in waiver cases appear more problematic than that in other matters... (p. 110).

In the past, legislatures erred, if not misrepresented, in suggesting that all decisions in JC should be made in the youth's BI. That is unrealistic and unreasonable. It was also unrealistic and unreasonable to suggest that it was only treatment, and never punishment, that was in play in the JJ system. The only discretion that seems to bother Zimring is that in the transfer decision. For more than six decades decisions, such as detaining, adjudicating and incarcerating juveniles, occurred in nearly every JC with absolute judicial discretion (and by probation officers--POs, too). Ironically, the first- and only-time juvenile defendants experienced constitutional rights during that era was *after* they had been transferred to CC. To some extent, that extreme discretion still exists in JC (see Sanborn, 1994b; Sanborn & Salerno, 2005).

Zimring (1998a) and others ridiculed judges' transferring for the most prevalent reason — i.e., beyond treatment (which he had accepted as plausibly valid on the previous page 110):

A second group of cases involved juveniles with extensive records of arrest and juvenile court sanctions who had ***exhausted the patience*** *of a juvenile court judge when rearrested... (p. 111, emphasis added).*

****

[T]he majority of juveniles transferred to adult courts are typically chronic, petty property offenders sent there by judges often ***fed up*** *with seeing them returning time and time again (D'Ambra, 1997, p. 278, emphasis added).*

****

Nonamenability to treatment, maturity, and predictions of future dangerousness should not be aggravating factors pursued by the prosecutor, because there is no reliable scientific measure of these factors (Hoeffel, 2013, p. 66).[3]

Fagan and Zimring (2000) portrayed amenability as "when words lose their meaning:"

Of course, one could construct an amenability-to-treatment argument out of the accusation of a serious crime by suggesting that to commit the offense was inconsistent with the type of responsiveness to treatment that makes youngsters appropriate subjects for juvenile court treatment. To similar effect, a history of frequent offending could be read as evidence that the youth in question was not amenable to any treatment in the arsenal of juvenile justice. Indeed, ***a rebellious attitude, an inappropriate haircut, or anything else that provokes a negative response from a juvenile court judge*** *can be marshalled as evidence that treatment won't work.* ***Everything can be grist for the theoretical mill of finding a youth not amenable to treatment*** *if the term acquires a sufficiently loose meaning and standardless practice (pp. 5-6, emphases added).*[4]

Finally, Fagan and Zimring (2000) condemned the amenability factor altogether:

[I]t is ***disingenuous and distortive****. It often* ***misstates the real reasons*** *why decisions to transfer are made, the motives that have produced the decision to transfer* ***well before*** *the nonamenability label has been pasted on the defendant. And it assumes under the umbrella category of nonamenability a miscellaneous collection of situations that do not fit a single meaning. The precedents that accumulate under the heading of nonamenability will give ample authority for application of the label (and achievement of the waiver result) in future cases. But the word has* ***lost any distinctive conceptual meaning****. The label will be applied whenever the result must be achieved. There is no value added by labored transformation of the* ***diverse motives*** *for waiver into a* ***distended*** *amenability category. What the process loses is candor and clarity (p. 6, emphases added).*

****

[T]he nonamenability rationale for waiver...provided a ***counterfeit*** *account of the reasons for transfer decisions... (T)he problem with* ***phony accounts*** *of the reasons for transfer is the* ***reality of transfer motive*** *... (Id., p. 8, emphases added; see, also, Zimring, 1981).*

****

The ***lawlessness*** *character of judicial waiver decisions is as easy to explain as it is difficult to remedy... (Zimring, 2000b, p. 220, emphasis added).*

****

The problematic nature of non-amenability to treatment as a justification for waiver may help explain the lack of probing analysis in judicial opinions about transfer from juvenile to criminal court. The obvious inconsistencies in the conceptual schema can generate feelings of insecurity about allowing deep inquiry into the foundations of transfer policy. If the ***underpinnings of transfer policy do not make sense,*** *then covering transfer discussions with huge grants of discretion to the decision-maker is one natural strategy to avoid confronting fundamental inconsistencies (Zimring, 2010, p. 3, emphasis added).*

Feld has joined the Fagan/Zimring crusade:

Judicial waiver criteria framed in terms of amenability to treatment or dangerousness give judges broad, ***standardless discretion.*** *Lists of substantive factors such as those appended to Kent do not provide adequate guidance.... The subjective nature of waiver decisions, the absence of effective guidelines to determine outcomes, and the lack of objective indicators or scientific tools with which to classify youths allow judges to make unequal and separate rulings without any effective procedural or appellate checks... Judges make individualized assessments of a youth's amenability to treatment and dangerousness even though they cannot make those decisions with any degree of accuracy, consistency, or uniformity... (Feld, 2000, p. 90, emphasis added).*

While amenability to treatment is evidently a fraud, Fagan and Zimring never explained, let alone detailed, the "real reasons," "real" motives, "counterfeit" reasons or "fundamental inconsistencies" that supposedly plague JT.[5]

Historically, in JT, prosecutors (perhaps a PO) put forth a transfer motion. That launches a PO report on the suitability for transfer. Offense details, delinquent record, previous treatment history, detailed reports from all previous dispositions/treatment programs, facilities available to address the youth's problems, and the PO recommendation are given to the judge/both counsels. At the amenability stage (part 2) of the transfer hearing, the prosecution argues for transfer; the defense gets to argue against transfer. The judge weighs the evidence/testimony disclosed during the PH (part 1 of the JT), the PO report, and counsels' arguments before making the transfer decision. Failure to produce PC during the PH should make the amenability stage irrelevant.[6]

That there are other "real reasons" or "motives" behind transfer, beyond actual or perceived non-amenability is intriguing. Impugning decision makers' integrity demands these so-called real reasons and motives be disclosed and corroborated. If the authors are referring to a nefarious motive, such as punishment (or deterrence or incapacitation), then there should be a straightforward acknowledgement of such.[7] Also unclear is how the decision to transfer is made "well before the nonamenability label has been pasted on the defendant." In JT, the judge makes the transfer call and attaches the official nonamenability/transfer label. No meaningful decision is possible prior to the judge's. Any and all "decisions" made prior to that time are advisory at most; prosecutors and POs are not empowered to make *the* decision. The judge is free to accept or decline the PO report and/or the prosecutor's motion to transfer. Just because the prosecutor and the PO favor and plead for transfer does not mean that will be the result. A PO's recommendation for transfer is by no means a done deal. The judge can always prefer to take "one more chance" with the juvenile. But, if the PO report calls for retention in JC, transfer does become much more difficult. Judges would need to explain why they are deviating from the expert's advice. So, it appears that only the decision to *deny* transfer has a chance of being known well before "any label has been pasted on the defendant." Thus, it remains unclear when or why or how the nonamenability "result must be achieved" prior to the judge's ultimate ruling. So much of this setup favors the juvenile offender it is difficult to discern the cause of Zimring's, Fagan's and Feld's vociferous objections to traditional JT. Actually, the more pro-juvenile, anti-transfer likelihood of judges' rulings would seem to be very attractive to these ATC members. And, indeed, maybe they are, and the objection is simply and only to having judges consider amenability factors.

Fagan and Zimring may not discern "any distinctive conceptual meaning" to nonamen-ability, but JC workers comprehend the concept. Opposing counsel will challenge the concept. Prosecutors who petition for transfer want the power granted to them and do not want to be forced to prove nonamenability. Unless defense attorneys favor transfer, no juvenile client is seen by them as nonamenable. While dimensions of nonamenability as a concept are known, there will be disagreements whether any one youth deserves the title. The same disagreements appear in talks on justice, fairness, due process, abortion, and the death penalty, among others.

Why a serious or violent crime cannot lead workers to conclude that a particular offender could not be successfully rehabilitated (especially an older youth) is unclear. Why a chronic offender who has accumulated a dozen or more adjudications and has experienced many, if not every, JC program cannot be considered to be beyond the help of JC is also unclear. Why workers cannot reasonably think the presence of a hardened juvenile offender would disrupt, and perhaps derail, the rehabilitation of other "more salvageable" juvenile offenders is also unclear. Since the prosecutor, PO, service providers, and the judge must agree that the offender is beyond the JC's help for transfer to occur, why is the concept of nonamenability disingenuous and distortive? Many questions remain unanswered as to exactly why JT lacks "candor and clarity."[8]

The pro JT/anti-amenability contingent of the ATC has constructed what they hope is a double insularity against transfer to CC. Most critically, prosecutors are removed from the equation, while only offense and/or record are legitimate criteria. The threat posed by alleged amorphous, ill-defined and malleable amenability criteria has been neutralized. For Zimring, this translates into (only) some murder charges' being subject to transfer, with the decision made by a judge, who ideally would not look at any potential homicide charge with the eyes of a prosecutor.

JT May Be Improper, But It Is Allegedly Superior to PT and The Only Acceptable Transfer Method

While the ATC unanimously endorses JT (see Brink, 2003-04), they offer inconsistent statements offered about the appropriateness of the amenability factor. Some ATC members appear to accept the same elements of the traditional version of JT they also condemn. Zimring wanted JT to focus only on needed punishment and any gap between JC and CC sentencing.

A clear focus on desert will reduce the probability that a judge will be distracted by heavy emphasis on other aspects of the case. Of course, ***many of the same characteristics that judges would consider in decisions about a juvenile's sophistication, attitude, or amenability to treatment will also be relevant to questions of the deserved punishment,*** *but continual emphasis on desert can reduce to* ***some extent*** *the capacity for confusion and self-delusion that accompany traditional juvenile court code words like "amenability and "sophistication," and long laundry lists of criteria for waiver (Zimring, 2000b, p. 221, emphases added).*

Somewhat puzzling, Zimring is strangely confident that judges who get "confused and self-delusional" using traditional JT criteria when evaluating amenability will avoid these issues (at least "to some extent") using the very same JT criteria when evaluating punishment and the appropriateness of transfer.

Equally remarkable, Feld and Fagan, who have forcefully condemned the ambiguity and discrimination potential of the amenability criteria, have included *amenability-oriented factors* as elements that are said to *prove the superiority of JT over PT*. These newly endorsed elements involve the *same ambiguity* and open the *same door to discrimination* as the traditional JT focus.

Unlike a judge, who has the benefit of judicial waiver hearings, however, where clinicians and court services personnel can provide information about a youth's maturity, sophistication, or amenability to treatment based on clinical evaluations, social service reports, interviews, and the like, prosecutors typically lack access to such personal information (Feld, 2000 p. 99).

****

As a matter of sentencing policy, the question recurs whether prosecutors will make better-informed and more appropriate decisions under such circumstances than would judges in an adversarial waiver hearing guided by appropriate waiver criteria (Id, p. 119).

****

(U)nlike judges they (prosecutors) lack any access to clinical information or the personal background of the youth, other than the prior juvenile or criminal record... (Id., p. 127).

****

The weight of evidence points toward returning to juvenile court judges the discretion to select juveniles for transfer. The evidence also points toward basing that selection on more criteria than age and offense. Using Kent-like criteria and new scientific knowledge of adolescent development in an open and transparent forum, judges, who are less influenced than legislators by the politics of crime and by electoral pressures, should be able to decide which adolescents should be transferred. A jurisprudence of discretionary decision making on transfer would promote two ancillary goals. It would restore the accountability that is diffused when legislators surgically remove entire classes of offenders from the juvenile court. And it would take seriously the responsibility for mistakes on both sides of the decision threshold (Fagan, 2008, p. 38, citation omitted).

In other words, although some of the ATC acknowledge the alleged shortcomings of JT, they are willing to tout those same characteristics as demonstrations of its superiority over PT. Most critical, perhaps, is the mischaracterization of OE by the ATC as mandatory, automatic, and non-discretionary (see Chapter 6). OE and direct file are every bit as discretionary as judicial transfer. Thus, emphasizing the discretionary character of JT as the reason for its supposed superiority over either form of PT is either a product of serious misunderstanding or a calculated misrepresentation.

For example, to establish the superiority of JT, Zimring falsely claimed OE is bound by "categorical rules," while with JT

***case-by-case determinations** for making transfer decisions are far superior to binding **categorical rules,** so that extensive discretionary power is necessary in transfer decision-making. For this reason, the real choice is not between rule-based and discretionary selection but rather between prosecutorial discretion and judicial discretion... (Zimring, 1998a, p. 109, emphases added; see, also, Hoeffel, 2013, p. 65).*

Fagan shares Zimring's misunderstanding of OE and came to a similar faulty conclusion:

*Returning to discretionary transfer rather than **"wholesale waiver"** would limit the number of youth subjected to criminal court prosecution while identifying those whose plasticity warrants juvenile court intervention. Yet it would also ensure proportional punishment for adolescents whose crimes are too serious to be adjudicated in the juvenile court (Fagan, 2008, p. 38, emphasis added).*

Both critics, among many others (see, also, Table 38 (E) in Chapter 6), misrepresent OE as "rule-bound" and "wholesale." Moreover, neither of these opponents of OE's supposed, inflexible transfer decision making explain why JT would be preferable to direct file (DF). DF is equally discretionary and involves an individualized analysis of the current offense and prior record (perhaps exclusively), without any amenability to treatment entanglements.[8]

The ATC contends JT is preferable to PT for numerous reasons. According to Allen (2000),

the waiver decision, involving as it does the weighing of multiple competing considerations of individual equity and social interests, is of the sort that experienced judges are most familiar with. One may fairly expect, therefore, that informed and unpartisan decisions are most likely to result from the exercise of judicial discretion (p. xv).

Zimring (1998a) shared this opinion as to the superiority of judges' making these decisions:

*Substantial discretion is a necessary element in determining the justice system's response to violent acts by adolescent offenders. The important issue is who should decide on the particular outcome of criminal charges. The competition for discretionary power is between prosecutors and judges. To the extent that judges are the **appropriate holders of discretionary power,** there is the further question of whether the power to determine transfer should be given to judges of the juvenile court or of the criminal court (p. 125, emphasis added).*

Why judges are evidently the only "*appropriate* holders of discretionary power" is not explained. Why prosecutors are not *equally gifted in exercising discretion* is not explained either; these officials are the benefactors of *incredible* discretion in the *charging process* in the criminal justice system, which Zimring ultimately conceded:

*The discretionary power of the public prosecutor is substantial in all criminal cases, and no realistic rearrangement of authority in juvenile or criminal courts would significantly limit the authority of prosecutors to determine and modify criminal charges. With respect to waiver, the field of choice is between systems of judicial waiver or transfer, in which the prosecutor would share power, and systems of **automatic transfer,** in which the **prosecutorial power to choose the forum operates without judicial review.** The important substantive issue is whether the transfer power is better exercised by **prosecutors alone***

or shared by prosecutors and judges. *The decisive consideration is whether the skills and perspectives of a judge improve the quality of decision in transfer cases (Id., emphases added).*

There are many sources of misinformation here. JT *does* bring about a significant and "realistic rearrangement of authority…to determine and modify criminal charges." JT strips prosecutors of meaningful charging authority and grants that authority to judges who are authorized to determine the forum of prosecution; prosecutors are restricted to picking a charge. Second, in JT, the power is *not shared* between prosecutors and judges. Prosecutors must *ask* judges to transfer a case; prosecutors enjoy neither veto power nor appellate challenge over a judge's transfer decision. Third, in neither form of PT is the transfer "automatic;" prosecutors must always *choose the charges in a case*, a *very discretionary choice*. Fourth, neither form of PT lacks "judicial review;" that incorrectly suggests that PT is abusive and unreviewable. Most states provide for CC judges to essentially nullify PT discretion and to return the case to JC via, in effect, their own charging authority (commonly referred to as "reverse waiver"). Moreover, a finding by a juvenile or CC judge that there is no probable cause for an excluded offense in OE either prevents the transfer from occurring in the first place or nullifies the transfer by forcing the case back to JC. The stripping of judicial power in PT is limited to the transfer decision itself.

Fifth, while the policy argument is irrelevant to the few jurisdictions that allow only JT, more than 40 legislatures have granted direct transfer power to prosecutors via the two forms of PT, purposely withholding from judges the authority to make this critical decision. Sixth, the claim that "the skills and perspectives of a judge improve the quality of decision in transfer cases" is patently false. The seasoned prosecutor certainly knows the ins and outs of charging better than the rookie (and perhaps veteran) judge.[9] Prosecutors are much more likely than JC judges to have a better take on charges that are appropriate for CC prosecution since they are the gatekeepers for CC prosecution. Plus, the prosecutor has access to particulars in the details of the crime that the judge will lack. Prosecutors have investigated the crime and know the case; judges appropriately have been kept in the dark to retain their objectivity should they have to adjudicate the case.[10] Seventh and finally, since Zimring (and others) want the amenability consideration removed from the transfer analysis, a charging decision, alone, is what would determine the outcomes of future transfers. Considering the history of this country's prosecution of criminal offenses, it can hardly be argued that judges' performance in making charging-oriented transfer decisions would be superior to those of prosecutors. The legitimacy of such an arrangement also would be questionable since it would constitute a violation of the separation of powers.

The ATC and Zimring do not want to "improve the quality of decision in transfer cases." They want the decision to transfer to be *less likely*, which is *more likely* with judges in charge.

Zimring (1998a) promoted another false premise's leading to another false conclusion:

Two types of argument favor allocating discretionary power to judges: considerations of competence and of perspective. If it is correct to regard the waiver question in ***serious crime*** *as a particularized determination of the* ***minimum punishment the community would tolerate,*** *is this type of determination more within the competence of prosecutors or of judges? If the issue of minimum desert is essentially a political one, a popularly elected prosecutor might be in a better position to make such a political judgment than an appointed judge, who operates at some remove from political sentiments of a particular community. But if the determination of just deserts involves balancing elements like the defendant's immaturity and the extent of the defendant's participation against the particular harm of the crime committed, this task*

***seems very similar to sentencing,** and judges would seem to be better equipped than prosecutors to take the substantive responsibility for sentencing decisions (pp. 125-126, emphases added).*

There are myriad problems with this argument. Two problems are that transfer is neither limited to serious crimes nor simply/only about minimum punishment calculations, although Zimring is lobbying for both. Third, what the "community would tolerate" likely is and arguably should be irrelevant to the transfer decision. The vast majority of juvenile crime, serious, violent, or chronic is off the media's and the community's radar, purposely. Fourth, it is ironic that Zimring sees just deserts as more compatible with JT than PT. Just deserts emerged as a subset of the retribution sentencing philosophy in the 1970s as an explicit reaction against and rejection of excessive judicial discretion, and the wide variation in sentences handed out to apparently equally situated offenders (obtained through employment of deterrence, incapacitation, and, especially, rehabilitation sentencing theories). Just deserts purposely limited the variables eligible for impacting the sentence to the current offense and record, and purposely removed the individual, personal considerations that had led to sentencing disparities (see Von Hirsch, 1976). Sentencing guidelines that emerged from just deserts allow for levels of offender responsibility to be considered in charging and sentencing decisions, but the ambiguous nature of offender "immaturity" created by the DPs would certainly reopen the door for the type of charging and sentencing variation just deserts vehemently contested. Assuming prosecutors are riveted to crime and record, as the ATC complains, just deserts virtually screams for their control over transfer, especially in cases of serious/violent or chronic crime.

Fifth, transfer involves charging, not sentencing. Prosecutors are better equipped than judges to determine the appropriate outcomes in serious crimes. Prosecutors have a better understanding of the particulars of the crime; they represent the community/victim, which is not the judge's responsibility. Finally, it is laughable that prosecutors supposedly lack some vital attribute in making sentencing-like decisions. Charging involves considerations similar to sentencing. The question as to what a "case is worth" and what the defendant "deserves" dominate the charging (and sentencing) decision. Most criminal court cases result in being either *nol prossed* or plea bargained. In making these charging choices, prosecutors utilize sentencing-oriented decisions, choosing exactly which outcome will attend which offense and record. Judges are completely removed from the *nol pros* decisions and are effectively neutralized in plea bargains. They typically merely ratify or reject plea offers, rarely serving as an umpire. The prevalence of sentence bargaining means prosecutors are intimately familiar with making sentencing decisions.[11]

Most important in charging and its relation to transfer is that prosecutors are trained to charge the highest feasible offense. If a defendant is undercharged, charges cannot be adjusted to a more serious level once jeopardy has attached.[12] We want an adversary at this point, which is why prosecutors charge offenders and are properly granted transfer power. Considering the realities of the work involved in resolving criminal cases, it cannot be seriously argued that judges enjoy a hegemony over the qualifications (and even experience) needed to sentence (or transfer) offenders. If the ATC claim is true, that "judges are better at making charging-oriented transfer decisions" than prosecutors, why are not criminal court judges allowed to make charging decisions in the CJ system? Despite these realities, Zimring (1998a) clamored for an *umpire* at the transfer decision (see, also, Artega, 2002, p. 1067).

The second dimension concerns the appropriate perspective for making waiver decisions. Both judges and prosecutors are public servants, but they represent the public interest in different ways. The judicial role is umpiral, whereas the prosecutorial perspective is adversarial. The judicial responsibility is to take into account everything of relevance when making a decision on waiver. The prosecutor's responsibility is to give emphasis to those considerations that will enhance punishment and the suppression of crime. This contrast in perspective explains most of the debates about waiver policy. Those who favor judicial control over waiver favor an umpiral perspective. Once that premise is granted, a conclusion of judicial superiority is inevitable. But if one believes that a decision should enhance only the crime-controlling capacity of the system, the prosecutorial advantage is just as obvious. Without doubt an umpiral perspective is something of an impediment in maximizing the crime control potential of criminal court transfer (p. 126; see, also, Zimring, 2000b, pp. 218-19).

****

(E)ven if the major element (of transfer) were the character and seriousness of the offense, the proper punishment response to a specific offense might more appropriately be decided by a judge than a prosecutor (Zimring, 1998a, pp. 126-27).

There are myriad problems with this view. Just deserts would be further undermined (beyond evaluating immaturity) by being required "to take into account everything of relevance when making a decision on waiver." It is true that "those who favor judicial control over waiver favor an umpiral perspective." Judicial superiority is neither inevitable nor universally supported, however. Ironically, judges are frequently prevented from acting in an umpire-like fashion even in JC. Assuming there is not a plea bargain (see Sanborn, 1985), POs are often the power brokers behind the disposition. They have performed all of the work in assembling a pre-disposition report that identifies the appropriate sentence. The judge's selecting an outcome harsher than the PO's version, is unlikely, if not constrained by statute/court rule. Judges are free to enter a less harsh disposition, but that rarely happens. Judges routinely sign off on the PO recommendation (see Sanborn & Salerno, 2005). Judges are properly umpiral *after all* of the facts/evidence have been admitted and there is a conviction. Charging occurs *before* the matter is litigated. The only way for judges to be truly umpiral is to wait for every consideration to be exhausted, which often will not happen until after a guilty plea or trial is completed, which is why this role is limited to sentencing. Umpires do not make charging decisions (except in JC), advocates do; judges are not supposed to be advocates, but this is exactly why the ATC wants JT, and not PT.

Fourth, (especially) when the crime is a serious one, granting transfer power to the individual responsible to "enhance punishment and the suppression of crime" (the prosecutor), is appropriate and the specific legislative design in PT. It reasonably can be argued that legislatures have spoken clearly in PT that they want prosecutors, and not judges, to make these calls to "enhance punishment and suppress crime." Fifth, since Zimring insists that JCs represent an embodiment of diversion from CCs, it is odd that he argues judges, and not prosecutors, must control the transfer decision (Zimring, 1998a). Judges are not authorized to divert cases from CC when adult offenders are involved (because the decision involves charging that specifically belongs to prosecutors), so why should they be able to act in this manner when juvenile offenders are involved in being diverted from CC. Sixth, although it is important, enhancing crime control is not the only reason PT is desirable. In serious crime cases, the best interests of the youth are, or should be, minimized, and the best interests and protection of the community should be paramount. When serious crime is at hand, the community needs an advocate on its side, not an umpire.

Seventh, POs are typically responsible for most of the heavy lifting in JT. If the PO recommends retention in the JJ system, statutes and/or court rules could prevent the judge from rejecting a retention recommendation. If the PO recommends transfer, the judge can veto that conclusion. Exactly how much a judge can be said to act like an umpire in the JT context is debatable. In many respects, the PO is the actual power source in JT. Eighth, multi-offender cases are plentiful in juvenile crime (Zimring, 1991, 1998a, 2000a, 2000b, 2019), forcing prosecutors to expend considerable energy in sifting through the various levels of culpability and appropriate punishment among the offenders. Transfer decisions are made according to the discovery of the particulars of the crime (and prior records) and weighing alternatives to seeking transfer, such as pursuing a plea bargain with one of more of the defendants. The last thing the JJ or CJ systems or society needs is to require this analysis receive the approval of a less informed umpire.[13] It would also be unseemly and impractical for judges to perform all of the legwork prosecutors perform in these contexts.

Meanwhile, Flesch (2004), Sabo (1996) and Coupet (2000) declared juvenile offenders' best interests and amenability should be the *only* considerations in JT; these considerations are seemingly absent from PT, which, again, supposedly demonstrates the superiority of JT (see, also, IJA/ABA, 1980; Stamm, 1973). Sabo (1996) also found JT to be preferable to PT because the latter is supposedly inappropriate since it allows prosecutors to choose *both charge and forum* (pp. 2446, 2449-2451).

No situation exists in the criminal system analogous to the unfettered discretion many prosecutors enjoy in choosing the forum in which to try a juvenile.... Additionally, prosecutorial waiver allows the party with an interest in conviction the discretion to pick the court which provides harsher penalties... (Id., p. 2447, footnote omitted).

****

(PT) ***erroneously collapses two decisions into one.*** *Waiver is a distinct and unique function. Charging a juvenile suspect with a crime involves examining the juvenile's age and the type of offense she has allegedly committed. Waiving juvenile court jurisdiction entails an additional determination, after the charge, of the forum in which to try the case...(Id., p. 2449, emphasis added, footnotes omitted)*

Feld echoed Sabo's complaint about DF that prosecutors lack forum-selecting experience:

While prosecutors possess expertise to evaluate the sufficiency of evidence and to select charges, they do not bring any professional insight to the forum selection decision whether to try a youth as a juvenile or as an adult. (Feld, 2000, p. 98, citing Sabo, 1996).

With offense exclusion (OE), the prosecutor's first (albeit not exclusive) focus is on the charge. By selecting the appropriate charge, the prosecutor simultaneously selects the forum. With direct file (DF), which seems to bother Sabo more than OE does, prosecutors select the charge *and then* choose the forum, in a sequential manner. Both forms of PT, nevertheless, involve the same decision making in terms of *both charge and forum*; one set of decisions is simultaneous (OE), while the other is sequential (DF). Additionally, there is every possibility that the prosecutor has done rotation work and has seen both JC and CC up close and personally. JC judges may lack previous exposure to CC or may have forgotten that experience. More important, when it comes to OE (and perhaps somewhat less in DF) the legislatures have prioritized the offense in affecting the forum decision, making the prosecutor the obvious choice, according to both Sabo's and Feld's logic! Also lost on the ATC critics of PT is that prosecutors make the very same estimates and calculations as to both the proper charge and forum in judicial transfer, too. The only difference, here, is that in JT, prosecutors can do no more than *request* a transfer decision rather than *impose* a transfer outcome, authorized in PT.

Charging necessarily involves prosecutors' selecting the charges to file and determining the level of penalties that should be pursued. Moreover, there actually is a "choosing the forum" analogy in most states. Most states have trial courts of limited vs. general jurisdiction. When prosecutors elect to fully charge a suspect with a felony they channel the case to the general jurisdiction trial court or they undercharge (assuming a felony) the case as a misdemeanor in order to steer it to the limited jurisdiction court (where there will be limited constitutional rights and limited punishment compared to the general jurisdiction court). This choice of limited vs. general jurisdiction courts is staggeringly similar to the choice between JC and CC. Prosecutors are well versed in selecting the charges as well as the forum for criminal offenders in most states.

So, according to many in the ATC, judges do a horrible job in transferring juvenile offenders under the current regime (deciding amenability to treatment). The judges' performance is so wanting that they demand the transfer focus be limited to the offense, and perhaps record, according to Feld and Zimring. Obviously, the ATC's thinking is that transfer should be reduced to gauging two of the elements that are critical to charging. But these scholars then insist that only the judge is qualified to make this charging/transfer decision, which is misidentified by them as sentencing. *This* is the analysis of transfer that results in "confusion."

If we restrict the transfer debate/discussion to a matter of charging, that screams for the prosecutor to make the call. If society's interests should prevail in cases that arguably qualify for transfer, that similarly screams for the prosecutor to make the call since it is the prosecutor, and not the judge, who is responsible for protecting society and its interests.

REFERENCES

Allen, F. A. (2000). Forward. In J. Fagan & F. E. Zimring (Eds.), *The changing borders of juvenile justice: Transfer of adolescents to the criminal court* (pp. ix–xvi). University of Chicago Press.

Artega, J. A. (2002). Juvenile (in)justice: Congressional attempts to abrogate the procedural rights of juvenile defendants. *Columbia Law Review, 102*(4), 1051–1088. doi:10.2307/1123650

Arya, N. (2010). Using *Graham v. Florida* to challenge juvenile transfer laws. *Louisiana Law Review, 71*, 99–156.

Bishop, D. M. (2000). Juvenile offenders in the adult criminal justice system. In M. Tonry (Ed.), *Crime & Justice: A Review of Research, 27, 81-167.* IL University of Chicago Press. doi:10.1086/652199

Brink, D. O. (2003-2004). Immaturity, normative competence, and juvenile transfer: How (not) to punish minors for major crimes. *Texas Law Review, 82*, 1555–1585.

Carroll, J. E. (2009). Rethinking the constitutional criminal procedure of juvenile transfer hearings: *Apprendi*, adult punishment, and adult process. *The Hastings Law Journal, 61*, 101–153.

Comment. (1973). Youthful offenders and adult courts: Prosecutorial discretion vs. juvenile rights. *University of Pennsylvania Law Review, 121,* pp. 1184-1193.

Coupet, S. M. (2000). What to do with sheep in wolf's clothing: The role of rhetoric and reality about youth offenders in the constructive dismantling policy of the juvenile justice system. *University of Pennsylvania Law Review, 148*(4), 1303–1346. doi:10.2307/3312844

Cross, K. S. (1998). When juvenile delinquents are treated as adults: The constitutionality of Alabama's automatic transfer statute. *Alabama Law Review, 50*, 155.

D'Ambra, L. (1997). A legal response to juvenile crime: Why waiver of juvenile offenders is not a panacea. *Roger Williams University Law Review, 2*, 277–303.

Deitch, M., Barstow, A., Lukens, L., & Reyna, R. (2009). From time out to hard time: Young children in the adult criminal justice system. Special Project Report. Lyndon B. Johnson School of Public Affairs, University of Texas at Austin.

Fagan, J. (2008). Juvenile crime and criminal justice: Resolving border disputes. 18 *The Future of Children* 81-118 (Pages numbered 1-48 in Columbia Law School Working Paper).

Fagan, J., & Zimring, F. E. (2000). Editors' Introduction. In Fagan, J., & Zimring, F.E. (Eds.), The changing borders of juvenile justice: Transfer of adolescents to the criminal court (pp. 1-10). University of Chicago Press.

Feld, B. C. (1978). Reference of juvenile offenders for adult prosecution: The legislative alternative to asking unanswerable questions. *Minnesota Law Review, 62*, 515–618.

Feld, B. C. (1998). Juvenile and criminal justice systems' responses to youth violence. *Crime and Justice, 24*, 189–261. doi:10.1086/449280

Feld, B. C. (2000). Legislative exclusion of offenses from juvenile court jurisdiction: A history and critique. In J. Fagan & F. E. Zimring (Eds.), *The changing borders of juvenile justice: Transfer of adolescents to the criminal court* (pp. 83–144). University of Chicago Press.

Flesch, L. M. (2004). Juvenile crime and why waiver is not the answer. *Family Court Review, 42*(3), 583–596. doi:10.1177/1531244504042003l4

Flicker, B. (1981). Prosecuting juveniles as adults: A symptom of a crisis in the juvenile courts. In J. C. Hall, D. M. Hamparian, J. M. Pettibone, & J. L. White (Eds.), *Major issues in juvenile justice information and training: Readings in public policy* (pp. 351–377). Academy for Contemporary Problems.

Frost Clausel, L. E., & Bonnie, R. J. (2000). Juvenile justice on appeal. *The changing borders of juvenile justice: Transfer of adolescents to the criminal court*, 181-206.

Garner, M. C. Jr. (1973). Due process and waiver of juvenile court jurisdiction. *Washington and Lee Law Review, 30*, 591–613.

Gimbel, V. N. (2015). There are no children here: DC youth in the criminal justice system. *The Georgetown Law Journal, 104*, 1307–1344.

Green, S. T. (2005). Prosecutorial waiver into adult criminal court: A conflict of interests violation amounting to the states' legislative abrogation of juveniles' due process right. *Penn State Law Review, 110*, 233–282.

Hamack, B. (2014). Go directly to jail, do not pass juvenile court, do not collect due process: Why waiving juveniles into adult court without a fitness hearing is a denial of their basic due process rights. *Wyoming Law Review*, *14*, 775–828.

Hirase, J. (1992). State ex. rel. v. EGT: Waiving childhood goodbye. *Journal of Contemporary Law*, *18*, 159–175.

Hoeffel, J. C. (2013). The jurisprudence of death and youth: Now the twain should meet. *Texas Tech Law Review*, *46*, 29–69.

IJA/ABA. (1980). Institute of Judicial Administration/American Bar Association. *Standards relating to transfer between courts*. Ballinger Publishing Company. Juvenile Justice Standards Project.

In re Gault. (1967). 387 U.S. 1.

In re Winship. (1970). 397 U.S. 358.

Jacobs, R. (2012). Waiving goodbye to due process: The juvenile waiver system. *Cardozo JL & Gender*, *19*, 989–1107.

Kent v. United States. (1966). 383 U.S. 541.

Kimbrell, M. (2015). It takes a village to waive a child-or at least a jury: Applying *Apprendi* to juvenile waiver hearings in Oregon. *Willamette Law Review*, *52*, 61–98.

Linares, H., & Bunton, D. (2010). An open door to the criminal courts: Analyzing the evolution of Louisiana's system for juvenile waiver. *Louisiana Law Review*, *71*, 191–230.

Manning, F. A. (2020). When prosecutors act as judges: Racial disparities and the absence of due process safeguards in the juvenile transfer decision. *Virginia Journal of Criminal Law*, *8*, 1–34.

McCarthy, F. B. (1994). The serious offender and juvenile court reform: The case for prosecutorial waiver of juvenile court jurisdiction. *Saint Louis University Law Journal*, *38*, 629–671.

Mlyniec, W. J. (1976). Juvenile delinquent or adult convict—The prosecutor's choice. *The American Criminal Law Review*, *14*, 29–57.

Notes. (2002). For the good of the child, for the good of society: Using Scotland and Jamaica as models to reform U.S. juvenile justice policy. *Harvard Law Review, 115,* 1964-1987.

Park, J. (2007). Balancing rehabilitation and punishment: A legislative solution for unconstitutional juvenile waiver policies. *The George Washington Law Review*, *76*, 786–818.

Quinn, M. C. (2015). In loco juvenile justice: Minors in munis, cash from kids, and adolescent pro se advocacy-Ferguson and beyond. *Brigham Young University Law Review*, 1247–1308. doi:10.2139srn.2614552

Rosenberg, I. M. (2000). Teen violence and the juvenile courts: A plea for reflection and restraint. *Houston Law Review*, *37*, 75–96.

Sabo, S. (1996). Rights of passage: An analysis of waiver of juvenile court jurisdiction. *Fordham Law Review*, *64*, 2425–2454.

Sanborn, J. B., Jr. (1985). *Plea negotiation in juvenile court*. [Unpublished doctoral dissertation, SUNY Albany, Albany, NY., United States].

Sanborn, J. B. Jr. (1996b). Policies regarding the prosecution of juvenile murderers: Which system and who should decide? *Law & Policy*, *18*(1-2), 151–178. doi:10.1111/j.1467-9930.1996.tb00168.x

Sanborn, J. B. Jr, & Salerno, A. W. (2005). *The juvenile justice system: Law and process*. Roxbury Publishing Company. Oxford University Publishing.

Schornhorst, T. F. (1967). The waiver of juvenile court jurisdiction: Kent revisited. *Indiana Law Review*, *43*, 583–613.

Schulhofer, S. J. (1997). Youth crime—And what not to do about it. *Valparaiso University Law Review. Valparaiso University. School of Law*, *31*, 435–447.

Snyder, H. N., & Hutzler, J. L. (1981). *The serious juvenile offender: The scope of the problem and the response of juvenile courts*. National Center for Juvenile Justice.

Stamm, M. J. (1973). Transfer of jurisdiction in juvenile court: An analysis of the proceeding, its role in the administration of justice, and A proposal for the reform of Kentucky law. *Kentucky Law Journal (Lexington, Ky.)*, *62*, 122–199.

Szymanski, L. A. (2007). *"Once an adult/always an adult" (2007 update). NCJJ Snapshot 12(4)*. National Center for Juvenile Justice.

Szymanski, L. A. (2008). *Once an adult/always an adult (2008 update). NCJJ Snapshot 13(4)*. National Center for Juvenile Justice.

Szymanski, L. A. (2009). *Once an adult/always an adult (2009 update). NCJJ Snapshot 14(5)*. National Center for Juvenile Justice.

Szymanski, L. A. (2010a). *Can juveniles transferred for criminal prosecution be held for pre-trial detention in adult jails? NCJJ Snapshot 15(8)*. National Center for Juvenile Justice.

U.S. v Bland. (1973). 472 F2d 1329 (DC Cir 1972), *cert denied*, 412 U.S. 909 (1973).

Vannella, D. M. (2006). Let the jury do the waive: How *Apprendi v. New Jersey* applies to juvenile transfer proceedings. *William and Mary Law Review*, *48*, 723–770.

Vitiello, M. (1976). Constitutional safeguards for juvenile transfer procedure: The ten years since Kent v. United States. *De Paul Law Review*, *26*, 23–53.

Von Hirsch, A. (1976). *Doing justice: The choice of punishments*. Hill and Wang.

Zimring, F. E. (1981). Notes on the jurisprudence of waiver. In J. C. Hall, D. M. Hamparian, J. M. Pettibone, & J. L. White (Eds.), *Major issues in juvenile justice information and training: Readings in public policy* (pp. 193–205). Academy for Contemporary Problems.

Zimring, F. E. (1991). The treatment of hard cases in American juvenile justice: In defense of discretionary waiver. *Notre Dame Journal of Law, Ethics & Public Policy*, *5*, 267–280.

Zimring, F. E. (1998a). *American youth violence*. Oxford University Press.

Zimring, F. E. (2000a). Penal proportionality for the young offender: Notes on immaturity, capacity, and diminished responsibility. In T. Grisso & R. G. Schwartz (Eds.), *Youth on Trial: A Developmental Perspective on Juvenile Justice* (pp. 271–289). University of Chicago Press.

Zimring, F. E. (2000b). The punitive necessity of waiver. In J. Fagan & F. E. Zimring (Eds.), *The Changing Borders of Juvenile Justice: Transfer of adolescents to the criminal court* (pp. 207–224). University of Chicago Press.

Zimring, F. E., & Fagan, J. (2000). Transfer policy and law reform. In J. Fagan & F. E. Zimring (Eds.), *The changing borders of juvenile justice: Transfer of adolescents to the criminal court* (pp. 407–424). University of Chicago Press.

ENDNOTES

1 Many states inferred *Kent* to be constitutional and revised their JT statutes to include the *Kent* rights. Once *Kent* was proven not to be constitutional, coupled with the rise of violent juvenile crime, most states adopted PT (especially OE) or expanded its and DF's scope.

2 This comment was repeated in 2008, 2009 and 2010; the only difference's being that the word, *treatment*, was replaced with *case handling* (Szymanski, 2008, 2009, 2010a).

3 Repeated commission of crimes and repeated failures at rehabilitation are legitimate reasons for transfer (as proof of nonamenability). To suggest that transfer occurs in this context due to "exhausting the patience" of judges, who are "fed up" with seeing them return rather than to juvenile offenders' "exhausting treatment options" are simply gratuitous insults of JC judges.

4 An "inappropriate haircut?" Fagan and Zimring trash their own plausible examples of JT, and then follow up by throwing judges under the bus. It certainly cannot be proved that this scenario has *never* occurred in the history of JC, but to suggest it is common or a norm in JT decisions is an unsubstantiated smear. It certainly cannot capture those judges who denied transfer, the majority outcome, and the same judges who likely granted transfer petitions on other occasions. It is puzzling that Fagan and Zimring would want any offenders prosecuted in JC since youths would be at the mercy of these same fickle judges at critical stages. The authors begin by saying nonamenability findings can be feasible for serious/chronic offenders, but then disregard its reasonableness by launching into attacking JC judges for their alleged fickleness.

5 Prosecutors might be disgusted with/angry at an offender's crime and criminal history and believe CC prosecution is warranted and be upset about lacking direct transfer power. POs might consider an offender too much to handle in JC's programs, as being too much of a threat to other inmates, as having exhausted all treatment programs, or as not being worth the expense of a JC commitment. Perhaps these are what the authors meant by "a miscellaneous collection of situations that do not fit a single meaning." There are many possible motives that can be reflected in a finding of nonamenability. Why nonamenability is required to involve only a single meaning to be legitimate is not explained. It could be the authors/ATC do not want transfer to be afforded more than a single meaning. Simply because a finding of nonamenability can serve an abundance of motives/objectives does not mean the concept is "disingenuous" or "distortive." Any varied motives are irrelevant in JT; only the judge's motives ultimately rule and matter.

6 For first offenders, about the only way in which transfer occurs is when the offense is very serious or the defendant is near the maximum retention age of JC, suggesting this youth is beyond the help of JC. For recidivists, the decision will rest upon the seriousness of the current offense, the past criminal record and the success or failure of previous treatment efforts. Although recidivism connotes a lack of treatment effectiveness, the conduct and attitude of the youth during previous treatment programs can have an independent, advantageous/deleterious effect on the outcome. Depending upon how the hearing transpires, how the information in the report is perceived, and the perspective of the judge, the transfer motion is granted or denied.

7 JC has been imposing punishment on juvenile offenders in some form or other from the first days (Allen, 2000, p. x). Incapacitation is always a by-product of institutionalization. That JJ would be tainted by punishment is hardly surprising, especially considering its clientele. Recognition of the punitive nature of JC led the U.S. Supreme Court to intervene into the JC network in *In re Gault* (1967) and *In re Winship* (1970). It granted juvenile defendants several constitutional rights so they could defend themselves against that punishment potential. Punishment is an integral part of JJ and of "amenability to treatment." Juvenile offenders are institutionalized in a context, one that typically offers one or more treatment programs in a punitive setting. Amenability to treatment is not solely about the offender's fit (or lack of fit) into a guided group interaction program. Treatment considerations also include, among other items, the security of the facility, the classification of juvenile offenders already in that program, and, the length of time until this offender reaches the maximum retention age of JC. Any of these could lead to a finding of nonamenability; the merits of punishment could play a key role. By the time juvenile offenders are transfer-eligible, punishment is certainly a relevant consideration. Just deserts likely would influence a prosecutor's take on a particular offender and the merits of that offender's transfer and could influence POs and judges as well. If this reference explains the authors' comment, then they should have disclosed it, together with an explanation as to why it is conclusively irrelevant to the concept of nonamemability.

8 Inasmuch as Zimring is a major party to this condemnation of JT, it is puzzling that he insists JT is the only acceptable transfer method. Similarly, since Zimring is ready to condemn JT and amenability considerations, why does he oppose OE, which is a cleaner consideration of offense and record? Once upon a time, Feld (1978) vigorously promoted OE. There is a clear indication of nonamenability: the recidivist who has experienced every treatment program in the JJ system and has continuously failed to benefit from them. A proof of nonamenability, here, is the dozens of rearrests and a failure to desist following those programs. The potential of eventual desistance, together with disregard of present and/or past crimes is what can be termed disingenuous and distortive. These youths exist in serious numbers, especially in urban centers. Even Fagan and Zimring (2000) give a nod to the "history of frequent offending" that could legitimately establish nonamenability (p. 5). They then denigrate the concept. While reality and statistics probably explain the authors' initial nod, the high number of youths who would qualify for transfer probably explains the authors' objection to the concept. Lost in all the rhetoric surrounding the alleged problems presented by nonamenability findings is that Fagan and Zimring write as though the JC is the only stakeholder in transfer; they imply JC created itself with a universal/unidimensional mandate and promise to treat all juvenile offenders. However, legislatures authorized JCs' introduction/operation and legislatures have directed some juveniles should be rejected by JCs and that prosecutors should

prevent some violent juvenile offenders from enjoying immunity from criminal prosecution. Zimring and Fagan (2000) also wrote: (L)*egislation must delegate the power to decide in individual cases either to judges or prosecutors. We believe an explicit delegation of authority is superior to formal statements that prescribe transfer but leave practical authority with prosecutors. As between prosecutors and judges, our preference would rest with the judiciary. But the need for discretion and to restrict legislative standards to necessary conditions is independent of the discretionary agency one chooses to carry out this vital function* (pp. 416-17). The delegation of transfer authority is the same for both judges and prosecutors; neither authority is categorical or mandatory, regardless of how explicit the delegation is. Prosecutors are charged with focusing primarily on offense/record, while judges focus primarily on amenability. The "command" (on both) is the same as is the discretion (for both). It is unclear whether Zimring and Fagan misunderstand discretion or simply fear PT because prosecutors *will* transfer. Transfer rules are as "binding" on judges as they are on prosecutors. Finding nonamenability "demands" judges transfer as much as "finding" an excluded offense "demands" prosecutors transfer. Judges can avoid the "command" by denying a lack of amenability; prosecutors can avoid the "command" by selecting a non-excluded offense. The difference between the two lies solely in the subject matter upon which they are required to focus. Both have the discretion to reach "findings" contrary to the "evidence;" neither can be forced to find anything or transfer anyone. Their endorsement of JT, minus amenability, is a rejection of PT, fearing prosecutors will exercise their explicit discretion to transfer chronic/violent juveniles.

9 JC Judges often are less experienced than CC prosecutors when it comes to charging (see Sanborn & Salerno, 2005).

10 This issue is particularly relevant to JCs that have only 1 judge (which is most JCs). In these locations, JT requires the eventual trial judge to hear inadmissible evidence during the transfer hearing, and then to ignore the same during the trial. This is why judges do not charge in CC (or in JC, except in the transfer context). Also, there may be sensitive evidence/information that prosecutors want to hold close to the vest until trial (e.g., witness protection could be vital and threatened by disclosure of witness identity). Forcing prosecutors to disclose that evidence at a transfer hearing could do severe damage to the case, including delaying or damaging sensitive plea negotiations or threatening the lives of necessary witnesses and victims.

11 While the U.S. Supreme Court has replaced judges with juries in death penalty sentencing, prosecutors still choose the cases they believe qualify for the ultimate punishment.

12 If the defendant is overcharged, judges or juries can reduce it to the proper level; the reverse is not constitutionally permitted.

13 Of course, jurisdictions with only JT force this scenario upon all transfer decisions.

Section 3
Analysis

Chapter 12 addresses the research that has purportedly examined transfer to CC. Just about all research has been limited to gauging deterrence. The research results have been mixed; some studies have found greater deterrence served by transfer, others have found less. Other studies have found sentences in CC that were longer than what JC could have imposed, others have found sentence shorter than the maximum JC disposition. The ATC uses the latter situation to "prove" that transfer is unnecessary. This chapter discloses the shortsightedness of the research, plus the serious methodological problems that compromise the findings, especially in matched-pair studies. Also identified are the very relevant factors that are typically ignored in the research. The chapter explains the promise of better constructed propensity-score research, which controls more factors and has found greater deterrence through transfer. The chapter finishes on a cautionary note to pro-transfer types not to expect stellar results from transfer.

Chapter 12
Research Addressing Transfer to CC

ABSTRACT

Chapter 12 addresses the research that has purportedly examined transfer to criminal court (CC). Just about all research has been limited to gauging deterrence. The research results have been mixed; some studies have found greater deterrence served by transfer, others have found less. Other studies have found sentences in CC that were longer than what juvenile court (JC) could have imposed, and still others have found sentence shorter than the maximum JC disposition. The anti-transfer crowd (ATC) uses the latter situation to "prove" that transfer is unnecessary. This Chapter discloses the shortsightedness of the research, plus the serious methodological problems that compromise the findings, especially in matched-pair studies. Also identified are the very relevant factors that are typically ignored in the research. The Chapter explains the promise of better constructed propensity-score research, which controls more factors and has found greater deterrence through transfer. The Chapter finishes on a cautionary note to pro-transfer types not to expect stellar results from transfer.

THE NUMBERS AND THE AGES

It is difficult to get am accurate count on the number of prosecutorial transfers (PTs); judicial transfers (JTs) have been the only figures that have been regularly available. Not surprising, the increase in the number of JTs from the mid-1980s to the mid-1990s was daunting. Between 1985 and 1994, the numbers steadily climbed from 7,200 in 1985 to 12,300 in 1994 (DeFrances & Strom, 1997, pp. 4-5), the height of the surge in juvenile violence. The yearly average of transfers for that 10-year period was 8,520. These numbers would also be high due, in part, to the absence of widespread availability of PT those years. PT became much more prevalent after (and, in part, as a response to) that period's severe increase in juvenile violence.

During these years JTs ranged from 1.2% to 1.4% of all juveniles petitioned in JC. That figure ignores the youths who were informally processed, meaning there was an even lower percentage of transferred juveniles among *all* offenders' having contact with JC. The percentage of transfers involving those sixteen

DOI: 10.4018/978-1-7998-7923-7.ch012

years of age and older ranged from a high of 94% in 1985 to a low of 88% in 1994. During these years, compared to larger JCs, smaller JCs had a higher percentage of juveniles prosecuted in CC (see Id). This would make sense since previous research among urban, suburban, and rural JCs has revealed that the smaller locations operate with fewer rungs of the disposition ladder within the JC sentencing structure (see Sanborn, 1985; Sanborn & Salerno, 2005). That means juvenile offenders in these areas have fewer opportunities (i.e., rungs of the ladder) to avoid climbing to the top of the ladder (i.e., transfer). Whereas an urban JC could use multiple stages of probation before reaching an officially designated *intensive* level (involving increasing levels of community controls over youths), suburban and rural JCs might use only one level before probation becomes *intensive*.[1] Also, first-degree felonies could be viewed as less acceptable in smaller JCs (see Sanborn & Salerno, 2005).

More recently, JT numbers have ranged from a low of 3,200 in 2015 to a high of 4,200 in 2014. Between 2013 and 2017, the percentage of juveniles transferred to CC following a petition to JC remained at a consistent 1% (Furdella & Puzzanchera, 2015; Hockenberry, 2018, 2019a, 2019b; Hyland, 2018). Data from 2005 to 2017 show a general reduction in JTs (in part explained by the more cases of PT) and a consistent dominance of older offenders (i.e., 15 years of age and older) among the transfer population (see Sickmund, Sladky & Kang, 2019; Table 43; see, also Synder et al., 2000). Not surprising, research has found older age to be associated with the likelihood of transfer (Bishop, 2000; Bishop & Frazier, 2000; Myers, 2001, 2005, 2016; Sickmund & Puzzanchera, 2014), while younger age has been linked with a greater likelihood of decertification (or reverse transfer) to JC (Snyder et al., 2000; Jordan, 2006; Jordan and Myers, 2007). Nearly all transfers involved youths older than 12 years of age (99.73%).[2]

THE FACTORS

Besides age, the two factors that have been most consistently played the most prominent role in the transfer decision are the seriousness of the current offense and the extent of the JC history (see Synder et al., 2000; Griffin et al, 2011). The serious offense can involve both person and property crimes, but the former is more prominent. Weapons, guns, and firearms, together with severe injury, have been especially influential in the transfer decision (Burrow, 2008b; Jordan & Myers, 2007; Myers, 2001, 2003. 2005). The number of offenders in the criminal incident has also been important, particularly if a gang was involved. Drug offenses have historically been found to increase the likelihood of transfer as well (see Snyder et al., 2000).

The critical impact of offense seriousness should not be surprising since a serious and/or violent offense could be seen as warranting a disposition beyond what is available to JC, especially if the offender is near the maximum retention age of the juvenile justice (JJ) system. This offender would fit squarely within the *greater-punishment* group that consistently has been a transfer target. To the extent that an extensive JC history is consistent with repeated failures at rehabilitation attempts, these offenders would also be transfer targets, hailing from the *beyond-treatment* group. The more adjudications offenders have, the more likely they are to experience transfer. Fewer adjudications appear to be needed in person-related offenses than in property ones for transfer to occur. Snyder and colleagues (2000) found five adjudications to be particularly significant in explaining decisions to transfer to CC; negative forecasts of amenability to treatment were related to the same outcomes as well (see Mulvey & Schubert, 2012).

While race has typically not been found to be related to transfer outcomes (Bortner, Zatz, & Hawkins, 2000; Burrow, 2008a, 2008b; Fagan & Deschenes, 1990; Fagan, Forst, & Vivona, 1987; Jordan & Myers 2007; Lemmon, Austin, Verrecchia, & Fetzer, 2005; Myers 2003; Podkopacz & Feld, 1995, 1996; Poulos & Orchowsky, 1994; Snyder et al. 2000), minority youth are overrepresented (Bortner, et al., 2000; Burgess-Proctor, Holtrop, & Villarruel, 2008; Hess, Furr, Armstrong, Francis, & White, 2010; Juszkiewicz, 2000; Males and Macallair, 2000; Olson, 2004; Poe-Yamagata and Jones, 2000; Smith, 2013; Tashea & Passarella, 2014; Zeidenberg, 2001). Gender has been found related to transfer outcomes; transfer, by far, is a male-thing (Snyder et al., 2000)

THE OUTCOMES

Depending upon the offense examined, CC sentencing outcomes for transfers vary considerably. It would not be rare to find some transferred property offenders' receiving shorter prison sentences than they *might have* received in JC. "Shorter" is speculative. There is no way to know for certain whether these offenders would have received *any* JC prison term, let alone a longer one.

For years, longer sentences for transfers in CC have been found via research.[4] Many transfers receive prison terms.[5] In fact, juvenile offenders have been found to experience higher rates of incarceration in CC (Spelman, 2000). It is also not uncommon for juveniles to receive harsher sentencing than adults (Jordan & Myers, 2011; Lemmon et al., 2005; Myers, 2003; cf., Kupchik, 2006). Violent gun users have been found to receive more immediate attention and severe sanctions in CC, as do juveniles with more serious and extensive offending backgrounds (Myers, 2001, 2005). The ATC also complains that juveniles receive harsher punishment in CC (see Mulvey & Schubert 2012), but that's kind of the point. This ATC sentence outcome demand places transfer supporters in a Catch-22/no-win position. If the transfer receives a sentence in CC that is shorter than could have been received in JC, the ATC insists the transfer is illegitimate and obviously did not need to occur. If the sentence is longer than the JC disposition could or would have been, this sentence is unfair and cruel due to the offender's likely *PRIC* traits.

Transfers that involve violent crimes have received sanctions far more severe than the vast majority of JCs could impose (Bishop, 2000; see, also, Kupchik, Fagan & Liberman 2003; Kurlychek & Johnson, 2004; Myers, 2003; Redding, 1999). Rudman and colleagues (1986) found that violent youth in CC received sentences five times longer than violent youth in JC.[6] Again, for violent offenders, longer institutional sentences have been common for a long time.[7] As Fagan (2008) noted:

The likelihood of incarceration was the same in juvenile and criminal court, but the juveniles waived to criminal court received longer sentences — almost always in adult prison — because there was no upper age boundary for incarceration… (p. 30).

While some research has discovered that transfers were more likely to receive prison sentences than young adults (see, e.g., Steiner, 2009; Jordan, 2014), other research has found transfers less likely to be incarcerated than adults, but given longer sentences; trial conviction was associated with longer incarceration sentences for transfers.[8] Some of the most interesting findings from the early 1990s were reported by Griffin and colleagues (2011). Overall, 68% of transfers received jail or prison, while only 40% of retained youths were institutionalized. For violent offenses, the incarceration rate was 79% for transfers and 40% for retained youths. Even transferred property offenders were more likely to experience confinement than those processed in JC (57% versus 35%). Data from later in the decade revealed violent-oriented transfers received *mean maximum* sentences of 118 months in prison, eight months in jail, and 55 months on probation; for property offenders the numbers of months for the three dispositions were 39, six, and 43, respectively (see Id.). What is interesting is not only that the length of incarceration sentences was considerably longer than any available in JC, but also the duration of mean probation sentences went well beyond the norm of community alternatives utilized in JC (see Sanborn & Salerno, 2005).

Important to remember is that most research on outcomes dates to the 1980s and 1990s. Considering the number of states that have recently allowed JC records to be factored into CC sentencing (see Sanborn, 1998, 2000), mostly since those studies were conducted, it is likely that the current sentencing of transfers in CC has become lengthier, even for property offenses.

THE TARGETED RESEARCH

Most quantitative research has been looking for evidence of deterrence via transfer to CC. The pivotal research question is, does transfer discourage offenders from committing more crimes (i.e., specific deterrence) and/or convince non-transfers from committing crimes to avoid transfer (i.e., general deterrence). Specific deterrence dominates the inquiry. That's certainly not an unwarranted focus, but it should not be the only focus. Not all of transfer's eggs are situated in deterrence's basket. A lack of deterrence has also been associated with prison and the criminal justice (CJ) system. Those realities have not led to a call to eliminate them. Deterrence is important and desirable, but it is not the *only* objective behind transfer to CC. Arguably, deterrence is not even the *most* important objective for most of them. Nevertheless, the ATC is desperate to conjure something to "prove" the inappropriateness of transfer. When worse recidivism/less deterrence is associated with transferred juvenile offenders, the ATC believes that the case against transfer has been made. While greater recidivism for transfers is not to be welcomed, the case that there actually is less deterrence for this group has not been satisfactorily made as of this date. This would not be the first agenda-driven, erroneous claim that has been forwarded by the ATC.

The findings on deterrence/recidivism have been mixed. Studies have discovered *less general and/or specific deterrence*, *no difference* in these categories, and *greater deterrence* among transfers. Barnoski (2003) found transfers had a 51% rate of recidivism and retained youth had an 81% rate (see, also, Jordan, 2012). On some occasions, the findings depended upon the offenses examined (which is why the outcomes of some studies are listed in more than one category, see Table 44).

Due to the prevalence of negative findings, the ATC asserts, generally, that transfer to CC results in offenders' being arrested more quickly and for more serious offenses than allegedly comparable offenders retained in JC. Rather than recommending longer sentences in CC, the ATC has concluded that *transfer* to CC compromises the safety of the community (and not the CC itself, interestingly). From that conclusion emanates the equally unsurprising ATC policy recommendation that the availability of transfer to CC should be severely restricted, if not eliminated, altogether.

THE METHODOLOGY

Deterrence/recidivism research results vary tremendously. One characteristic of most transfer research that does not vary, however, is the methodological deficiency with which most studies have been conducted.

In the end, contrary to the claims of the ATC, we really do not know more than we do know about the supposed effects of transfer on recidivism.

Despite the wealth of research, the fact remains that we know relatively little about the true effects of waiver (Mears, 2003, p. 157).

Perhaps the most workable inference/observation/bottom line is that we should not expect much deterrence regarding transfers (Fagan, 2008). Unfortunately, the studies also consistently show that we should not expect much deterrence payback via offenders prosecuted in JC, either. Some observers question whether juvenile offenders can be deterred by either JC or CC.[9]

What also seems important is that the findings often are based on relatively short follow-ups on respondents (e.g., 18 months in Myers, 2003). Even the renowned Bishop, et al. research that found a 54% recidivism rate among transfers (compared to only a 32% rate for the retained group) after one year (1996), found only a 1% difference after seven years, with transfers registering slightly better results than the retained population (Lanza-Kaduce, Frazier, Lane, & Bishop, 2002). Interesting, Jordan (2012) found a 31% difference in favor of transfers after an eight-year follow-up (see, also, Fagan, 1996). It is also pretty clear that the type and length of disposition matters (but is frequently ignored in research). Myers (2001) found that transfers with longer prison sentences had a lower recidivism rate upon release than those incarcerated for shorter periods. Similarly, Fagan (1996) found that transfers sentenced to probation had substantially higher recidivism rates than offenders institutionalized via JC.

To measure deterrent effect, researchers have compared the fate of "equal" offenders to see how they fare with rearrest after processing in both systems. The factors most frequently controlled are seriousness of the offense and prior record to see, for example, how transferred burglars with three adjudications in JC fare in the future. One of the most expansive and detailed matched pair studies was conducted on direct file (DF) by Bishop and colleagues in Florida. The researchers found 2,738 matched pairs. The researchers utilized seven factors: most serious offense; number of counts; most serious prior offense; number of prior referrals; age; gender; and, race (Winner, Lanza-Kaduce. Bishop, & Frazier, 1997).

The only reliable factors here are age, gender, and race. The others are problematic, and possibly misleading. Controlling for the most serious offense is fraught with potential serious misperceptions (see below); the number of current counts offers a bare number without any quality context. For example, *four transferred counts* (armed robbery, coupled with two burglary charges and a felony assault) are importantly different from *four retained counts* (armed robbery, coupled with two retail theft charges and a trespassing charge). Prior referrals are incomplete without a reference to their nature: *four transferred prior referrals* (a graduation through *all* the levels of JC dispositional alternatives, including a juvenile prison) are importantly different than *four retained prior referrals* (only multiple probation-level sentences). The most serious prior offense has the same problem as the most serious current offense (see below). Any matching that actually occurred here would seem to have required an act of God, more than researcher insight.[10]

It is remarkable that these researchers were not concerned by finding so many allegedly matched offender pairs, half transferred and the other half retained. One matched pair would seem to scream as a denial of equal protection, if not unfairness. It would imply prosecutors selectively, if not arbitrarily, transferred some offenders who had committed the same offense, having the same delinquent history, as others who were permitted to remain in the friendly confines of JC.

THE FRAGILITY/FALLIBILITY OF AGGREGATE AND MATCHED PAIRS RESEARCH

There could be two reasons why research has found retained youths' faring better in recidivism compared to transfers, especially when it comes to DF (as well as to JT).

One is that there could be (and, ideally, should be) a substantive difference between the two populations, despite the apparent similarity in offenses; the same observation applies to similar records. Juveniles transferred via DF likely reflect the prosecutor's evaluation that these youths are "worse" offenders that merit prosecution in CC. Uniquely, however, the selected charge for CC will not necessarily communicate a "worse" offender compared to those retained in JC. Offenses with the same title can be prosecuted in either JC or CC under DF (and JT). With concurrent jurisdiction, a first-degree robbery charge can be prosecuted in *both* courts.

The same applies to JT. Probation officer's (PO's)/prosecutorial requests of a judge to transfer a case involve offenses that can be heard in both JC and CC. If the offenses cannot be heard in JC (offense exclusion or OE), then the prosecutor would have the authority to transfer the case independently and would not need a judge's permission. If the case cannot be heard in CC, any transfer request would be moot. POs and judges could see a considerable difference in criminality between two offenders charged with the same robbery and recommend/choose only one of them for transfer due to the nature of that offender's behavior, among other factors; this outcome could occur even if the delinquent records of the two juveniles were similar. Thus, just as in DF, two youths charged with the same transferrable offense legitimately could be treated much differently in JT, reflecting the PO's/Judge's perceiving greater criminality in the transferred offender due to a very different criminal profile.[11]

In OE, if first-degree robbery is excluded, a prosecutor's deciding to charge that offense, thereby transferring the case, suggests the prosecutor thinks the offender truly merits CC prosecution due to having committed an actual first-degree robbery. Other negative offender characteristics could convince the prosecutor not to "look the other way;" *but for* those characteristics the prosecutor might have "undercharged" the offender to retain the youth in JC. Excluded offenses cannot be prosecuted in JC so research studies should not make a mistake in comparing the fate of an excluded offense in both JC and CC. Charging the excluded offense should speak for itself.[12]

Again, with DF and JT, the apparent similarity of retained vs. transferred charges (they are all robberies) enables researchers to collect 100 robbery cases from JC and to contrast them against 100 supposedly equal robbery cases from CC.[13] Should the two groups actually be equal the most pressing question should be why were they treated differently? This comparability issue is never addressed by the ATC. Of course, the absence of any actual match between the two groups could help explain the lack of concern among the ATC. Experts have noted:

Aggregate studies don't control for between offense variation — just collective whole that may hide important differences among juvenileoffenses (Mulvey & Schubert, 2012, p. 9; see, also, Monahan, Steinberg, & Piquero, 2015).

Complicating the selection of the charges designated for JC prosecution is that it is hazardous to rely upon JC records to reflect the true nature of the charges for which the defendant was adjudicated.

This could affect research on the effects of DF and JT. JCs do not always (and some JCs never) exercise care in either determining or recording precisely the charges attending the adjudication. For decades, JCs were not obligated to observe due process or much in the way of legal exactness/scrutiny. Even today, JC dispositions are not inextricably linked to the level or number of offenses in many jurisdictions. Juvenile offenders in many states can go to any facility for an unspecified length of time (until the maximum retention age), regardless of the offense (and often the record) (see Sanborn, 1985; Sanborn & Salerno, 2005). Whereas a first degree or Class A felony has serious sentencing/record ramifications in a CC conviction, the same usually cannot always be said of a JC adjudication, at least in terms of the immediate sentence (see Sanborn, 1993a). What was carefully and accurately identified as a first-degree robbery CC conviction may be much more serious than (and not a match for) a first-degree robbery adjudication in JC.

Similarly, attempting to hold prior record constant can fail by assuming JC records reflect all the nuances of previous crimes. While JC records will likely identify previous delinquencies in a generic sense, they typically will not provide a full capturing of what this particular offender actually did in those crimes. Police reports, witness statements, trial/hearing transcripts would need to be consulted to acquire a true appreciation of this offender's criminal performance. Just as with current offenses, not all *prior* robberies (robberies, burglaries, auto thefts, etc.) are equal.

Attempting to hold previous treatment experiences constant is hazardous as well. This is particularly relevant to JT. While JC records will disclose the location and identity of treatment programs, a deeper dive into the file is needed to fully understand this offender's character and performance in past treatment programs. Not all treatment performances are equal. Juveniles' demonstrating some success in previous treatment efforts could receive benefit of the doubt and be retained in JC. Those who have constantly failed at all facilities could be fast-tracked for transfer. Not wanting to waste more resources on offenders who seem destined to fail (again) in another treatment program would be a legitimate concern of the JC workers (see Table 45). Retaining these nonamenable offenders means fewer beds available for those offenders who need and could benefit from treatment, and could compromise the treatment of other more salvageable youths (see Id.). These developments can give treatment (yet another rehabilitation failure) and JC (should have known better than to keep this kid in JC) a bad name. Thus, although some retained offenders might have similarly equal (i.e., failing) track records on paper as some transfers, it is highly likely that both POs and judges (and perhaps prosecutors) will regard the two sets of offenders much differently. It is also highly unlikely that researchers will perform this beyond-the-JC-record examination to fully understand the nature of the offender who has been transferred (or retained); this analysis is simply too labor intensive, while simple record searches via datasets are quick and relatively easy, if not uninformative. Again, perhaps the only factors that can be kept truly constant with confidence in the JC situation are age, race, and gender.[14]

Myers (2016) offered that increased recidivism could be a result of transfer but admits that transferred offenders "are systematically different in more ways than just their court of prosecution (p. 929)." He and others gave potential credit to JC judges:

It is also possible that juvenile court judges simply are effective in sending the highest risk or "worst" offenders to the adult system; after which, these youth exhibit greater recidivism (i.e., selection bias is the major explanation for the findings) (Id., p. 930; see, also, Redding, 2016, pp. 942-43).

******

(J)udicial waiver may be a more selective mechanism of transfer that places higher risk youth in the adult system. From that perspective, the increased recidivism would not be causal; instead, research on judicial transfer may not have sufficiently addressed selection effects associated with transfer (Zane et al., 2016, p. 916).

******

Moderator analysis revealed that studies of judicial waiver were associated with the highest recidivism level. One explanation for that finding is that judicial waiver does not act as a specific deterrent. Another is that the finding is spurious, a result of unaddressed selection effects. If judicial waiver is a more selective transfer mechanism, it may send higher risk juvenile offenders (i.e., more likely to recidivate) to criminal court. Indeed, this use represents the traditional role of judicial transfer... (Id., p. 920).

****

To the extent that those transferred are more serious offenders, transferred youth would be expected to have greater risks of subsequent violence, independent of any effect of their experience with the adult criminal system... (McGowan et al., 2007, p. S12).

****

Researchers have yet to examine recidivism in a study fully controlling for case and offender seriousness. Even research that has attempted to study comparable groups (matched samples, for example) of transfers and delinquents retained in juvenile court has not been able to control for many of the factors that might make the transfers a more serious group. Thus, it remains unclear whether the reason harsher sanctions are more likely and reoffending is higher among transfers is because these juveniles are more serious offenders... (Snyder et al., 2000, p. 7).

These observations make sense. Typically, in JT (and often in PT) for transfer to occur, the offender must have racked up a significant history of offenses as well as bad performances in previous treatment attempts, leading to negative projections for any future treatment attempts. That chronic-prone property offenders are more likely to see CC via JT than PT, combined with relatively lenient sentences often awaiting these "innocuous" offenders, nearly guarantee higher recidivism rates. There is even a possibility that having yet another pair of eyes/expert opinion (viz., the PO's) sign off on the need for transfer would solidify its appropriateness and a reason to believe that the chronic criminal behavior of the youth will not desist after transfer.[15]

Consequently, *selection bias* has undermined the value of most transfer research to date, especially concerning JT and DF (see Zane et al., 2016). As Loughran and colleagues (2010) noted:

A comparison of offenders who do and do not get transferred to adult court... involves a contrast of two groups that are inherently different in important, preexisting ways which may affect any comparison of the groups' patterns of re-offending. Consequently, observed differences (e.g., higher recidivism rates) in the transferred population cannot be accurately attributed to the transfer experience itself, as long as these differences in outcomes might also be partially or fully attributable to fundamental differences between the transferred and retained youth (p. 477).

Zane and colleagues (2016) completed this observation with:

Failing to control for differences between transferred and nontransferred juveniles may bias estimates of the effect of transfer on reoffending (Mears, 2003; Nagin et al., 2009). It may even lead us to confuse cause and effect: If waived juveniles are sent to adult court because of their higher risk, the increased likelihood of reoffending might be better described as a cause, rather than as an effect, of transfer (p. 905).

Another possible reason for different outcomes could be that judges' and prosecutors' removal of truly bad actors from JC facilitates and enhances the rehabilitation experience for retained youths. The ATC is convinced that poor performance of transferred youths in CC is due to rubbing elbows with adult offenders. The corollary is also possible. Treatment for retained offenders is benefited by not forcing the redeemable to be housed with the irredeemable.[16]

Regardless of the explanation(s) for higher recidivism rates found among transfers, there is no way to have confidence in the construction of most research studies. As Loughran and colleagues (2010) stated, finding greater recidivism rates related to transfer are not to be trusted:

The existing research behind this conclusion, however, is limited by its inability to address adequately the issue of heterogeneity in adolescents transferred to adult court. It is debatable whether this research has fully addressed the issue of sample selection when assessing the impact of being transferred to adult court or retained in juvenile court. Several factors, including but not limited to age, offense, and number of prior petitions, may influence the likelihood that an individual's case is transferred to criminal court. Furthermore, some of these same factors associated with transfer may also be associated with higher levels of future recidivism. A comparison of offenders who do and do not get transferred to adult court thus involves a contrast of two groups that are inherently different in important, pre-existing ways which may affect any comparison of the groups' patterns of re-offending. Consequently, observed differences (e.g., higher recidivism rates) in the transferred population cannot be accurately attributed to the transfer experience itself, as long as these differences in outcomes might also be partially or fully attributable to fundamental differences between the transferred and retained youth.... It is unclear, however, whether or not the statistical controls used to adjust for selection bias in these investigations achieved their goal. Many data sources are necessarily limited in their ability to characterize an adolescent offender's background or current functioning, and there is the possibility that some important group difference between the transferred adolescents and their juvenile court counterparts might be producing some of the observed effects. It is difficult to know with certainty if selection bias can be properly accounted for by matching cases on a limited range of potential confounders (pp. 477-478).

These researchers ultimately identified what they called a "differential effect of transfer." Some transfers had worse recidivism rates than retained offenders, but some scored markedly better, depending upon the base offense and the CC sentence (community or institutional corrections) as well as its length (see Id.). Although the rearrest results for property offenders were slightly (not significantly) worse for transfers, *there is a significant reduction in offending associated with transfer for those who engage in person crimes, even when controlling for primary selection factors.... The differential effects suggest that transferred adolescents charged with person crimes show lower rates of re-arrest, even after controlling for those covariates which are statistically significantly different between the adult and juvenile groups... (Id., pp. 484, 486).*[17]

THE GENERATION OF IMPROVED TRANSFER RESEARCH

Recent research has utilized more advanced and comprehensive research methodology that has found better transfer recidivism results. These studies employed propensity score matching (accounting for and then matching/scoring more background characteristics); they have been more comprehensive in including and examining the factors concerning retained and transferred populations and their rate of recidivism. These "improved" research efforts have found more positive results attending the future criminal behavior of transferred offenders (see Loughran et al., 2010; Mulvey & Schubert, 2012; Jordan, 2012; Zane et al., 2016).[18]

(T)he propensity-score matching analyses, when coupled with potentially more and better variables to address confounding, in fact provided more accurate estimates of impact. If so, then the true effect of transfer may be that it decreases recidivism... (Zane et al., 2016, p. 917).

Not surprising, propensity score research has been recognized as the current preferred method of analysis (see Myers, 2016), while the limits of previous research have finally been called out.

Earlier studies, which analyzed a limited number of variables, likely did not include important variables that may have significantly affected the results (Redding, 2016, p. 943).

******

(I)t would behoove researchers and advocates to exercise humility when discussing the state of our scientific knowledge on the effects of transfer... (Id., p. 944).[19]

THE TYPICALLY IGNORED FACTORS

Loughran and colleagues (2010) compiled 59 variables to gauge the effect of transfer on recidivism. They included "demographic, family history, peer, legal, psychological, substance abuse, psychosocial maturity, and prior adjustment factors." Improvements in constructing some factors occurred.[20] These researchers examined a wide and varied array of factors (see, Mulvey, Steinberg, Piquero, Besana, Fagan, Schubert, & Cauffman, 2010; Mulvey & Schubert, 2012). Virtually every other previous transfer study pales in comparison to the comprehensiveness of the work of Loughran and colleagues (2010).[21]

Results might be different if a truly comprehensive list of factors were included in the research, such as the following (which studies identified in the parentheses have included):

- offender's age at the decision on transfer/retention (i.e., months/years remaining for a JC disposition to be enforceable since offenders could be substantially older at this time than at the time of the crime and now be close to the maximum retention age) (see Fagan, 1990; Semple & Woody, 2011);
- offender's age at beginning of criminal "career" (see D'Angelo, 2007; Durose & Antenangeli, 2021; Myers & Kiehl, 2001; Snyder, 1996);
- offenders' (and families') history of dependency/previous non-delinquent history in JC or "cross-over" youth (see D'Angelo, 2007; MST Services, 2018; Kolivoski, Goodkind, & Shook, 2017; Loughran, Brame, Fagan, Piquero, Mulvey, & Schubert, 2015; Vidal, Prince, Connell, Caron, Kaufman, & Tebes, 2017);
- offenders' perception of risk or threat of sanctions/certainty of arrest (see Anwar & Loughran, 2011; Cauffman & Steinberg, 2012; Loughran et al., 2015; Loughran, Piquero, Fagan, & Mulvey, 2012; Matthews & Agnew, 2008; Millstein & Halpern-Felsher, 2002; Myers, 2016; Redding, 2003; Reyna & Farley, 2006; Scott, Reppucci & Woolard, 1995; Scott & Steinberg, 2008; Steinberg, 2007; Steinberg & Cauffman 1996);
- offenders' knowledge of the law and possible transfer/penalties/prison (see Doob & Webster, 2003; Glassner, Ksander, Berg, & Johnson, 1983; Kleck, Sever, Li, & Gertz, 2005; Mears, 2003; Miner-Romanoff, 2014; Redding, 2005, 2008, 2010; Redding & Fuller, 2004; Robinson & Darley, 2004);
- offenders' belief that transfer and CC punishment will be applied to them (see Miner-Romanoff, 2014; Redding, 2010);
- extent of "legal cynicism" and perceived unfairness (see Fagan & Tyler, 2008; Miner-Romanoff, 2014; Woolard, Harvell, & Graham, 2008);
- offenders'estimated life expectancy (see Knowles, Rowan, Frick, Steinberg, & Cauffman, 2022);
- offenders' living arrangement, especially whether living with one or both parents (see Cheeseman, Waters, & Hurst, 2010; D'Angelo, 2007);
- offenders currently enrolled in school (see Chessman et al., 2010);
- offenders' previous transfer history (see Cheeseman et al. 2010);
- previous detention/correctional experience in juvenile justice (JJ) (see DeLisi, Hochstetler, Jones-Johnson, Caudill, & Marquart, 2011; Myers & Kiehl, 2001; Sridharan, Greenfield, & Blakley, 2004);
- previous detention/correctional experience in criminal justice (CJ);
- home environment, previous violence/victimization in home, community, and JJ system D'Angelo, 2007; Horowitz, 2000; Podkopacz & Feld, 1996; Myers & Kiehl; Singer, 1993);
- decertification/reverse transfer from CC (see Hess et al., 2010; Jordan, 2006; Jordan & Myers, 2007, 2011; Tashea & Passarella, 2014);
- PO's report on amenability as well as PO's estimate on availability/plausibility of JC treatment options;
- POs' nature and tendencies in supervising probationers and parolees in JC/CC;
- length of probation and jail/prison terms (see Loughran and colleagues, 2010) ;
- conditions associated with sentence (especially probation) (see Zane et al., 2016);
- level of offender's threat to victim/community;
- does a JC prosecution undervalue the offense/record;

- weapon use (see Annino, 2000; Burrow, 2008b; D'Angelo, 2007; Jordan & Myers, 2007; Myers, 2001, 2003. 2005; Myers & Kiehl; Snyder et al., 2000; Sridharan et al., 2004);
- juvenile offenders' sensitivity to rewards/incentives, but not to disincentives/punishments (see Cohen et al., 2016);
- actual length of sentence served, as opposed to original sentence, meaning time at risk (see Fritsch, Caeti, & Hemmens, 1996; Zane et al., 2016);
- level of culpability in the crime(s);
- number and nature of co-defendants, especially older juveniles, adults and/or gang (see Annino, 2000; Cheeseman et al., 2010; D'Angelo, 2007);
- proportion of minorities in the community and any impact of race/minority threat theory (see Anderson & Ouellette, 2019; Jordan & Maroun, 2010; Lowery, Burrow, & Kaminski, 2018);
- various attitude measures, such as remorse, willingness to participate in rehabilitation programs (see Redding, 2016; Zane et al., 2016);
- extent of offender's criminal peers;
- person initiating the transfer pursuit, PO versus prosecutor;
- judge involved in the transfer decision (see Burrow, 2008a; D'Angelo, 2007; Keenan, Rush, & Cheeseman, 2015; Shook, 2004);
- method of transfer (see Verrecchia, 2011; Zane, 2017);
- extent of victim injury, impact of crime on victim and community (see Sridharan et al, 2004; Cheeseman et al., 2010);
- number of victims (see Redding, 2016);
- victim characteristics (such as age, race, gender) (see Sridharan et al., 2004;
- victim's impact statement;
- victim's position on transfer;
- arresting officer's position on transfer;
- type of defense attorney (public defender vs private counsel) (see Redding, 2016);
- JC obligation to factor in protection of the victim/community (see Sanborn, 1994d);
- escalation vs de-escalation in crime severity history;
- complete dispositional history (highest rung of the disposition ladder attained);
- sequence of JC sanctions (see Zane et al., 2016; Johnson, Lanza-Kaduce & Woolard, 2011);
- severity of JC sanctions vs. CC sentencing (see Levitt, 1998);
- performances in previous treatment programs;
- mental health treatment history (see Cheeseman et al., 2010);
- substance abuse history (see D'Angelo, 2007; Sridharan et al., 2004);
- school attendance/performance/drop out history (see D'Angelo, 2007; Myers & Kiehl, 2001; Podkopacz & Feld, 1996; Singer, 1993; Sridharan et al., 2004)
- adjustment(s)/modification(s) of the disposition of retained offenders;
- location of the JC, different states with different laws, etc. (see Burrow, 2008a; Cauffman, Piquero, Kimonis, Steinberg, Chassin, & Fagan, 2007; Cheeseman et al., 2010; Feld, 1984b, 1989, 1993a; Myers & Kiehl, 2001; Poulos & Orchowsky, 1994; Smith & Paternoster, 1990; Sridharan et al., 2004; Zane et al., 2016);
- any impact of the "liberation hypothesis" (see Beaudry-Cyr, Leibe, Brubaker, & Jaynes, 2020);
- type of JC (urban vs suburban vs rural) (see Sanborn, 1994a);
- was a plea bargain offered and accepted/refused (see Burrow & Lowery, 2015);

- nature of the disposition ladder of the JC (such as the number of rungs on the ladder) (see Sanborn, 1985; Sanborn & Salerno, 2005);
- system and community resources available to the JC (see Mulvey & Reppucci, 1988; Shook, 2004);
- parent(s) criminality and parental willingness to assist JC;
- neighborhood (and possible effect on post-release experience); and,
- community risk and protective factors/resources (see Redding, 2016; Zane et al., 2016);

The list of relevant, impactful, and typically ignored variables is virtually endless. For example, POs in JJ can be social work-oriented (but perhaps not in every JC); some JCs require POs to have an MSW. Does that requirement distinguish the behavior of POs in these JCs versus those who work in JCs without such a requirement? POs in CC tend to be law enforcement-oriented (but perhaps not in every CC); many are frustrated would-be cops. The variation among JCs and CCs can lead to serious differences in the willingness and readiness of POs to violate and rearrests probationers, and maybe parolees as well. The length of the sentences can be important, too. Probation in JC tends to be short-term. The thinking is that juveniles either will straighten out (and be discharged from probation as early as possible to keep caseloads manageable) or will need more intensive supervision and an adjustment of the disposition, including perhaps a commitment. Unlike CC sentences, JC dispositions can be relatively easily modified; *perhaps the disposition has been adjusted rather than registered as an instance of recidivism.* JC even has review hearings regularly scheduled to see how the disposition is working (or not) (see Sanborn and Salerno, 2005). Probation in CC, on the other hand, can range for years, if not decades, and is not nearly as malleable due to an adult probationer's having a right to liberty. The effects, if any, that the PO's orientation, the length of time and the ability to adjust conditions have on POs in CC have not been evaluated in the context of transfer. These differences could impact rates of recidivism and rearrest in unexplored ways.[22]

In a rare display of victim and public/community awareness, Pennsylvania JC judges are instructed to factor all of the following into transfer decisions:

(I)n making its "public interest" determination in a transfer proceeding, the court is required to give careful consideration to victim impact evidence. The extent to which the victim has been harmed by the offense is one basic measure of its seriousness. Moreover, the degree of harm suffered by the victim should have considerable bearing on the court's assessment of the adequacy of a juvenile disposition to meet the case. Accordingly, in the course of the transfer hearing, evidence should be presented on the physical, emotional, and financial impact of the offense on the victim, and such evidence should be weighed appropriately in the court's decision. Where necessary, as in a disposition hearing, the court should make its own inquiries regarding the victim's feelings, concerns, and wishes regarding transfer (PA Judges, 2018, pp. 114-115).[23]

Thus, whether a victim was present at a transfer hearing or collaborated with a prosecutor in a DF consideration, and whether the victim submitted (or read) a victim impact statement could have a central, but unknown effect on the decision made in a JT or DF case.

Besides the relative dearth of factors examined in most transfer research, typically the research omits any consideration of the most violent offenses, such as rape, murder, and arson. Loughran and colleagues

(2010) conceded that a limitation of their study is that these most serious crimes were ignored. They explain that to include them would bias results and is of little concern:

Another possible limitation is the screening of the most serious offenders from the sample (i.e., those charged with murder, rape, or arson, all of whom spent the entire recall period in confinement), as it may be creating a biased estimate of the overall treatment effect of transfer. We argue, however, that this is not problematic, since ***there is little ambiguity regarding the issue of transfer for these individuals.*** *Indeed, an individual in this age group charged with such a serious crime will almost always be transferred to adult court, regardless of the statutory scheme governing this practice. Thus, while the treatment effect we estimate does not include these individuals, it is unlikely that knowing the effect of transfer on this specific group would carry much sway in a discussion about recalibrating the transfer policy (p. 486, emphasis added).*

It is telling that this work, as well as so many others, did not examine offenders *most worthy of transfer*, and the ones most likely to receive *very lengthy prison sentences*, preventing recidivism and rearrests for a lengthy period. While apparently sincere, it is humorous that these researchers claim that "there is little ambiguity regarding the issue of transfer for these individuals." One would have to assume Loughran and colleagues either have not consulted the transfer literature or have not talked among themselves. To their credit, nevertheless, the researchers announced that their work was intended to stimulate "discussion of *how to reform, rather than refute*, the practice of transferring juveniles to the adult court system (Id., p. 487, emphasis added)." Even this statement is far afield from the positions assumed in the vast majority of transfer literature.

OTHER METHODOLOGICAL WEAKNESSES/CONCERNS/UNCERTAINTIES

Incomplete factors and limited traditional research methodologies are certainly problematic when examining the impact of transfer to CC on deterrence. Perhaps even worse is including "transfer" respondents who were not actually transferred to CC. For example, Fagan purported to study the differences between two populations of juvenile offenders who had been transferred to CC in New Jersey and New York. While the New Jersey sample had actually experienced transfer, the New York youths had been subjected to mandatory exclusion (ME). The latter had exceeded the maximum JC age. Although it may be fruitful to compare the fates of two sets of youths in this manner, comparing transfer between two jurisdictions did not occur here. Fagan compared how JCs and CCs handled possibly "comparable" offenders (see Bishop, 2000, p. 131).

Similarly, McGowan and colleagues (2007) declared that "(f)or the purposes of (their) review, 'transfer' refers to placing juveniles under the jurisdiction of the adult criminal justice system, rather than the juvenile justice system (p. S7)." All youths prosecuted in CC via either the two versions of ME or due to a transfer to CC were identified as transfers by the researchers. That is wrong and inaccurate. How many other transfer studies copied this approach is uncertain. For those that did, the findings and accompanying policy recommendations are compromised.[24]

Sometimes when factors are compared, they are not equal between JJ and CJ. JC dispositions have a finite character due to the maximum retention age, which typically translates to three-to-six years in length at most. Meanwhile in CC the finite can be incarceration of the offender for a number of years staggeringly higher than anything JCs have to offer. In order to achieve comparability, very lengthy sentences, such as (but not only) life without parole, are omitted from research, giving a very biased account of the numbers on specific deterrence.[25]

Another factor-related weakness of transfer research is that all studies claim to examine recidivism but control for no factors that would be critical to post-release behavior; recidivism-related variables are ignored. Transfer research has been more focused upon who ends up being transferred, but not so much on the factors associated with post-release success/failure. For example, do longer probation/incarceration sentences available in CC (perhaps many years) compared to JC (perhaps only one or two years) result in closer scrutiny of probationers for a longer time in CC, affecting the detection of recidivism? While some factors can surface in both contexts, such as gang affiliation and delinquent peers, some factors are likely to surface only after the sentence is served. Ignored are factors directly connected to the post-release world into which probationers and inmates find themselves, such as family dynamics and capabilities, neighborhood, community support programs/abilities, etc. Even the location of the JC can be critical in diverse ways: it is about what the court environment is like, such as the disposition ladder and available programs. On the post-sentence side it could be more about family, job programs and community support, etc. The post-release experience can vary, depending upon whether it occurs in a rural vs suburban vs urban environment; no two JCs are alike (Rothman, 1980; Sanborn & Salerno, 2005). The school record that can be critical to disposition, could easily be mostly disregarded during the transfer decision, only to reemerge at the post-sentence stage as of vital importance.[26]

THE LESSONS THAT CAN BE LEARNED FROM TRANSFER RESEARCH

We learn valuable information via research on deterrence, but hardly enough to develop sound transfer policy. The researchers have warned us to not expect much in terms of better results to flow from transfer. There is no reason to expect much deterrence in JC, either. Just because transferred offenders receive prison sentences longer than were available in JC, that does not mean there will be less recidivism among these offenders, eventually.

We lack equally important information from transfer research, however, besides that already mentioned. We do not know how much, if at all, JJ facilities and JC dispositions, in general, contribute to juveniles' failing to develop a sense of risk or fear in committing crime.[27]

At the same time, we do not know how much adult prisons fail to impress juveniles transferred to the CJ system. Scared Straight programs convinced some youths that prisons were not only survivable, but also were not much to fear. Between JJ facilities and CJ prisons there may truly be a criminogenic effect that explains the lack of subsequent deterrence. But the criminogenic effect may have more to do with facilities' being too "doable," especially the JJ versions, than with learning more tricks of the trade from fellow inmates.

Even the better constructed propensity-score-oriented research, which typically happens to find more positive findings on recidivism among transferred offenders, cannot examine recidivism associated with the lengthy sentences imposed on some transferred offenders in CC.

Another problem with developing policy in light of deterrence research is that, much like studies on offender desistance, most insights about prospective recidivism/criminal careers can be gleaned only after offenders' histories have run their course. This research parallels career criminal studies conducted in the 1970s, which resulted in the serious, but short-lived, attractiveness of selective incapacitation as a sentencing philosophy.[28]

It is not possible to predict, with certainty, those who will recidivate (or will be deterred). If that were possible, we could fashion appropriate/effective sentences (or transfers) that would disproportionately affect repeat-prone criminals, furthering the cause of crime reduction. We can generate transfer policies/ strategies based on offenders' tendencies (the way selective incapacitation did with targeted sentencing), but that would produce both false positives and negatives (the way selective incapacitation did), while also possibly producing grossly disproportionate and discriminatory transfers and outcomes (the way selective incapacitation did).[29]

Finally, basing any relevant transfer policy upon the "potential" behavioral forecasts of likely eventual adherence to law-abiding behavior is not only dangerous, but also unethical. Instead, behavior is serving as a guide for accountability and the systems' reactions to that behavior, juvenile offenders would be handled in light of their statistical recidivist (or desistance, perhaps) likelihoods, relating to an arbitrary, and possibly incomplete or overinclusive set of factors. The implications of deterrence research are that juvenile offenders will be transferred or not according to some statistical formula that is incomplete at best, and inaccurate at worst.[30]

CONCLUSION

One ATC member has conceded that transfer research may be so flawed as to not adequately inform about recidivism, etc.; also, that processing in JC actually may not be associated with a lower probability of reoffending (Bishop, 2000, p. 150).

Other ATC-inclined researchers echo that transfer research has not made a case for lesser deterrence resulting from CC prosecution of juvenile offenders:

To date, no studies of juvenile transfer seem to have fully captured the ways in which transferred and nontransferred youth may be different. The challenge of comparability is not unique to transfer research and represents a larger obstacle in studying juvenile court sanction effects (Zane et al., 2016, p. 916, citing Mears, 2003).

****

What emerges from this present review is that, after nine strong research evaluations of transfer have been undertaken, there is no reliable basis on which to argue that scientific evidence "now" exists for or against transfer as a policy of specific deterrence. Rather, the evidence is that transfer may decrease recidivism, but it also may increase it. The precise conditions under which such effects might arise remain unknown (Zane et al., 2016, p. 917).

****

Extant research does not provide a clear or consistent basis for determining whether transfer increases, decreases, or has no effect on recidivism (Id., p. 918).

Perhaps most remarkable is the resiliency of the ATC in condemning transfer despite acknowledging the faulty nature of research as well as the lack of evidence showing a lesser deterrence result (their go-to reason to oppose transfer to CC). This maneuver is made while ignoring the plethora of factors that most transfer research studies have completely ignored, the very positive recidivism reduction found for transfers via propensity-scoring research, and, the myriad other reasons/purposes served by transfer to CC beyond reducing recidivism (see Chapters 13-15).

So, for example, following the admissions noted above, Zane and colleagues (2016) claimed:

The continued lack of empirical evidence poses some concern given the importance of developing a coherent legal rationale for juvenile transfer (Zimring, 2010). It remains possible that transfer achieves appreciable reductions in juvenile crime rates; however, little empirical basis exists to support that claim. If in fact transfer does not have a general or specific deterrent effect, then its continued use may be questionable. At the same time, it is conceivable that even if transfer has no effect on juvenile crime, it may enable the juvenile court to operate more effectively and in keeping with its original mission focused on child welfare. No empirical studies have assessed that possibility. Given the considerable growth of the juvenile justice system in recent decades and the fact that only a small percentage of court referrals are transferred, it seems unlikely that such a benefit exists... (p. 919).

Even more remarkable, Zane and colleagues admitted there might be other reasons for transfer, but then disregard all of them because they have never been researched.[31] McGowan and colleagues, although aware of the limitations and findings of transfer research, simply asserted:

Transferring juveniles to the adult justice system is counterproductive as a strategy for deterring subsequent violence. (McGowan et al, 2007, p. S15).

Nevertheless, four pages after this declaration this group conceded:

It is not clear whether the effect of increased violence among juveniles who experience the adult versus the juvenile justice system is attributable to the overall judicial process, to the differences in sanctions experienced, or to some other component of the process... (Id., p. S19).

Seeming to reverse course yet once again, these researchers concluded with:

Overall, available evidence indicates that use of transfer laws and strengthened transfer policies is counterproductive for the purpose of reducing juvenile violence and enhancing public safety (Id., p. S20).

Ideology, rather than adequate research or comprehensive thought and analysis, appears to steer ATC policy considerations.

REFERENCES

Angell, K. M. (2004). The regressive movement: When juvenile offenders are treated as adults, nobody wins. *Southern California Interdisciplinary Law Journal, 14*, 125–144.

Andersen, T. S., & Ouellette, H. M. (2019). Juvenile court outcomes following youth's first arrest: A national test of the racial and ethnic threat hypothesis. *Crime and Delinquency*, *65*(2), 183–214. doi:10.1177/0011128718793616

Annino, P. G. (2000). Children in Florida adult prisons: A call for a moratorium. *Florida State University Law Review. Florida State University. College of Law*, *28*, 471–490.

Anwar, S., & Loughran, T. A. (2011). Testing a Bayesian learning theory of deterrence among serious juvenile offenders. *Criminology*, *49*(3), 667–698. doi:10.1111/j.1745-9125.2011.00233.x

Barnes, C., & Franz, R. (1989). Questionably adult: Determinants and effects of the juvenile waiver decision. *Justice Quarterly*, *6*(1), 117–135. doi:10.1080/07418828900090071

Barnoski, R. P. (2003). *Changes in Washington state's jurisdiction of juvenile offenders: Examining the impact*. Washington State Institute for Public Policy.

Beaudry-Cyr, M., Leiber, M., Brubaker, S. J., & Jaynes, C. (2020). The liberation hypothesis perspective and juvenile court outcomes: Implications for an understanding of the interplay between offender and offense characteristics. *Crime and Delinquency*, *66*(6-7), 806–836. doi:10.1177/0011128719894916

Bishop, D. M. (2000). Juvenile offenders in the adult criminal justice system. In M. Tonry (Ed.), *Crime & Justice: A Review of Research, 27, 81-167.* IL University of Chicago Press. doi:10.1086/652199

Bishop, D. M., & Frazier, C. E. (2000). Consequences of transfer. In J. Fagan & F. E. Zimring (Eds.), *The changing borders of juvenile justice: Transfer of adolescents to criminal court* (pp. 227–276). University of Chicago Press.

Bishop, D. M., Frazier, C. E., & Henretta, J. C. (1989). Prosecutorial waiver: A case study of questionable reform. *Crime and Delinquency*, *35*(2), 179–201. doi:10.1177/0011128789035002001

Bortner, M. A. (1986). Traditional rhetoric, organizational realities: Remand of juveniles to adult court. *Crime and Delinquency*, *32*(1), 53–73. doi:10.1177/0011128786032001004

Bortner, M. A., Zatz, M. S., & Hawkins, D. F. (2000). Race and Transfer: Empirical Research and Social Context. In J. Fagan & F. E. Zimring (Eds.), *The changing borders of juvenile justice: Transfer of adolescents to the criminal court* (pp. 277–320). University of Chicago Press.

Brown, J. M., & Langan, P. A. (1998). *State court sentencing of convicted felons, 1994.* U.S. Department of Justice, Office of Justice Programs, Bureau of Justice Statistics.

Burgess-Proctor, A., Holtrop, K., & Villarruel, F. A. (2008). *Youth transferred to adult court: Racial disparities*. Campaign for Youth Justice.

Burrow, J. D. (2008a). Examining the influence of Matza's principles of justice and their impact on reverse waiver decisions: Has Kadi-(In) justice survived? *Youth Violence and Juvenile Justice*, *6*(1), 59–82. doi:10.1177/1541204007308422

Burrow, J. D. (2008b). Reverse waiver and the effects of legal, statutory, and secondary legal factors on sentencing outcomes for juvenile offenders. *Crime and Delinquency*, *54*(1), 34–64. doi:10.1177/0011128707306687

Burrow, J. D., & Lowery, P. G. (2015). A preliminary assessment of the impact of plea bargaining among a sample of waiver-eligible offenders. *Youth Violence and Juvenile Justice*, *13*(3), 211–227. doi:10.1177/1541204014537089

Butts, J. A., & Connors-Beatty, D. J. (1992). *A comparison of juvenile court's and criminal court's response to violent offenders: 1985-1989*. National Center for Juvenile Justice.

Cauffman, E., Piquero, A. R., Kimonis, E., Steinberg, L., Chassin, L., & Fagan, J. (2007). Legal, individual, and environmental predictors of court disposition in a sample of serious adolescent offenders. *Law and Human Behavior*, *31*(6), 519–535. doi:10.100710979-006-9076-2 PMID:17245634

Cauffman, E. E., & Steinberg, L. (2012). Emerging findings from research on adolescent development and juvenile justice. *Victims & Offenders*, *7*(4), 428–449. doi:10.1080/15564886.2012.713901

Champion, D. J. (1989). Teenage felons and waiver hearings: Some recent trends, 1980-1988. *Crime and Delinquency*, *35*(4), 577–585. doi:10.1177/0011128789035004005

Cheesman, F. L., & Waters, N. L., & Hurst, H. (2010). Who gets a second chance? An investigation of Ohio's blended juvenile sentence. *Journal of Health and Human Services Administration*, 406–450. PMID:21329194

Clarke, E. E. (1996). A case for reinventing juvenile transfer. *Juvenile & Family Court Journal*, *47*(4), 3–22. doi:10.1111/j.1755-6988.1996.tb00757.x

Cohen, A. O., Bonnie, R. J., Taylor-Thompson, K., & Casey, B. J. (2016). When does a juvenile become an adult: Implications for law and policy. *Temple Law Review*, *88*, 769–788.

Coupet, S. M. (2000). What to do with sheep in wolf's clothing: The role of rhetoric and reality about youth offenders in the constructive dismantling policy of the juvenile justice system. *University of Pennsylvania Law Review*, *148*(4), 1303–1346. doi:10.2307/3312844

D'Angelo, J. M. (2007). The complex nature of juvenile court judges' transfer decisions: A study of judicial attitudes. *The Social Science Journal*, *44*(1), 147–159. doi:10.1016/j.soscij.2006.12.011

Dawson, R. O. (1992). An empirical study of *Kent* style juvenile transfers to criminal court. *St. Mary's Law Journal*, *23*, 975–1054.

DeFrances, C. J., & Strom, K. J. (1997). Juveniles prosecuted in state criminal courts, 1994. BJS Bulletin, U.S. Department of Justice, Office of Justice Programs.

DeLisi, M., Hochstetler, A., Jones-Johnson, G., Caudill, J. W., & Marquart, J. W. (2011). The road to murder: The enduring criminogenic effects of juvenile confinement among a sample of adult career criminals. *Youth Violence and Juvenile Justice*, *9*(3), 207–221. doi:10.1177/1541204010396107

Doob, A. N., & Webster, C. M. (2003). Sentence severity and crime: Accepting the null hypothesis. *Crime and Justice*, *30*, 143–195. doi:10.1086/652230

Durose, M. R., & Antenangeli, L. (2021). *Recidivism of prisoners released in 34 States in 2012: A 5-year follow-up period (2012–2017)*. U.S. Department of Justice, Office of Justice Programs. Bureau of Justice Statistics.

Eigen, J. P. (1981a). The determinants and impact of jurisdictional transfer in Philadelphia. In J. C. Hall, D. M. Hamparian, J. M. Pettibone, & J. White (Eds.), *Major Issues in Juvenile Justice Information and Training: Readings in Public Policy* (pp. 333–350). Academy for Contemporary Problems.

Eigen, J. P. (1981b). Punishing youth homicide offenders in Philadelphia. *The Journal of Criminal Law & Criminology, 72*(3), 1072–1093. doi:10.2307/1143276

Fagan, J. (1990). Social and legal policy dimensions of violent juvenile crime. *Criminal Justice and Behavior, 17*(1), 93–133. doi:10.1177/0093854890017001007

Fagan, J. (1996). The comparative impacts of juvenile and criminal court sanctions on adolescent felony offenders. *Law & Policy, 18*, 77–114. doi:10.1111/j.1467-9930.1996.tb00165.x

Fagan, J. (2008). Juvenile crime and criminal justice: Resolving border disputes. 18 *The Future of Children* 81-118 (Pages numbered 1-48 in Columbia Law School Working Paper).

Fagan, J., & Deschenes, E. P. (1990). Determinants of juvenile waiver decisions for violent juvenile offenders. *The Journal of Criminal Law & Criminology, 81*(2), 314–347. doi:10.2307/1143909

Fagan, J., Forst, M., & Vivona, T. S. (1987). Racial determinants of the judicial transfer decision: Prosecuting violent youth in criminal court. *Crime and Delinquency, 33*(2), 259–286. doi:10.1177/0011128787033002004

Fagan, J., & Tyler, T. (2005). Legal socialization of children and adolescents. *Social Justice Research, 18*(3), 217–242. doi:10.100711211-005-6823-3

Feld, B. C. (1984b). The decision to seek criminal charges: Just deserts and the waiver decision. *Criminal Justice Ethics, 3*(2), 27–41. doi:10.1080/0731129X.1984.9991756

Feld, B. C. (1988). The juvenile court meets the principle of offense: Punishment, treatment, and the difference it makes. *Boston University Law Review. Boston University. School of Law, 68*, 821–915.

Feld, B. C. (1989). Bad law makes hard cases: Reflections on teen-aged axe-murderers, judicial activism, and legislative default. *Minnesota Journal of Law & Inequality, 8*, 1–101.

Feld, B. C. (1993a). Criminalizing the American juvenile court. In M. Tonry (Ed.), *Crime & Justice: A Review, 17, 197-280.* doi:10.1086/449214

Fisher, W. S., & Teichman, L. (1986). Juvenile waivers to adult court: A report to the New Jersey state legislature. *Criminal Justice Quarterly, 9*, 68–103.

Fritsch, E. J., Caeti, T. J., & Hemmens, C. (1996). Spare the needle but not the punishment: The incarceration of waived youth in Texas prisons. *Crime and Delinquency, 42*(4), 593–609. doi:10.1177/0011128796042004006

Furdella, J., & Puzzanchera, C. (2015). *Delinquency cases in juvenile court, 2013.* Office of Juvenile Justice and Delinquency Prevention.

Gillespie, L. K., & Norman, M. D. (1984). Does certification mean prison: Some preliminary findings from Utah. *Juvenile & Family Court Journal, 35*(3), 23–34. doi:10.1111/j.1755-6988.1984.tb00541.x

Glassner, B., Ksander, M., Berg, B., & Johnson, B. D. (1983). A note on the deterrent effect of juvenile vs. adult jurisdiction. *Social Problems, 31*(2), 219–221. doi:10.2307/800213

Greenwood, P. W., Abrahamse, A., & Zimring, F. E. (1984). *Factors Affecting Sentencing Severity for Young Offenders*. National Institute of Justice.

Griffin, P., Addie, S., Addie, B., & Firestine, K. (2011). *Trying juveniles as adults: An analysis of state transfer laws and reporting*. U.S. Department of Justice, Office of Justice Programs, Office of Juvenile Justice and Delinquency Prevention.

Hess, W., Furr, L., Armstrong, K., Francis, S., & White, A. (2010). *Just kids: Baltimore's youth in the adult criminal justice system. A report of the just kids partnership to end the automatic prosecution of youth as adults*. Just Kids Partnership.

Hockenberry, S. (2018). *Delinquency cases in juvenile court, 2015*. Office of Juvenile Justice and Delinquency Prevention.

Hockenberry, S. (2019a). *Delinquency cases in juvenile court, 2016*. Office of Juvenile Justice and Delinquency Prevention.

Hockenberry, S. (2019b). *Delinquency cases in juvenile court, 2017*. Office of Juvenile Justice and Delinquency Prevention.

Horowitz, M. A. (2000). Kids who kill: A critique of how the American legal system deals with juveniles who commit homicide. *Law and Contemporary Problems, 63*(3), 133–177. doi:10.2307/1192328

Houghtalin, M., & Mays, G. L. (1991). Criminal dispositions of New Mexico juveniles transferred to adult court. *Crime and Delinquency, 37*(3), 393–407. doi:10.1177/0011128791037003006

Hyland, N. (2018). *Delinquency cases in juvenile court, 2014*. Office of Juvenile Justice and Delinquency Prevention.

Johnson, B. D., & Kurlychek, M. C. (2012). Transferred juveniles in the era of sentencing guidelines: Examining judicial departures for juvenile offenders in adult criminal court. *Criminology, 50*(2), 525–564. doi:10.1111/j.1745-9125.2011.00270.x

Johnson, K., Lanza-Kaduce, L., & Woolard, J. L. (2011). Disregarding graduated treatment. *Crime and Delinquency, 57*(5), 756–777. doi:10.1177/0011128708328867

Jordan, K. L. (2006). *Violent youth in adult court: The decertification of transferred youth*. LFB Scholarly.

Jordan, K. L. (2012). Juvenile transfer and recidivism: A propensity score matching approach. *Journal of Criminal Justice, 35*, 53–67.

Jordan, K. L. (2014). Juvenile status and criminal sentencing: Does it matter in the adult system? *Youth Violence and Juvenile Justice, 12*(4), 315–331. doi:10.1177/1541204013505298

Jordan, K. L., & Maroun, R. (2016). Minority threat and criminal sentencing: Examining juveniles in the adult criminal justice system. *Journal of Criminal Justice, 39*, 41–54.

Jordan, K. L., & McNeal, B. A. (2016). Juvenile penalty or leniency: Sentencing of juveniles in the criminal justice system. *Law and Human Behavior*, *40*(4), 525–564. doi:10.1037/lhb0000186 PMID:26974365

Jordan, K. L., & Myers, D. L. (2007). The decertification of transferred youth: Examining the determinants of reverse waiver. *Youth Violence and Juvenile Justice*, *5*(2), 188–206. doi:10.1177/1541204006295150

Jordan, K. L., & Myers, D. L. (2011). Juvenile transfer and deterrence: Reexamining the effectiveness of a "get-tough" policy. *Crime and Delinquency*, *57*(2), 247–270. doi:10.1177/0011128708319111

Juszkiewicz, J. (2000). *Youth crime/adult time: Is justice served?* Building Blocks for Youth.

Keenan, S. J., Rush, J. P., & Cheeseman, K. A. (2015). Judicial waiver decisions in two southern states: A study of judicial perceptions. *American Journal of Criminal Justice*, *40*(1), 100–115. doi:10.100712103-014-9241-y

Kinder, K., Veneziano, C., Fichter, M., & Azuma, H. (1995). A comparison of the dispositions of juvenile offenders certified as adults with juvenile offenders not certified. *Juvenile & Family Court Journal*, *46*(3), 37–42. doi:10.1111/j.1755-6988.1995.tb00821.x

Kleck, G., Sever, B., Li, S., & Gertz, M. (2005). The missing link in general deterrence research. *Criminology*, *43*(3), 623–660. doi:10.1111/j.0011-1348.2005.00019.x

Knowles, A., Rowan, Z., Frick, P. J., Steinberg, L., & Cauffman, E. (2022). Examining the relation between estimated life expectancy and delinquency across development: An examination of adolescent males following their first arrest. *Journal of Developmental and Life-Course Criminology*, *8*(1), 1–24. doi:10.100740865-021-00177-5

Kolivoski, K. M., Goodkind, S., & Shook, J. J. (2017). Social justice for crossover youth: The intersection of the child welfare and juvenile justice systems. *Social Work*, *62*(4), 313–321. doi:10.1093wwx034 PMID:28957574

Kupchik, A. (2006). *Judging juveniles: Prosecuting adolescents in adult and juvenile courts*. New York University Press.

Kupchik, A., Fagan, J., & Liberman, A. (2003). Punishment, proportionality, and jurisdictional transfer of adolescent offenders: A test of the leniency gap hypothesis. *Stanford Law & Policy Review*, *14*, 57–83.

Kurlychek, M. C., & Brian, D. (2004). The juvenile penalty: A comparison of juvenile and young adult sentencing outcomes in criminal court. *Criminology*, *42*(2), 485–515. doi:10.1111/j.1745-9125.2004.tb00527.x

Kurlychek, M. C., & Johnson, B. D. (2010). Juvenility and punishment: Sentencing juveniles in adult criminal court. *Criminology*, *48*(3), 725–758. doi:10.1111/j.1745-9125.2010.00200.x

Lab, S. P., & Whitehead, J. T. (1988). An analysis of juvenile correctional treatment. *Crime and Delinquency*, *34*(1), 60–83. doi:10.1177/0011128788034001004

Lanza-Kaduce, L., Frazier, C. E., Lane, J., & Bishop, D. M. (2002). *Juvenile transfer to criminal court study: Final report*. Floria Department of Juvenile Justice.

Lehmann, P. S., Chiricos, T., & Bales, W. D. (2018). Juveniles on trial: Mode of conviction and the adult court sentencing of transferred juveniles. *Crime and Delinquency*, *64*(5), 563–586. doi:10.1177/0011128717714203

Lemmon, J. H., Austin, T. L., Verrecchia, P. J., & Fetzer, M. (2005). The effect of legal and extralegal factors on statutory exclusion of juvenile offenders. *Youth Violence and Juvenile Justice*, *3*(3), 214–234. doi:10.1177/1541204005276263

Levitt, S. D. (1998). Juvenile crime and punishment. *Journal of Political Economy*, *106*(6), 1156–1185. doi:10.1086/250043

Loughran, T. A., Brame, R., Fagan, J., Piquero, A. R., Mulvey, E. P., & Schubert, C. A. (2015). Studying deterrence among high-risk adolescents. Juvenile Justice Bulletin. August 2015. U.S. Department of Justice, Office of Justice Programs. OJJDP.

Loughran, T. A., & Mulvey, E. P. (2010). Estimating treatment effects: Matching quantification to the question. In *Handbook of quantitative criminology* (pp. 163–180). Springer. doi:10.1007/978-0-387-77650-7_9

Loughran, T. A., Mulvey, E. P., Schubert, C. A., Chassin, L. A., Steinberg, L., Piquero, A. R., Cota-Robles, S., & Cauffman, E. (2010). Differential effects of adult court transfer on juvenile offender recidivism. *Law and Human Behavior*, *24*(6), 476–488. doi:10.100710979-009-9210-z PMID:20195895

Loughran, T. A., Piquero, A. R., Fagan, J., & Mulvey, E. P. (2012). Differential deterrence: Studying heterogeneity and changes in perceptual deterrence among serious youthful offenders. *Crime and Delinquency*, *58*(1), 3–27. doi:10.1177/0011128709345971

Lowery, P. G., Burrow, J. D., & Kaminski, R. J. (2018). A multilevel test of the racial threat hypothesis in one state's juvenile court. *Crime and Delinquency*, *64*(1), 53–87. doi:10.1177/0011128716678192

Males, M., & Macallair, D. (2000). *The color of justice: An analysis of juvenile adult court transfers in California*. Building Blocks for Youth.

Matthews, S. K., & Agnew, R. (2008). Extending deterrence theory: Do delinquent peers condition the relationship between perceptions of getting caught and offending? *Journal of Research in Crime and Delinquency*, *45*(2), 91–118. doi:10.1177/0022427807313702

Mays, G. L., & Houghtalin, M. (1992). Trying juveniles as adults: A note on New Mexico's recent experience. *Justice System Journal*, *15*(3), 814–823. doi:10.1080/23277556.1993.10871163

McGowan, A., Hahn, R., Liberman, A., Crosby, A., Fullilove, M., Johnson, R., Moscicki, E., Price, L., Snyder, S., Tuma, F., Lowy, J., Briss, P., Cory, S., & Stone, G. (2007). Effects on violence of laws and policies facilitating the transfer of juveniles from the juvenile justice system to the adult justice system: A systematic review. *American Journal of Preventive Medicine*, *32*(4), S7–S28. doi:10.1016/j.amepre.2006.12.003 PMID:17386331

Mears, D. P. (2003). A critique of waiver research: Critical next steps in assessing the impacts of laws for transferring juveniles to the criminal justice system. *Youth Violence and Juvenile Justice*, *1*(2), 156–172. doi:10.1177/1541204002250876

Millstein, S. G., & Halpern-Felsher, B. L. (2002). Perceptions of risk and vulnerability. *The Journal of Adolescent Health, 31*(1), 10–27. doi:10.1016/S1054-139X(02)00412-3 PMID:12093608

Miner-Romanoff, K. (2014). Juvenile offenders tried as adults: What they know and implications for practitioners. *Northern Kentucky Law Review, 41*, 205–224.

Monahan, K., Steinberg, L., & Piquero, A. R. (2015). Juvenile justice policy and practice: A developmental perspective. *Crime and Justice, 44*(1), 577–619. doi:10.1086/681553

Services, M. S. T. (2018). Multisystemic Therapy. *Do we know the full extent of juvenile recidivism?* info.mstservices.com, November 1, 2018.

Mulvey, E. P., & Reppucci, N. D. (1988). The context of clinical judgment: The effect of resource availability on judgments of amenability to treatment in juvenile offenders. *American Journal of Community Psychology, 16*(4), 525–545. doi:10.1007/BF00922769 PMID:3189236

Mulvey, E. P., & Schubert, C. (2012). *Transfer of juveniles to adult court: Effects of a broad policy in one court. Juvenile Justice Bulletin. December 2012*. U.S. Department of Justice, Office of Justice Programs. Office of Juvenile Justice & Delinquency Prevention.

Myers, D. L. (2001). *Excluding violent youths from juvenile court: The effectiveness of legislative waiver*. LFB Scholarly Publications.

Myers, D. L. (2003). The recidivism of violent youths in juvenile and adult court: A consideration of selection bias. *Youth Violence and Juvenile Justice, 1*(1), 79–101. doi:10.1177/1541204002238365

Myers, D. L. (2005). *Boys among men: Trying and sentencing juveniles as adults*. Praeger Publishers.

Myers, D. L. (2016). Juvenile transfer to adult court: Ongoing search for scientific support. *Criminology & Public Policy, 15*(3), 927–938. doi:10.1111/1745-9133.12232

Myers, D. L., & Kiehl, K. (2001). The predispositional status of violent youthful offenders: Is there a "custody gap" in adult criminal court? *Justice Research and Policy, 3*(1), 115–143. doi:10.3818/JRP.3.1.2001.115

Myers, D. L., Lee, D., Giever, D., & Gilliam, J. (2011). Practitioner perceptions of juvenile transfer in Pennsylvania. *Youth Violence and Juvenile Justice, 9*(3), 222–240. doi:10.1177/1541204010391216

Mulvey, E. P., Steinberg, L., Piquero, A. R., Besana, M., Fagan, J., Schubert, C., & Cauffman, E. (2010). Trajectories of desistance and continuity in antisocial behavior following court adjudication among serious adolescent offenders. *Development and Psychopathology, 22*(2), 453–475. doi:10.1017/S0954579410000179 PMID:20423553

Nagin, D. S., Piquero, A. R., Scott, E. S., & Steinberg, L. (2006). Public preferences for rehabilitation versus incarceration of juvenile offenders: Evidence from a contingent valuation survey. *Criminology & Public Policy, 5*(4), 627–651. doi:10.1111/j.1745-9133.2006.00406.x

Olson, J. K. (2004). *Waiver of juveniles to criminal court: Judicial discretion and racial disparity* [Unpublished doctoral dissertation, University of Nevada-Las Vegas, Las Vegas, Nevada].

Judges, P. A. (2018). *PA judges benchbook*. Pennsylvania Juvenile Court Judges' Commission.

Paternoster, R. (1989a). Absolute and restrictive deterrence in a panel of youth: Explaining the onset, persistence/desistance, and frequency of offending. *Social Problems*, *36*(3), 289–309. doi:10.2307/800696

Paternoster, R. (1989b). Decisions to participate in and desist from four types of delinquency: Deterrence and the rational choice perspective. *Law & Society Review*, *23*(1), 7–40. doi:10.2307/3053879

Podkopacz, M. R., & Feld, B. C. (1995). Judicial waiver policy and practice: Persistence, seriousness, and race. *Minnesota Journal of Law & Inequality*, *14*, 73–178.

Podkopacz, M. R., & Feld, B. C. (1996). The end of the line: An empirical study of judicial waiver. *The Journal of Criminal Law & Criminology*, *86*(2), 449–492. doi:10.2307/1144033

Poe-Yamagata, E., & Jones, M. A. (2000). *And justice for some: Differential treatment of minority youth in the justice system*. Building Blocks for Youth.

Poulos, T. M., & Orchowsky, S. (1994). Serious juvenile offenders: Predicting the probability of transfer to criminal court. *Crime and Delinquency*, *40*(1), 3–17. doi:10.1177/0011128794040001001

Redding, R. E. (1999). Examining legal issues: Juvenile offenders in criminal court and adult prison. *Corrections Today*, (April), 92–123.

Redding, R. E. (2003). The effects of adjudicating and sentencing juveniles as adults: Research and policy implications. *Youth Violence and Juvenile Justice*, *1*(2), 128–155. doi:10.1177/1541204002250875

Redding, R. E. (2005). Adult punishment for juvenile offenders: Does it reduce crime? In Dowd, N. Singer, D., & Wilson, R. (Eds.), Handbook of children, culture, and violence (Chapter 19). Sage Publications.

Redding, R. E. (2008). *Juvenile transfer laws: An effective deterrent to delinquency*. U.S. Office of Juvenile Justice and Delinquency Prevention.

Redding, R. E. (2010). *Juvenile transfer laws: An effective deterrent to delinquency?* U.S. Department of Justice, Office of Juvenile Justice & Delinquency Prevention.

Redding, R. E. (2016). One size does not fit all: The deterrent effect of transferring juveniles to criminal court. *Criminology & Public Policy*, *15*(3), 939–948. doi:10.1111/1745-9133.12239

Redding, R. E., & Fuller, E. J. (2004). What do juvenile offenders know about being tried as adults? Implications for deterrence. *Juvenile & Family Court Journal*, *55*(3), 35–44. doi:10.1111/j.1755-6988.2004.tb00167.x

Reyna, V. F., & Farley, F. (2006). Risk and rationality in adolescent decision making: Implications for theory, practice, and public policy. *Psychological Science in the Public Interest*, *7*(1), 1–44. doi:10.1111/j.1529-1006.2006.00026.x PMID:26158695

Robinson, P. H., & Darley, J. M. (2004). Does criminal law deter? A behavioral science investigation. *Oxford Journal of Legal Studies*, *24*(2), 173–205. doi:10.1093/ojls/24.2.173

Roysher, M., & Edelman, P. (1981). Treating juveniles as adults in New York: What does it mean and how is it working? In J. C. Hall, D. M. Hamparian, J. M. Pettibone, & J. L. White (Eds.), *Major Issues in Juvenile Justice Information and Training: Readings in Public Policy* (pp. 265–293). Academy for Contemporary Problems.

Rudman, C., Hartstone, E. C., Fagan, J., & Moore, M. (1986). Violent youth in adult court: Process and punishment. *Crime and Delinquency*, *32*(1), 75–96. doi:10.1177/0011128786032001005

Sanborn, J. B., Jr. (1985). *Plea negotiation in juvenile court.* [Unpublished doctoral dissertation, SUNY Albany, Albany, NY., United States].

Sanborn, J. B. Jr. (1994a). Certification to criminal court: The important policy questions of how, when, and why. *Crime and Delinquency*, *40*(2), 262–281. doi:10.1177/0011128794040002007

Sanborn, J. B. Jr. (1994d). The juvenile, the court, or the community: Whose best interests are currently being promoted in juvenile court? *Justice System Journal*, *17*(2), 249–266. doi:10.1080/23277556.1994.10871207

Sanborn, J. B. Jr. (1998). Second-class justice and first-class punishment: The use of juvenile records in sentencing adults. *Judicature*, *81*, 206–213.

Sanborn, J. B. Jr. (2000). Striking out on the first pitch in criminal court. *Barry Law Review*, *1*, 7–61.

Sanborn, J. B. Jr, & Salerno, A. W. (2005). *The juvenile justice system: Law and process.* Roxbury Publishing Company. Oxford University Publishing.

Schneider, A. L., & Ervin, L. (1990). Specific deterrence, rational choice, and decision heuristics: Applications in juvenile justice. *Social Science Quarterly*, *71*, 585–601.

Schubert, C. A., Mulvey, E. P., Loughran, T. A., Fagan, J., Chassin, L. A., Piquero, A. R., Losoya, S. H., Steinberg, L., & Cauffman, E. (2010). Predicting outcomes for transferred youth: Implications for policy and practice. *Law and Human Behavior*, *34*, 460–475. doi:10.100710979-009-9209-5 PMID:20204478

Scott, E. S., Reppucci, N. D., & Woolard, J. L. (1995). Evaluating adolescent decision making in legal contexts. *Law and Human Behavior*, *19*(3), 221–244. doi:10.1007/BF01501658

Scott, E. S., & Steinberg, L. (2008). *Rethinking juvenile justice.* Harvard University Press.

Semple, J. K., & Woody, W. D. (2011). Juveniles tried as adults: The age of the juvenile matters. *Psychological Reports*, *109*(1), 301–308. doi:10.2466/07.17.PR0.109.4.301-308 PMID:22049670

Shook, J. J. (2004). *Treating juveniles as adults in the justice system: A case study of decision making and case processing.* [Unpublished doctoral dissertation, University of Michigan, Ann Arbor, MI].

Sickmund, M., & Puzzanchera, C. (2014). *Juvenile offenders and victims: 2014 national report.* National Center for Juvenile Justice.

Sickmund, M., Sladky, A., & Kang, W. (2019). *Easy access to juvenile court statistics: 1985-2017. Online.* National Center for Juvenile Justice. https://www.ojjdp.gov/ojstatbb/ezajcs/ .

Singer, S. I. (1993). The automatic waiver of juveniles and substantive justice. *Crime and Delinquency*, *39*(2), 253–261. doi:10.1177/0011128793039002009

Smith, C. K. (2013). Nothing About Us Without Us! The failure of the modern juvenile justice system and a call for community-based justice. *The Journal of Applied Research on Children*, *4*(1), 11.

Smith, D. A., & Paternoster, R. (1990). Formal processing and future delinquency: Deviance amplification as a selection artifact. *Law & Society Review*, *24*(5), 1109–1131. doi:10.2307/3053663

Snyder, H. N. (1996). The juvenile court and delinquency cases. *The Future of Children*, *6*(3), 53–63. doi:10.2307/1602593 PMID:9117366

Snyder, H. N., Sickmund, M., & Poe-Yamagata, E. (2000). *Juvenile transfers to criminal court in the 1990s: Lessons learned from four studies*. U.S. Department of Justice, Office of Justice Programs, Office of Juvenile Justice and Delinquency Prevention.

Spelman, W. (2000). What recent studies do (and don't) tell us about imprisonment and crime. *Crime and Justice*, *27*, 419–494. doi:10.1086/652204

Sridharan, S., Greenfield, L., & Blakley, B. (2004). A study of prosecutorial certification practice in Virginia. *Criminology & Public Policy*, *3*(4), 605–632. doi:10.1111/j.1745-9133.2004.tb00067.x

Steinberg, L. (2007). Risk-taking in adolescence: New perspectives from brain and behavioral science. *Current Directions in Psychological Science*, *16*(2), 55–59. doi:10.1111/j.1467-8721.2007.00475.x

Steinberg, L., & Cauffman, E. (1996). Maturity of judgment in adolescence: Psychosocial factors in adolescent decision making. *Law and Human Behavior*, *20*(3), 249–272. doi:10.1007/BF01499023

Steiner, B. (2009). The effects of juvenile transfer to criminal court on incarceration decisions. *Justice Quarterly*, *26*(1), 77–106. doi:10.1080/07418820802119943

Strom, K. J., Smith, S.K., & Snyder, H.N. (1998). *Juvenile felony defendants in criminal courts. State court processing statistics, 1990-94*. U.S. Department of Justice. Office of Justice Programs. Bureau of Justice Statistics Special Report.

Tashea, J. R., & Passarella, A. (2015). Youth charged as adults: The use and outcomes of transfer in Baltimore City. *University of Maryland Law Journal of Race, Religion. Race, Gender, & Class*, *14*, 273–302.

Thomas, C. W., & Bilchik, S. (1985). Prosecuting juveniles in criminal court: A legal and empirical analysis. *The Journal of Criminal Law & Criminology*, *76*(2), 439–479. doi:10.2307/1143613

Thomas, C. W., & Bishop, D. M. (1984). The effect of formal and informal sanctions on delinquency: A longitudinal comparison of labeling and deterrence theories. *The Journal of Criminal Law & Criminology*, *75*(4), 1222–1245. doi:10.2307/1143384

Torbet, P. M., Gable, R., Hurst, I. V. H., Montgomery, I., Szymanski, L. A., & Thomas, D. (1996). *State responses to serious and violent juvenile crime*. Office of Juvenile Justice and Delinquency Prevention.

Verrecchia, P. J. (2011). The effect of transfer mechanism from juvenile court on conviction on a target offense in criminal court. *Contemporary Justice Review*, *14*(2), 189–201. doi:10.1080/10282580.2011.565976

Vidal, S., Prince, D., Connell, C. M., Caron, C. M., Kaufman, J. S., & Tebes, J. K. (2017). Maltreatment, family environment, and social risk factors: Determinants of the child welfare to juvenile justice transition among maltreated children and adolescents. *Child Abuse & Neglect*, *63*, 7–18. doi:10.1016/j.chiabu.2016.11.013 PMID:27886518

Whitehead, J. T., & Lab, S. B. (1989). A meta-analysis of juvenile correctional treatment. *Journal of Research in Crime and Delinquency*, *26*(3), 276–295. doi:10.1177/0022427889026003005

Winner, L., Lanza-Kaduce, L., Bishop, D. M., & Frazier, C. E. (1997). The transfer of juveniles to criminal court: Reexamining recidivism over the long term. *Crime and Delinquency*, *43*(4), 548–563. doi:10.1177/0011128797043004009

Woolard, J. L., & Harvell, M. P. P. (2008). Anticipatory injustice among adolescents: Age and racial/ethnic differences in perceived unfairness of the justice system. *Behavioral Sciences & the Law*, *26*, 207–226. doi:10.1002/bsl.805 PMID:18344171

Zane, S. N. (2017). Do criminal court outcomes vary by juvenile transfer mechanism? A multi-jurisdictional, multilevel analysis. *Justice Quarterly*, *34*(3), 542–569. doi:10.1080/07418825.2016.1190395

Zane, S. N., Welsh, B. C., & Mears, D. P. (2016). Juvenile transfer and the specific deterrence hypothesis: Systematic review and meta-analysis. *Criminology & Public Policy*, *15*(3), 901–925. doi:10.1111/1745-9133.12222

Zeidenberg, J. (2001). *Drugs and disparity: The racial impacts of Illinois' practice of transferring young drug offenders to adult court*. Building Blocks for Youth.

ENDNOTES

1. Urban JCs could adopt this practice to prevent rapid ascensions up the ladder by multitudes of juveniles; also, suburban, and rural JCs should have fewer probationers assigned to each PO, which can allow probation to be an intensive experience there earlier than in urban JCs.
2. By that age, a youth's "performance of simple cognitive tasks reaches adultlike performance in speed and accuracy (Cohen et al., 2016, p. 779, citations omitted)." A 2006 qualitative study of JC workers found interesting views of the appropriate qualifying age for transfer. Not surprising, public defenders scored the highest desired age (16.93 mean age), while judges registered the second highest at 15.95. POs were third in the ranking at 15.78, while prosecutors recommended the lowest age (14.09). Not surprising was the strongest opposition to offense exclusion (OE) being claimed by the public defenders; judges, however, considered OE to be effective, perhaps suggesting a willingness on their part to surrender control of the transfer decision in serious cases to prosecutors. Most intriguing was the fact that those who had worked in JC longer supported a lower age of criminal responsibility (see Myers. Lee, Giever, & Gilliam, 2011, pp. 229-234; see, also, Sanborn, 1994a).
3. See Champion, 1989; Clarke, 1996; Coupet, 2000; Feld, 1988; Gillespie & Norman, 1984; Houghtalin & Mays, 1991; Kinder, Veneziano, Fichter, & Azuma, 1995; Podkopacz & Feld, 1995, 1996; Roysher & Edelman, 1981; Thomas & Bilchik, 1985.
4. See Barnes & Franz, 1989; Barnoski, 2003; Bortner, 1986; Dawson, 1992; Eigen 1981a, 1981b; Fisher & Teichman, 1986; Greenwood, Abrahamse & Zimring, 1984; Houghtalin & Mays, 1991; Mays & Houghtalin, 1992; Myers, 2001; Podkopacz & Feld, 1995, 1996; Thomas & Bilchik, 1985.
5. See Bishop et al, 1989; Butts & Connors-Beatty, 1992; Dawson, 1992; Houghtalin & Mays, 1991; Podkopacz & Feld, 1995, 1996; Redding. 2003; Strom, Smith & Snyder, 1998.

6 For comparable results, see; Brown & Langan, 1998; Fagan, Forst & Vivona, 1987; Rudman, Hartstone, Fagan, & Moore, 1986; Torbet et al., 1996).

7 Keeping in mind that the typical, maximum potential commitment disposition in JC would be four or five years, at least for older offenders, it would not be surprising to find longer six-to-ten years prison terms (and even much longer) being imposed on violent juvenile offenders in CC.

8 See, e.g., Johnson & Kurlychek, 2012; Jordan & McNeil, 2016; Lehmann, Chiricos, & Bales, 2018.

9 See Angell, 2004; Kurlychek & Johnson, 2004, 2010; Lab & Whitehead 1988; Paternoster, 1989a, 1989b; Redding, 2003; Schneider & Ervin, 1990; Thomas & Bishop, 1984; Whitehead & Lab, 1989.

10 Bishop (2000) later admitted they did not consider "jurisdictional variations in community context," or the "considerable variation in crime rates as well as practices of crime control," and they "controlled for many, but certainly not all, of personal offender and offense characteristics that affect the risk of recidivism. It is possible that the two groups differ(ed) in terms of factors such as mental health, family background, or neighborhood, which were not controlled." Bishop was convinced, nevertheless, that there was "minimal bias from such sources (pp. 132- 133)."

11 Feld and Zimring emphasized the wide variation in assault and robbery charges and how that creates an opportunity to abuse discretion. Just as important, it points to the incredible unreliability of research that uses matched samples. Not all burglaries/assaults are created equal. The surprise, here, is that these two ATC members are willing to characterize OE as categorical and as establishing binding rules. It seems, then, to these scholars OE can be simultaneously discretionary and nondiscretionary.

12 Direct file (DF) is usually possible for broad categories of crimes, such as all degrees of robbery (see Sanborn & Salerno, 2005). The DF crime, alone, does not explain why the case is being prosecuted in CC. With OE, when two defendants are arrested for first-degree robberies, the prosecutor's choosing only one of them for transfer should reflect that the transfer is "criminally worse" than the retained youth. That trait could lead to OE transfers' being more disposed to criminality compared to retained offenders; this trait could also account for transfers' acting on that inclination quicker and more often than retained youths. Nevertheless, comparing the outcomes of OE transfers versus retained offenders should be impossible since there is no charge-oriented comparable retained group.

13 This problem of selection bias potential has not been lost on some critics: (I)*t is debatable whether this research has fully addressed the issue of sample selection when assessing the impact of being transferred to adult court or retained in juvenile court. A comparison of offenders who are transferred to adult court and those who are not transferred involves two groups that are inherently different in important ways that predate incarceration and that may affect any comparison of the groups' patterns of reoffending. Consequently, observed differences (e.g., greater arrest rates) in the transferred population cannot be accurately attributed to the transfer experience itself as long as these differences in outcomes might also be partially or fully attributable to fundamental differences between the transferred and retained youth…* (Mulvey & Schubert, 2012, p. 7).

14 Implicit in the presence of the charge in CC is some element of the robbery (such as aggravated circumstances of the crime, the role played by this offender, the number of fellow participants, the gang nature of the offense, the victim's position) plus, perhaps, some factor(s) of the youth's background that makes the prosecutor believe that prosecution in JC undervalues the crime and record and/or overestimates the rehabilitation capacity of the offender. Important variables that

influenced the prosecutor's transfer decision are most likely unknown to the researcher, especially if there has been total reliance on a JC dataset.

15 Maybe judges (and perhaps prosecutors) transfer the worst offenders. Unfortunately, it is not possible to conduct the best research here since that would involve random assignment to the two groups (see Loughran & Mulvey, 2010; Mulvey & Schubert 2012; Zane, Welsh & Mears, 2016), which creates serious ethical problems; no such study has been conducted. The greater recidivism rates among transfers could be explained, in part, by prosecutors' and judges' making prescient choices as to which juveniles are not likely to stop their criminal behavior.

16 This second reason/observation has special applicability to JT. The transfer of non-amenable types and avoidance of overcrowded facilities has helped the JJ system's helping retained offenders to some degree. The more lenient the CC sanction, the more recidivism must be expected/invited since CC leniency would inform offenders that neither system treats them harshly. That awareness must contribute to a lack of any deterrent effect.

17 They concluded transfer may contribute to *differential deterrence* (see Loughran et al., 2010; and Loughran et al, 2015). Considering how chronic property offenders tend to be, it is no surprise that these offenders would continue offending after transfer to CC. Schubert and colleagues (2010) found when all transfers were examined together there was no effect on rearrests, but when person offenses were isolated, there was a lower rearrest for transfers. These researchers claim that examining aggregate umbers, as most transfer research has done, confounds results.

18 Jordan's work has produced the most encouraging findings, using this approach: a 31% lesser recidivism rate among transfers, with an eight-year post-release tracking period.

19 Selection bias will still occur and can never be fully eliminated, but propensity scoring is an improvement since it includes more critical variables and reduces selection bias.

20 The number of priors was divided into: ever; past year; and past six months. Also, the age at first prior petition was examined as was the number of early onset behavioral problems. Gang membership and any overnight stays in a facility were included as were total anxiety score and several risk-need variables. Remaining factors included: IQ, employment status, community service history, alcohol/drug use/dependency, mental health diagnosis, psychopathy factors, multiple measures of ethnic identity, exposure to violence as either a victim or a witness, several Weinberger-related items, psychosocial maturity, resistance to peer influence, self-regulation ability, several social and personal costs/rewards of punishment measures, legal cynicism, domains of social support, motivation to succeed, moral disengagement, involvement in community activities, number of unsupervised routine activities, and social capital and social ties.

21 Besides finding less recidivism among person-crime transfers (greater recidivism for property crimes and an overall null effect of transfer), researchers found significant differences between the retained vs transfers in 3 factors rarely, if ever, measured elsewhere: offenders' perceptions of punishment as less certain; stronger sense of ethnic identity and greater exposure to violence.

22 Cohen and colleagues (2016) may be on to something: "teens show enhanced performance on decision-making tasks when either money or points are at stake and dependent on their performance (pp. 781-82, citations omitted)." If this attribute is widespread among juveniles, it could help explain urban youths' chronic burglaries, robberies, and auto thefts. That property crime is the most difficult to deter among juveniles, whether they are prosecuted in JC or in CC, would be in sync with this finding. A 2011 study in King County, WA found, in a 2-year span, nearly two-thirds of offenders had experience in the child welfare system; an extensive history in that system

led to greater likelihood reoffending than without a history (70% versus 34%); girls' recidivism rate difference was the same (63% versus 27%) (see MST Services, 2018, p. 2).

23 The PA Judges' Benchbook recognizes a "public interest" in transfer and expounds upon the JC's obligation to consider the victim and the community. *A victim of a juvenile offense has the right to notice of any hearings related to the transfer of a juvenile to and from criminal proceedings and may decide to participate in the proceedings. As noted above, in making its "public interest" determination in a transfer proceeding, the court is required to give careful consideration to victim impact evidence. The* **extent to which the victim has been harmed** *by the offense is one basic measure of its seriousness. Moreover, the* **degree of harm suffered by the victim** *should have considerable bearing on the court's assessment of the adequacy of a juvenile disposition to meet the case. Accordingly, in the course of the transfer hearing, evidence should be presented on the* **physical, emotional, and financial impact of the offense on the victim,** *and such evidence should be weighed appropriately in the court's decision. Where necessary, as in a disposition hearing, the court should make its own inquiries regarding the victim's feelings, concerns, and wishes regarding transfer....* **Accountability to victims and victim restoration** *are among the Pennsylvania juvenile justice system's primary goals... The law requires the court, in weighing a request for transfer to or from criminal proceedings, to* **take into account any impact the offense has had on the community and any threat to the community's safety** *that may be posed by the juvenile...* (PA Judges, 2018, Section 6.8, emphases added, citations omitted). This Benchbook reveals the potential impact of the victim and community on transfer.

24 Although the number is small, some transfers are in CC by virtue of a self-transfer.

25 Perhaps it is not the transfer that failed to deter but rather the experiences in CC that encouraged the recidivism. If CC continues to impose the relatively lenient sentencing some offenders have already experienced in JC, perhaps no deterrent effect should be expected. If so, it is the CC that has failed society, not transfer. Research has taught us transfers allowed back into the community in relatively brief time cannot be trusted to be law abiding (the same for retained juveniles). Ignoring the possibility that short CC sentences could explain the deterrence problem, the ATC instead blames transfer.

26 The list could be expanded considerably. Even if transfer does not deter, that does not mean we should abolish transfer. That prison does not deter does not mean we should close prisons.

27 Perhaps feelings of fealty towards JC explain the findings of Bishop and Frazier that transfers are angry and resentful when prosecuted in CC; they see unfair CC sentences and a less caring system (Bishop & Frazier, 2000; see Winner et al., 1997). Transfers regard JC fondly. It is small wonder that offenders prefer the JJ system's shorter sentences and more hospitable facilities. Some juveniles who would rule in JJ facilities, will not be able to do the same in prisons. Perhaps many of the intimidators in JJ morph into the intimidated in CJ. It might not be the CC process that juveniles perceive as injustice (see Bishop & Frazier, 2000; Winner et al., 1997), but rather a feeling of denied entitlement since JC does not get to "coddle" them once again. It could be the fond feelings toward JC that help explain the high recidivism rates among retained juveniles. While the answer is not to make JJ a worse/harsh, non-rehabilitative experience to prepare offenders for CJ, the answer is equally not to eliminate transfer so as not to disappoint/offend transfers.

28 Selective incapacitation supporters promised numerous risk factors could identify and selectively incarcerate offenders predicted to have the most prolific criminal futures. Supporters predicted a serious reduction in the crime rate; the results never matched the promise.

29 These concerns apply equally to rehabilitation; it created the same problems inherent in selective incapacitation, such as discrimination. That disappointed some rehabilitation types, which led to their launching the Just Deserts movement, a subset of the retribution philosophy.

Most transfer studies claim definitive answers of its findings in CC only to have them refuted by later improved methodologies. The crystal ball might become less opaque over time with better understanding of the factors that must be examined to better comprehend transfer and its results. Nevertheless, the ball will never be crystal clear. Nor does it help when findings are qualified with words, such as "tendencies," "might," "could be," "most," "less," etc.; that is also characteristic of DPs' research on CST. That necessary couching lends to a lack of confidence as to how any group of offenders, let alone any individual juvenile, will perform in the future.

30 Using the findings from these (deterrence/desistance) research efforts to inform prevention strategies and treatment modalities (and perhaps JC dispositions) certainly can benefit both the JJ system and offenders. Employing them to determine who does and who does not get transferred (or how they are sentenced there) has significant legal ramifications, and potential discriminatory results, that should cause hesitancy in adopting them. The same (potential) discrimination witnessed when rehabilitation and selective incapacitation determined sentencing in CC testifies to the need for an appropriate level of hesitancy in their use in transfer. The same variability and discriminatory outcomes that concerned Feld and Zimring when amenability-oriented JT is utilized should raise similar reactions here. Perhaps these potential differential outcomes are inevitable whenever utilitarian goals in transfer and sentencing are pursued. These potential differential outcomes convince retributionists not to have their philosophy tethered to any utilitarian mission.

31 Many of the benefits identified in Chapters 13, 14 and 15 are difficult, if not impossible, to measure. Not only are the benefits not prone to empirical verification, given the state and ideology of academia, there is little chance they will ever be acknowledged, let alone examined.

What seems lost on the ATC is that retaining only a few violent offenders can alter JC's character detrimentally (reducing the JC's maximum age) or fatally (abolishing JC). Keeping transfer eligible juveniles can ruin JJ facilities, cause overcrowding/trickle-down effect, or launch a case where "serious, older offenders represent a danger to other juveniles (Zane et al., 2016, p. 919)," The ATC criticizes the safety valve reason and then purposely invites it.

CHAPTER 12 TABLES

Table 43.[*] *Judicial Transfers to CC by Age, 2005-2017*

Age	# and % of Total Transfers	# and % of Formal Cases	# and % of Formal & Informal Cases
< 12	67 .1% 5.2/year	67/203,211 .03%	67/569,524 .012%
12	112 , 17% 8.6/year	112/312,498 .04%	112/710,058 .016%
13	240 .36% 18.5/year	240/718,565 .03%	240/1,445,296 .017%
14	1,286 1.9 98.9/year	1,286/1,313,189 .1%	1,286/2,449,934 .05%
15	5,728 8.5% 440.6/year	5,728/1,969,750 .3%	5,728/3,480,430 .16%
16	19,588 29.1% 1,506.8/year	19,588/2,290,844 .9%	19,588/4,012,986 .5%
17	35,408 52.6% 2,723.7/year	35,408/1,806,278 1.96%	35,408/3,069,594 1.2%
>17	4,905 7.3% 377.3/year	4,905/281,441 1.74%	4,905/419,869 1.2%
<12/12	179 .27%	179/515,709 .03%	179/1,279,582 .01%
13+	67,155 99.73%	67,155/8,149,533 .82%	67,155/14,888,109 .45%
14+	66,915 99.4%	66,915/7,430,968 .9%	66,915/13,442,813 .5%
15+	65,629 97.5%	65,629/6,117,779 .75%	65,629/10,992,879 .6%
16+	59,901 89%	59,901/4,148,029 1.1%	59,901/7,502,449 .8%
Total	67,334 100% 5,179.5/year	67,334/8,665,242 .78% 5,179.5/666.557.1 .78%	67,334/16,167,691 .42% 5,179.5/1,243,668.5 .42%

[*]Adapted from Sickmund, Sladky & Kang, 2019.

Table 44. Transfer research findings on recidivism/deterrence

Worse results (i.e., may be increase in crime or worse; specific and/or general deterrence):
Bishop, (2000)
Bishop & Frazier, (1996)
Cohn & Mialson, (2008)
Drake, (2013)
Fagan, (1991), (1995), (1996)
Fagan, Kupchik, & Liberman, (2007)
Hahn et al., (2007)
Jensen & Metsger, (1994)
Lanza-Kaduce et al., (2002)
McGowan et al., (2007)
Myers, (2001), (2003)
Podkopacz & Feld, (1995), (1996)
Redding, (2008), (2016)
Risler, Sweatman, & Nackerud, (1998)
Singer, (1996b)
Singer & McDowell, (1988)
Steiner, Hemmens, & Bell (2006)
Steiner & Wright, (2006)
Winner et al., (1997)
None/Same results (or no significant reductions in recidivism):
Barnoski, (2003)
Fagan, (1996)
Fagan et al., (2007)
Farrington et al., (2012)
Hoeffel, (2013)
Loughran et al., (2010)
McGowan et al., (2007)
Mulvey & Schubert, (2012)
Myers, (2003)
Podkopacz & Feld, (1995), (1996)
Steiner, Hemmens, & Bell, (2006)
Steiner & Wright, (2006)
Winner et al., (1997)
Zane, Welsh, & Mears, (2016)
Zimring & Rushin, (2013)
Better results (or less recidivism):
Barnoski, (2003)
Cohn & Mialson, (2008)
Hansen, Thayer, Feldstein Ewing, Sabbineni, & Bryan, (2018)
Jordan, (2012)
Loeffler & Grunwald, (2015).
Loughran et al., (2010)
Steiner, Hemmens, & Bell (2006)
Steiner & Wright, (2006)

Table 45. Sources for a No-Transfer Policy Leading to: Waste of resources and/or Contamination of Salvageable Youths

Bishop & Frazier, (1991)
Bishop, Frazier, & Henretta, (1989)
Bortner, (1986)
Bove, (1991)
Browne, (1977)
Comment, W., (1966)
Comments, C., (1973)
Edwards, (1977)
Fagan & Deschenes, (1990)
Feld, (1978)
Forst & Blomquist, (1991)
Ganzfried, (1972)
Gasper & Katkin, (1980)
Gillespie & Norman, (1984)
Grisso, (2000)
Grisso, Tomkins, & Casey, (1988)
Grundfest et al., (1981)
Hogan, (1974)
Kozich, (1980)
McNulty, (1996)
Mears, (2003)
Mears et al., (2014)
Mountford & Berenson, (1969)
Notes, (1966)
Notes & Comments, (1967)
Parker, (1976)
Polen, (1987)
Reiney, (1966)
Stamm, (1973)
Steward-Lindsey, (2006)
Thomas & Bilchik, (1985)
Zane, Welsh, & Mears, (2016)
Zimring, (1981)

Table 43 References

Sickmund, M., Sladky, A., & Kang, W. (2019). *Easy access to juvenile court statistics: 1985-2017. Online*. Available: https://www.ojjdp.gov/ojstatbb/ezajcs/ National Center for Juvenile Justice.

Table 44 References

Bishop, D. M. (2000). Juvenile offenders in the adult criminal justice system. In Tonry, M. (Ed.) Crime & Justice: A Review of Research, 27, 81-167. Chicago, IL University of Chicago Press.

Bishop, D. M., & Fraizer, C. E. (1996). Race effects in juvenile justice decision-making: Findings of a statewide analysis. *The Journal of Criminal Law & Criminology*, *86*, 392–414.

Cohn, J.M., & Mialson, H.M., (2008). The relationship between tougher juvenile transfer laws and juvenile crime rates. *Paper delivered by Emory University*, 33pp. SSRN 1289963.

Drake, E. (2013). *The effectiveness of declining juvenile court jurisdiction of youth*. Washington State Institute for Public Policy.

Fagan, J. (1991). *The comparative impacts of juvenile court and criminal court sanctions on adolescent felony offenders*. Final Report to the National Institute of Justice. U.S. Department of Justice.

Fagan, J. (1995). Separating the men from the boys: The comparative advantage of juvenile versus criminal court sanctions on recidivism among adolescent felony offenders. In J. C. Howell, B. Krisberg, J. D. Hawkins, & J. J. Wilson (Eds.), *Serious, Violent, and Chronic Juvenile Offenders: A Sourcebook* (pp. 238–260). Sage Publications.

Fagan, J. (1996). The comparative impacts of juvenile and criminal court sanctions on adolescent felony offenders. *Law & Policy*, *18*, 77–114.

Fagan, J., Kupchik, A., & Liberman, A. (2007). Be careful what you wish for: Legal sanctions and public safety among adolescent offenders in juvenile and criminal court. *Columbia Law School, Pub. Law Research Paper* 03-61.

Farrington, D. P., Loeber, R., & Howell, J. C. (2012). Young adult offenders: The need for more effective legislative options and justice processing. *Criminology & Public Policy*, *11*, 729–750.

Hahn, R., McGowan, A., Liberman, A., Crosby, A., Fullilove, M., Johnson, R., Moscicki, E., Price, L., Snyder, S., Tuma, F., Lowy, J., Briss, P., Cory, S., & Stone, G. (2007). Effects on violence of laws and policies facilitating the transfer of youth from the juvenile to the adult justice system: A report on recommendations of the Task Force on Community Preventive Services. *Morbidity and Mortality Weekly Report: Recommendations and Reports*, *56*(9), 1–11.

Hansen, N. S., Thayer, R. E., Feldstein Ewing, S. W., Sabbineni, A., & Bryan, A. D. (2018). Neural correlates of risky sex and response inhibition in high-risk adolescents. *Journal of Research on Adolescence*, *28*, 56–69.

Hoeffel, J. C. (2013). The jurisprudence of death and youth: Now the twain should meet. *Texas Tech Law Review*, *46*, 29–69.

Jensen, E. L., & Metsger, L. K. (1996). A test of the deterrent effect of legislative waiver on violent juvenile crime. *Crime and Delinquency*, *40*, 96–104.

Jordan, K. L. (2012). Juvenile transfer and recidivism: A propensity score matching approach. *Journal of Criminal Justice*, *35*, 53–67.

Lanza-Kaduce, L., Frazier, C. E., Lane, J., & Bishop, D. M. (2002). *Juvenile transfer to criminal court study: Final report*. Floria Department of Juvenile Justice.

Loeffler, C. E., & Grunwald, B. (2015). Decriminalizing delinquency: The effect of raising the age of majority on juvenile recidivism. *The Journal of Legal Studies*, *44*(2).

Loughran, T. A., Mulvey, E.P., Schubert, C.A., Chassin, L.A., Steinberg, L., Piquero, A.R., Cota-Robles, S., & Cauffman, E., & Losoya. (2010). Differential effects of adult court transfer on juvenile offender recidivism. *Law and Human Behavior*, *24*, 476–488.

McGowan, A., Hahn, R., Liberman, A., Crosby, A., Fullilove, M., Johnson, R., Moscicki, E., Price, L., Snyder, S., Tuma, F., Lowy, J., Briss, P., Cory, S., & Stone, G. (2007). Effects on violence of laws and policies facilitating the transfer of juveniles from the juvenile justice system to the adult justice system: A systematic review. *American Journal of Preventive Medicine*, *32*, S7–S28.

Mulvey, E. P., & Schubert, C. (2012). *Transfer of juveniles to adult court: Effects of a broad policy in one court. Juvenile Justice Bulletin. December 2012*. U.S. Department of Justice, Office of Justice Programs. Office of Juvenile Justice & Delinquency Prevention.

Myers, D. L. (2001). *Excluding violent youths from juvenile court: The effectiveness of legislative waiver*. LFB Scholarly Publications.

Myers, D. L. (2003). The recidivism of violent youths in juvenile and adult court: A consideration of selection bias. *Youth Violence and Juvenile Justice*, *1*, 79–101.

Podkopacz, M. R., & Feld, B. C. (1995). Judicial waiver policy and practice: Persistence, seriousness, and race. *Law & Inequality*, *14*, 73–178.

Podkopacz, M. R., & Feld, B. C. (1996). The end of the line: An empirical study of judicial waiver. *The Journal of Criminal Law & Criminology*, *86*, 449–492.

Redding, R. E. (2008). *Juvenile transfer laws: An effective deterrent to delinquency? Juvenile Justice Bulletin, August*. Office of Juvenile Justice and Delinquency Prevention.

Redding, R. E. (2016). One size does not fit all: The deterrent effect of transferring juveniles to criminal court. *Criminology & Public Policy*, *15*, 939–948.

Risler, E. A., Sweatman, T., & Nackerud, L. (1998). Evaluating the Georgia legislative waiver's effectiveness in deterring juvenile crime. *Research on Social Work Practice*, *8*, 657–667.

Singer, S. I. (1996b). *Recriminalizing delinquency: Violent juvenile crimes and juvenile justice reform*. Cambridge University Press.

Singer, S. I., & McDowall, D. (1988). Criminalizing delinquency: The deterrent effects of the New York juvenile offender law. *Law & Society Review*, *22*, 521–535.

Steiner, B., Hemmens, C., & Bell, V. (2006). Legislative waiver reconsidered: General deterrent effects of statutory exclusion laws enacted post-1979. *Justice Quarterly*, *23*, 34–59.

Steiner, B., & Wright, E. (2006). Assessing the relative effects of state direct file waiver laws on violent juvenile crime: Deterrence or irrelevance? *The Journal of Criminal Law & Criminology*, *96*, 1451–1477.

Winner, L., Lanza-Kaduce, L., Bishop, D. M., & Frazier, C. E. (1997). The transfer of juveniles to criminal court: Reexamining recidivism over the long term. *Crime and Delinquency*, *43*, 548–563.

Zane, S. N., Welsh, B. C., & Mears, D. P. (2016). Juvenile transfer and the specific deterrence hypothesis: Systematic review and meta-analysis. *Criminology & Public Policy*, *15*, 901–925.

Zimring, F. E., & Rushin, S. (2013). Did changes in juvenile sanctions reduce juvenile crime rates? A natural experiment. *Ohio State Journal of Criminal Law*, *11*, 57–69.

Table 45 References

Bishop, D. M., & Frazier, C. E. (1991). Transfer of juveniles to criminal court: A case study and analysis of prosecutorial waiver. *Notre Dame Journal of Law, Ethics & Public Policy*, *5*, 281–302.

Bishop, D. M., Frazier, C. E., & Henretta, J. C. (1989). Prosecutorial waiver: A case study of questionable reform. *Crime and Delinquency*, *35*, 179–201.

Bortner, M. A. (1986). Traditional rhetoric, organizational realities: Remand of juveniles to adult court. *Crime and Delinquency*, *32*, 53–73.

Bove, C. M. (1991). The child-adult: Michigan waiver law. *Detroit College of Law Review*, *1991*, 1071–1096.

Browne, E. W. (1977). Guidelines for statutes for transfer of juveniles to criminal court. *Pepperdine Law Review*, *4*, 479–495.

Comment, W. (1966). Criminal offenders in the juvenile court: More brickbats and another proposal. *University of Pennsylvania Law Review*, *114*, 1171–1220.

Comments, C. (1973). Juvenile justice—Statutory exclusion from the juvenile process of certain alleged felons. *Boston University Law Review. Boston University. School of Law*, *53*, 212–225.

Edwards, L. (1977). The case for abolishing fitness hearings in juvenile court. *Santa Clara Law Review*, *17*, 595–630.

Fagan, J., & Deschenes, E. P. (1990). Determinants of juvenile waiver decisions for violent juvenile offenders. *The Journal of Criminal Law & Criminology*, *81*, 314–347.

Feld, B. C. (1978). Reference of juvenile offenders for adult prosecution: The legislative alternative to asking unanswerable questions. *Minnesota Law Review*, *62*, 515–618.

Forst, M., & Blomquist, M. E. (1991). Cracking down on juveniles: The changing ideology of youth corrections. *Notre Dame Journal of Law, Ethics & Public Policy*, *5*, 323–375.

Ganzfried, J. J. (1972). Double jeopardy and the waiver of jurisdiction in California's juvenile courts. *Stanford Law Review*, *24*, 874–902.

Gasper, J., & Katkin, D. (1980). A rationale for the abolition of the juvenile court's power to waive jurisdiction. *Pepperdine Law Review*, *7*, 937–951.

Gillespie, L. K., & Norman, M. D. (1984). Does certification mean prison: Some preliminary findings from Utah. *Juvenile & Family Court Journal*, *35*, 23–34.

Grisso, T. (2000). What we know about youths' capacities as trial defendants. In T. Grisso & R. G. Schwartz (Eds.), *Youth on Trial: A Developmental Perspective on Juvenile Justice* (pp. 139–171). University of Chicago Press.

Grisso, T., Tomkins, A., & Casey, P. (1988). Psychosocial concepts in juvenile law. *Law and Human Behavior*, *12*, 403–437.

Grundfest, A. R., Paskow, A. C., Szabo, H. E., & Williams, R. J. (1981). Trial of juveniles in adult court: The prosecutor's perspective. In Hall, J.C., Hamparian, D.M., Pettibone. J.M., & White, J.L. (Eds.), Major issues in juvenile justice information and training: Readings in public policy (pp. 321-332). Academy for Contemporary Problems.

Hogan, C. (1974). Waiver of juvenile jurisdiction and the hard-core youth. *North Dakota Law Review*, *51*, 655–677.

Kozich, S. D. (1980). A model for the transfer of juvenile felony offenders to adult court jurisdiction. *Journal of Juvenile Law*, *4*, 170–186.

McNulty, E. W. (1996). The transfer of juvenile offenders to adult court: Panacea or problem? *Law & Policy*, *18*, 61–75.

Mears, D. P. (2003). A critique of waiver research: Critical next steps in assessing the impacts of laws for transferring juveniles to the criminal justice system. *Youth Violence and Juvenile Justice*, *1*, 156–172.

Mears, D. P., Cochran, J. C., Stults, B. J., Greenman, S. J., Bhati, A. S., & Greenwald, M. A. (2014). The "true" juvenile offender: Age effects and juvenile court sanctioning. *Criminology*, *52*, 169–194.

Mountford, H., & Berenson, H. S. (1969). Waiver of jurisdiction: The last resort of the juvenile court. *University of Kansas Law Review. University of Kansas. School of Law*, *18*, 55–70.

Notes. (1966). Juvenile delinquents: The police, state courts, and individualized justice. *Harvard Law Review, 79*, 775-810.

Notes & Comments. (1967). Separating the criminal from the delinquent: Due process in certification procedure. *Southern California Law Review*, *40*, 158–164.

Parker, D. B. (1976). Juveniles in the criminal courts: A substantive view of the fitness decision. *UCLA Law Review. University of California, Los Angeles. School of Law*, *23*, 988–1016.

Polen, C. A. P. (1986). Youth on death row: Waiver of juvenile court jurisdiction and imposition of the death penalty on juvenile offenders. *Northern Kentucky Law Review*, *13*, 495–517.

Reiney, C. W. (1966). Problem of age and jurisdiction in the juvenile court. *Vanderbilt Law Review*, *19*, 833–864.

Stamm, M. J. (1973). Transfer of jurisdiction in juvenile court: An A\analysis of the proceeding, its role in the administration of justice, and A proposal for the reform of Kentucky law. *Kentucky Law Journal (Lexington, Ky.)*, *62*, 122–199.

Steward-Lindsey, S. (2006). Fulfilling the promise of *Kent:* Fixing the Texas juvenile waiver statute. *American Journal of Criminal Law*, *34*, 109–126.

Thomas, C. W., & Bilchik, S. (1985). Prosecuting juveniles in criminal court: A legal and empirical analysis. *The Journal of Criminal Law & Criminology*, *76*, 439–479.

Zane, S. N., Welsh, B. C., & Mears, D. P. (2016). Juvenile transfer and the specific deterrence hypothesis: Systematic review and meta-analysis. *Criminology & Public Policy*, *15*, 901–925.

Zimring, F. E. (1981). Notes toward a jurisprudence of waiver. In J. C. Hall, D. M. Hamparian, J. M. Pettibone, & J. L. White (Eds.), *Major issues in juvenile justice information and training: Readings in public policy* (pp. 193–205). Academy for Contemporary Problems.

Section 4

Benefactors of Transfer to Criminal Court (CC): The Case for Transfer

Transfer to CC has received much attention, especially from the ATC, nearly all of which has been negative. The nature and operation of transfer have been vilified, explaining why most ATC accounts call for its being severely restricted, if not abolished. These assaults are especially relevant, but not limited, to prosecutorial transfer (PT).

Most states' offense exclusion and "direct file" laws do not provide either a jurisprudential rationale nor a principled legal answer to the question of which youths states should prosecute as adults... (Feld, 2001, p. 18).

This Section identifies the benefits attending transfer for JCs (Chapter 13), defendants (Chapter 14), and society (Chapter 15). In addition, the situations in which transfer to CC is not only appropriate but also necessary are identified. Jurisprudential rationales and principled legal answers in support of transfer and stating which youths should be prosecuted "as adults" are provided as well.

Disparaging observations regarding transfer have been, most often, significant distortions, if not purposeful misrepresentations, which already have been disclosed, addressed and resolved. Defenses of transfer are rare. The fact that transfer has been adopted in one or both forms (i.e., judicial transfer--JT and/or prosecutorial transfer — PT) in every jurisdiction likely explains why articulating its multiple benefits and purposes has been rare, if not non-existent. A policy so widely practiced does not need to be defended. It would seem all critical players, particularly lawmakers and judicial actors, must support it (with the notable exception of defense attorneys). A detailed explanation of the benefits and purposes behind transfer is critical, however. Its alleged problems are claimed to be plentiful and are broadcasted extensively by the ATC. The reduction/elimination of transfer may be within the ATC's reach. It would not be strange for this one-sided, ill-informed, and agenda-driven monologue from the ATC to derail what is a vital aspect of JC's operation (and survival).

Now that the misrepresentations have been neutralized, the benefits attending and purposes served by transfer to CC can be fully explicated. The next three chapters will reveal the multi-faceted dimensions of transfer together with its many benefits and benefactors.

REFERENCES

Feld, B. C. (2001). Race, youth violence, and the changing jurisprudence of waiver. *Behavioral Sciences & the Law*, *19*(1), 3–22. doi:10.1002/bsl.427 PMID:11241678

Chapter 13
Benefits to Juvenile Court (JC)

ABSTRACT

Chapter 13 details how transfer to criminal court (CC) benefits juvenile courts (JCs). The first benefit deals with JCs' maintaining a positive public image (and acceptance). Simply put, transfer allows JC to avoid claims of being a never-ending-revolving-door for juvenile offenders or a place where juveniles get away with murder. Unlike CCs, JCs need that positive image because they are not indispensable. As important, transfer helps JCs' operation by preventing them from becoming even more punitive (and criminalized), which would likely require an increase in the rights afforded to defendants. Transfer also helps the image of rehabilitation, critical to the preservation of JCs; it allows rehabilitation (a reward of sorts) to be denied to rapists and murderers (among others). Rehabilitation's operation is also benefitted by not losing resources that would be spent for increased rights in JC, and by not having violent and chronic offenders clogging up facilities and compromising the treatment of salvageable youths.

INTRODUCTION

The first benefactor is JC whose image and rehabilitation mission are aided by transfer.

Part 1: Helping the JC's Image and Operation

a) Transfer Aids the Public's Perception and Societal Acceptance

Preserving the JC's image is no small measure or mission. Transfer helps JCs to better maintain their commitment to the BI of the youth, and to project that commitment credibly to the community. Transfer allows JCs to avoid criticism for not prioritizing society's/the victim's best interests (BI) since only *relatively* non-chronic/violent offenders are prosecuted there. The public can perceive that JCs are all about helping kids; rehabilitation is given a real and meaningful chance. JCs are not forced to severely punish juvenile offenders since transfer removes most that deserve that outcome. Transfer communicates to the public that society's interests are considered and influence the prosecution of some chronic/violent offenders via transfer. Transfer promotes JC's credibility that it can exist with its mission (a

DOI: 10.4018/978-1-7998-7923-7.ch013

system that attempts to help *most* offenders and serves as a CC diversion project) without demanding unrealistic, unnecessary, extreme and dangerous sacrifices from the public for its safety. Transfer makes it palatable that JCs should be and can afford to be helping children and most adolescents more than protecting society, per se, that it can and should address juvenile delinquency and not youthful chronic and wanton criminality.

Transfer also enables offenders to retain a positive attitude towards JC. Bishop has found that offenders processed in JC regard it fondly, compared to transfers who dislike just about everything in CC. This makes sense since JC is mostly about relatively benign treatment of juveniles, while CC is not. As Bishop (2000) pointed out, JCs are nicer, more concerned about their clientele, and offer better rehabilitation programs compared to CCs (pp. 136-137). Transfer brings about some nasty realities of punishment and reactions to chronic and violent crime. What is not acknowledged by the ATC is that transfer is what allows JCs to remain mostly faithful to their original design, and that the removal of the bad eggs helps JCs to do their rehabilitation job.

Transfer for the truly criminal juvenile offender allows for the *condemnation* of that behavior to occur in its proper forum; JC does not have to condemn its population. Fagan and Zimring were disturbed that JCs abandoned their non-blameworthy perception of juveniles not long after JCs were launched, but are willing now to force JCs to process the most blameworthy juveniles. Similarly, as then pro-transfer Feld (1987) noted 36 years ago, transfer supports and reaffirms fundamental norms. JCs should be spared mostly from having to fulfill this task.

Besides providing solace that juveniles will not get away with murder, etc. (see Welch, Butler, & Gertz, 2019, p. 474), transfer makes the pursuit of juveniles' BI more likely and more palatable. Total retention would make pursuit of a juveniles' BI-only policy more problematic, more dangerous, and less credible. It seems disingenuous to argue that the BI of brutal juvenile rapists and wanton juvenile murderers should be paramount, anywhere! To contend that JCs will commit to juveniles' BI (and to only this) in this context strains credibility. Transfer allows JCs to better retain community support and confidence that JCs are doing the right things by offenders (i.e., mostly treatment or only minimum punishment), while allaying fears that JCs are threatening the safety of the community by adhering to this approach since "bad kids" are transferred to CC.

Unlike indispensable CCs, JCs mostly persist at the sufferance and deference of the legislature (and society). At any time, a state legislature can severely modify or even abolish JC. Cases unwisely and unnecessarily kept in JC (e.g., heinous rape/murder charges) and/or blatant treatment failures (e.g., a chronic violent offender who commits yet another highly publicized violent crime despite several previous JC rehabilitation efforts) can put JC's remaining intact, or surviving, in jeopardy. Comparable failures in the CJ system can and have led to modifications (e.g., all those new laws named after victims failed by the system), but the survival of the court, itself, has never been seriously challenged. A lack of viable alternatives prevents the destruction of CC. Since CCs are a viable Plan B should JCs be abolished, and surely not the reverse, the latter do not enjoy invincibility.

This was recognized as early as a century ago when JCs were almost brand new:

In the 1920s and 1930s, the charge that juvenile courts coddled criminals was a much greater threat to the legitimacy of these courts than scattered procedural critiques by academics and judges. The "soft on crime" argument was dangerous because it threatened devastating political consequences... (Tanenhaus, 2000, p. 27).

Benefits to Juvenile Court (JC)

Dawson (2000) also tied the need for transfer to political realities and concerns (and a safety valve):

(Transfer) is necessary in order to preserve the juvenile justice system politically within the context of modern penological expectations (p. 45).

Even Fagan and Zimring (2000) acknowledged the need for at least some transfer to be available:

Even when public opinion is tolerant of juvenile delinquency, the teen killer is the nightmare case for the juvenile justice system.... (T)he deep-end adolescent offender is a particular threat to public acceptance of the mission and objectives of juvenile justice... (p. 1).

Feld (2000) agreed but he saw transfers as victims not the perpetrators of chronic and violent crimes.

*(Transfer mechanisms) provide a safety valve that permits the **expiatory sacrifice** of some youths, (and) quiet political and public clamor...(p. 83, emphasis added).*[1]

Some of the ATC has admitted that retaining serious and violent juvenile criminals might be seen by the public as a reason to doubt JC's legitimacy and rehabilitation mission (see Bishop, 2000; Bortner, 1986; Feld, 1978; Sargent & Gordon, 1963; Zimring, 1981, 2000a, 2000b). These high-profile cases are rare, nevertheless. The public is largely unaware JC's internal workings. But what these cases lack in quantity can be compensated by quality. Even a few retained murder or aggravated rape cases could cause the JC a serious public relations nightmare The ATC is wrong, however, in arguing that this so-called safety valve reason is a primary transfer purpose.

What seems to gain little traction in ATC literature is any consideration of the actual impact of an all-inclusive policy (i.e., no or hardly any juvenile offender is transferrable) on the JCs and their perception in the public's eyes. It would appear incumbent upon those who adamantly insist that no one (or almost no one) be transferred to CC to discuss and to anticipate any deleterious effects (unintended consequences by the ATC, perhaps) on the court, which they say must address all juvenile crime. The entire focus of the ATC is on the plight of transfers. Nary a word or thought is granted to JC or to retained juveniles. A theory or two, here, proffered by the ATC might enhance the richness of the transfer debate.[2]

Retaining the option to transfer chronic and serious/violent juvenile offenders to CC has aided JCs to mostly retain their rehabilitation identity despite the complaints, launched mostly by the ATC, ironically, that JCs have become so punitive as to have abandoned rehabilitation (see Table 41 A in Chapter 7). Not only is this assertion an exaggeration, but it can also contribute to critics' attempts to abolish JCs.[3]

It is critical to keep strong boundaries between JC and CC, which is why Blended Sentencing is problematic: it blends (or bridges) the two systems together. That might be in the interests of the ATC since arguably transfer is less likely when blended sentencing is possible. It does not appear that fewer transfers have resulted from the inclusion of blended sentencing, however (which is beyond the focus of this book). Regardless, blended sentencing and the resulting changes required in JC procedure have yielded negative results for the JCs' images. Blended sentencing means JCs are that much closer to being a partner of and conduit to CC. JCs are CCs in drag: false promises together with confusion and disappointment. It is in the BI of JC to be perceived as different from CC in as many ways as ethically and plausibly possible. Being all about rehabilitation (or at least as much as feasible) is perhaps the most critical feature of JC, which is most threatened by an all-inclusive policy. JCs have already become more-punitive and less-rehabilitation focused due to the dramatic changes in crimes and offenders (as well as the volume of both) they process. But, so far, *less rehabilitation* has not meant *no rehabilitation.* Bishop (2000) verified this claim:

Despite the punitive rhetoric of juvenile justice in Florida in 1997, the juvenile institutions we visited were clearly treatment oriented...(p. 141).

Perhaps the reason Bishop found this situation in juvenile institutions was due to the high rate of transfers for which Florida is famous. This facet of transfer outcomes has been neither acknowledged nor addressed by the ATC. Keeping all juvenile offenders in JC would stretch, if not obliterate, that rehabilitation image (as well as the public's acceptance of its true uniqueness and commitment to rehabilitation), if that image has not already been obliterated (due, in some part, to ATC exaggerations).

Remembering the JC founders' views might help reinforce this issue. According to the grand JC design, defendants were to be denied constitutional rights for an abundance of reasons; the lack of rights soon became a trademark of JCs. One of the easily forgotten concerns of the founders was that granting rights in JC would lead to an assumption in public circles that JCs were treating their defendants the same as CCs were treating theirs. That public "misperception" was seen as an existential threat to JCs' survival (see Sanborn & Salerno, 2005). Although the granting of constitutional rights to JC defendants has contributed to the criminalization of JCs, there has not been a complete merger of rights or identity between JCs and CCs, so far.

The best way for contemporary JCs to maintain their unique rehabilitation identity/image and to continue to receive support from the public is to not to have to adjudicate and sentence juvenile murderers, brutal rapists, chronic armed robbers, repeat residential burglars, etc.

b) Transfer Assists the JC's Operation in Numerous Respects

Also ignored by the ATC is the atmosphere, operation, and the internal dynamics of JC. Beyond the parameters of JC, total retention will invite legislatures to add even more CC-like purposes to JC Purpose Clauses. A no-transfer policy would contribute to JC's criminalization.

The more JC becomes a clone of CC, by retaining all juvenile offenders (or even transferring *only* the worst of the worst), the more complete that cloning becomes, and the more JC would be instructed to adopt more CC-oriented purposes. Accompanying this cloning would be a lesser emphasis of JC's rehabilitation mission and identity. JCs have already witnessed significant changes in their purpose clauses due to both increased legalization of the court and increased severity in the volume and nature juvenile crime (see Sanborn, 1994c). By transferring most of the chronic, serious/violent juvenile offenders JCs can avoid being forced to become even more focused on societal protection, more sympathetic to victims' rights and vindication, as well as more punishment-oriented. Ironically, transfer has been decried by the ATC as another example of the criminalization of JC, when just the opposite is the case.

A no-transfer policy would likely require increasing JC's punishment capacity, meaning increasing the retention age would be inescapable. Bishop (2000) proposed a "modest" extension of the "upper boundary of the juvenile court's continuing jurisdiction (p. 86; see, also, Redding, 1997, p. 709)." The current typical retention age of 21 would never be appropriate for 16- and 17-year-old murderers. By the time an adjudication would likely be achieved, that limit would translate into two-, three- or four-year sentences for chronic, serious/violent offenders. Total retention would then initiate a drive for increased constitutional rights in JC. For juvenile offenders to face very serious JC dispositions without proportionate constitutional rights would create complaints of a lack of due process and equal protection (Feld, 1997). The atmosphere within JC would become more adversarial, while the BI of juvenile defendants would be mostly sacrificed to the interests of justice, victims, court workers, and the community.[4] One JC abolitionist observed that JCs become irrelevant when they sentence like CCs (Ainsworth, 1991).

Transfer allows JCs to avoid extended sentences, permitting them to retain their mostly rehabilitation image and commitment. Extended sentences may be an alternative to transfer, but they also result in embracing incapacitation in lieu of treatment, which will not be beneficial to JCs. Extended sentences will also threaten non-transferrable offenders, who would otherwise not be vulnerable to lengthy sentences. Of course, that may not be possible if there is a logjam at juvenile justice (JJ) facilities. Nevertheless, perhaps that logjam will never materialize, if legislatures decide to reduce the maximum JC jurisdictional age. Transfer allows legislatures to avoid pressure to lower the maximum JC age due to some violent crimes being committed by older offenders. Recently, most states that formerly had a maximum age of 15 or 16 have joined the long-standing majority by adopting a maximum JC age of 17. The possibility of transfer may have convinced legislatures that raising the maximum age could be safely done since any truly bad offenders could be sent to CC (see Sanborn, 2003). If appellate courts were ever to force a no-transfer dictate on JCs (or perhaps even a JT-only policy), angered legislatures could respond with an age-reduction move.[5] Of course, legislatures could also eliminate transfer. If that were to happen, it would not be surprising for those legislatures to reduce the maximum JC age as a reaction to the profound changes/consequences attending a no-transfer legislation.

It is not only lengthier sentences that would likely result from a total retention policy:

Total retention also could wreak havoc with the internal dimensions of juvenile court sentencing. That is, prosecuting all juvenile offenders in juvenile court could encourage greater adoption of minimum, mandatory and longer (but within the upper age limit) sentences, provisions that historically are more characteristic of criminal court (Sanborn, 2003, p. 206).

It is quite possible that the drive for enhanced sentences would continue unabated:

Historically, juvenile courts have been able to maintain a mostly rehabilitative and mostly moderate dispositional scheme (together with a mostly best-interests-of-the-child focus) because the most problematic/violent youth have been subject to transfer to adult court. The abolition of exclusion certainly could prompt legislatures to restructure juvenile court dispositions so as to resemble a mini-criminal court. This increased criminalization development would appear to be unavoidable. As word would spread through the neighborhood that no youth will ever again be prosecuted in criminal court, chances are that some juveniles would perceive no disincentive (or at least much less of one) to committing crime. The likely reaction within the juvenile justice system would be to raise the ante for punishments a youth could receive in that forum (Id.).

Total retention would trigger a renewed edition of the domino theory that influenced the Supreme Court in *McKeiver v. Pennsylvania* (1971). In *McKeiver*, the Court declined to grant defendants a right to jury trial in JC for fear of equating JC and CC (which it arguably would). The Court saw that equality as a threat to the survival of the JC. The Court's theory was that there would be no need for the separate existence of two courts that were so similar that one could be described as the clone of the other. The

Court's fear/theory is plausible. Should JC become a truly veritable clone of CC, it would not be unreasonable or strange to question its need to exist separately from CC. The logical extreme of criminalization (via the granting of rights, etc.) is the elimination of JCs. The *McKeiver* Court observed 40 years ago:

If the formalities of the criminal adjudicative process are to be superimposed upon the juvenile court system, there is little need for its separate existence. Perhaps that ultimate disillusionment will come one day, but for the moment we are disinclined to give impetus to it (1971, p. 551).

More than 35 years ago, Feld (1987) highlighted how criminalized JCs had already become at that point and warned that increased criminalization of JC could bring about its demise.

As juvenile courts base sentencing decisions more frequently on the basis of the principle of offense rather than individualized justice, the McKeiver Court's "treatment" rationale becomes less tenable, and the continued existence of a separate juvenile court appears more questionable (p. 487).

Feld was an abolitionist then so this observation may have been wishful thinking.

Even Zimring opposed increasing the sentences/punishment available to JCs as an alternative to a no-transfer policy. He maintained that position because he acknowledges that there is an insufficient due process foundation in JC to sustain increased potential sentences, and possibly even for sentence possibilities that already exist. More important, extended sentences are inconsistent with the premise and philosophy of JC (Zimring, 1998a, p. 169; 2000b, p. 209). Zimring's points are spot on; he is correct in being apprehensive about a no-transfer setup. His error is in thinking that a (only some) murderers-only policy will suffice to ward off the very outcomes he fears will hurt, if not destroy, JCs. It is puzzling that he is not equally concerned about and fails to foresee that the retention of vicious, and chronic, would-be killers, rapists, armed robbers and home invaders will encourage, if not force, legislatures to require JCs to lengthen sentences considerably, particularly for older juvenile criminals, which could then trickle-down to younger offenders.

The most intriguing question never asked by the ATC is exactly how much more punitive would JCs need to become, exactly how much higher must the JCs' retention age be raised to accommodate juvenile murderers, brutal rapists, and chronic armed robbers/residential burglars? What if there were multiple rape victims or an offense that involved 15 shooting victims who fortunately did not die? Would an upper age of 25 be sufficient to deal with a murderer who just turned eighteen or nineteen? That would amount to a six- or seven-year sentence. Would the age need to be thirty or thirty-five, which would still mean only a 12- or 17-year sentence for the older juvenile murderer? At what hyper-extended retention age would it be impossible to assert that JC was really addressing a "juvenile" offender? Would it matter when more than one-half of the sentence (and perhaps as much as eighty percent) affected a chronological adult (i.e., time served after the offender's turning eighteen)? Even with lengthened sentences there could easily remain extreme distress in the community (and even more so among victims) that the most chronic and violent juvenile offenders would serve relatively little time for their crimes.

Even if lengthy sentences did not occur via total retention, there could be other criminalization effects of a no/limited-transfer regime. Victims and the public could be dissatisfied that serious, non-rehabilitated offenders would depart from JJ without a criminal record. Failing that, JC records could become permanent and public. A no/limited-transfer policy could create more pressure to develop victims' rights in JC (see Sanborn, 2001b). The increase in victims' rights, in turn, could bring about more pressure on prosecutors to refrain from (or be prevented from) filing a *nol pros* and/or to pressure JC judges to impose a more severe disposition than that recommended by the PO. Chances are increased rights will result in an increase in wrongful acquittals and non-prosecutions, which had prompted the founders to adopt a no-rights policy in the early JCs. Even post-conviction remedies, such as motions for re-trials and appeals would become more relevant. Besides the pressure to add more rights to JC's adjudicatory hearing, other trial-related protections (such as bail) will also likely become relevant. The lack of bail in JC has prompted some of the ATC to argue that a no-transfer policy better protects society precisely because dangerous juveniles do not tend to enjoy pre-trial freedom. It is curious, then, that the ATC apparently has not considered this potential boomerang impact to a no/limited-transfer policy.

Total retention could create more demand that the identity of chronic/violent offenders be revealed to the community. JC hearings might be unable to maintain their mostly non-public operation, while the media and others could demand permission to attend hearings (see Sanborn & Salerno, 2005). The retention of chronic/violent offenders could create extra pressure for an increased use of the JC record in CC sentencing, which could also adversely affect the non-transferred offenders. Increased CC use of the JC record would also increase pressure to add more rights in JC to a point of full replication of CC criminal procedure. There have already been dramatic developments in factoring the JC record into CC sentencing. In some jurisdictions, offenders can carry two strikes from JC and strike out on the first pitch in CC, even while being a chronological juvenile. There are constitutional problems with this, not yet acknowledged by appellate courts (see Sanborn, 1998, 2000). Total retention will likely only exacerbate this situation, culminating in the wholesale absorption of juveniles' JC records into sentences in CC.

Part 2: Helping the JC's Rehabilitation Mission[4]

a) Transfer Aids the Image of Rehabilitation

Helping the court's image simultaneously helps the court's rehabilitation mission. Rehabilitation is, arguably, the *reason d'etre* of JC.[6] This is still the case even with the JCs' evolution that introduced older, more chronic, and more violent juvenile offenders to the system (see Chapter 5). It is difficult to exaggerate how important rehabilitation's image is to JC.

(I)n terms of the prospect of rehabilitation, total retention likely guarantees the poorest results possible for the success of treatment programs, which, in turn, threatens the credibility and survival of juvenile court. Research that has examined the recidivism rates of somewhat comparable, serious young offenders prosecuted in juvenile and criminal courts has discovered very poor results in both systems (Bishop et al., 1996; Fagan, 1991; Winner et al., 1997). Not surprisingly, retaining the worst criminals in the juvenile system portends poor treatment outcomes, at least as measured by recidivism rates. Whereas the rehabilitative prowess of criminal court has never been the justification of its existence, the same cannot be said of juvenile court. Its separate existence relies largely, if not primarily, upon its ability to successfully rehabilitate young criminals. Unlike criminal court, then, the more the juvenile system fails to stem the tide of juvenile crime, the more counterproductive and unreasonable it can seem to continue to divert offenders to it from criminal court (Sanborn, 2003, p. 204).

The failure of rehabilitation is worse than the failure of punishment. That means that recidivism after treatment efforts in JC looks worse than recidivism after failed punishment in CC. Retribution is non-utilitarian, contrary to the claims and desires of some in the ATC (see Chapter 10). It does not promise more than simple and straight punishment. No "extra" reward is promised, and none should be expected, apart from imposing punishment, while fulfilling the social contract that promised punishment for committing crimes. By design, punishment has been achieved *once the sentence has been served*, as the offender is released from probation or incarceration after having experienced punishment. The true measure of punishment is gauged (and satisfied) by merely *completing the sentence*. By design, rehabilitation has not been achieved (or is not truly relevant) *until after the offender has served the sentence*, depending, in other words, upon how this person fares once back in the community. The true measure of rehabilitation is *refraining from committing crime following release from a sanction*. Show me the rehabilitation!!

So, when CC punishment fails to prevent recidivism, the validity of punishment, per se, is not called into question, with the one notable exception of crimes threatened with the death penalty. Punishment just will not stop some offenders unless and until they are physically prevented from committing crime. Rehabilitation is utilitarian and the utility involves a promise to cure of the offender, potentially at significant cost (i.e., expensive treatment programs), while sacrificing the formal imposition of punishment. When the cure fails the validity of rehabilitation is called into question; promises have not been kept, hopes and expectations have been dashed. While an offender can always "be punished" whether that ultimately works or not, some offenders may not "be treatable" so why waste the effort/expense and sacrifice the condemnation/punishment? The more these ideas/questions infect the view of JCs in general, the more reasonable it could appear to question rehabilitation's actual utility (i.e., curing juvenile offenders). Since rehabilitation failures matter, minimally JCs should not be forced to burden themselves by having to treat incorrigible, chronic juvenile offenders. Recidivism by juvenile murderers/rapists will indelibly tarnish the reputation (and apparent utility) of rehabilitation and JC interventions.

Adding more elements of criminalization that will require the extension of more rights will result in taking resources away from rehabilitation programs, a major reason rights were denied by the original JCs. JCs will likely become less rehabilitation-focused. Assuming there's any merit to the *McKeiver* prediction, adopting more criminalization will exacerbate the threat to JC's survival. There is still more criminalization possible; the more this occurs the further JCs are removed from their rehabilitation mission.

In other words, the less juvenile court is about rehabilitation, the less reason for its existence

Historically, JC dispositions can be perceived as a *reward* for misbehaving; the original JC design was to be ameliorative, not punitive. Community and institutional corrections in JJ were mostly addressing offenses that were self-destructive. To be sure, there were burglary, rape and robbery charges processed in JC; some homicide cases also ended up there, but so many of them ended in adjustments or probation, it is questionable whether an actual homicide was at hand or was a legitimate charge in the first place. These behaviors destroy others, not just the offender. Importantly, however, the vast majority of youths subjected to JC intervention had committed truancy or running away from home, and incorrigibility (see Chapter 4).

Adding these non-offenses to the plethora of playing ball in the street and stealing rides cases, etc. (see Chapter 4) meant JCs dealt mostly with *innocuous* misbehaviors. These behaviors could lead to worse behavior, which was the motivation behind JC intervention. Nevertheless, none of these offenses had left victims bleeding-out in the streets. Offering these "offenders" preventive, rehabilitation-oriented dispositions made sense and likely forced no one to recoil at the thought of "rewarding" their misconduct (e.g., commit truancy and get a high school diploma; run away from home and enjoy your new foster home). However, extending the same courtesies and rewards to those committing violent, societal threatening conduct (e.g., rape or kill a co-ed, get a high school diploma) could easily result in quite a different reaction from the public. As the severity of the crime or the chronicity of the record increases, the appropriateness of extending rewards to these misbehaviors as well can seem grossly inappropriate.

It reasonably could be argued that JC is already pushing the envelope, and its rightful boundary, in prosecuting the many chronic (some JCs allow seemingly unlimited recidivism) and violent offenders (some courts have no necessary exclusion of brutal rape and homicide charges). It is difficult to estimate how much the modern JC jurisdiction has cost it in terms of perceived commitment to rehabilitation. Some ATC members have argued that JCs only punish and do not even attempt to rehabilitate. These claims greatly exaggerate and do a disservice to the sincere efforts of many JCs to help improve juveniles' lives and to preserve life chances. Curtailing transfer to CC will result in greater stretching of rehabilitation resources and image, perhaps to a final breaking point.

Adjudicating brutal rapists and would-be murderers in JC is not the only way to threaten the image of rehabilitation. Having supposedly rehabilitated chronic serious/violent offenders, which is implied by having released them from a treatment program, only to have them recidivate damages rehabilitation's reputation and standing. That "failure" leads to questioning the effectiveness of treatment and the appropriateness of JC processing in general. Failure of treatment can undermine treatment and lead to doubts of its efficacy altogether. Similarly, the "failure" of treatment with chronic offenders can suggest JCs just do not know how to rehabilitate or when to give up on trying. The worse the example of retention becomes (in terms of quality and quantity of offenses), the worse both JCs and rehabilitation look.

b) Transfer Assists the Operation of Rehabilitation Programs

It may seem counterintuitive, but transfer helps the operation of treatment programs as well. Transfer helps decrease the JC's caseload (Bishop, 2000, p. 127), and frees resources to address the younger and beginning less serious juvenile offender, which was the original design of JC. Treatment resources could become even more valuable and scarce due to being severely depleted by the costs of additional due process measures, should a no/limited-transfer policy be adopted.

Total retention, especially for the chronic offenders, would likely be a waste of valuable resources as well as a source of contamination of more salvageable kids; successful rehabilitation of the later could be compromised. The original JCs disqualified the older delinquents due to this fear that the younger population could be adversely affected by the presence of older youths. Even the ATC admits the possibility of the waste and contamination effects (see Table 45 in Chapter 12). JC workers have overwhelmingly endorsed this view as well (see Sanborn, 1994a, p. 275).

Retention of serious and violent delinquents in juvenile corrections also increases the potential for the victimization of other inmates/staff. That could also lead to disruption of the facility's operation (see Butts & Mitchell, 2000; Mears, 2003; Redding, 2003; Trulson et al., 2011), meaning that even if programs are not overwhelmed, their day-to-day operation could be compromised.

Keeping all youth regardless means valuable, limited treatment resources will be wasted and/or that warehousing (at least some) youth will be encouraged. Moreover, total retention of dangerous, intractable youthful criminals threatens not only the rehabilitation but also the physical welfare of youth who have a chance of being helped by the system. Again, rehabilitation cannot be the primary purpose under such a scheme (Sanborn, 2003, p. 204; see, also, Forst & Blomquist, 1991, p. 334).

It is interesting that the ATC is willing to point out the troubles facing juvenile offenders incarcerated in the CJ system (see, e.g., Bishop, 2000, pp. 144-146), but never considers the harmful effect chronic/violent offenders could have upon retained youths in JJ facilities (see, e.g., Id.). The ATC is committed to keep status offenders away from delinquents due to the adverse effect the latter can have on the former, but refuse to consider a parallel effect chronic/violent/older offenders can have on younger, less chronic/serious juvenile offenders. So many of the ATC that are so enamored of rehabilitation in JC refuse to acknowledge how retaining all juvenile-aged offenders in the JJ system does a serious disservice to that very same mission.

Programs' availability could be at risk. Nearly all of the would-be transfer population would be destined for an institution, assuming an adjudication. If these offenders would qualify for transfer, they would likely also qualify for placement, most likely at the highest levels of juvenile facilities. Total retention would result in many more serious offenders serving longer sentences in the JJ system. An absence of transfers could easily lead to serious overcrowding in JJ facilities. There would likely be a logjam at the highest levels of juvenile facilities, which would then create a trickle-down effect. As the top-tier facilities fill, those who cannot be placed in one of them will bleed down to the next lower level, etc. Inasmuch as JJ facilities are notorious for being limited in capacity (to give rehabilitation programs a fighting chance), it would not require retaining very many of the should-be transferred group to create havoc in the JJ system.

If increased sentences are a result of the no-transfer policy, the logjam created at the top-level facilities would be that much worse, exacerbating the trickle-down effect so as to possibly prevent the JJ system's addressing the delinquencies of rookie juvenile offenders, the primary original target of JC. Total retention could create a no-room-at-the-inn phenomenon. Delinquents who could have been helped will have no place to go (except home, perhaps) to receive that help. For those below-the-radar offenders there might be only probation available; there could be no ability to offer inpatient help and to remove of the salvageable offender from a negative home and neighborhood. Chronic, but still salvageable, offenders will be able to experience probation at most, and might have to be continued on that disposition for perhaps several subsequent offenses, jeopardizing any possible crime deterrent effect. The trickle-down facility effect will bleed all the way to the community. Probation rolls, meanwhile, will likely be swamped, undermining the chances for successful treatment experiences in the community as well.

Even if the facility logjam is not overwhelming, it is almost impossible for it to not be significant. Overcrowding will not only adversely affect treatment initiatives, but it will also threaten an essential element of behavioral control in JJ facilities. Total retention will make it more difficult to control the behavior of lower and mid-level commitments. Compliance among inmates is necessary for rehabilitation to have any chance to succeed. Compliance, by itself, may be insufficient for success, to be sure. Nevertheless, the inability to curtail overt resistance and belligerence or incorrigibility by program participants will likely result in treatment failures for those individuals and others. Currently, compliance in JJ institutions is facilitated by a threat that acting out (running away, attacking fellow inmates or staff) and/or failure to cooperate in and complete a program will lead to removal from the facility and a transfer to a higher-level facility (perhaps to a juvenile prison). Crowded higher level institutions can effectively neutralize that threat. The trickle-down effect could remove any consequences for failure to comply with probation conditions, too. POs may have no viable threats to keep their charges in line; filing violations of probation may be pointless and threats of same may be laughable and known to the probationer.

The atmosphere of the facilities will likely change due to a total retention approach. The depreciation in rehabilitation efforts/programs could convert true treatment facilities into warehouses. Incapacitation and custody will become the norm. That may already be the norm at the highest-level juvenile facilities (i.e., a levell-10 or the juvenile prison), but this norm could easily become a facet of the trickle-down effect to lower-level facilities currently offering real rehabilitation. JJ facilities will mirror criminal prisons, thereby completing the criminalization effect and the existential threat to JCs' survival.

Other negative treatment outcomes are possible. The upper age limit of JC jurisdiction, typically 21 years of age, is a hard boundary. Any treatment program that is incomplete at the expiration of JC's retention age will necessarily remain in that condition (see Trulson et al., 2011). For juvenile offenders that require sustained treatment intervention, CC may be the only available option, especially when older offenders are involved (see Grisso, 2000).

Each of these benefits (as well as detriments) is additive, not mutually exclusive. One benefit might be more apparent in a particular case, and not all will be present in every case. Nevertheless, all of them can be realized via transfer, all of them threatened via the elimination of transfer. Contrary to what the ATC insists, there is no (and should be no) requirement that all benefits surrounding transfer must attend every juvenile offender transferred to CC.

This observation is important because a regular tactic of the ATC is to try to present the mention of one of these benefits as a replacement of another or as a contradiction of another/rest of the benefits. For example, Tanenhaus reported a history of pro-transfer explanations in 1930s Illinois. After mentioning that some JC judges defended transfer to protect other inmates at JJ facilities, Tanenhaus explains that later, judges were contending that transferred juveniles were not amenable to treatment. Tanenhaus saw these as contradictory reasons. They are not mutually exclusive, let alone contradictory. Instead of allowing for varied reasons behind transfer for varied times and different cases/problems presented by different and evolving juvenile offender populations, Tanenhaus (2000) opined: "The threat to public safety, no longer the safety of children in reform schools, had become the justification for waiver (p. 29)." According to Tanenhaus' account, the second reason *replaced* the first. Evidently, Tanenhaus believed there could not be more than one reason supporting transfer, regardless of the likelihood of differences among cases. The implication is that JC judges at that time were fickle in defending transfer; or, that they originally supported a later discarded (and now believed to be an) inappropriate reason for transfer. A broader implication is that all defenders/defenses of transfer are fickle. This could be a *divide* (the benefits/arguments) *and conquer approach*. Instead, it is more than merely reasonable, it is a fact, that there are myriad reasons for, and myriad benefits derived from transfer that can be identified.

As a concluding comment for the discussion in this chapter, five observations should be noted: first, much like JCs were started primarily to keep adult offenders away from corrupting juvenile delinquents, transfer extends this logic to keeping the worst juvenile delinquents (i.e., most chronic and violent) away from salvageable juvenile offenders. Second, in this context, a longer sentence in CC is not primary, negating the ATC contention that transfer is *only* about longer sentences. The ATC makes this contention because that reason can easily be weaponized. Third, deterrence, although always desired, is not in the forefront of concerns in preserving-the-JCs/rehabilitation contexts. Most of transfer's benefits for JCs have nothing to do with the deterrence objective. In addition, the ATC rarely, if ever, considers the impact of a no-transfer policy on JCs. Fourth, basically all of the benefits attending transfer for JCs also serve to benefit juvenile offenders retained in the JJ system (see Chapter 14). The preservation of

JCs and their mostly-rehabilitation policy benefits the vast majority of juvenile offenders who are not transferred to CC. The ATC never factors the plight of retained juveniles into their no-transfer formula. Finally, and very important, essentially all of the benefits transfer extends to JCs are immeasurable via social science research methods.

REFERENCES

Ainsworth, J. E. (1991). Re-imagining childhood and reconstructing the legal order: The case for abolishing the juvenile court. *North Carolina Law Review*, *69*, 1083–1133.

Bishop, D. M., & Frazier, C. E. (2000). Consequences of transfer. In J. Fagan & F. E. Zimring (Eds.), *The changing borders of juvenile justice: Transfer of adolescents to criminal court* (pp. 227–276). University of Chicago Press.

Bishop, D. M., Frazier, C. E., Lanza-Kaduce, L., & Winner, L. (1996). The transfer of juveniles to criminal court: Does it make a difference? *Crime and Delinquency*, *42*(2), 171–191. doi:10.1177/0011128796042002001

Bonnie, R. J. (1989). Juvenile homicide: A study in legal ambivalence. In E. P. Benedek & D. G. Cornell (Eds.), *Juvenile homicide* (pp. 185–217). American Psychiatric Press.

Bortner, M. A. (1986). Traditional rhetoric, organizational realities: Remand of juveniles to adult court. *Crime and Delinquency*, *32*(1), 53–73. doi:10.1177/0011128786032001004

Butts, J. A., & Mitchell, O. (2000). Brick by brick: Dismantling the border between juvenile and adult justice. *Criminal Justice*, *2*, 167–213.

Dawson, R. O. (2000). Judicial waiver in theory and practice. In J. Fagan & F. E. Zimring (Eds.), *The changing borders of juvenile justice: Transfer of adolescents to the criminal court* (pp. 45–81). University of Chicago Press.

Fagan, J. (1991). *The comparative impacts of juvenile court and criminal court sanctions on adolescent felony offenders*. Final Report to the National Institute of Justice. U.S. Department of Justice.

Fagan, J., & Zimring, F. E. (2000). Editors' Introduction. In Fagan, J., & Zimring, F.E. (Eds.), The changing borders of juvenile justice: Transfer of adolescents to the criminal court (pp. 1-10). University of Chicago Press.

Feld, B. C. (1978). Reference of juvenile offenders for adult prosecution: The legislative alternative to asking unanswerable questions. *Minnesota Law Review*, *62*, 515–618.

Feld, B. C. (1987). The juvenile court meets the principle of the offense: Legislative changes in juvenile waiver statutes. *The Journal of Criminal Law & Criminology*, *78*(3), 471–533. doi:10.2307/1143567

Feld, B. C. (1997). Abolish the juvenile court: Youthfulness, criminal responsibility, and sentencing. *The Journal of Criminal Law & Criminology*, *88*(1), 68–136. doi:10.2307/1144075

Feld, B. C. (2000). Legislative exclusion of offenses from juvenile court jurisdiction: A history and critique. In J. Fagan & F. E. Zimring (Eds.), *The changing borders of juvenile justice: Transfer of adolescents to the criminal court* (pp. 83–144). University of Chicago Press.

Feld, B. C. (2001). Race, youth violence, and the changing jurisprudence of waiver. *Behavioral Sciences & the Law, 19*(1), 3–22. doi:10.1002/bsl.427 PMID:11241678

Forst, M. L., & Blomquist, M. E. (1990). Cracking down on juveniles: The changing ideology of youth corrections. *Notre Dame Journal of Law, Ethics & Public Policy, 5*, 323–375.

Grisso, T. (2000). What we know about youths' capacities as trial defendants. In T. Grisso & R. G. Schwartz (Eds.), *Youth on Trial: A Developmental Perspective on Juvenile Justice* (pp. 139–171). University of Chicago Press.

Kent v. United States. (1966). 383 U.S. 541.

McKeiver v. Pennsylvania. (1971). 403 U.S. 528.

Mears, D. P. (2003). A critique of waiver research: Critical next steps in assessing the impacts of laws for transferring juveniles to the criminal justice system. *Youth Violence and Juvenile Justice, 1*(2), 156–172. doi:10.1177/1541204002250876

Redding, R. E. (1997). Juveniles transferred to criminal court: Legal reform proposals based on social science research. *Utah Law Review, 1997*, 709–763.

Redding, R. E. (2003). The effects of adjudicating and sentencing juveniles as adults: Research and policy implications. *Youth Violence and Juvenile Justice, 1*(2), 128–155. doi:10.1177/1541204002250875

Sanborn, J. B. Jr. (1994a). Certification to criminal court: The important policy questions of how, when, and why. *Crime and Delinquency, 40*(2), 262–281. doi:10.1177/0011128794040002007

Sanborn, J. B. Jr. (1994c). Remnants of *parens patriae* in the adjudicatory hearing: Is a fair trial possible in juvenile court. *Crime and Delinquency, 40*(4), 599–615. doi:10.1177/0011128794040004008

Sanborn, J. B. Jr. (1998). Second-class justice and first-class punishment: The use of juvenile records in sentencing adults. *Judicature, 81*, 206–213.

Sanborn, J. B. Jr. (2000). Striking out on the first pitch in criminal court. *Barry Law Review, 1*, 7–61.

Sanborn, J. B. Jr. (2001b). Victims' rights in juvenile court: Has the pendulum swung too far? *Judicature, 85*, 140–146.

Sanborn, J. B. Jr. (2003). Hard choices or obvious ones: Developing policy for excluding youth from juvenile court. *Youth Violence and Juvenile Justice, 1*(2), 198–214. doi:10.1177/1541204002250879

Sanborn, J. B. Jr, & Salerno, A. W. (2005). *The juvenile justice system: Law and process*. Roxbury Publishing Company. Oxford University Publishing.

Sargent, D., & Gordon, D. H. (1963). Waiver of jurisdiction: An evaluation of the process in the juvenile court. *Crime and Delinquency, 9*(2), 121–128. doi:10.1177/001112876300900202

Tanenhaus, D. S. (2000). The evolution of transfer out of the juvenile court. In J. Fagan & F. E. Zimring (Eds.), *The changing borders of juvenile justice: Transfer of adolescents to the criminal court* (pp. 13–43). University of Chicago Press.

Trulson, C. R., Caudill, J. W., Belshaw, S. H., & DeLisi, M. (2011). A problem of fit: Extreme delinquents, blended sentencing, and the determinants of continued adult sanctions. *Criminal Justice Policy Review, 23*(3), 263–284. doi:10.1177/0887403410370618

Welch, K., Butler, L. F., & Gertz, M. (2019). Saving children, damning adults? An examination of public support for juvenile rehabilitation and adult punishment. *Criminal Justice Review, 44*(4), 470–491. doi:10.1177/0734016819833141

Winner, L., Lanza-Kaduce, L., Bishop, D. M., & Frazier, C. E. (1997). The transfer of juveniles to criminal court: Reexamining recidivism over the long term. *Crime and Delinquency, 43*(4), 548–563. doi:10.1177/0011128797043004009

Zimring, F. E. (1981). Notes on the jurisprudence of waiver. In J. C. Hall, D. M. Hamparian, J. M. Pettibone, & J. L. White (Eds.), *Major issues in juvenile justice information and training: Readings in public policy* (pp. 193–205). Academy for Contemporary Problems.

Zimring, F. E. (1998a). *American youth violence.* Oxford University Press.

Zimring, F. E. (2000a). Penal proportionality for the young offender: Notes on immaturity, capacity, and diminished responsibility. In T. Grisso & R. G. Schwartz (Eds.), *Youth on Trial: A Developmental Perspective on Juvenile Justice* (pp. 271–289). University of Chicago Press.

Zimring, F. E. (2000b). The punitive necessity of waiver. In J. Fagan & F. E. Zimring (Eds.), *The Changing Borders of Juvenile Justice: Transfer of adolescents to the criminal court* (pp. 207–224). University of Chicago Press.

ENDNOTES

1. Transfer in limited situations can be a safety valve (see Chapter 7). A complete lack of transfer capability could cause public outcry. Inasmuch as most transfers occur off the radar, however, it is difficult to perceive it, at its core, as serving to "quiet political and public clamor."
2. Perhaps Fagan and Zimring had this void in the ATC conversation in mind while bemoaning the absence of debate in transfer. The ATC avoids any discussion on possible deleterious effects of their no-transfer policy on other non-transferrable juvenile offenders, victims, JC, and society. The entire ATC focus is riveted to the possible bad things awaiting transfers. They completely ignore any benefits attending the transfer population, as well.
3. Feld was once the most vocal advocate of the JC's abolition (see Feld, 1997). Feld alleged JCs had abandoned rehabilitation and had adopted too many punitive measures without extending proportionate constitutional rights. That development led him to advocate abolition. His point about the lack of proportionate rights was reasonable; his "no-rehabilitation in JC" and his abolition solution were unreasonable. Feld is correct JCs can go only so far in punishments without also granting

rights. This valuable lesson seems to have been ignored or forgotten by the ATC (and now perhaps by Feld) in insisting that (virtually) no juvenile should be transferred.

4 As Sanborn (2003) noted two decades ago: *Traditionally, supervision over juveniles did not extend beyond the youth's 21st birthday. Typically, this age limit provided ample opportunity for juvenile court to attempt the rehabilitation of older delinquents retained in the system. Of course, the very violent youth, whether pretty young or very near the upper age limit of the court's jurisdiction has long been a candidate for transfer to adult court, especially when juvenile court authorities believed they lacked sufficient time to work with the offender. The inability to send this offender to criminal court would exert pressure on legislatures to exceed 21 years of age as the upper retention limit of juvenile court jurisdiction.... Being forced to prosecute seventeen-year-old murderers in juvenile court would induce many jurisdictions... to maintain sentencing authority over youth until well into their adulthood. The problem with this formula is fourfold. First, giving juvenile courts the power to sentence youth to institutionalization for up to 10 years or more... smacks of punishment and not of rehabilitation. Second, such extended sentencing power raises serious questions as to why offenders should be diverted from criminal court and criminal liability when very lengthy state control (and punishment) is believed necessary to correct/prevent their misbehavior. Third, developing extended dispositional options invites their corruption by exposing some youth whose behavior was not especially chronic/violent to be sentenced to the same outcomes (Zimring, 1998). Fourth, the vast majority of juvenile courts do not provide anywhere near adequate due process in order to sustain such a substantial exertion of state control and punishment.* (Sanborn, 2003, p. 205, footnote omitted).

5 After the Supreme Court decided *Kent v. U.S.* (1960), Congress adopted offense exclusion (OE) for serious crimes by older offenders, embracing PT and bypassing *Kent* requirements altogether.

6 One ATC member has identified a non-rehabilitation justification for JCs. (JC's) *separate existence is warranted not because of proven rehabilitative success but because leniency toward the young is morally justified and because the risk of failure is worth taking* (Bonnie, 1989, p. 206). Retaining *all* juvenile offenders in JC is neither morally justified nor worth the risk of failure.

Chapter 14
Benefits to Defendants

ABSTRACT

Chapter 14 demonstrates the myriad ways in which transfer benefits juvenile offenders, especially, but not only, those retained in juvenile court (JC). The anti-transfer crowd (ATC) completely ignores the fate of these juveniles; the ATC's focus, instead, is towards transfers exclusively. The JJ system remains more able to be committed to offering rehabilitative services because the worst of the worst, in terms of violent and chronic offending, are denied those services. Retained youths benefit from this. Jurisdictions' practicing OE offer retained offenders the potential benefit of facing a reduced charge that was arranged to keep the case in JC. Contrary to ATC assertions, some offenders will benefit from transfer, especially because of the increase in due process protections they should experience in CC; some youths might transfer themselves. Some adult defendants can also benefit by not looking as chronic and/or violent in their offending, and could experience greater opportunities for leniency as a result.

INTRODUCTION

Part 1: Benefits to Juvenile Court's (JC's) Retained and Transferred Offenders

It is possible to identify ways in which youthful offenders retained in JC can benefit from transfers made to CC in ways that differ from the benefits the transfers, themselves, can realize. It is also possible to identify how both groups equally reap benefits from cases' being sent to CC.

The ATC is hyper-focused on the plight of transfers, disregarding all other considerations. Completely lost on the ATC is that the vast majority of transfers will have experienced JC (perhaps several times) prior to being transferred; first-time violent offenders are relatively rare among transfer cases. All of the benefits that apply to retained youths and to JC benefit future transfer-bound youths as well, often for years on end. In other words, transfer to CC helps JCs persevere, offering significant, multiple opportunities for reform to offenders, or, in Zimring's words, to preserve life chances. Most transfers have had those still available JJ opportunities and have failed to take advantage of them; their negative evolution relates to only a minority of juvenile offenders, however. For most transfers, criminal behavior and court experiences would be much worse if JCs cease to exist. The ATC's rigid focus on those im-

DOI: 10.4018/978-1-7998-7923-7.ch014

mediately threatened with transfer results in their ignoring retained offenders who will eventually desist under the auspices of JC and will avoid transfer due to that JC experience. Perhaps the threat of transfer helped some offenders, otherwise bound to be transfer material, to avoid that outcome due to fearing a CC prosecution and sentence.

Transfer takes pressure off legislatures to reduce the maximum age of JC jurisdiction (see Feld, 2000, p. 83), which seems unnecessary, if not completely inappropriate when transfer exists: why is it necessary to remove *all* offenders below a reduced age when only a relatively few of them merit prosecution in CC? Perhaps this realization is what led ten states recently to raise their maximum JC age to from 15- and 16-years-old to 17-years-of-age. On the other hand, the elimination/serious reduction of transfer availability makes the reduction of the maximum age seem very desirable, if not inevitable. Having to keep all juvenile offenders, regardless of crime and record is self-defeating, dangerous and unacceptable. Retained and future transfers benefit from having a longer time (higher maximum age) within which to misbehave before being held criminally accountable.

Transfer to CC also allows for less pressure on legislatures to expand the problematic policy of factoring the JC record into subsequent CC sentencing (which could mean serious outcomes awaiting the offender after this transfer to CC). Sanborn (2003) noted 20 years ago, the lack of transfer could have serious impacts:

[T]otal retention likely would expand the recent tendency to allow juvenile court adjudications to be factored into subsequent criminal court sentencing, following eventual conviction in that forum. Currently, many jurisdictions permit adult court judges to significantly enhance the sentence offenders will receive in criminal court due to their juvenile court records.

In some situations, juveniles effectively can carry two strikes from juvenile court and "strike out" on their first "pitch" (or conviction) in criminal court (Sanborn, 1998, 2000). Removing transfer to adult court would create even greater pressure to not ignore the indiscretions of youth, marked by adjudications in juvenile court. The desire to "get even" with youth who continue to commit crime as adults, after having been given repeated, considerable leniency (and complete immunity from criminal liability throughout their juvenile years), would seem to be irrepressible. Allowing a juvenile court record to have such an impact in criminal court when that record was secured without serious due process in that forum only serves to exacerbate the relatively weak foundation of justice in juvenile court. Of course, the challenges to due process that have been identified by individuals who endorse the total exclusion position could prompt legislatures to convert juvenile court into the functional equivalent of criminal court, complete with the procedural rights granted adult defendants. Of course, juvenile court also could adopt a sentencing response similar to adult court and completely abandon any pretense at rehabilitation or legislatures could perceive this evolution of juvenile court as a signal of the time for its abolition. Arguably, a good deal of the recent criminalization of juvenile court can be explained by the retention of too many serious juvenile criminals (p. 206).

What seems lost on the ATC in the transfer "debate" is that transfers are not the only ones benefitted by restricting the use of the JC record in CC sentencing. Some youths (retained in JC for the time being) will age out of the JJ system and then commit another crime (their first) as a chronological adult. These never-transferred youths would be equally threatened with disastrous results via JC record use in CC sentencing via a no-transfer policy. Current transfer candidates are not the only juveniles that stand to be disadvantaged if transfer is eliminated. All juvenile offenders, whether future transfer candidates, or not, benefit from a viable JC/JJ system.

Part 2: Benefits to Defendants Retained in JC

Although it would be relevant to the benefits retained offenders realize via transfer, Chapter 13's treatment of JCs' benefits from transfer will not be reprinted in toto here. A few observations bear repeating, however. Transfer translates into retained youths' receiving better JC treatment. Transfer means there will be more resources for the (more) amenable group, including fewer residents in facilities, which avoids overcrowding and the trickle-down effect on institutionalization. Beds will be more available, and finances will be better able to keep up with demand. Finances will benefit from not having to divert resources to pay for the expanded due process rights that would have to accompany the increases in JC sentencing. Removal of the "top" echelon of juvenile offenders also allows the JC to initiate an earlier and more intensive start on treating the early starters in juvenile delinquency, which was what the original JCs aimed to do (see Chapters 2 and 4). The "nicer" character the JJ system can maintain due to the existence of transfer will more likely produce favorable attitudes of juvenile offenders toward the system, critical in furthering the cause of rehabilitation in JC. Bishop (2000) linked her findings of better recidivism rates in retained versus transferred juveniles with that better, favorable attitude, much of which could be attributable to the lack of transfers in JJ facilities.

Transfer simply makes the rehabilitation mission that much more likely to succeed in JC. The possible contamination of younger offenders by their older counterparts motivated the founders to not invite 16- and 17-year-olds to JC jurisdiction in the first place. "True" juveniles were the ones originally removed from the reaches of CC. Nevertheless, even within the friendly confines of JCs, it was recognized early in the day that older youths would contaminate the rehabilitation of younger, more amenable/vulnerable offenders. Historically, JCs embraced this reason behind transfer and considered it critical. The first JC soon supported this perspective.

A child, a boy especially, sometimes becomes so thoroughly vicious and is so repeatedly an offender that it would not be fair to the other children in a delinquent institution who have not arrived at his age of depravity and delinquency to have to associate with him (Judge Merritt Pinckney, Cook County Juvenile Court, 1911, cited in Tanenhaus, 2000, p. 13).

JC judges in Cook County let prosecutors go after older recidivists so as to not contaminate younger kids in reformatories (Tanenhaus, 2000, pp. 20-21); the benefits applied also to the facility/staff.

By the late 1920s, it appears that a local culture of waiver had developed in Chicago. Judges continued to acquiesce in the informal system of concurrent jurisdiction and still explained the active transfer decision as a means of protecting children housed in reform schools. Concerns about the manageability of older adolescents in the state's juvenile reform schools, which were designed for malleable delinquents, not hardened criminals, triggered the transfer decision (Id., p. 23).

Cook County judges held the view "that these older boys were considered to be a threat to younger ones in the state's juvenile reformatories… (Id., p. 21)."

Benefits to Defendants

Numerous studies have found that compared to transfers, offenders retained in JC fare better when recidivism is measured (see Chapter 12). Retained youths are allowed to remain in JC, in part, because they do not project as criminal an orientation as those selected for transfer. Retained youth can also benefit from removing perhaps the most criminal-looking offenders (via transfer) and in having the adjudicatory hearing (AH) transpire without the latters' contamination of the proceedings. Defense attorneys (of the retained defendants, at least) would welcome having the trial of the most criminal-and violent-looking offenders occur in CC, perhaps making all of the defendants in JC look good in comparison. Judges and prosecutors may actually be selecting the appropriate candidates for transfer, assuming a criminogenic character is an appropriate candidate for transfer. The ATC does not address this potential. Also ignored is that perhaps retained offenders do better with rehabilitation programs and with recidivism numbers because the negative influences of chronic and violent offenders have been removed from JC treatment programs via transfer; there are not as many "bad" offenders to corrupt the treatment experiences of less chronic/violent offenders.

ATC members highlight the plight of juveniles incarcerated with adults in becoming potential victims of adults. That is understandable and needs attention and remedy where the problem exists. Two interesting points, however. First, there could be an appreciable number of adults in prison who are going to be threatened by the presence of some juvenile inmates. Second, and more important, there seems to be zero concern among the ATC for the plight of much less violent juvenile inmates in facilities that are forced to accommodate otherwise transferrable juveniles. Transfer allows for less physical victimization and less disruption in JJ facilities (see Butts & Mitchell, 2000; Mears, 2003; Redding, 2003; Trulson et al., 2011). But it is not just/only about the physical safety of salvageable juvenile inmates. It is also about room in the facilities; the trickle-down effect of total inclusion is a serious threat. Transfer means the salvageable will not lose access to JJ institutions overcrowded with chronic/violent juveniles.

The ATC's disregard of total inclusion's effect on less chronic/violent offenders is remarkable since the original JCs excluded the older youths who were (and still are) most likely to dominate both the chronic and violent offender groups. If staying true to the original JC design is so sacrosanct to the ATC, completely disregarding this exclusionary aspect of the original design is puzzling. The ATC endorses only original characteristics that are consistent with a no-transfer policy.

The ATC also ignores the theory and concerns/objectives linked to the removal of status offenders (SOs, such as truancy, incorrigibility, running away from home) from the JCs' delinquent jurisdiction. Originally, *all* juvenile "offenders" received a delinquent label (see Chapter 4). By the 1960s, juvenile delinquents (JDs) were thought of as young criminals. The prosecution of some chronic and violent offenders in JC made that thinking understandable. In the 1970s, reformers did not want SOs to be thought of in the same terms as delinquents. The momentum behind this latter-day separation was three-fold, two of which directly benefitted the SO population.[1] Separation (together with a newly minted SO title) spared SOs from the stigma associated with a delinquent label. Truants and incorrigibles (SOs) did not deserve a harsh/disadvantageous label.

More important, separation also provided SOs separate treatment programs and facilities. SOs were placed in more benevolent and treatment-oriented programs, disassociated from more punitive delinquent facilities/programs. SOs were also spared the corrupting influence resulting from being institutionalized with JDs. SO facilities also have a less harsh atmosphere and a less security-oriented operation and construction. If it makes sense to separate SOs (mostly hurting themselves) from JDs (mostly hurting others), then why is it not appropriate to separate chronic (either committed to crime and/or already failures at JC programs) and violent (ready and willing to seriously hurt others) from the relatively non-chronic and the non-violent who have not adopted these profiles yet? This separation of SOs from JDs mirrored the original separation of juvenile offenders from adult criminals. This second separation was simply at the lower level of JJ/juvenile offenders.[2]

As one ATC member noted:

(S)tatus offenders were subject to incarceration together with delinquents in secure correctional facilities where they were often subjected to brutal conditions and given lessons in serious criminal behavior.... The current trend is to treat status offenders differently and to keep them separate from delinquents... (Rosenberg, 2000, pp. 85-86, citations omitted).

A legitimate question is: since we do not want SOs to be mixed with delinquents, fearing the latter will corrupt the former, why is not there a concern with mixing the less chronic/violent juvenile offenders with transfer-eligible juvenile offenders? Separation is needed also at the higher/upper level of JJ, which is provided by transfer. Removing the chronic and violent offenders from JC performs a similar service for retained offenders. Transfer allows JCs to maintain a lesser stigma for delinquents processed in JC. Transfer permits JCs to maintain a delinquent essence and label as well as to avoid the wanton criminal label for retained offenders by sending the wanton criminals to CC. It is difficult, if not impossible, to refer to chronic armed robbers/residential burglars, brutal rapists, and wonton murderers as *delinquents*. Transfer also allows JCs to avoid the pressure to increase sentences, which will hurt JCs' image and operation, while also exposing the non-transfers to harsher JC outcomes.

Zimring (2000b) admitted that transfer allows JCs to stay relatively non-punitive, and that the need to limit JC disposition power creates pressure to transfer.

The reason for this dual importance is that the mix of sanctions limited in this way is the best result for the overwhelming majority of all youth law violations, but a serious problem for the very few of the most serious of juvenile crimes. If the unwillingness of a juvenile court to disfigure is a defining character of its orientation to its subjects, the very serious crime committed by a sixteen—or seventeen-year-old is exactly the kind of hard case that the juvenile court cannot easily accommodate while preserving its nondestructive mandate (p. 210).

The Potential Special Benefit Attending Offense Exclusion (OE)

OE forces prosecutors to be extra vigilant and to more carefully analyze and choose the charges since selecting the charge simultaneously selects the forum. Defendants cannot be charged with an excluded offense and remain in JC. Prosecutors that want to retain a youth in JC, must "undercharge" youths to keep them in JC. Retained youths thus benefit from being "undercharged," or perhaps from *being more accurately charged*, in order to be kept in JC. This is, in effect, a "free" charge reduction. Even when the youth may have committed the excluded offense, technically, OE forces the prosecutor to ignore this technical qualification if a CC prosecution is not desired. An excluded robbery 1 charge that might have been either too high to begin with or is higher than it needed to be, might be reduced to robbery 2 to keep the youth in JC.[3] Without OE there is every possibility the youth would have been charged with and maybe adjudicated of robbery 1 in JC. That cannot happen with OE for those retained in JC. Moreover, prosecutors must be careful in selecting an excluded offense. Comparable charging carefulness is not necessary in JC. With OE, if the charge is too high, the prosecutor is threatened with not being able to establish PC for the charge, and it gets bounced back to JC (or never leaves JC in some states). Defense attorneys would also like OE since their JC clients have their cases initiated at a point below OE and at least a facing a less serious charge either in trial or more critically in plea bargaining.[4]

Miscellaneous Benefits to Retained Juveniles

A study on plea negotiation in JC found an abundance of it, but, unlike CC, no trial penalty. JCs did not need to punish their defendants for exercising a right to trial (Sanborn, 1985). One reason was that a relative lack of trials, coupled with a quick conclusion for those cases that are formally resolved removes the need for prosecutors to threaten dire consequences for non-compliance from juvenile defendants (i.e., insisting upon going to trial). Given adequate resources, on both prosecutorial and defense sides, there could be little pressure to avoid adjudicatory hearings. Adding chronic and serious/violent offenses to the case list, together with lengthy sentences, however, could result in a serious increase in JC trials. Jurisdictions under pressure to informally resolve cases due to a lack of adequate staffing could experience an increase in that pressure. That increase in pressure, in turn, could result in a trial penalty, placing more stress on retained offenders to plea bargain to avoid that trial penalty.

Finally, depending upon the ages selected for transfer eligibility, the presence of transfer can result in less pressure on (especially younger) juvenile gang members to be the forced by older gang members to be the ones who commit the most serious/violent offenses.

Part 3: Benefits to Defendants Transferred to CC

Best Interests (BI) Served by Transfer to CC

The ATC considers the BI only of transfers and is short-sighted, too (see Zimring & Fagan, 2000); only negative outcomes are perceived for transfers. The BI of transfers is a two-edged sword. Best interests in JC have two foci: treatment and legal interests. Treatment interests involve the help/therapy/program youths need to become whole and to stop committing crime. While it is reasonable to think the JC would serve those interests better than CC would, that may not be the case 100% of the time. For youths who need an extended period of help, it is very possible that only CC can provide that sustained assistance. Additionally, there could be some programs in CC, simply unavailable in JJ, that could rehabilitate the youths. It is wrong to assert that the juveniles' BI, including treatment ones, are *always* served better in JC (see Sobol, 2022). Transfer encourages the development of individual responsibility and informs youths that criminal behavior is indeed their fault and responsibility as well as unacceptable. JC likely spared them of that reckoning.

Similarly, it is certainly true that adjudication in JC serves juveniles' legal BI better than conviction in CC; having a JC record is preferable to having a CC record. Having said that, while legal BI are disadvantaged by conviction in CC, an enhanced constitutional rights status in CC can serve as a "better" way to avoid being found guilty, compared to prosecution in JC. For those who can be vindicated, transfer to CC could also serve juveniles' legal BI.

The Reasons Juvenile Offenders Welcome Transfer to CC

There are myriad reasons as to why juvenile offenders would want to have their prosecutions occur in CC. Generally, it is the presence of greater due process in CC that explains the benefits of being prosecuted there. The abolitionists have cited greater justice as a benefit to transfers (see Ainsworth, 1991; Federle, 1990; Feld, 1990, 1993b).[5]

Defendants in CC have a right to bail. That right is typically denied to defendants in JC. This is not always a disadvantage for youths in JC. Many states operate with a presumption of release to the parents, which is better than being able (or forced) to post bail since the former situation does not require any funds to be posted to gain release. Nevertheless, there are many juveniles for whom neither posting bail in the JJ system nor release to parents is an option. These youths are likely destined for detention. Detention can cause defendants in JC serious disadvantage in later stages of the JC proceedings, perhaps even worse than the disadvantages in CC (see Sanborn, 1992a, 2001a; Sanborn & Salerno, 2005, Chapter 10).[6] Being transferred and gaining pre-trial release creates a "custody gap" and provides these defendants a better chance to prepare a defense.

There are also numerous elements of the CC trial that could lead juvenile offenders to prefer prosecution there. Most obvious is the ability to demand a trial by jury, constitutionally denied defendants in JC (see *McKeiver v. Pennsylvania*, 1970); some states do extend this right to defendants in JC, but its exercise is rare and barely, if ever, reported. Juries are known for convicting less often than judges.[7]

Less obviously valuable is the right to a public trial, which some defendants could prefer to the very private nature of the AH.[8] Public trials afford a better chance to control judges' overstepping and exceeding their authority, which is characteristic of some JCs (see Sanborn, 1985, 1994c). Youths could pursue transfer to secure a defense attorney in CC that is more competent than the one who would be likely to represent them in JC, and who would be less likely to want to help convict youths (of something) to guarantee they receive beneficial treatment following conviction. *Guardian* defense attorneys pursue the youth's treatment interests (not fighting for a complete acquittal of the case) instead of their legal interests (which is always a complete acquittal); they regularly appear in some JCs (Sanborn, 1994c; Sanborn & Salerno, 2005).

Parens patriae judges, the judicial version of the guardian defense attorney, also want youths adjudicated so they receive JC's help. To prevent acquittal, these judges will:

- rule against a legitimate motion to suppress;
- adjust the rules of evidence, perhaps allowing hearsay (such as a mother's observations as to the child's behavior at home);
- not recuse themselves despite having had access to inadmissible, prejudicial evidence via a previous hearing in this case or previous dealings with the defendant/family;
- allow the prejudicial joining of matters: trial on this matter plus sentencing on another case or two, and/or review of yet another case already sentenced;
- seek inadmissible, prejudicial information (the youth's court file);
- take command of the trial, shutting down a defense attorney trying too hard for an acquittal or a prosecutor not trying hard enough;
- reduce the standard of proof for adjudication (i.e., below beyond a reasonable doubt) (see Sanborn, 1994c).

Even the atmosphere of JC can work against the ability to receive a fair trial. That JC pursues the rehabilitation of the child, primarily, coupled with the objective of improving the child's life can affect how adversarial the trial is. This mandate potentially impacts how much of a fight the defense attorney (even if not a guardian) will raise, and how demanding the judge will be in ensuring that opposing counsel do their jobs (see Sanborn, 1994c).

A "better" trial may not be the only reason prosecution in CC is welcomed by juvenile offenders. If convicted, some juvenile offenders fare better in CC than they would have fared in JC. Even non-serious first offenders may face harsher dispositions in JC, compared to CC, due to their being sentenced in a context in JC: family, neighborhood, school, etc. Relatively innocuous offenders can receive serious JC dispositions either immediately at disposition or later via a review hearing, gauged by their condition/status as opposed to their behavior. More equitable handling of a case is possible in CC since sentencing often must be based on crime and record. The younger the offender is, the greater the possible sentence disparity (i.e., the greater the potential disposition in JC).

More lenient CC sentencing also could be the case when juveniles have experienced several previous adjudications in JC. Remaining in JC under these circumstances could result in a relatively long disposition in a prison-like juvenile facility. The more offenses committed, especially after several treatment efforts, there typically results an escalation in dispositions through the system's correctional network. The higher youths climb the court's dispositional ladder, the less rehabilitation-oriented and more prison-like the facilities become (see Sanborn, 1985; Sanborn & Salerno, 2005). In CC, however, youths might receive a less harsh sentence, especially if the JC record cannot be factored into the CC sentence (see Sanborn, 1998, 2000). If the JC record cannot be used, the chronic juvenile offender still may be seen as a "lesser" offender and could be in CC for a "first" offense. Also contributing to a lesser sentence could be: conviction on a non-serious offense (youths were considered beyond treatment and were transferred for that reason, not due to committing serious or violent crimes); youths appear to be relatively innocuous to the prosecutor and/or judge due to a young age (even relatively serious offenders might qualify here); youths were able to secure a favorable plea bargaining for several possible reasons (shaky evidence, testifying against co-defendants in CC, etc.); the judge or jury convicted on an offense less serious than that which triggered transfer; or youths simply met a judge accustomed to lenient sentencing, perhaps especially for younger offenders.

To be sure, prosecution in CC has serious liabilities for defendants, in terms of the potential sentence and the CC record. Just as sure, however, when the ATC condemns transfer across the board, suggesting *all* transfers are disadvantaged and damaged by sending a case to CC, many offenders and many situations must be ignored to reach that sweeping conclusion.

That juveniles would want to self-transfer or to not fight the state's transfer would probably be rare (due to the possible severe consequences identified above) but would not be unheard of.

Part 4: Benefits to Adult Defendants

There is also a possible trickle-down effect in CC that means transfer will benefit adult offenders as well. The increased load presented by transfer cases could add pressure for more diversion in CC. The relatively better-looking adult offenders, compared to the chronic and serious/violent juvenile transfers, can make possible an expansion of diversion for beginning adult criminals (who look good in comparison), more lenient sentencing for the same group for the same reason, and more favorable plea bargains due to caseload pressures. The inclusion of juvenile-aged transfers into the prison population can also lead to adding more education and treatment programs and more emphasis on rehabilitation.

REFERENCES

Ainsworth, J. E. (1991). Re-imagining childhood and reconstructing the legal order: The case for abolishing the juvenile court. *North Carolina Law Review*, *69*, 1083–1133.

Bishop, D. M. (2000). Juvenile offenders in the adult criminal justice system. In M. Tonry (Ed.), *Crime & Justice: A Review of Research, 27, 81-167*. IL University of Chicago Press. doi:10.1086/652199

Butts, J. A., & Harrell, A. (1998). *Delinquents or criminals: Policy options for young offenders. Crime & Policy Report, June 1998*. The Urban Institute.

Federle, K. H. (1990). The Abolition of the juvenile court: A proposal for the preservation of children's legal rights. *Journal of Contemporary Law*, *16*, 23–51.

Feld, B. C. (1990). The punitive juvenile court and the quality of procedural justice: Disjunctions between rhetoric and reality. *Crime and Delinquency*, *36*(4), 443–466. doi:10.1177/0011128790036004002

Feld, B. C. (1993b). Juvenile (in)justice and the criminal court alternative. *Crime and Delinquency*, *39*(4), 403–424. doi:10.1177/0011128793039004001

Feld, B. C. (2000). Legislative exclusion of offenses from juvenile court jurisdiction: A history and critique. In J. Fagan & F. E. Zimring (Eds.), *The changing borders of juvenile justice: Transfer of adolescents to the criminal court* (pp. 83–144). University of Chicago Press.

Hughes v. State. 1994. 653 A.2d 241. Delaware Supreme Court.

McKeiver v. Pennsylvania. (1971). 403 U.S. 528.

Mears, D. P. (2003). A critique of waiver research: Critical next steps in assessing the impacts of laws for transferring juveniles to the criminal justice system. *Youth Violence and Juvenile Justice*, *1*(2), 156–172. doi:10.1177/1541204002250876

Redding, R. E. (2003). The effects of adjudicating and sentencing juveniles as adults: Research and policy implications. *Youth Violence and Juvenile Justice*, *1*(2), 128–155. doi:10.1177/1541204002250875

Rosenberg, I. M. (2000). Teen violence and the juvenile courts: A plea for reflection and restraint. *Houston Law Review*, *37*, 75–96.

Sanborn, J. B., Jr. (1985). *Plea negotiation in juvenile court*. [Unpublished doctoral dissertation, SUNY Albany, Albany, NY., United States].

Sanborn, J. B., Jr. (1992a). Detention in juvenile court: Adequate protection or arbitrary decision making? (Paper presentation). Academy of Criminal Justice Sciences. Pittsburg, PA, United States.

Sanborn, J. B. Jr. (1993b). The right to a public jury trial: A need for today's juvenile court. *Judicature*, *78*, 230–238.

Sanborn, J. B. Jr. (1994c). Remnants of *parens patriae* in the adjudicatory hearing: Is a fair trial possible in juvenile court. *Crime and Delinquency*, *40*(4), 599–615. doi:10.1177/0011128794040004008

Sanborn, J. B. Jr. (1996a). Factors perceived to affect dispositions in juvenile court: Putting the sentencing decision into context. *Crime and Delinquency*, *42*(1), 99–113. doi:10.1177/0011128796042001006

Sanborn, J. B. Jr. (1996b). Policies regarding the prosecution of juvenile murderers: Which system and who should decide? *Law & Policy*, *18*(1-2), 151–178. doi:10.1111/j.1467-9930.1996.tb00168.x

Sanborn, J. B. Jr. (1998). Second-class justice and first-class punishment: The use of juvenile records in sentencing adults. *Judicature*, *81*, 206–213.

Sanborn, J. B. Jr. (2000). Striking out on the first pitch in criminal court. *Barry Law Review*, *1*, 7–61.

Sanborn, J. B. Jr. (2001a). A *parens patriae* figure or impartial fact finder: Policy questions and conflicts for the juvenile court judge. *Criminal Justice Policy Review*, *12*(4), 311–332. doi:10.1177/0887403401012004004

Sanborn, J. B. Jr. (2003). Hard choices or obvious ones: Developing policy for excluding youth from juvenile court. *Youth Violence and Juvenile Justice*, *1*(2), 198–214. doi:10.1177/1541204002250879

Sanborn, J. B. Jr, & Salerno, A. W. (2005). *The juvenile justice system: Law and process*. Roxbury Publishing Company. Oxford University Publishing.

Sobol, S. (2022). Rethinking juvenile rehabilitation: Presumptive waiver and alternative sentencing in Indiana. *Indiana Law Journal (Indianapolis, Ind.)*, *97*, 365–391.

Tanenhaus, D. S. (2000). The evolution of transfer out of the juvenile court. In J. Fagan & F. E. Zimring (Eds.), *The changing borders of juvenile justice: Transfer of adolescents to the criminal court* (pp. 13–43). University of Chicago Press.

Trulson, C. R., Caudill, J. W., Belshaw, S. H., & DeLisi, M. (2011). A problem of fit: Extreme delinquents, blended sentencing, and the determinants of continued adult sanctions. *Criminal Justice Policy Review*, *23*(3), 263–284. doi:10.1177/0887403410370618

Zimring, F. E. (2000b). The punitive necessity of waiver. In J. Fagan & F. E. Zimring (Eds.), *The Changing Borders of Juvenile Justice: Transfer of adolescents to the criminal court* (pp. 207–224). University of Chicago Press.

Zimring, F. E., & Fagan, J. (2000). Transfer policy and law reform. In J. Fagan & F. E. Zimring (Eds.), *The changing borders of juvenile justice: Transfer of adolescents to the criminal court* (pp. 407–424). University of Chicago Press.

ENDNOTES

1 Separation spared JCs from having to provide SOs with the same constitutional rights (i.e., the *Gault/Winship* holdings) as delinquents. The rights granted to delinquents by the Supreme Court were based on criminal acts; status offenders can be denied comparable rights.

2 SOs and JDs are also separated from dependent/neglected youths for similar reasons.

3 Prosecutors could also exploit this charge "reduction" to complete a plea negotiation.

4 Direct file (DF) lacks this lesser-charge benefit since prosecutors can charge the same offense in both JC and CC. The higher charges that DF prosecutors elect to keep in JC could result in defendants' being adjudicated on those higher, offenses otherwise excluded in OE.

5 Pro-JC types and non-abolitionists agree (see Sanborn, 1993b, 1996b).

6 Juveniles held in custody until the AH are disadvantaged. The trial judge knows the youth has a problem, likely with the home, or he/she would not have been detained. By the time of trial, two people, the intake worker who detained and then the detention hearing judge who upheld that decision, have decided that the youth could not be released to the parent(s). Money would not have been the issue since bail was not an alternative anyway. It is worse when there have been several days without a release to the parent(s). That means detention was not due to simply an inability to contact a parent or a parent's initial refusal to take the child home during the arrest stage. More important, detention then suggests the youth needs help. This can prejudice the trial judge who knows an acquittal could mean the youth's problem goes unaddressed. In a close case, these youths should experience a greater likelihood of adjudication compared to those released pending trial. If youths continue in custody after adjudication, a similar prejudice arises at disposition since they have not been home to demonstrate that they can be safely released to the community. For youths who return home and proceed later to court without a rearrest, it would seem cruel or arbitrary/illogical to impose a commitment; why is commitment necessary? A second issue is that it is less psychologically damaging to a judge to commit a detained youth. That youth has already been temporarily removed from the home so commitment here would merely be a continuation of institutionalization. Holding offense and record constant, these detained youths should experience harsher outcomes at disposition compared to those youths who were released pending sentencing, which is what the data show (see Sanborn, 1992a, 1994c, 1996a; Sanborn & Salerno, 2005).

7 Defense attorneys might push for the advantages/rights attending CC prosecution.

8 Public trial joins jury trial as a Sixth Amendment right. Ironically, the *McKeiver* Court rejected the juvenile's jury trial request, in part, because granting jury trial would trigger a right to a public trial. The fear of operationalizing one constitutional right was used as an excuse for not granting another constitutional right. The ominous character of the public trial in CC was similarly used as a reason the Delaware Supreme Court did not accept the validity of an early example of OE (see *Hughes v. State*, 1994). What really underscores the irony is that the right to a public trial is the *only* trial-related constitutional right that is non-waivable; even the rights to silence, counsel, and to trial, itself, are waivable.

Chapter 15
Benefits to Society

ABSTRACT

Chapter 15 itemizes the benefits transfer offers society. Like the benefits associated with juvenile court (JC) and defendants, the benefits society realizes are mostly, if not completely, immeasurable; and, not surprisingly, have not been researched. One critical benefit is that transfer allows for a balance of society's and the juvenile's best interests (BI). If the no-transfer policy prevails and JC becomes all and only about juvenile offenders, there is little likelihood that the juveniles' BI will be operationalized in JC. Transfer allows a realistic prospect that JCs' and retained juveniles' BI can co-exist, which, in turn, serves society's BI. Transfer also promotes community protection, with the ability for CC to impose lengthy sentences for the severely violent and seriously chronic juvenile offender. Transfer and prosecution in CC also serves numerous important concepts and pursuits, such as justice, moral condemnation, proportionality, incapacitation, deterrence and retribution. The Chapter concludes by explaining how prosecutors benefit by transfer.

INTRODUCTION

Benefits accruing to the JC and to retained juvenile offenders apply equally to society, which can retain confidence that the juvenile justice (JJ) system is doing the right thing to both retained and transferred offenders. JCs can continue to receive the support of the community. A no/limited-transfer policy would have to appear both dangerous and unacceptable to the general population.

Transfer Promotes a Proper Balance of Best Interests (BI)

At some point in the spectrum of juvenile criminal behavior, society's and victims' interests must be vindicated (PCC, 1967, p. 81; Springer, 1991, p. 6); some ATC members acknowledge this (Zimring, 2000a, 2000b). Above a certain threshold of chronic and violent juvenile criminality it simply should not be all about the juveniles' BI. That simply sends the wrong message to JCs, youths and society.

Although it is rare, some of the ATC have admitted that society can support JCs' both transferring dangerous juvenile offenders and promoting the rehabilitation of other offenders.

DOI: 10.4018/978-1-7998-7923-7.ch015

The poll data indicate strong support for juvenile justice reforms that respond to public safety concerns and simultaneously advance improved treatment for juvenile offenders (Krisberg & Austin, 1993, p. 4).

Transfer puts proper emphasis on society's BI and gives more reassurance to everyone in the community that society can afford the best interests of juveniles' being the primary focus of JC; it is a matter of reasonableness and acceptability. JC can do its job with the 90% or more of the juvenile offender population retained in JC without much push back because society is not asked to tolerate too much.

The problem (with total criminal immunity) becomes expecting society to have none of its interests served or protected in juvenile court, which would be a result of total retention. Diverting every young criminal from criminal court asks society always to look the other way, again regardless of the circumstances.... (Recently there has been a) revision of juvenile court purpose clauses so as to include protecting the public and promoting society's interests. These purposes become more pivotal to juvenile court proceedings when violent/chronic offenders are processed there. These purposes do not appear to be served by total retention, and it does not seem reasonable or plausible to simply ignore or marginalize society's interests, especially when it comes to serious criminal behavior. It certainly does not seem unreasonable to question whether only the juvenile's best interests should be served when serious, chronic or violent crimes are at hand, and to doubt whether the juvenile system can maintain a one-dimensional, imbalanced purpose in this situation (Sanborn, 2003, pp. 204-05).

Transfer Furthers Community Protection

Perhaps the most frequently acknowledged purpose served by transfer is the potential enhancement of community protection (Wizner, 1995). Both pro-transfer types and the ATC tend to offer only this purpose.[1] Feld (2000) suggested that OE and DF "symbolize a fundamental change in juvenile justice...from amenability to treatment to public safety... (pp. 128-29). Ironically, transfer allows JJ systems to remain mostly faithful to "amenability to treatment," consigning to CCs/CJ systems the primary responsibility of "public safety;" JCs can largely duck the latter.

Discussions aimed at the *greater-punishment* group have gone astray, mostly due to a narrow explanation of PT. Protecting society was likely the reason prosecutors cited for seeking more transfer power via PT.[2] The ATC has taken advantage of this narrow perspective and has emphasized how CC does not do a better job than JC in protecting society from chronic or violent juveniles.

It is critical for pro-transfer types to acknowledge that transfer will not better protect society in *every* case, and that prosecution in JC can *at times* better serve the protection of society. The greater likelihood of a transfer's securing bail in CC can threaten the protection of society (Myers, 2001; Redding, 2003). There is, indeed, a "custody gap" between JC and CC Myers & Kiehl, 2001). Moreover, unlike in CC, preventive detention is constitutionally recognized and openly practiced in JC (*Schall v. Martin*, 1984). CCs usually provide the accused the opportunity to post bail and to gain freedom pending trial, increasing the potential for these pre-trial releases to end in criminal behavior. The abundance of cases and cumbersomeness of prosecutions in CC could encourage more *nol pros* outcomes for transfers who appear less threatening to prosecutors than adult offenders. Substantive and procedural rights in the CC make acquittals more possible. Depending upon the circumstances, sentences in CC may not be as harsh/long as JC dispositions (see Chapter 12).[3]

Most of the dialogue and research on transfer has focused on the relative punishments meted out by both systems. The ATC points to the possibility of a *leniency* or *punishment gap* between juvenile and criminal courts. Juveniles who accumulate a considerable record in JC could be destined for a significant period of incarceration in the JJ system, whereas their first appearance in CC could result in probation (or minimal jail/prison time) due to their "rookie" status there. Historically, JC records could not be directly factored into CC sentencing due to the limited due process attending JC adjudications and the limited responsibility of juvenile offenders. Chronic juvenile offenders were "virgins" at their first appearance in CC. Even first-time violent transfers may appear to be relatively innocuous to a CC judge and may not receive serious punishment. Several ATC folks maintain this punishment gap calls into question the legitimacy of transfer.[4]

Many problems mar this criticism. Serious dispositions of incarceration for chronic and violent offenders are never certain in most JCs, regardless of the crime and delinquent record. Most transfers have been aimed at the *beyond-rehabilitation* group for whom longer sentences in CC are neither desired nor likely (and dominate research). The punishment gap is largely irrelevant to these transfers. Even for the *greater-punishment* group, the failure of the CC to deliver a harsh sentence does not retroactively invalidate the transfer. This position means JC policies must be held hostage to CC practices.[5] To the extent that lengthy sentences are desired/warranted, JC cannot be relied upon to significantly punish young offenders without running afoul of its treatment mission and without undermining the limited due process provided in the adjudicatory hearing (AH) (Feld, 1984a; Zimring, 1981, 1991). A JC sentence of more than two/three years calls into question how much rehabilitation influenced the outcome (or was it all about incapacitation?). The ATC is unaware of or unconcerned by a potential surge in relatively lengthy JC dispositions and their effect on the image/purpose of JC. Many studies have found more punitive sanctions for juveniles in CC (see Chapter 12).[6] This is especially true for serious violent crimes, such as murder (Benedek & Cornell, 1989; Eigen, 1981a, 1981b; Rudman et al., 1986). Finally, to eliminate the punishment gap and ensure lengthier sentences, JC records would have to be factored directly and more heavily into CC sentencing. This way, juveniles in CC for the first time *would be* considered recidivists due to their JC record. This practice, which has now been adopted by many jurisdictions, presents very serious constitutional problems, however (see Sanborn, 1998, 2000).

Critical to remember is that transfer to CC will not always produce a longer sentence than could/might have been obtained in JC. That reality should encourage prosecutors (or judges) to exercise care and guarded discretion in making the transfer decision, and to not oversell the idea that greater justice or punishment will prevail by transferring the case to CC. Nevertheless, in those cases in which (perhaps much) longer sentences *are warranted, pursued, and obtained*, that *cannot/will not happen in the absence of the transfer* of chronic and violent juvenile offenders.

Having acknowledged the reality that transfer does not always serve to protect society, it is time to emphasize how transfer can aid that mission. Transfer can and has resulted, appropriately, in longer sentences, which are served in more secure adult facilities, compared to juvenile institutions. Society has been the benefactor of the availability of transfer. Even Feld (2000, p. 111), Zimring (1981, 1991) and other ATC members have admitted as much.[7] Grisso (2000) conceded that transfer "allows juvenile courts to waive jurisdiction over juveniles for whom rehabilitation by the time of required release is considered unlikely… (p. 324)," as well as providing for the continued secured custody of "…youths who present a high risk of violence (and) may run away from juvenile facilities, thereby presenting a threat to the community (Id.)." Redding (2016) explained "transfer may be useful as a way of keeping older juveniles who would age out of juvenile justice jurisdiction under continuing justice system supervision… (p. 945)."

Transfer also helps community protection through public awareness of chronic/violent youths. Transfer to and conviction in CC results in public records that allow greater exposure of these criminals at both conviction and release from sanctions. Public records also let future employers know prospective employees have a criminal background, helping to protect customers and guarding employers against lawsuits.

Transfer Serves Penal Policy Elements of: Justice, Moral Condemnation, Proportionality, Incapacitation, Deterrence and Retribution

A clever ATC tactic is to claim that transfer either cannot serve *any* of the four major sentencing objectives (i.e., rehabilitation, deterrence, incapacitation, and retribution), or it must serve *more than one*, or even that it must serve *all four* objectives simultaneously to be legitimate. Brink claims that transfer "is inconsistent with retributive, rehabilitative, and deterrent rationales for punishment… (Brink, 2003-04, p. 1585)." It seems incapacitation has escaped his consideration.

Another tactic is to suggest that JCs' explanations or justifications for transfer are ever-shifting and nefarious, possibly even insincere. Zimring (1998a) was critical of JCs' pursuit of transfer and alleged abandonment of rehabilitation, its sworn and apparently solitary original design and mission (consider Chapter 2):

When the formal jurisprudence of the juvenile court emphasized the treatment of delinquency, the official reason for waiving jurisdiction was often that the juvenile was not suitable for or amenable to treatment. As the court's rationale has become more ***eclectic,*** *the official reasons for passing juveniles onto criminal courts have become somewhat more* ***diverse…*** *(p. 109, emphases added; see, also, 1998b).*[8]

As juvenile crime soon and gradually became more chronic, serious, and violent (perhaps more eclectic, too?), the naivete/unbridled optimism of the founders was exposed, as well. The original anticipated "failures" of the JC mission were those who committed repeated innocuous offenses (e.g., could not remain at home or faithfully attend school) and would not stop despite the JCs' multiple efforts to reform. That anticipation was shortsighted. Transfer, rare in the early days, meant JCs ultimately believed some serious offenders were so determined to misbehave that they were simply beyond the help of JC. As JCs became more inclusive, in terms of older and more serious offenders, explanations of transfer shifted to the need to protect society. Arguably, the need to protect society was neither pressing nor obvious in the early years of JC. Eventually, protecting society *joined*, rather than *replaced*, rehabilitation as the responsibility of JCs. The naivete of the founders was indeed exposed. In recognition of the fundamental change in juvenile offending (see Chapter 5), and in response to U.S. Supreme Court's intervention into JC procedure, legislatures refashioned JC purpose clauses to reflect the need to defend society against some juvenile offenders, to impose punishment, and to hold juvenile offenders accountable (see Sanborn, 1994d). Forcing JCs to become more diverse in serving multiple purposes did not mean JCs were no longer about rehabilitation or that they were only to punish, etc. Meanwhile, JC workers realized, long before legislatures did, that JCs could no longer be (if they ever were) unidimensional in their response to juvenile criminals, and that the more chronic, serious and violent needed to be prosecuted in CC. Later-in-the day, prosecutors would join the JC workforce (in the post-*Gault* era), would see increasing severity in juvenile crime, would understand the deficiencies of JC sanctions in addressing, treating, and controlling chronic, serious and violent juvenile offending, and would lobby for more control of the transfer decision since judges were more erratic and hesitant in transferring worthy offenders.

JC workers and pro-transfer types could be blamed for not providing a more thoughtful and comprehensive analysis/defense of transfer. To date, that treatise does not exist, which makes this work that much more relevant and necessary. Even still, the ATC refuses to acknowledge that transfer accomplishes all four sentencing objectives, simultaneously allows JCs to remain mostly rehabilitative, and helps JCs avoid greater pressures to adopt even more punitive/retributive measures than those that surfaced during the get-tough movement. That transfer allows JCs to avoid becoming more punitive and retributive (and more criminalized) appears to be lost on the ATC.

The good news for JCs is that the public strongly supports rehabilitation for juvenile offenders (Applegate, Davis, & Cullen, 2009; Welch, Butler, & Gertz, 2019). The bad news for the ATC is that the public also strongly supports punishment, especially for chronic and violent juvenile offenders (Mears, Pickett, & Mancini, 2015; Welch et al., 2019; Zimring, 2000a, 2000b).

The ATC implies that any single transfer that lacks a connection to a sentencing objective is illegitimate and holds that if there is *one* transfer that lacks legitimacy, then *all* transfers lack legitimacy. Of course, this ATC position begs the question as to why transfer must satisfy *any* sentencing objective to be considered necessary or legitimate. Transfer produces numerous, multi-faceted benefits that go beyond sentencing objectives (see Chapters 13 and 14).[9] Transfer furthers all four sentencing objectives (and more), just not simultaneously or in every case.

Improvement in the operations and outcomes of rehabilitation programs was addressed in the previous chapter. Promoting rehabilitation is not the primary goal of every transfer case; it may be irrelevant in any particular case, such as some chronic offenders who appear to be incorrigible and non-amenable. At the same time, a transfer in this context should be considered a pro-rehabilitation result for retained juvenile offenders. Nevertheless, contrary to ATC assertions, rehabilitation does not have to be a concern in *every* transfer to be listed as a reason behind transfer. The ATC tactic is to highlight one of more cases where the cause of rehabilitation was not served (or pursued) as proof that transfer *never* furthers rehabilitation. That tactic might score propaganda points, but it does not advance an honest debate on transfer, which might just be the point of the propaganda.

Objectives accomplished in one transfer might not surface in every transfer. The benefits enumerated in this book do not need to be realized in every transfer to be necessary or legitimate. Transfer might achieve retribution, but not deterrence; a CC sentence might achieve proportionality, but not assist rehabilitation. Transfer might satisfy justice, but not deter. A single transfer might not promote more than one, let alone all, of the sentencing objectives; that does not translate into not satisfying *any* sentencing objective or some other worthy cause. One transfer might not satisfy any of the sentencing objectives but still be legitimate.

One global statement is correct, however. Eliminating (or too narrowly restricting) transfer will reduce, if not erase, the potential benefits identified in Chapters 13, 14 and 15.

Justice

JCs were founded on the principle that juvenile offenders needed the state's help in avoiding a criminal career. There was never a commitment to looking the other way for each and every juvenile offender, regardless of the severity of the crime or the chronicity of the behavior. Simply put, violent crimes, such as brutal rapes and homicides, plus serious chronic ones, such as robbery and residential burglary should not be classified as delinquency. That label does a disservice to the actual outcomes of those crimes. The JC's position on these crimes was evident as far back as 1937 in a case from a New Jersey appellate that upheld the exclusion of a murder charge from JC.

We think that a charge which is in effect that of murder cuts so deeply into human emotions, collides so violently with life's experiences fair expectations, and is so horrible in fact and in contemplation of society, that it remains a crime within the purview of the Constitution, whatever treatment may be appended to it by the Legislature (Ex parte Mei, 1937: 83, cited in Tanenhaus, 2000, pp. 28-29).

Zimring (1998a) agreed that murder is beyond the capacity of JC and conceded that the juveniles' BI sometimes needs to yield to the quest for and imposition of justice and deserved punishment.

When there is unavoidable conflict between the objectives of youth policy and the minimum demands for deserved punishment, the latter should carry the day.... However, when desert and youth support conflict, electing the minimum punishment becomes the sad necessity of the sentencing court (p. 143, emphases added).[10]

Similarly, Feld (2000) acknowledged that transfer provides for the reaffirmation of fundamental norms as well as for maintaining the integrity of the substantive criminal law (p. 111).

Transfer also avoids the problem when there is no place to prosecute, not due to a statute of limitations obstacle (which prevents *any* prosecution), but because the offender is not arrested or prosecuted until after the expiration of the JC maximum age or there is a minimum age for transfer for a murder committed by a juvenile younger than the eligible age. Assuming it is known or suspected that the offender was a juvenile, the crime, itself, might even not be investigated either immediately or afterwards due to realizing "nothing" can be done to the offender. This will likely not "sit well" with the victim(s) or the community.

To be sure, as the ATC likes to highlight, the status of a juvenile (the ATC prefers using the word, child) does not simply evaporate when the offender is prosecuted in CC, but, at the same time and simply put, the ATC chooses to ignore:

The quest of and need for justice do not evaporate simply because the offender is a juvenile.

Moral Condemnation

At some point of criminal offending, whether due to the severity of the crime and/or the chronicity of the offending, society needs and wants to be able to condemn criminal behavior. This reaction to crime rightfully belongs in CC, not in JC (as much as can be reasonably avoided).

(Transfer is) .... a moral judgment of the same nature as represented in the codification of the criminal law; obviously, exclusion means that the criminal law will be vindicated in criminal rather than in juvenile court....

The moral condemnation involved in the prosecution of criminal law has belonged historically to criminal courts. Juvenile courts were designed to prosecute youthful defendants without a clear declaration of culpability. Discretionary exclusion allows juvenile courts to remain mostly true to their original design by relinquishing to adult courts those candidates worthy of moral condemnation (lengthier sentences, etc.). That juvenile courts have become less rehabilitative or benign in orientation and operation recently probably speaks mostly to their attempting to accommodate too many offenders who actually warrant the criminal court's retribution and condemnation (Sanborn, 1996b, p. 160).

****

(A) state might feel very strongly that an individual who is morally responsible for his conduct committed an act which requires a very clear statement of its wrongfulness, even if no enormous penalty is to be executed.... (Transfer amounts to a) desire to reinforce the moral order through a clear declaration of culpability. Some juvenile offenders, of course, are morally responsible, criminally blameworthy actors, who happen to be statutorily defined as children... (McCarthy, 1994, p. 661; see, also, Wizner, 1995, p. 1034).

Preventing proper CC condemnation of criminals opens JCs to deleterious effects.

Total retention encourages condemnation to become a part of juvenile court processing, which, in turn, promotes more punishment and warehousing (and less treatment) of juvenile offenders, and greater promise to protect society through juvenile court intervention .... (T)otal retention creates added pressure to invite the victim to become a significant and perhaps determining voice in juvenile court proceedings, as has occurred in much juvenile justice legislation recently. This potentially hostile party can further undermine and derail the rehabilitative focus of juvenile court, and can introduce a more punitive atmosphere and its attending consequences into the proceedings (Sanborn, 2003, p. 205, citing Sanborn, 2001b).

Even though juveniles may be "less culpable" than adults, generally, not all juveniles are less culpable nor equally culpable among themselves. Some warrant condemnation greater than that available in JC, even when some juveniles may not be equally culpable as some adults.

Finally, flipping the moral condemnation coin, excluding the most chronic and violent offenders from JC both helps prevent moral decay and advances moral reaffirmation among law-abiding juveniles. Probably the last event society needs developing among adolescents, who are supposedly busy learning the elements and requirements of morality, is the idea that chronic violations of the criminal law or violent acts perpetrated against others are "okay." That would seem to be a reasonable conclusion for youths to draw if society's response to these behaviors is ambiguous, or worse, rewarding, as represented in immunity from criminal prosecution via processing in JC. Perhaps this inference already operates among some juveniles and explains their moral ambiguity, defiance, or rejection. Perhaps it is not an inability to learn or respect moral requirements, but rather seeing rewards extended to situations of moral depravity. That would be a natural response to observing fellow neighborhood young criminals' expressing gratitude for their visits to Bulls, Bears, Black Hawks, and Cubs games thanks to their JC dispositions. Youths prone to obeying the law, or at least not committing the number and kind of offenses meriting transfer, are rewarded, to some extent, by the current availability of transfer to CC. At least they witness serious unlawful behavior incurring the wrath and condemnation of society via prosecution in CC; they can even share in that condemnation.

Again, simply put, the ATC chooses to ignore:

The quest of and need to condemn some chronic and violent criminal behavior do not evaporate simply because the offender is a juvenile.

Proportionality

Although it can be regarded as a subset of retribution (as in Just Deserts), proportionality is served by transfer as well. Unless the JC sanction involves the highest level of JJ facilities (i.e., a juvenile prison), it can reasonably be asserted that proportionate punishment for crime (at least for those who commit serious/violent felonies) simply cannot occur in JC. A lack of proportionate punishment is not only the specific design of JC, but also appropriate, and should remain that way. Transfer helps JC to maintain that character by allowing JC to remain mostly true to its original design.

Transfer allows for a graduated transition from juvenile to adult offender, should criminal behavior continue into adulthood. The ATC supports graduated sanctions for offenders, provided *all* of the sanctions *remain within JC*. Requiring such means there will be a serious backlog at the top of the JJ disposition ladder/sanctions. That backlog means that proportionality will have to expire at some point if transfer does not exist.

Once JJ dispositions are maxed out the juvenile offender can segue via transfer rather than quantum leap into CC sanctions. The fact that not all transfers receive lengthier sentences is actually a good thing. One of the problems with factoring the JC record into CC sentencing is that there can be a serious gap between the previous JJ disposition and the initial CJ sanction (see Sanborn, 1998, 2000). It is arguably unfair for juvenile offenders to experience repeated leniency via JC handling, and to build significant JC records due to not being transferred, only to have those voluminous JC records slam them on their first visits to CC. Perhaps the silver lining for some chronic offenders that do not receive lengthier CC sentences is that at least they have been warned that, even when not extreme, CC punishment will no longer replicate the JC dispositions. Recidivism at this stage suggests that the offenders are truly committed to a criminal lifestyle and/or that they have not been impressed/deterred by either JC or CC sanctions.

Again, simply put, the ATC chooses to ignore:

The quest of and need for proportionate sanctions/punishments for chronic and violent crimes do not evaporate simply because the offender is a juvenile.

Incapacitation

The ATC criticizes transfers in which longer sentences do not occur. Research has verified that many transfers end up sentenced to incarceration for longer periods than would have been possible in JC (see Chapter 12); the ATC ignores these transfers. Meaningful incapacitation of some offenders results from transfer (Bishop, 2000, p. 85). The abundance of juvenile offenders' serving life without parole speaks to the incapacitation potential in CC completely absent from JCs. Perhaps the ATC's criticism of an insufficient number of longer sentences should be aimed at the CCs that perhaps fail to take juvenile offenders seriously enough and/or against the states that have not authorized sufficient impact of the JC record in CC sentencing.

Again, simply put, the ATC chooses to ignore:

The quest of and need for the incapacitation of some chronic and violent criminals do not evaporate simply because the offender is a juvenile.

Deterrence

The ATC does recognize the deterrence outcome resulting from transfer.[11] If nothing else, rather lengthy CC sentences guarantees incapacitation and specific deterrence (at least during the duration of the sentence). Although he does not mention deterrence, Feld conceded transfer opens the door for general societal protection through greater certainty and visibility of consequences (2000, p. 111).[12]

JC was set up to be rehabilitative and reformative. In some (hopefully most) jurisdictions JC is still just that. We want JC to be and stay that way, often offering a setting and workers that are superior to the offender's previous experiences, better than the family/peers with whom the offender has interacted. This is the ideal of JJ that should not change simply so as to retain chronic and violent juvenile offenders. The entire disposition structure (apart from the most severe juvenile prisons, which are still superior to their adult counterparts) can be regarded as a reward for committing a crime.[13] It is little wonder that juvenile delinquents are not deterred.

JC was not designed for deterrence, per se, although prevention (and implicitly deterrence) was certainly a major goal. Most dispositions available to JC speak to leniency, if not benevolence, more than to punishment. Deterrence should not be expected from JC dispositions. If deterrence is desired, then fewer "rewards" and more punishment should be implemented in JC. That some juvenile offenders finally get the message and desist after "one more" JC sanction, as research suggests, is not surprising. Discerning exactly when in a specific offender's life that desistance message will be acted upon is impossible; tendencies are the best we can gauge. That some juvenile offenders continue to recidivate after experiencing a CC sanction is also not unexpected. That tendency speaks to a punishment message being rejected by the offender, perhaps after too many kind and compassionate sanctions in JC, followed by a too lenient/not sufficiently serious initial sanction in CC.

A no-transfer policy would likely lead some JCs to impose no or token dispositions on juveniles when offenders have exhausted all available programs. This is possible even when transfer is available. Some juvenile offenders fall between the cracks of the two systems. They are not really 'transfer material' (the offender is chronic, but has not committed a serious offense), but, at the same time, they are not suitable candidates for probation or a JJ facility. All available dispositions could reasonably be regarded as a waste of resources and/or as undermining the treatment of other juvenile offenders. It would not be unusual for this offender to be simply let go without any sanction or a relatively meaningless one, such as a fine or community service (see Sanborn, 1985).

While having transfer might not deter a juvenile offender committed to committing crimes, a total lack of a transfer threat could be successful in opening the floodgates. A no/limited-transfer policy could incentivize crimes by the newly non-transferrable population, especially, but not only, if the current/future offenses would result in a no-disposition outcome in JC.

As word would spread through the neighborhood that no youth will ever again be prosecuted in criminal court, chances are that some juveniles would perceive no disincentive (or at least much less of one) to committing crime (Sanborn, 2003, p. 206).

Again, simply put, the ATC chooses to ignore:

The quest of and need for pursuing some deterrence do not evaporate simply because the offender is a juvenile.

Retribution

Retribution has received the most ATC attention in the transfer discussion. The ATC grants little credibility to deterring juvenile offenders. Incapacitation succeeds but often fails, in the eyes of the ATC, when longer sentences do not result in CC. The ATC simply cannot wrap its collective mind around rehabilitation's ever being served. It ignores the plight of retained juveniles and, it summarily dismisses the CJ system's rehabilitating any offender. That leaves only retribution to be addressed as a necessary or legitimate reason behind transfer. Slobogin (2013) does not hesitate in claiming that retribution is the *only* plausible reason for transfer, and that it simply *fails* to justify or explain transfer (pp. 107, 127; see, also, Sellers & Arrigo, 2009: 439). Zane and colleagues (2016) announced retribution is possible via transfer, but then claimed that what society wants in this regard is unclear and that transfer does not guarantee that punishment will occur. Inasmuch as prosecution of adult offenders in CC also "does not guarantee that punishment will occur," it is puzzling why only the prosecution of juveniles offenders in CC (via transfer, of course) must be held hostage to this expectation/standard.

Zane and colleagues (2016) concluded that even if transfer satisfies retribution, recent U.S. Supreme Court decisions in *Roper v. Simmons* (2005), *Graham v. Florida* (2010), and *Miller v. Alabama* (2012) (CC sentencing-oriented cases involving juveniles) can be interpreted as any retributive rationale for transfer "appears to be tenuous (Zane et al., 2016, p. 920)." Other ATC members, however, admit that retribution can result from transfer (Bishop, 2000: 86; Loughran, Reid, Collins, & Mulvey, 2016; Redding, 2016, p. 939), conceding it is possible "that transfer achieves a more appropriate level of retribution, one more consistent with what society may view as desirable… (Zane et al., 2016, p. 920)."

Perhaps recognizing this view led Feld (1987) to spend considerable time and energy in trying to disconnect transfer from any contribution to the cause of retribution. Feld initially conceded retribution's connection to transfer but ultimately decimated any legitimate connection between them.

Retribution ***alone,*** *however, is* ***an inadequate theory*** *for the selection of waiver criteria both because it is overly inclusive and because the infliction of harm without any* ***offsetting utilitarian gain*** *is undesirable. Consistent with the the underlying rationale for waiver, selective incapacitation is an appropriate theory to couple with retribution because there is a limited class of offenders whose persistent history of wrongdoing is also indicative of the inadequacy of the sanctions available in the juvenile court… (p. 495, emphases added, citation omitted).*[14]

****

(A) retributive rationale alone may be overly inclusive and inflict penal harm ***without any offsetting utilitarian gain,*** *because violent offenders desist at about the same rate as do other youths… (Feld, 2000, p. 111, emphasis added).*

****

Retribution limits severe sanctions to the ***most culpable and blameworthy,*** *imposes a degree of proportionality and determinacy on decisions, and* ***restricts eligibility for waiver only to the most serious crimes…*** *(Id., emphases added).*

There are myriad problems with Feld's arguments. First, there is no reason why retribution would have to stand "alone" or even be the primary rationale for a transfer; it might be irrelevant or of secondary importance in any one transfer. It co-exists with other rationales (and situations) in justifying transfer. In addition, retribution is not beholden to achieving any "utilitarian gain" to be legitimate or appropriate; it is decidedly and purposely non-utilitarian. Retribution is the one *non-utilitarian* sentencing rationale; it is purely backwards-looking and is not future-oriented. That means retribution is not swayed by the potential or promise or rates of desistance. Except for achieving/imposing justice, retribution does not look for a payback. Simply following through with the promise of punishment for being proved to have responsibly committed crime satisfies the elements of retribution. If a retributive reaction to the offense also scares this offender or other potential offenders sufficiently to not commit crimes (deterrence), and/or prevents this offender from committing crime while on probation or incarcerated (incapacitation), and/or convinces this offender that crime is wrong (rehabilitation), these outcomes would simply be collateral/bonus utilitarian paybacks.[15] Once the validity and accuracy of the current offense and prior record are determined, and an equal and proportionate (commensurate) retributive-driven sentence is imposed, retribution has been achieved and satisfied. The only relevant future aspect is serving out the sentence.

Second, crimes also do not need to be serious to qualify for either retribution or for punishment beyond JCs capabilities, especially, but not only, with older offenders. Accepting Feld's (and Zimring's) *longer-sentence rationale,* it still takes a quantum leap to also embrace *only the most serious crimes limitation* for transfer eligibility. The most serious crimes might engender demands for retribution and the lengthiest sentences, but even the stolen automobile can evoke cries for retribution. Lengthy probation qualifies as retributive, but it is not a severe sanction. Most important, allowing that a CC sentence must exceed the maximum available JC sentence to qualify for transfer does not mean the CC sentence would have to be particularly severe/lengthy. Older juvenile offenders (95% or more of the targets of transfer are 15 years of age/older) have less than six years of JC sanction available; 17-year-olds have less than four years remaining. Feld has eliminated juvenile offenders "requiring" six or more years of incarceration, hardly a severe sanction, from his (and Zimring's) transfer criteria.

Third, retribution is also not restricted to either severe sanctions or to the "*most* culpable and blameworthy." Retribution is eligible/deserving for any responsible offender; we simply choose (with merit) to ignore this in allowing most juveniles to escape *retributive-oriented* punishment and to enjoy immunity from criminal prosecution by remaining in JC. Nearly all transfer-eligible juveniles satisfy the age/mental capacity variable to be considered responsible. If not, permitting 16-year-olds to be licensed to drive a lethal weapon is beyond irresponsible on society's part; providing 15-year-olds with learner's permits simply takes society's irresponsibility to yet another level. Moreover, chronic offenders merit retribution even when their repeated criminal behavior is not serious/violent. Interesting, Feld saw persistent offenders as not meriting retribution, despite multiple warnings and consequences (which would seem to enhance the appropriateness of retribution), while more violent types are equally not seen by him as deserving of retribution because their crimes do not tend to be chronic (see Id., and below).[16]

Due to offense exclusion's (OE's) strong connection to retribution, Feld (2000) saw OE as problematic to JC's image.

Legislative offense exclusion laws that ***define chronological juveniles as adults*** *on the basis of a serious offense reflect a retributive, just deserts alternative to individualized, rehabilitative juvenile justice jurisprudence (p. 103, emphasis added).*

OE does not define chronological juveniles as adults; it defines certain offenses/records *as criminal rather than as delinquent* (see Chapter 6). Moreover, OE involves both serious offenses *and* chronic offenders. It is puzzling that Feld lamented OE's representing an alleged transition from "individualized, rehabilitative juvenile justice jurisprudence" to retribution since he has long asserted that JCs operate without any serious commitment to rehabilitation (see Chapter 7). Another puzzling feature of Feld's stance is that he evidently gives judicial transfer (JT) a pass when it, too, in Feld's words, "define(s) chronological juveniles as adults."

Contrary to Feld's assertions, OE is as individualized as rehabilitation. Feld's claim presumes prosecutors never consider youth's rehabilitation potential/past. It is not that prosecutors *cannot or will not* consult the JC records; rather, OE means they *do not have to* consult them. OE simply removes the amenability barrier to transfer. The rehabilitation history and potential will lead prosecutors to "undercharge" some juveniles to keep them in JC or, in Feld's words, to commit "subterfuge." How, then, prosecutors can be guilty of purposely engaging in subterfuge and in the undercharging of (at least some) juvenile offenders that qualify for OE while not simultaneously conducting any individualized analysis via OE is puzzling, indeed. Moreover, prosecutors need to know the record as a measure of self-defense. To transfer a juvenile offender lacking a sufficient JJ history can come back to haunt prosecutors via reverse transfer. In addition, knowing prior records/treatments helps prosecutors gain PB leverage, fulfilling a need to know, as completely as possible, offenders' backgrounds and situations.

Prosecutors must carefully scrutinize charges and records to see if juvenile offenders qualify for the excluded offense. Comparing the requirements needed to pursue rehabilitation and retribution demonstrate that while the ends are different (treatment versus punishment), the means are much the same (individualized consideration of the merits). OE is more about *who* should make the transfer choice and *who* is ineligible for immunity from criminal prosecution.

Feld (2000) accused OE of engaging in unethical futuristic criminality predictions:

Moreover, given the likelihood of errors, overprediction, and "false positives," to preventively incarcerate people on the basis of what they might do in the future rather than for what they already have done poses extraordinary ethical and legal problems. Moreover, the best indicator of future criminality, an extensive prior record, provides an imperfect indicator of active criminality because only a small proportion of actual crimes result in arrest and conviction. Finally, young career offenders require time to accumulate an extensive prior record and thereby to distinguish themselves from their desisting contemporaries, a criminological luxury seldom available to judges and prosecutors (p. 106, citation omitted).

Feld's claims are completely baseless. "False positives" are not relevant to OE since it considers *only* past behavior (offense and record) and age. Feld's condemnation is directed at sentencing (incarcerating), not charging/transfer. Sentencing juvenile offenders in CC can, indeed, become unclear and hazardous considering the ambiguity of delinquent careers, as Feld suggested. In that context, his concerns are on point. Associating those concerns with OE, however, is where Feld misleads. There is *simply no such thing* as either an error or a "false positive" present with OE. OE does not involve any prediction, unlike amenability determinations made via JT do. OE is completely backwards-looking (as is all of retribution). Ironically, Feld criticized the spread of OE (a transfer method he originally enthusiastically endorsed) as being rigidly focused on offense and record (which involves, necessarily and exclusively, matters that have already occurred), on the one hand, and then reverts to attacking OE for being future-oriented. Nothing could be farther from the truth. Ironically, many chronic offenders that qualify for OE (and DF) have already racked up "an extensive prior record" and are transferred to CC on that basis. Feld believed that many juvenile offenders commit many crimes for which they are never caught or prosecuted. If nothing else, this "truth" should encourage prosecutors to engage in transfer with more confidence that they are doing the right thing since this current case could easily be only the tip of the crime-oriented iceberg. Feld's moral appears to be:

since you have gotten away with committing many crimes without being caught, once you are caught that is justification for not transferring you.

Finally, it is puzzling Feld was concerned prosecutors are basing their OE transfer decisions on future offending prospects when he has criticized them for focusing exclusively on the crime and record, which is a matter of the past, not the future.

Legislative offense exclusion that focuses primarily on the seriousness of the present offense rather than on chronic offending fosters an over- and underinclusive response to the problems posed by young career criminals. Such a policy punishes severely one youth's serious, albeit isolated act of violence, while nominally sanctioning less severely a chronic offender's current, less serious property crime (Id.)

Apparently, Feld believed OE provisions are too narrow in some states and need to be expanded, particularly to include more chronic offenders. Feld was wrong in trying to inextricably link OE with career offender sentencing. OE involves charging, not punishment. How transfers are sentenced in CC depends upon, among other things, the severity of crimes and prior records and what the statute allows for factoring the prior JC record into CC sentencing. More important, an "isolated" act of violence can be seen as deserving more retribution than a less serious chronic offender. While OE is usually associated with serious/violent crime, it is also linked with chronic offending of less serious crime (see Sanborn & Salerno, 2005). Moreover, some less serious chronic offenders can experience more serious punishment than some "nominal" sanction. Whether that punishment occurs in CC depends largely upon what CC judges and prosecutors believe about juvenile offending, and what legislatures allow in CC sentencing. Regardless, the need for and justification of transfer is not beholden to either those CC officials or that legislative policy choice. Feld's concern about potential punishment gaps and what constitutes less-than-ideal-sentencing of career juvenile offenders (versus those that will desist offending) is a problem separate from transfer that calls for a separate solution, as well (such as factoring the JC record into CC sentencing).

Again, simply put, the ATC chooses to ignore:

The quest of and need for the punishment of chronic and violent offenders do not evaporate simply because the offender is a juvenile.

Transfer Benefits Prosecutors

There are several ways prosecutors benefit from PT. Transfer enhances prosecutors' power to plea bargain (see Bishop, 2000; Dawson, 2000; Redding and Howell, 2000; Krisberg and Austin, 1993); prosecutors have more leverage with a threat to transfer non-cooperative defendants. Also, as Zimring (2010) noted, PT "decreases the workload necessary to produce a waiver outcome… (p. 9)." PT does decrease prosecutors' transfer workload since it dispenses with their having to counteract a potential PO's anti-transfer recommendation, prepare witnesses for a transfer hearing, participate in the transfer hearing, and secure the agreement of a judge. More important than workload considerations, however, PT increases the likelihood of transfer, which, of course, is why the ATC is so adamant about eliminating it.

Transfer also allows the prosecution of all co-defendants in CC, which even the *Kent* criteria acknowledge. In addition, even if prosecutors desire a longer sentence that never materializes in CC, they can draw some satisfaction that the offender's criminal record begins now, instead of waiting for additional crimes to be committed. Sanborn (1993c) noted 30 years ago:

It should be remembered that prosecutors can consider transfer a victory even if the serious offender is treated more leniently in criminal court, because at least the youth's adult liability has begun at that point instead of at some later date, perhaps after additional serious crimes have been committed (p. 120).

REFERENCES

Applegate, B. K., Davis, R. K., & Cullen, F. T. (2009). Reconsidering child saving: The extent and correlates of public support for excluding youths from the juvenile court. *Crime and Delinquency*, *55*(1), 51–77. doi:10.1177/0011128707308104

Barnes, C., & Franz, R. (1989). Questionably adult: Determinants and effects of the juvenile waiver decision. *Justice Quarterly*, *6*(1), 117–135. doi:10.1080/07418828900090071

Benedek, E. P., & Cornell, D. G. (Eds.). (1989). *Juvenile homicide*. American Psychiatric Press.

Bishop, D. M. (2000). Juvenile offenders in the adult criminal justice system. In M. Tonry (Ed.), *Crime & Justice: A Review of Research, 27, 81-167.* IL University of Chicago Press. doi:10.1086/652199

Bishop, D. M., & Frazier, C. E. (1991). Transfer of juveniles to criminal court: A case study and analysis of prosecutorial waiver. *Notre Dame Journal of Law, Ethics & Public Policy*, *5*, 281–302.

Bishop, D. M., Frazier, C. E., & Henretta, J. C. (1989). Prosecutorial waiver: A case study of questionable reform. *Crime and Delinquency*, *35*(2), 179–201. doi:10.1177/0011128789035002001

Bortner, M. A. (1986). Traditional rhetoric, organizational realities: Remand of juveniles to adult court. *Crime and Delinquency*, *32*(1), 53–73. doi:10.1177/0011128786032001004

Bove, C. M. (1991). The child-adult: Michigan waiver law. *Detroit College of Law Review*, *1991*, 1071–1096.

Brink, D. O. (2003-2004). Immaturity, normative competence, and juvenile transfer: How (not) to punish minors for major crimes. *Texas Law Review*, *82*, 1555–1585.

Champion, D. J. (1989). Teenage felons and waiver hearings: Some recent trends, 1980-1988. *Crime and Delinquency*, *35*(4), 577–585. doi:10.1177/0011128789035004005

Champion, D. J., & Mays, G. L. (1991). *Transferring juveniles to criminal courts: Trends and implications for criminal justice*. Praeger Publishers.

Dawson, R. O. (1992). An empirical study of *Kent* style juvenile transfers to criminal court. *St. Mary's Law Journal*, *23*, 975–1054.

Dawson, R. O. (1992). An empirical study of *Kent* style juvenile transfers to criminal court. *St. Mary's Law Journal*, *23*, 975–1054.

Dawson, R. O. (2000). Judicial waiver in theory and practice. In J. Fagan & F. E. Zimring (Eds.), *The changing borders of juvenile justice: Transfer of adolescents to the criminal court* (pp. 45–81). University of Chicago Press.

Eigen, J. P. (1981a). The determinants and impact of jurisdictional transfer in Philadelphia. In J. C. Hall, D. M. Hamparian, J. M. Pettibone, & J. White (Eds.), *Major Issues in Juvenile Justice Information and Training: Readings in Public Policy* (pp. 333–350). Academy for Contemporary Problems.

Eigen, J. P. (1981b). Punishing youth homicide offenders in Philadelphia. *The Journal of Criminal Law & Criminology*, *72*(3), 1072–1093. doi:10.2307/1143276

Ex parte Mei. (1937). 122 N.J. Eq. 125, 192 Atl. 81. N.J. Court of Errors and Appeals.

Fagan, J., & Deschenes, E. P. (1990). Determinants of juvenile waiver decisions for violent juvenile offenders. *The Journal of Criminal Law & Criminology*, *81*(2), 314–347. doi:10.2307/1143909

Feld, B. C. (1978). Reference of juvenile offenders for adult prosecution: The legislative alternative to asking unanswerable questions. *Minnesota Law Review*, *62*, 515–618.

Feld, B. C. (1984a). Criminalizing juvenile justice: Rules of procedure for the juvenile court. *Minnesota Law Review*, *69*, 141–276.

Feld, B. C. (1984b). The decision to seek criminal charges: Just deserts and the waiver decision. *Criminal Justice Ethics*, *3*(2), 27–41. doi:10.1080/0731129X.1984.9991756

Feld, B. C. (1987). The juvenile court meets the principle of the offense: Legislative changes in juvenile waiver statutes. *The Journal of Criminal Law & Criminology*, *78*(3), 471–533. doi:10.2307/1143567

Feld, B. C. (1989). Bad law makes hard cases: Reflections on teen-aged axe-murderers, judicial activism, and legislative default. *Minnesota Journal of Law & Inequality*, *8*, 1–101.

Feld, B. C. (2000). Legislative exclusion of offenses from juvenile court jurisdiction: A history and critique. In J. Fagan & F. E. Zimring (Eds.), *The changing borders of juvenile justice: Transfer of adolescents to the criminal court* (pp. 83–144). University of Chicago Press.

Fisher, W. S., & Teichman, L. (1986). Juvenile waivers to adult court: A report to the New Jersey state legislature. *Criminal Justice Quarterly*, *9*, 68–103.

Forst, M., & Blomquist, M. E. (1991). Cracking down on juveniles: The changing ideology of youth corrections. *Notre Dame Journal of Law, Ethics & Public Policy*, *5*, 323–375.

Gasper, J., & Katkin, D. (1980). A rationale for the abolition of the juvenile court's power to waive jurisdiction. *Pepperdine Law Review*, *7*, 937–951.

Gillespie, L. K., & Norman, M. D. (1984). Does certification mean prison: Some preliminary findings from Utah. *Juvenile & Family Court Journal, 35*(3), 23–34. doi:10.1111/j.1755-6988.1984.tb00541.x

Glassner, B., Ksander, M., Berg, B., & Johnson, B. D. (1983). A note on the deterrent effect of juvenile vs. adult jurisdiction. *Social Problems, 31*(2), 219–221. doi:10.2307/800213

Graham v. Florida. (2010). 560 U.S 48, 2010.

Greenwood, P. W., Abrahamse, A., & Zimring, F. E. (1984). *Factors Affecting Sentencing Severity for Young Offenders*. National Institute of Justice.

Grisso, T. (2000). What we know about youths' capacities as trial defendants. In T. Grisso & R. G. Schwartz (Eds.), *Youth on Trial: A Developmental Perspective on Juvenile Justice* (pp. 139–171). University of Chicago Press.

Grundfest, A. R., Paskow, A. C., Szabo, H. E., & Williams, R. J. (1981). Trial of juveniles in adult court: The prosecutor's perspective. In Hall, J.C., Hamparian, D.M., Pettibone. J.M., & White, J.L. (Eds.), Major issues in juvenile justice information and training: Readings in public policy (pp. 321-332). Academy for Contemporary Problems.

Houghtalin, M., & Mays, G. L. (1991). Criminal dispositions of New Mexico juveniles transferred to adult court. *Crime and Delinquency, 37*(3), 393–407. doi:10.1177/0011128791037003006

In re Gault. (1967). 387 U.S. 1.

Kozich, S. D. (1980). A model for the transfer of juvenile felony offenders to adult court jurisdiction. *Journal of Juvenile Law, 4*, 170–186.

Krisberg, B., & Austin, J. (1993). *Reinventing juvenile justice*. Sage Publications. doi:10.4135/9781483326450

Loughran, T. A., Mulvey, E. P., Schubert, C. A., Chassin, L. A., Steinberg, L., Piquero, A. R., Cota-Robles, S., & Cauffman, E. (2010). Differential effects of adult court transfer on juvenile offender recidivism. *Law and Human Behavior, 24*(6), 476–488. doi:10.100710979-009-9210-z PMID:20195895

Loughran, T. A., Reid, J. A., Collins, M. E., & Mulvey, E. P. (2016). Effect of gun carrying on perceptions of risk among adolescent offenders. *American Journal of Public Health, 106*(2), 350–352. doi:10.2105/AJPH.2015.302971 PMID:26691293

Mays, G. L., & Houghtalin, M. (1992). Trying juveniles as adults: A note on New Mexico's recent experience. *Justice System Journal, 15*(3), 814–823. doi:10.1080/23277556.1993.10871163

McCarthy, F. B. (1994). The serious offender and juvenile court reform: The case for prosecutorial waiver of juvenile court jurisdiction. *Saint Louis University Law Journal, 38*, 629–671.

Miller v. Alabama. (2012). 132 S Ct. 2455.

Myers, D. L. (2001). *Excluding violent youths from juvenile court: The effectiveness of legislative waiver*. LFB Scholarly Publications.

Myers, D. L., & Kiehl, K. (2001). The predispositional status of violent youthful offenders: Is there a "custody gap" in adult criminal court? *Justice Research and Policy*, *3*(1), 115–143. doi:10.3818/JRP.3.1.2001.115

PCC. (1967). *President's Crime Commission on Law Enforcement and Administration of Justice. The Challenge of Crime in a Free Society*. U.S. Government Printing Office.

Podkopacz, M. R., & Feld, B. C. (1995). Judicial waiver policy and practice: Persistence, seriousness, and race. *Minnesota Journal of Law & Inequality*, *14*, 73–178.

Podkopacz, M. R., & Feld, B. C. (1996). The end of the line: An empirical study of judicial waiver. *The Journal of Criminal Law & Criminology*, *86*(2), 449–492. doi:10.2307/1144033

Polen, C. A. P. (1986). Youth on death row: Waiver of juvenile court jurisdiction and imposition of the death penalty on juvenile offenders. *Northern Kentucky Law Review*, *13*, 495–517.

Redding, R. E. (2003). The effects of adjudicating and sentencing juveniles as adults: Research and policy implications. *Youth Violence and Juvenile Justice*, *1*(2), 128–155. doi:10.1177/1541204002250875

Redding, R. E. (2016). One size does not fit all: The deterrent effect of transferring juveniles to criminal court. *Criminology & Public Policy*, *15*(3), 939–948. doi:10.1111/1745-9133.12239

Redding, R. E., & Howell, J. C. (2000). Blended sentencing in American juvenile courts. In J. Fagan & F. E. Zimring (Eds.), *The changing borders of juvenile justice: Transfer of adolescents to the criminal court* (pp. 145–180). University of Chicago Press.

Roper v. Simmons. (2005). 543 U.S. 551.

Rudman, C., Hartstone, E. C., Fagan, J., & Moore, M. (1986). Violent youth in adult court: Process and punishment. *Crime and Delinquency*, *32*(1), 75–96. doi:10.1177/0011128786032001005

Sagatun, I., McCollum, L. L., & Edwards, L. P. (1985). The effects of transfers from juvenile to criminal courts: A loglinear analysis. *Crime and Justice*, *8*(1), 65–92. doi:10.1080/0735648X.1985.9721310

Sanborn, J. B., Jr. (1985). *Plea negotiation in juvenile court*. [Unpublished doctoral dissertation, SUNY Albany, Albany, NY., United States].

Sanborn, J. B. Jr. (1993c). Review of the book, *Transferring juveniles to criminal courts: Trend and implications for criminal justice*, by Champion, D.J., & Mays, D.G. Praeger Publishers, 1991. *Criminal Justice Review*, *18*, 118–120. doi:10.1177/073401689301800128

Sanborn, J. B. Jr. (1994a). Certification to criminal court: The important policy questions of how, when, and why. *Crime and Delinquency*, *40*(2), 262–281. doi:10.1177/0011128794040002007

Sanborn, J. B. Jr. (1994d). The juvenile, the court, or the community: Whose best interests are currently being promoted in juvenile court? *Justice System Journal*, *17*(2), 249–266. doi:10.1080/23277556.1994.10871207

Sanborn, J. B. Jr. (1996b). Policies regarding the prosecution of juvenile murderers: Which system and who should decide? *Law & Policy*, *18*(1-2), 151–178. doi:10.1111/j.1467-9930.1996.tb00168.x

Sanborn, J. B. Jr. (1998). Second-class justice and first-class punishment: The use of juvenile records in sentencing adults. *Judicature*, *81*, 206–213.

Sanborn, J. B. Jr. (2000). Striking out on the first pitch in criminal court. *Barry Law Review*, *1*, 7–61.

Sanborn, J. B. Jr. (2001b). Victims' rights in juvenile court: Has the pendulum swung too far? *Judicature*, *85*, 140–146.

Sanborn, J. B. Jr. (2003). Hard choices or obvious ones: Developing policy for excluding youth from juvenile court. *Youth Violence and Juvenile Justice*, *1*(2), 198–214. doi:10.1177/1541204002250879

Schall v. Martin. (1984). 467 U.S. 253.

Scialabba, N. (2016). Should juveniles be charged as adults in the criminal justice system? *American Bar Association. 3*.

Sellers, B. G., & Arrigo, B. A. (2009). Adolescent transfer, developmental maturity and adjudicative competence: An ethical and justice policy inquiry. *Criminology*, *29*, 435–488.

Springer, C. E. (1991). Rehabilitating the juvenile court. *Notre Dame Journal of Ethics & Public Policy*, *5*, 397–420.

Stamm, M. J. (1973). Transfer of jurisdiction in juvenile court: An A\analysis of the proceeding, its role in the administration of justice, and A proposal for the reform of Kentucky law. *Kentucky Law Journal (Lexington, Ky.)*, *62*, 122–199.

Tanenhaus, D. S. (2000). The evolution of transfer out of the juvenile court. In J. Fagan & F. E. Zimring (Eds.), *The changing borders of juvenile justice: Transfer of adolescents to the criminal court* (pp. 13–43). University of Chicago Press.

Thomas, C. W., & Bilchik, S. (1985). Prosecuting juveniles in criminal court: A legal and empirical analysis. *The Journal of Criminal Law & Criminology*, *76*(2), 439–479. doi:10.2307/1143613

Welch, K., Butler, L. F., & Gertz, M. (2019). Saving children, damning adults? An examination of public support for juvenile rehabilitation and adult punishment. *Criminal Justice Review*, *44*(4), 470–491. doi:10.1177/0734016819833141

Wizner, S. (1984). Discretionary waiver of juvenile court jurisdiction: An invitation to procedural arbitrariness. *Criminal Justice Ethics*, *3*(2), 41–50. doi:10.1080/0731129X.1984.9991757

Wizner, S. (1995). On youth crime and the juvenile court. *Boston College Law Review. Boston College. Law School*, *36*, 1025–1035.

Zane, S. N., Welsh, B. C., & Mears, D. P. (2016). Juvenile transfer and the specific deterrence hypothesis: Systematic review and meta-analysis. *Criminology & Public Policy*, *15*(3), 901–925. doi:10.1111/1745-9133.12222

Zimring, F. E. (1981). Notes on the jurisprudence of waiver. In J. C. Hall, D. M. Hamparian, J. M. Pettibone, & J. L. White (Eds.), *Major issues in juvenile justice information and training: Readings in public policy* (pp. 193–205). Academy for Contemporary Problems.

Zimring, F. E. (1991). The treatment of hard cases in American juvenile justice: In defense of discretionary waiver. *Notre Dame Journal of Law, Ethics & Public Policy*, *5*, 267–280.

Zimring, F. E. (1998a). *American youth violence*. Oxford University Press.

Zimring, F. E. (1998b). Toward a jurisprudence of youth violence. *Crime and Justice*, *24*, 477–501. doi:10.1086/449285

Zimring, F. E. (2000a). Penal proportionality for the young offender: Notes on immaturity, capacity, and diminished responsibility. In T. Grisso & R. G. Schwartz (Eds.), *Youth on Trial: A Developmental Perspective on Juvenile Justice* (pp. 271–289). University of Chicago Press.

Zimring, F. E. (2000b). The punitive necessity of waiver. In J. Fagan & F. E. Zimring (Eds.), *The Changing Borders of Juvenile Justice: Transfer of adolescents to the criminal court* (pp. 207–224). University of Chicago Press.

Zimring, F. E. (2010). The power politics of juvenile court transfer: A mildly revisionist history of the 1990s. *Louisiana Law Review*, *71*, 1–15.

ENDNOTES

1 Only a minority of JC workers identified protecting society as a primary reason for transfer in one research study (Sanborn, 1994a, p. 271).

2 Asking for more transfer power to preserve JC and to increase treatment effectiveness for retained juveniles would likely have been met with skepticism, if not derision. As JC aged, especially in the 1960s and after, the rise in serious/violent crimes committed by older offenders brought more pressure to expand those eligible for transfer. Joining the rise in violent, serious and chronic juvenile crime was the "rehabilitation doesn't work" hysteria. Prosecutors, frustrated at being unable to transfer themselves, and encountering judges who would not transfer, lobbied state legislatures to grant them the power to transfer. This lobbying met with significant success after the mid-1980s to mid-1990s increase in juvenile violence. Justifications for transfer kept pace with expansions in violent crime by juveniles. Nothing complex or nefarious here. It was reasonable to give prosecutors direct transfer control over the most chronic, older, serious and violent juveniles, especially given the uncertainty of rehabilitation measures.

3 Gerry Gault's two-month maximum jail sentence in the CJ system pales compared to the potential five-year incarceration he faced in the JJ system (*In re Gault*, 1967). Otherwise, (b)*acklog in criminal court and the presence of more obstacles to conviction than in juvenile court (jury trial, for example) could easily force the criminal court to be lenient with, to plea bargain with, and perhaps even to ignore large numbers of juveniles to be transferred there for prosecution. Thus, even youths who are targeted for heavy punishment by juvenile court officials and who are transferred for that reason alone may not experience severe punishment in the adult system...* (Sanborn, 1993c, p. 119).

4 See Bortner, 1986; Champion, 1989; Champion & Mays, 1991; Feld, 1984, 1987; Gasper & Katkin, 1980; Gillespi & Norman, 1984; Sagatun, McCollum & Edwards, 1985.

5 CCs fail to convict/punish many adult offenders but does not mean police should not arrest adult criminals or that these offenders should not be prosecuted. The ATC wrongly insists "the legitimacy of juvenile court (transfer) policy is subject to the idiosyncrasies of criminal court processing.... (Sanborn, 1993c, p. 119)."

6 See Barnes & Franz, 1989; Dawson, 1992; Fisher & Teichman, 1986; Greenwood, Abrahamse & Zimring, 1984; Houghtalin & Mays, 1991; Mays & Houghtalin, 1992; Podkopacz & Feld, 1995, 1996; Thomas & Bilchik, 1985.

7 See Bishop & Frazier, 1991; Bortner, 1986; Bove, 1991; Fagan & Deschenes, 1990; Feld, 1978, 1984b, 1987, 1989; Forst & Blomquist, 1991; Gasper & Katkin, 1980; Gillespi & Norman, 1984; Kozich, 1980; Stamm, 1973; Wizner, 1984.

8 Andrew Goldin was only 11 years old when he pulled a fire alarm to flush out the students and teachers at his middle school in Jonesboro, AR, in 1998, and proceeded to murder four students and a teacher. His young age prevented transfer (Arkansas minimum transfer age at that time was 14). He was institutionalized by the JC until the age of 21, whereupon he was released to society with a clean record.

9 Transfer's joining all defendants in a CC prosecution does not satisfy any sentencing objective, per se. That and other examples demonstrate the speciousness of the ATC claim.

10 Zimring simply believed that only (some) murder charges fit this description.

11 See Bishop, 2000; Bishop, Frazier & Henretta, 1989; Bortner, 1986; Bove, 1991; Gasper & Katkin, 1980; Glassner, Ksander, Berg & Johnson, 1983; Grundfest, Paskow, Szabo, & Williams, 1981; Loughran et al., 2010; Polen, 1986; Redding, 2003, 2016.

12 Sciaballa (2016) insisted that transfer was implemented solely for the purpose of deterrence, which has failed.

13 While conducting my dissertation data collection (1979-1981) in Philadelphia's JC, I heard several defendants say they committed an offense hoping to be committed to Glen Mills, until recently, considered the premier juvenile facility in the country, having an exemplary program, with buildings and lodgings that rivaled any private prep school. The sports program won state championships in numerous sports against competitive public and private schools. The school offered trips to professional sporting events and Disney World; one graduate became the captain of the West Virginia University football team. Youthful offenders who have experienced commitments to this facility and many others have not learned deterrence. One could argue they have been rewarded for committing crimes. It is against this background that many serious offenders recidivate. They can hardly be blamed for their not learning a lesson in deterrence.

14 Feld (1987) limited justifications for transfer to two sentencing rationales: retribution and incapacitation. Why neither deterrence nor rehabilitation can be furthered by transfer was not addressed by Feld. This is puzzling since Feld said transfer does deter due to an "increased general prevention through greater certainty and visibility of consequences… (p. 49)."

15 Retribution's lack of utilitarian goals is likely why Feld tried to reformulate it.

16 Seemingly, one-murder-only is insufficient to qualify for retribution.

17 All of these courtroom interactions and agreements must happen for JT to result.

Section 5
Policy Development

A popular R&B song from the early 1970s, written by Philly's Gamble and Huff, *"Now That We Found Love What Are We Gonna Do With It?"* was recorded by Philly-based *The O'Jays* on their *Ship Ahoy* album (reprised by both *Third World* and *Heavy D & the Boyz*). So, with the viability and the desirability of CC transfer established, what are we gonna do with it?

REEXAMINING JUVENILE COURT (JC) AND PUTTING TRANSFER TO CRIMINAL COURT (CC) IN CONTEXT

Initially, it is time to recognize that the conceptualization of juvenile vis-à-vis adult that was prominent until the mid-20th century has evolved, much like the JC. Today's is a different world than that existing while the founders created JC. Harkening back to the original JC cannot contribute to the transfer debate. It is time to put the image of JC's original purpose to rest.

That JCs and juvenile offenders are different from the original days does not mean either must be or should be abandoned. That JCs have become more punitive in reaction to offenders' becoming more violent and chronic does not mean JC should be considered as a failure or as devoid of rehabilitative efforts. Accepting that *most* juveniles *can and will be helped* does not require an assumption that *all* offenders *will be or should be helped*. Some chronic, serious and violent juvenile offenders are beyond the capacity of JC, which is where transfer to CC comes in.

Although JCs will not address all offenders, the JC experiment should not be abandoned. JC can still be regarded as a valuable diversionary destination even when 100% of juveniles will not benefit from diversion. Simply because not every juvenile offender merits immunity from criminal prosecution does not mean the 90-95% that do should be denied this legacy of leniency.

We do not have to insist upon the demise of JC due to a due process deficiency (Federle, 1990; Feld, 1990) or due to a rethinking of the nature of juvenility (Ainsworth, 1991).[1] Despite the changing nature of juveniles and their crimes together with some JC shortcomings, JC still has (and deserves) public support and belief in the efficacy of rehabilitation.[2] At the same time, it needs to be recognized that there is also public support for transfer to criminal court, especially for violent and chronic offenders.[3] While the public wants rehabilitation, it also wants public safety, punishment, and accountability (Bolin, Applegate, & Oullette, 2019; Mears, Pickett, & Mancini, 2015; Miller & Applegate, 2015; Myers, 2016; Welch et al., 2019), which is where transfer comes in.

Chapter 16
Developing Transfer Policy and Integrating JCs and CCs

ABSTRACT

Chapter 16 begins by very briefly revisiting the misinformation that dominates the transfer literature (see Chapters 6-11), and by briefly reaffirming the dimensions of transfer identified in Chapter 3. The Chapter then explains the three tasks associated with developing transfer policy: 1) choosing an option, such as no transfer, no transfer, but serious modifications to JC, selective transfer, or total transfer (abolition of JC); 2) selecting a transfer method, such prosecutorial transfer (PT) and/or judicial transfer (JT) (assuming transfer is the option chosen); and, 3) discussing implications associated with the available policies. The Chapter concludes by attempting to accomplish reconciliations in three contexts: whether there is a lack of fit between transfer and CC/CJ System outcomes; whether transfer should be backwards-looking (based on current offense and/or delinquent/treatment record) or forward-looking (based on future behavior forecasts, such as future dangerousness or desistance from crime); and, whether reverse transfer from CC should be available.

Three tasks surround the creation of transfer policy. The ***first task*** is to select the proper policy among the four available: 1) no transfer to CC or total retention of all juvenile offenders; 2) no transfer, but serious modifications to JC; 3) selective transfer to CC, via JT and/or PT, with or without modifications; and, 4) total or complete transfer to CC (or total exclusion), meaning the abolition of JC. The fourth option will be mostly ignored here since it would end JC.

Some from the anti-transfer crowd (ATC) suggest that JC abolition and/or reducing the maximum JC age, a partial abolition, is less radical than transfer. These critics suggest that it would be more "honest" to reduce the JC's maximum age or to abolish JC completely than to selectively transfer.

(T)he abolitionist reform preserves the traditionalist's insistence that, all else being equal, juveniles are less culpable for the harm they cause than their adult counterparts, and so are deserving of less punishment; whereas, the transfer trend rejects this commitment to differential desert and punishment. From this perspective, the transfer's trends reforms are much more radical than the abolitionist reforms. Because

DOI: 10.4018/978-1-7998-7923-7.ch016

the abolitionist reforms do not threaten differential desert and punishment, they are less threatening to the traditional rationale for a separate juvenile court... (Brink, 2003-2004, p. 1580).

Abolition of JC does not guarantee a youth discount sentence, however; Brink admits that two pages later (Id., p. 1582). Discounts across-the-board have not happened to date, and arguably present problems of their own (see Zimring, 1998a). Transfer does not rely upon any particular CC sentencing model. Transfer only sometimes means a longer CC sentence, which often is not the goal of transfer.

The ***second task*** arises if the second or third policy choices are adopted and that task is to select the proper method(s) for transferring juvenile offenders to CC: judicial transfer (JT) and/or prosecutorial transfer (PT).

Finally, the ***third task*** involves discussing the implications of the four policy choices.

Task # 1: Selecting the Proper Transfer to CC Policy

Accounting for the Misinformation

Before adopting policy, it is important to reiterate that mandatory exclusion (ME) measures exist independently of transfer provisions and considerations. Whether the maximum JC jurisdictional age should be 15, 16, or 17 requires a separate conversation. Whether prior transfers to and/or convictions in CC should permanently disqualify a juvenile defendant from JC prosecution also requires a separate conversation. Suffice it to say, a maximum JC age of 17 makes sense, especially (but perhaps only) if transfer to CC remains an option. Not allowing juvenile offenders to return to JC from CC, especially (but perhaps only) when there has been a CC conviction, also makes sense.

It is also beneficial to briefly revisit the take-aways from Section II. First, *all* transfer (both JT and PT) is *discretionary*. Adjectives such as *nondiscretionary*, *mandatory,* and *automatic* should be banned from *all* conversations regarding transfer. There are *only two* forms of transfer, JT and PT, each of which has two versions. JT is either *regular* (amenability burden on state) or *presumptive* (amenability burden on defendant). While a JT hearing may be called mandatory, it really is not because it depends completely on a prosecutor's charging the qualifying offense. No such charge means no such hearing. Moreover, judges cannot be forced to transfer anyone.

PT is either concurrent jurisdiction (or direct file — DF) or offense exclusion (OE), which is not mandatory, etc. In DF, the prosecutor can charge qualifying offenses in *either* JC *or* CC. It is no more or less discretionary than OE. OE means that a prosecutor's charging the excluded offense requires that offense be prosecuted in CC. The prosecutor *can never be forced* to charge an excluded offense so there is nothing mandatory about the decision. The prosecution *must occur* in CC, but *only if* the excluded offense is charged. OE is not a third version of transfer and should never be referred to as legislative or statutory since *all* transfer is legislatively authorized and all transfer provisions are in a statute (are statutorily based). Employing these terms adds to the confusion in the literature. While the legislature is the source transfer power, it cannot exercise the power itself; it can only delegate that authority to judges and prosecutors. It should be called OE because it is the offense that is excluded from JC jurisdiction.

Hyperbole must be removed from the discussion. The debate is not furthered when the ATC portrays transfer candidates as *children* who have done virtually *nothing wrong*, and that transfer amounts to an "attack upon unsuspecting, mere mistake-prone youth (Sanborn, 2003, p. 211)." Adolescent offending is portrayed as simply committing mistakes during a period in which juveniles are simply learning rules.

At the heart of this process is a notion of adolescence as a period of learning by doing, when competence in decision making can be achieved only by making decisions and ***making mistakes****. For this reason, adolescence is a period that is mistake-prone by design. The special challenge here is to create safeguards in the environment of adolescents that reduce the permanent* ***costs of mistakes****. Two goals of legal policy are to facilitate learning by doing and to reduce the hazards associated with* ***expectable errors****. One important hallmark of adolescence is* ***survival to adulthood,*** *preferably with one's life chances intact (Zimring, 1998a, pp. 81-82, emphases added).*

According to this thinking, rape can be cast as learning interpersonal relations, and murder as discovering the limits of human survival. We are left to wonder what makes an action a mistake: committing an offense or getting caught? Also of wonder is what constitutes a mistake? Is a brutal rape (or series of such) or wanton murder a mistake only? Considering that juveniles are the most likely victims of juvenile violence, one also must wonder whether a *victim's survival to adulthood* gets equal play as *offenders* in Zimring's formula. Most important, while aging, the relevant *learning tasks* are *not stealing* from or *not assaulting* others, unambiguous conduct for which learning begins (or should have begun) years ago, either at home, in school, or, failing that, via previous arrests for crimes. The learning and mistakes do not involve something new and novel, such as taking apart and reassembling a car engine or effecting air conditioning repairs. Mistakes during the latter learning episodes are understandable and necessary to permit growth in expertise. Learning not to rip off or injure others should be old hat by adolescence, although a history in JC processing could muddle that learning. What may be new to some adolescents, depending on the state's reaction to previous misconduct, is that the state demands respect for the property and physical integrity of others, and will not tolerate youths' doing whatever pleases them. What also is likely a learning experience for some adolescents is how to deal with the anger of either not being able to commit crimes to get what they want or getting caught committing the crime.[4]

Zimring's (1998a) take on juvenile misconduct led him to ponder that "major interventions may not be necessary to reorient offenders. The central notion of what has been called adolescent-limited offending is that the cure for youth crime is growing up (p. 82, citation omitted)." Zimring (1998a) did not apply his formula to murder, however. Sure, the 90% to 95% of juvenile offenders who do not commit chronic or violent crimes are allowed to grow up in JC. The problem is often we do not know which of the other 5-10% society can afford to let "grow up" until it is too late to do any good.[5] Zimring (1998a) posited, "there is the worry that drastic countermeasures, those that inhibit the natural transition to adulthood, may cause more harm than they are worth… (p. 82)." There is great reliance here that desistance will come naturally and soon. Ignored are the effects the presence of transfer historically has had on desistance (and what removing the threat of transfer will produce), the victims that occur in the interim, and the fact that for some "the natural transition to adulthood" involves committing many more crimes (and not stopping until they are physically prevented).

Zimring's characterization does a disservice to the stakes involved. The vast majority of transfers are at least 15 years old (and nearly none younger than 13), and the *offenses are* typically chronic/serious/violent and *offenders are* typically chronic, barring significant violence. In OE, the crimes, records, and ages typically required before prosecutors are authorized to transfer prevent their being able to reach far down the juvenile offender age/behavior spectrum. Transfer does not involve trying a child as an adult. Transfer means the youth is prosecuted as a criminal instead of as a delinquent; immunity from criminal prosecution is denied due to serious/violent/chronic behavior.

The ATC claim that transfer to CC does not contribute to a reduction in crime has already been addressed in Chapter 12. Good crime reduction rates have been found in recent propensity score research. Also, research has found high recidivism rates in both JCs and CCs (Bishop et al., 1996; Fagan, 1991; Winner et al., 1997); neither system does a good job in deterring juveniles. The CC/CJ system likely shoots itself in the foot when it imposes lenient sentences or allows early releases (see Fritsch et al., 1996a, 1996b; Redding, 2008), especially after a JC history of leniency.

Prosecutors and other pro-transfer types make a strategic mistake when they defend transfer by placing total reliance upon its protecting society better than prosecution in JC. This is foolish and sometimes very incorrect. The better prospect for an acquittal in CC, the possibility of judicial or jury nullification or a sweet plea bargain or a judge enamored of lenient sentences are just some of the reasons CC conviction could end up less onerous than a JC adjudication (see Sanborn, 1994b, 2001a). Research has found that substantially lengthy sentences of incarceration helped decrease the recidivism rate among transfers (Sanborn, 2003, p. 208, citing Myers, 2001).

Option #1: Total Inclusion/Zero Transfer to CC

ATC extremists demand no transfer or total inclusion of juvenile offenders within JC, particularly if they are amenable to JC treatment (see Arya, 2010; Baruwa, 2013; Beatty, 1995; Cohen et al., 2015; Edwards, 1977; Flesch, 2004; Gasper & Katkin, 1980; Giardino, 1996; Hess, Furr, Armstrong, Francis, & White, 2010; Liwanga & Ibe, 2021; Marrus, & Rosenberg, 2005; Martin, 1992; Pagnanelli, 2007; Pollitt, 2004; Sargent & Gordon, 1963; Sarri & Shook, 2005; Slobogin, 2013; Smith, 1995; Smith, 2013; Stamm, 1973; Wizner, 1995). They emphasize: transfer's limited purpose and "poor" results experienced in CC. All the possible negatives attending CC prosecution and punishment are also trumpeted. These extremists do not tend to concede that any other serious alteration of JC policy or practice is either necessary or desirable.

The ATC criticizes the lack of separate housing units/special programs for juveniles in adult facilities (Angell, 2004; Austin, Johnson, & Gregoriou, 2000; Bishop, 2000; Redding, 2003; Reddington & Sapp, 1997), higher rates of misconduct, assaults, and suicide among youths in the CJ system (see Austin et al., 2000; Beck & Harrison, 2008; Bishop, 2000; Goetting & Howsen, 1986; Myers, L.B. & Levy, 1978; Memory, 1989), all of which lead to managerial problems (Bishop, 2000, p. 123). CC conviction causes civil disabilities in employment opportunities and disruptions in "personal development identity formation, relationships, learning, growth in skills and competencies, and positive movement into adult status (Mulvey & Schubert. 2012, p. 1; see, also, Scott & Steinberg, 2008)." Also possible are "modeling and learning of criminal behaviors from adult inmates; stigmatization; humiliation; loss of self-respect; attenuation of guilt or shame; hardening of the delinquent self-concept; weakening of ties to family, prosocial peers, and community; and diminishment of jobs and educational prospects (Redding, 2003, p. 136)." Myers (2005) added resentment, feelings of injustice and decreased rehabilitation chances.

The ATC's concerns are noteworthy, and suggest caution in transferring youths and warnings to the CJ system to adequately prepare for a unique/different population. But they also reflect a bias. Chronic and violent juvenile transfers are juxtaposed against adult offenders, not other juveniles. While some transfers may be victim-prone in adult settings (and must be prevented), there is also a likelihood that they could victimize adults. The potential for violence in prison flows in more than one direction. If retained, these should-be transfers could wreak havoc and destruction in juvenile facilities (Redding, 2003, p. 139), harming more salvageable youths, and not just physically. The ATC ignores the latter potential in their no/limited-transfer formula.[6]

Even though chronic offenders tend to dominate transfer, the ATC never considers the numerous possible traits that could be found among transfers *preceding* transfer to CC, such as: a defined criminal self-concept; criminal behavior modeling; broken family ties (if one exists); no pro-social peers and community; and, not going to school or working. What is found among many transfers may have nothing to do with being prosecuted in CC. Not surprising, some transfers are angry at their handling in CC and the CJ system. This could be especially prevalent among offenders with a JC/JJ history. That prosecution in CC no longer means "it is all about you" could be infuriating to these transfers.

ATC complaints that transferred offenders are incompetent to stand trial (IST) or not culpable have been dealt with earlier. Since the overwhelming majority of transfers are 15 years of age or older, both competent to stand trial (CST) standards and the concept of responsibility must be stretched beyond reason/recognition to serve as categorical barriers to transfer. It also bears repeating that anyone truly concerned about CST should welcome CC prosecution since that is where CST will be given a broader and more honest interpretation/application (see Sanborn, 2003, p. 206; Sanborn, 2009a). Similar arguments about lack of impulse control, risk aversion and understanding long-term consequences, and the influence of peer pressure, if valid and applicable, would explain why an individual juvenile cannot/should not be transferred. None of these acts as a categorical prohibition against the transfer of groups of juvenile offenders; like CST, these are individual and not collective or group measures.[7]

As important, many of these supposedly debilitating traits can be found among adult offenders, too, which speaks more to their being characteristics of some criminals than it does to some immutable qualities of juveniles since most juveniles are never on transfer's radar. "These characteristics are certainly not necessary to or universal in adolescence (Sanborn, 2003, p. 206)."

A disturbing anti-transfer claim is that prosecution in CC could be too costly.

Criminal prosecutions demand more resources than juvenile ones. They require more hearings, involve more attorney preparation, call on more investigative resources, are more likely to result in jury trials, and take at least twice as long to process as comparable cases in juvenile court.... (Bishop, 2000, p. 123).

That the greater cost of affording constitutional rights to accused offenders in CC compared to JC should constitute an obstacle to transfer speaks volumes about both JC and the ATC.

Option #2: No Transfer but JC Modifications Required

Some ATC members have suggested replacing transfer with a more serious embracing of restorative justice and a balanced approach (or graduated sanctions) to juvenile delinquency (Coupet, 2000; Danziger, 2003; Redding, 2016; Pagnanelli, 2007: Sellers & Arrigo, 2009; Smith, 2013). JCs have adopted these policies, but they have never been the exclusive policy of any JC because they need to be balanced with "victim restoration and community protection," as identified in the Pennsylvania JC Act. JCs are to be congratulated for adopting these measures and attempting to reconcile offenders and victims. But while this approach may work for first offenders (McGarrell & Hipple, 2007), there is little chance such measures would be plausible for chronic and violent juveniles. For these crimes it is not only about the offender and the victim and their attempt to reconcile the injury inflicted on the victim. Society's interests also require consideration and input, here. The same applies to pleas for diversion/prevention (see Angell, 2004; Scott, 2013), greater use of community-based programs (Notes, 2002), linking JC with courts, such as drug, gun, teen, community courts (Butts & Harrell, 1998), or adopting a family-focused approach (Gilbert, Grimm & Parnham, 2000; Kumpfer & Alvarado, 1998; Pagnanelli, 2007; Redding, 2016; Smith, 2013). These are services that should, when appropriate, be operationalized in addition to transfer, not in lieu of transfer.

Imposing longer sentences in JC to alleviate the need to transfer (Martin, 1992; McGee, 1989; Myers, 2001; Park, 2007; Pollitt, 2004; Redding, 2003; Slobogin, 2013; Wizner, 1984, 1995) or extending the "upper boundary" of JC jurisdiction (Arya, 2010; Bishop, 2000; Bonnie, 1989; Burke, 1995; Prescott, 2000), even as until twenty-five years of age (Marrus & Rosenberg, 2005; Myers, 2005; Pagnanelli, 2007; Smith, 1995), does not solve the transfer "problem." In many, if not most, transfers the issue is not the need for longer sentences. Moreover, some offenders could "require" sentences beyond *any* plausible maximum retention age. Increasing the maximum retention age also contributes to the criminalization of JC, undermining the system's ability to help retained juveniles and making the denial of some due process elements much more problematic. This move also opens the door to sentencing less serious offenders to longer dispositions (see Zimring, 1998a),[8] which would further exacerbate the previous issues. Some states increased their retention age in the 1990s, answering the spike in juvenile violence. Allowing JCs to sentence juvenile offenders to 15 years of incarceration strains the legitimate boundaries of JC/JJ beyond recognition or acceptance.

When the juvenile court becomes the instrument of open-ended incapacitation, the damage is to its core commitment; the court has not shot itself in the foot, it has shot itself in the heart (Zimring, 2000b, p. 216).

Option #3: Selective/Discretionary Exclusion: Supporting Transfer to CC

Theories/Principles Supporting Transfer to CC

The case *for transfer* to CC has been extensively revealed in Chapters 13-15. The benefits derived from and purposes served by transfer are numerous and significant. They deserve consideration for constituting a theoretical support and practical diagram for transfer.

Zimring has thrown down a gauntlet in this theory-related arena:

But those who wish to retain the traditional features of juvenile court for most 13-to-17-year-olds accused of felonies but exclude either some or all violent offenders must offer distinctions between them. This demands an explicit theory of the kind of case and the kind of young offender that the juvenile court should retain and treat in traditional fashion... (Zimring, 1998a, p. 161).

This exercise is not problematic. A distinction can be readily recognized in an *intent to inflict* and *produce harm* (which Zimring embraced as a concept but then ignored in developing policy). Offending that satisfies this criterion due to being violent, serious and/or chronic means that society's best interests (BI) should prevail. Barring a *true lack of responsibility* (not just irresponsibility attributed to age groups), harmful intent/product easily qualify for denying offenders immunity from criminal prosecution; legislatures should make the broad eligibility call and authorize judges/prosecutors to make the ultimate individual decision. Both quantity and quality of juvenile misbehavior can be factored into the calculation of harmful intent and product. The less harmful the offense is, the more chronic the criminal behavior should be to qualify for transfer. The more harmful the offense is, the less chronic the criminal behavior can be to qualify for transfer; perhaps no prior record is necessary, here, given a particularly violent current offense.

Similarly, Fagan and Zimring (2000) contended:

The reality is that most decisions about transfer standards are made on an ad hoc basis without any reference to general notions about the competence or limits of juvenile courts. Decisions are made as an aspect of policy toward crime, but not as a self-conscious act of constructing or elaborating a theory of juvenile justice... (p. 3).

This observation is inaccurate. The dispositional limits of JCs have directly influenced prosecutorial transfer (PT). The severity of the current offense, coupled perhaps with age and prior record, impact prosecutors' transfer power. The JC's treatment limits in addressing chronic offenders or limited prospects for a one-time violent offender have historically played a role in judicial transfer (JT). In the latter case, crime severity is usually as major a consideration as are prior criminal and treatment records. The treatment and time limits have been recognized and accepted from the very first days of JC. The dispositional limits were always present but became more glaring and troubling as juvenile crime involved more serious and violent (and chronic) offenses committed by older and older juveniles well before the notorious spike in juvenile violence in the mid-1980s-to-mid-1990s. Legislatures were informed:

- a good bit of juvenile crime is serious, violent and chronic;
- juvenile court has limited sanctions and abilities to successfully address some juvenile offenders, especially regarding older and chronic ones;
- judges resist transfer altogether or will not transfer frequently enough;
- sometimes the offense/record should dominate the transfer consideration (and not amenability to treatment or only chronic offending); and,
- prosecutors and not judges should make the transfer decision when serious/violent and some chronic offenders make themselves known to JC.

These truths/opinions led to a remarkable expansion of the ability to transfer chronic, serious and violent juveniles. Prosecutors experienced the greater amount of power expansion, but judges were also granted more authority (see Sanborn, 1996a). Prosecutors lobbied the legislatures for more power, complaining about reluctant judges and violent/chronic youths' being beyond the capacity of JC. They stated when serious and violent crimes are at issue, the offense and record should dictate the transfer outcome and that prosecutors were the best determiners of the appropriateness of transfer in this context.

Fagan and Zimring complained all of these developments occurred without constructing or *elaborating a theory of juvenile justice (JJ)*. There was a theory expressed by those seeking increased transfer power. Fagan and Zimring (among other ATC members) just do not like the theory. The theory is that JCs, as currently constructed and properly operating, are not equipped to handle the severity of crimes committed by some youths due to a lack of programs, resources, and/or time, and sometimes also due to a lack of sufficient punishment or an ability to condemn behavior. It was hardly inappropriate or irrational for prosecutors to argue that they, and not judges, should be the primary gatekeepers to CC, especially when the crime is serious or violent. PT is even more appropriate when the irrefutable is understood and accepted that *transfer is charging*.

Zimring is correct that we should do our best to avoid destroying youths' life chances; the more kids we keep in the relatively law-abiding camp, even if that requires not overreacting to a few offenses, the better for the youths and society. It certainly speaks to the benefit of promoting prevention and diversion programs in JC. At the same time, there needs to be an agreement that some youths will not stop doing serious crime until they are forcibly stopped. There are juveniles

who are angry, frequently in pain, and too often unattached to other human beings due to experiences in their home and neighborhood environments.... Many of these youths lack...the resources to improve their lives.... As a result, many juveniles today are living under extreme stress and are severely alienated.... Often chronically bored, they... commit crimes for fun. They live in the moment. To them, thrills — and lives — are cheap (Heide, 1999, p. 49).[9]

This, together with the possibility that *PRIC* characteristics drive some juvenile offenders, should give us pause in granting these youths immunity from criminal prosecution and in granting them access to other youths who are not yet so damaged.

It is possible that the JJ system has more positive attributes to offer than the homes or neighborhoods of some offenders. This is appropriate, was a vital part of the original design, and should not be changed. It should also be acknowledged that this status possibly acts as an incentive for some youths to commit crime.

Principles for Selecting Those Eligible for Transfer

To develop policy, five interrelated, critical factors must be weighed: the culpability of the offender; the harm represented in this and previous behavior(s); the interests that should dominate the proceedings; the amount of justice that should be available to the accused; and, the extent of condemnation and punishment (versus tolerance and rehabilitation) that is deserved.[10] Legislatures need to establish proportionality among the three major variables: behavior; punishment; and, process; each ends up triggering the other. As the criminal behavior becomes more chronic/serious/violent, the state's response appropriately becomes more exacting (punitive), which, in turn, necessitates affording rights commensurate/proportionate to the state's response.

There are degrees of support for selective exclusion. Even some of the developmental psychologists (DPs)/ATC will allow some modified transfer. Some ATC members tolerate transfer, provided judges control it (Frost Clausel & Bonnie, 2000).[11] Some ATC folks have decided to accept transfer by circling the transfer wagons around the narrowest possible substantive basis of selective exclusion. Zimring (1998a) insisted that transfer is justifiable only when (some) murders are charged. Zimring is not wrong in choosing murder; he is simply too stingy in identifying it as the sole qualifying crime/circumstance. To bolster his claim, Zimring tried to write off juvenile violence as a natural and expected. This is partly correct: just about all juveniles commit at least one offense before and/or during adolescence. That speaks loudly to maintaining JC for most juveniles. Zimring's tactic succeeds when it comes to preserving the status quo, which is disqualifying the bottom 90% or more of juvenile offenders from transfer. Zimring's policy fails with the upper 10%, however. Although murder harms, it is certainly not the only offense (or collection of offenses) that harms and it, just as certainly, is not the only time society's BI should prevail over the juvenile's BI. Society should be able to express moral condemnation of chronic/serious/violent juvenile offenders in CC.

What is also correct, and what Zimring ignored, is that only relatively few juveniles will be so chronic/serious/violent in their criminality to fall within the crosshairs of transfer statutes. That point is not conceded by Zimring or other ATC types because it weakens, if not destroys, their argument of the supposed universality and normality of juvenile *violence*. That truth, nevertheless, speaks volumes for denying JC access to these relatively few chronic, serious and violent juvenile offenders. Some serious and violent juvenile crimes constitute sufficient harm to justify transfer for a single offense (and to deny immunity from criminal prosecution), while chronic crime ultimately culminates in the same way. There is simply no reason, apart from a *judgment call* or *personal preference*, to restrict transfer narrowly to what *might appear* to be *the most* serious/violent offense. It is easy to imagine serious and violent encounters that result in significant harm, even though no one died (yet, perhaps).[12]

The qualifying harm can stem from a victim's/community's being directly physically harmed, which is where juvenile violent crime comes in. There is no reason the harmed victim cannot also include JC, the JJ system, and retained offenders. Even some ATC members acknowledge the appropriateness of transfer for chronic and generally violent juvenile offenders:

(I)t is difficult to support continued efforts to treat chronic offenders who have been unresponsive to efforts to rehabilitate them. Similarly, it is difficult to justify a rehabilitative posture toward youths — even first offenders — who have committed serious violent crimes that provoke strong societal indignation and fear for public safety. These concerns...are not easily assuaged within the range of dispositional alternatives traditionally available to the juvenile court.... (Bishop & Frazier, 1991, p. 282).

It is pretentious to identify crime-by-crime or record-by-record which juveniles should be eligible for transfer; this is the legislatures' province, probably best determined after holding hearings to hear from all sides of the issue. Inasmuch as PT and/or JT exist(s) in every jurisdiction, there may be no need to reconsider transfer statutes. If it is not broken, why fix it?

For jurisdictions wishing to revisit their statutes, the mission would seem to be two-fold. It would seem profitable to divide the transfer-eligible offender population into the two general groups: the *greater-punishment group* where offense and record dominate the decision and the *beyond-treatment group* where a lack of amenability to treatment rules.

Probably the first task connected to the greater-punishment group is to determine whether there are crimes that simply do not belong in JCs; First-degree/Class A felonies are examples. Perhaps some offenses would require only one count (e.g., murder), while less serious/violent crimes might require multiple counts; the same considerations apply as to whether a prior record and/or a minimum age would be required for any of the offenses (perhaps neither for murder).

Probably the first task connected to the beyond-treatment group would be to summon representatives from the JC network, including judges, prosecutors, defense attorneys, POs, and service providers, to get their insight as to what nonamenability to JC treatment means in their jurisdiction and to draw some usable formula for all JCs in the jurisdiction, such as:

(T)o be adjudged nonamenable to treatment the record must reveal at least three prior adjudications of delinquency and at least one prior commitment to a residential treatment program. (Bishop & Frazier, 1991, p. 301).[13]

Sensitivity needs to be provided to differing JCs. Not all JCs are equal. While demanding equality *within* each JC seems reasonable and just, demanding the same *among* all JCs does not. Not all JCs operate with the same number of levels on their disposition ladder, nor do they graduate offenders from one level to the next higher one (or always in the same upward direction, for that matter; see Sanborn, 1985) at the same speed. Probably the wisest and most appropriate method of identifying the nonamenability criteria is to presumptively require offenders exhaust all available treatment options/programs on the JC's disposition ladder. Any exception to this general standard could require POs, service providers, and judges to sign off on the exception and explain why rehabilitation is not considered plausible. Limits to the length of remaining time in JC's authority over the youth, lack of program fit, and concern for the safety of staff and fellow inmates, among other considerations, could be statutorily identified as grounds for exceptions to the general rule. For first offenders, exceptional reasons could be required for transfer.

Task #2: Selecting the Proper Method(s) for Transferring Offenders to CC

The transfer formula currently practiced in most states appears to be a compromise and to make the most sense (see Sanborn, 2003). The compromise has prosecutors' transferring the most serious/violent crimes, and perhaps the most chronic offending, too. The statutory focus on offense and record speaks to the legislatures' commitment to prosecutors' making the transfer call in these cases. These cases represent a threat to society and call for the imposition of punishment. Society's BI should be paramount, and society's representative should make the call (i.e., the prosecutor). The wisest approach would seem to be to establish a threshold that divides crime severity into two levels: above the threshold would mean the prosecutor chooses the court (the way OE operates), while below the threshold would mean the judge controls the decision. The threshold could also be configured to accommodate multiple counts of less serious offenses, prior delinquent and treatment records and age. A second-degree felony could "belong" to the prosecutor due to multiple counts, 5 previous adjudications and/or 3 prior placements, and/or advanced offender age. Regardless of the matrix/division, whatever is above the threshold means society's BI prevail and the prosecutor is in charge to operationalize those BI.[14] Although they are not constrained by amenability, here, prosecutors cannot completely ignore it, either.[15] PT saves JC from much work and avoids violating separation of powers by not having judges charge (i.e., transfer) juveniles.

PT is also preferable for the most serious/violent/chronic offenses because, unlike JT, the decision can be centralized in the prosecutor's office (DeFrances, 2002; Perry, 2006), advancing "the objectives of consistency and accountability in the system's operations (Allen, 2000, p. xiv)." The charging unit will have knowledge of what offenses/records go to which court, abundant experience in charging (and in finding the particulars of crimes via interviewing witnesses and arresting officers, etc.), and consistency since it will be acting in accord with office policies (see Hoeffel, 2013). Judges cannot offer anything comparable to prosecutors' expertise in these capacities. One reason Feld and Zimring have been dissatisfied with JT is that JC judges have different perspectives and can respond very differently to the same transfer-eligible scenario. PT offers a greater chance for equal and proportionate handling of cases (see Zimring & Fagan, 2000, p. 411); discriminatory charging via PT after arrest is easier to track. JT allows extra-legal variables, such as the juvenile's character and needs, family situation, among others, to influence the outcome and expands the potential for disparate treatment. JT is also problematic because

> *judicial transfer makes mental health professionals and probation officers responsible for the evaluative amenability decision that is critical to the transfer outcome. For crimes of the nature and seriousness*

of murder, the moral, social, and legal judgment involved as to which court should prosecute the case belongs to the official who is directly responsible to the public: the prosecutor... (Sanborn, 1996b, pp. 170-171, citation omitted).

****

[P]robation officers and/or clinicians form the most critical appraisals of the youth's amenability to treatment, which typically convince the judge as to the appropriateness of transfer. This relationship effectively transfers the transfer decision to court officials and private citizens who are neither elected by nor accountable to the public. This arrangement is inappropriate when society's interests should be vindicated (Sanborn, 2003, p. 209).

Judges also get to hide behind the opinions and conclusions of civil servants. Zimring and Feld want JT, minus amenability, reducing the judge's role to evaluating charges/future prospects of desistance. If that is to be the focus of JT, judicial charging should have no bearing in these cases.

The second part of the method question is a choice between offense exclusion (OE) and direct file (DF) for the serious, violent, and chronic offenses. If the threshold idea holds, OE is the preferred version of PT. It

draws a clear line or boundary as to where criminal court jurisdiction legitimately begins, and where diversion to juvenile court is not acceptable. For example, it seems to make sense to assert that murder (perhaps depending upon age) simply should not be subject to juvenile court processing and should be excluded thereby. Here, offense exclusion makes an unequivocal statement that society's interests must prevail when prosecutors determine that a murder charge is the correct allegation (Id., p. 210).

DF would seem to be a less suitable PT method when the stakes are highest because it allows the prosecution of some murderers in JC (Sanborn, 1996b, p. 171), and, worse, perhaps, it

can raise issues of ambiguity, equality, and legitimacy. That is, why is it acceptable to prosecute some seventeen-year-old murderers in juvenile court, while other seventeen-year-old murderers can be prosecuted in criminal court ... (Sanborn, 2003, p. 210)?

DF thus appears vulnerable to an equal protection challenge (see Sanborn, 1996b, p. 171). That research studies supposedly could find hundreds of "matched pairs" prosecuted in juvenile and criminal courts bears witness to the vulnerability of DF.

It is possible that some jurisdictions would want to subdivide the offenses/records above the threshold. In these cases, some legislatures could determine that DF would be suitable.

Less serious (or maybe younger serious) and chronic offenders... would appear to be the most suitable candidates for concurrent jurisdiction. These youth do not appear to be as far above the threshold that automatically triggers society's interests, as are youth who murder and rape. Although their fate belongs within a charging rather than a treatment amenability framework since they, too, are above the threshold, there is a logic to allowing the prosecutor to determine that some of these youth do not require criminal court prosecution; diversion to juvenile court is still a prospect for some (Id.).

Legislatures in many states have chosen both OE and DF in this arrangement. In the alternative, jurisdictions could place all above the threshold within OE and then place those below the threshold within the reach of judicial transfer (JT). In states with both PT and JT, "judges have been granted transfer authority over less violent youth who are nevertheless not likely to be rehabilitated by the juvenile system (Id.)." These offenders can be less chronic and younger, too.

Judicial transfer should be utilized for youth whose behavior has not been sufficiently serious or chronic so as to trigger society's concerns and interests, but who still may not be amenable to juvenile court intervention.... Assumedly, this allocation of authority also would involve minimum ages, offenses, and records, which is typical in the legislation of most states. The presumption in these cases is that the youth's best interests should dominate the decision making, which is why it is proper to entrust it to a judge. Nevertheless, the presumption is not absolute and can be overcome by the judge's decision to certify the youth to adult court due to the youth's lack of amenability (Id., pp. 209-210).

While some ATC support traditional JT (see Hoeffel, 2013), Zimring (1998a) objected to the juvenile's maturity and sophistication criterion determined in JT.

In statutes providing for waiver to criminal courts, juvenile court judges are asked to decide whether particular accused persons are mature. If they are, they can be punished as adults... (p. 73, citation omitted)

The DPs/ATC insist that *immaturity is a major reason for staying in JC,* but pro-transfer advocates are not allowed to consider *maturity as a reason for transfer*. Zimring (1998a) explained:

The problem with withdrawing the protections of juvenile justice only when the subject is mature and sophisticated is that the ***most serious*** *cases are not the* ***most mature*** *offenders. The empirical pattern is, if anything, to the contrary. The most serious acts of violence are committed by youths with* ***lower levels*** *of educational attainment, less capacity for mature judgment, and* ***less understanding of the world*** *around them than others of the same chronological age... (p. 75, emphases added).*

Zimring simply wanted it both ways: employing interpretations of (im)maturity (or an absence of maturity) are permissible when it will help his cause in seeking to avoid transfer, but using interpretations of maturity (maturity actually exists) will not have a chance to backfire on him since they cannot be used in a similar fashion to support transfer.

More important, not all of the "most serious acts of violence" are committed by the type of youth Zimring envisioned. Those *not fitting* his description do not deserve his literal get-out-of-jail-card. Zimring based his claim on these juveniles' not being "the *most* mature," or having "*lower levels* of educational achievement," "*less* capacity" for moral judgment and "*less* understanding of the world." Zimring employed relatives to accomplish a categorical (no transfer). He did not claim that these juveniles have no (or even an insufficient) level of educational achievement, have no (or even insufficient) maturity, have no (or even an insufficient) capacity for moral judgment or have no (or even an insufficient) understanding of the world to make it impossible for them to be found criminally responsible. Neither juvenile nor adult offenders have ever been required to demonstrate "mature judgment" or an "understanding of the world around them," whatever that means, to stand trial in CC. JC statutes have listed the maturity and sophistication factors for decades and were cited with approval in the 1966 *Kent* decision. The factors relate to the level of maturity reflected in the youth's choices and criminal behavior (especially, but not only, over a period of time) and to the sophistication disclosed in how the offense was committed. Both elements can be relevant to determining amenability and the fit of treatment programs, both in substance and in terms of effect on fellow inmates. Even more critical, both elements can be relevant to the appropriate level of punishment as suggested by the way in which the crime(s) unfolded. Moreover, maturity and sophistication are *only two*, not *the only* criteria used in judicial transfer. Zimring used a double false premise to create a false categorical. He implied that *all* serious/violent juvenile offenders fit his description, and that the *entirety of* amenability revolves around mature judgment/understanding of the surrounding world variables.[16] Neither position is accurate.

Feld and Zimring tried to eliminate nonamenability as a legitimate transfer factor. Feld (1987, 1995) focused on the ambiguity/discriminatory potential of JT's focus on this variable. Zimring (1998a) emphasized that not all violent offenders are nonamenable. Since violent offenses do not lend to *nonamenability findings* on a *categorical level* he argued the former cannot be of a valid part of transfer policy.[17] Zimring and Feld ended up retaining JT, but eliminating amenability.

No categorical findings of either high or low amenability to treatment have been issued for entire subclasses of violent offenders...But the absence of valid generalizations gives us a finding of some importance to the policy process. Since category-wide generalizations are not valid, no general policy toward violent offenders can be justified on amenability grounds (Zimring, 1998a, p. 164).

Of course, transferring violent offenses neither depends upon nor requires justification via amenability considerations. OE, in fact, eliminates the amenability factor (at least as an obstacle to transfer). Plus, Zimring merely stated "no general policy" for violent offenses can be justified based on amenability. That does not convert to violent offenses' never qualifying for transfer via nonamenability findings. Zimring suggested (perhaps inferred) that a general policy requiring JT for violent offenses due to nonamenability results in the "automatic" transfer of all violent offenses. The most that Zimring's policy qualification means is that pro-transfer types cannot argue *all* of those who commit violent offenses are nonamenable, which is true and should not require comment. They can argue, however, that violent offenses do not deserve immunity from criminal prosecution, regardless of amenability capacity. Most important, most pro-transfer types advocate violent offenders *should be* transferred. Those who understand transfer realize that *should be* is not equivalent to *must be* transferred, and that *mandatory transfer* is an oxymoron.

More critical, amenability is simply one factor that can be cited in favor of not transferring. There is no reason violent offenses cannot qualify for transfer via retributive or incapacitation, justice, condemnation, etc. considerations, and all be given priority over amenability in violent offenses. Unlike amenability, retribution, and incapacitation (etc.) *can be generally prescribed.* The latter do not require analysis apart from severity of offense (and perhaps record). So, for example, all juveniles who commit a first-degree felony (perhaps with a previous felony adjudication) can be preordained via retribution or incapacitation (etc.) criteria to qualify for CC prosecution, regardless of amenability. Thus, a general offense (and record) condition can indeed lead to a general transfer policy.

Associating amenability with transfer does not require the conclusion Zimring draws. All transfer is discretionary. General policies authorizing the transfer of violent offenses due to nonamenability can be and have been drafted without doing violence to the transfer concept. A general policy does not preordain a particular, required result. In JT statutes, there can be a "general policy" that youths charged with violent offenses (combined with whatever other factors) merit an amenability analysis, which, if (but only if) that culminates in a nonamenability finding, transfer will occur.

Zimring proffered a solution in search of a problem. Actually, Zimring created an unnecessary problem and then crafted a solution that just so happened to be in sync with his general anti-transfer ideology. He suggested that all of the eggs surrounding the transfer of violent offenses are in amenability's basket. However, transfer power over violent offenders is most often granted to prosecutors who are not burdened by having to prove nonamenability. A general policy of PT for violent offenses is easily constructed, as the OE law in most states today reveals.

In violent offenses, society's/victim's interests should prevail over the juvenile's BI, and the youth's amenability to treatment should be irrelevant. In other words, the criminal behavior (and perhaps criminal history) should be the number one consideration. PT should control in these cases.

Task #3: Implications for Developing Transfer to CC Policy

The implications of the *No Transfer/Total Inclusion* policy are numerous and serious. The first is the effect on juvenile offenders. Transfer cannot rely on promoting deterrence but stripping JCs of all transfer power could open a Pandora's Box. Individual offenders could wreak havoc without fear of much in the way of consequences. Gangs could pressure younger members to do the heavy crime-lifting, perhaps encouraging even more gang violence with so relatively little in consequences at stake. Although public sentiment is not the primary consideration in defending transfer, a lack of transfer options could easily trigger an incredibly hostile public sentiment towards JCs. The perceived lack of justice by victims and community members could lead to a cry for the abolition of JCs. Even some ATC folks acknowledge this. Given a sufficient extent of/increase in juvenile violence attributed to this policy, the survival of JCs could easily be in question.

Even if JCs were not destroyed from the outside, an absence of transfer could fatally ruin the JCs from the inside. Maintaining any allegiance to the juvenile's BI would seem tenuous. Increasing JCs' sanctioning power, seemingly inevitable, would necessarily contribute to the criminalization of JC. Allowing JCs to impose easily foreseeable 20 to 30 years sentences could raise serious and legitimate questions as to why we need/have a JC. Making these sentence adjustments without an accompanying increase in the constitutional rights of juvenile defendants would seem unlikely, if not impossible. *Gault*, Part 2, would almost have to transpire; arguably, it already should have occurred (see Sanborn, 1993b). These developments would *have to* result in JCs' being seen as *nothing* other than CCs for younger offenders. The addition of would-be transfers to juvenile facilities would clog up perhaps *all* levels of facilities (especially considering the lengthier sentences), making any institutional help for salvageable juveniles unlikely at all (or at least not until it is too late). The chances of any meaningful rehabilitation programs being offered in these facilities would decrease substantially, if not disappear altogether. Maintaining a JC/JJ system lacking rehabilitation and the BI of juveniles as its focus, with punitiveness and inefficiency comparable to CC/CJ system would seem unnecessary, undesirable, and unlikely. Adopting a no-transfer policy would likely culminate in the demise of the JC experiment.

Selective exclusion/transfer as a policy has more promise for all parties. Supporting OE for crimes such as murder and rape, etc. does not amount to a repudiation of JC's mission to rehabilitate children; the opposite is true. The legislature can believe JC exists to promote the youths' BI and rehabilitation, and due to that belief, it will exclude murder, etc., from JC's jurisdiction. Legislatures can also believe acts that serious require putting the BI of the victim, community, and other juveniles ahead of the murderer/

rapist and require prosecution in CC. JC's rehabilitation mission and procedural atmosphere is simply too benevolent and relatively due process free to accommodate the prosecution of behaviors as serious, detrimental, and repugnant as murder and rape. Once upon a time, Feld also believed the limits in JC's due process limited the number of the prosecutions of some juvenile offenders that should occur there.

Legislatures have long adhered to this view. Even when JCs were first implemented, and enjoying the height of popularity, murder was often excluded from their jurisdiction. Excluding murder and rape, etc., can also promote JC's credibility that it can pursue its mission without demanding unrealistic, unnecessary, and dangerous sacrifices from the public. OE makes it more palatable that JC should be and can afford to help juveniles more than protect society because JC is addressing *juvenile delinquency*, not *wanton youth criminality*. Retaining these youths requires a stronger adjudicative process and longer sanctions that would not be treatment-oriented.

Last-Minute Reconciliations

Reconciling the Supposed Lack of Fit between Transfer and CC Outcomes

Three items remain to be reconciled. The first is the supposed lack of fit between transfer and CC/CJ outcomes. Transfer is not accountable for all the problems manifesting in CC, such as prison conditions, assaults, suicide, etc. These outcomes reflect a failure of the CJ system and are not the fault of transfer to CC. Legislatures need to follow through and complete transfer policy by mandating age segregation, protection from older prisoners, counseling, educational programs, special mental health services, among other considerations (see Zimring, 1998a, p. 145). Juvenile-centered post-release programs should also be available to transfers. While forcing transfer-eligible offenders into juvenile facilities is problematic, community programs with expertise in working with youths can be fruitful. These programs should extend services to transfers following the expiration of a CC sentence (and perhaps during a probationary/parole period from JC or AC) (Cf., Zimring, 2000b, p. 209).

Feld (1999) focused on CC and blames a general "lack of fit" in CC outcomes on transfer.

Discretionary and idiosyncratic prosecutorial and judicial waiver decisions exacerbate the "lack of fit" between transfer and criminal court sentencing practices and undermine the rationality of social control... (p. 231).

****

The lenient responses to many young career offenders when they first appear in criminal courts occur because the criteria for removal from juvenile court and adult court criminal sentencing practices often lack congruence. Several studies of the criminal sentences imposed on judicially waived juveniles report a "lack of fit" between waiver decisions and criminal sentencing practices. The "punishment gap" allows chronic and active young offenders to fall between the cracks of the two justice systems. The punishment gap occurs because waiver decisions involve two somewhat different but overlapping populations of young offenders — older chronic offenders currently charged with a property crime ***and*** *violent youths, some of whom also are persistent offenders. Criminal courts respond differently to chronic offenders currently charged with a property crimes (sic) and those charged with violence because of the seriousness of their present offense... (Feld, 2000, p. 107, emphasis in original, citations omitted).*

Transfer is not the source or cause of any so-called lack of fit. The gap between JC records and dispositions and CC sentences is the source, which has no necessary relationship to transfer. Aging out of juvenile delinquency/JC and "starting over" as an adult criminal (without having been transferred) produces the same punishment gap. It is the possible lack of integration between the two systems that accounts for the lack of fit, regardless of whether transfer explains the offender's presence in CC.

The *irrationality of social control* would be allowing all offenders to remain in JC until adulthood. Transfer policies and mechanisms are not to blame for illogical/unsatisfactory CC sentences; legislatures and CC officials are. The punishment gap was set due to the insufficiency of due process in JC, and to allow offenders to graduate from JC without a criminal history; they got to start over in CC. There is also no lack of fit in different sentencing outcomes for chronic versus violent offenders. The latter can receive a lengthy sentence due to the penalty attached to the current offense *alone*. Chronic juvenile offenses, most of which are property-oriented, do not tend to carry the same hefty outcomes because of the relative non-seriousness of the offense, and probably because the youth does not appear violent/ dangerous to decision makers. The statute or the CC prosecutor/judge likely accounts for the leniency granted these transfers (see Kupchik, 2003). Feld is aware of this. This was simply his attempt to invalidate and prevent most, if not all, chronic non-violent offender transfers. Again, it is not transfer policy that causes the gap. It is an inability (or unwillingness) to factor the previous JC adjudications sufficiently into CC sentencing. To reduce the gap, prior JC adjudications would have to be factored directly into CC sentencing and would also have to be adopted and implemented by CC officials. This has happened in many states (see Sanborn, 1998, 2000), which likely accounts for the lengthier sentences being imposed currently on these transfers. The gap is not a reason to deny/delay transfer. All that accomplishes is to have the "inappropriate" CC sentence occur later in the day, after the juvenile possibly has committed more crimes, making a bad situation and lack of fit even worse. Even Feld (2000) conceded the appropriateness of transferring chronic offenders.

The small group of chronic offenders also may deserve or require longer minimum sentences than the maximum sanctions available in juvenile court because of their persistent offending… (p. 111).

Feld's solution to the lack of fit was to provide a youth discount, categorically by age. In 1995, he maintained 14-year-olds should get 33% of the "adult" sentence, 16-year-olds should get 66%, and 18-year-olds should get the same as adults (which has not varied over time) (p. 1127). By 1997, things improved for transfers: 14 meant between 25 and 33%, and 16 meant between 50 and 60% (1997, p. 118). By 2013, 14 meant between 20 and 25%, and 16 meant the judge could not impose a maximum sentence greater than 50% (2013a, p. 323, 2013b, p. 141-142).[18] Feld (2013a) used the Supreme Court's adoption of categorical prohibitions against the juvenile death penalty and life without parole sentences in certain situations (see *Roper v. Simmons*, 2005; *Graham v. Florida*, 2010; *Miller v. Alabama*, 2012) as support for his proposal and argued that it is a "way for legislatures to recognize juveniles' *categorical diminished responsibility* and to incorporate youthfulness as a mitigating factor in sentencing (pp. 263-264, emphasis added)." The absence of any actual "*categorical* diminished responsibility" among juvenile offenders, however, depreciates the relevance and utility of this proposal. This formula does not advance justice since not all offenders of the ages he identified deserve such a break; some youth even could deserve and warrant harsher sentences than some adult criminals.

Even if maturation is reasonably regular, so that there is a significant correlation between age and maturity, there will be individual variance. Some 16-year-olds will have as much normative competence as the normal 18-year-old, and some 16-year-olds will have as much normative competence as the normal 14-year-old. So adoption of a categorical age-based discount will be both under-punitive and over-punitive, relative to the demands of individualized justice (Brink, 2003-2004, p. 1584).

Zimring (1998a) rejected Feld's solution because it could lead to expanding potential range of sentences (p. 148). Moreover, Zimring doubted

whether even advanced knowledge of adolescent development and the particular characteristics of young violent offenders will produce a satisfactory schedule of punishments normed to age or prior offenses. The range of individual variation among youths of the same age is notoriously large... The significant variables in determining the proper punishment for a teen killer will not fit comfortably into a two-dimensional grid... (Id.).[19]

Probably the only way to bridge the lack of fit is to integrate sentencing between the two systems. Factoring the JC record into CC sentencing has gone too far in some jurisdictions.[20] But allowing offenders to "start over" in CC, despite a significant JC history, is self-defeating and contrary to society's BI. Transfers should receive credit for both their criminal history, as an aggravating factor, and their youth, as a mitigating factor. Minimally, offenders with a JC history should be denied probation and qualify for a presumptive sentence of incarceration. Following a JC history of leniency with continued lenience in CC invites continued disrespect from juveniles, likely manifesting in continued crime; this could easily explain greater recidivism among transfers that some research has found. Imposing "adult"-like sentences on all transfers can be unfair and unjust. Depending upon their history, they should receive a lesser sentence than a comparably behaving adult. A happy medium can be reached here; aggravation and mitigation can be individually administered. The extremes and any categoricals, here, are wrong.

Reconciling the Utilitarian vs Non-Utilitarian Considerations Underlying Transfer: Should Transfer Be Backward or Forward-Looking?

A second, contentious question is whether transfer eligibility and policy should be fact-based/backward-looking or a matter of potential-prospect/forward-looking?

Zimring (1998a) based his general no/limited-transfer (only some murders) policy upon a premise:

Adolescence is a period of human development that is notorious for the tendency to change quickly.... This dynamic quality makes it less likely that patterns of deviance will become ingrained and inevitably be repeated. Because the adolescent is changeable, his or her previous criminal activity is less predictive of future criminal activity... (pp. 165-166).

Zimring was basing transfer eligibility on utilitarian considerations or future prospects, such as offenders' desisting? But this is why we have JC prosecute the vast majority of offenders. At a certain offense level — chronic or serious/violent — it is about society and not the juvenile (which Zimring partially accepted), whether or not the offender will change. Even if youths will change (which, beyond a simple statistic and tendencies, we cannot definitively know until they get there), they *have already earned* CC punishment and denial of JC processing. Transfer needs to be based upon what the offender has already done, not what they might or might not do in the future. Not too long ago, Feld (1984b, p.32) adamantly insisted upon this focus. Meanwhile, Zimring's formula makes transfer ripe for unequal outcomes and discrimination (which he supposedly decries), rather than on more equitable notions, such as past behavior.

Ironically, Zimring (and Feld) condemned the amenability to treatment component of JT due to its ambiguity and ability to discriminate only to embrace other utilitarian aspects that contain the very same prospects for discrimination. This approach is calculated to cut down on the number of transfers, which it likely would, but it will also promote a serious potential for discrimination. Chronic criminal behavior (even in non-serious crime) is a legitimate/good indicator of a commitment to criminal activity (until forcibly prevented from continuing, perhaps). Zimring's approach forces us to rely on tendencies while he wants transfer decisions to be based on predicting desistance. Correctly predicting desistance (i.e., offender will recidivate as predicted) creates no horror since the offender has already earned the punishment by virtue of prior conduct. Incorrectly predicting desistance (i.e., offender will recidivate despite a prediction of desistance) means yet another victim (and society) will pay for the offender's crime. Incorrect predictions do not help JC's survival chances.

When the ATC dislikes transfer categoricals (even though *none exists,* as in offense exclusion — OE), they denigrate them. When they like categoricals, they readily embrace them, even when that embrace requires engaging in misrepresentations, such as alleging across-the-board juvenile incompetence to stand trial (IST) and diminished responsibility (DR). Similarly, the ATC decries the lack of individualization (again, incorrectly perceived in OE), but embrace it when it promotes their cause (age-based prohibitions against transfer). At best, these maneuvers are bold, disingenuous, and simple attempts to further an ideological bent. At worst, they promise success to would-be career juvenile criminals who, without transfer, can enjoy immunity from criminal prosecution until they reach adulthood at the expense of JCs, retained juveniles, and society.[21]

Reconciling CC's Back-door JC Re-entry Measure: Eliminating the Reverse Transfer Option for CC Judges in Offense Exclusion Cases

A final consideration involves whether CC judges should be able to return the defendant to JC for prosecution via a *reverse transfer* (or decertification). This can happen even when a JC judge has found the accused an unfit candidate for JJ treatment (see Sanborn & Salerno, 2005, Chapter 12), which does not seem to make much sense. Admittedly, the existence of this transfer contradicts an earlier assertion in this text that judicial charging does not occur in CC. A reasonable policy position would be to stop this possibility. JC judges should be granted priority in making amenability determinations (meaning their decision to transfer stands), and "reversals" of this decision should be allowed for abuse of discretion situations only.

The reverse transfer potential not surprisingly is more prevalent in jurisdictions with PT, where DF and/or OE are practiced (see Id.). A plausible defense of this in DF cases is that prosecutors could have been unaware of, or could have chosen to ignore, the offender's rehabilitation potential. In light of that possibility, juveniles are permitted to challenge the transfer to CC; both courts share jurisdiction over those cases. Statutes then place the treatment burden on the defense (the equivalent of presumptive transfer in JC) in CC to send the case back to JC, which hardly seems unreasonable or inappropriate. Even still, the statute should then allow the prosecutor to petition the JC judge to transfer the case back to CC, much like a regular JT would allow. Amenability factors, such as a lack of available treatment programs could have been unknown or miscalculated by the CC judge, calling for a "better expert" to reverse that reversal.

The OE situation is completely different, however (and may represent another way in which OE is "wiser" and more straightforward/less complicated than DF). With OE the legislature has made a clear and unequivocal statement that juveniles facing certain charges, perhaps having reached a certain age, and having accumulated a certain record, do not belong in JC. In these situations, legislatures have proclaimed that society's BI prevail over the juveniles' BI. Allowing reverse transfer, here, directly undermines and counteracts the intent and import of the OE legislation. It effectively empowers CC judges to engage in JT based on their read of the offense/record/age variables or "something else" altogether in deciding a JC prosecution is warranted. Reverse transfer in this context enables CC judges to charge the most serious juvenile offenders, which worsens the already tenuous violation of separation of powers.

When prosecutors elect to charge a qualifying excluded offense, that decision should speak for itself, and should be reversible only when there is a lack of probable cause for the excluded offense. As society's representatives, prosecutors are elected/appointed to make precisely those decisions. This situation is not one calling for a neutral CC umpire.

REFERENCES

Ainsworth, J. E. (1991). Re-imagining childhood and reconstructing the legal order: The case for abolishing the juvenile court. *North Carolina Law Review*, *69*, 1083–1133.

Angell, K. M. (2004). The regressive movement: When juvenile offenders are treated as adults, nobody wins. *Southern California Interdisciplinary Law Journal*, *14*, 125–144.

Applegate, B. K., Cullen, F. T., & Fisher, B. S. (1997). Public support for correctional treatment: The continuing appeal of rehabilitative ideal. *The Prison Journal*, *77*(3), 237–258. doi:10.1177/0032855597077003002

Applegate, B. K., Davis, R. K., & Cullen, F. T. (2009). Reconsidering child saving: The extent and correlates of public support for excluding youths from the juvenile court. *Crime and Delinquency*, *55*(1), 51–77. doi:10.1177/0011128707308104

Arya, N. (2010). Using *Graham v. Florida* to challenge juvenile transfer laws. *Louisiana Law Review*, *71*, 99–156.

Austin, J., Johnson, K. D., & Gregoriou, M. (2000). *Juveniles in adult prisons and jails: A national assessment*. U.S. Department of Justice, Office of Justice Programs.

Baruwa, B. (2013). Should juveniles be transferred to adult criminal court in the criminal justice system. *Tennessee Journal of Race Gender & Social Justice*, *2*, 101–127.

Beatty, H. (1994). Is the trend to expand juvenile transfer statutes just an easy answer to a complex problem. *University of Toledo Law Review. University of Toledo. College of Law*, *26*, 979–1025.

Beck, A. J., & Harrison, P. M. (2008). *Sexual victimization in local jails reported by inmates, 2007*. US Department of Justice, Office of Justice Programs, Bureau of Justice Statistics.

Beck, A. J., Harrison, P. M., & Guerino, P. (2010). Sexual victimization in juvenile facilities reported by youth, 2008-09. Bureau of Justice Statistics Special Report. NCJ 228416. US. Department of Justice (NJ1).

Bishop, D. M. (2000). Juvenile offenders in the adult criminal justice system. In M. Tonry (Ed.), *Crime & Justice: A Review of Research, 27, 81-167.* IL University of Chicago Press. doi:10.1086/652199

Bishop, D. M., & Frazier, C. E. (1991). Transfer of juveniles to criminal court: A case study and analysis of prosecutorial waiver. *Notre Dame Journal of Law, Ethics & Public Policy*, *5*, 281–302.

Bishop, D. M., Frazier, C. E., Lanza-Kaduce, L., & Winner, L. (1996). The transfer of juveniles to criminal court: Does it make a difference? *Crime and Delinquency*, *42*(2), 171–191. doi:10.1177/0011128796042002001

Bolin, R. M., Applegate, B. K., & Oullette, H. M. (2019). Americans' opinions on juvenile justice: Preferred aims, beliefs about juveniles and blended sentencing. *Crime and Delinquency*, *57*, 1–25.

Bonnie, R. J. (1989). Juvenile homicide: A study in legal ambivalence. In E. P. Benedek & D. G. Cornell (Eds.), *Juvenile homicide* (pp. 185–217). American Psychiatric Press.

Bouley, E. E. Jr, & Wells, T. L. (2001). Attitudes of citizens in a southern rural county toward juvenile crime and justice issues. *Journal of Contemporary Criminal Justice*, *17*(1), 60–70. doi:10.1177/1043986201017001006

Brink, D. O. (2003-2004). Immaturity, normative competence, and juvenile transfer: How (not) to punish minors for major crimes. *Texas Law Review*, *82*, 1555–1585.

Burke, M. K. (1994). This Old Court: Abolitionists Once Again Line Up the Wrecking Ball on the Juvenile Court When All It Needs Is a Few Minor Alterations. *University of Toledo Law Review. University of Toledo. College of Law*, *26*, 1027–1055.

Butts, J. A., & Harrell, A. (1998). *Delinquents or criminals: Policy options for young offenders. Crime & Policy Report, June 1998.* The Urban Institute.

Cohen, A. O., Bonnie, R. J., Taylor-Thompson, K., & Casey, B. J. (2015). When does a juvenile become an adult: Implications for law and policy. *Temple Law Review*, *88*, 769–788.

Coupet, S. M. (2000). What to do with sheep in wolf's clothing: The role of rhetoric and reality about youth offenders in the constructive dismantling policy of the juvenile justice system. *University of Pennsylvania Law Review*, *148*(4), 1303–1346. doi:10.2307/3312844

Cullen, F. T., Golden, K. M., & Cullen, J. B. (1983). Is child saving dead? Attitudes toward juvenile rehabilitation in Illinois. *Journal of Criminal Justice*, *11*(1), 1–13. doi:10.1016/0047-2352(83)90093-4

Cullen, F. T., Skovron, S. E., Scott, J. E., & Burton, V. S. Jr. (1990). Public support for correctional treatment: The tenacity of rehabilitative ideology. *Criminal Justice and Behavior*, *17*(1), 6–18. doi:10.1177/0093854890017001003

Danziger, G. (2003). Delinquency jurisdiction in a unified family court: Balancing intervention, prevention, and adjudication. *Family Law Quarterly*, *37*, 381–401.

DeFrances, C. J. (2002). *Prosecutors in state courts, 2001*. U.S. Department of Justice, Office of Justice Programs, Bureau of Justice Statistics. doi:10.1037/e387402004-001

Edwards, L. (1977). The case for abolishing fitness hearings in juvenile court. *Santa Clara Law Review*, *17*, 595–630.

Fagan, J. (1991). *The comparative impacts of juvenile court and criminal court sanctions on adolescent felony offenders*. Final Report to the National Institute of Justice. U.S. Department of Justice.

Fagan, J. (2008). Juvenile crime and criminal justice: Resolving border disputes. 18 *The Future of Children* 81-118 (Pages numbered 1-48 in Columbia Law School Working Paper).

Fagan, J., & Zimring, F. E. (2000). Editors' Introduction. In Fagan, J., & Zimring, F.E. (Eds.), The changing borders of juvenile justice: Transfer of adolescents to the criminal court (pp. 1-10). University of Chicago Press.

Federle, K. H. (1990). The Abolition of the juvenile court: A proposal for the preservation of children's legal rights. *Journal of Contemporary Law*, *16*, 23–51.

Feld, B. C. (1984b). The decision to seek criminal charges: Just deserts and the waiver decision. *Criminal Justice Ethics*, *3*(2), 27–41. doi:10.1080/0731129X.1984.9991756

Feld, B. C. (1987). The juvenile court meets the principle of the offense: Legislative changes in juvenile waiver statutes. *The Journal of Criminal Law & Criminology*, *78*(3), 471–533. doi:10.2307/1143567

Feld, B. C. (1990). The punitive juvenile court and the quality of procedural justice: Disjunctions between rhetoric and reality. *Crime and Delinquency*, *36*(4), 443–466. doi:10.1177/0011128790036004002

Feld, B. C. (1995). Violent youth and public policy: A case study of juvenile justice law reform. *Minnesota Law Review*, *79*, 965–1128.

Feld, B. C. (1997). Abolish the juvenile court: Youthfulness, criminal responsibility, and sentencing. *The Journal of Criminal Law & Criminology*, *88*(1), 68–136. doi:10.2307/1144075

Feld, B. C. (1999). *Bad kids: Race and the transformation of the juvenile court*. Oxford University Press.

Feld, B. C. (2000). Legislative exclusion of offenses from juvenile court jurisdiction: A history and critique. In J. Fagan & F. E. Zimring (Eds.), *The changing borders of juvenile justice: Transfer of adolescents to the criminal court* (pp. 83–144). University of Chicago Press.

Feld, B. C. (2013a). Adolescent criminal responsibility, proportionality, and sentencing policy: Roper, Graham, Miller/Jackson, and the youth discount. *Law & Inequality*, *31*, 263–330.

Feld, B. C. (2013b). The youth discount: Old enough to do the crime, too young to do the time. *Ohio State Journal of Criminal Law*, *11*, 1–148.

Flesch, L. M. (2004). Juvenile crime and why waiver is not the answer. *Family Court Review*, *42*(3), 583–596. doi:10.1177/1531244504042003 14

Forst, M., Fagan, J., & Vivona, T. S. (1989). Some paradoxical effects of the treatment-custody dichotomy for adolescents in adult prisons. *Juvenile & Family Court Journal*, *40*(1), 1–15. doi:10.1111/j.1755-6988.1989.tb00634.x

Fritsch, E. J., Caeti, T. J., & Hemmens, C. (1996a). Spare the needle but not the punishment: The incarceration of waived youth in adult prisons. *Crime and Delinquency*, *42*(4), 593–609. doi:10.1177/0011128796042004006

Fritsch, E. J., Hemmens, C., & Caeti, T. J. (1996b). Violent youth in juvenile and adult Court: An assessment of sentencing strategies in Texas. *Law & Policy*, *18*(1-2), 115–136. doi:10.1111/j.1467-9930.1996.tb00166.x

Frost Clausel, L. E., & Bonnie, R. J. (2000). Juvenile justice on appeal. *The changing borders of juvenile justice: Transfer of adolescents to the criminal court*, 181-206.

Garbarino, J. (1999). *Lost boys: Why our sons turn violent and how we can save them.* The Free Press.

Gasper, J., & Katkin, D. (1980). A rationale for the abolition of the juvenile court's power to waive jurisdiction. *Pepperdine Law Review*, *7*, 937–951.

Giardino, L. F. (1996). Statutory rhetoric: The reality behind juvenile justice policies in America. *Journal of Policy & Law*, *5*, 223–276.

Gilbert, J., Grimm, R., & Parnham, J. (2000). Applying therapeutic principles to a family-focused juvenile justice model (delinquency). *Alabama Law Review*, *52*, 1153–1212.

Goetting, A., & Howsen, R. M. (1986). Correlates of prisoner misconduct. *Journal of Quantitative Criminology*, *2*(1), 49–67. doi:10.1007/BF01064595

Graham v. Florida. (2010). 560 U.S 48, 2010.

Hart, T. C. (1998). Causes and consequences of juvenile crime and violence: Public attitudes and question-order effect. *American Journal of Criminal Justice*, *23*(1), 129–143. doi:10.1007/BF02887287

Heide, K. M. (1999). *Young killers: The challenge of juvenile homicide.* Sage Publications.

Hess, W., Furr, L., Armstrong, K., Francis, S., & White, A. (2010). *Just kids: Baltimore's youth in the adult criminal justice system. A report of the just kids partnership to end the automatic prosecution of youth as adults.* Just Kids Partnership.

Hoeffel, J. C. (2013). The jurisprudence of death and youth: Now the twain should meet. *Texas Tech Law Review*, *46*, 29–69.

Horowitz, M. A. (2000). Kids who kill: A critique of how the American legal system deals with juveniles who commit homicide. *Law and Contemporary Problems*, *63*(3), 133–177. doi:10.2307/1192328

Jan, I.-F., Ball, J. D., & Walsh, A. (2008). Predicting public opinion about juvenile waivers. *Criminal Justice Policy Review*, *19*(3), 285–300. doi:10.1177/0887403407307431

Kumpfer, K. L., & Alvarado, R. (1998). *Effective family strengthening interventions. Juvenile Justice Bulletin. Nov. 1998.* Office of Juvenile Justice & Delinquency Prevention.

Liwanga, R. C., & Ibe, P. (2021). Transfer of child offenders to adult criminal courts in the USA: An unnecessary exercise, unconstitutional practice, international law violation, or all of the above? *Georgia Journal of International & Comparative Law*, *49*, 99–128.

Marrus, E., & Rosenberg, I. M. (2005). After *Roper v. Simmons*: Keeping kids out of adult criminal court. *San Diego L. Rev., 42*, 1151-1182.

Martin, G. A. Jr. (1992). The delinquent and the juvenile court: Is there still a place for rehabilitation? *Connecticut Law Review*, *25*, 57–63.

McCarthy, F. B. (1994). The serious offender and juvenile court reform: The case for prosecutorial waiver of juvenile court jurisdiction. *Saint Louis University Law Journal*, *38*, 629–671.

McGee, C. M. (1989). Measured steps toward clarity and balance in the juvenile justice system. *Juvenile & Family Court Journal*, *40*(3), 1–23. doi:10.1111/j.1755-6988.1989.tb00656.x

Mears, D. P. (2001). Getting tough with juvenile offenders: Explaining support for sanctioning youths as adults. *Criminal Justice and Behavior*, *28*(2), 206–226. doi:10.1177/0093854801028002004

Mears, D. P., Hay, C., Gertz, M., & Mancini, C. (2007). Public opinion and the foundation of the juvenile court. *Criminology*, *45*(1), 223–257. doi:10.1111/j.1745-9125.2007.00077.x

Mears, D. P., & Pickett, J. T. (2019). Voting preferences and perceived juvenile crime trends: Examining racial and political preferences. *Criminal Justice Policy Review*, *30*(6), 840–861. doi:10.1177/0887403417729879

Mears, D. P., Pickett, J. T., & Mancini, C. (2015). Support for balanced juvenile justice: Assessing views about youth, rehabilitation, and punishment. *Journal of Quantitative Criminology*, *31*(3), 459–479. doi:10.100710940-014-9234-5

Memory, J. M. (1989). Juvenile suicides in secure detention facilities: Correction of published rates. *Death Studies*, *13*(5), 455–463. doi:10.1080/07481188908252324

Miller, R. N., & Applegate, B. K. (2015). Adult crime, adult time? Benchmarking public views on punishing serious juvenile felons. *Criminal Justice Review*, *40*(2), 151–168. doi:10.1177/0734016814546039

Miller v. Alabama. (2012). 132 S Ct. 2455.

Mulvey, E. P., & Schubert, C. (2012). *Transfer of juveniles to adult court: Effects of a broad policy in one court. Juvenile Justice Bulletin. December 2012*. U.S. Department of Justice, Office of Justice Programs. Office of Juvenile Justice & Delinquency Prevention.

Myers, D. L. (2001). *Excluding violent youths from juvenile court: The effectiveness of legislative waiver*. LFB Scholarly Publications.

Myers, D. L. (2005). *Boys among men: Trying and sentencing juveniles as adults*. Praeger Publishers.

Myers, D. L. (2016). Juvenile transfer to adult court: Ongoing search for scientific support. *Criminology & Public Policy*, *15*(3), 927–938. doi:10.1111/1745-9133.12232

Myers, L. B., & Levy, G. W. (1978). Description and prediction of the intractable inmate. *Journal of Research in Crime and Delinquency*, *15*(2), 214–228. doi:10.1177/002242787801500207

Pagnanelli, E. (2007). Children as adults: The transfer of juveniles to adult courts and the potential impact of Roper v. Simmons. *The American Criminal Law Review*, *44*, 175–194.

Park, J. (2007). Balancing rehabilitation and punishment: A legislative solution for unconstitutional juvenile waiver policies. *The George Washington Law Review*, *76*, 786–818.

Perry, S. W. (2006). *Prosecutors in state courts, 2005*. US Department of Justice, Office of Justice Programs, Bureau of Justice Statistics.

Pollitt, B. (2004). Buying justice on credit instead of investing in long-term solutions: Foreclosing on trying juveniles in criminal court. *Journal of Law & Family Studies*, *6*, 281–300.

Prescott, M. M. (1999). Another option for older, nonviolent juveniles: Statutory retention of juvenile court jurisdiction past the age of majority. *Iowa Law Review*, *85*, 997–1033.

Redding, R. E. (2003). The effects of adjudicating and sentencing juveniles as adults: Research and policy implications. *Youth Violence and Juvenile Justice*, *1*(2), 128–155. doi:10.1177/1541204002250875

Redding, R. E. (2008). *Juvenile transfer laws: An effective deterrent to delinquency? Juvenile Justice Bulletin, August*. Office of Juvenile Justice and Delinquency Prevention.

Redding, R. E. (2016). One size does not fit all: The deterrent effect of transferring juveniles to criminal court. *Criminology & Public Policy*, *15*(3), 939–948. doi:10.1111/1745-9133.12239

Redding, R. E., & Howell, J. C. (2000). Blended sentencing in American juvenile courts. In J. Fagan & F. E. Zimring (Eds.), *The changing borders of juvenile justice: Transfer of adolescents to the criminal court* (pp. 145–180). University of Chicago Press.

Reddington, F. P., & Sapp, A. D. (1997). Juveniles in adult prisons: Problems and prospects. *Journal of Criminal Justice*, *20*, 139–152.

Roper v. Simmons. (2005). 543 U.S. 551.

Ruttenberg, H. (1994). The limited promise of public health methodologies to prevent youth violence. *The Yale Law Journal*, *103*(7), 1885–1912. doi:10.2307/797016

Sanborn, J. B., Jr. (1985). *Plea negotiation in juvenile court*. [Unpublished doctoral dissertation, SUNY Albany, Albany, NY., United States].

Sanborn, J. B. Jr. (1993b). The right to a public jury trial: A need for today's juvenile court. *Judicature*, *78*, 230–238.

Sanborn, J. B. Jr. (1994a). Certification to criminal court: The important policy questions of how, when, and why. *Crime and Delinquency*, *40*(2), 262–281. doi:10.1177/0011128794040002007

Sanborn, J. B. Jr. (1994b). Constitutional problems of juvenile delinquency trials. *Judicature*, *76*, 230–238.

Sanborn, J. B. Jr. (1996b). Policies regarding the prosecution of juvenile murderers: Which system and who should decide? *Law & Policy*, *18*(1-2), 151–178. doi:10.1111/j.1467-9930.1996.tb00168.x

Sanborn, J. B. Jr. (1998). Second-class justice and first-class punishment: The use of juvenile records in sentencing adults. *Judicature*, *81*, 206–213.

Sanborn, J. B. Jr. (2000). Striking out on the first pitch in criminal court. *Barry Law Review, 1*, 7–61.

Sanborn, J. B. Jr. (2001a). A *parens patriae* figure or impartial fact finder: Policy questions and conflicts for the juvenile court judge. *Criminal Justice Policy Review, 12*(4), 311–332. doi:10.1177/0887403401012004004

Sanborn, J. B. Jr. (2003). Hard choices or obvious ones: Developing policy for excluding youth from juvenile court. *Youth Violence and Juvenile Justice, 1*(2), 198–214. doi:10.1177/1541204002250879

Sanborn, J. B. Jr. (2009a). Juveniles' competency to stand trial: Wading through the rhetoric and the evidence. *The Journal of Criminal Law & Criminology, 99*, 135–214.

Sanborn, J. B. Jr, & Salerno, A. W. (2005). *The juvenile justice system: Law and process*. Roxbury Publishing Company. Oxford University Publishing.

Sargent, D. A., & Gordon, D. H. (1963). Waiver of jurisdiction: An evaluation of the process in the juvenile court. *Crime and Delinquency, 9*(2), 121–128. doi:10.1177/001112876300900202

Sarri, R., & Shook, J. (2005). Juvenile justice in the United States: Adherence to Human Rights Conventions. In M. Ensalaco & L. C. Majka (Eds.), *Children's human rights: Progress and challenges for children worldwide* (pp. 218–240). Rowman and Littlefield Publishers.

Schwartz, J. S. (1982). The youth offender: Transfer to the adult court and subsequent sentencing. *Criminal Justice Journal, 6*, 281–313.

Scott, E. S. (2013). Miller v. Alabama and the (past and) future of juvenile crime regulation. *Law & Inequality, 31*, 535–558.

Scott, E. S., & Steinberg, L. (2008). *Rethinking juvenile justice*. Harvard University Press.

Sellers, B. G., & Arrigo, B. A. (2009). Adolescent transfer, developmental maturity and adjudicative competence: An ethical and justice policy inquiry. *Criminology, 29*, 435–488.

Slobogin, C. (2013). Treating juveniles like juveniles: Getting rid of transfer and expanded adult court jurisdiction. *Texas Tech Law Review, 46*, 103–132.

Smith, A. (1994). They dream of growing older: On kids and crime. *Boston College Law Review. Boston College. Law School, 36*, 953–1024.

Smith, C. K. (2013). Nothing About Us Without Us! The failure of the modern juvenile justice system and a call for community-based justice. *The Journal of Applied Research on Children, 4*(1), 11.

Stamm, M. J. (1973). Transfer of jurisdiction in juvenile court: An A\analysis of the proceeding, its role in the administration of justice, and A proposal for the reform of Kentucky law. *Kentucky Law Journal (Lexington, Ky.), 62*, 122–199.

Steinberg, L., & Piquero, A. R. (2010). Manipulating public opinion about trying juveniles as adults: An experimental study. *Crime and Delinquency, 56*(4), 487–506. doi:10.1177/0011128708330179

Sundt, J. L., Cullen, F. T., Applegate, B. K., & Turner, M. G. (1998). The tenacity of the rehabilitative ideal revisited: Have attitudes toward offender treatment changed? *Criminal Justice and Behavior, 25*(4), 426–442. doi:10.1177/0093854898025004002

Tripplett, R. (1996). The growing threat: Gangs and juvenile offenders. In T. J. Flanagan & D. R. Longmire (Eds.), *Americans view crime and justice: A national public opinion survey* (pp. 137–150). Sage Publications. doi:10.4135/9781483326900.n10

Trzcinski, E., & Allen, T. (2012). Justice towards youth: Investigating the mismatch between current policy and public opinion. *Children and Youth Services Review*, *34*(1), 27–34. doi:10.1016/j.childyouth.2011.07.014

Welch, K., Butler, L. F., & Gertz, M. (2019). Saving children, damning adults? An examination of public support for juvenile rehabilitation and adult punishment. *Criminal Justice Review*, *44*(4), 470–491. doi:10.1177/0734016819833141

Winner, L., Lanza-Kaduce, L., Bishop, D. M., & Frazier, C. E. (1997). The transfer of juveniles to criminal court: Reexamining recidivism over the long term. *Crime and Delinquency*, *43*(4), 548–563. doi:10.1177/0011128797043004009

Wizner, S. (1984). Discretionary waiver of juvenile court jurisdiction: An invitation to procedural arbitrariness. *Criminal Justice Ethics*, *3*(2), 41–50. doi:10.1080/0731129X.1984.9991757

Wizner, S. (1995). On youth crime and the juvenile court. *Boston College Law Review. Boston College. Law School*, *36*, 1025–1035.

Wu, B. (2000). Determinants of public opinion toward juvenile waiver decisions. *Juvenile & Family Court Journal*, *51*(1), 9–20. doi:10.1111/j.1755-6988.2000.tb00014.x

Zimring, F. E. (1998a). *American youth violence*. Oxford University Press.

Zimring, F. E. (1998b). Toward a jurisprudence of youth violence. *Crime and Justice*, *24*, 477–501. doi:10.1086/449285

Zimring, F. E. (2000b). The punitive necessity of waiver. In J. Fagan & F. E. Zimring (Eds.), *The Changing Borders of Juvenile Justice: Transfer of adolescents to the criminal court* (pp. 207–224). University of Chicago Press.

Zimring, F. E., & Fagan, J. (2000). Transfer policy and law reform. In J. Fagan & F. E. Zimring (Eds.), *The changing borders of juvenile justice: Transfer of adolescents to the criminal court* (pp. 407–424). University of Chicago Press.

ENDNOTES

1 Cf., Ainsworth (1991) contended changes in juveniles means JCs should be abolished: *Having an autonomous juvenile justice system with its own distinctive procedures made sense in a world that viewed the categories of "child" and "adult" as inherently antithetical in their essential attributes. Once the imagined nature of childhood changed and the child-adult dichotomy blurred, however, the ideological justification for a separate juvenile jurisprudence evaporated. With its philosophical underpinnings no longer consonant with the current social construction of childhood, the juvenile court now lacks a rationale for its continued existence other than sheer institutional inertia. All*

things being equal, inertia might not be an insupportable basis for maintaining the juvenile court. After all, dismantling the system would entail at least some political and economic costs. Indeed, overcoming the vested interests of such an entrenched institution could take a heroic political effort of will. Yet all things are not equal. Perpetuating an anachronistic juvenile court exacts its own costs, both ideological and practical. These costs compel me to conclude that the juvenile court ought to be abolished (p. 1118).

2 See Applegate, Cullen & Fisher, 1997; Cullen, Golden & Cullen, 1983; Cullen, Skovron, Scott & Burton, 1990; Mears, Hay, Gertz & Mancini 2007; Sundt, Cullen, Applegate & Turner, 1998; Trzcinski & Allen, 2012.

3 See Applegate, Davis & Cullen, 2009; Bouley & Wells, 2001; Hart, 1998; Jan, Ball & Walsh, 2008; Mears, 2001; Mears, Hay, Gertz & Mancini 2007; Mears & Pickett, 2019; Schwartz, J. S., 1992; Steinberg & Piquero, 2010; Tripplett 1996; Wu, 2000.

4 Zimring relied on the "high prevalence of offenses in the teen years" that are reported in self-report studies. From this Zimring (1998a) perceived "criminal offenses as a *more or less* normal adolescent phenomenon…. (p. 82, emphasis added), suggesting that criminal behavior can be a "transitory phenomenon" for many, and perhaps most, juveniles. Criminal behavior is more of a lifestyle for some juveniles, and less for others. Many of the former tend to end up in JC or CC, while some of the latter desist without being caught. Most, but not all, youths will do *something* criminal prior to reaching adulthood. But Zimring's theories and policy recommendations are directed at "youth violence" and are not aimed at juvenile delinquency. The important omission/misrepresentation in Zimring's comments is that the overwhelming majority of youths do not commit the type of serious, violent, or chronic offenses that are the targets of transfer. There is a serious disconnect between Zimring's take on the nature of juvenile offending, in general, and the kind of criminal behavior that merits transfer consideration. Unless and until (God forbid) chronic and violent behavior is a norm among juveniles, that behavior should not be regarded as "a byproduct of the same transitional status that increases traffic accidents, rates of accidental pregnancy, and suicidal gestures (Id.)." Entirely missing in these false analogies (of supposedly typical juvenile conduct) is the ever-important variable of *intent to harm* that is recognized elsewhere by Zimring as vital to the transfer conversation.

5 The same problem arose with the plausibility of selective incapacitation.

6 Violence in juvenile facilities can be as bad (Beck, Harrison, & Guerino, 2010) or worse (Fagan, 2008; Forst, Fagan & Vivona, 1989) than what transpires in adult facilities. In the end: *Antiexclusionists have a valid point in criticizing adult penal policy that does not prevent the harmful mixture of youth with adult criminals. Of course, this is a (typically ignored) two-way street. Age is only one criterion by which to gauge the "right fit" of incarceration. Some adults can be harmed by an inappropriate mixture with violent juveniles, just like youth retained by the juvenile system can be harmed by these same violent juveniles were they to be retained as well (which the ATC typically ignores, as well). In fact, some states provide for youth convicted in criminal court to serve any sentence of incarceration in a juvenile facility at least while they are still of a juvenile age (usually until 16 or 18 years of age). The wisdom of this policy is not beyond scrutiny, albeit this is not an issue that has received much, if any, attention in the literature. Although adult penal policy certainly should aim to protect the physical safety of excluded youth, lapses in this policy do not invalidate exclusion policy in general or the prosecution of any particular juvenile in criminal*

court. The same logic applies to victimized adult inmates and the validity of their prosecution in criminal court (Sanborn, 2003, p. 207).

7 As Sanborn (2003) noted: (A)*ccepting the relative immaturity of youth converts, at best, to granting (only) qualifying youth what some have called "diminished" culpability.... Importantly, diminished culpability (or penal proportionality) does not convert into criminal immunity for all (even qualifying) youth. While it may justify a reduction in the criminal court's response to the offender, it does not automatically and categorically justify the elimination of a response from this court altogether* (p. 207, citation omitted).

8 Adopting Extended Jurisdiction/Blended Sentencing does not alleviate pressures to transfer the most chronic/violent offenders, and opens the doors to reaching juveniles currently below/off the transfer radar (see Redding & Howell, 2000, p. 151; Zimring, 1998a, 2000b).

9 Similarly, Garbarino stated: *Children who kill have often failed to receive love, support, or faith they needed in the first years of their lives. As a result, these children have.... "damaged souls" and are "unable to connect with love to the world around them." These children "often lack the emotional fundamentals for becoming a well-functioning member of society and are more prone to become infected with whatever social poisons are around them. In short, they have trouble learning the basics of empathy, sympathy, and caring." They feel no connection to their homes, their parents, or their surroundings, and so society's social conditions do not get "incorporated into the ways (the) kids think and feel about the world, about* **their** *world, and about themselves." Because they do not feel connected to society, these children do not incorporate society's definitions of "right" and "wrong" into their daily lives* (Horowitz, 2000, p. 154, citing Garbarino, 1999, pp. 36-38, 19, emphasis in original). Horowitz (2000) wrote that youths' experiencing domestic and neighborhood violence regularly means they could "come to accept violence as natural and inconsequential." Meanwhile, risky behavior becomes appealing, while violence is acceptable behavior. Horowitz warns us these youths will not respond to punishment (p. 156). Ruttenberg (1994) opined "many American children and youths today see their future prospects as so bleak that potential criminal sanctions seem meaningless. Some take it for granted that they will not live past their twentieth birthdays (p. 1908)." It is highly unlikely that any system response will deter these youths — incapacitation (together with treatment programs) may be the only course of plausible action, one that is often likely to take much longer to accomplish than what the JJ system has in its arsenal.

10 The more irresponsible youths are and the more their behaviors do not seriously harm society, then the youths' interests should be paramount, and society should be willing to show tolerance and compassion, to preserve youths' "life chances," and to promote their rehabilitation within the relatively friendly confines of JC. The more culpable youths are and the more their behaviors harm society, then society's interests should dominate, and society is justified in seeking the condemnation and punishment of those offenders, which means the greater equality and justice available in CC make it the proper/necessary prosecution forum.

11 Some DPs/ATC simply dislike the legislative/democratic process: *The decision whether a youth should be treated as a juvenile or an adult lies within the virtually unreviewable discretion of legislators (who draw unreviewable classifications based on age, offense, and perhaps offense history), prosecutors (who need to give no reasons at all), or judges (who must give a reason compatible with whatever the legislature has prescribed in the statute)* (Frost Clausel & Bonnie, 2000, p. 198). These DPS see everyone acting unfavorably and inappropriately (seemingly DPs, alone, should

make the call, if ever). Presumably, all appellate courts are at fault, too, since they have unanimously upheld PT.

12 Zimring (1998a) fronted a false equivalency between youth violence and youth-precipitated traffic accidents (pp. 85-86), suggesting that if society accepts the damage inflicted by youth traffic accidents without banning juveniles' use of automobiles, it should accept the damage inflicted by juvenile violence without banning (transferring) offenders. There is comparability between the two sets of youths in that people can be injured or die from both actions, but zero comparability between youth violence and youths' lawfully/productively operating a vehicle, however. While the latter is lawful and provides substantial benefits (driving mom to the doctor), there is nothing legal or positive in the former. More important, the vehicle example *is* equivalent to youth violence *but only when* the vehicle is used effectively as a weapon, when there is an illegal intent (or recklessness/negligence), which, like youth violence, is criminal and unacceptable, and very possibly transferrable to CC! Zimring has already constructed a distinction between murder (which is transferrable in his view) and other examples of juvenile violence. Zimring's theory on juvenile violence simply needs to be broadened. The harm from an armed robbery of a single victim can be distinguished from a shooting, involving an attempt to kill 5 pedestrians where serious and near fatal injuries occurred. While the former could reasonably be disqualified from transfer (depending upon prior record), the latter screams for transfer (even as a first offense), all based on the intent to inflict and produce harm. Nevertheless, the shooting incident could not result in transfer, according to Zimring's policy, since no one died (and maybe even if someone had died). Seemingly, even permanent paralysis or blindings suffered by multiple shooting victims would not suffice for transfer in Zimring's policy.

13 There is nothing magical about these criteria, of course, but, ironically, while these criteria were offered as a safeguard against transfer, in most, and perhaps all, urban centers, thousands of offenders still would satisfy these standards annually.

14 Sanborn (2003) argued years ago: (T)*he central and pivotal question in transfer is whether the youth should be diverted from criminal court via a referral to juvenile court or should be prosecuted in criminal court. This choice properly belongs to the prosecutor, especially when serious/violent offenses are involved and/or when the defendant's prior record is lengthy. It is appropriate for legislatures to identify a threshold associated with crimes that are too serious and/or too numerous to be diverted to juvenile court... Prosecutors are charged with representing society's interests, which is why they should control the determination of when youth have exceeded that threshold. Unlike judges, prosecutors are experienced in evaluating charges and cases that should be filed (or diverted). In addition, judges do not have access to witnesses and arresting officers so as to be able to gauge the appropriate level of charge to file. Moreover, judges are known to be less likely than prosecutors to transfer youth (McCarthy, 1994; Sanborn, 1994a) and thus they would be more likely to undercharge offenders so as to keep youth in juvenile court. That is not the proper orientation with which to initiate charging decisions, particularly when serious and violent crimes or chronic offenders are at hand. Finally, it is inappropriate, and arguably a violation of separation of powers, to invest judges with the executive branch-based authority of charging offenders* (p. 209).

15 Contrary to ATC suggestions, prosecutors do face boundaries to transfer beyond those specifically identified in the statute. Prosecutors must engage in
a scrutiny of both the offense and the offender. Even prosecutors must be sensitive to both elements if for no other reason than subjecting either the wrong crime or the wrong criminal to

trial in adult court easily could result in acquittal or in judicial or jury nullification in that forum (Sanborn, 2003, p. 211).

16 Zimring has moved the goalposts in redefining juveniles' maturity to mirror philosopher kings who have "mature judgment" and, a "full understanding of the world around them," whatever that means. Of course, since the ATC interprets having mature judgment and fully understanding the surrounding world as *not committing crimes*, especially violent ones, Zimring's criteria establish an impenetrable shield against transfer, which was the objective. It seems inconsistent that he allows the transfer of murderers since they likely can project neither their conception of mature judgment nor a full understanding of the world around them. Why these violent juvenile offenders differ significantly, if at all, from other violent juvenile offenders, such as serial and multiple stabbers, armed robbers, and brutal rapists is not addressed. Considering the number of adult offenders that lack "mature judgment" and an "understanding of the world around them," perhaps no offender could be prosecuted in CC under Zimring's maturity standard. Is it accident, irony, or something else altogether that the *rights of passage* the ATC endorses as reasons to excuse juvenile crime, even chronic and violent crime, by not transferring youths to criminal court are the same *rights of passage* violent gangs demand from their pledges' behavior as the latter are interning with in the hope of joining the violent gang?

17 Inasmuch as amenability is an individualized analysis, rather than a categorical one, there is no reason that judges cannot make the call, especially when they already do for non-violent offenses. Most important, amenability in violent behavior cases can be a criterion and lead to transfer especially when previous attempts at treatment have failed, the defendant is considered too violent for inclusion within a juvenile offender population, the violent behavior may be considered non-treatable or require many years of intervention, which cannot be attained within the constraints of the JJ system. The last item would seem to synchronize well with Zimring's longer sentence rationale.

18 Between 1995 and 2013 Feld's sentence discount for 14-year-olds decreased a total of 13% (from 33 to 20) or .72% per year; for 16-year-olds the decrease was minimally 16% (from 66 to *not more than* 50%; there was no minimum sentence identified) or .88% per year. Using that discount formula and extrapolating Feld's discount to today (2023), 14-year-olds would warrant between 5% and 13% and 16-year-olds would receive between 25% and 35%. By mid-century, 16-year-olds would receive no more than 17%, and 14-year-olds would receive approximately -7%, suggesting they would qualify for a sincere apology, a high school diploma, a college scholarship, and an automobile (not including the one they are charged with stealing).

19 Zimring (1998a) pointed to the large variation in levels of culpability, explaining that *age is an incomplete proxy for levels of maturity during the years from age 12 to 18. The variation among individuals of the same age is great, and individual determinations of immaturity are thus superior to averages bases on aggregate patterns. Second, the vulnerabilities associated with early and middle adolescence play a more important part in explaining some patterns of homicide than others....Moreover, the large variation in the level of achieved maturity interacts with the differential vulnerabilities found in different circumstances to present a complicated landscape, one much too complex for an age-determined series of presumed discounts from a standing price list of penalties.* (pp. 150-151, citation omitted).

20 In some jurisdictions, juveniles can carry two strikes (adjudications or convictions) from JC and "strike out" on their first conviction in CC (see Sanborn, 1998, 2000),

21 Transfer policy should avoid extremes and categoricals: not subject all juveniles (especially 15 and older) to CC punishment for all offenses even though they are culpable and are competent to stand trial. Instead, let JCs address their crimes without obliterating their life chances. But, at the same time, do not give all juveniles (or those below an arbitrarily selected age) immunity from criminal prosecution due to a possible developmental deficiency that still did not render their choices to commit chronic, serious, and violent crime involuntary, incompetent or irresponsible.

Glossary: The Meaning of Acronyms Utilized in the Text

AC = Adjudicative Competence

AH = Adjudicatory Hearing

ATC = Anti-Transfer Crowd

CC = Criminal Court

CJ = Criminal Justice (System)

CST = Competency to Stand Trial

DF = Direct File

DP(s) = Developmental Psychologist(s)

DR = Diminished Responsibility

EP = Effectiveness of Participation

IST = Incompetent to Stand Trial

JC = Juvenile Court

JD = Juvenile Delinquent

JJ = Juvenile Justice (System)

JT = Judicial Transfer

LR = Legal Responsibility

MR = Moral Responsibility

OE = Offense Exclusion

PC = Probable Cause

PH = Preliminary Hearing

PRIC = *P*eer pressure; lack of *R*isk aversion; lack of *I*mpulse control; and, no ability to consider long-term *C*onsequences

PT = Prosecutorial Transfer

SO = Status Offender/Offense(s)

About the Author

Joe Sanborn earned a B.A. in Sociology from Villanova University in 1973, and a M.A. (1974) and PhD (1984) in Criminal Justice from SUNY Albany (University at Albany). His Dissertation topic was titled, Plea Negotiation in Juvenile Court, which remains the only comprehensive examination of this important subject. The data for the Dissertation were derived from 265 days observing case dispositions in court and interviewing hundreds of juvenile court workers in Philadelphia's Juvenile (Family) Court; more than 10,000 cases were included in the study.

Joe researched and taught juvenile justice at the college level for more than four decades: Glassboro State College/Rowan University (1979-1994), Department Chair (1989-1992), Law and Justice Studies Department; Villanova University (1985-1994) Adjunct, Graduate Human Organization Sciences Department; West Chester University (1985-1994) Adjunct, Undergraduate, Criminal Justice Department; and University of Central Florida (1994-2017), Undergraduate Coordinator, Graduate Coordinator, PhD Coordinator, Assistant Chair.

At these Universities, Joe taught a variety of courses, including: juvenile justice, prosecution and adjudication, criminal law, constitutional law, human rights and criminal justice, seminar in law, seminar in social justice, criminal procedure, legal aspects of policing, and legal aspects of the criminal court.

Joe is the author of two books, *The Juvenile Justice System: Law and Process* (Oxford University Press; co-author Anthony W. Salerno); and, *The Legal Aspects of Policing* (West Academic Publishing) and numerous articles that have appeared in *Journal of Criminal Law and Criminology*; *Justice Quarterly*; *Judicature*; *Crime & Delinquency*; *Youth Violence and Juvenile Justice*; *Law & Policy*; *The Justice System Journal*; *Criminal Justice Review*; *Criminal Justice Policy Review*; *Criminal Law Bulletin*; and *Barry Law Review*. Many of the articles were included in subsequent anthology publications.

Joe is a previous President, Southern Criminal Justice Association (SCJA, 2002), and long-time member of the Academy of Criminal Justice Sciences (ACJS) and the American Society of Criminology (ASC). Joe retired from UCF (and from college teaching) after the Fall 2017 semester.

Index

P

R

S

T

Z

www.ingramcontent.com/pod-product-compliance
Lightning Source LLC
LaVergne TN
LVHW081328021026
849161LV00010BA/2364
9781799879237